UNDERSTANDING

A2 level COMPUTING for AQA

Ray Bradley

Published in 2005 by:
Nelson Thornes Ltd
Delta Place
27 Bath Road
CHELTENHAM
GL53 7TH
United Kingdom

05 06 07 08 09 / 10 9 8 7 6 5 4 3 2 1

A catalogue record for this book is available from the British Library

ISBN 0 7487 7704 0

Page make-up by Mathematical Composition Setters Ltd

Printed and bound in Great Britain by Scotprint

Acknowledgements

We are grateful to the following awarding body for permission to reproduce questions from their past examinations:
Assessment and Qualifications Alliance (AQA)
All answers provided for examination questions are the sole responsibility of the author.

Contents

How to make the best use of this A2 level book

Introduction and resources

Although this book is written specifically for the **AQA Computing** Subject Specification, it should prove extremely useful for Computing and Computer Science related examinations for other boards, and similar examinations held at this level. This is the second of two books in this series. The first, *Understanding AS level Computing for AQA*, covers the AS Level course. This book completes the material needed for the full A level Computing course. A useful set of **Examination Hints and Tips** is included, together with key words that often need to be understood in the context of an AQA examination. There is a separate glossary of AS and A2 level computing terms for AQA, *The Ultimate Computing Glossary for Advanced Level*, which is also available from Nelson Thornes.

Numerous margin entries offer helpful advice in the form of 'hints and tips'. Both the AS and A2 books are in full colour, and the **bold green entries** flag terms that have corresponding entries in the comprehensive 88-page glossary mentioned above. This glossary is special because it is written specifically with AS and A2 computing students in mind. It is not burdened with unnecessary terms or with over-complicated definitions. It thus makes definitions much easier to learn and provides a comprehensive snapshot of the material which needs to be covered. Each glossary entry has a colour which flags it as belonging to the AS or the A2 course, and it is therefore ideally mapped to both the AS level and A2 level Computing for AQA books.

An 88-page glossary of AS level and A2 level computing terms for AQA is available in addition to this A2 book.

Electronic resources

In addition to the above three books there are two sets of **interactive electronic resources**, one for **AS level Computing** and one for **A2 level Computing**. There is also a website (www.revisecomputing.com) which offers additional help and information, including careers advice for students thinking of pursuing a career in Computer Science or a related subject.

There is also an AS level book, interactive electronic resources and a revision website.

Modular structure

This book is arranged in a **modular** fashion, which corresponds to the **three AQA modules**, as follows:

- Module 4 – *Processing and Programming Techniques*
- Module 5 – *Advanced Systems Development*
- Module 6 – *The Practical Project*

The material is split up into easy-to-digest chapters, many of which can be studied independently of each other. At the beginning of each chapter you are told which **key concepts** are going to be covered, and whether the material you are reading depends on material in other chapters. The **end-of-chapter exercises** will check that you have understood the work just covered, and there are **comprehensive answers** to each of these exercises at the end of this book. Two further chapters on **examination questions** for modules 4 and 5 complete the range of material available for the theoretical modules.

A real AQA A2 computing project has been analysed, developed and tested in this book.

This is used to give invaluable project advice for A2 students.

Project work

AQA module 6 consists of an appropriate open-ended real problem to which the student provides a suitable solution. An actual **AQA project** has been undertaken in great detail in module 6. It fully covers the **analysis**, **design**, **technical solution**, **system testing**, **system maintenance**, **user manual** and **appraisal** of the project, including a fully worked **sample write up**.

Keep up to date

It is not possible for any book to keep you right up to date, and you must therefore read **computer magazines**, **newspapers**, watch the **news** and look at **specialist programmes** which cover computer-related material. This will help considerably with the **moral**, **ethical**, **social**, **cultural** and other issues about which you are expected to be able to comment in a knowledgeable fashion.

The subject specification, mark schemes and Examiners' reports for AQA A2 computing are all available from www.aqa.org.uk.

Set up an effective revision schedule

Before you take your A2 examinations it is essential to be organised. *Start weeks before the examinations are due*. AQA Computing is usually taken in June, so March/April is a good time to start thinking about building up your revision schedule.

Download a copy of the current **AQA Computing specification** from the Internet. *Remember to download the correct one for the year in which your examination will take place*. You can search for the current Computing specification on the AQA Internet site which is at **www.aqa.org.uk**.

After you have downloaded the **pdf file**, print it out, and then work through Module 4 using a highlighter pen. Highlight any topics which you do not understand, then use this book or get your teacher to go through them. You will find that the **glossary** for this course (mentioned at the beginning of this chapter) is particularly useful for revision purposes. You could make use of the glossary to test your friends and classmates. Do the same with Module 5. Remember also that there are likely to be synoptic elements. This means that work covered in your AS level modules 1, 2 and 3 might also form part of a question at A2.

You will need Adobe Acrobat Reader, a free program available on the web (from www.adobe.com), to read the pdf (portable document format) files containing information for AQA A2 level Computing.

Find a revision pattern which works for you

Work out suitable time slots which are best suited to *your* revision routine. Some students get up at the crack of dawn, and others prefer to work late into the night. Make sure that the work you are doing is productive. If you get stuck for long periods of time or find yourself doing nothing, then stop and do something completely different. There is no substitute for writing things down, e.g. highlighting key points. Simply looking through a book is not necessarily good enough for most students. Make notes in your own words, then categorise the material into manageable sections.

Do as many past papers as possible

At the time of writing, A2 Computing has been undertaken for a number of years. Remember that there are **AQA A2 Computing examinations** in both **January** and **June**. Make sure that you get all the papers that are available, and many can be downloaded from the web. In addition to the actual papers you will need access to the **mark schemes**, which are also available on the web. This will save your teachers/lecturers a lot of time, and *you will be able to see what the examiners are looking for*. Finally, get access to the **Report on the Examination**. This is where the Principal Examiners write down where many of the candidates go wrong or lose marks each year. *You can learn an enormous amount from reading this material and by learning from the mistakes that students have made in the past*.

Make use of the past examination questions in this book, but most importantly of all, save one or two papers to do *under timed examination conditions*. It is only by doing this that you will really know what you are capable of.

Examination hints and tips for AQA A2 level computing

Examination technique

Good grades in examinations are usually the result of **good examination technique**. *A good knowledge of the theory may not be enough to get you a top grade unless you know the rules.*

Examination jargon

It is important to know what the examiners expect, and the list of **key words** produced by AQA is essential reading. These key terms, referring to the key words used in AQA examinations are as follows.

Name (What is the name of?) Usually requires a technical term or its equivalent. Answers to this type of question normally involve no more than one or two words.

List A number of features or points, each often no more than a single word, with no further elaboration of detail required.

Define (What is meant by?) 'Define' requires a statement giving the meaning of a particular term. 'What is meant by ... ?' is used more frequently as it emphasises that a formal definition as such is not required.

Outline A brief summary of the main points is required. The best guide to the amount of detail required lies in the mark allocations; approximately one to one-and-a-half minutes should be allowed per mark. This generally works out at around two or three lines in a standard answer booklet for each mark.

Describe Means no more than it says, that is, 'Give a description of ... '. So, 'Describe one feature of a graphical user interface (GUI) which is likely to be helpful to a non-technically minded user' requires a description of a feature such as a pictorial icon in terms of making the selection and execution of a program easier. 'Describe one relationship that can be inferred from the data requirements' means supplying its name and degree.

Explain This creates major difficulties for many candidates. A reason or interpretation must be given, not a description. The term 'Describe' answers the question 'What?', and the term 'Explain' answers the question 'Why?' or 'How?'.

Suggest 'Suggest' is used when it is not possible to give the answer directly from the facts that form part of the subject material detailed in the specification. The answer should be based on the general understanding rather than on recall of learnt material. It also indicates that there may be a number of correct alternatives.

Give evidence for (Using examples from ...) Answers to questions involving these phrases must follow the instructions. Marks are always awarded for appropriate references to the information provided. General answers, however comprehensive, will not gain maximum credit.

Calculate This term is used where the only requirement is a numerical answer expressed in the appropriate units.

State 'State' falls short of 'Describing' and amounts to no more than making bullet points. For example, for the question, 'State one advantage of writing a program as a collection of modules,' the answer might be, 'Teams of programmers are able to work on producing individual modules at the same time.'

The definitions shown on this page have been produced by AQA examiners.

Understand these terms and you can maximise your chance of getting a good grade in the examination.

Computing content

Some computing questions are difficult to answer for the following reasons:

- innovations happen so quickly that old criteria may no longer apply
- the number of ways of doing things is so vast that it is difficult to mark some of the material.

The AQA and other boards have their work cut out to make sure that all questions are still relevant. Not many subjects have to check for possible new responses so close to producing the mark schemes for the examinations.

Answer your questions wisely and stick to the specification

Do not try to be too clever when you answer questions, and go for the obvious answers if you have a choice. Consider, for example, the following question:

Hard disks and floppy disks are both secondary storage media; state three differences between these two devices.

There are many ways that different concepts can be explained in computing.

Using the AS level and A2 level glossary will give you a feel for the depth that is required for the AQA Computing specification. (See 'How to make the best use of this A2 level book' above.)

Three 'correct' answers could be as follows:

- A floppy disk has a read/write protect tab.
- A floppy disk does not rotate very quickly; a hard disk does.
- A hard disk is sealed; a floppy disk is open to the elements.

Better answers, containing more obvious differences, would be as follows:

- A hard disk is able to store a huge amount of data compared with a floppy disk.
- Data may be read much more quickly from a hard disk.
- A hard disk is usually fixed; a floppy disk is usually portable.

All bulleted points above are 'correct', but the second batch would probably be in the mark scheme, along with others such as 'A hard disk is more reliable than a floppy disk'.

Students at A level, especially those who know a great deal about computers, think that the required answers are 'obvious', there must be a catch! Some of the simpler questions at A2 level are obvious, and it is important to realise that details about the technical intricacies of the hardware are not usually required but information about the functionality of the hardware is.

Check what you need to know from the AQA A2 level computing subject specification. It seems unfair, but 'right answers' may gain no marks because they are not in the specification, and hence not in the mark scheme. Sensible suggestions are usually in the mark scheme, so make sure that your answers are sensible in the context of what you are meant to know.

Remember, carefully following the guidance given here could gain you a grade or even two.

1 The microprocessor and its register set

In this chapter you will learn about:

- A simplified microprocessor with a typical set of registers
- The factors that affect speed of operation like bus width and word length
- The role played by some of the common registers in a simple microprocessor
- The Accumulator, ALU and Control Unit
- What an interrupt is
- Simple interrupts, the vectored interrupt mechanism and interrupt priorities

A simplified microprocessor system

Microprocessors are very complex, but they all share a common heritage, making use of the **stored program concept**, enabling a **program** (or *sequence of instructions*) stored in memory (**RAM**) to be run. In the simplified system shown in Figure 1.1, instructions are processed one at a time by **fetching** each instruction from memory, **decoding** it (*deciding what to do*) and finally **executing** the instruction (*carrying out what the instruction has asked the microprocessor to do*). This is called the **fetch-decode-execute cycle**, which is often shortened to the **fetch-execute cycle**. Programs will often need **data** too, and this must be stored along with the program in a different part of the RAM.

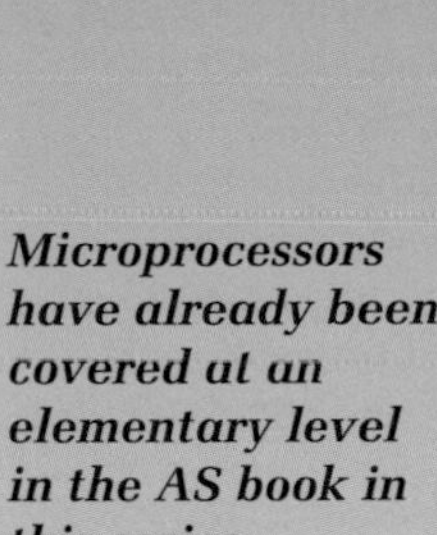

Microprocessors have already been covered at an elementary level in the AS book in this series.

The stored program concept was invented in the 1940s by John von Neumann, a Hungarian mathematician who was living in the US at the time.

If a microprocessor is switched on, then it is simply going through the fetch-execute cycle.

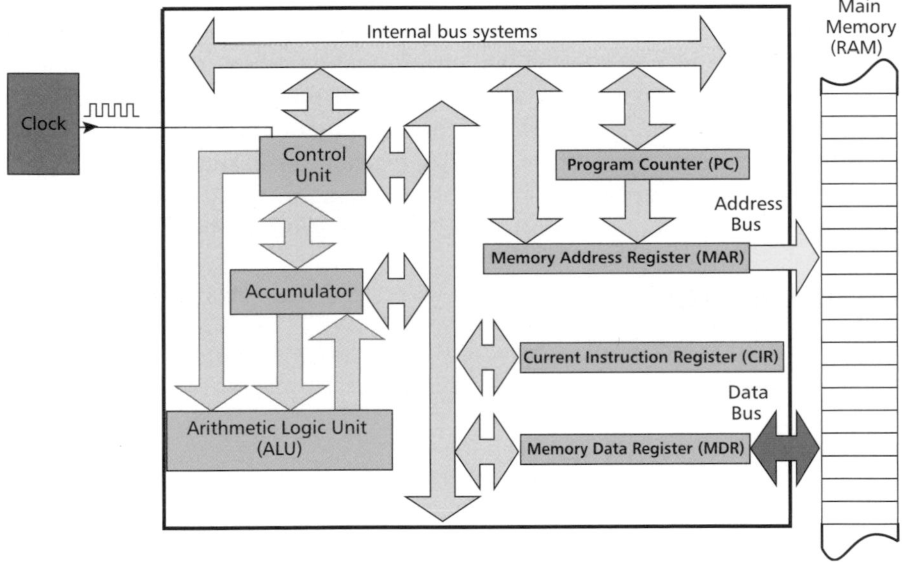

Figure 1.1 A simplified microprocessor system

Factors affecting the speed of operation

The rate at which operations are carried out by a microprocessor is governed by a number of important factors: namely the **clock** speed, the width of the **data bus** and the **word** length. On modern computer systems the speed of the clock is usually measured in GHz (1 GHz is 1 000 000 000 cycles per second).

A faster clock rate does not necessarily mean that information is processed more quickly. The *width* of the data bus is also important because a wider data bus means that more bits of data can be processed (fetched from memory or placed back into memory) at the same time. A 32-bit data bus is common, but 64-bit microprocessors (this means that the data bus is 64 bits wide) are also available. Even wider data buses may be used on specialist computers like **supercomputers**. The term **word** refers to the number of bits that a microprocessor can typically handle in one chunk and this is dictated by the size (*number of bits*) of the **registers** (see below) inside the microprocessor.

The word length is usually the same as the width of the data bus.

A microprocessor with a 64-bit word length would usually have a 64-bit data bus, and registers capable of dealing with 64 bits (or multiples of this) at the same time.

A typical microprocessor might have between 32 and 64 registers, but powerful microprocessors used to create supercomputers may have well over 100 registers.

Example

Two computer systems have been set up in which the width of the data bus and the word length are identical. They are also clocked at the same speed. When running identical software one system is faster than the other. Outline one possible factor which may account for this discrepancy, explaining why this is so.

Solution

One possible factor could be that one of the systems is using faster computer memory. This means that the time taken to read data from the memory or write data to the memory is less, and thus the system will get through the fetch-execute cycle more quickly.

The microprocessor register set

Each microprocessor has a different set of registers, or places (memory) *inside* the microprocessor where data (in the form of a set of **binary digits**) may be stored. All share a common heritage and similar principles, although the latest microprocessors will inevitably have advanced features not available on the earlier models.

Registers may be divided into **special purpose registers** such as a **flag register** (see chapter 2) *dedicated* to the task of holding bits of information which reflect the state of various operations inside the microprocessor, and **general purpose registers** such as a register which may have its function assigned by the programmer. Figure 1.1 shows a microprocessor with a simple register set; the flag register, for example, is not shown. To understand the functions carried out by these registers we will run a very simple **assembly language program**, but first let us consider each register in detail.

A good analogy exists with a railway network. If the data, address and control buses are equivalent to railway lines, then the control unit would be equivalent to the signal box operating all the points, making sure that they open and close at the right moments in time. The whole 'network' must all be run to a strict timetable – which is dictated by the clock.

The accumulator (ACC)

The **accumulator** is used to accumulate results. It is the place where the answers from many operations are stored temporarily before being used for some other process.

The Arithmetic Logic Unit (ALU)

The **Arithmetic Logic Unit** or **ALU** is the unit that carries out **arithmetical** (+, – etc.) and **logical** (AND, OR and NOT etc.) **operations** on the data inside it. The ALU provides answers which are normally placed into the accumulator (ACC) register.

The control unit

The **control unit** is literally in control. It acts under the direction of the clock (see Figure 1.1), and by decoding the program instructions it sorts out the internal paths inside the microprocessor to make sure that data is moved from and placed in the right place. It also instructs the ALU which arithmetical or logical operation is to be performed.

If you imagine the clock to be a metronome going tick-tock tick-tock etc., then the control unit is equivalent to the conductor in an orchestra. The control unit makes sure that the different sections of the microprocessor are in time. Some internal connections from the control unit have not been shown in Figure 1.1 for the sake of simplicity.

The program counter (PC)

The **program counter** (PC), or **Sequence Control Register** (SCR), determines the sequence in which program instructions are to be executed. In our simple system, this is just one after the other. We start by setting up the PC to point to the memory location where the beginning of the program can be found. After the first instruction has been fetched, we increment the PC by 1; this is so that the next instruction to be fetched from memory can be accessed very easily. The program counter is fundamental to the **stored program concept** mentioned above.

The Current Instruction Register (CIR)

The **Current Instruction Register** (CIR) is a place where the current instruction (i.e. the instruction which has just been fetched from memory) is placed. The binary digits representing the most-recently-fetched instruction are held here so that the instruction decoder inside the **control unit** can decode them. It is important to realise that as far as the microprocessor is concerned, data (numbers and letters etc.) and instruction codes look the same; they are all groups of binary digits. The programmer must make sure that instructions are put into the appropriate places in memory. If data intended for other purposes gets interpreted as an instruction, then the computer will probably crash.

The memory data register (MDR)

The **memory data register** (MDR) holds the data that was either read from or written to the main memory the last time a read/write operation was carried out. You will recall from reading the above that data and instructions all look similar. In fact, the codes used by some instructions are bound to be identical to the codes used for some of the data. If the program is being interpreted correctly, a copy of the instruction will be transferred to the CIR register, whereas ordinary data would not.

The memory address register (MAR)

The **memory address register** (MAR) holds the address of the data (or instruction) currently being accessed. It is used to alter the address bus without affecting the PC.

A simple program

We now use the microprocessor shown in Figure 1.1 to run the **assembly language** program shown in Table 1.1. It will appear to be a long process, but *bear with it and you will understand a great deal about machine code and microprocessor operations*.

In practice, memory locations with addresses as low as 10, 11 and 12 would not be used to store users' programs. These would be reserved for special purposes. However, using low numbers in this program example makes this work easier to understand.

Table 1.1 A simple assembly language program

The example program which is used over the next few pages			
Instructions			**Comments**
LOAD	A	[10]	; LOAD the Accumulator with the data from memory location 10
ADD	A	[11]	; ADD data from memory location 11 to the number already in the Accumulator and put the result in the Accumulator
STORE	A	[12]	; STORE the result from the Accumulator in memory location 12

The program shown in Table 1.1 will LOAD the accumulator with the number contained inside memory location 10 (the brackets around the numbers in the program indicate this). It will then ADD this to the number contained in memory location 11, and finally STORE the result into memory location 12. If 3 is placed in location 10 and 2 is placed in location 11, then the answer (2 + 3) placed in location 12 would obviously be 5; but let us see how the microprocessor shown in Figure 1.1 would do this.

Setting up the program and data

The program in Table 1.1 would have to be stored in memory because this is the stored program that will control the microprocessor. It should not be stored in locations 10, 11 or 12 because these locations have already been used for storing the data and reserving a place for the answer. Assume that the program will be stored starting at Address 100. Being three lines long, and assuming that the code for each instruction will fit into a single memory location (in some real systems it may not), we end up with the important parts of our **memory map** shown in Figure 1.2. We have assumed that the contents of all irrelevant memory locations have been set to zero – but in practice the contents of these memory locations are of no consequence.

*A **memory map** is a map of how the memory is being used. The memory map in Figure 1.2 shows where the program and data needed by the program are stored.*

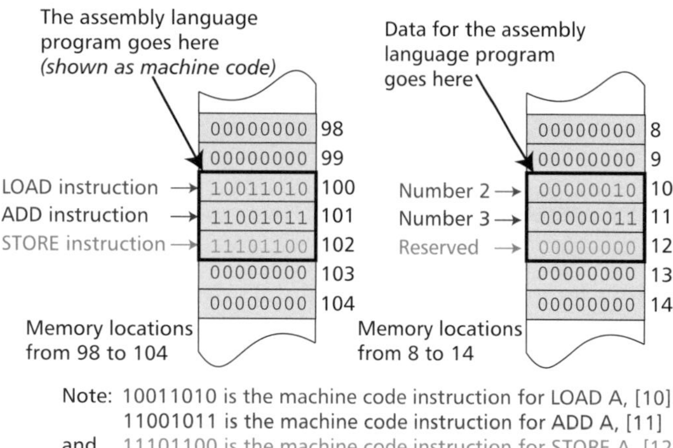

Figure 1.2 Program and data memory maps

The numbers to be added are stored using pure binary, but each program instruction needs a code (**machine code**) too. These are assigned by the microprocessor manufacturer. Our simplified instructions are explained in more detail in Table 1.2.

In our system the memory location is contained in the same byte as the code – more than one byte would be needed in practice for a greater variety of instructions and a sensible addressing range (see later in this chapter).

Table 1.2 The machine code instruction format

A detailed look at how the codes relate to what has to be done										
Instructions			**The binary codes**							
LOAD	A	[10]	1	0	0	1	1	0	1	0
			Code for LOAD A [memory location]				Binary code for memory location 10			
ADD	A	[11]	1	1	0	0	1	0	1	1
			Code for ADD A [memory location]				Binary code for memory location 11			
STORE	A	[12]	1	1	1	0	1	1	0	0
			Code for STORE A [memory location]				Binary code for memory location 12			

A unique code is assigned to each operation, together with a means of identifying the source or destination of data (memory locations). We now investigate the role played by each of the registers during the execution of the program shown in Table 1.1. This is covered in the next few sections.

Setting up the registers

The first stage is to make sure that the **program counter** (**PC**) is set to **100**, as shown in Figure 1.3(a). The binary number for 100 is shown in the PC register.

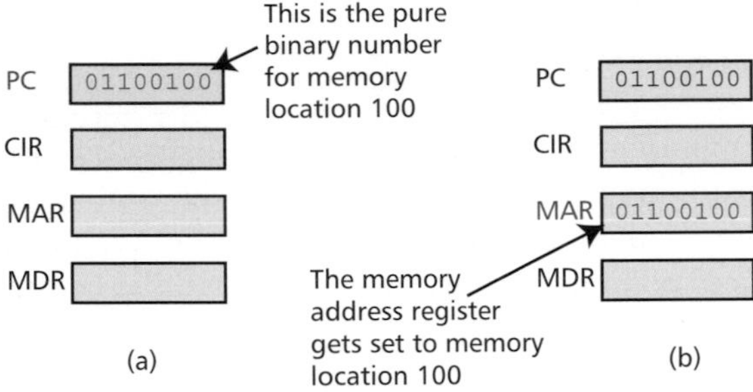

Figure 1.3 Setting up the initial registers

Next the memory address register (MAR) is set up to contain the binary code for 100, obtained from the contents of the PC – this is so that the **address bus** can be set to access the correct location in memory (see Figure 1.3(b)). We are now ready to run the program.

The first instruction – LOAD A [10] – is fetched

The data from memory location 100 is fetched and loaded into the CIR via the MDR because the microprocessor must assume that the first piece of code encountered in a program is a valid instruction. Figure 1.4(a) shows that the data representing this instruction ends up in the Current Instruction Register. The next *vital step* is to increment the PC by 1 to 101 as shown in binary in Figure 1.4(b). This ensures that the right instruction is fetched next time in the fetch-execute cycle.

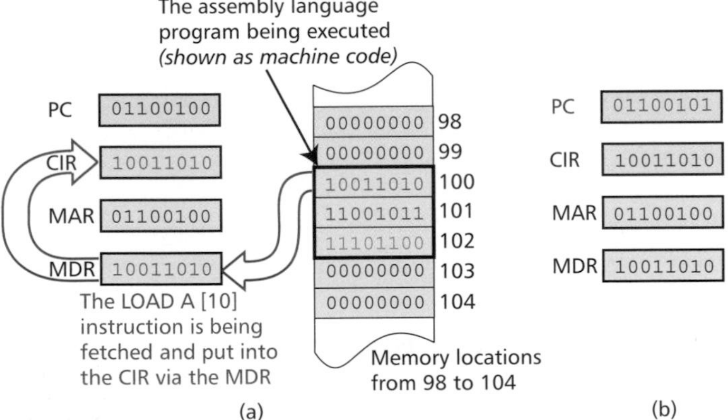

Figure 1.4 The fetch phase for the first instruction and incrementing the PC

The first instruction – LOAD A [10] – is decoded

The next phase involves decoding the instruction and is done automatically by the decoder electronics inside the microprocessor's control unit. The idea can be thought of as shown in Figure 1.5, but the control paths indicated here are not shown in Figure 1.1.

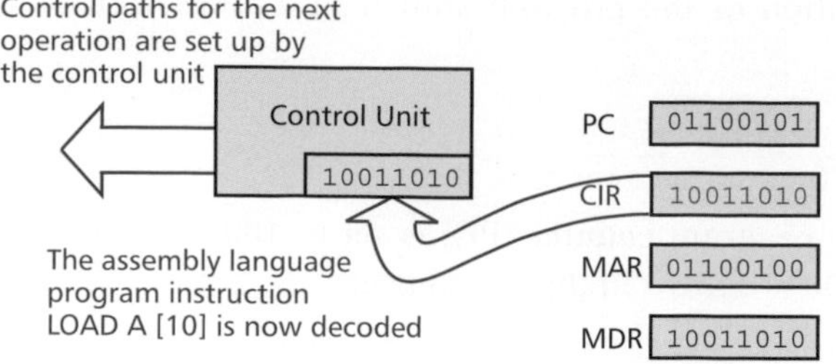
Control paths for the next operation are set up by the control unit
Control Unit
10011010
PC 01100101
CIR 10011010
MAR 01100100
MDR 10011010
The assembly language program instruction LOAD A [10] is now decoded

Figure 1.5 The instruction just fetched is decoded by the microprocessor

During the decoding process the digits representing this machine code instruction are analysed electronically, and the control paths are set up to make sure that 'the contents of memory location 10 will be loaded into the accumulator' during the next execution phase. To do this the MAR will have to be set up to point to memory location 10 and the control unit must set up the memory for a read operation.

The first instruction – LOAD A [10] – is executed

This is the phase during which the instruction LOAD A [10] is actually carried out. The contents of memory location 10 will be placed into the **accumulator** as shown in Figure 1.6.

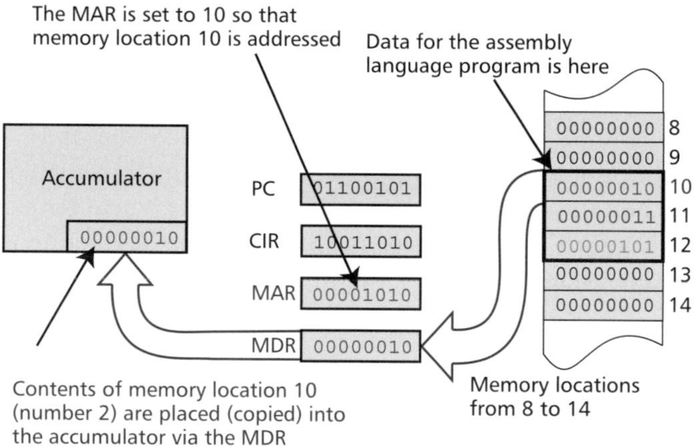
The MAR is set to 10 so that memory location 10 is addressed
Data for the assembly language program is here
Accumulator
00000010
PC 01100101
CIR 10011010
MAR 00001010
MDR 00000010
00000000 8
00000000 9
00000010 10
00000011 11
00000101 12
00000000 13
00000000 14
Contents of memory location 10 (number 2) are placed (copied) into the accumulator via the MDR
Memory locations from 8 to 14

Figure 1.6 The first instruction is executed

We have now worked through one complete phase of the fetch-execute cycle and have carried out just *one* machine code instruction, namely LOAD A [10].

At this stage you should find these processes become easier to understand. You should even be able to start guessing what will actually happen next.

The second instruction – ADD A [11] – is fetched

The program counter (PC) has already been incremented and therefore points to the place from where the next instruction is to be fetched. The MAR is set to 101 (the contents of the PC) and the data from memory location 101 is loaded into the CIR via the MDR as shown in Figure 1.7(a). As before, we automatically increment the PC ready for the next fetch phase, and this action is shown in Figure 1.7(b).

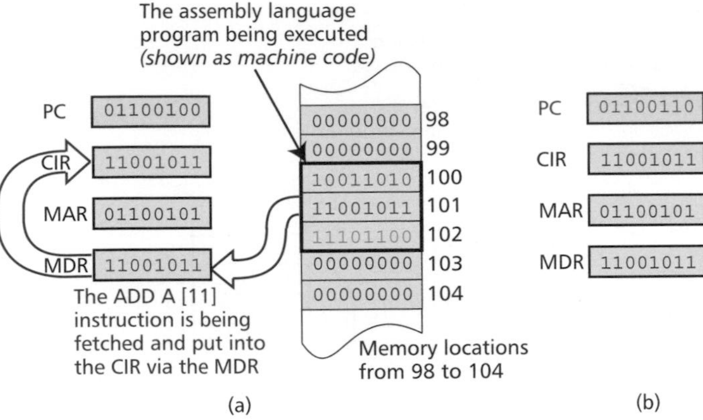

Figure 1.7 The fetch phase for the second instruction and incrementing the PC

There is lots of work for the control unit to do here – going back to the railway analogy, many levers would have to be pulled in the right sequence to make sure that the data trains do not go down the wrong track!

The second instruction – ADD A [11] – is decoded

The second instruction (ADD A [11]) is now decoded as shown in Figure 1.8. The decoding electronics decides that it is an ADD instruction. The electronic paths are then set up so the number already in the accumulator has the number contained in memory location 11 added to it. The result of this operation is then stored inside the accumulator.

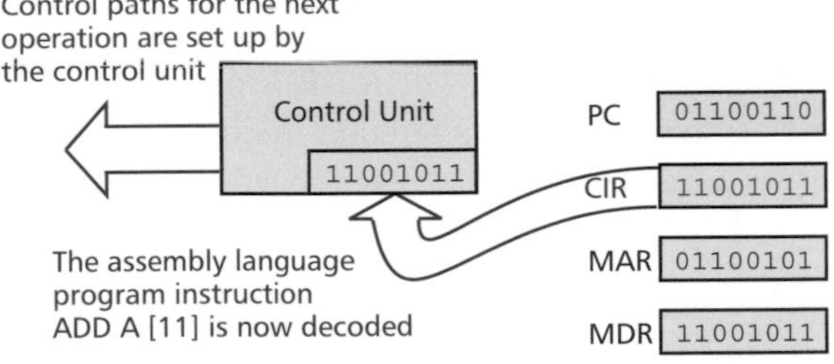

Figure 1.8 The instruction just fetched is decoded by the microprocessor

On first reading, microprocessor operations might appear to be complex, but they do give a very good indication of what is actually going on inside a typical microprocessor. Binary digits are constantly being fetched from memory, manipulated by using the registers inside the microprocessor, and then the results get put out to memory again. In practice there would be a lot more registers than are present inside the microprocessor shown in Figure 1.1, but the principles are very similar.

The second instruction – ADD A [11] – is executed

This process is a little more complex than previous ones because we are operating on two items of data (the numbers to be added) and the result (the answer to the sum). The control unit instructs the ALU to do an 'ADD operation'. This is indicated by the part of the internal **control bus** shown as a single connection between the control unit and ALU in Figure 1.9.

The numbers to be added are contained in memory location 11 and the **accumulator**. The first number from the accumulator gets transferred to a register inside the ALU. Next the **MAR** is set to the binary pattern for 11, and the number from memory location 11 is transferred into the accumulator, where it is then combined, by addition, with the first number already in the ALU register. This produces the sum, which is then about to be put back into the accumulator, thus overwriting the old contents of the accumulator with the answer. In Figure 1.9 the overwriting part of this operation has not been shown.

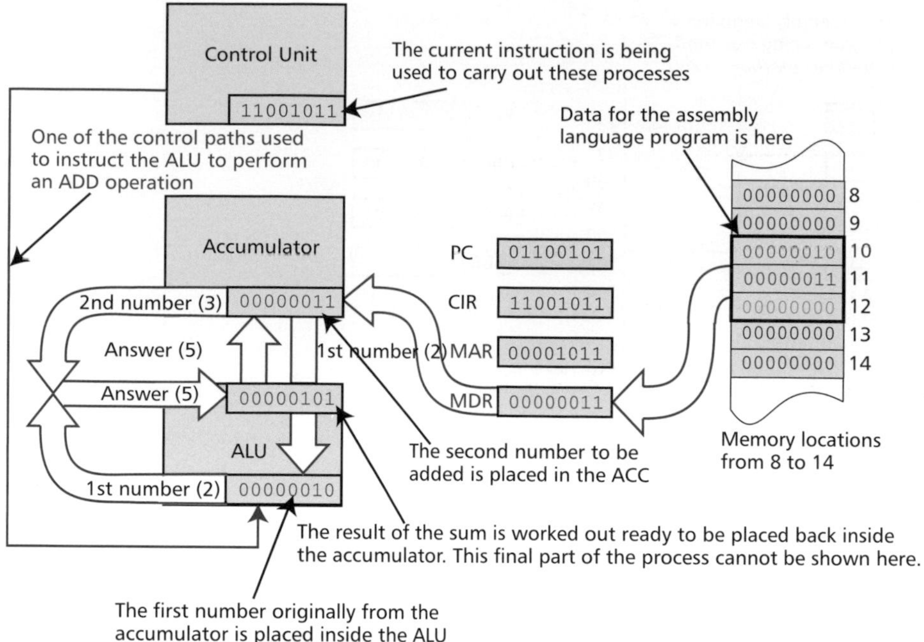

Figure 1.9 The arithmetical instruction ADD A [11] is now being executed

The third instruction – STORE A [12] – is fetched

We are now ready to complete the final part of the program. The MAR is now set to the contents of the PC, and the data from memory location 102 is fetched. As before, the PC contents are incremented by 1, ready for the next instruction. These stages are shown in Figures 1.10 (a) and (b) respectively.

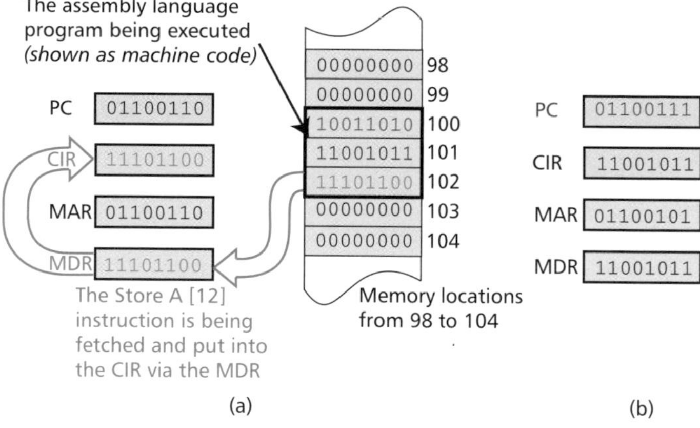

Figure 1.10 The fetch phase for the third instruction and incrementing the PC

You should note that when numbers are transferred from one location to another a copy of the original is being taken, thus leaving the original contents unchanged.

The third instruction – STORE A [12] – is decoded

The final instruction is now decoded, and the electronic decoder inside the control unit decides that the current contents of the accumulator should be stored in memory location 12. The appropriate registers and control paths are now set up for this operation as shown in Figure 1.11.

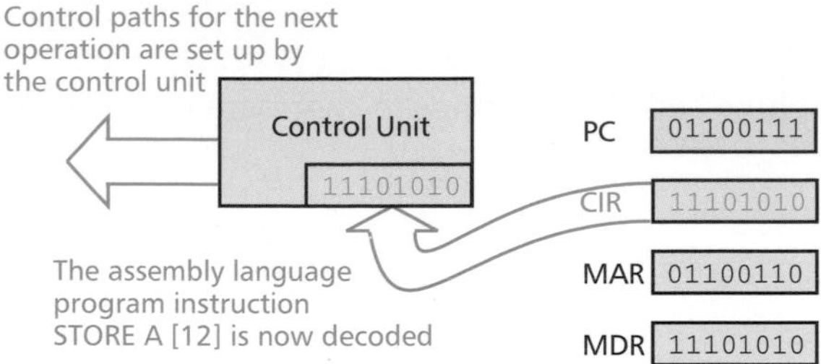
Control paths for the next operation are set up by the control unit
Control Unit
11101010
PC 01100111
CIR 11101010
MAR 01100110
MDR 11101010
The assembly language program instruction STORE A [12] is now decoded

Figure 1.11 The STORE A [12] instruction is decoded by the microprocessor

The third instruction – STORE A [12] – is executed

The final stage of the entire process is to put the answer inside the accumulator into memory location 12. This is shown in Figure 1.12. We have now worked out 2 + 3, made the answer equal to five and stored this answer in the main memory.

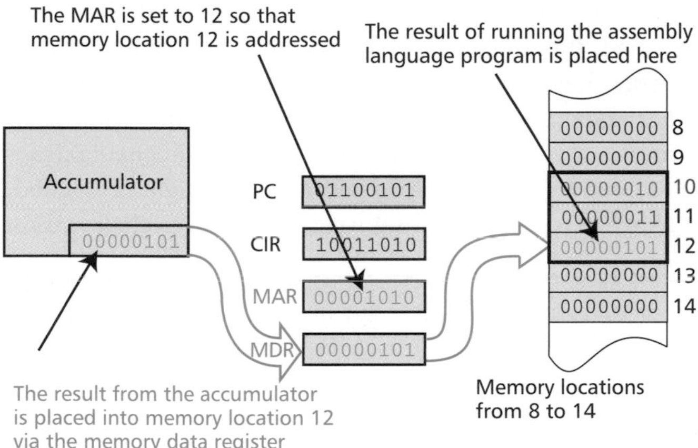
The MAR is set to 12 so that memory location 12 is addressed
The result of running the assembly language program is placed here
Accumulator
00000101
PC 01100101
CIR 10011010
MAR 00001010
MDR 00000101
00000000 8
00000000 9
00000010 10
00000011 11
00000101 12
00000000 13
00000000 14
The result from the accumulator is placed into memory location 12 via the memory data register
Memory locations from 8 to 14

Figure 1.12 The STORE A [12] instruction just fetched is now being executed

Don't forget that all computer operations from 'creating sound' to 'computer art' are just manipulation of binary digits.

If you have understood this work, you should now have a better understanding of how a microprocessor could do any arithmetic or logical operation, and hence how microprocessors could be used in anything from the control of a washing machine to creating animation for full-length feature films.

The next instruction is fetched!

You will recall that a **microprocessor** has just one purpose in life – to **fetch**, **decode** and **execute** instructions just like the ones we have been carrying out. The PC has already been set up, so the microprocessor *will* fetch the next piece of data from memory location 103, attempt to decode it and then attempt to execute it. What happens next could be literally anything. The machine which is being controlled by the microprocessor would certainly crash as it runs through all of the remainder of the memory desperately trying to carry out what it 'thinks' is the rest of the program.

In practice, any program run in this way would need a machine code instruction which returns control back to what the microprocessor was doing before the program counter was set to 100 in Figure 1.3 to embark on our program. On a real machine, control would be returned back to the **operating system**.

The register set for the ×86 range of microprocessors is covered in detail in chapter 2 when assembly language is considered. The register set used in this chapter is simplified for the purpose of understanding this material.

Example

Briefly explain how it is possible for machine code instructions to represent operations such as 'ADD', 'SUBTRACT' and 'OR'.

Solution

Each machine code instruction can perform just one simple operation. The microprocessor manufacturer assigns a unique code for each operation, like 'ADD' and 'SUBTRACT', which it is then possible for a particular microprocessor to carry out. The binary digits which make up these special machine codes are decoded by the microprocessor to determine which particular operation is to be carried out. It usually takes one complete fetch-decode-execute cycle to do this.

Different microprocessor systems

Modern microprocessors often employ more advanced techniques to increase the speed with which a program may be executed. **Pipeline architectures** are used in which different instructions may be fetched whilst others are being decoded and yet other instructions are being executed. Assuming that the next instruction required is the one that came after the previous one, then this increases the speed considerably. However, if the next instruction is not the one that is required (a jump to a different place in memory might be needed, for example) then the pipeline will have to be flushed and the system is slowed to less than optimum speed.

To achieve a much faster rate, more than one processor can be employed. This literally means that more than one thing can be done simultaneously. In very powerful computers many processors are used simultaneously, and this technique is described by the term parallel processing. To take full advantage of these more sophisticated systems *both* the operating systems and **application software** must be capable of making use of more than one processor at the same time.

Special-purpose registers

Two important special-purpose registers are the **flag register** and the **interrupt register**. The flag register contains a number of **bits** used to **flag** special situations like 'errors occurring with arithmetic', or to 'flag if an **interrupt** has occurred'. An example of part of a typical flag register can be seen in Figure 1.13.

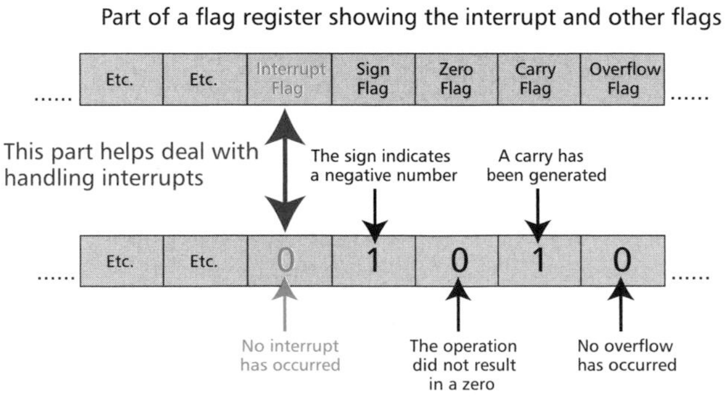

Part of a flag register showing the interrupt and other flags

......	Etc.	Etc.	Interrupt Flag	Sign Flag	Zero Flag	Carry Flag	Overflow Flag	......
......	Etc.	Etc.	0	1	0	1	0	......

This part helps deal with handling interrupts

The sign indicates a negative number

A carry has been generated

No interrupt has occurred

The operation did not result in a zero

No overflow has occurred

Figure 1.13 A flag register

From Figure 1.13 we are able to deduce that 'no interrupt has occurred', assuming that the **interrupt flag** is set to a '1' if an interrupt needs attention. From here you can see that an interrupt is really just a *signal, which is used to get the microprocessor's attention*.

***Interrupts** usually happen many times a second inside a typical computer system. They are therefore a common operation which happens during the normal execution of a program. However, interrupts are also used for errors and emergency situations such as an imminent power failure.*

Introduction to interrupts

So far we have implied that computer programs are executed in linear fashion from beginning to end. In practice, most programs are usually interrupted many times each second, so that other programs may be run too. Both **hardware** and **software** may cause these interrupts to happen, and the mechanisms for doing this will vary. In computing, the general name for temporarily halting a process so that some other process may be carried out is called an interrupt. Many things will cause interrupts to happen, but typical examples are 'data arriving at a network interface card (NIC)', 'updating the real-time clock' or 'a printer running out of paper'.

How a simple interrupt is handled

A microprocessor can be interrupted in the middle of whatever it is doing. It must therefore 'make a note' of what is happening at this moment in time, and it does this by saving the contents of important **registers** like the PC, ALU and flags etc. onto the **LIFO stack** (see the first (AS) book in this series). It must then service the interrupt by setting the PC to point to the new program to be executed (the **interrupt handler** routine), and then carry on in the ways described earlier in this chapter. After the interrupt handler has been run, a return is made to the original program which was previously interrupted. Before control is returned to the next instruction in the original program, the registers like the PC, ALU and flags etc. are put back to their previous states. This is done by popping the contents of these registers off the stack, and the original program can then carry on as though no interrupt had ever occurred. These ideas are shown in Figure 1.14.

Pay particular attention to the type of diagram shown in Figure 1.14. You may need to produce something similar when asked to explain how interrupts work.

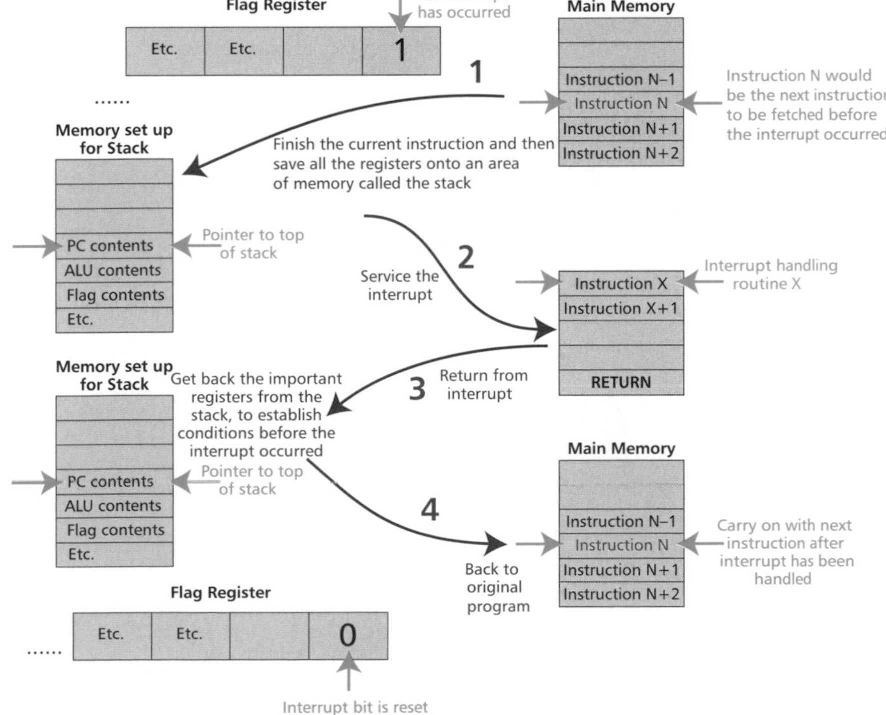

Figure 1.14 A simple interrupt is handled by a microprocessor

To work through what happens, let us assume that instruction N–1 (shown at the top of Figure 1.14) is currently being executed. An interrupt (indicated by the interrupt bit in the flag register being set to '1') occurs, and so instruction (N–1) is completed because you cannot interrupt a microprocessor in the middle of a fetch-decode-execute cycle. This is not a problem as it only takes a fraction of a billionth of a second to accomplish. The contents of all the appropriate microprocessor registers are then saved onto the LIFO stack.

Next the interrupt is handled by the interrupt handler routine. This is shown by routine X in the right-hand middle of Figure 1.14. In practice the stack would probably be used by this interrupt handling routine, and other interrupts may also occur during this period. This would involve using **interrupt priorities** (see later in this chapter).

When the interrupt has been handled, a RETURN (shown at the end of routine X) is executed, causing the contents of the stack (the microprocessor register set before the interrupt occurred) to be loaded back into the microprocessor. When this has happened the PC is set to point to instruction N (shown in red at the bottom of Figure 1.14) and the microprocessor can now carry on in blissful ignorance of the fact that an interrupt has actually occurred. Note that the interrupt flag inside the flag register has now been reset so that another interrupt may occur and be processed in the same way.

The vectored interrupt mechanism

Many different interrupts may need processing, and a method is needed to sort out which interrupt handler should be run. The **vectored interrupt** mechanism is a way of doing this, by using a **vector** (a number stored in memory) to point to the memory location which contains the routine (machine code) to handle the interrupt. Figure 1.15 shows two interrupt-handling routines, labelled X and Y.

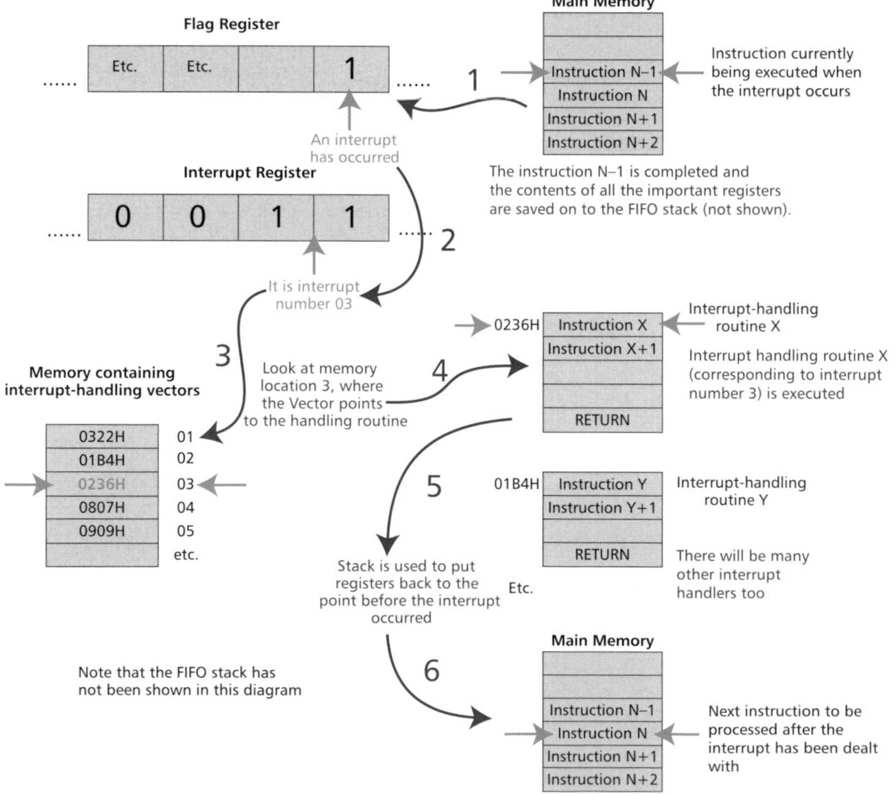

Figure 1.15 The vectored interrupt mechanism in use

From Figure 1.15 we see that an interrupt flag in the flag register has been set. The processor finishes the fetch-execute cycle for instruction (N–1) currently being executed, then dumps the contents of important registers like the PC, ALU and flags etc. to the LIFO stack. By examining bits in the interrupt register, we can see that interrupt number 3 (binary 0011) is demanding attention. For the sake of argument assume that memory location 3 contains a pointer (vector) which represents the memory location (0236 Hex) where the interrupt handler for interrupt number 3 resides.

The PC (program counter) can now be put equal to (0236 Hex), and the processor will begin the fetch-execute cycle for interrupt handler X. On completion of this, the RETURN instruction at the end of routine X causes the register information previously put onto the stack to be placed back inside the microprocessor registers. After the interrupt has been handled, the PC is put back to its old value (N in this case). The registers are now returned to their previous states, and the microprocessor can continue with the original task it was doing before the interrupt occurred.

Example

A higher-priority interrupt occurs when another interrupt is in the middle of being processed. Explain how the use of a FIFO stack helps the computer to keep track of what is happening. Include the route by which the computer would service both routines and get back to the program that was being run before any interrupts occurred.

Solution

To service the first interrupt the contents of the registers are saved onto a LIFO stack. This means that the contents of the PC, ALU etc. pertinent at the time just before the interrupt occurred are saved. The microprocessor is currently servicing the first interrupt when a second more important interrupt occurs, and thus the contents of the registers at this moment in time are dumped onto the LIFO stack. The microprocessor can now service the new interrupt, and when a RETURN is encountered, the register contents are popped off the stack, and the microprocessor is back into the position of servicing the first, less important interrupt. When a RETURN from this interrupt is encountered, the contents of the registers are popped off the stack and the microprocessor is back to the main task.

Interrupt priorities

Modern processors need to be able to deal with **nested interrupts** (i.e. interrupts that occur when other interrupts are in the middle of being processed). Let us assign four numbers (representing interrupt priorities), where the magnitude of the numbers reflects their importance. Here we will make 1 the highest and 4 the lowest.

In practice the operating system itself would also cause interrupts to happen. Examples of this could be controlling resources like 'processor time' or 'peripheral equipment'. The work covered here is closely related to the work on operating systems in chapter 8.

In practice both hardware and software may cause interrupts, and Table 1.3 shows a typical scenario in which four different interrupts happen at different moments in time. For simplicity we assume that there are four devices labelled 1 to 4, where the number of the device reflects the interrupt priority number as described above. The Processor Activity column shows what the processor is actually doing at any particular moment in time. The letter M has been assigned to the main task, which is the program being executed by the processor when no interrupt has occurred.

Table 1.3 How a microprocessor deals with different interrupt priorities

Interrupts are assigned priorities 1 to 4, with 1 being the most important					
Devices causing the interrupts (Numbers indicate the priority)				Processor activity	Comments
Device 1	Device 2	Device 3	Device 4		
–	–	–	–	MMM	Main task is being carried out.
–	–	–	–	MMM	Main task is being carried out.
–	–	–	*	444	Device 4 receives processor attention.
–	–	–	–	MMM	Device 4 is serviced, the main task is reinstated.
–	*	–	–	222	Device 2 receives processor attention.
–	*	*	–	222	Device 3 requests processor attention but is ignored.
–	*	*	–	222	Device 2 still being processed.
–	–	*	–	333	Device 2 is serviced, device 3 now gets attention.
–	–	–	–	MMM	Device 3 is serviced, the main task is reinstated.
–	*	–	–	222	Device 2 receives processor attention.
*	*	–	–	111	Device 1 overrides the current priority 2 interrupt.
*	*	–	*	111	Device 4 is ignored as it is of lower priority.
–	*	–	*	222	Device 1 is serviced, device 2 is reinstated.
–	*	*	*	222	Device 3 requests processor attention but is ignored.
–	–	*	*	333	Device 2 is serviced; device 3 now gets attention, even though device 4 requested attention some time ago.
–	–	–	*	444	Device 3 is serviced; device 4 now receives attention at last.
–	–	–	–	MMM	Device 4 is serviced, the main task is reinstated.

From Table 1.3 we see how a processor handles a multitude of interrupts, each with a different priority level. It is up to the operating system software to handle these queues and to make sure that lower priority interrupts do not get stuck in the system (i.e. they might never get serviced based on the scenario shown here).

Example

(a) What is meant by nested interrupts?

(b) A microprocessor is set up to handle interrupts with different levels of priority. However, many of the devices have the same priority level. Suggest a way that the processor could handle nested interrupts with the same level of priority.

Solution

(a) A nested interrupt is an interrupt that happens when another interrupt is in the middle of being serviced.

(b) To handle nested interrupts of the same priority a queue of these devices could be formed, with the operating system sequentially working through the queue. Higher and lower priority interrupts will still be handled in the same way.

Self-test questions

1 Explain the meaning of the following terms indicating the function of each.

(a) Microprocessor	(b) The fetch-execute cycle	(c) ALU
(d) Register	(e) Program counter	(f) Address bus
(g) MAR	(h) MDR	(i) CIR
(j) Data bus	(k) Control bus	(l) Internal bus.

2 What is the difference between machine code and assembly language? Is there a relationship between the two? If so, what is it?

3 List four different factors that would improve the speed of a program running on a particular microprocessor.

4 Why is the clock speed insufficient to compare the speed of different microprocessors?

5 What is the difference between general and special-purpose registers?

6 Microprocessors operate on the stored program concept. What is meant by this?

7 In addition to writing to the computer's memory, we have to write to hardware like disk drives, USB ports and printers. As far as the microprocessor is concerned, what is the difference between writing to RAM and writing to these hardware devices?

8 A microprocessor is clocked at 5 GHz. What is the function of this clock and what type of signal is output from it?

9 What is meant by the term memory map? Why is it necessary to have a map?

10 How does a microprocessor determine the difference between program instructions and data?

11 A microprocessor is able to perform a set of instructions which include the following: LOAD, STORE, ADD, SUBTRACT, MULTIPLY, DIVIDE.
Using these instructions as a guide, explain the typical processes that would have to go on at machine code level for the computer to work out the cumulative total of five numbers contained in five consecutive memory locations. (You do not need to draw diagrams or use all the instructions given.)

12 Explain what is meant by an interrupt. How would a simple interrupt be processed?

13 A LIFO stack is used when handling interrupts. Why is this data structure useful?

14 What is meant by the vectored interrupt mechanism? State two advantages that this mechanism has over simpler interrupt-handling systems.

15 Explain the role played by the flag register and interrupt register when interrupts are processed.

16 What is an interrupt priority? How do interrupt priorities help the operating system to manage many different tasks all requesting attention at the same time?

17 Using three different interrupt priority levels as an example, with 1 being the highest priority and 3 being the lowest level, show how the processor would handle the following scenario. Assume that a level 3 interrupt occurs first, followed by a level 2 interrupt happening before the level three interrupt has been completely serviced.

2 Assembly language

In this chapter you will learn about:

- What assembly language is
- Modes of addressing and a typical register set
- Arithmetical, logical and shift operations
- The concept of masking
- Jump instructions
- Assembly language program examples
- The assembler and the assembly process
- Calls to the operating system

Assembly language

The ';' in the comments column is used to denote the start of a comment. When the assembler comes to assemble the code (change it into machine code) the characters after the ';' will be ignored. However, they will appear on the source code listing to help program readability.

You may recall from your AS course (see the first book in this series) that **assembly language** is a **second-generation low-level language** made up from **mnemonics** which can be used instead of **machine code** because it is easier to use. The format of an assembly-language instruction consists of four parts, shown in Figure 2.1, but the labels are not needed for all instructions and the comments are optional.

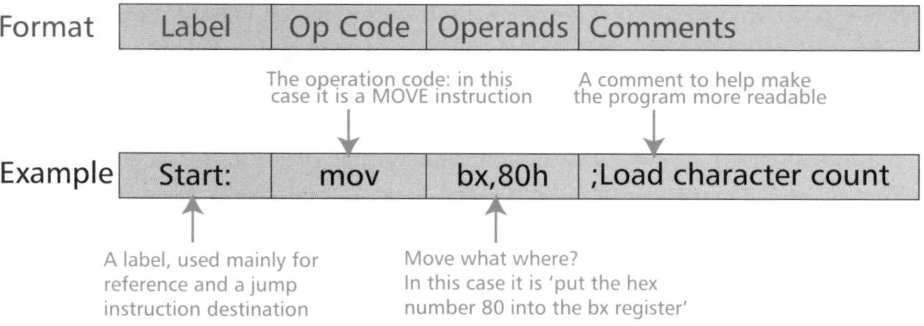

Figure 2.1 The format of an assembly-language instruction

The **label** is used as a reference and is useful when calculating relative jumps, for example. The **operation code** contains the **mnemonic** (a mnemonic to **MOV**e data in Figure 2.1) which describes the operation being carried out. The **operands** describe the *source* and *destination* of the data to be operated on (the source is the number 80 and the bx register is the destination). The **comments** are a convenience for the programmer, and help aid readability.

Example

Assembly language is difficult and time consuming compared with a high-level language. Explain why effort put into this sort of programming is still a viable proposition.

Solution

Writing assembly language could give an important speed advantage compared with the same application written in a high-level language. If your application is used frequently, and undertakes intensive and time-consuming processes, then your application, which does exactly the same job as the others but two or three times quicker, may have the edge. Assembly language enables access to registers and exact memory addresses.

Most modern processors would have registers which are longer than a single byte.

Addressing modes

Understanding assembly language is intimately tied up with **addressing modes**. These are related to physical attributes like the **registers** available and the **word length**. If, for example, you have a single-byte register in which to store information for a jump instruction, then you can jump a maximum of 255 memory locations because this is the largest number that will fit in this location. Double the length of the location, and you could jump 65 536 locations, or from +32 767 to −32 768 if **two's complement** numbers are used. The most common addressing modes are outlined below, where the popular Intel ×86 family of microprocessors is used as an example.

Look at chapter 1 in the AS book in this series if the numeric calculations presented here seem difficult.

Register addressing

If data is transferred from a source register to a destination register, then this is an example of **register addressing**.

Table 2.1 Register addressing

Label	Op Code	Operands	Comments
	mov	ds, ax	;An example of register addressing

Here the ax register is the *source* of the data and the ds register is the *destination*. After execution of this instruction a copy of the ax register would be placed in the ds register (see margin entry).

A key point to realise when we have two operands as shown here is the source and destination of the data.

For the work covered in this chapter, it is always as follows.

Operands
destination, source

Immediate addressing

This is where the data appears *immediately* after the op code, as part of the instruction, like the number 20 in this example.

Table 2.2 Immediate addressing

Label	Op Code	Operands	Comments
	mov	ax, 20	;An example of immediate addressing

Here, the decimal number 20 is to be placed into the ax register. **Immediate addressing** is a very convenient way of putting numbers into registers by specifying the number as one of the operands.

Therefore, the immediate addressing example shown here moves the source (the number 20) into the destination, the 8-bit ax register.

Do not confuse the position of the destination and source or your code will not work properly.

Direct addressing

Direct addressing refers directly to a specific memory location.

Table 2.3 Direct addressing

Label	Op Code	Operands	Comments
	mov	ax, [myData]	;An example of direct addressing

Here the contents of the memory location, in this case specified by a label named myData, is copied into the ax register.

Indirect addressing

Indirect addressing uses a number inside a register (usually an **index register**) to point to the memory location of interest where the actual data can be found.

Table 2.4 Indirect addressing

Label	Op Code	Operands	Comments
	mov	ax, [bx]	;An example of indirect addressing

In this example the brackets around the bx register indicate that the memory location pointed to by the bx register, and not the actual number inside the bx register, will be used. In this case the data in the memory location pointed to by the bx register is copied to the ax register.

Indexed addressing

For **indexed addressing** a number contained in one register is usually used in combination with the number in another register to point to the actual memory location where the data is stored.

Table 2.5 Indexed addressing

Label	Op Code	Operands	Comments
	mov	cx, [bx + di]	;An example of indexed addressing

In this example, the number in the bx register is combined with the number in the di register. As with indirect addressing, the square brackets indicate that this points to the memory location from where the actual data to be put into the cx register can be obtained.

Base register and base indexed addressing

You may also come across the terms **base register addressing** and **base indexed addressing**. Consider the following two examples.

Table 2.6 Base register and base indexed addressing

Label	Op Code	Operands	Comments
	Ld	&10 [ax]	;An example of base register addressing
	mov	cx, [bx + di]	;An example of base indexed addressing

In the first entry an address is held in the base register, in this case the ax register, and an offset (the hex number 10) is added to it. The second entry is useful for handling arrays, and is shown in more detail in the next example.

Example

By means of an example, show a typical use for a base indexed addressing mode.

Solution

A classic example of indexed addressing is setting up an array in memory. Consider the two-dimensional array, as shown in the following example.

$$\begin{bmatrix} 10 & 11 & 12 \\ 21 & 22 & 23 \\ 31 & 32 & 33 \end{bmatrix}$$

This could be mapped onto the memory locations as shown in Figure 2.2.

A linear sequence of memory locations is mapped onto a two-dimensional array by using two index registers, namely the base-index and destination-index registers. One register

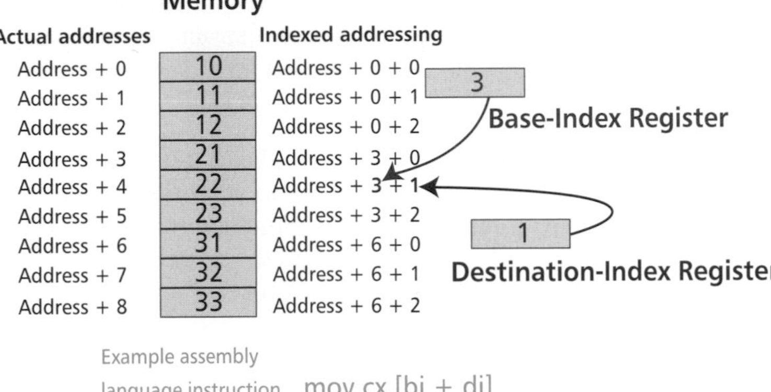

Figure 2.2 An example making use of indexed addressing

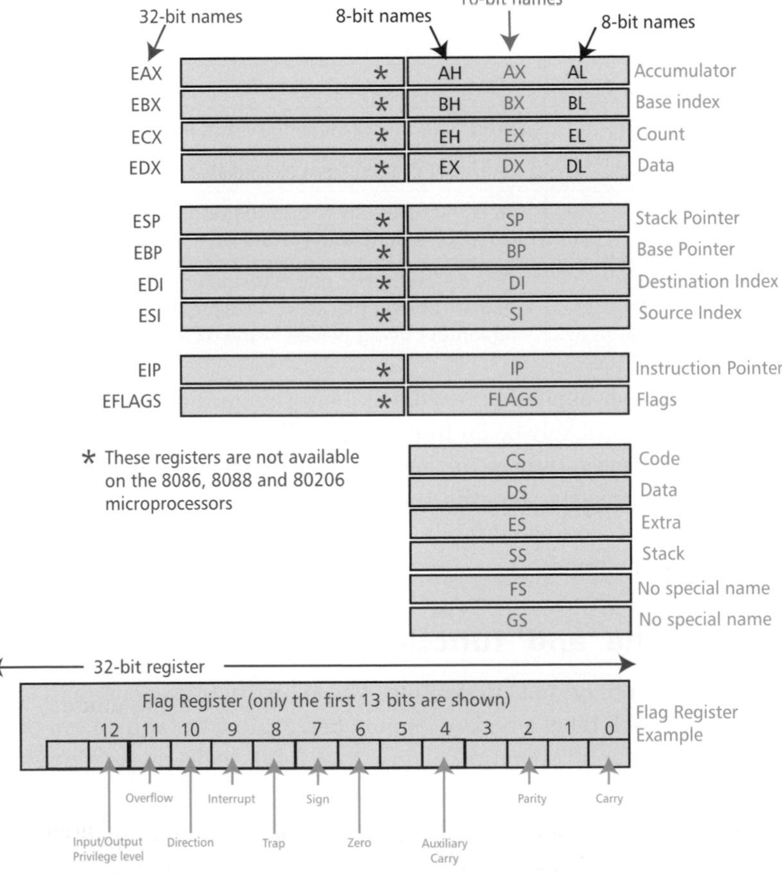

Figure 2.3 The ×86 register set and part of the flag register

No particular processor need be studied for your A2 examination, but the 80 × 86 processor shown here is typical of what is required.

In your A2 examination a made-up language could be used, but the principles are the same.

Figure 2.3 shows a popular set of registers, many of which are still retained in the Pentium and AMD processors. Compatibility with earlier processors is maintained by having the smaller registers still available, e.g. the AL register is eight bits long, the AX register is 16 bits long and the EAX register is 32 bits long.

is used for each dimension of the array. The example shows how the fifth element in the array (i.e. 22) is accessed by putting the base index register to a value of 3, and the destination index register to a value of 1. In this case the fifth element (do not forget we start at 0) is accessed, and the number 22 is placed in the cx register.

Typical assembly language instructions

The register set inside a microprocessor gives us a convenient mental model about what is going on inside.

You should be aware of typical assembly language instructions, and be able to write elementary programs using them. Instructions are made up of **logical operations** like 'AND', 'OR' and 'NOT', shift left and shift right instructions, **rotate instructions**, **arithmetical instructions**, bit **set** or bit **reset** instructions, and program-control instructions like **jumps**. Making sensible use of this involves understanding the **register set** for a particular processor, and the register set for the Intel ×86 range of 32-bit processors is shown in Figure 2.3.

At first sight, register sets may appear daunting, but they are just places into which binary digits can be stored temporarily ready for processing, or places to store results after the binary digits have been processed. Assembly language programming involves carrying out operations like those described in the last sections, and then passing control to different routines depending on the results of various flags. We will now take a more detailed look at some typical assembly language instructions.

Arithmetical operations

Typical of the arithmetical operations are 'addition', 'subtraction', 'multiplication' and 'division'. A few typical instructions for the ×86 microprocessor set would be as follows.

Table 2.7 Instructions for ×86 mircoprocessor

Label	Op Code	Operands	Comments
	add	al, bl	;Add bl to al and store the result in al
	sub	ax, 08h	;Subtract 8 (hex) from ax and store the result in ax
	mul	bl	;al is multiplied by bl and the result is stored in ax Note: ax is double the width of al and bl
	div	cx	;The dx-ax register pair is divided by the cx with the quotient being placed in the ax register and the remainder being placed in the dx register

Most microprocessors are able to do arithmetic on decimal, binary, and hex numbers. Most modern microprocessors allow you to do arithmetic in BCD too. (See the AS book in this series.)

The complexity of each operation depends on what is being done. For example, when dividing two numbers there will probably be an integer answer (called the **quotient**) and a **remainder**. When multiplying two numbers the register length needed for the result is probably much larger than the register lengths that hold the original numbers. Other factors, like the number base used, coding methods, and whether 8-, 16- or 32-bit numbers are needed further complicate the issues.

Logical operations – the 'and' function

The logical operations include **and**, **or**, **not** and **xor** etc. These instructions operate in what is called **bitwise mode**, where each bit of a register is matched against the equivalent bit in another register. Consider the 'and' operation using two 8-bit registers as shown in Figure 2.4.

The table on the left of Figure 2.4 shows what is meant by a **logical 'and' operation**; an output of 1 is produced only when both inputs (i.e. al AND bl) are 1. Using this information, and matching the bits in the al and bl registers (i.e. bit 0 in the al with bit 0 in the

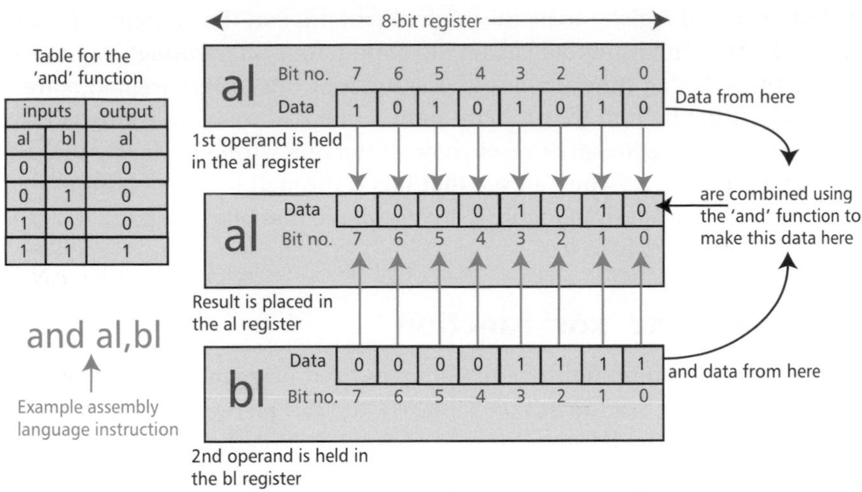

Figure 2.4 The logical operation 'and' performed using the al and bl registers

You should remember the table for the 'and' operation. Remember an output of 1 is produced only when input1 AND input2 are both at 1. The outputs are 0 under all other conditions.

bl register) we get the result in the middle of the diagram which should be the final state of the al register, where the answer has overwritten the original operand inside the al register. The 'and' function is useful for **masking** (see below).

Logical operations – the 'or' function

Figure 2.5 shows how a **logical 'or' function** is carried out. The two sources for this operation are the al and bl registers, and the result of the 'or' operation is placed into the al register. The table for the 'or' operation is shown on the left-hand side of Figure 2.5.

You should remember the table for the 'or' operation. Remember an output of 1 is produced if one input OR the other input OR both inputs are at 1.

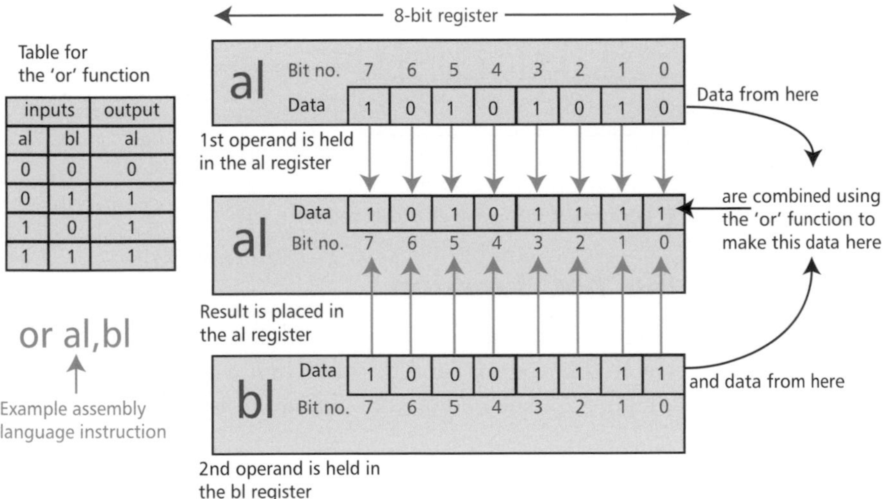

Figure 2.5 The logical operation 'or' performed using the al and bl registers

As you can see from Figure 2.5, the output from a logical 'or' is a 1 if either al OR bl OR both inputs are a 1.

Masking

The bit patterns chosen in Figures 2.4 and 2.5 have not been chosen at random but to illustrate an important concept called **masking**. When using the logical 'and' and 'or' functions, we can create a **mask** which either lets a pattern of bits through, or blocks them. If you consider the contents of the al register to be the original pattern, and the contents of the bl register to be the mask. The 'and function' has let the bottom four bits 'through', and reset the top four bits, whereas the 'or' function has let the top four bits of the original pattern 'through' and blocked off the bottom four bits by setting them all to 1s. Masking is used extensively in assembly language to set or reset some of the bits without altering the patterns of other bits. From Figure 2.5 you can see that bits 0 through to 3 (the bottom four bits) have been set (made to 1), and from Figure 2.4 you can see that bits 4 through to 7 (the top four bits) have been reset (made to 0).

Masking is particularly useful when using a microprocessor for control purposes, or for managing networks using IP addresses.

Logical operations – the 'xor' function

Figure 2.6 shows a **logical 'xor' function**. The two sources for this operation are the al and bl registers, and the result of the 'xor' operation is placed into the 'al' register. The table for the 'xor' operation is shown on the left-hand side of Figure 2.6. Note how similar the 'xor' operation is to the 'or' operation. Indeed the only difference between these two logical functions is that the 'xor' or 'exclusive or' function excludes producing an output of 1 when both the inputs are 1.

Table for the 'xor' function

inputs		output
al	bl	al
0	0	0
0	1	1
1	0	1
1	1	0

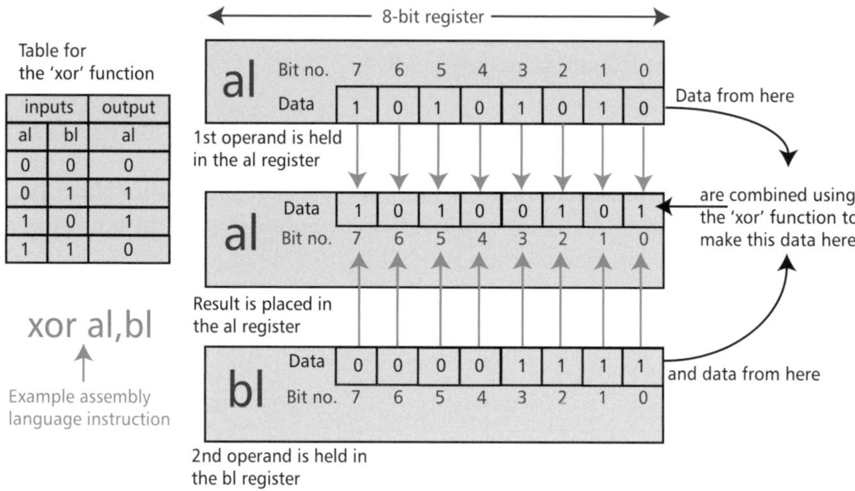

Figure 2.6 The logical operation 'xor' performed using the al and bl registers

Logical operations – the 'not' function

This operation is very simple indeed and needs only one source of data. The bits are inverted ('not' means 'the inverse' in this context) and thus bits that were 0 become 1 and any bits that were 1 become 0. Figure 2.7 shows how this operation is used in assembly language programming.

Table for the 'not' function

input	output
al	al
0	1
1	0

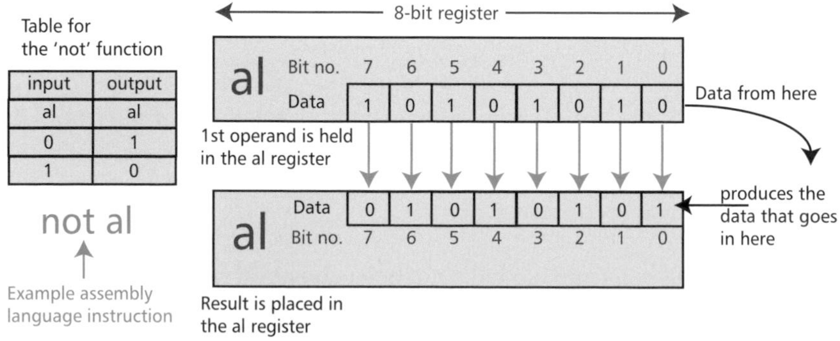

Figure 2.7 The logical operation 'not' performed using the al register

Example

A central-heating system consists of eight different zones. Each zone is controlled by a bit held in an 8-bit register using the following specification.

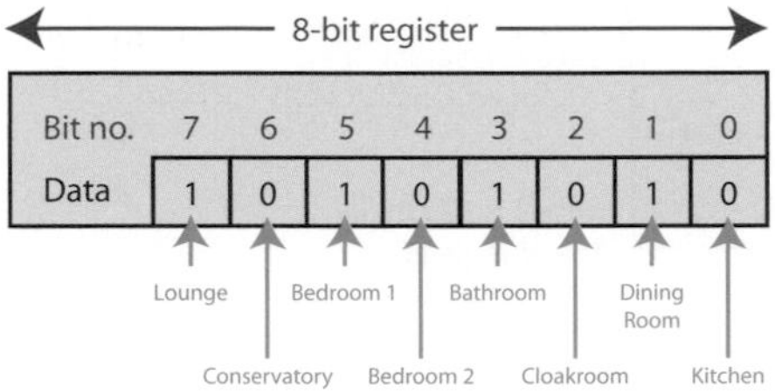

Figure 2.8 The assignments of bits for the central heating system

Assuming that the bit pattern shown above reflects the current state of the central heating (1 means 'on' and 0 means 'off'), show how masking might be used to switch on the kitchen and conservatory without affecting all the other rooms.

Solution

To switch something on, we need a function which, when combined with whatever bit is present produces a 1. The logical operation 'or' is ideal for this, because anything combined with a 0 will remain the same, and anything combined with a 1 will either remain a 1 or be turned into a 1. Therefore this will ensure that whatever state is originally present will remain unless it is combined with a 1. The solution shown here would therefore solve the problem.

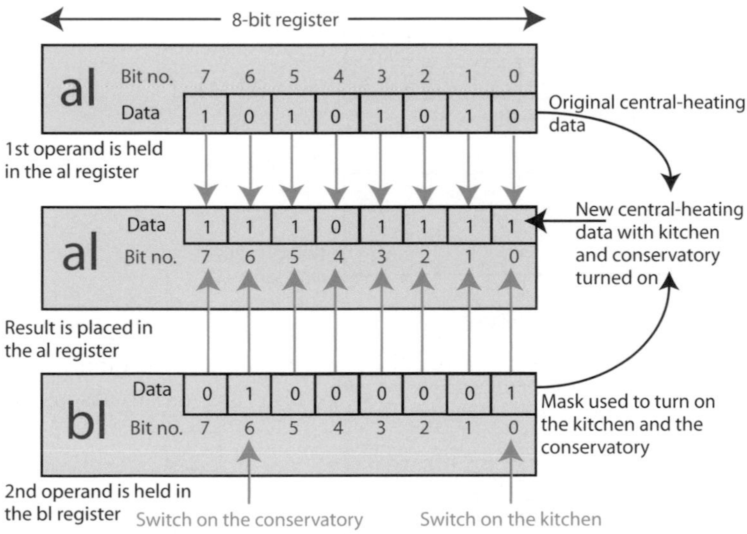

Figure 2.9 Switching on the kitchen and the conservatory heating using a mask

Shift operations – logical shift (left or right)

There are two types of shift operation, an **arithmetical shift** (see below) and a **logical shift**. A shift operation involves moving bits left or right making use of a register. Figure 2.10 shows a **logical shift left** by just one bit. The original bits in the al register (at the top of the diagram) are marched to the left, with the most significant bit falling off the left-hand side

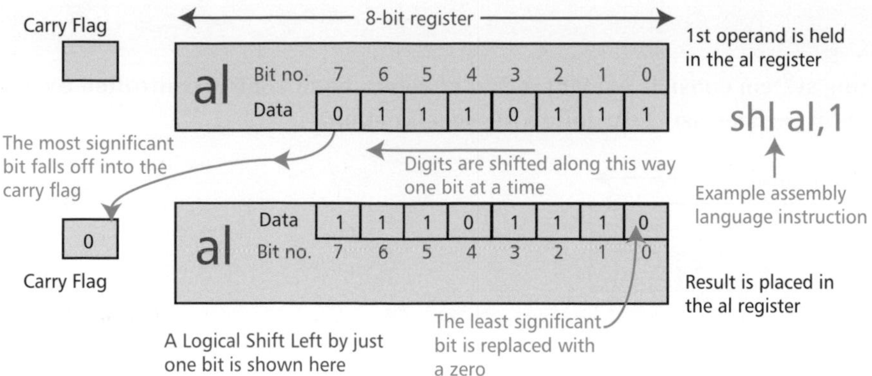

Figure 2.10 Logical shift left

and being placed into the 'carry flag' (i.e. the 'carry' in the **flag register** shown in Figure 2.10). Bit zero in the register is vacated and is replaced with a zero if a logical shift operation is being performed. A **logical shift right** is similar in principle, and if carried out the bit on the right-hand side of the al register would get placed in the carry flag, and bit 7, becoming vacated in these circumstances, would be replaced with a 0.

Shift operations – arithmetical shift (left or right)

An **arithmetical shift** operation preserves the sign of the number. You should recall from your work with binary numbers (see the AS book in this series) that a shift right would

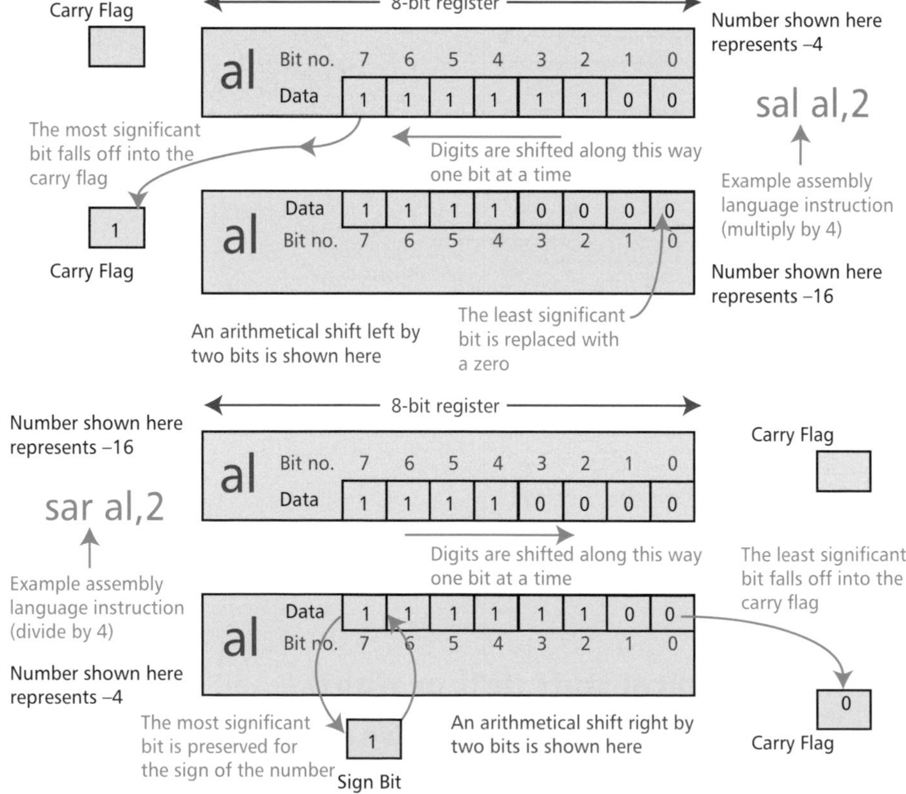

Figure 2.11 Examples of arithmetical shift left and arithmetical shift right

multiply a number by two and a shift left would divide the number by two. However, the sign bit (if **two's complement** is used) must be preserved, or negative numbers may change into positive numbers and vice versa when these multiplication or division operations are being carried out.

The sign bit must therefore be preserved, and this is the difference between a **logical shift** (which does not preserve the sign) and an arithmetical shift (which does). Figure 2.11 shows an arithmetical shift left (by 2 bits) and an arithmetical shift right (by 2 bits).

At the top of Figure 2.11 you can see the effect of an arithmetical shift left on the binary number which represents –4 (8-bit two's complement). After shifting two places left (equivalent of multiplying by 4) you see that the result represents the two's complement number for –16.

Rotate instructions

We can make use of **rotate instructions** to look at numbers which are too big to be contained in a single register (some microprocessors allow you to rotate register pairs). This scenario still applies even if the larger 32-bit registers are being used. An example using a 'Rotate Right 4-bits' instruction is shown in Figure 2.12. Instead of the digits 'falling off' the end, they are directed round the path shown by the arrows and redirected into the other end of the register.

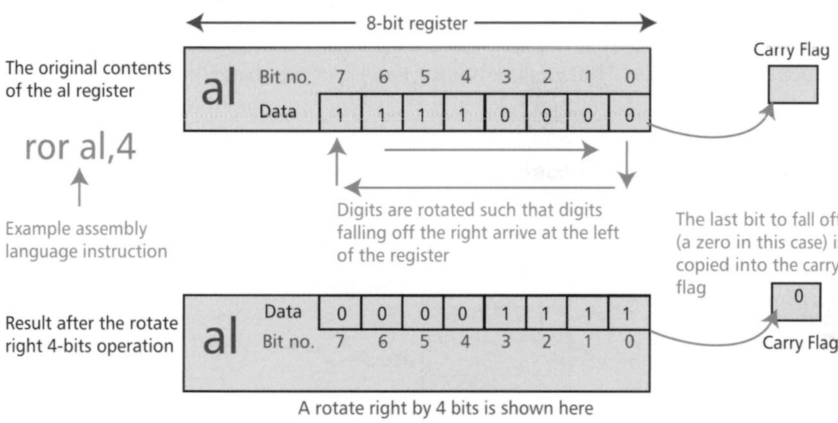

Figure 2.12 An example of a rotate instruction

It is not usually necessary to remember the syntax of any particular assembly language.

Note that the carry flag in Figure 2.12 is acting as a copy of the last digit to be shifted round from the end. There may be some instructions available in which the carry flag acts as a 1-bit extension to the register itself. Nevertheless, the ideas associated with the rotate instruction are quite simple to understand, and therefore we will not bother showing the rotate-left instruction format too.

Other basic instructions

In an examination you would probably be given all the instructions you need to use in your program. They may be different to the ones shown here, but the principles are identical.

There are many other assembly language instructions, but any instructions likely to be encountered in an A2 examination would be a variation on the themes already covered. You might, for example, encounter a **compare instruction** (**cmp** *destination*, *source* in the instruction set being considered here). This particular instruction could, for example, compare the contents of two registers and, based on the results in the flag register, you can send control to a different part of the program. The **zero flag** is set if the *destination* = *source*, or the **carry flag** is set if the *destination* < *source*. You could then use a jump instruction (see below) to send control to a different part of the program depending on the original comparison. This is how the 'if-then-else' type statements are used in assembly language, and there are some examples of doing this below.

Program control instructions

If no syntax is given in an examination, then use the syntax of the instructions with which you are most familiar.

An assembly language program which could only operate in a serial fashion (one instruction after another) would not be very powerful, and would mean that there is no decision-making element. We obviously need to control programs in more sophisticated ways than this, and instructions are therefore required to divert the flow of the program to different parts depending on the state of some particular condition. These essential and important assembly language instructions are known as the **jump instructions**.

Unconditional jumps

This type of instruction forces an unconditional jump to some other part of the program, usually identified by means of a label. The **mnemonic** representing the op code (operation code) for this is 'jmp', and we have chosen a label called 'next'.

Table 2.8 Unconditional jump

Label	Op code	Operands	Comments
	jmp	next	;This is an example of an unconditional jump to a label called 'next'

You will recall that the first part of the assembly language instruction format (not used so far in this chapter) enables us to use a label which is simply a tag placed at some other part of the program pointing to a particular place in memory where some alternative assembly language instructions can be found and therefore executed. Figure 2.13 shows how an

Using non-relocatable code is usually not a good idea because of the lack of transferability of the software when run on machines with different memory maps.

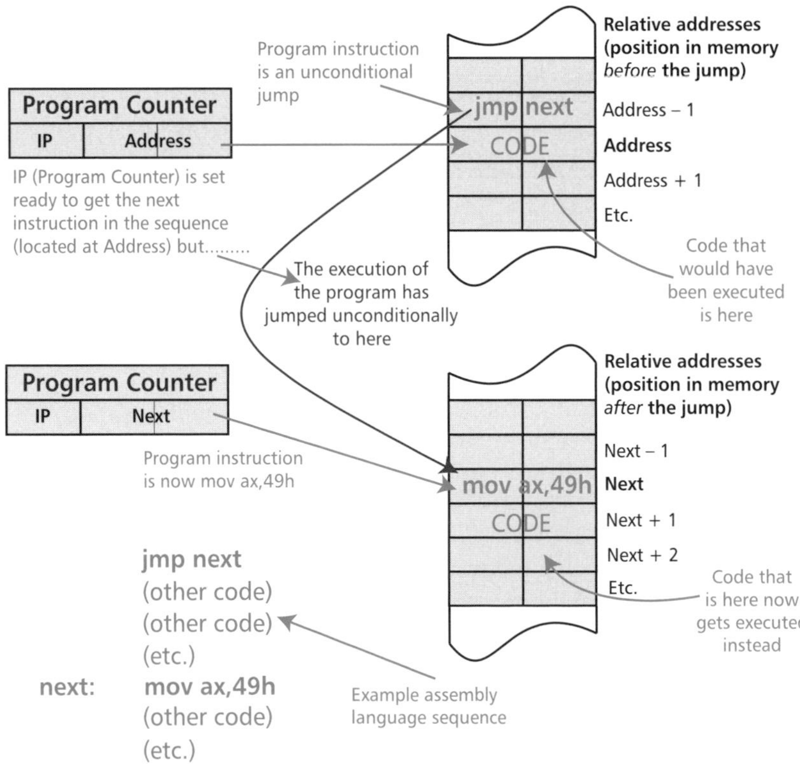

Figure 2.13 An unconditional jump alters the next code to be executed

unconditional jump would be used in practice. When the 'jmp next' instruction is encountered, the program counter (called the IP register in the assembly language resister set that we are currently using) gets put to whatever address is identified by the label 'next'.

From the top half of Figure 2.13 you can see how the unconditional jump, the instruction currently being executed by the microprocessor, causes the program counter to be put equal to the value of the memory location which is labelled 'next'. Although physically possible to do so, it is not usually good practice to specify an absolute value for the address of a particular memory location – it is far better to use a label instead. This practice usually enables us to relocate the code more easily (i.e. run it in any part of the memory).

Conditional jumps

Many different types of jump command are available, and this variety stems from the multitude of ways in which most microprocessors can address different areas of memory, as shown at the beginning of the chapter. The deciding conditions as to whether or not the jump is made usually stem from examination of the state of the flags inside the flag register (see the following).

Table 2.9 Conditional jumps

Label	Op code	Operands	Comments
	jno	next	;Jump if no overflow (i.e. the 'O' flag = 0)
	js	next	;Jump on a sign bit (i.e. S = 1)
	jcxz	Next	;Jump if the cx flag is zero (i.e. CX = 0)

It would take too long to demonstrate them all, but it is important to appreciate some typical jump conditions. You will recall that a flag register exists to flag different conditions happening inside the processors, so it is not surprising, therefore, to find that the flag register plays a pivotal role in helping to decide if jumps are to take place. Therefore, conditions like 'jump if no overflow' or 'jump if carry set', for example, are typical of the types of conditions which may be used. The actual distance over which a jump may take place depends on how many bytes are used to hold the jump address. For example, if 1 byte is used, then a jump to +127 or −128 with respect to the current location could be made. However, if a 2-byte address is used, then we can go to +32 767 or −32 768. (See the first AS book in this series.) Four bytes would be needed to cover the full 4 Gigabyte range possible on a microprocessor with a 32-bit address bus.

Some assembly language examples

For the purpose of the A2 examination you will probably be given a list of assembly language instructions (not necessarily with the same **syntax** shown in this chapter) and be expected to solve some relatively simple problems making use of your knowledge of addressing modes, arithmetical and logical instructions, jump instructions and labels.

Some typical examples now follow. They are *not* fully blown programs. In practice you would have to assemble them using an assembler like **MASM** (Microsoft's assembler), and also provide extra information like 'where in memory the program is to be run'. This is covered briefly later in this chapter. You will recall that all high-level languages must eventually be turned into machine code to run on the computer, and the first couple of examples show how this might be accomplished.

Example

You should be familiar with high-level language statements. The following code, written in Basic, tests to see if the value of a variable called 'result' is equal to 40 and, if true, sets a variable called 'answer' to have a value of 50, else the value of the variable 'answer' is set to zero.

```
If result = 40 THEN
   answer = 50
Else
   answer = 0
EndIf
```

The code shown above now needs to be translated into some equivalent assembly language instructions. Suggest how this might be done by using some of the following instructions and the 32-bit register set shown in Figure 2.3.

Table 2.10 Assembly language instructions

Label	Op code	Operands	Comments
	mov	destination, source	;Move the value of 'source' into the destination
	cmp	destination, source	;Compare the value of the source with the destination. (The zero flag is set if they are the same, or the carry flag is set if source < destination)
	jnz	label	;Jump to a label if the zero flag is not set
	jz	label	;Jump to a label if the zero flag is set
	jc	label	;Jump to a label if the carry flag is set

Solution

First let's *assume* that the result is contained in a memory location with a label called 'result'. The assembly language code, designed to produce the same results as the multiple if-then-else statements shown above could be as follows. Copious comments are given to explain how this particular snippet of assembly language would work.

Table 2.11 Assembly language instructions

Label	Op code	Operands	Comments
	mov	eax, 40	;Move the value '40 decimal' into the eax register. This is the 32-bit name for the 8-bit ax register used earlier
	cmp	eax, result	;Compare the value of 40 (the destination), with the value of the result (the source)
	jz	same	;Jump to the label called 'same' because the result is equal to 40, if the zero flag is set, because the answer needs putting equal to 50
	mov	eax, 0	;We have arrived here because the result is not 40, therefore we set eax to 0
	jmp	next	;Unconditional jump to last part of the program to save us inadvertently altering the value to 50
same:	mov	eax, 50	;We have arrived here because the result is 40, therefore we set eax to 50
next:	mov	answer, eax	;The contents of the eax register are stored in a memory location labelled 'answer'

You should note that this is only one of a possible range of solutions to this problem. By **dry running** the above assembly language code, you should be able to see that the eax register contains the answer, which is either 0 or 50, depending on the comparison made. Do not confuse the destination and source (outlined earlier when addressing modes were considered). The content of the eax register (0 or 50) is placed into a memory location labelled answer.

Example

Loop structures are common in all high-level languages. Suggest how the following structure could be implemented making use of assembly language.

```
while temperature <= 100 do
   temperature = temperature + 1
endwhile
```

The following assembly language instructions would be suitable for the above task.

Table 2.12 Assembly language instructions

Label	Op code	Operands	Comments
	inc	eax	;Increment the contents of the eax register by 1
	cmp	destination, source	;Compare the value of the source with the destination. (The zero flag is set if they are the same, or the carry flag is set if source < destination)
	jbe	label	;Jump to the label if the unsigned value of the destination is less than or equal to the value of the source
	jmp	label	;Jump to a label unconditionally

Solution

The 'jbe' jump instruction is the key to the solution of this problem. Therefore, we need to set up the destination to be the eax register and the source to be the value of the temperature. The unconditional jump instruction will enable us to go round the loop until the condition is true.

Table 2.13 Assembly language instructions

Label	Op code	Operands	Comments
	mov	eax, temperature	;Put the value of the memory location labelled 'temperature' into the eax register
begin:	cmp	eax, 100	;Compare the eax (destination) with the value 100 (source)
	jbe	next	;Jump to next (i.e. exit the loop) if this is true. (If the unsigned value of the destination is less than or equal to the value of the source)
	inc	eax	;Increment the value of the temperature, stored in the eax register
	jmp	begin	;Go round the loop again
next:			

We will assume that the current temperature is stored in a memory location labelled 'temperature'.

You should note that this is only one of a possible range of solutions to this problem. By **dry running** the above assembly language code, you should be able to see that the loop is being continually executed until the appropriate condition is met, in which case we exit the loop.

The assembler

An **assembler** is software that converts the assembly language mnemonics (the instructions used in the last few examples) into machine code ready for execution on the **target machine** (i.e. the machine on which the program will be run). Without an assembler you would have to translate each assembly language mnemonic into machine code by hand; a tedious and error-prone task.

If hand assembly is undertaken, we would have to decide exactly where the instructions would be placed in memory.

With an assembler, provided it has information about where in the memory to start the object code, it takes care of the positioning of all the code for you. This is a big bonus because you can make good use of labels, as demonstrated in the last example.

The assembly language mnemonics would normally have to be written using a **text editor**. The listing of the **assembly language mnemonics** is called the **source code** or the **source program**. After the assembly process has been carried out, we end up with the machine-code program which is called the **object code** or the **object program**. These processes are shown in Figure 2.14.

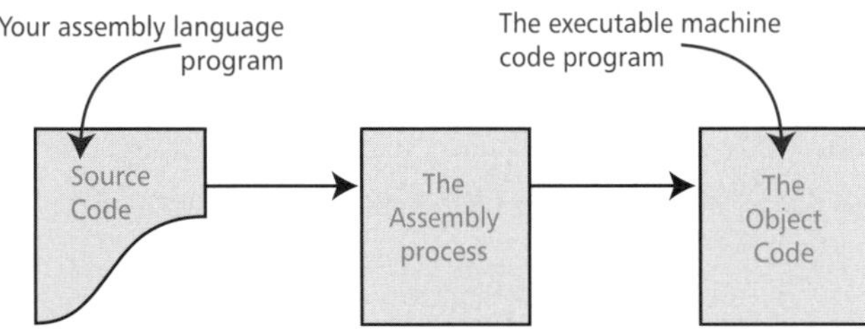

Figure 2.14 The process of assembly

The main features of a typical assembler

Besides obvious features, such as translating the source code into the object code, the main features of an assembler (*not in any order of importance*) are:

- Use of **symbolic addressing**, i.e. the assembler will work out the address values for any labels that have been correctly used in the source program. You can give names to specific memory locations where data is to be found.
- It performs arithmetic by including the appropriate signs in the source code listing.
- Use of different bases, e.g. base two, eight, 16 and decimal (denary) are often supported.
- It alerts the user to any errors during the assembly process, such as incorrect instructions or other errors in syntax.
- The user can tell the loader program (see below) where parts of the program or data should be placed inside the computer's memory.
- It produces a listing of the source code or object code, together with error messages, formatted to the user's requirements. It produces a listing with comments enabling you to work manually through parts of the program to sort out any **bugs**.
- It works out all the necessary forward and backward references such as jumps and subroutines. This is a *very* tedious process if carried out manually.
- It may use just one instruction to define a sequence of other instructions. It then converts these instructions into the equivalent set of machine-code instructions. These are called **macros**.

Some of the above operations, such as allocating areas of memory are not translated into machine-code instructions. These extra instructions are called **assembler directives** or **pseudo-operations** because they are really instructions to the assembler and not actual code to be executed on the target machine.

The last few sections here outline typical processes that have to be carried out when assembling the source code, but we do not go into detail about using any particular assembler. However, if you have access to MASM (Microsoft's Assembler) or something similar, do make use of it because the material covered in this chapter will be a lot easier to understand. Typical methods used are shown in Figure 2.15, and are outlined in more detail here. This numbered section shows how to start the problem, what is typically covered at each stage of the solution, and what has to be done in the event of any errors being encountered.

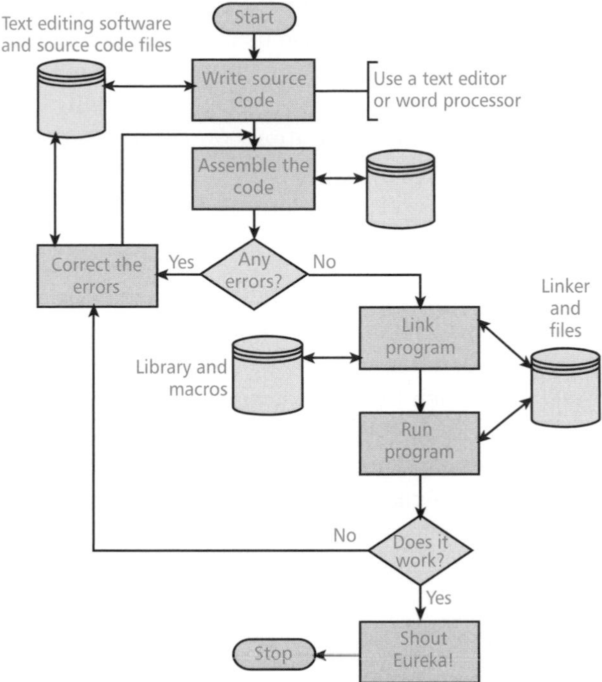

Figure 2.15 Assembling an assembly language program using a typical assembler

Assembling an assembly language program

We have covered a lot of complex and detailed information in this chapter. It is important to get clear in your own mind exactly what has to happen when you go through the assembly process, i.e. what do you *actually have to do* to get an assembly language program working?

1 The problem to be solved must be broken down into a suitable form, making use of **flowcharts**, **pseudocode**, or a clear set of written statements.

2 Code the problem by making use of assembly language mnemonics. The code must be written either by making use of a text editor or a word processor that can produce ASCII text. This code must be combined with all the appropriate directives and macros etc. (see below) that will make it run on the actual target machine.

3 Assemble the program using the source code produced above by making use of an appropriate assembler for your particular machine.

4 If the assembler produces any errors these must be corrected by going back to step 2, changing the source code, and re-assembling. Errors detected at this stage would include invalid instructions or other **syntax errors**.

5 Link the code and add any macros. These are pre-written routines which typically can be called up from a **library**. The source code is then converted into **executable code**, i.e. the code that can be run on a particular machine, which is finally linked to any other code that might be needed by using the **linker program**.

6 If any execution errors are encountered, or the program assembles incorrectly (i.e. it is not syntactically correct), your solution will not produce the desired results. If this is so

then you will have to return to step 2 yet again, find the errors, alter the source code, then re-assemble and run the linking programs again.

It is most advisable to save your program on disk *before* running it. This is because certain errors can cause the machine to crash, thus destroying your program. Such errors are called **fatal errors**. On many systems there are also **debuggers** that help you to single-step through assembly language code as it is being run. Without these useful **utilities** it is often difficult, if not impossible, to see why a program does not produce the desired output. The only alternative would be to do a very tedious **dry run** manually. The exact details to be carried out on particular machines vary, but they are all variations on the above theme. The above ideas are summarised in Figure 2.15.

Directives and pseudo-operations

These are operations that *do not form part of the actual program*. They are not assembly language instructions in the normal sense but instructions to the assembler. They will not produce machine code that forms part of your program. For example, in the MASM system, the END command tells the assembler when to stop assembling. There are many other uses of pseudo-ops and directives such as telling the assembler the position in memory at which the code is to start being assembled, or convenient ways to define bytes and words. Without help such as this, assembly language programs would be much more tedious and difficult to write. However, remembering such details is best left to the reader when an individual assembly language (or subset of one) is studied.

Do make use of an actual assembler; it makes the work covered here much easier to understand.

An enormous amount of satisfaction can be gained from being able to control a microprocessor at a fundamental level.

Calling operating system functions

Other basic operations must also be carried out. Examples would be printing characters on the screen, getting characters from the keyboard, opening or closing a file, or any of the many chores that might need to be done. It would be inefficient if you had to write all these routines from scratch. Therefore, most computer systems have ways of calling up the appropriate subroutines that reside somewhere inside the **operating system**. Calls to these operating system routines often make use of **interrupts** (see chapter 1), i.e. your program is interrupted to call a routine that resides somewhere else in the computer. After carrying out the required task, control is passed back to your original program. These calls let the user have access to routines, which saves them the bother of having to work out the sequence of instructions that would be necessary to carry out the same tasks routinely carried out by the operating system.

Example

When writing assembly language programs, *macros*, *assembler directives* and *calls to the operating system* are frequently encountered. Explain the terms in *italics*, and give an example of where each may typically be used.

Solution

When using assembly language, a macro is the name given to a single instruction which can be replaced by a large number of pre-written instructions. It saves the programmer the bother of having to type the same code again and again. A macro can literally be anything, but typically a macro might be some code used to read data from a bar-code reader.

An assembler directive is an instruction to the assembler rather than source code which is to be assembled into object code. Assembler directives provide a whole host of extra functionality like telling the assembler where to assemble the code in the computer's memory or defining bytes and words.

Remember that the operating system itself is just a large number of assembly language routines working together. It would be silly to have to reinvent the wheel to accomplish mundane tasks like sending characters to a printer or reading characters from a disk, for example. Therefore, calls are made to operating system routines by name, and parameters may be passed over to them and retrieved from them. Without hundreds of these operating system calls, writing assembly language programs would be very much harder and more tedious to do.

Self-test questions

1 Most low-level programming is carried out using assembly language. What typical scenario might mean that a program has to be written in machine code?

2 Why do assembly language instructions written for one type of machine not run on another?

3 What is the purpose of the following parts of a typical assembly language instruction?
(a) Label (b) Operation code (c) Operands (d) Comments.

4 Why are different modes of addressing encountered when programming in assembly language? Explain what is meant by immediate, direct, indirect and indexed addressing.

5 An assembly language instruction set may be broken down into subsets like 'logical', 'arithmetical' and 'control'. Making use of the arithmetical subset outlined in this chapter, show how two simple one-byte integer binary numbers may be added together.

6 Explain how a mask may be used to prevent alteration of the top (most significant) three bits and the bottom (least significant) two bits but set the rest of the bits in the register to 1.

7 Carefully explain the difference between an arithmetical and a logical shift operation. Show, by making use of the 16-bit shift register in the following diagram, how the contents of the register would be altered by the operations shown after the diagram.

16-bit register

Bit numbers															
15	14	13	12	11	10	9	8	7	6	5	4	3	2	1	0
1	1	1	1	0	0	0	0	1	1	1	1	0	0	0	0

(a) Logical shift left by 3 places
(b) Arithmetical shift left by 3 places
(c) Logical shift right by 2 places
(d) Arithmetical shift right by 2 places

8 Explain, by using examples, how logical operations like 'AND' and 'OR' may be carried out by using the registers inside a typical microprocessor.

9 (a) What is an assembler?
(b) Outline four advantages that using an assembler will give over manually creating the equivalent machine code.

10 (a) What is meant by the term 'source code'?
(b) What is meant by the term 'object code'?
(c) Outline the typical stages that need to be carried out to convert source code into object code when using a typical assembler.

11 What is the function of a debugger when using an assembler?

12 What is meant by the term 'pseudo-operation' or 'assembler directive' when using an assembler?

13 Why is it useful to link assembly language routines to routines that make up the operating system? Outline three typical routines that might be called up in this way.

14 Making use of the syntax used for assembly language in this chapter, write an assembly language program to test the value of the contents of a 16-bit accumulator. You should jump to a routine labelled 'accumzero' if it is zero, or jump to a routine called 'accumnonzero' in all other cases. Make sure that you provide a variety of suitable comments to explain your methods.

3 Programming concepts

In this chapter you will learn about:

- An introduction to high-level languages and their development
- Generations of languages
- The characteristics and classification of high-level languages
- Which programming language is best for developing particular applications
- Programming paradigms, imperative and declarative languages
- Structured programming
- Logic programming with examples using Prolog
- Object-oriented programming

Introduction to high-level languages

You should already have considerable experience of programming in at least one high-level language (see the AS book in this series).

At A2 level we need to take a more formal look at high-level languages, and classify them according to their main schemes of working.

What a fabulous contribution high-level languages have made. Without them we would be programming computers using low-level languages like the machine code and assembly language covered earlier. Without high-level languages the development of the computer would be decades behind the current levels of performance.

When humans solve problems we operate in ways very different to the ways in which a machine would operate to solve the same problem. The further we can get from the **bits** and **registers** used in the computer's architecture the better, especially if the path taken gets us closer to the way in which humans prefer to think. Such human-oriented methods include *mathematics*, *logic*, *English-like statements*, or any method that enables us to concisely and elegantly communicate with the computer without having to 'speak' to the computer in its primitive low-level language. Remember that the computer's language may be primitive, but what you can achieve with it is not!

Natural or formal languages

Due to current limitations of computer hardware and software, computer languages are much more restrictive than human language. Human languages such as English and French belong to a class of *context-sensitive languages* or **natural languages**. This is because the meaning (**semantics**) of these languages depends upon the context being used, and is not just based on the legal arrangement (syntax) of the words.

Computer languages are *context free*, which means that they are easier to analyse by machine. Each line of a program must be precisely defined and unambiguous. We are still a long way from being able to have prolonged and intelligent conversations with a computer system, especially one which will allow for the idiosyncrasies in our context-sensitive speech. Context-free languages (computer-type languages) are also known as **formal languages**, and much work has gone into the development of these.

High-level language development

It is important to realise that the path of high-level language development has been neither straight nor smooth. *Political decisions*, *monetary considerations* and other factors have had just as great an impact on development as advances in methodology! The language **C**,

Remember that the criteria for choosing a language must also include factors like politics, economics, availability and experience. These are in addition to the technical considerations that will be covered below.

for example – although a superb language in its own right – proved to be very popular because it was intimately connected with **Unix**, which was, and still is, one of the most powerful operating-system platforms (Linux is derived from Unix).

Many languages have come and gone because they were not accepted in tightly controlled **hardware**, **software** and **operating system** environments. You should realise that people are quite naturally reluctant to relearn methods just because a different language comes along. This is one of the main reasons why **COBOL** has reigned supreme for such a long time – the enormous investment in programs already written, the billions of dollars that are controlled by COBOL programs each day, and the huge number of programmers that have been appropriately trained, are factors which obviously cannot be ignored. There must be very compelling reasons indeed for the professionals to start again with any new language. It is also important to realise that most languages pass through *stages of evolution*. Languages which have stood the test of time have probably been redefined (usually by adding new and better features) at least several times.

Programming paradigms

When students are asked to describe a particular paradigm, or to give an example of a language which belongs to a particular paradigm, some degree of confusion exists.

To solve this dilemma you should always choose the main paradigm, and give far less importance to other paradigms embedded within it. Therefore, C++ rightly belongs to the object-oriented programming group, even though it is also a procedural language.

A **programming paradigm** is the name given to the *main* method (ideas, concepts or models) that is used to solve a problem using a particular programming language. **C++**, for example, is a language that is best suited to solutions making use of the concept of **objects**, *because* C++ has been designed using an **object-oriented programming** paradigm.

The methods used to solve a problem in one language may therefore be very different to solving the *same problem* using a language which utilises a completely different paradigm. Different levels of abstraction are important because different paradigms have been leading the way to developing more sophisticated systems with fewer errors, greater complexity and less development time. Programming paradigms represent a *level of abstraction* that is further removed from the bits and registers inside the actual machine.

As you read through the following material you will realise that most languages have elements of different paradigms embedded within them. This is because of the historical ways in which these languages have been developed. C++, for example, is both **procedural** *and* **object oriented**.

Imperative programming – introduction

The **imperative programming** paradigm typifies languages like machine code, assembly language, **DML** (a **data manipulation language** from **SQL**) and the very early versions of the high-level language **Basic**. It involves writing sequences of instructions (called **imperatives**), which directly control the state of the system. It is up to the programmer to control the system in more rudimentary ways, compared to using a **procedural language** like **Pascal**, **FORTRAN**, **COBOL** and later versions of **BASIC**. The imperative programming style consists of writing sequences of imperative statements, and is often more difficult to follow because of this. Control structures (like For-to-next and Repeat Until) would have to be built up from the simpler imperative statements, and Assembly-Language programmers are very adept at doing this, making use of a huge variety of standard routines which have been developed over the years (see example on page 29).

It should be realised that the hardware inside the computer will only be able to run code written in imperative form. This is because machine code is an imperative language, and this represents the *only* programming paradigm that will actually run at low level on the computer. Other programming paradigms are just different levels of abstraction for the convenience of humans.

The early versions of imperative languages, like the original versions of Basic, had few control structures, which therefore forced programmers to make excessive use of unconditional jumps like the 'GOTO'. Some code is shown here; it is badly written and illustrates non-structured programming in an imperative style, using an early version of Basic.

It is important to realise that the programs given here are for illustrative purposes only to compare the imperative and procedural paradigms. You should note that a procedural program does not have to make use of procedures as in the example shown here. Procedures have been used because it illustrates the stark contrast between the facilities available to programmers if procedural programming is used.

This is a simple program which responds with 'woof' if 'dog' is input or 'meow' if 'cat' is typed in. However, as you can see from this small piece of code, the logic is not too easy to follow. Imagine a project with 'half a million lines of code' written in the same style! It would be almost impossible to debug because the logic would be so convoluted. It was against this background that **procedural programming** was developed.

Some code written in an imperative programming style

```
10 INPUT A$
20 IF A$ = "DOG" THEN GOTO 40
30 GOTO 60
40 PRINT "WOOF"
50 GOTO 90
60 IF A$ = "CAT" THEN GOTO 80
70 GOTO 90
80 PRINT "MEOW"
90 END
```

Advantages of imperative programming

Imperative programming has no advantages over the other paradigms outlined in the following sections because imperative programming was the first paradigm to be developed and other paradigms were invented to get over its limitations.

Procedural programming – introduction

Procedural programming still involves writing sequences of instructions to solve a problem, but much better structures are available like control loops and splitting up the problem into smaller self-contained units which are called **procedures** or **subroutines**. Modern procedural programming languages like FORTRAN, COBOL and Basic *support procedural programming methods*, and students of today are indeed fortunate that they have such a rich variety of functionality from which to choose.

Modern procedural languages are well structured and have a good variety of control structures and other features which aid readability and maintenance.

Procedural programming is ideal for solving problems expressed hierarchically, by means of a **hierarchical diagram**. By careful use of procedures, and passing parameters by value or by reference, **algorithms** may be modularised, and thus many people can be set to work on large systems. (See the first AS book in this series.) However, imperative and procedural programming methods alone become increasingly ineffective when systems become overly complex, and this is one of the reasons why other paradigms like object-oriented programming, logic programming and functional programming have been developed.

Some code written in a procedural programming style

```
Input animal$
Proc animal_noise(animal$)
End

Defproc animal_noise(animal$)
   If animal$ = "Dog" then print
   "Woof"
   IF animal$ = "Cat" then print
   "meow"
End Proc
```

The same program, written in a procedural style can be seen here. The part of the program which analyses the input to determine which noise should be made is *explicitly clear* from the procedure definition. Two 'if then' control structures and sensible variable names have also been used, just to make the point that this program is a much better **structured**

program (see below) than the one shown in the imperative programming paradigm section above.

Advantages of procedural programming

Some of the advantages of procedural programming are that problems may be structured more carefully compared with imperative methods. One way of doing this is by splitting up the problem into more manageable modules. These modules may then be joined together to form the complete solution. A number of people may therefore work on the same overall problem, each with the task of tackling a particular sub-problem.

At present, for the purpose of A2 computing, you are not expected to be able to write any code using a functional language.

Coding in languages like Clean and Haskell is more appropriate for Computer Science at degree level.

Functional programming – introduction

This method involves describing what must be achieved by writing the problem as though it were a series of mathematical or *other types* of functions. This paradigm evaluates functional expressions rather than 'sequences of commands', which typifies the imperative method. Part of the power of this method derives from the fact that functions can act as inputs to other functions, and elegant methods of solution to some types of problem are possible compared with the same problems expressed imperatively. For purely functional languages there are also fewer side effects because *function calls do not modify variables in other parts of the program*. Inadvertently messing up global variables is a common problem with imperative and procedural programming.

Languages which typify this programming paradigm are **LISP**, **Clean** and **Haskell**. Functional programming is much more complex than the simple ideas conveyed here. You should recall that these ideas are similar to those regarding mathematical functions covered in elementary mathematics. The following example shows how $f(x)$, a function of x, is evaluated for a particular value of x.

$$f(x) = x^2 + 1$$

In the above case, if $x = 2$, then $f(2)$ is evaluated by putting 2 into the function to get $2^2 + 1 = 5$. Therefore, 5 is output when 2 is input to this function. Similar ideas can easily be translated to demonstrate a few functional programming techniques shown by the small snippet of code.

The top part of the code shows a couple of function definitions which are written to sum integer numbers from n down to and including zero. i.e. $n + (n - 1) + (n - 2) + \ldots + 3 + 2 + 1 + 0$.

```
Code written in a functional
programming style
Sum(0) = 0
Sum(n) = n + Sum(n - 1)

A dry run of how the above
function works out Sum (3)
Sum (3) = 3 + Sum (2)
Sum (3) = 3 + 2 + Sum(1)
Sum (3) = 3 + 2 + 1 + Sum(0)
Sum (3) = 3 + 2 + 1 + 0
Sum (3) = 6
```

Although the computer would probably add the numbers as it goes along, the explanation at the bottom of the code shows how repeated calls to the function Sum(n) are evaluated by a technique called **recursion**. The early imperative languages that supported function calls did not allow them to operate recursively, but recursion is one of the cornerstones of functional programming. When solving this sort of problem, functional programming provides elegant solutions with the minimum amount of code.

You would be right in assuming that the function definitions above could be accomplished by calling functions recursively in a procedural language that supports these features (most modern procedural languages do). However, the logic behind functional languages like Clean and Haskell are beyond the scope of this book at A2 level.

Functional languages are not limited to processing numerical data like the example shown here. Whole structures can be defined to process just about any information that can be defined on a computer because virtually anything can be defined as a function. Functional languages like Clean provide excellent interactive interfaces to current versions of operating systems such as Windows and Linux, for example.

Advantages of functional programming

Functional programming promotes fast development time because problems can usually be expressed with fewer lines of code compared with procedural programming. The compiled code is extremely fast, and the execution of applications developed with functional programs tends to be more efficient compared with those that were developed using a procedural paradigm. Functions can be used to build up and process very large structures with appropriate input and output.

Logic programming – introduction

Logic programming concentrates on the descriptive side of defining **relationships**. To get output from a logic program we ask sets of **questions** by defining **queries** to interrogate the **knowledge base** built from our relationship definitions. In this type of programming environment we do *not* have to write sequences of instructions (**imperatives**) which tell the computer exactly what to do, and *this level of abstraction helps us to concentrate on the solution itself, rather than the steps necessary to get to the solution.*

The **logic programming paradigm** derives from the sort of arguments you may hear when two people are having a conversation using conventional logic. You might, for example, use statements like, 'If that is true then we can deduce that this is true too'. *Logic programming revolves around 'declaring* **facts**', *'defining* **rules**' *and 'asking* questions' (see below). There is a sound mathematical basis behind these rules of logic called 'predicate calculus', but *at A2 level you have only to understand a few simple principles, involving* facts, questions, rules, lists *and the technique of* recursion.

You need to cover logic programming in more detail.

Examination questions may be asked on this programming paradigm, and without any practice you will be seriously disadvantaged.

Some excellent Prolog compilers are available free on the Internet.

Logic programming – Prolog facts

A fact is used to declare *something that is unconditionally true*. In **Prolog** a fact is made up of a 'name' or a **predicate**, and a number of **arguments** or 'objects', which could be zero. Examples of simple facts are as follows.

```
parent(tom,dick).          % Tom is a parent of Dick
like(ray,food).            % Ray likes food
man(spencer).              % Spencer is a man
mother(sue,veron).         % Sue is the mother of Veron
```

All the predicates *must begin with a lower-case letter*, and the arguments *must also begin with a lower-case letter*. This is why people's names are spelt using a lower-case letter at the beginning. If you start an argument name with an upper-case letter it becomes a **variable**, as you will see in the next section. You should note that there are no correct or incorrect ways of ordering the arguments, but the fact '`likes(mary,tom)`', for example, meaning that 'Mary likes Tom' does not imply that 'Tom likes Mary'. It is up to the programmer to make sure that consistency is applied regarding the ways in which the rules

A single-line comment in Prolog starts off with a % sign.

%this is a comment

An alternative is to use a multi-line comment which starts with '/*' and ends with '*/'.

/* this is a comment too /*

are defined and used. If we wish for Tom to like Mary too, then another program statement is needed to explicitly state this fact, or we could define a new rule. No spaces are allowed in predicate names or argument names, but the underscore character can be used in exactly the same way as it is used in other high-level languages. Therefore a predicate name such as 'author_of_fiction' would be valid in the language Prolog.

Example

Making use of Prolog, define the following simple facts.

(a) Mickey Mouse is a cartoon character.

(b) Donald can play football.

(c) Bert is 75 years old.

(d) Samantha has four children called Dotty, Spotty, Lotty and Potty.

Solution

(a) cartoon_character(mickey_mouse).

(b) play_football(donald).

(c) age(bert,75).

(d) children_of(samantha,dotty,spotty,lotty,potty)./* This predicate is defined such that Samantha is the parent, and the four arguments that follow represent her children.*/

In part (d) of the last example, it is up to the programmer to interpret the results properly according to the ways in which the facts have been defined.

Logic programming – Prolog rules

Note how easy it is to build up 'rules' from the limited number of statements we have covered already.

A rule is *used to specify the condition(s) that must be satisfied if something is to be regarded as being true*. Consider the rule for defining the relationship 'brother_of'. It would seem to be quite logical to say that 'X is a brother of Y' if 'X is male' and 'X has the same parents as Y'. In Prolog, this rule could be written as follows, but this is not actually the best definition (see the section which deals with Prolog questions for an explanation of this!). Note that capital letters (X, Y, M and F) are being used here because they represent variables.

```
brother_of(X,Y) :-      % x is a brother of y if
  male(X),              % x is male and
  parents(X,M,F),       % x has mother m and father f and
  parents(Y,M,F).       % y has mother m and father f
```

Failing to appreciate Prolog's naming convention will often be the source of errors in your Prolog programs.

Consider the statement 'brother_of(X,Y) :-'. This is the head of the **rule** and is called the *conclusion*; the other three statements in the main body of the rule are called the *conditions*. You should note that condition (1) *and* condition (2) *and* condition (3) must all apply for the conclusion at the head of the rule to be true. The 'AND' function is implied by the use of the comma at the end of each condition, and the full stop at the end of the last condition denotes the end of the rule. Rules can be written horizontally if the correct syntax is used. The above rule could therefore have been entered into a **Prolog compiler** as:

```
brother_of(X,Y) :- male(X),parents(X,M,F),parents(Y,M,F).
```

X, Y, M and F in the above program are all variables because they start off with a capital letter. If lower-case letters are used then X would not be a variable, for example, but could be somebody with the name 'X'! *This naming convention is important.*

The ',' represents an 'AND' operation but a ';' can be used to represent an 'OR' operation (see the next margin entry).

Example

Making use of the logic programming language Prolog, define the following rules:
(a) 'Mother of' (b) 'Grandfather of'

Solution

(a) 'X is a mother of Y' if 'X is the parent of Y' and 'X is female'. In Prolog this rule could be written as:

```
Mother(X,Y) :- female(X), parent(X,Y).
```

(b) This is a lot more complex. To solve this problem you should think about a family tree structure like that shown in Figure 3.1. Here GF represents the grandfather on the father's side, and GM represents the grandfather on the mother's side.

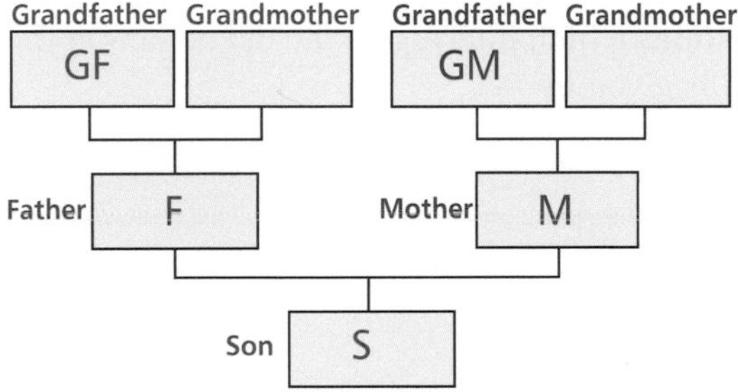

Figure 3.1 Part of a family tree for the relationship 'grandfather'

In the last example, part (b), in addition to this rule we would obviously have to add some additional names using facts like 'parent_of' to make the rule work in an actual Prolog program, and this is covered below when dealing with Prolog questions.

There are two possible sets of rules for grandfather, one on the father's side (the first condition) and one on the mother's side (the second condition).

```
Grandfather_of(GF,S) :-
 male(GF), parent_of(GF,F), parent_of(F,S);
 male(GM), parent_of(GM,M), parent_of (M,S).
```

Note that the ';' at the end of the second line represents 'OR', and the ',' represents 'AND' as described above.

Logic programming – Prolog questions

Having established a **knowledge base** of facts and rules we can now ask simple questions, but first we put in a few extra facts which will reflect the family tree shown in Figure 3.2. This is shown in the first eight lines of the following Prolog code.

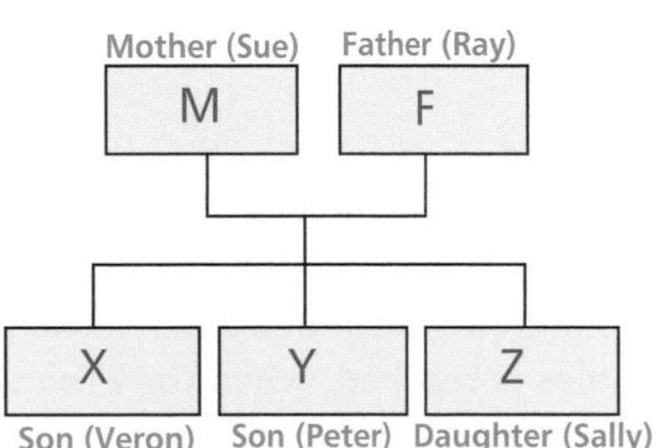

Figure 3.2 A family tree showing the relationship 'Brother of'

The relationship 'brother_of' involves the person concerned being a male and having the same parents. From Figure 3.2 we can see that 'X is a brother of Y' and 'X is a brother of Z'. Also 'Y is a brother of X' and 'Y is a brother of

Z'. This is true because X, Y and Z have the same parents M and F. Expressing this in Prolog leads to the rule shown at the end of the following Prolog code.

```
female(sue).                       % enter all data for Figure 3.2
male(ray).
male(veron).
male(peter).
female(sally).
parents_of(veron,sue,ray).
parents_of(peter,sue,ray).
Parents_of(sally,sue,ray).
brother_of(X,Y) :-                 % x is a brother of y if
  male(X),                         % x is male and
  parents_of(X,M,F),               % x has mother m and father f and
  parents_of(Y,M,F).               % y has mother m and father f
```

Note that the variables (in the rule definition at the end) start with an upper-case letter, and the arguments in the initial list of facts start with a lower-case letter.

We can now get Prolog to interrogate the knowledge base by asking questions in a variety of formats. We start off with some simple questions which interrogate the list of facts at the beginning of the program. The Prolog prompt is given by '?-'.

```
? - female(sue).
yes
? — male(ray).
yes
? — male(sally).
no
```

The first question asks if Sue is a female, and Prolog responds with the answer 'yes', because of line 1 in the previous program. The second question is true because of line 2, and the final question is false because Sally has not been defined to be a male.

Questions may be framed in a variety of different ways and the following is just one example.

```
? — male(Who).
Who = ray ;
Who = veron ;
Who = peter ;
? -
```

The first question is using a variable called 'Who' to find out the complete set of males within the knowledge base. Prolog responds first with 'ray', then the user types in a semi-colon, and Prolog responds with 'veron'; the user continues in this way until the end of the set of males is reached, when the Prolog prompt is returned.

More complex questions can be asked, and the following are typical of some of the techniques that may be used.

```
? - brother_of(veron, Who).
Who = veron ;
Who = peter ;
Who = sally
? -
```

This question interrogates the knowledge base to see who Veron is the brother of. Prolog responds with 'veron', then the user types in a ';', and Prolog responds with 'peter'. After the user types in a ';' again, Prolog responds with Sally because all these facts fit the description that a brother is a male and shares the same parents! This means that 'Veron' is his own brother, and thus our definition of 'brother_of' needs to be tightened up!

You can now see why the 'brother of' definition used on page 40 needs to be rewritten.

We need to fine tune our definition of 'brother_of' to include the situation where X and Y are *not* the same person. We thus need to express the fact that if 'X and Y are the same' the 'brother_of' is not true. In our original definition of 'brother_of', a new rule can be added called 'not_the_same', as shown in the following code.

```
brother_of(X,Y) :-        % x is a brother of y if
  male(X),                % x is male and
  not_the_same(X,Y),      % x is not the same person as y
  parents_of(X,M,F),      % x has mother m and father f and
  parents_of(Y,M,F).      % y has mother m and father f
```

We need to instruct Prolog what is meant by the rule 'not_the_same(X,Y)', and this can be achieved in many versions of Prolog by use of the following syntax.

```
not_the_same(X,Y) :-
   not(X = Y).
```

This rule may be added to the end of the above program, which will resolve the silly condition where Veron is his own brother, encountered earlier. The modified program responds to the following three questions as shown.

```
?- brother_of(veron,sally).
yes
?- brother_of(veron,peter).
yes
?- brother_of(veron,veron).
no
```

Prolog is a compiled language, not an interpreted language like Basic.

This means that Veron is a brother of Sally and Peter, but not his own brother. The actual program to accomplish this is shown running in Figure 3.3.

Here the WinProlog system is being used on a computer at the author's school. The program is shown at the top, and the console, which is the place where the user may interrogate the knowledge base, is shown at the bottom.

Colour is used to good effect to show the different components like 'comments' and 'variables'. The compiled code is displayed in a different colour to the code that has not been compiled. This helps to save time if you make a slight alteration to the code and then forget to recompile it!

Figure 3.3 The 'Brother of' program running in the author's WinProlog system

Logic programming – Prolog clauses

The facts, rules and questions considered in the last three sections are all examples of **clauses**. *A Prolog clause consists of a body and a head*, like the rule used to define a 'brother_of' covered above.

```
brother_of(x,y) :-     % This is an example of the head.
  male(x),             % This is
  not_the_same,        % an
  parents(x,m,f),      % example of
  parents(y,m,f).      % the body.
not_the_same(X,Y) :-   % This is another head.
  not(X=Y).            % This is another body.
```

A fact is simply *a clause without a body* (no *conditions*), a question is *a clause without a head* (a condition only), and a rule is a clause with *both* a head and a body.

Backtracking

In the last section, when asking Prolog questions about the data contained in the **knowledge base**, we had particular goals to satisfy like 'is Veron a brother of Sally?' or 'is Veron a brother of Peter?', for example. More complex Prolog programs may have many such goals, and Prolog attempts to satisfy them by going through a list. As each goal is satisfied, the variables become instantiated (*instances of the variables are created*) and Prolog then goes on to the next goal. If a goal cannot be satisfied, then Prolog will attempt to find a different route by backtracking to the previous goal, removing the instances of the variables previously created and then trying again. This is called **backtracking**.

It is common practice in examinations to give a set of numbered rules which build up things like 'valid sentences', 'valid program statements' or 'valid characteristics of animals' etc., and an example is shown below.

Examples

Consider the following very simple definitions for a sentence in the English language.

1 **sentence → noun_phrase, verb_phrase.**

2 **sentence → noun_phrase, verb_phrase, noun_phrase.**

3 **noun_phrase → determiner, noun.**

4 **verb_phrase → verb.**

5 **verb_phrase → verb, noun_phrase.**

6 **determiner → [the].**

7 **determiner → [a].**

8 **adjective → [big].**

9 **noun → [banana].**

10 **noun → [orang_utan]**

11 **verb → [eats].**

12 **adverb → [quickly].**

(a) **Draw a tree structure showing how the sentence 'the orang-utan eats the banana' would be constructed.**

(b) **Write a Prolog program which implements these simple rules.**

(c) **Which rules have been used in the production of the above sentence? Show the order in which the rules would probably have been applied.**

(d) **The sentence 'the orang-utan eats the big banana' will not be valid according to the above rules. Write a new rule that will make this so.**

Solution

(a) The tree structure for the construction of the sentence 'the orang-utan eats the banana' is shown in Figure 3.4.

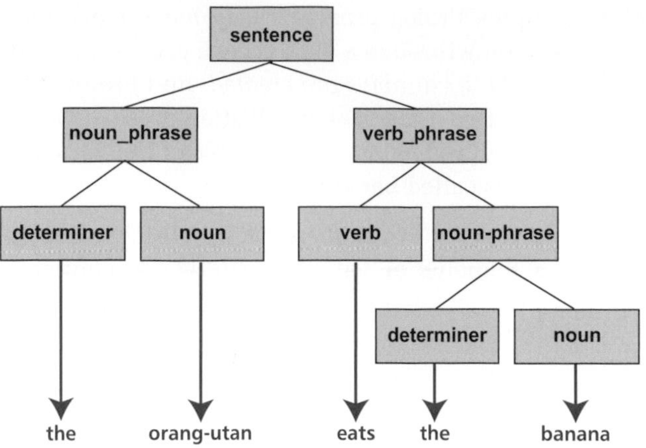

Figure 3.4 A tree structure showing the creation of the first sentence

(b) A simple Prolog program to implement these rules could be as follows.

```
determiner(a).           %these are the atomic 'text name' values
determiner(the).
adjective(big).
noun(orang_utan).
noun(banana).
verb(eats).
adverb(quickly).

noun_phrase(X,Y) :-      % noun_phrase >- determiner AND noun
  determiner(X),
  noun(Y).

verb_phrase(X) :-        % verb_phrase >- adverb AND verb OR verb
  adverb(X),
  verb(X);
  verb(X).

verb_phrase(X,Y) :-      %verb_phrase >- verb AND noun_phrase
  verb(X),
  noun_phrase(Y).

sentence(A,B,C,D,E) :- %sentence >- noun_phrase AND verb_phrase
  noun_phrase(A,B),      % AND noun_phrase
  verb_phrase(C),
  noun_phrase(D,E).
```

(c) The rules used in the production of the above sentence are as follows.

Table 3.1 Rules to produce sentence using the rules given above for the definition of a simple sentence

Rule number	Rule	Explanation
(2)	sentence (A,B,C,D,E).	A = the, B = orang_utan, C = eats, D = the, E = banana
(2)	noun_phrase(A,B).	First part of rule two being analysed.
(3)	noun_phrase(X,Y).	X = the,Y = orang_utan
(3)	determiner(X).	First part of rule 3 being analysed.
(6)	determiner(X).	X = the, goal is therefore satisfied, first part of rule 3 has been successfully completed.
(3)	noun(Y).	Second part of rule 3 is being analysed.
(10)	noun(Y).	Y = orang_utan, goal is therefore satisfied. Second part of rule 3 successfully completed, and hence rule 3 has been successfully completed.
(2)	verb_phrase(C).	Return to the second part of rule 2.
(4)	verb_phrase(X)	X = eats.
(11)	verb[eats].	First and only part of rule is satisfied because 'eats' is defined as a verb by rule 11.
(2)	noun_phrase(D,E)	Return to the third part of rule 2. D = the, E = banana
(3)	noun_phrase(X,Y).	X = the,Y = banana
(3)	determiner(X).	First part of rule 3 being analysed.
(6)	determiner(X).	X = the, goal is therefore satisfied, first part of rule 3 has been successfully completed.
(3)	noun(Y).	Second part of rule 3 being analysed.
(10)	noun(Y).	Y = banana, goal is therefore satisfied. Second part of rule 3 successfully completed, and hence rule 3 has been successfully completed.
(2)	sentence(A,B,C,D,E).	Return to sentence rule with all conditions satisfied, therefore 'the orang-utan eats the banana' is a valid sentence.

(d) We need a new rule for a sentence containing six words as follows:

```
sentence(A,B,C,D,E,F) :-
  noun_phrase(A,B),
  verb_phrase(C),
  determiner(D),
  adjective(E),
  noun(F).
```

We need to introduce a rule for 'adjective' here.

Remember from your English lessons that an adjective is a term used to modify a noun.

and the following rule for the case when a noun_phrase can be a single noun:

```
noun_phrase(X) :-
  noun(X).
```

This is needed to describe parts of a sentence like 'big banana', because the adjective 'big' describes in more detail the noun banana.

Logic programming – creating and processing lists in Prolog

A list is represented in Prolog as having a **head** and a **tail**. The *first item* is called the head of the list and *the remaining part of the list* is called the tail. Therefore, in the following ordered list of computer hardware,

[disk, dvd, keyboard, mouse, printer, vdu]

disk is the head and the list *[dvd, keyboard, mouse, printer, vdu]* represents the tail.

A list may be empty (i.e. have no elements), it may have one element (in which case the tail is empty) or, as in the above case, it may have many elements. Prolog is good at processing data structures like **lists** and **trees**, and a list is really only a special case of a **binary tree**.

An empty list in Prolog is written as `[ ]`. Remember that a list has a head and a tail, so an empty list would have an empty head and an empty tail. A list consisting of just one element 'disk' can be written as `(disk, [])` in which case the head is 'disk' and the tail is an empty list.

To output data from Prolog we use the command 'write'. Hence, in the true 'Hello World' tradition, to write 'Hello World' the following syntax may be used.

```
write('Hello World'),nl.
```

Prolog will respond with something like the following.

```
Hello World
```

It is best to use a 'nl' (new line) command too, or the Prolog response 'yes' gets mixed up with your output and you end up with 'Hello Worldyes' which looks a little ridiculous when you wanted 'Hello World' to be printed. To write out the contents of a list requires recursion, and this is covered below.

List processing is really powerful in Prolog. The simple examples given here do not do justice to the language.

If you are interested in using Prolog then this would make a good A2 project. However, be prepared to put in a lot of extra effort learning new techniques.

If you use the Prolog keyword 'write' to print out a "string" (note the double quotes) you would end up with a sequence of ASCII values in square brackets separated by commas, which is obviously not too helpful to read the text!

Recursion using Prolog

Let us suppose we want to get Prolog to print a list of the names shown here.

[disk, dvd, keyboard, mouse, printer, vdu]

The most common way of doing this is to define a procedure, give it a sensible name like 'writelist', and use the built-in Prolog procedure 'write' to actually output the data. This is typically done in the following way.

```
writelist([]).

writelist([Head|Tail]):-
  write(Head), nl,
  writelist(Tail).
```

After compilation, if you call the 'writelist' procedure with the data shown here (note that `[]` are used around the list)

```
?- writelist([disk, dvd, keyboard, mouse, printer, vdu]).
```

then Prolog will respond with the following data, all on separate lines, and followed by the now familiar 'yes'.

```
disk
dvd
keyboard
mouse
printer
vdu
yes

?-
```

The procedure is defined by '`writelist([])`'., and the rule which is defined within the body of the procedure initially has the head = `disk` and the tail = `dvd, keyboard, mouse, printer, vdu`.

Line 2 of the procedure writes the Head of the list (disk) and prints a new line. Finally, the procedure is called recursively, with the Tail of the list becoming the new list to be printed. The second time this procedure is called head = `dvd` and the tail = `keyboard, mouse, printer, vdu`. These recursive calls to '`writelist([]).`' continue until the entire list has been printed.

Prolog has enormously powerful list processing capabilities, including searching for items in a list, adding or deleting items and concatenating lists (joining different lists together). These processes are also available with files, which are treated in ways identical in principle to the lists described above.

Advantages of logic programming

An advantage of logic programming is the ability to concentrate on the declarative view of the problem and not on the imperative solution. You can set up the system using knowledge-based reasoning. Logic programming has a close relationship to mathematical logic, and this is useful for solving problems which can be expressed using mathematical logic. You do not have to tell the machine how to solve a problem using the language of the computer. Programs written in Prolog are, on average, between five and 10 times smaller than the equivalent programs written using a procedural language.

Declarative programming – introduction

A **declarative language** is a generalised term covering both **functional programming** and **logic** (or relational) **programming**, which have both been described in this chapter. Good examples of declarative programming languages are Prolog and Haskell. Remember that declarative languages concentrate on the logic of the problem (rules and facts etc.) and not on the mechanics of writing sequential programming statements to solve a problem. Logical programming languages like Prolog can do this because they have a built-in **inference engine** which helps to manage the interrogation of the **knowledge base**. Functional programming languages like Clean evaluate expressions which are formed using mathematical and other types of functions.

Object-oriented programming – introduction

Object-oriented programming methods are able to model real-world scenarios using concepts such as 'objects' and 'classes'. To be recognised as fully object oriented, a computer language should support **objects**, **classes**, **polymorphism**, **encapsulation** and **inheritance** (see below). Object-oriented programming methods have gained great popularity because they are ideally suited to modelling extremely complex applications in which teams of people may work on the same overall problem. It is this paradigm that enables time devoted to development and testing to be reduced considerably compared with imperative and declarative programming techniques. It does this by enabling much code to be shared or reused in many different ways.

Object-oriented programming – classes and objects

Before an object can be created a class definition must be written. This is shown using the C++ code in the first program.

The keyword 'void' is used if no parameters are passed back to the calling routine.

A **class** is just an **abstract data type**. A class is defined by making use of a class definition, (a *self-contained structure*) which is really a *blueprint* or *prototype* for an **object** (see below). When defining a class in a language like C++, it is important to realise that you are not creating an actual instance (or *an example*) of the class.

An object can be anything from a 'teapot' to an 'abstract mathematical concept'. An object will become a member of a particular class after an instance of that object has been created (called **instantiation**). However, a more abstract class may be used simply to pass on some of its characteristics to other classes. An object contains both the '**functions** and **procedures**' and 'other attributes' like the variables and data that support the object. This means it contains both the routines to solve a particular problem (called the **methods**) *and* the attributes (called the **members**) associated with these routines.

The mechanisms enabling us to *combine both the data and methods (functions and procedures)* into one single unit called a class, and then to *hide the internal workings* of this mechanism from other parts of the program unless the appropriate methods are used to access them is called **encapsulation** or containment. The following code shows how a class is defined, and how an object is created by using an instance of the class. The syntax used is that of the language C++, and the class being defined is called 'Robot'.

Some code written in an object-oriented programming style (creating a simple class definition for a robot)

```
class Robot
{
   public:
   void terminator();   //declares a function which accepts and
                        //returns no arguments (parameters)
   int weapons;         //The number of weapons – maximum of
                        //three
   int speed;           //speed in km/h
   string weapon1;
   string weapon2;
   string weapon3;
   string intelligence; //Three levels – 'high', 'medium' and
};                       //'low'
```

An instance of the 'Robot class' is created by running the following code, which also includes the class definition shown above, together with some necessary prelims. The actual object is a robot called 'Terminator3' which belongs to the 'Robot class'.

```
Some code written in an object-oriented programming style
(creating an instance of the Robot class – i.e. creating a
Robot object)
#include <string>
#include <iostream>
using namespace std;

class Robot
{
  public:
  void terminator();    //declares a function which accepts and
                        //returns no arguments (parameters)
  int weapons;          //The number of weapons – maximum of
                        //three
  int speed;            //speed in km/h
  string weapon1;
  string weapon2;
  string weapon3;
  string intelligence;   //Three levels – 'high', 'medium' and
                         //'low'
};

int main()
{
  Robot Terminator3;
  Terminator3.weapons = 3;
  Terminator3.speed = 150;
  Terminator3.weapon1 = "Rotary Cannon";
  Terminator3.weapon2 = "Laser Guided Missile";
  Terminator3.weapon3 = "Smart Bomb";
  Terminator3.intelligence = "High";
  cout << "The Terminator 3 robot has the following
          specification" \n;
  cout << "Terminator 3 has" << Terminator3.weapons "weapons"
          \n;
  cout << "Terminator 3's first weapon is a" <<
          Terminator3.weapon1 \n;
  cout << "Terminator 3's second weapon is a" <<
          Terminator3.weapon1 \n;
  cout << "Terminator 3's third weapon is a" <<
          Terminator3.weapon1 \n;
  cout << "Terminator 3 has" << Terminator3.intelligence
          "intelligence" \n;
  return 0;
};
```

Although this is a simple example, you can see how the class 'Robot' has been defined, and how an object, or *instance of that class* (in this case a Robot called 'Terminator3'), has been assigned 'Rotary Cannons', 'Laser Guided Missiles', 'Smart Bombs' and 'High Intelligence'. We have not made use of private data and extra functions have not been used in this program, only instances of simple data types. The code at the bottom of the second program prints out information about our Terminator 3 Robot's specification.

Object-oriented programming – inheritance

Inheritance in **object-oriented programming** is a useful technique in which a **derived class** can inherit properties from a **base class**. The base class is the original class definition, and other classes (called the derived classes) can selectively inherit some or all of the properties from the base class, governed by permissions from the base class, using keywords like **public**, **private** and **protected**.

Figure 3.5 shows a base class with three characteristics which may be inherited. Any **private** data would *not* be inherited by this mechanism because it is private. Instead of making data **public**, with the consequent availability to other classes (we do not normally wish to do this as this bypasses the good encapsulation ideas mentioned earlier) there is a **protected** data area in which data may only be inherited by a derived class.

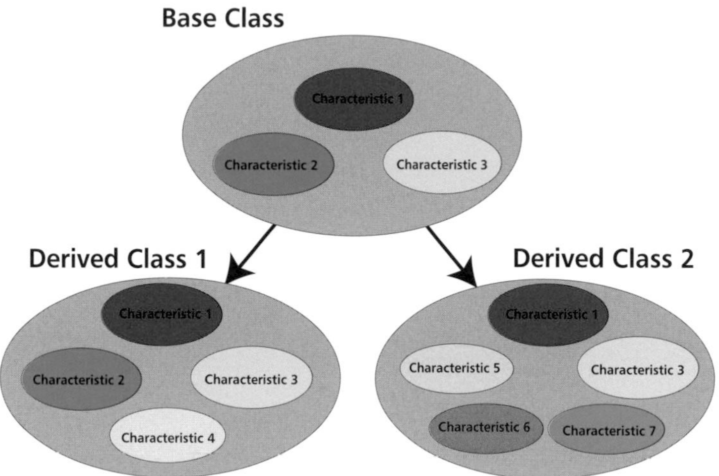

Figure 3.5 The concept of inheritance in object-oriented languages

Figure 3.5 shows two derived classes. 'Derived class 1' has inherited all the characteristics from the base class and has defined a new characteristic called Characteristic 4. 'Derived class 2' has inherited Characteristic 1 and Characteristic 3 from the base class, but has also defined three others, called Characteristics 5, 6 and 7.

Example

Making use of an object-oriented language like C++, explain the concept of a class, clearly stating how encapsulation is used. Show, in principle, how public and private data may be defined within a class.

Solution

A class is a data type that encapsulates both functions and data. The concept of encapsulation is an important one in object-oriented programming, because we can tightly control access to our methods and data, and therefore others cannot inadvertently mess up the data or methods by running any new code that they may write.

The data inside the class is more secure because it is not directly accessible to members outside this class. Members outside the class may access public data but not private data. Therefore the class definition controls which classes have access to which data by the use of these public and private sections, as shown in the following C++ code.

```
class Example
{
public:
  //This section contains the data that is accessible to all
classes

private:

  //This section contains the data that is accessible only to the
derived class
}
```

The importance of **inheritance** in object-oriented programming is obvious – it is easier to reuse code than to reinvent similar code from scratch. Both the methods (functions etc.) and other attributes associated with the base class can all be reused in the derived class. We can selectively decide what is and what is not inherited (controlled from the base class), and we can add extra characteristics. The new derived classes can also be used as a base class from which other derived classes may be made. This helps us to build up powerful objects with great sophistication, mirroring real-world concepts and applications. (See question 15 in the self-test questions at the end of this chapter.)

Example

A database has been set up for a library by using an object-oriented programming language like C++. The database was originally designed just for books, but now has to cope with similar information stored on other media such as CD-ROMs and DVDs. You do not wish to alter any of the original code by adding extra fields as the database has been working perfectly for years. What property of an object-oriented language could be used to overcome this problem?

The second example shown here underlines the importance of object-oriented programming techniques in practice.

Solution

A new derived class can be established by the process of inheritance. We can inherit all of the properties and methods that would be common to books, CD-ROMs and DVDs like 'title', 'subject', 'publisher' etc. The new derived class inherits properties and methods from the base class (by inheriting the protected data areas). Other properties which are pertinent to the new media, like 'format' and 'playing time' etc., may now be added to the new derived class. In this way, by the process of inheritance, the new database does not inadvertently mess up any of the existing database methods or data.

The older parts of the program have not been modified and therefore do not have to be retested.

Object-oriented programming – polymorphism

Polymorphism literally means 'many forms'. In object-oriented programming languages like C++, it refers to *entities behaving differently according to the context in which they are being used*. When dealing with numeric expressions in other programming languages, you have probably encountered a simple form of polymorphism without even realising it! The minus sign in the expression '–3', for example, indicates the sign of the number, but in another expression like '5 – 3' the *same sign* is used to represent a *different operation*, namely the subtraction of two numbers. Using polymorphism in this simplified way is called **overloading** in C++.

Polymorphism may also be used in more sophisticated ways, specifically by using references to a base class that can behave differently when used in a derived class, and the ability to decide which method is actually used at run time (i.e. *not* at the time when the program is compiled). This might not sound too revolutionary but it is, because we can then use the same compiled code to provide a huge variety of different functionality with the base class providing the foundation on which the other methods in the derived classes are based.

Object-oriented programming – a polymorphism example

A classic example of polymorphism in action occurs when using an object-oriented programming language to draw simple shapes like lines, rectangles, circles, ellipses and triangles etc. To save re-inventing the wheel, you could create a base class called 'Shapes' which acts as a generalised building block on which the other shapes outlined are based. The base class may be inherited by the other derived classes, and thus the derived classes are being used in *many forms* (polymorphism).

Imagine a user is constructing a drawing. The shapes drawn so far might be stored in a list (on file or in memory) which represents the current state of the drawing. This list would be needed in the event of a 'redraw' (e.g. the window containing the drawing might have been obscured by another window) or 'loading the drawing again'. All the shape objects need to reference the base class 'Shape', because the lines, rectangles and ellipses etc. are derived from it.

When a 'redraw' is being carried out, your program might need to call the 'Draw() method for a circle object', the 'Draw() method for a line' and the 'Draw() method for an ellipse' etc. depending on what objects have been chosen by the user of the program. These objects are not known at compile time because your interactive program is a dynamic entity with objects being created on the fly (randomly). The list produced for the redraw will be a list in which each entry has a reference to the base class, but the method used depends on the object being drawn. This idea, where the calls to the base class may take on many different forms (line, circle, rectangle etc.) is called polymorphism. In C++ polymorphism is accomplished by using the additional keyword 'virtual' in front of the function definition in the base class.

Structured programming – introduction

This is not usually regarded as being a different programming **paradigm**, but is more concerned with methods to modularise and aid readability. It is therefore intimately tied up with, and is really an extension of, procedural programming. One of the first languages to typify a more rigorous structured approach was Pascal. As more people saw the benefits, other languages followed suit. Basic, for example, which was highly *unstructured* in its original form, joined the structured programming way of working. Modern systems extend these ideas into **structured design**, mainly using the **top-down design method** (splitting up the system into a hierarchical structure) and **computer aided software engineering** or **CASE**.

High-level languages which have stood the test of time have usually been through several versions and are inevitably well structured. Well-structured languages have a rich variety of control structures, support procedure calls which pass parameters by reference or by value, insist on variable declaration, have a rich variety of different data types, encourage the use of comments and thus provide ample support for the top-down design methods mentioned above. Some of the well-structured languages which supported good procedural programming paradigms have now been developed into fully object-oriented languages, and Visual Basic.NET is a good example of this.

Event-driven programming – introduction

In the early days of computing a program took over the entire machine. This meant that the user could do only one thing at a time. We could, for example, use a word processor, and then quit the word processor and use a spreadsheet. Modern operating systems allow users to run a **virtual machine** inside a window. Using the same example, we could have a word processor running in one window and a spreadsheet running in another. The user can switch between the two windows by clicking with the mouse to activate either the word processor or the spreadsheet. If the user is able to use an 'event' like a mouse click to activate some task, then this is an example of event-driven programming.

Writing **event-driven programs** is more complex than writing programs that sequentially run through a task where no interruption from the user is possible. These programs must continually poll the tasks that are being run and be able to respond to a huge variety of different events, many of which can be controlled by the user and others which are controlled by the operating system. Modern languages like Visual Basic and C++ are ideally suited to the Windows environment where event-driven programming is the norm.

In what area is each paradigm particularly useful?

For the purpose of the A2 examination you should be able to quote applications which are typically developed making use of each paradigm described in this chapter. Table 3.2 shows a list of typical applications for one language within each paradigm.

Table 3.2 Applications, the language used and the paradigm

Language	Paradigm	A few typical application areas
FORTRAN	Procedural	Weather forecasting and other highly mathematical applications such as magnetohydrodynamics, work on electromagnetism and many other scientific areas of research.
COBOL	Procedural	Mission-critical business and banking applications.
Visual Basic	Procedural	Many general-purpose applications have been written in VB including web applications, databases, applications for Word, Excel, Access and PowerPoint etc.
Clean	Functional	Compiler design, editors, drawing tools, control systems and computer games etc.
Prolog	Logical	Artificial intelligence, expert systems, data mining, graphical applications, deductive databases etc.
C++	Object oriented	Operating system design, graphics applications like Adobe's Photoshop, Illustrator and Acrobat, search engines (the Google search engine was written in C++) and even SETI (the search for extra terrestrial intelligence) etc.
Pascal	Structured	Many modern languages are now well structured. This involves having a rich variety of loops, long variable names, code which can be identified with a beginning and an end etc. This enables different people to work on different parts of the program more easily.
Visual Basic.NET	Event driven	Many modern languages are event driven, which means they respond to external 'events' like the click of a mouse. This enables two or more programs to run at the same time. Before event-driven programming, a single program would take over the entire machine.

As you can see from Table 3.2, typical application areas for each of the above paradigms are vast. The list shows those which have actually been developed rather than generalised theoretical ideas.

Generations of programming languages

Languages are classified into **generations** according to major changes in methodology. **Machine code** (the *pure binary digits*) is a **first-generation language** (1GL), and was *the* first language to be developed. Programming using this method is a tedious, error-prone and time-consuming task.

The **second-generation languages** (2GL) are assembly languages which are translated by the assemblers (like MASM outlined in chapter 2). Assembly language consists of mnemonics which represent machine code equivalent instructions. They are much easier to use than machine code because of the increased functionality which comes with the assembler.

Third-generation languages (3GL) are the **procedural** (see earlier in this chapter) high-level languages like the current versions of Pascal and Basic. Some are more structured than others (see **structured programming** techniques) and the more recent evolutions of these languages have provided more structured facilities. **Object-oriented** languages (see above) belong to a separate class of their own.

You should note that the generation to which a particular language belongs does not refer to when the language was actually developed.

A version of Visual Basic, for example, developed in 2000 is a third-generation language, but Prolog, developed in the 1970s, is a fifth-generation language!

The **fourth-generation languages** (4GL) are languages with the all-powerful commands like the **SQLs** considered in chapter 10, or the languages that accompany spreadsheets and a whole host of other applications. Commands such as 'SORT' are a lot easier than writing your own sort procedures using typical third-generation languages. However, most 4GLs are very specific in the tasks that they can perform easily.

Fifth-generation languages (5GL) are languages like Prolog (covered in this chapter) which are often regarded as very high-level languages, but expert systems, often written in Prolog, also belong to this class of language definition.

Languages have gone through a slow metamorphosis starting with machine code, and have developed in different directions according to specialist needs. This metamorphosis proceeds through assembly language and all the different versions of the high-level languages, to arrive at today's extremely powerful object-oriented languages and other equally successful paradigms. Each generation is further removed from the ways in which the computer operates and is nearer to the ways that humans like to work.

Self-test questions

1 What is the difference between a natural and a formal language?
2 The first programming paradigm to be developed was imperative programming. What is meant by a 'programming paradigm' and what is 'imperative programming'?
3 List two advantages of procedural programming over imperative programming.
4 Name three high-level programming languages which belong to the procedural programming paradigm.
5 Functional programming enables algorithms to be expressed in terms of functions.
   (a) What is a function?
   (b) What is the main mode of operation of a functional programming language?
   (c) List two advantages of functional programming compared with procedural programming.
6 Logical programming and functional programming both belong to which programming paradigm?

7 Solving a problem using a logical programming paradigm requires you to structure the problem in ways very different to an imperative or procedural style. Outline how a problem has to be structured to be solved using a logical programming paradigm.

8 State three advantages that a logical programming paradigm has over a procedural programming paradigm.

9 Define the following terms used in the logic programming language Prolog.
(a) A fact (b) A rule (c) List (d) Head (e) Tail.

10 What criteria does a language have to meet to be fully object oriented?

11 Define the following terms used in object-oriented programming.
(a) Class (b) Object (c) Encapsulation (d) Inheritance
(e) Instantiation (f) Base class.

12 Why have object-oriented programming methods proved to be so popular?

13 What is meant by the term polymorphism? Give an example of its use.

14 Write a class definition for a 'teapot' using some data of your own choosing.

15 Using the class definition of 'teapot' from question 14 write a derived class for 'teapot with stand', which enables the combination to inherit all the attributes of a 'teapot'.

4 Data structures

In this chapter you will learn about:

- What a data structure is
- Linear lists
- Tree structures and the concept of pointers
- Circular lists and queues
- Static and dynamic data structures
- Stacks
- Linked lists

If you have time it is useful to turn the pseudocode shown here into a suitable high-level language and run it on a computer.

This will give you a better understanding of the work being covered in this chapter.

What is a data structure?

A **data structure** is an abstract set of data, organised in an efficient way so that the data contained in it can be manipulated to process or extract information. From your work on AS computing, you will recall that information may be extracted from data if structure is applied to it. At A2 level we look at increasingly sophisticated data structures, each of which are ideal for modelling common data processing operations as shown in Table 4.1.

Table 4.1 Common data processing operations

Data processing operation	Examples
Traversing a structure	Moving round a data structure, possibly listing or processing the data within the structure as we proceed with the traversal.
Adding data to a structure	Inserting data into the right place in a sorted list, or adding an item of data to the beginning or end of a list.
Deletion of data from a structure	Removing unwanted data from a list, and freeing up the space occupied by the old data.
Sorting data in a structure	Putting something in alphabetical or numeric order. Some clever structures enable us to do this without moving the data.
Searching a structure	Looking for a particular item of data in a list, and determining if it is there or not.
Merging data in two different structures	Joining together different structures so they become one data structure containing all the previous data in the right order.

Linear list

A **linear list** is an *ordered set of elements*. For example, the following set of data

`{dog, cat, bird, mouse, pig}`

forms an ordered list. This list is not in any *particular* order, but it is ordered. Such lists could be the product of **transactions** carried out in a shop during the day. However, we will use a simple list of

```
Pseudocode to print the
contents of a linear list.
Set pointer to beginning of
list
Repeat
  Read  list item
  Print list item
  Pointer = Pointer + 1
Until end-of-list
```

animals for all our examples. Linear lists are very easy to process; to display the contents of this list we could use the **pseudocode** shown above.

If we wish to **search** for an item of data contained in a linear list, it is a case of looking at every element in the list until the item of interest is found, or found not to be in the list. The second pseudocode algorithm shown here will do this. Notice that all the data items are read until we find the desired item. However, if it is not in the file or data structure, the loop will be exited and a message printed out.

Linear lists may be implemented in memory by using **arrays**, or they may be implemented via **files** stored on secondary storage media like tape or disk.

Data structures are easier to understand if you can visualise them, and a linear list can be viewed as a one-dimensional array, as shown in Figure 4.1. You can see the original list, shown in green, the list with one extra item added, shown in red, and the state of the list after all available 'memory' slots have been filled.

Pseudocode to search for and print out a particular data item from a linear list.

```
Set pointer to beginning of list
Input desired_item
Repeat
  Input list_item
  If list_item = desired_item
then
    Print "Item found"
  Exit procedure
  Else
    Pointer = Pointer + 1
Until end-of-list
Print "Item was not found"
```

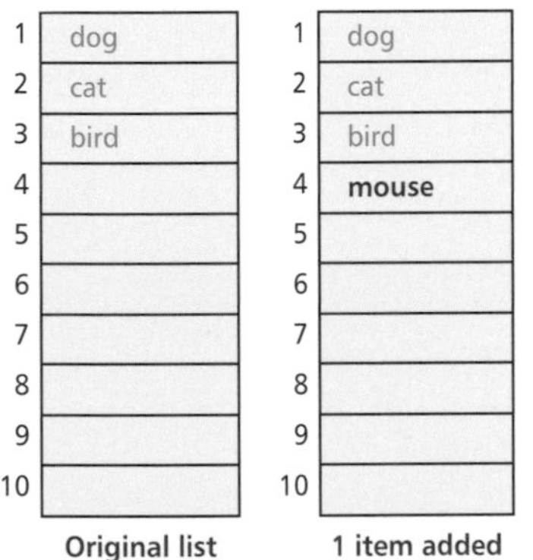

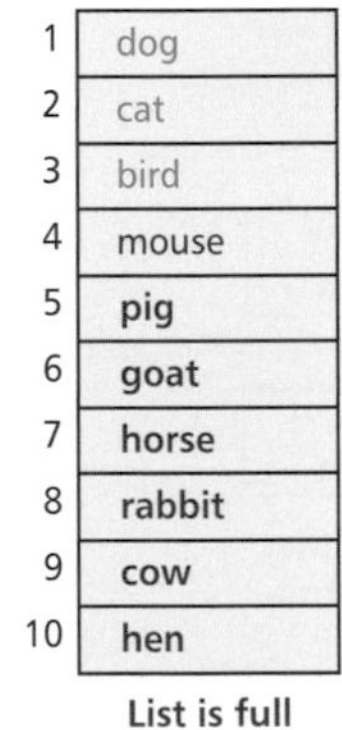

Figure 4.1 Visualising a linear list

The numbers shown in Figure 4.1 could represent memory locations inside the computer, or be used as the subscript number in a subscripted variable using an array. We could set up the list by using a subscripted variable called List(N), e.g. List(1) ... to List(10). N = 5 would be the number used to point at the fifth element, which in this case contains the data 'pig'.

Example

Using pseudocode, show how a one-dimensional array, consisting of 10 elements, can be set up as linear list data structure. Assume that the start data consists of 'dog', 'cat' and 'bird'. Show how this array may be set up and the original list created. Your algorithm must allow the user to add data to the list and should cope if the list is full.

Solution

The original list may be created, using an array called A, as follows:

```
Rem reserve the storage locations for an array
Dim (10)
Rem create the original three entries
```

```
A(1) = dog
A(2) = cat
A(3) = bird
```

We will now need some sort of pointer, pointing to the next element of the array which is used to store the next data entry. If the magnitude of this pointer exceeds the dimension of the array then no more data can be stored. The idea is as follows:

```
Rem set up pointer to point to next free space
Pointer = 4
Repeat
  Input "Enter data"; data
  If Pointer > 10 then
    Print "No room left"
    Exit this Procedure
  Else
      A(Pointer) = data
      Pointer = Pointer + 1
  Endif
Until false
```

From the above code you can see that if the Pointer > 10, a 'No room left' message is printed, and the procedure is exited, else the data is stored in the appropriate part of the array called 'A' and the pointer is incremented ready for the next input.

Tree data structures

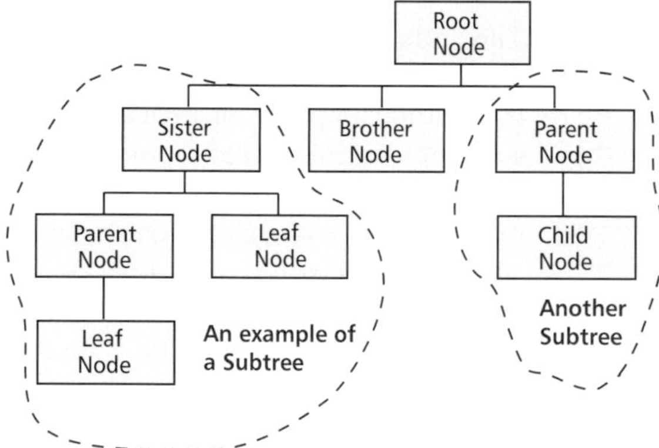

Figure 4.2 A tree structure

The concept of a tree structure is of fundamental importance at A2 level. These data structures form the root of many different types of problem.

Time spent understanding these important data structures should be well rewarded.

A **tree** structure is a **hierarchical data structure**. Many things can be modelled using this structure and a general tree structure, together with an explanation of the terminology used, is shown in Figure 4.2.

Each represents some *data* and/or *pointer information* (see below). Each of the boxes in the tree is called a **node**. A **pointer** is needed to **traverse** (or *move*) from one item of data to the next. In this context a pointer is a number used to point to the place where the next node is stored.

The first node at the base (top!) of the tree is called the **root node**. The names given to the other nodes are derived from the position of the node within a family tree. A **parent node**, for example, is one that has a child. **Brother** and **sister nodes** are nodes which share a common parent. As you can imagine, nodes can be named in different ways according to the point of reference. Therefore, the same node may be a 'parent', 'child' and 'brother', all at the same time, depending on the other nodes to which they refer.

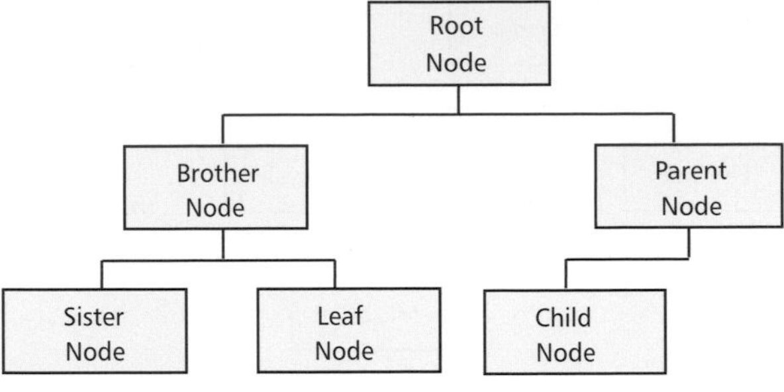

Figure 4.3 A binary tree

The implementation of tree structures depends upon the programming language being used to model it. Languages like Prolog and Lisp, for example, are particularly efficient at doing this. You will also need to be familiar with methods to implement these structures using **procedural languages** like Pascal or Basic. The following methods, used to model these structures, are common to most of the modern **procedural languages**.

Binary trees

A **binary tree** is a tree structure in which a parent is allowed to have *a maximum of two children*. The idea is shown in Figure 4.3. As you can see, no parent has more than two children. The brother node has two children, the parent node has just one child and the sister node has no children. The tree structure is therefore a binary tree. A binary tree uses '**left**' and '**right**' **pointers** to point to the child nodes, and could be built up by using relationships such as '<' or '>' (less than or greater than). If data, built up by using these relationships has been inserted into the tree (e.g. in alphabetical order using the pointers as shown in the next example) then it is called an **ordered binary tree**.

Example

Using the data in the following list, create an ordered binary tree by using the first element as the root node. The other elements must be placed in the tree by using the rule 'if name to be entered is < name in node then follow left pointer, else follow the right pointer'.

List = {microfilm, firewall, processor, memory, heap, stack, queue, backup}

Solution

The first item of data forms the root as shown in Figure 4.4a. Next 'Firewall' is read from the linear list, and because 'Firewall < Microfilm', (as the letter F comes before the letter M) the left pointer (left-hand path in the binary tree structure) is followed to store the data, which is also shown in Figure 4.4a. Next 'Processor' is read from the list, and compared with the data in the root. As 'Processor > Microfilm', the right-hand path is taken and the data is inserted as shown in Figure 4.4b.

Get lots of practice building up ordered binary trees like the one shown here.

Next 'Memory' is read from the list and compared with the data in the root. As 'Memory < Microfilm', the left-hand pointer is followed. Next 'Memory' is compared with 'Firewall', the next node in the tree. As 'Memory > Firewall', the right-hand path is followed, and the data placed accordingly. The final binary tree is shown in Figure 4.4c.

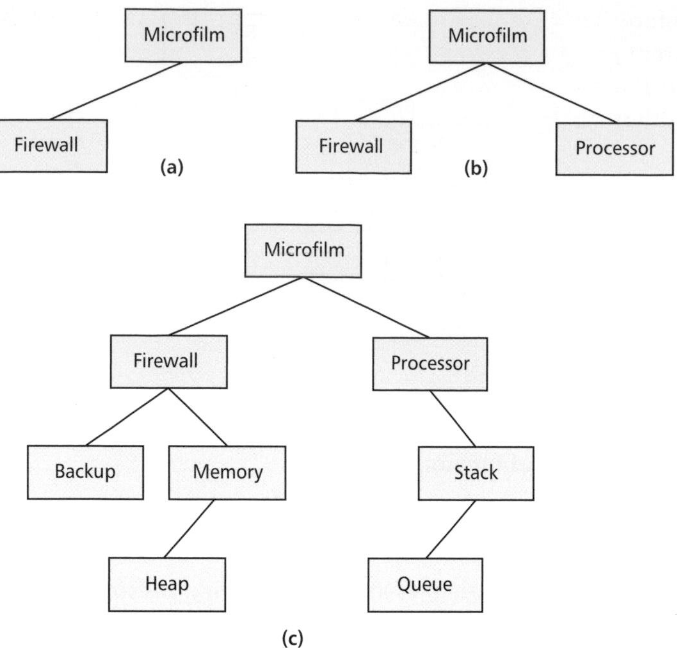

Figure 4.4 An *ordered binary tree* for the computing terms in the list

Once mastered, these techniques are an easy way to gain marks in your A2 examination.

Queues

A **queue** can be thought of like a queue in a shop. Because of this, the first item put in the queue (equivalent to the first person in a shop) must be processed (*served*) first. An alternative name for a queue is a **FIFO data structure** (*First In First Out*). The organisation of a queue is controlled by two pointers, the **start pointer** and the **end pointer**, respectively pointing to the beginning and end of the queue. From Figure 4.5 you can see how the pointers are used. The start pointer and end pointer are sometimes called the **header** and **footer**, indicating the head and foot of the queue.

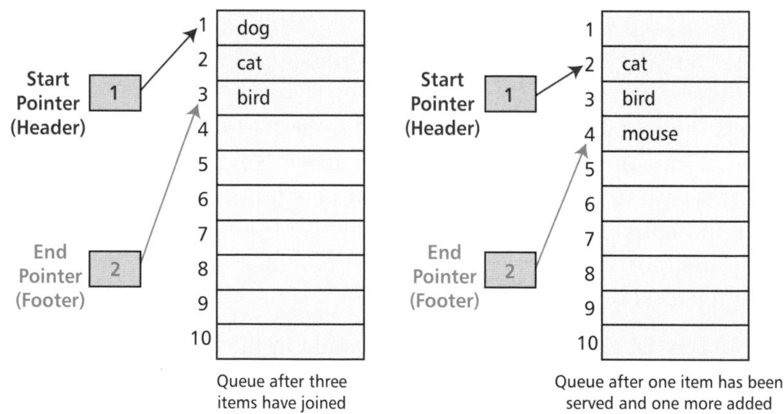

Figure 4.5 Pointers are used to manage a queue

The data structure outlined in Figure 4.5 has only 10 storage locations available; therefore, the programmer must manage the situation when the queue is full. Another problem arises as data is removed from the queue: the entire data set creeps down the data structure!

Therefore, we could set up a **circular queue** but manage the pointers effectively to maintain the beginning and ends of the queue as shown in Figure 4.6.

You need to be able to reproduce diagrams like these to show that you understand how queues and circular queues are implemented in practice, making use of pointers to implement the headers and footers in a list.

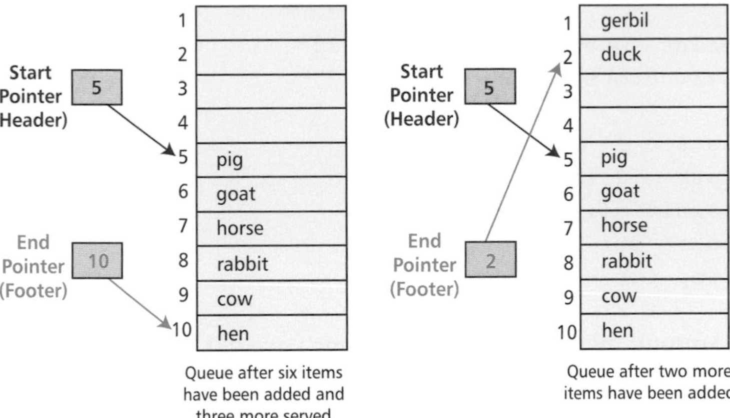

Figure 4.6 Pointers used to create a circular queue

From Figure 4.6 you can see that the pointers manage the positions in the queue very effectively. By crossing over, we have established a circular queue, but still have a 10-item limitation due to the physical size of the data structure.

Example

By making use of pseudocode, show how a circular queue might be managed if it consists of 10 elements stored in an *array*. You need to be able to *add* and *delete* items from the queue. You must not allow an element to be added to a full queue, and must not allow an element to be removed from an empty queue.

Solution

The structure of the queue can be visualised as shown in Figure 4.6. We therefore need a couple of variables called 'start_ptr' and 'end_ptr', which represent the 'start pointer' and 'end pointer' respectively. As we must not allow data to be added to a queue when it is full, we need to detect when the queue is full by examination of the pointers. Figure 4.6 shows that two conditions must be checked to see if the queue is actually full. These two conditions can be summarised as follows.

```
If start_ptr = 1 and end_ptr = 10        If start_ptr = end_ptr + 1
```

The first condition checks when the pointers are not crossed and the second condition checks if they are crossed. Therefore, we need to string these two conditions together with an OR function in our code. If the queue is not full, we insert an item at the end of the queue, and update the end_ptr to reflect the new end of the queue. If the end_ptr gets to 10, then we put it back to 1 to start at the beginning of the array, thus forming a circular queue.

At the start of the program the pointers need setting up because the queue is initially empty. This is achieved by putting the start and end pointers both equal to 0. We will assume that the item to be inserted is called 'data'. The pseudocode for the algorithm that adds data to the queue is as follows:

```
Procedure ADD
        (*Check to see if queue is full*)
        If start_ptr = 1 and end_ptr = 10 or start_ptr = end_ptr
        + 1 then
                Print "Queue is already full"
                Exit Procedure
        Endif
        (*Check to see if queue is empty*)
        If start_ptr = 0 then
                (*initialise queue*)
                start_ptr = 1
                stop_ptr = 1
        else
                (*queue not empty, update pointers*)
                If end_ptr = 10 then end_ptr = 1
                        else
                        end_ptr = end_ptr + 1
                endif
        endif
        (*store data in the array*)
        Queue(stop_ptr) = data
End Procedure
```

We could make the procedure more general by supplying the array size and pointers as parameters passed over to it. In this way the same procedure could be used to update many different queues. The code to delete an item of data is developed in a very similar way and is shown in the following pseudocode procedure:

```
Procedure REMOVE
        (*check to see if the queue is empty*)
        if start_ptr = 0 then
                Print "queue is empty"
                Exit Procedure
        else
                (*get data from front of queue*)
                Data = Queue(start_pointer)
                if start_ptr = end_ptr then
                        (*one item of data in queue*)
                        start_ptr = 0
                        end_ptr = 0
                        Exit Procedure
                endif
                (*more than one item in queue*)
                if start_ptr = 10 then
                        start_ptr = 1
                        else
                        star_ptr = start_ptr + 1
                endif
        endif
End Procedure
```

In practice, to get the above two procedures working they would need to be put inside a loop which is repeated for as long as the user wishes to enter the data. The array Queue(10) would also need dimensioning (setting up) at the beginning of the program. These additions are trivial, and the code has therefore not been listed again to include these.

Stacks

You have already seen a **FIFO data structure**, or queue, earlier in this chapter. A similar structure, called a **LIFO** (last in first out) or **stack** is of paramount importance in computer science. The **LIFO stack** is very similar in operation to a queue, with the exception that the last element put onto the stack is the first element that is removed from the stack. Although unfair from a conventional queue point of view, this is ideal for many computer problems like how to handle interrupts for example (see chapter 1).

Make sure that you can write pseudocode to implement stacks and queues.

These two data structures are extremely important at A2 level.

Try to implement these pseudocode algorithms making use of a high-level language to which you have access.

The LIFO structure typifies trying to remember what you were doing if you get interrupted. For example, you might be in the middle of a conversation and the telephone rings, you stop what you are doing to answer the phone. After dealing with the phone, you get back to the conversation. However, you might not remember what you were talking about, and this is the essence of the LIFO stack. When the phone rings, you pop some information regarding your position in the conversation onto the stack. You then forget about the conversation, deal with the phone call, and then retrieve the information back from the stack when the phone call is over. The last bit of information put onto the stack (about the original conversation) is the first to be removed from the stack – hence the name LIFO stack. If, during your phone call, the doorbell interrupted you, then you could put the phone information onto the stack, and so on. Inside computers many interrupts may be processed in this manner by saving register information onto an area of memory set up to be a stack and by retrieving this information when the interrupt has been serviced.

Example

(a) Draw a diagram to illustrate how a LIFO stack may be set up in memory. Show how pointers may be used to maintain this data structure. Illustrate your answer by pushing six items onto the stack and then removing three.

(b) Write some pseudocode to manage a stack of 10 elements. You must show how items may be added or removed from the stack. Your code must cope if the stack becomes full or if the stack is empty.

Solution

(a) A typical LIFO data structure is shown in Figure 4.7. Here you can see that the stack pointer is pointing to 6, being the last item put onto the stack, and therefore this will be the first item to be removed. After three further items have been removed, the stack pointer is now pointing to 3.

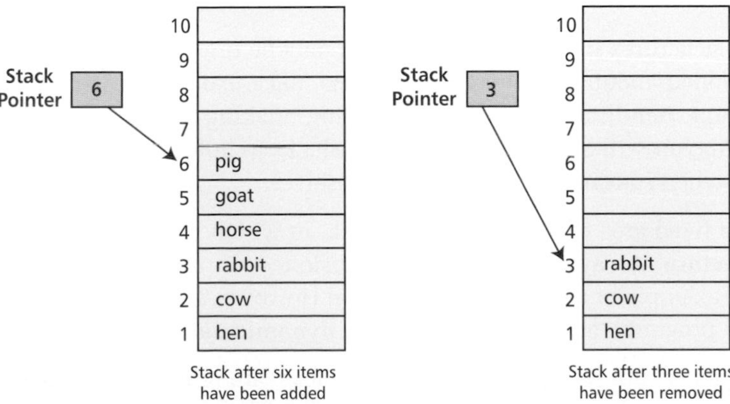

Figure 4.7 An example of a stack or LIFO structure for part (a)

(b) The code should be reasonably self-explanatory. The procedure to add an item onto the stack needs to check if it is full, and the procedure to remove an item from the stack needs to check if it is empty. The pointer will be called 'stack_ptr'. The data to be put onto or removed from the stack is called 'data'. The array, set up to simulate the area of memory is an array called 'Stack'. The pseudocode is as follows:

The term 'PUSH' is often used to place an item on the stack and the term 'POP' is often used when an item is removed from the stack.

```
Procedure PUSH
        If stack_ptr = 10 then
                (*stack is full*)
                Print "no room on stack*)
                Exit Procedure
        Else
                (*push data onto the stack*)
                stack_ptr = stack_ptr + 1
                Stack(stack_ptr) = data
        endif
End Procedure
```

The principles of removing data from a FIFO stack are just as simple, and the code is as follows.

```
Procedure POP
        If stack_ptr = 0 then
                (*stack is empty*)
                Print "stack is empty"
                Exit Procedure
        Else
                (*pop data off and alter pointer)
                data = Stack(stack_ptr)
                stack_ptr = stack_ptr - 1
        endif
End Procedure
```

To get the above two procedures working they would need to be put inside a loop, which is repeated for as long as the user wishes to enter the data. The array Stack(10) would also need dimensioning (setting up) at the beginning of the program. These additions are trivial, and the code has therefore not been listed again to include these.

Static and dynamic data structures

You have just seen how structures like stacks and queues may be organised in memory. You have also been reminded about how operating systems make use of such structures when organising interrupt handling. When programming making use of recursive techniques (see chapter 5), you will also be making use of stacks to hold information that needs to be remembered when routines make calls to themselves.

It is possible to allocate a fixed area of memory to the stack, in which case this would be called a **static data structure**. **Arrays** cannot be redimensioned during execution of a program and are another example of a **static data structure**. However, files may get larger during the execution of a program and are an example of a **dynamic data structure**.

More general areas of memory, not set up specifically for stacks, are referred to as **heaps**. A heap can therefore be regarded as a *temporary storage area*. The operating system or some of your programs will probably make use of the area of memory called the heap, and different parts of the system would need to use different parts of the heap according to what is happening at the time. The idea is very similar indeed to the organisation of memory on a disk. Bits needed by one process might be allocated to one part of memory, and other processes might not be able to fit into the available space. Fragmentation of the memory (heap) occurs, and it becomes less efficiently used because of the large number of small spaces available. At some stage it might be necessary to clean up the heap, or you will get 'heap full' messages occurring. This process is called defragmentation.

Errors in programs (such as infinite recursive calls, for example) might cause stacks and heaps to overflow, irrespective of how much memory your system has.

Example

Give one example of a static data structure and one example of a dynamic data structure.

Solution

If you dimension an array in a program, then its size is fixed for the duration of the running of that program. For example 'DIM A(100) As Integer' might be the method used in a high-level language to reserve 100 memory locations (101 if you count location zero) into which integer numbers may be stored. This is an example of a static data structure because you cannot allocate more space to the array during the execution of the program.

If you are creating a file on a direct-access media such as disk, for example, then you can store as much data in that file as is available on your disk. Making the file bigger or smaller may be done dynamically during the execution of a program, and this is therefore an example of a dynamic data structure.

Linked lists

Linked lists are established and managed by pointer systems. As with the **linear list**, they may be implemented in main memory by using structures like arrays, or implemented on direct-access storage media such as disks by using data structures such as files.

The idea of a linked list is to have fast access to data via pointer systems. Just like the binary tree structure mentioned above, clever insertion and deletion methods ensure that the data structures do not have to be radically altered when new data is entered or old data is removed. A linked list must have a start pointer (or header), which points to the head of the list. The idea is shown in Figure 4.8.

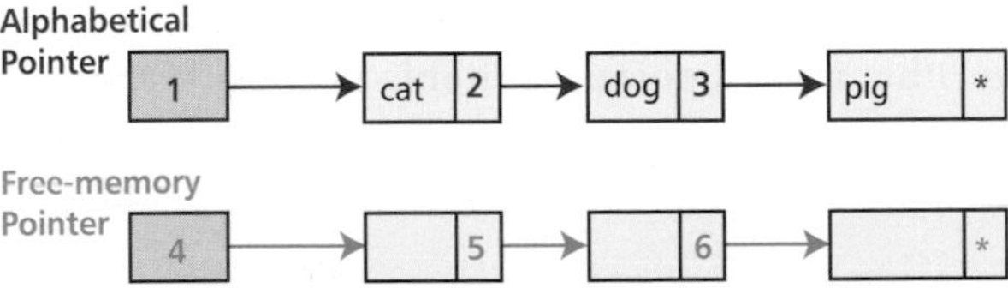

Figure 4.8 Data structures like linked lists can be set up using arrays

You can imagine this data to be set up in a two-dimensional array, where data, like 'cat' and 'dog' for example, is stored along with the pointer information like '2' and '3', which point to the next items in the linked list. Here, we have used alphabetical pointers to make the system very easy to understand. At the end of the list, the pointer does not contain a

Inserting data into a linked list is important at A2 level.

Make sure you can draw diagrams showing how the original list and free-space pointer systems are maintained.

It is also an advantage to be able to reproduce pseudocode to implement these algorithms.

number used to go to the next item, but has some indication that the list has ended. ('*' or '–1', for example, are quite common.) This is shown at the right-hand side of the pig node in Figure 4.8.

If data needs to be added to the list, then we need some extra storage locations, and the 'free-memory' pointer, which points to the next free space, indicates this. Because the free space list is also finite, this too must have an end-of-list marker, which may be used to determine if the list is full. If we wish to insert a 'cow' into the appropriate place in the list, then the start pointer must be consulted, which points to the beginning of the list. The pointers are then followed, and the 'node data' is compared to the data we wish to insert. In this case, 'cow' is compared with 'cat', and because 'cow > cat', we follow cat's pointer to dog. As 'cow < dog', we have established the alphabetical position in the list at which we insert the word 'cow' (i.e. between cat and dog).

To actually insert the data, 'cow' must be put into the node pointed to by the free-memory pointer, and all the pointers altered accordingly. The linked list structure after the insertion of the 'cow' node is shown in Figure 4.9.

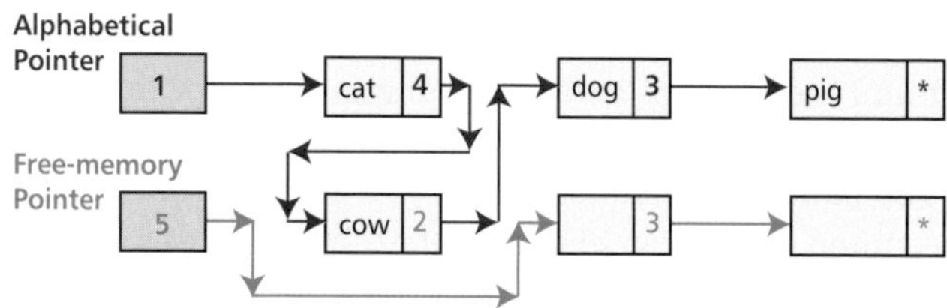

Figure 4.9 The new structure after the 'cow' node has been inserted

Note that the data 'cat', 'dog' and 'pig' etc. are stored at positions '1', '2' and '3' respectively. After the insertion of the 'cow' node, the data at the old positions are not altered, only the pointers are. Therefore, the pointer stored along with 'cat' now has to point to node '4', the position where 'cow' has been inserted. The pointer stored along with 'cow' is altered to point to '2', the position where 'dog' is stored. The free memory pointer must also be updated to the next free location, which is now pointing to location '5'.

When data structures are very large, it is not efficient to move large quantities of data just to insert one or two new items into a list. With a linked list, only the pointers are altered, and the operation can thus be achieved with far less processing. Nevertheless, the end result is the same as if all the data had been moved, and this is why the linked-list data structure is so useful.

Example

Write an algorithm using pseudocode to search for an item of data in a linked list, like the one shown in Figure 4.8. Your algorithm must display a suitable message if the desired data cannot be found.

Solution

The algorithm is quite simple. We need to follow the pointers from the beginning of the list (i.e. by looking at the start pointer) and then sequentially going through the list, examining items of data until the desired item is found. If we reach the end of the list, then the desired item is not present. The code is as follows, and we assume that the start pointer in the list is represented by the variable start_ptr. Assume also that the item to be found is represented by the variable 'data'. Finally, we will assume that the list is held in an array called List, and the pointers are held in an array called Link(pointer). Each data item can be examined by the variable List(pointer).

```
Procedure Search
        (*Point to beginning of list*)
        Pointer = start_ptr
        Repeat
               If data = List(pointer) then
                       (*data found - print it out*)
                       Print List(pointer)
                       Exit Procedure
               Else
                       Pointer = Link(pointer)
               Endif
        Until Pointer = "*"
        (*last node found - desired data not in list*)
        Print "No match can be found"
End Procedure
```

As the list is already ordered, it may not be necessary to search to the end of the list before an item is found or found not to be in the list. A very simple modification of the code shown here will do this. Try to work out which line needs to be altered and what modification would have to be made.

Two-way linked lists

We have already seen how a **linked list data structure** is useful for traversing data making use of a pointer system, and Figure 4.8 shows a typical example of this. It is possible to set up a variety of different pointer systems on the *same data structure*, and a two-way linked list is a good example. If the pointer system was set up alphabetically, then a reverse pointer system could be set up to traverse the list backwards, as shown in Figure 4.10. Note that two pointers are now needed for each node. Complex linked lists may have many pointer systems, representing a variety of things from 'best sales' to 'most absent' for example, depending on what data is present in a particular list.

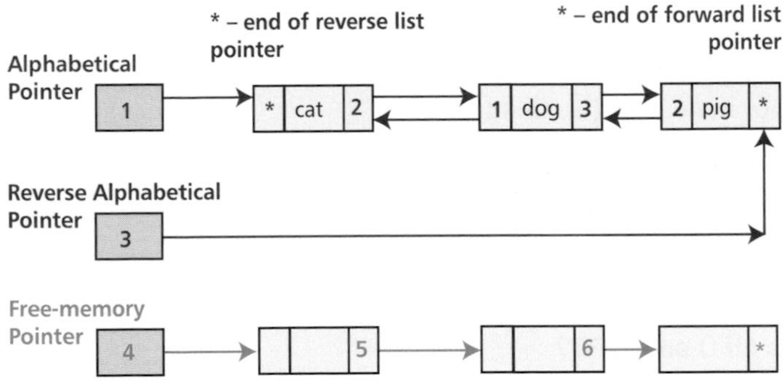

Figure 4.10 A two-way linked list system

Example

A sentence needs to be stored in such a way that it may be altered by the insertion or deletion of whole words only. It is also necessary to join sentences together to form larger units. It is suggested that a linked-list data structure be used to store the words in each sentence. Explain, with the aid of diagrams, how a linked-list structure may be used to store each sentence.

Solution

The following diagram shows two sentences stored as a linked list.

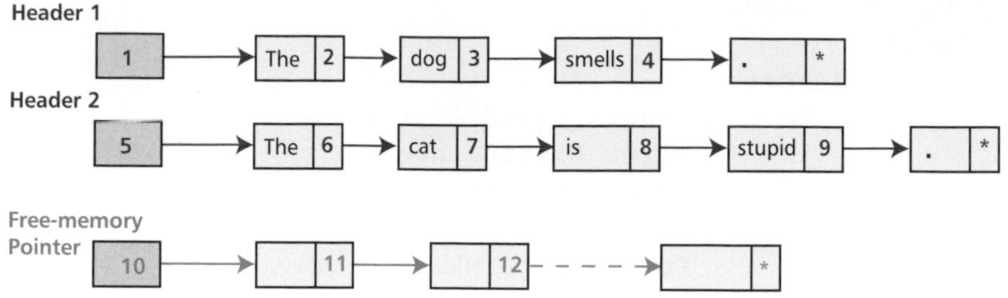

Figure 4.11 A possible data structure for storing sentences using a linked list

Each sentence is assigned to the next available memory storage in the structure. Therefore the header for sentence 2 starts at 5, the next available memory location because locations 1 to 4 inclusive are used to store the first sentence.

The free pointer system is shown starting at memory location 10, because memory locations 1 to 9 have been used to store the sentences. The addition of any new words would involve altering the pointers in ways similar to those shown in Figure 4.9.

Self-test questions

1. Explain what is meant by a data structure?
2. A linear list may be implemented by the use of pointers. What is a linear list, and how do pointers help to implement it?
3. What is a tree structure? Why are tree structures important in computer science?
4. Draw a tree structure containing data elements of your choice. On the tree structure label the following terms clearly.
   (a) Node (b) Root node (c) Child node
   (d) Parent node (e) Leaf node (f) Subtree.
5. What is the main difference between a tree and a binary tree?
6. (a) What is an ordered binary tree?
   (b) Why are ordered binary tree structures important?
7. Explain how a binary tree may be used to store data in alphabetical order.
8. What is meant by the terms LIFO and FIFO?
9. (a) What is an alternative name for a LIFO data structure?
   (b) What is an alternative name for a FIFO data structure?
10. Pointers play an important role when implementing queues and stacks. Explain the role of these pointers when implementing each of these data structures.
11. What is the difference between a dynamic and static data structure?
12. Explain what is meant by a linked list.
13. Show how a two-way linked list may be set up by the use of pointer systems. Give an example (other than a simple alphabetical one) of why a two-way linked list might be used in practice.
14. Outline the difference between a stack and a heap. For what purposes are heaps used?

5 Further data structures

In this chapter you will learn about:

- Pre-order, in-order and post-order traversal of binary trees
- Pseudocode algorithms for traversing tree structures
- Recursion
- Maintenance of tree structures

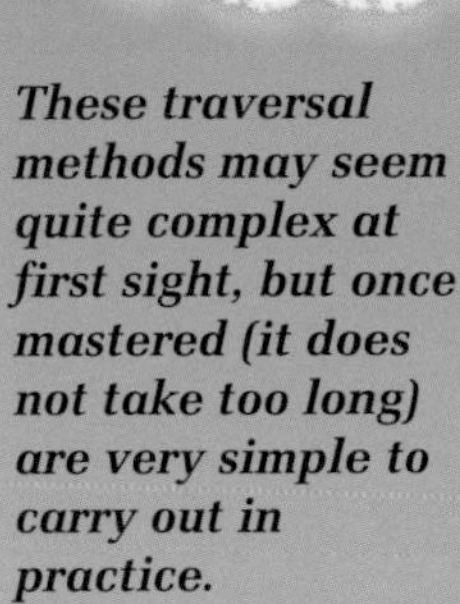

Traversing binary trees

Traversing a tree structure means 'walking' around the structure such that each node in the tree structure is visited once. The idea is usually to find, process or insert data associated with the tree structure. There are three ways to traverse a tree structure, namely **pre-order traversal**, **in-order traversal** and **post-order traversal** and these three methods refer to the position in which the root node is visited relative to the rest. These ideas are relatively simple, and the tree structure shown in Figure 5.1 will be used as an example.

These traversal methods may seem quite complex at first sight, but once mastered (it does not take too long) are very simple to carry out in practice.

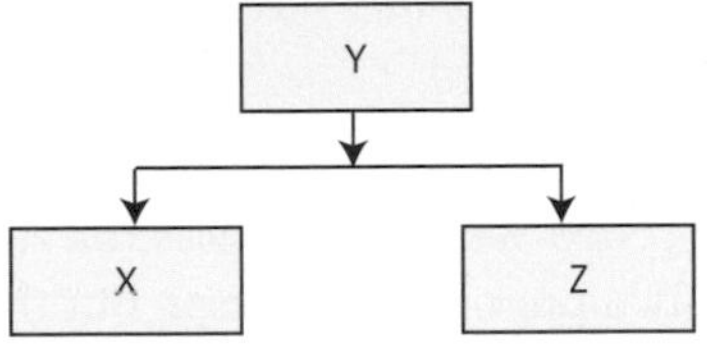

Figure 5.1 Simple tree for traversal methods

For pre-order traversal, the root node is visited *first* (hence the term *pre*). This means we list the data in the order 'root', 'left subtree' then 'right subtree' giving Y, X, Z.

For in-order traversal, the root node is visited in the *middle* (hence the term *in*). This means we list the data in the order 'left subtree', 'root' then 'right subtree' giving X, Y, Z.

For post-order traversal, the root node is visited *last* (hence the term *post*). This means we list the data in the order 'left subtree', 'right subtree' then 'root' giving X, Z, Y.

Only single nodes were present in the subtrees shown above. Subtrees will usually consist of other trees, which also have subtrees. Methods must be applied recursively (see **recursion**) if this is the case, and then the sophistication of these methods becomes clear.

Example

Consider the tree structure shown in Figure 5.2. List the data in this tree by applying (a) pre-order (b) in-order and (c) post-order traversal methods.

Given that this tree is an ordered binary tree, what is special about the in-order traversal mechanism carried out in part (b)?

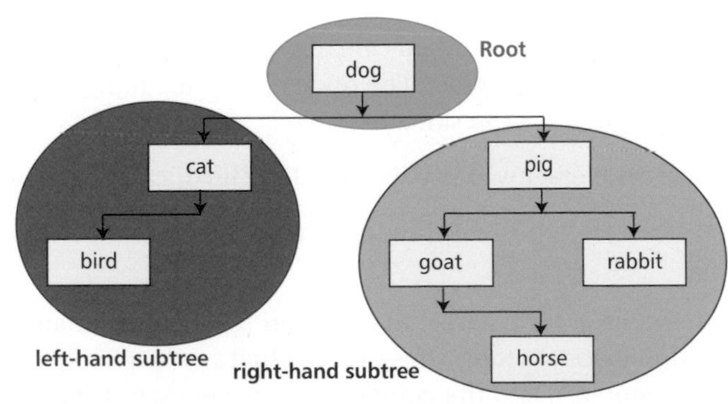

Figure 5.2 A complex ordered binary tree

Solution

It is far easier to carry out these processes than to explain what is happening. Therefore, we will carry out the pre-order traversal in great detail.

(a) Pre-order traversal involves visiting the root, left-subtree and then the right-subtree. First we list the data at the root node in Figure 5.2; the list starts off with **{dog}**.

Next we visit the left-hand subtree, shown in red in Figure 5.2. Now this data itself is a tree structure, and so we must apply pre-order traversal again. (This is called recursion.)

To traverse the red left-hand tree by pre-order traversal, we visit the root node first, and extract the data 'cat'. We add this to our original list (just 'dog' at the moment), and the new list now becomes **{dog, cat}**.

Next we visit the left-hand subtree of the red subtree, which consists only of 'bird'. As this is not a tree itself, but a leaf node, we simply list the data.
The list now becomes **{dog, cat, bird}**.

Next we visit the right-hand subtree of the red subtree. As there is no data here, we have finished the red subtree, and have now visited the root and left-hand subtree in the original tree structure.

So far we have processed the root and left-hand red subtree in our pre-order traversal of the entire tree. Next we must process the right-hand subtree, shown in blue in Figure 5.2. Again we apply a pre-order traversal, but this time operating on the blue tree. (This is another example of a recursive call.) We must process the root, therefore 'pig' gets added to the list, and the list now becomes **{dog, cat, bird, pig}**.

Next we process the left-hand subtree of the blue tree. This is yet another tree, and we apply a recursive call yet again, and traverse this by pre-order traversal. We visit the root, which finds 'goat', and so this is added to the list **{dog, cat, bird, pig, goat}**.

Next we traverse the left-hand subtree, which does not exist; therefore, we traverse the right-hand subtree, and find 'horse'. The list now becomes **{dog, cat, bird, pig, goat, horse}**.

Having traversed the left-hand subtree of the blue tree, we now traverse the right-hand subtree. This consists only of 'rabbit', and so this data is added to the list **{dog, cat, bird, pig, goat, horse, rabbit}**.

We have traversed the entire right-hand subtree, which was the final part of the original tree traversal, and have therefore produced the list of data for the entire tree, using pre-order traversal. The final list is, therefore, as follows.

{dog, cat, bird, pig, goat, horse, rabbit}

The next two traversal methods are almost identical in principle and therefore will not be explained in much detail. The node data will simply be listed. However, make sure that you can produce the same lists.

(b) In-order traversal will produce the list **{bird, cat, dog, goat, horse, pig, rabbit}**

(c) Post-order traversal will produce the following list **{bird, cat, horse, goat, rabbit, pig, dog}**.

Being an ordered binary tree, the in-order traversal mechanism has produced a list of data in alphabetical order, thus proving that new alphabetical data may be inserted into a tree (see chapter 4) and the contents of the tree may still be listed alphabetically without moving any of the existing data.

Recursion

You have already seen how recursive techniques are used when traversing tree structures. We now need to formalise these methods, and show how to apply recursion to a variety of different problems. More formally a recursive method is *one which is allowed to call itself.* Elegant and complicated techniques can be carried out with a minimum of code compared with the same algorithms implemented non-recursively.

Example

The factorial of a number N is written as N!
N! is simply a number, worked out as follows:

N! = N × (N – 1) × (N – 2) × ... 3 × 2 × 1, also, 1! = 1 and 0! = 1. Therefore, 5! = 5 × 4 × 3 × 2 × 1 = 120. Write two routines to work out a factorial N, one that uses recursion and one that does not.

Solution

(a) First, consider writing the code without the use of recursion. Here a loop structure is used, with special cases to determine the answer if N = 0 or N = 1.

```
(*non-recursive procedure*)
Input N
If N = 1 Or N = 0 Then
factorial = 1
Else
  count = 2
  factorial = 1
  Repeat
    factorial = factorial*count
    count = count + 1
  Until count = N+1
Endif
```

Here the variable called 'factorial' returns the value required.

(b) A recursive routine (one that can call itself) is as follows.

```
Procedure Factorial(N)
  If N = 1 Or N = 0 Then
    Factorial = 1
    Exit Procedure
  Else
    Factorial = N*Factorial(N-1)
  Endif
End Procedure
```

Here you can see the elegance of the recursive method. A parameter, in this case N, is passed over to the procedure. If N = 1 or N = 0, then the factorial is trivial, and after assigning a value the procedure is exited. However, if N > 1, then the procedure calls itself at line 6. The number of times it does this recursive call depends on how big N is. The data structure called a stack (see chapter 8) usually manages these recursive calls.

A binary tree example

In chapter 4 you saw how binary trees can be set up by inserting data items into an ordered list (i.e. if data to be inserted is alphabetically greater than the data in the root node, then the right-hand pointer of that node is followed, otherwise the left-hand pointer is followed etc.).

We will now develop some pseudocode to create a binary tree using the following list as data. Furthermore, the pseudocode will make good use of recursive routines.

{Maths, Geography, Physics, Computing, Technology, History, English}

First, let us create the binary tree. The first data item, being 'Maths' in the above list, is set up as the root node. This is shown in Figure 5.3a. The left and right pointers are set to null because they do not go anywhere yet.

Next the data item 'Geography' is to be inserted. As (Geography < Maths), then the left pointer from 'Maths' is set up to point to Geography, and the 'Geography' data item is stored as shown in Figure 5.3b.

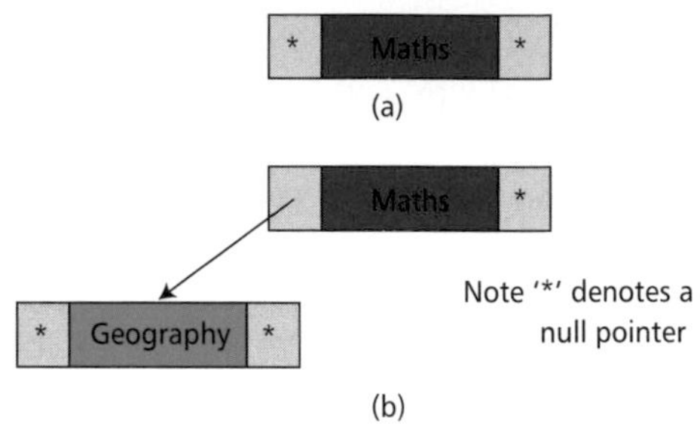

Figure 5.3 Initial construction of the binary tree

We now continue to build the tree, where each data item in the ordered list is compared with the data in the root node, and then the appropriate pointer is followed or set up, until the place where the data needs to be stored is encountered. The final tree, using the given data, is shown in Figure 5.4.

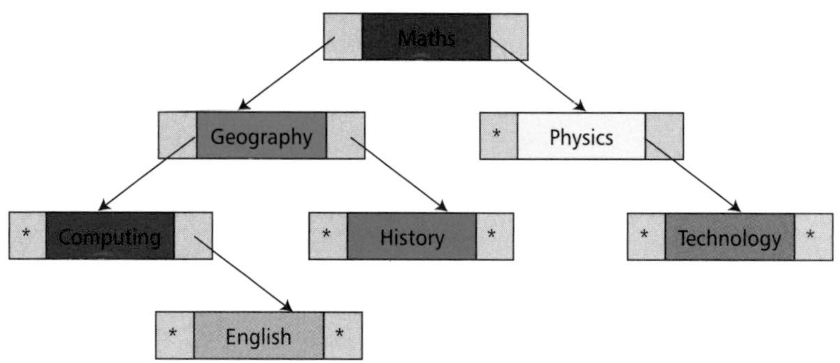

Figure 5.4 The completed binary tree for the subjects list

Next consider the data shown in Table 5.1, taking particular note of the three columns to the right which contain the left pointer, actual data and right pointer respectively. The colours for each data item match the tree in Figure 5.4, and were inserted into the data structure in the order given by the original list. You should be able to build up a table like this yourself. For example, as 'Geography' < 'Maths', and 'Geography' is the second data item to be inserted, 'Geography' is physically put into position number 2, and the left pointer belonging to 'Maths' gets set to 2, being Geography's position in the list.

We can store the data and pointers in three arrays, called 'Left_Pointer', 'Data' and 'Right_Pointer' respectively. Therefore, Right_Pointer(4) is Computing's right pointer, or Data(3) is the actual data 'Physics', for example. We also need some sort of pointer like 'Position', to determine the actual address in the arrays where new data may be stored.

If the binary tree structure is empty, then the first node to be inserted, ('Maths' in this case) is special as there are no left or right pointers set up to follow. Therefore, we set up the root node by inserting the data, updating the position pointer to 2, and setting the left and right pointers to null (*).

Having initialised the binary tree by creating the root node, we need to develop the algorithm for inserting the next items of data.

We must basically find the place in which to store the new node and add it onto the existing tree structure, maintaining the pointers as we go.

Table 5.1 The same binary tree stored using arrays

Position	Left pointer	Data	Right pointer
1	2	Maths	3
2	4	Geography	6
3	*	Physics	5
4	*	Computing	7
5	*	Technology	*
6	*	History	*
7	*	English	*
8	*		
9	*		
10	*Etc.*		*Etc.*

There are basically two stages to the algorithm, depending on whether we follow a left pointer or a right pointer. These are as follows.

1 Check to see if the data we need to insert is alphabetically *less than* the data in the node being considered. If it is, we look at the left pointer of the current node, which is either empty, in which case we insert the new node here, or we have to follow the left pointer and call this routine again.

2 Check to see if the data we need to insert is alphabetically *greater than* the data in the node being considered. If it is, we look at the right pointer of the current node, which is either empty, in which case we insert the new node here, or we have to follow the right pointer and call this routine again.

You should check to see that you agree with the above reasoning, then apply it to constructing the tree in Figure 5.4 to make sure you understand these principles.

The clever part comes from treating any subtree as though it were another binary tree; therefore, the root of the subtree can be treated as though it were the root of the main tree for our **recursive algorithm**. This idea of treating any new node as being the root node of a new subtree is essential to understanding the following algorithm. A variable called 'Root' will be set up to maintain the root of the subtree currently under examination.

Developing the pseudocode

We now need to turn the above statements into **pseudocode**. We will call the routine INSERT_NODE, and pass the parameters 'root' and 'data' over to it. Root is a variable which acts as a pointer to the root node of the binary tree currently being considered, and 'data' is the actual data to be inserted.

As an example, let's insert 'Geography'. As the only entry so far is 'Maths', we may call the insert-node routine as follows:

```
INSERT_NODE(1,Geography)
The pseudocode to insert the nodes is as follows:
(* Initialise binary tree *)
Dim Left_Pointer(10)
Dim Right_Pointer(10)
Dim Data(10)
```

```
Root = 1
Position = 1
Input data
(* Create root node as tree is empty *)
Left_Pointer(root) = *
Data(root) = data
Right_Pointer(root) = *
Position = 2

(* Create the rest of the tree *)
While data <>"999" Do
  Input data
  Call INSERT_NODE(root,data)
End While
End

(* node creation procedure based on the algorithms just developed
*)
INSERT_NODE(root,data)
(* left-hand subtree search *)
IF data<Data(root) THEN
  IF Left_Pointer(root)= * THEN
    (*Insert new terminal node here *)
    Data(position) = data
    Left_Pointer(position)= *
    Right_Pointer(position) = *
    (* update root pointer *)
    Left_Pointer(root) = position
    Position = Position + 1
  ELSE
    CALL INSERT_NODE(Left_Pointer(root)
                                        ,data)
  ENDIF
ELSE
  EXIT procedure
ENDIF

(* right-hand subtree search *)
IF data>Data(root) THEN
  IF Left_Pointer(root)= * THEN
    (*Insert new terminal node here *)
    Data(position) = data
    Left_Pointer(position)= *
    Right_Pointer(position) = *
    (* update root pointer *)
    Right_Pointer(root) = position
    Position = Position + 1
  ELSE
   CALL INSERT_NODE(Right_Pointer(root)
                                        ,data)
  ENDIF
```

You would not be expected to produce all the pseudocode shown here in an A2 examination question, but you may be expected to produce a small part of it, or explain some of the principles of the algorithms being described here for the maintenance of ordered binary trees.

```
ELSE
  EXIT procedure
ENDIF
END PROCEDURE
```

Few of the marks will be awarded for perfectly working code. Indeed, few students will actually get perfect pseudocode under examination conditions, and this is why the problems in examinations are kept reasonably simple. It may even be worth learning the methods until you are confident using them.

The next example demonstrates how a student, who finds writing pseudocode difficult, can gain marks by attempting to answer the 'creation of a binary tree example' covered in the last section. You must still understand the principles of the creation of a binary tree (which are trivial), and how this relates to storing data in an array like that shown in Table 5.1, which is also relatively easy to understand.

Some students find work on recursion quite difficult. If you are good at programming then the work will be relatively straightforward, but if you find programming difficult, you may never be able to achieve a good result in a limited amount of time. If you are in the latter position then concentrate on the principles of what is happening, draw pictures, and support your arguments with straightforward statements.

Example

An array/s needs to be set up to store data held in a binary tree. The data itself needs to be stored, as do the left and right pointers. Therefore, you will need three separate parts of the array/s, called 'Left Pointer', 'Data' and 'Right Pointer'. The data should be inserted into the correct position in the array by using a pointer called 'Position' – these ideas are shown in Table 5.1. Develop some pseudocode to outline these principles.

Solution

The pseudocode code to accomplish this could be as follows:

```
Set up a 10 x 3 array to store data and pointers
Set up left and right pointers

As the tree is initially empty, read first item of data and store
in the root (i.e. put 'Maths' into data position number 1).

While there is more data to be read

  READ next item of data
  Call INSERT ROUTINE (sending pointer parameters)

End While loop

INSERT ROUTINE (With pointer data and actual data passed over to
it)

  IF data just read < current data Then
       Search the left subtree and process data by altering the
       pointers or by calling this routine again.

  ELSE
       Search the right subtree and process data by altering the
       pointers and calling this routine again.

END INSERT ROUTINE
```

The above routine outlines the main principles, which, together with a few tree diagrams and Table 5.1 would get you most of the marks. It illustrates the recursive calls, but does not go into detail regarding the complex parameter passing.

Maintenance of tree structures

We now continue to develop algorithms for binary tree structures using the techniques of **recursion**. Some of the techniques covered here are not easy, and you may need to go over this work several times. The data for the example that follows is the same set of data that was used earlier in this chapter. The following example will take up most of the rest of this chapter. However, the work covered should help to explain recursion, enabling you to answer examination questions with a greater confidence, and make use of these techniques in your project work if necessary.

Example

Develop an algorithm to delete a node from an ordered binary tree structure like that shown in Figure 5.4. Explain your algorithm with reference to the deletion of the 'English', 'Physics' and 'Geography' nodes shown in Figure 5.4. What happens if we want to delete Maths?

Solution

The ordered binary tree maintenance algorithms shown here will be developed throughout the remainder of this chapter.

There are a number of different cases to be considered here.

1 The node to be deleted must be found, or an appropriate error message displayed. Therefore, we will need an algorithm to search the binary tree. If the node to be deleted cannot be found, then an error message must be displayed.

2 If the node to be deleted is a terminal node (i.e. having null left- and right-hand pointers), then the node may be deleted, and the pointer to this node from its parent set to null. This is shown in Figure 5.5.

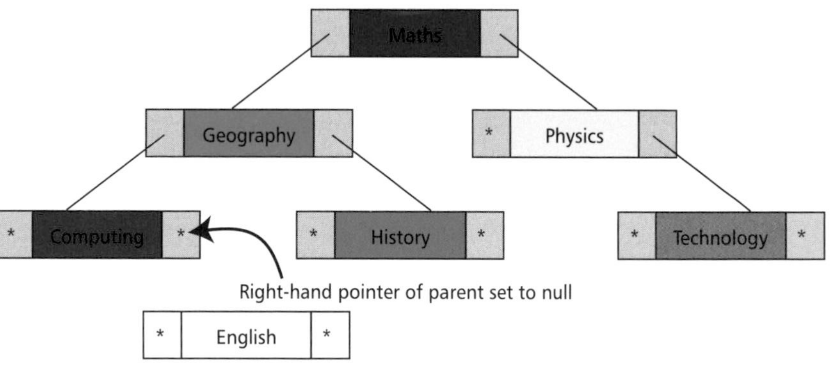

Figure 5.5 The 'English' node has been deleted

3 If the root node is to be deleted, then this is a special case and we need to create a parent for the deleted root node. A dummy node, containing no data but still maintaining the left-hand and right-hand pointers to the remaining tree structure, can do this.

4 If the node to be deleted has a null left-hand pointer, then the right-hand subtree can be joined on to the parent, as shown in Figure 5.6.

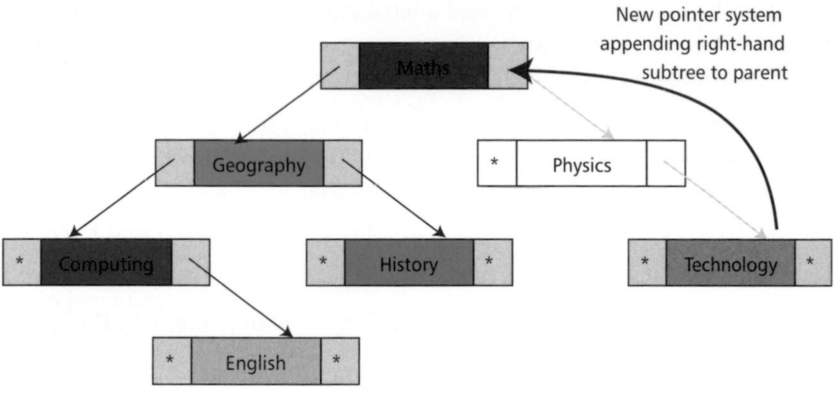

Figure 5.6 Deletion of the 'Physics' node

5 If the node to be deleted has a null right-hand pointer, then the right-hand subtree is empty, and the left-hand subtree can be joined to the parent in a similar way to that outlined in 4.

The final part of the algorithm is a little more complex and therefore needs a considerable amount of explanation. It will be covered in two parts.

(a) The case where the node to be deleted is a parent of its in-order successor.

The original list of data is as follows.

{Maths, Geography, Physics, Computing, Technology, History, English}

After being put into the binary tree (using < and > as before), the data would be in alphabetical order.

{Computing, English, Geography, History, Maths, Physics, Technology}

Now deletion of Geography should result in a tree structure which, when processed by in-order traversal (see the beginning of this chapter), results in the following list.

{Computing, English, History, Maths, Physics, Technology}

The important point to consider here is the parent of Geography in the tree, namely Maths, and the in-order successor to Geography, namely History. The new tree will be as shown in Figure 5.7 if 'Geography' were to be deleted.

The term 'in-order successor' denotes the node that comes after another node in the order used to create the binary tree.

An interactive project covering this important topic may be found on the Understanding Computing Interactive A2 CD-ROM.

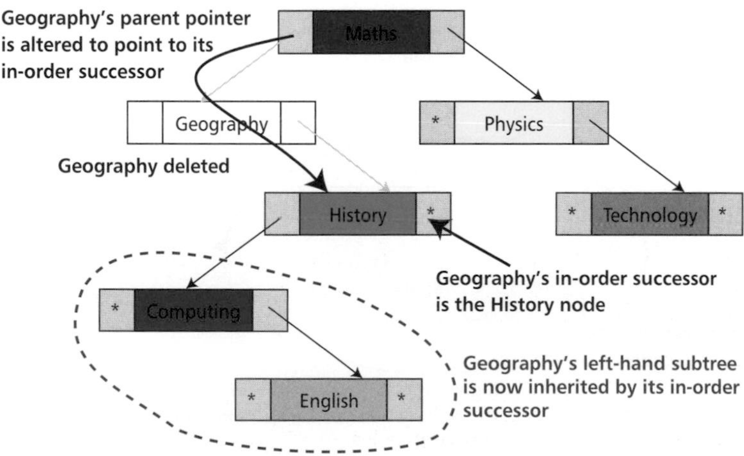

Figure 5.7 The 'Geography' node was the parent of its in-order successor

You should note that if the node 'History' had a left-hand subtree already (it did not in this case shown in Figure 5.6), then the 'Computing' and 'English' subtree would have to be added on to the extreme left of History's left-hand subtree.

(b) If the node to be deleted is not a parent of its in-order successor, then we need to do things in a slightly different way. We will run through a couple of examples to establish how the binary trees must be altered in this case.

To demonstrate this, we need a few more subjects added to the original list. Let us add Biology, Chemistry and Drama; the original (unordered) list now becomes:

{Maths, Geography, Physics, Computing, Technology, History, English, Biology, Chemistry, Drama}

The new tree structure, showing the left subtree only, is shown in Figure 5.8.

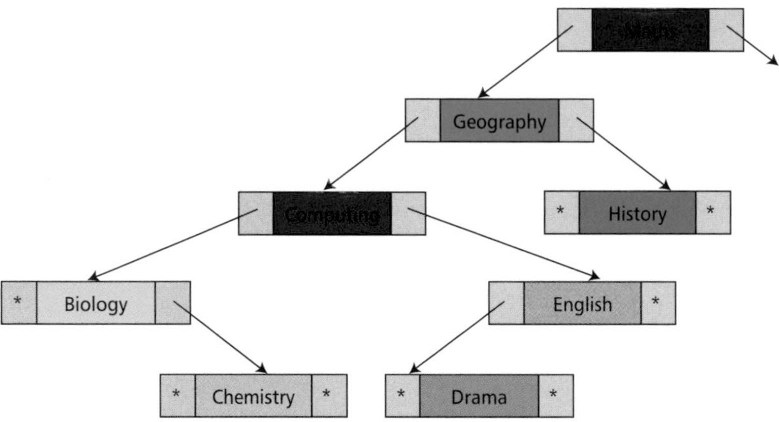

Figure 5.8 A few extra subjects are added

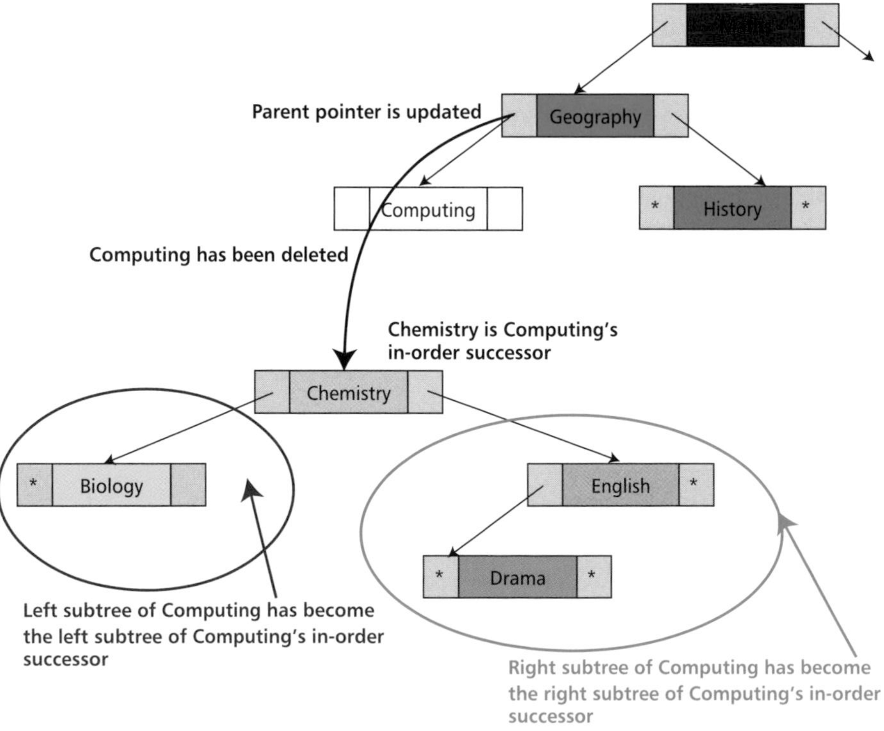

Figure 5.9 The binary tree after the deletion of the 'Computing' node

Let us suppose, for the sake of argument, that we wish to delete the node 'Computing'. Here, 'Computing' is not a parent of its in-order successor, namely 'Drama'. The simple algorithm developed for the deletion of 'Geography' will therefore not work in this case.

We must now alter the binary tree to that shown in Figure 5.9. If you perform an in-order traversal of the tree, you will find that the data is listed properly in alphabetical order.

From Figure 5.9 we can see that the right subtree of 'Computing' (as seen in Figure 5.8) has become the right subtree of 'Chemistry', the in-order successor to 'Computing'. The left subtree of 'Computing' has become the left subtree of 'Chemistry', the successor of 'Computing'. This is a little easier to handle because the node 'Chemistry' has no subtrees attached in Figure 5.8. However, if it did, then there would be one extra stage – that of attaching the subtree to the parent of the deleted node, and this is considered next.

As this is a complicated procedure, we will do one more deletion as a final example to establish the pattern of what is happening. Consider the brand new tree shown in Figure 5.10, which has been set up for the sole purpose of this last part of our example.

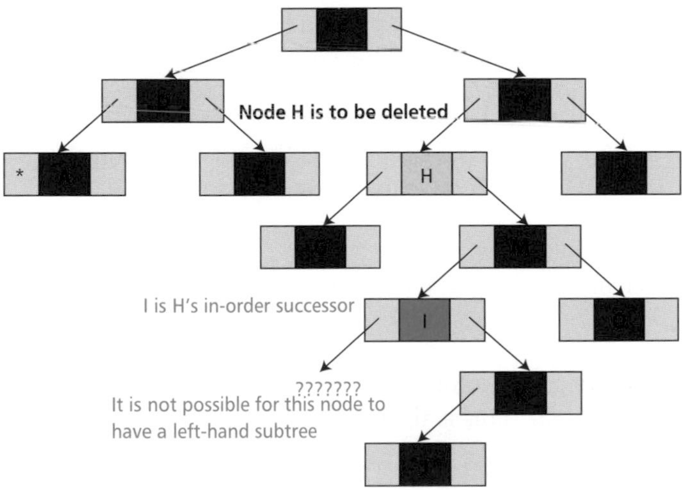

Figure 5.10 The in-order successor cannot possibly have a left-hand subtree

If we are to delete the H node in Figure 5.10, then H is *not* the parent of its in-order successor I. Also, H has left and right subtrees, and the successor I also has a subtree. In this case, we must change the tree to that shown in Figure 5.11.

If you perform an in-order traversal of the binary tree in Figure 5.11, you should find that you get an alphabetical listing, with node H missing. Note also the important point that the in-order successor node cannot possibly have a left-hand subtree because the node to be deleted is the one before this one!

To achieve all of this we had to carry out the processes outlined in detail in Figure 5.11.

We may now finalise the last stage of the algorithm (following on from stage 5 developed above) as follows.

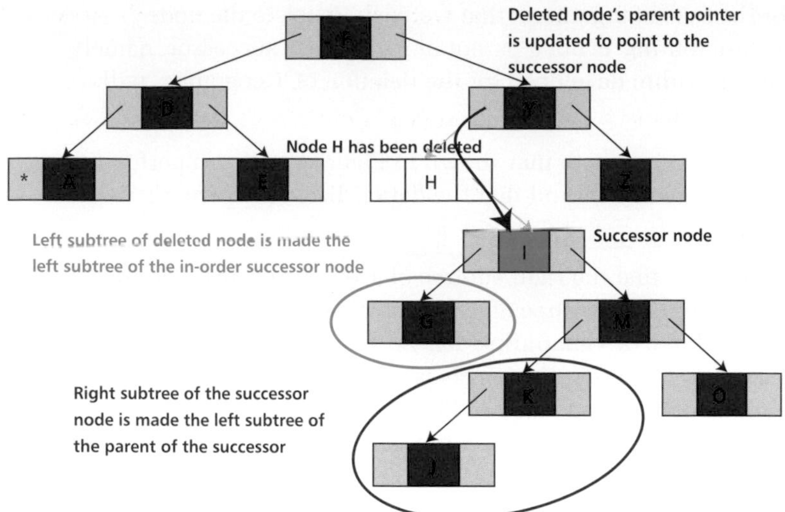
Deleted node's parent pointer is updated to point to the successor node
Node H has been deleted
H
Left subtree of deleted node is made the left subtree of the in-order successor node
Successor node
I
Right subtree of the successor node is made the left subtree of the parent of the successor

Figure 5.11 The binary tree after the deletion of the 'H' node

6 If the node to be deleted is a parent node of the successor, then we put the left-hand subtree of the deleted node onto the extreme left-hand side of the subtree of the in-order successor. (See example shown in Figure 5.7.) However, if the node to be deleted is not the parent of its successor, as was the case in Figure 5.11, then we perform the methods outlined in parts 7, 8 and 9.

7 We make the right subtree of the in-order successor's node the left subtree of the in-order successor's child. (See how J and K have moved in Figure 5.10 and Figure 5.11.)

8 We make the left-hand subtree of the node to be deleted the left-hand subtree of the in-order successor.

9 Finally, we must not forget to update the pointers for the parent of the deleted node to point to the in-order successor. This is the same for Figure 5.11 and Figure 5.7.

Self-test questions

1 **There are various ways of traversing tree structures including:**
(a) Pre-order traversal.
(b) In-order traversal.
(c) Post-order traversal.
Using the tree structure shown here, write down the order in which the node data would be listed using the three traversal mechanisms described above.

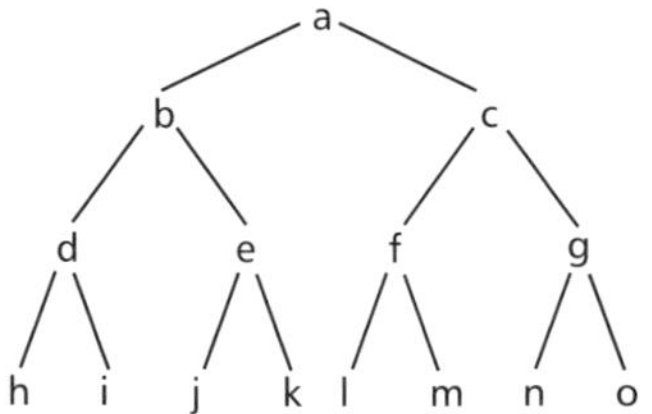
a
b
c
d
e
f
g
h
i
j
k
l
m
n
o

2 Using a suitable language, develop algorithms and produce code to solve the following problems.

(a) Create a binary tree using the names of people in your class. Choose a suitable root node (i.e. someone whose name is roughly in the middle of the alphabet) and create an ordered binary tree.

(b) Perform an in-order traversal of the binary tree to check that the names come out in the correct alphabetical order.

6 Sorting and searching algorithms

In this chapter you will learn about:

- Standard sorting and searching techniques
- The insertion sort
- The bubble sort
- The linear search technique
- The binary search technique

Standard sorting and searching techniques

When working through the following algorithms you will find it most useful to write down the numbers on separate pieces of paper and move them around as the algorithms proceed. In this way the author has found that students' understanding of the different sorting techniques is considerably improved. Try this method and see – you will not be disappointed.

Much data processing is concerned with **sorting** and **searching**. Sorting data requires putting raw data into some predetermined order, which could be alphabetical if the data is a set of words, or it might be ascending or descending numerical order for numbers. Searching simply means finding a specific item of data from a list of data.

The techniques used for these processes depend very much on the way in which the data is stored, and on particular aspects of the hardware. For example, is the data in main memory, or is it on disk or on tape? Can all the data fit into main memory at the same time? Factors like these, together with considerations such as speed and efficiency and amount of memory used, all play a part in deciding the most efficient algorithms to use.

Sorting

The following list of numbers will be used for the sort routines.

Table 6.1 The list of numbers that will be used in all the sort and search algorithms

N(1)	N(2)	N(3)	N(4)	N(5)	**N(6)**	N(7)	N(8)	N(9)	N(10)	N(11)	N(12)
27	48	13	50	39	**77**	82	91	65	19	70	66
Lower elements						Upper elements					

Throughout the following few sections we will talk about the elements in the above list and refer to them using subscripted variables like N(3) or N(7) for example. We will also talk about 'lower elements' and 'upper elements'. If we consider number 77 in the above list, all the elements before 77 (i.e. 27, 48, 13, 50 and 39) are called the 'lower elements'. Similarly, all the elements after 77 would be called the 'upper elements' as shown in the above table.

Algorithms in this chapter will be developed using a Pascal-like pseudocode. This can be contrasted with the Basic-like pseudocode developed in some other chapters. Both methods should be easily understood by students at A2 level. This will provide a pleasant alternative for those who do not have access to Basic, and will show a slight variation on writing pseudocode for those students that do.

Insertion sort

The **insertion sort** is the simplest sort algorithm and so will be covered first. It basically revolves around starting with a very small list containing just two numbers, and inserting the last number in the right place. We then consider the next number in the list to be sorted; this number then gets put into the right place, and the list gets longer and longer until the last number in the list has been considered, in which case the list is sorted. A typical algorithm, using the numbers in the above table, is as follows.

1 Start with the second number (48 in the above list). (If you do not start with the second number there would be nothing in the lower elements to compare it with!)
2 Compare the above number with all the lower elements and insert the number in the right place.
3 Repeat the above two stages, but moving to the third, fourth and fifth number etc., until the last number has been considered in stage 1.

Using the above algorithm, the list is sorted into ascending order as shown in Table 6.2.

Table 6.2 mirrors the movement of the pieces of paper mentioned previously.

The number shown in red is the current number being considered, and the numbers shown in green are the lower elements in the list.

When all the elements have been considered the list is sorted.

Table 6.2 The insertion sort

Sorting numbers using the INSERTION-SORT algorithm												Comments
27	48	13	50	39	77	82	91	65	19	70	66	Original list (start with the second number in the list).
27	48	13	50	39	77	82	91	65	19	70	66	48 compared with 27 (the lower elements) no changes necessary.
27	48	13	50	39	77	82	91	65	19	70	66	13 compared with 27 and 48. Number 13 inserted at beginning of list.
13	27	48	50	39	77	82	91	65	19	70	66	50 compared with 13, 27 and 50. No changes necessary.
13	27	48	50	39	77	82	91	65	19	70	66	39 compared with lower elements, number 39 inserted in correct place.
13	27	39	48	50	77	82	91	65	19	70	66	77 compared with lower elements ... no changes necessary.
13	27	39	48	50	77	82	91	65	19	70	66	82 compared with lower elements ... no changes necessary.
13	27	39	48	50	77	82	91	65	19	70	66	91 compared with lower elements ... no changes necessary.
13	27	39	48	50	77	82	91	65	19	70	66	65 compared with lower elements, number 65 inserted in correct place.
13	27	39	48	50	65	77	82	91	19	70	66	19 compared with lower elements, number 19 inserted in correct place.
13	19	27	39	48	50	65	77	82	91	70	66	70 compared with lower elements, number 70 inserted in correct place.
13	19	27	39	48	50	65	70	77	82	91	66	66 compared with lower elements, number 66 inserted in correct place.
13	19	27	39	48	50	65	66	70	77	82	91	Last number already considered.
13	19	27	39	48	50	65	70	77	82	82	91	**Numbers are now sorted in the correct order.**

The above table can be used to produce a pseudocode solution (and finally some real Pascal code) for the insertion-sort problem, but first let us introduce some extra terminology. Let current_position be a pointer to the number (initially set to N(2)) being used for comparison purposes, and let pointer_position be a pointer to the numbers that are being compared with the 'current_position number' in the above list. The argument will go along the following lines:

```
SET UP the current_position and pointer_position pointers.
Repeat
  Repeat
  Compare all elements in list below the current_pointer position
  Until
  N(pointer_position) > N(current_position)
  (In which case we INSERT and MOVE the elements as shown in the
  tables in the examples given above.)
  Or
  N(pointer_position) = N(current_position)
  (In which case no inserts or moves will be necessary.)
  Increment the current_position
  Reset the pointer_position
Until the current_position is at the maximum position in the
list.
```

Using Pascal, and assuming the numbers are stored in an array called N, we get the following program from the above description of the algorithm:

```
current_position: = 1;
REPEAT
  current_position : = current_position + 1; (* Set up pointers
  *)
  pointer_position : = 1;
  While pointer_position <= current_position Do
    Begin
      If N[pointer_position] > N[current_position] Then
      (* Insert necessary? *)
      Begin
        temp : = N[current_position]; (* Insert and move routine
        *)
        For count : = current_position Downto pointer_position +
        1 Do
          Begin
            N[count]: = N[count - 1]
          End;
        N[pointer_position] := temp;
      End;
    pointer_position : = pointer_position + 1; (*Move pointer*)
    End;
Until current_position = maximum;
```

A working version would obviously have to include declaring the variables, reading in the data and printing out the sorted list. A working version using **Pascal** is as follows:

```
Program insert sort (INPUT, OUTPUT);
Var current_position, pointer_position, maximum, temp, count:
Integer;
N: ARRAY [0..12] OF INTEGER;
Begin
 maximum : = 12;
 For count : = 1 To maximum Do      (* Get numbers to be sorted *)
   Begin
     Writeln('Please type in number', count);
```

```
      Readln(N[count]);
    End;
  Writeln ('Original list of numbers is');
  For count : = 1 To maximum Do       (* Print out numbers to be
                                      sorted *)
    Begin
      Writeln(N[count]);
    End;

  current_position : = 1;             (* Start insertion sort
                                      routine *)
  Repeat
    current_position : = current_position + 1;     (*Set up
                                                    pointers*)
    pointer_position : = 1;
    While pointer_position <= current_position Do
      Begin
        If N[pointer_position] > N[current_position] Then
          (* Insert necessary? *)
          Begin
            temp : = N[current_position];
            (*Insert and move routine*)
            For count: = current_position Downto pointer_position
                         + 1 Do
              Begin
                N[count] : = N[count - 1]
              End;
            N[pointer_position] : = temp;
          End;
        pointer_position : = pointer_position + 1     (* Move
                                                      pointer *)
      End;
  UNTIL current_position = maximum;

  Writeln('Sorted list');
  For count : = 1 To maximum Do      (* Print out sorted numbers *)
    Begin
      Writeln (N[count])
    End;
End.
```

Bubble sort

There are many other sort techniques, but a **bubble sort** is the only other technique required at A2 level. The name derives from the fact that the sorted item ‘floats’ to the top of the list like a bubble in water. We will use the same 12 numbers as before:

Table 6.3 Numbers for bubble sort

N(1)	N(2)	N(3)	N(4)	N(5)	N(6)	N(7)	N(8)	N(9)	N(10)	N(11)	N(12)
27	48	13	50	39	77	82	91	65	19	70	66

An algorithm for the bubble sort is as follows:

1 Start with the first pair of numbers in the list and compare N(1) with N(2).
2 If N(1) > N(2) then swap i.e. N(1) becomes N(2) and N(2) becomes N(1). If a swap was necessary then make a note of it (i.e. set a flag).
3 Go on to the next pair of numbers and repeat stages 1 and 2 using the next pair of numbers until the last pair of numbers in the list has been compared.
4 If a swap (one or more) took place (i.e. the flag set up in 2 is set), then reset the flag and repeat the entire procedure. If no swaps took place then END.

The flag must be reset (NOT SET) at the beginning of every pass, as shown in the tables. The first pass using the above algorithm is shown in Table 6.4.

During each pass the higher-value numbers are gradually floating to the top of the list.

Notice how the number 91 floated to the top of the list during the first pass shown in Table 6.4.

This is why the method is called the bubble sort.

Table 6.4 The first pass of the bubble sort algorithm

Sorting numbers using the bubble sort algorithm (FIRST PASS)												Comments	Flag
27	48	13	50	39	77	82	91	65	19	70	66	27 compared with 48, no swap is necessary, do not alter flag	NOT SET
27	48	13	50	39	77	82	91	65	19	70	66	48 compared with 13, swap necessary, flag is set.	SET
27	13	48	50	39	77	82	91	65	19	70	66	48 compared with 50, no swap necessary do not alter flag.	SET
27	13	48	50	39	77	82	91	65	19	70	66	50 compared with 39, swap necessary, flag is set.	SET
27	13	48	39	50	77	82	91	65	19	70	66	50 compared with 77, no swap necessary, do not alter flag.	SET
27	13	48	39	50	77	82	91	65	19	70	66	77 compared with 82, no swap necessary, do not alter flag.	SET
27	13	48	39	50	77	82	91	65	19	70	66	82 compared with 91, no swap necessary, do not alter flag.	SET
27	13	48	39	50	77	82	91	65	19	70	66	91 compared with 65, swap necessary, flag is set.	SET
27	13	48	39	50	77	82	65	91	19	70	66	91 compared with 19, swap necessary, flag is set.	SET
27	13	48	39	50	77	82	65	19	91	70	66	91 compared with 70, swap necessary, flag is set.	SET
27	13	48	39	50	77	82	65	19	70	91	66	91 compared with 66, swap necessary, flag is set.	SET
27	13	48	39	50	77	82	65	19	70	66	91	Last two numbers have been compared.	SET
												SWAPS were necessary, therefore another pass is needed. RESET the flag.	*NOT SET*

Swaps were necessary because the flag was set. Therefore we reset the flag and do another pass, as shown in Table 6.5.

Table 6.5 Part of the second pass of the bubble sort algorithm

Sorting numbers using the bubble sort algorithm (SECOND PASS)												Comments	Flag
27	13	48	39	50	77	82	65	19	70	66	91	27 compared with 13, swap is necessary, flag is set.	SET
13	27	48	39	50	77	82	65	19	70	66	91	27 compared with 48, no swap necessary, do not alter flag.	SET
13	27	48	39	50	77	82	65	19	70	66	91	48 compared with 39, swap is necessary, flag is set.	SET
The above processes continue until the end of the second pass													

After the second pass the numbers become:

Table 6.6 Numbers after second pass

N(1)	N(2)	N(3)	N(4)	N(5)	N(6)	N(7)	N(8)	N(9)	N(10)	N(11)	N(12)
13	27	39	48	50	77	65	19	70	66	82	91

Swaps were necessary so a third pass is needed.

After the third pass we get:

Table 6.7 Numbers after third pass

N(1)	N(2)	N(3)	N(4)	N(5)	N(6)	N(7)	N(8)	N(9)	N(10)	N(11)	N(12)
13	27	39	48	50	65	19	70	66	77	82	91

We proceed with as many passes as necessary until no swaps are recorded. In which case the list of numbers would be:

Table 6.8 No swaps recorded

N(1)	N(2)	N(3)	N(4)	N(5)	N(6)	N(7)	N(8)	N(9)	N(10)	N(11)	N(12)
13	19	27	39	48	50	65	66	70	77	82	91

Notice that all the lower-value elements are floating to the left and all the higher-value elements are floating to the right. Hence the name bubble sort.

The **pseudocode algorithm** for the bubble sort would therefore be as follows:

```
REPEAT
      RESET flag to zero.
      COMPARE all pairs of numbers and swap if necessary.
      IF a swap occurred set a flag,
UNTIL flag is not set.
```

The main Pascal code to achieve the above is shown, together with the input and output procedures for our 12 numbers:

```
PROGRAM bubble (INPUT, OUTPUT);
      VAR temp, count, flag, maximum, pointer: INTEGER;
      N: ARRAY [0..12] OF INTEGER;
      BEGIN
```

```
      maximum : = 12
      FOR count : = 1 TO maximum DO
      BEGIN
        WRITELN('Please type in number', count);
        READLN(N[count]);
      END;
      WRITELN('The original list of numbers is');
      FOR count : = 1 TO maximum DO
      BEGIN
        WRITELN([count]);
      END;
      REPEAT         (*Main routine*)
        flag : = 0;
        FOR pointer : = 1 TO maximum - 1 DO
        BEGIN
          WHILE N[pointer]>N[pointer + 1] DO
          BEGIN
            temp : = N[pointer + 1];
            N[pointer + 1] := N[pointer];
            N[pointer] : = temp;
            flag : = 1;
          END;
        END;
      UNTIL flag = 0;
      WRITELN('Sorted list');
      FOR count : = 1 TO maximum DO
      BEGIN
        WRITELN (N[count])
      END;
    END;
  END.
```

Search techniques

Searching means going through lists of data until one or more items of data that match some specified criteria can be found, or the data is found not to be in the list. In most systems we will probably be searching for some item of information that is contained in a key field within a file, and the enquiry will probably want the other data associated with this key field to be printed out also. However, during the following algorithms we will assume that only one item of information is associated with any search. The techniques of coping with the other information associated with the key field are already well established in other parts of this book.

In the solutions given to the following search techniques we will simply search through a list of numbers contained in the computer's main memory. The compilation of these lists is unimportant and therefore the list of numbers will be stored in an array called N. Hence the items in the array will be referred to as N[1], N[2], N[3] etc.

Search techniques are compared by considering the average number of comparisons that must be made to get to the desired item of data. This is referred to as the search length. If, for a certain list of data, an average of 250 comparisons must be made before an item of data is located, the search length would be given as 250. Another often-quoted parameter would be the search time. This is simply the average time taken to search for a given item of data.

The linear search

The simplest search technique is called the **linear search**, and this means examining each element in a list one by one until the desired element has been found! This is the method where the list is sequentially examined until the information required is obtained. Not much thought is needed for this one, and the following pseudocode should be quite obvious:

```
Begin
  Read required search criteria
  count := 1
  flag := 0
  While there is more data in the list to be read DO
    Begin
      Read element in list
      If criteria satisfied Then
        Begin
          Write information
          set flag
          increment count
        End;
    End;
End.
If flag is not set Then Write no match found in the list
```

The following Pascal program enables the user to find how many integer numbers of a particular size occur in a list of 20. The main algorithm is shown, and the other code is to enable the user to type in 20 numbers for test purposes.

```
Program linear search (Input Output);
Var count, test, flag : Integer;
N: Array [0..20] OF Integer;
Begin
  For count : = 1 To 20 Do
  Begin
    Writeln('type in number', count);
    readln(N[count]);
  End;
  Writeln('Please type in the search criteria');
  Readln(test);
  count : = 1;
  flag : = 0;

  While count < 21 Do
    Begin
    If test = N[count] Then
      Begin
        Writeln('criteria matched');
        Writeln(N[count]);
        flag : = 1;
      End;
    count : = count + 1;
  End;
```

```
    If flag = 0 Then Writeln('Sorry, no match found');
End.
```

The linear or sequential search is certainly not very efficient. If the item of data to be found is at the end of the list, then all previous items must be read and checked before the item that matches the search criteria is found. No structure was applied to the data in this simple case. The **search length** can easily be worked out by considering the following argument.

If, for example, there are only three data items in the list, then it could take one, two or three comparisons to find the required item of interest. Therefore, the average search length would be given by:

Average search length = (1 + 2 + 3)/3 = 2

Therefore, if there were N data items in the list, the average search length would be:

Average search length = (1 + 2 + 3 + 4 + ··· + N)/N

Using arithmetic progressions it can easily be shown that:

1 + 2 + 3 + 4 ... + N = N(N + 1)/2 therefore,
for the linear search, the average search length = N(N + 1)/2N = (N + l)/2

If the data has already been sorted (see beginning of this chapter) then much faster techniques for searching can be used.

Successfully locating the data is called a hit, and the hit rate is a measure of the success, or how many searches or accesses have to be done to find the data. A binary search algorithm should provide a better (lower) hit rate than a linear search algorithm because, on average, due to the structured data, the search length is less.

The binary search

The **binary search** relies on the data being **sorted** before it is searched. Therefore, some of the sort algorithms at the beginning of this chapter might have to be used before the binary search technique could be applied to a set of data.

The idea behind a binary search is quite simple. First compare our search criteria with the middle (the median) number in the list or with one number away from this middle number if there is an even quantity of numbers. Consider the ordered list shown in Table 6.9.

Table 6.9 An ordered list of numbers to demonstrate the binary search

Original ordered list of numbers used to demonstrate the binary-search techniques												
2	3	4	7	12	18	(23)	29	31	37	38	49	53
Left-hand list							Right-hand list					

The binary-search algorithm can be described by the following pseudocode:

```
Compare the desired number with 23 (the middle number in the
list)
If successful, Then
       A match occurs - we have completed the search
       Stop
Else
       If the desired number is less than the middle number Then
             Search the left-hand list
```

```
        Else
                Search the right-hand list.
        End
End.
```

The techniques used to search the left-hand and right-hand list are also a binary search. Hence the algorithm will call itself recursively (see **recursion** in chapter 5).

Table 6.10 The number 3 can be found by application of the binary search algorithm

1	2	3	4	5	6	7	8	9	10	11	12	13	**Index**
													Comments
2	3	4	7	12	18	23	29	31	37	38	49	53	Original numbers
2	3	4	7	12	18	23	29	31	37	38	49	53	INT((1 + 13)/2) = 7th
2	3	4	7	12	18	23	29	31	37	38	49	53	3 < 23 left-hand list is chosen
Left-hand list							Right-hand list						
2	3	4	7	12	18	23	29	31	37	38	49	53	INT((1 + 6)/2) = 3rd
2	3	4	7	12	18	23	29	31	37	38	49	53	3 < 4 left-hand list is chosen
Left-hand list			Right-hand list										
2	3	4	7	12	18	23	29	31	37	38	49	53	INT((1 + 3)/2) = 2nd
2	3	4	7	12	18	23	29	31	37	38	49	53	
	3												Number 3 has been found
Search has been stopped													

As an example of a binary search, consider finding the number 3 in the list shown in Table 6.9. The processes described in the binary search algorithm are actually carried out in Table 6.10. Note that only three comparisons are needed in the above case.

If we assume that the original list is simply 'integer numbers' in an array called N, then we can set up pointers to indicate the left- and right-hand numbers of each list.

The Pascal-like pseudocode algorithm can therefore be developed as follows:

```
maximum := number of elements in the array. (*Set up initial
conditions*)
left :=1
right maximum
middle := INTEGER((left + right)/2)
Read search criteria
PROCEDURE split (left, right, test)         (*Perform binary
split*)
  While (flag is not set)AND(middle >= 1)AND(middle <= max) Do
    Begin
      middle := Integer((left + right)/2)
      If N(middle) = search criteria Then
        Begin
```

The median or middle position from the numbers 1 to 13 can be found by using the formula

INT(1 + 13)/2 = 7

Similarly, for the numbers 1 to 6, the median or middle position can be found using the formula

INT(1 + 6)/2 = 3

```
          print out the search criteria
          set flag
        End Program
      Else
        Begin
          If search criteria > N[middle] Then
            Begin
              left := middle + 1
            End;
          Else
            Begin
              right := right - 1
            End;
        End;
      End;
    End;
  split (left, right, test)  (*Binary-split is called
recursively*)
End.
```

A complete Pascal program to perform a search on 20 numbers using the binary search now follows. The main algorithm is shown and the 20 numbers to search must be typed in order. If not, one of the sort procedures shown at the beginning of this chapter will have to be used.

```
Program binary-search (Input, Output);
Var right, left, maximum, middle, test, flag, count: INTEGER; 15:
Array [0..20] OF INTEGER;
PROCEDURE split-up (Var left, right, test: Integer);
Begin
  While (flag = 0) And (middle > 1) And (middle < maximum) Do
    Begin
      middle   Trunc((left + right)/2);
      If test N[middle]Then
        Begin
          Writeln('match found', N[middle]);
          flag := 1;
        End.
      Else
        Begin
          IF test > N[middle]Then
            Begin
              left := middle + 1;
            End;
          Else
            Begin
              right := middle - 1;
            End;
        End;
      End;
      split_up(left, right, test);
    End;
End;
```

```
Begin
  maximum := 10;
  left := 1;
  right      := maximum;
  flag := 0;
  middle := TRUNC((left + right)/2);

  For count := 1 To maximum Do
    Begin
      Writeln('Please type in number', count);
      Readln(N[count]);
    End;
  Writeln('Please type in search number');
  Readln(test);
  split-up(left, right, test);
  If flag = 0 Then
    Begin
      Writeln('Sorry, no match found in the list');
    End;
End.
```

The binary search is obviously much more efficient than the linear search, although it should be remembered that the data to be searched must be ordered. To get an idea of the **maximum search length** for a binary search, consider the following.

Suppose we wish to find the number 3 in the following lists by applying the binary search algorithms already well established:

1 (3)

Two elements would require just one comparison.

1 3 (5) 6   1 (3)

Four elements would require just two comparisons.

1 3 5 6 (8) 9 12 19   1 3 (5) 6   1 (3)

Eight elements would require three comparisons.

1 3 5 6 8 9 12 19 (23) 26 27 35 37 39 40 41
1 3 5 6 (8) 9 12 19
1 3 (5) 6
1 (3)

Sixteen elements would require four comparisons etc.

The above, together with the next few results are summarised in Table 6.11.

Table 6.11 Table showing the maximum number of comparisons needed in a binary search

Number of elements in the list	Maximum number of comparisons
2	1
4	2
8	3
16	4
32	5

The log of a number to any base is the power to which the base has to be raised to equal the given number.

This suggests a logarithmic relationship. If we use logs to base two then:

$\log_2(2) = 1$
$\log_2(4) = 2$
$\log_2(8) = 3$
$\log_2(16) = 4$ etc.

Therefore, in general, for N elements we require a maximum of $\log_2(N)$ comparisons.

Hence for a binary search, MAXIMUM SEARCH LENGTH = $\log_2(N)$.

Recursive algorithms using a logic programming language

So far in this chapter we have used **declarative programming** methods to demonstrate how numbers can be sorted or searched. As a comparison, we now show a **logic programming** algorithm using Prolog to perform the **insertion sort** covered in this chapter. You should refer to chapter 3, where Prolog programming was considered in detail.

Insertion sort

A typical insertion sort algorithm written in Prolog is as follows. The goal is to produce a sorted list, and this is accomplished by stripping successive numbers from the head of the list until the list is empty. Each number is then passed over to an 'insert' routine which inserts it in the right place and returns a modified list which is the sorted list. These processes are carried out by using recursive calls.

The Prolog programs shown here will make little sense unless you have worked through the Prolog material in chapter 3.

```
insertion_sort([X|Xs],Sorted)
          :-
          insertion_sort
          (Xs,Zs),
          insert(X,Zs,Sorted).

insertion_sort([],[]).

insert(X,[],[X]).

insert(X,[Y|Sorted],[Y|Zs]) :-
          X > Y,
          insert(X,Sorted,Zs).

insert(X,[Y|Sorted],[X,Y|Sorted])
:-
          X =< Y.
```

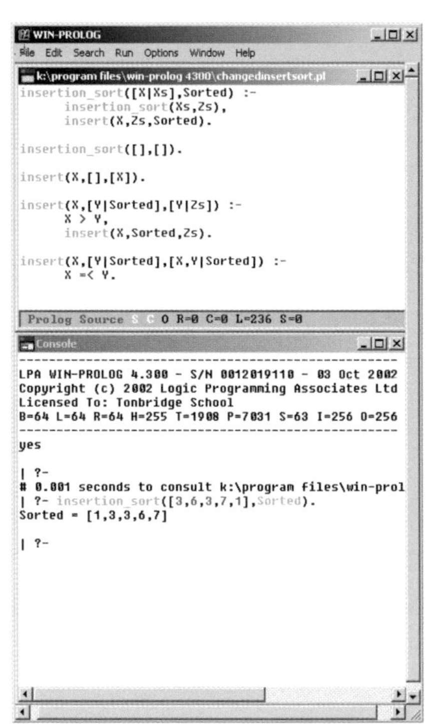

Figure 6.1 The 'insertion sort' algorithm being run on the author's machine

In Figure 6.1 the above routine is called by the user typing in the unsorted list 3, 6, 3, 7, and 1 using the syntax `"insertion_sort([3,6,3,7,1],Sorted)."`. The list is passed over inside square braces and 'Sorted' represents the variable (a list in this case), to be output by the Prolog compiler at the end of the program execution.

If you enter the code into your Prolog compiler and turn on trace, you will gain a good understanding of how the above routine works. The output is too long to show here, but a snippet is shown in Figure 6.2. Here you can see that the head of the list [3,6,3,7,1], has been stripped off the list and the tail of the list is the remaining numbers [6,3,7,1].

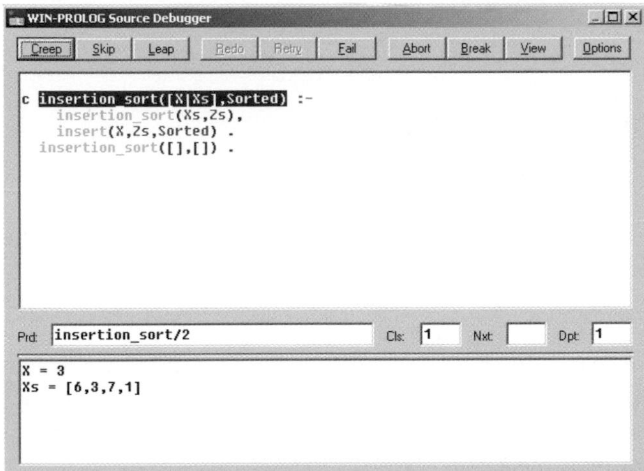

Figure 6.2 An early part of running a trace on the Prolog 'Insertion_sort' routine

Self-test questions

1. Sorting sets of data into some kind of order is important in the data-processing industry. An insertion sort is one way of accomplishing this task. Briefly outline the strategy to be undertaken when carrying out an 'insertion sort' on a computer.
2. Explain the concept of a 'bubble sort'. Outline the main stages to be undertaken if a bubble sort is to be carried out on a computer.
3. Explain what is meant by the terms 'linear search' and 'binary search'.
4. A linear or sequential search involves examination of each element within an array. This can be very slow if the desired elements are near the end of a long list. A better method is to make use of a binary search. This involves storing the data in order as a binary tree. Show how it is possible to search and find any element in a list of 1000 by examining at most only 10 of the elements.
5. Recursion is a theme common to many different computer-based algorithms. Explain what is meant by recursion and give an example of an algorithm that would benefit from using the technique of recursion.

7 Data representation in computers

In this chapter you will learn about:

- Number bases – binary, denary and hexadecimal
- Integer and real numbers
- Two's complementation to represent negative numbers
- Floating point numbers
- The need for normalisation

Number bases

You have already covered simple binary in the AS book in this series.

This chapter reinforces and extends this work, with particular emphasis on negative number representation using two's complement.

The important principles of normalisation are covered here too.

Computers work in binary or **base two**. You should recall that the principles are exactly the same as counting in **base ten** (*our normal system*) which is also known as the **decimal system** or **denary**. As a reminder, numbers in base two use only the set of digits {0,1}, and counting in binary is demonstrated in Table 7.1

Table 7.1 The idea of counting in binary

Decimal		Binary	Comments
1 decimal	is	1 binary	One lot of 1
2 decimal	is	1 0 binary	One lot of 2 and no lots of 1
3 decimal	is	1 1 binary	One lot of 2 and one lot of 1
4 decimal	is	1 0 0 binary	One lot of 4, no lots of 2 and no lots of 1

Table 7.2 Counting in decimal and binary numbers for numbers from 0 to 31

Decimal numbers		Equivalent 5-bit binary numbers					Decimal numbers (continued)		Equivalent 5-bit binary numbers				
Tens	Units	16s	8s	4s	2s	1s	Tens	Units	16s	8s	4s	2s	1s
0	0	0	0	0	0	0	1	6	1	0	0	0	0
0	1	0	0	0	0	1	1	7	1	0	0	0	1
0	2	0	0	0	1	0	1	8	1	0	0	1	0
0	3	0	0	0	1	1	1	9	1	0	0	1	1
0	4	0	0	1	0	0	2	0	1	0	1	0	0
0	5	0	0	1	0	1	2	1	1	0	1	0	1
0	6	0	0	1	1	0	2	2	1	0	1	1	0
0	7	0	0	1	1	1	2	3	1	0	1	1	1
0	8	0	1	0	0	0	2	4	1	1	0	0	0
0	9	0	1	0	0	1	2	5	1	1	0	0	1
1	0	0	1	0	1	0	2	6	1	1	0	1	0
1	1	0	1	0	1	1	2	7	1	1	0	1	1
1	2	0	1	1	0	0	2	8	1	1	1	0	0
1	3	0	1	1	0	1	2	9	1	1	1	0	1
1	4	0	1	1	1	0	3	0	1	1	1	1	0
1	5	0	1	1	1	1	3	1	1	1	1	1	1

You should also remember how binary numbers may be formed by considering the binary column headings 1s, 2s, 4s, 8s etc. Table 7.2 reminds you how to form binary numbers from their decimal equivalents by using the column headings.

Example

What pattern of binary digits represents the following decimal numbers?
(a) 27 (b) 100 (c) 255

Solution

The column headings for the binary numbers are needed up to and including 128, as follows.

Table 7.3 Binary column headings required

Question	Decimal number	Binary column headings								Comments
		128	64	32	16	8	4	2	1	Binary column headings
(a)	27	0	0	0	1	1	0	1	1	16 + 8 + 2 + 1 = 27
(b)	100	0	1	1	0	0	1	0	0	64 + 32 + 4 = 100
(c)	255	1	1	1	1	1	1	1	1	Easy to work out as it is '1 less than 256'

Conversion between decimal and binary numbers

To convert integer decimal numbers into binary we use the methods shown in the above table. Write down the binary column headings until they are of sufficient size, then work out how many headings are needed to make up the decimal number, putting a 1 underneath if a column heading is needed or a zero underneath if it is not. Conversion from binary to decimal is just as simple. Here we add up the column headings with a '1' underneath to obtain the decimal number. Some examples now follow.

Always use the simpler method to work out the answer if one is available.

Example

What decimal numbers do the following binary numbers represent?
(a) 1 0 1 (b) 1 0 0 0 1 0 0 0 (c) 1 1 1 1 1 1 1 1 1 1 1 1 1 1 1

Typical binary patterns where all the digits are '1' are examples of this as shown in two of the examples on this page.

Solution

(a)

4	2	1
1	0	1
4 + 0 + 1 = 5		

(b)

128	64	32	16	8	4	2	1
1	0	0	0	1	0	0	0
128 + 8 = 136							

(c)

2048	1024	512	256	128	64	32	16	8	4	2	1
1	1	1	1	1	1	1	1	1	1	1	1
2048 + 1024 + 512 + 256 + 64 + 32 + 16 + 8 + 4 + 2 + 1 = 4095 OR, because it is *much* easier to do, use $2^{12} - 1 = 4096 - 1 = 4095$											

Remember that binary column headings are easy to work out by raising two to the appropriate power, noting that $2^0 = 1$, $2^2 = 4$, $2^3 = 8$ etc., as shown in Table 7.4

Table 7.4 Powers of two represent the column headings in binary

Binary column headings													
Number	4096	2048	1024	512	256	128	64	32	16	8	4	2	1
Power of two	2^{12}	2^{11}	2^{10}	2^9	2^8	2^7	2^6	2^5	2^4	2^3	2^2	2^1	2^0

Therefore, in the last example, we used 2^{12} because this number would be one more than the binary number with 12 binary digits in it (remember we start off with 2^0).

Hexadecimal numbers

You will recall from your AS work that **hexadecimal**, (**hex**) or base sixteen numbers use the set of digits {0, 1, 2, 3, 4, 5, 6, 7, 8, 9, A, B, C, D, E, F} where 'A' represents '10', 'B' represents '11' up to 'F' which represents '15'. The headings are shown in Table 7.5.

Table 7.5 Powers of 16 represent the column headings in hexadecimal

Hexadecimal column headings				
Number	4096	256	16	1
Power of sixteen	16^3	16^2	16^1	16^0

Example

What are the decimal equivalents of the following hexadecimal numbers?
(a) 2A (b) 3ED

Solution

(a)

16	1
2	A
$2 \times 16 + 10 = 42$	

(b)

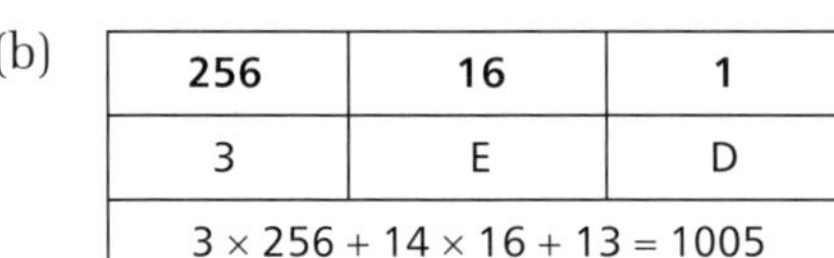

256	16	1
3	E	D
$3 \times 256 + 14 \times 16 + 13 = 1005$		

Hexadecimal is used because of the strong relationship between hex and binary, and the fact that it is easier for humans to use. Groups of four binary digits, representing the decimal numbers from 0 to 15, have a one to one relationship with a hex digit, also representing decimal numbers from 0 to 15. Therefore, groups of four binary digits may be replaced with the hexadecimal equivalent.

The number base subscript notation

When working in multiple bases, a subscript is used to identify the base, as shown here.

Decimal number	Hexadecimal number	Binary number
101_{10}	101_{16}	101_2

The first number represents 'one hundred and one', the second number is 'two hundred and fifty seven' and the third number is 'five'. Without subscripts, they all look like the same number. Subscripts are often omitted if the base being used is obvious.

Converting between number bases

Any number base can be converted to any other by first changing it into base ten. To convert binary into hex, we could first convert binary into base ten, and then convert the base ten numbers into hex using the methods described above. However, there is a much quicker method, and this should be used in preference to the long method. The methods are simple because of the strong relationship between binary and hex mentioned when hexadecimal numbers were considered above.

To change a binary number directly into hex without going via base ten first, we split up the binary number into groups of four digits. Starting at the right-hand side of the number, write down the hex equivalent for each group of four binary digits as follows:

Binary number	1 1	1 0 1 0	0 1 1 1	0 0 1 0
Hex equivalent	3	A	7	2

Therefore, $1\,1\,1\,0\,1\,0\,0\,1\,1\,1\,0\,0\,1\,0_2 = 3A72_{16}$

It is just as easy to convert from hex into binary; we simply reverse the process as follows.

Hex number	2	C	0	5
Binary equivalent	1 0	1 1 0 0	0 0 0 0	0 1 0 1

Therefore, $2C05_{16} = 1\,0\,1\,1\,0\,0\,0\,0\,0\,0\,0\,1\,0\,1_2$

When converting between binary and hex or hex and binary, the above methods should be used in preference to base ten.

Binary fractions

Binary fractions are used to represent the fractional part of a binary number. Consider the column headings for binary numbers. From left to right they get smaller by a factor of two (... 8s, 4s, 2s, and 1s). Continuing this process we get the fractional headings 1/2, 1/4, 1/8, 1/16 etc. The binary point separates the fractional and whole number.

Table 7.6 Binary fractions

Integer part of the number						Binary point	Fractional part of the number				
32	16	8	4	2	1	.	1/2	1/4	1/8	1/16	1/32
1	0	1	0	1	0	.	0	1	0	1	1

The number shown above must be treated in two parts, and the whole number or integer part can be treated using the methods of the previous sections.

To find the decimal value of the integer part we add:
$32 + 8 + 2 = 42$.
To find the value of the fractional part we add:
$1/4 + 1/16 + 1/32 = 11/32$

It is usual to express this fraction as a decimal: $0.25 + 0.0625 + 0.03125 = 0.34375$.
The fractional and integer values are added together to get 42.34375.
Therefore $101\,010.01011_2 = 42.34375_{10}$

Common binary fractions are shown for your convenience in Table 7.7.

Those of you undertaking mathematics at A level should appreciate the difference between the term 'real number' as used in computing and the term 'real number' as used in mathematics.

In computing a 'real number' is used to distinguish it from an integer, and real numbers are usually approximated as a 'floating point number' inside a computer.

Floating point numbers are considered later in this chapter.

Table 7.7 Some typical conversion factors

Binary fraction	Fraction	Decimal fraction	Binary fraction	Fraction	Decimal fraction
0.1	1/2	0.5	0.000001	1/64	0.015 625
0.01	1/4	0.25	0.0000001	1/128	0.007 812 5
0.001	1/8	0.125	0.00000001	1/256	0.003 906 25
0.0001	1/16	0.062 5	0.000000001	1/512	0.001 953 125
0.00001	1/32	0.031 25	0.0000000001	1/1024	0.000 976 562 5

Real numbers

In mathematics real numbers are made up of the set of **rational** and **irrational numbers**. Rational numbers *can be expressed as a fraction* (like 7/8 or 13/29) and irrational numbers *cannot be expressed as a fraction* (pi = 3.141592654...). In computing, a real number (or **real**) is the name given to a **data type** that includes both integer *and* fractional parts, like those just covered in the binary fractions section above. The term real is used to distinguish this data type from **integer** or whole numbers.

Negative binary numbers – two's complement

One of the most common methods used for negative numbers can be explained with reference to a counter. Let us assume that we have a three-digit counter as shown in Figure 7.1(a).

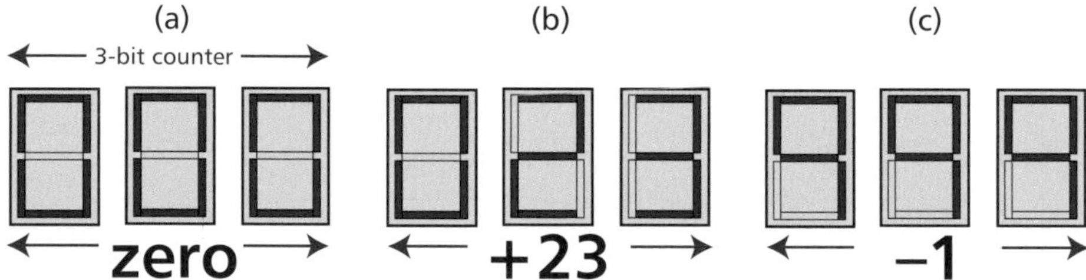

Figure 7.1 Using a three-digit counter

Start with the counter set to 000, as shown in Figure 7.1(a), then, after 23 counts, the counter would register 023 as shown in Figure 7.1(b). This system could record positive numbers up to and including 999. However, the system would break down if we counted to 1000 because the counter would read 000 again.

Let us now use the same counter, but invent a way to record negative numbers too. If we start again, but this time count backwards by one, the counter would read 999, as shown in Figure 7.1(c). This could, therefore, be a possible representation for –1. Of course we could not let 999 represent +999 in the forward direction as well, and so our range of numbers in the forward direction would now be more limited. Similar principles can be applied to a binary counter, as shown in Table 7.8. For simplicity our **register** will have just four **bits** (binary digits).

If a four-bit binary number were used in the conventional way, 0000 to 1111 would give us 16 different positive combinations of decimal numbers from 0 to +15. Using the above

Table 7.8 A four-bit binary counter used to represent negative numbers

	Register contents				Decimal equivalent
	1	0	0	0	−8
	1	0	0	1	−7
	1	0	1	0	−6
Negative numbers	1	0	1	1	−5
	1	1	0	0	−4
	1	1	0	1	−3
	1	1	1	0	−2
	1	1	1	1	−1
Start here	**0**	**0**	**0**	**0**	**0**
	0	0	0	1	1
	0	0	1	0	2
	0	0	1	1	3
Positive numbers	0	1	0	0	4
	0	1	0	1	5
	0	1	1	0	6
	0	1	1	1	7

method we still have 16 unique numbers (−8 to +7) but the range in the positive direction is reduced to +7. It is easy to distinguish positive and negative numbers because *all negative numbers* start off with *1* and *all positive numbers* start off with *0*. This method of representing numbers is called **two's complementation**.

Two's complementation is vitally important at A2 level.

Not only will you be able to understand positive and negative integers, but two's complementation is used for floating point numbers as well (see later in this chapter).

The idea of two's complementation is really quite simple. However, learn the quick method of working out the numbers as shown on this page. This is far less tedious than most other methods.

Two's complement – a quick method

It would be inconvenient to have to draw out tables similar to Table 7.8 simply to find the two's complement binary representation of a particular negative number. Suppose, for example, we wish to find the two's complement four-bit representation for −6. From the above table we can see that the answer is: 1010. However, consider the following method.

1 Write down the positive binary number using four bits, i.e. for −6, we would write the binary number for +6. Therefore 6 becomes 0110 using four bits.
2 Starting at the right-hand side, rewrite this number up to and including the first 1. For 0110 this would mean writing down 1 and 0. Therefore, the right-hand two digits only are written down: 10.
3 For the remainder of the number (i.e. all the digits to the left), change the 0s for 1s and 1s for 0s. Therefore, the number becomes 1010, which is the required answer.

Example

Write down the two's complement eight-bit representation for −39.

Solution

The column headings for the binary numbers are needed up to and including 128, as follows.

Table 7.9 Representation for −39

128	64	32	16	8	4	2	1	Binary column headings using eight bits
0	0	1	0	0	1	1	1	This is the binary number for +39
–	–	–	–	–	–	–	1	Write the number up to and including the first 1
1	1	0	1	1	0	0	1	Change all other 0s for 1s and 1s for 0s

Therefore $-39_{10} = 1\,1\,0\,1\,1\,0\,0\,1_2$ if eight-bit two's complement is used.

As well as representing negative numbers in binary, it is possible to subtract numbers by adding the complement, i.e. 59 + (−32) is the same as 59 − 32. All the electronic circuits designed for adding inside a computer chip can be used for subtraction as well. This is just one of the reasons why complementation is of such fundamental importance in computing.

Example

Show how a computer is able to use two's complementation to work out 38 – 27 by using addition only. You should show your working in binary using eight bits.

Solution

Using eight bits, +38 is 0 0 1 0 0 1 1 0. To work out the bit pattern for −27, use +27 and the quick rule mentioned earlier. +27 using eight bits is 0 0 0 1 1 0 1 1, therefore, −27 is 1 1 1 0 0 1 0 1. The sum, worked out by the computer will therefore be:

+38 =		0	0	1	0	0	1	1	0
−27 =		1	1	1	0	0	1	0	1
									+
This bit falls off the end!	1	0	0	0	0	1	0	1	1

Giving an answer of $0\,0\,0\,0\,1\,0\,1\,1_2$ which is +11, the right answer for 38 – 27. The most significant bit is lost (shown in red) because we only have eight bits available.

Fixed point binary numbers

Except when using two's complement notation, we have not been bothered about the number of digits required to represent a number, or the position of the binary point within the number. In practice the **register** holding the number is of fixed length, and therefore compromises may have to be made. The size of register will therefore affect the range of numbers that can be displayed. There are two major types of fixed point representation – **integer** and **fractional**. We now consider these two systems in detail.

Integer fixed point binary numbers

We will assume an eight-bit register (a sensible choice as many computers work in eight bits or multiples thereof) and two's complementation will be used throughout. The register can therefore be visualised as shown in Table 7.10.

Table 7.10 An eight-bit register

	An eight-bit integer fixed point register							
Register (Bit number)	8	7	6	5	4	3	2	1
Register contents	*	*	*	*	*	*	*	*

You need to be able to evaluate the limitations of such a system (e.g. what are the largest and smallest numbers?). This can easily be worked out by filling the register up with the appropriate bits and working out what happens. This is carried out in Table 7.11.

Table 7.11 The limitations of an eight-bit two's complement fixed point binary number

	An eight-bit integer fixed point register							
Register (Bit number)	8	7	6	5	4	3	2	1
Maximum positive number (+127) Most significant bit must be zero	0	1	1	1	1	1	1	1
Minimum positive number (+1)	0	0	0	0	0	0	0	1
Smallest magnitude negative number (−1) Look at Table 7.8 if this appears confusing	1	1	1	1	1	1	1	1
The largest magnitude negative number (−128) (First bit must be a 1 or it is not negative)	1	0	0	0	0	0	0	0

If we look at the above results we can see that the range of numbers (i.e. from largest to smallest) is +127 to −128 inclusive.
It would be more useful to express the relationship in terms of powers of two, because this can then be extended to evaluate the numbers for any register with N bits:

For an eight-bit register $-2^7 \leqslant \text{range} \leqslant 2^7 - 1$ (Using two's complement)
Therefore for an N-bit register $-2^{N-1} \leqslant \text{range} \leqslant 2^{N-1} - 1$ (Using two's complement)

Example

What is the 'maximum magnitude positive number' and the 'maximum magnitude negative number' that can be represented by using a 12-bit register if two's complement notation is used?

Solution

Using 12 bits, the maximum positive number would be $011111111111 = 2^{11} - 1 = 2047_{10}$
Using 12 bits, the maximum negative number would be $100000000000 = -2^{11} = -2048_{10}$

Fractional fixed point binary numbers

Two's complementation will be used, but this time the binary point is in the position shown in Table 7.12 (the binary point may be in any fixed position within the register).

Table 7.12 An eight-bit register

	An eight-bit fractional fixed point register								
Register (Bit number)	8		7	6	5	4	3	2	1
Register contents (• represents the binary point)	*	•	*	*	*	*	*	*	*

The limitations of this particular register layout are shown in Table 7.13.

As we are dealing with fractional numbers, there will be many numbers (an infinite number, actually) that cannot be represented exactly.

For example, the largest magnitude negative fraction that can be represented is 1.0000001. Working this out we get the following:

$0.1111111 = -(1 - 1/2^7) = -(1 - 1/128) = -0.992\,187\,5$

Therefore, numbers between this and −1 cannot be represented at all. The consequences of this are the introduction of errors, which can sometimes give misleading results to calculations performed on a computer system.

Table 7.13 The limitations of a fractional fixed point binary number system

	An eight-bit integer fixed point register								
Register (Bit number)	8		7	6	5	4	3	2	1
The maximum positive number $1 - 1/2^7 = 1 - 1/128 = 0.9921875$	0	•	1	1	1	1	1	1	1
The smallest positive number $1/2^7 = 1/128 = 0.0078125$	0	•	0	0	0	0	0	0	1
The smallest magnitude negative number $-1/2^7 = -1/128 = -0.0078125$	1	•	1	1	1	1	1	1	1
The largest magnitude negative number (−1)	1	•	0	0	0	0	0	0	0

Although it might seem strange at first sight, there are an infinite amount of numbers that computers will never be able to represent.

Remember that this is true for your calculator too. No calculator will give the exact answer to a simple sum like 1/3, because an infinite number of digits are needed to do this.

If enough digits are used, then the answers to most sums are well within acceptable limits.

The floating point numbers here are commonly used in science and engineering where very large or very small quantities are being processed.

Floating point representation of binary numbers

This is a more versatile system than fixed point representation considered above. To understand it you need to recall that numbers can be split into two parts called a **mantissa** and an **exponent**. As an example consider the following number written using a mathematical technique called standard form:

1.637×10^{60}

Here '1.637' is called the **mantissa**, and '60' is called the **exponent**. You will recall from your mathematics that such a number means that the decimal point in the mantissa has to be moved 60 places to the right (for a positive exponent). Therefore, the equivalent number to the above, written conventionally, would be:

1637000000000000000000000000000000000000000000000000000000000000

You will agree that the range is extended, but the precision with which the number can be represented has been sacrificed. It is usual to make a compromise between the bits used for the mantissa (more precision) and the bits used for the exponent (more range).

It is fortunate that it is unusual to require a vast range and to be highly precise at the same time. If you require such precision and range, as would be the case with calculation of large primary numbers, for example, then special assembly language or high-level language routines would have to be written. The term **floating point** is derived from the fact that to build up the final number (as above) the point floats along until it rests in the final place.

Consider an example, which uses a 16-bit **register**. We will assign 10 bits for the **mantissa** and six bits for the **exponent**. This is shown in Table 7.14, together with the bit pattern of numbers to be used in this particular example.

Table 7.14 A 10-bit fractional mantissa and a six-bit integer exponent

10-bit mantissa fractional (two's complement)												six-bit exponent integer – (two's complement)					
10		9	8	7	6	5	4	3	2	1		6	5	4	3	2	1
0	•	1	0	1	1	0	0	1	0	0		0	0	0	1	0	0

As can be seen, the mantissa has a 10-bit fractional representation using two's complement, and the exponent will use a six-bit integer two's complement representation. Therefore, the methods used will be a combination of the previous methods already covered in this chapter. The binary number contained in this 16-bit floating point register must be decoded in two parts.

1 The mantissa, 0.101100100, is simply rewritten in the same form.

2 The exponent '000100' is binary for +4. This means that the binary point in the mantissa has to be moved four places to the *right*, using the convention that + means move right and – means move left.

The final answer is therefore: 01011.00100 i.e. 11 1/8
Therefore: 0.101100100 | 000100 represents 11.125_{10}

Example

Using the same floating point representation as shown in Table 7.11, determine the decimal value of the following floating point number.

1.100110000 | 111100

Solution

This time the mantissa is a negative number (two's complement and the sign bit is 1). Therefore we will have a negative answer.
The two's complement of 1100110000 is 0011010000.
Therefore, the mantissa becomes –0.011010000
The exponent is also negative. Now the two's complement of 111100 is –000100 = –4.
Therefore, we move the binary point four places to the left.
Altering the original mantissa we get –0.00000110100.

Now 0.0000011010 = 1/64 + 1/128 + 1/512
= 0.015 625 + 0.007 812 5 + 0.001 953 125
= 0.025 390 625
Therefore: 1.100110000 | 111100 = –0.025 390 625

Normalisation of floating point numbers

Before looking at the range of numbers offered by floating point representations, consider the following three numbers represented using our 16-bit register shown in Table 7.14:

(a) 0.100000000 | 000010
(b) 0.010000000 | 000011
(c) 0.001000000 | 000100

Number (a) above is $0.100000000 \times 2^2 = 010.0000000 = 2$
Number (b) above is $0.010000000 \times 2^3 = 010.0000000 = 2$
Number (c) above is $0.001000000 \times 2^4 = 010.0000000 = 2$
They are all different representations of the same number 2!

Multiple representation of the same number is not satisfactory. Also, if there are leading zeros before the most significant figures, as in the (b) and (c) representations above, then it is possible that some less-significant digits will be lost, thus causing an unnecessary error. For example, if 0.100000101 had been used then this can be faithfully represented using (a), but not using (b) and (c) because the last digit would be lost. This would cause a slight difference in the value of the number, and is not sensible if it is not absolutely necessary to lose this digit. **Normalisation** is used to overcome these problems.

The precision of the floating point representations, like those described above, depends on the number of digits that can be held in the mantissa. For positive numbers, there must be no leading zeros to the left of the most significant bit. This obviously must exclude the sign digit or it would be a negative number! Thus (using 10 bits) the number:

0000011111 would be represented in the mantissa as 0.111110000

The exponent would obviously have to be altered to compensate for this shift or we would end up with a different number.

For negative numbers, there must be no leading 1s to the left of the most significant bit. (If you think about two's complement negative numbers then the '0' becomes the significant bit.) This must obviously exclude the sign bit or it would be a positive number. Thus (using 10 bits) the number:

1111100100 would be represented in the mantissa as 1.001000000

Again the exponent would have to be altered to compensate.

***Normalisation* ensures that the maximum possible accuracy with a given number of bits is maintained, and ensures that only a single representation of the number is possible, i.e. it is a standard form which optimises the way in which the number is stored. It can also be used to detect if error conditions such as 'underflow' or 'overflow' occur.**

It is essential to be able to determine the largest and smallest numbers that a given register combination can hold. The rules in the previous section on normalisation should be well understood.

Example

Using a 16-bit register (10-bit two's complement fractional mantissa, and six-bit two's complement integer exponent) as shown in Table 7.14, express the following numbers in normalised form:
(1) 123 (2) 0.1875 (3) −15/32

Solution

1 123 in binary is 0001111011 (10 bits). The normalised mantissa will be 0.111101100.
The binary point will have to be moved seven places to the right to make the normalised mantissa back into the original number. Therefore, the exponent will be 7, which in binary is 000111. Hence the normalised form for 123 is
0.111101100 | 000111

2 0.1875 = 1875/10000 = 75/400 = 3/16 = 2/16 + 1/16 = 1/8 + 1/16 = 0.001100000
Therefore, the normalised mantissa will be 0. 110000000.
The binary point will have to be moved two places to the left to make the normalised mantissa back into the original number. Therefore, the exponent will be −2. Now the exponent must be represented in two's complement integer notation using six bits.
Now 2 in binary (six bits) is 000010. Therefore, −2 = 111110. Therefore, the exponent will be: 111110. Hence the normalised form for
0.1875 = **0.110000000 | 111110**

3 −15/32 is a negative number, we therefore need the two's complement of +15/32 to represent it. Now +15/32 = 1/4 + 1/8 + 1/16 + 1/32 = 0.011110000 (10 bits). The two's complement of 0.011110000 is 1.100010000. Therefore, the normalised mantissa will be 1.000100000.
The binary point will have to be moved one place to the left to make the normalised mantissa back into the original number. Also, remember that if the number is negative, when the point is continuously moved to the left, leading 1s and not 0s would have to be introduced.
Therefore, the exponent will be −1. The two's complement of +1 (000001) using six digits is 111111. Therefore, the exponent will be: 111111.
Hence the normalised form for −15/32 = **1.000100000 | 111111**

Range of normalised floating point numbers

To keep the range of numbers to a reasonable level, let us consider a 10-bit register which uses six bits for the two's complement fractional mantissa, and four bits for the **two's complement integer exponent**, as shown in Table 7.15.

Table 7.15 A six-bit fractional mantissa and a four-bit integer exponent

six-bit mantissa fractional (two's complement)								four-bit exponent (integer – two's complement)			
6		5	4	3	2	1		4	3	2	1
*	•	*	*	*	*	*		*	*	*	*

The range for this floating point register will be considered in four parts.

1 First we look at the maximum positive number.
This will need the largest positive mantissa and largest positive exponent.

0.11111 | 0111

The exponent requires the binary point to be moved seven places to the right. Therefore, the mantissa now becomes:

01111100. = 124. Therefore, the largest positive number is +124.

2 Next we look at the minimum positive number.
This will be when the smallest positive mantissa and largest negative exponent occurs.

0.10000 | 1000

Note that (0.00001) is *not* a normalised number. The two's complement of the exponent is 1000, and thus the exponent requires that the binary point be moved eight places to the left. The mantissa now becomes 0.000000001 = 1/512 = 0.001 953 125. Therefore, the smallest positive number is +0.001 953 125.

3 The smallest-magnitude negative number can be found by having the smallest magnitude negative mantissa and the largest negative exponent.

1.01111 | 1000

Note that 1.01111 is the smallest possible negative mantissa in standard form. 111111 is *not* a normalised number. The exponent requires that the binary point be moved eight places to the left. Therefore the mantissa becomes 1.1111111101111.

Note 'leading 1s' are required for negative numbers. The two's complement of this number is 0.0000000010001.

This number is binary for +1/512 + 1/8192 = 17/8192 = 0.002 075 195 313 (to ten decimal places). Therefore, the smallest-magnitude negative number is approximately

−0.002 075 195 313.

4 Finally, the largest-magnitude negative number occurs with the largest-magnitude negative mantissa and the largest positive exponent.

1.00000 | 0111

The two's complement for the negative mantissa is 1.00000.

The exponent requires that the binary point be moved seven places to the right, therefore the mantissa becomes 10000000. = 128. Therefore, the largest-magnitude negative number is −128.

The range for the 10-bit register using a six-bit two's complement fractional mantissa and four-bit two's complement integer exponent is therefore:

$$-128 \leqslant \text{negative range} \leqslant -0.002\ 075\ 195\ 313$$
$$+0.001\ 953\ 125 \leqslant \text{positive range} \leqslant +124$$

Working through the above theory you may have lost sight of the fact that zero (000000) is not a normalised number! It does therefore not exist in normalised floating point numbers! To get over this problem, the computer will normally use the smallest positive number. In the above case this is only 0.001 953 125, a pitiful representation of zero! However, it is usual to have many more digits to represent floating point numbers, even on the humblest of microcomputers.

Self-test questions

1 Explain what is meant by a number base, using binary and denary as an example.

2 (a) Convert the following binary numbers into denary:
(i) 1010 (ii) 101000 (iii) 11111111 (iv) 010100111011
(b) Convert the following denary numbers into binary:
(i) 27 (ii) 128 (iii) 789 (iv) 65 535

3 Convert the following binary numbers into hexadecimal:
(a) 10101011 (b) 11110000 (c) 1001100101010100

4 Convert the following hexadecimal numbers into binary:
(a) 160 (b) 279 (c) FF60 (d) FBFF

5 Change the following decimal fractions into binary fractions:
(a) 0.25 (b) 0.031 25 (c) 1.5 (d) 15.375 (e) 12.015625

6 What is meant by two's complementation? Why is this system useful when working out numbers inside a computer system?

7 Represent the following decimal numbers using eight-bit two's complement representation:
(a) −4 (b) −13 (c) −69 (d) −123

8 Find the two's complement representation of the following real numbers: (use eight bits for the integer part and four bits for the fractional part)
(a) −63.25 (b) −17.625 (c) −113.1875

9 Explain why normalisation is needed when dealing with floating point numbers.

10 A floating point number is made up from a mantissa and an exponent. Explain what is meant by the terms 'mantissa' and 'exponent' when used in this context.

11 When a fixed length register is used to represent numbers, there are limitations on the types of numbers that can be stored according to the methods used. Comment on the limitations of the following systems:
(a) An eight-bit integer register.
(b) An eight-bit fractional register.
(c) A floating point register consisting of an eight-bit mantissa and a four-bit exponent.

12 Using an integer fixed point binary two's complement representation with a 12-bit register, work out the following:
(a) What is the maximum positive number that can be stored?
(b) What is the minimum positive number?
(c) What is the smallest-magnitude negative number?
(d) What is the largest-magnitude negative number?

13 Using a fractional fixed point binary two's complement representation and a 10-bit register, and assuming that the binary point is in the position shown:

* . * * * * * * * * *

if normalisation is *ignored*, work out the following:

(a) What is the maximum positive number that can be stored?
(b) What is the minimum positive number?
(c) What is the smallest-magnitude negative number?
(d) What is the largest-magnitude negative number?

14 Work out the following representations using a fractional floating point two's complement binary representation with a 16-bit register, split up into a 10-bit mantissa (two's complement fractional) and a six-bit exponent (two's complement integer). Assuming that your answers must be normalised work out the following:

(a) What is the maximum positive number that can be stored?
(b) What is the minimum positive number?
(c) What is the smallest-magnitude negative number?
(d) What is the largest-magnitude negative number?

8 Operating systems

In this chapter you will learn about:

- The classification of operating systems into batch, interactive and real time
- Job control languages and the mainframe computer environment
- Multiprogramming, multiuser and multitasking systems
- Client server, distributed file systems and network operating systems
- The user interface, memory management, file management and I/O management
- Process, process state, threads and scheduling in a multiprogramming OS

Some of today's modern operating systems like Windows XP professional, for example, consist of millions of lines of programming code.

The new 64-bit operating systems are even more complex.

It is a tribute to the ingenuity of the designers that such complex systems work efficiently for most of the time.

This chapter introduces you to some of the principles on which these systems are based.

Introduction

To a novice the **operating system** is probably the least-important part of the computer – but nothing could be further from the truth. Computers have now become so easy to use that beginners often do not realise the crucial role played by this vital piece of software. This is mainly due to the fact that on microcomputers, it is one of the jobs of a modern operating system to present the user with an easy-to-use interface.

Operating systems may be classified by the main uses to which they are put. Typical classifications include **batch**, **interactive**, **real time** and **network operating systems**. Some students find it difficult to appreciate concepts such as a 'batch operating system', because it is used mostly in a **mainframe** computer environment. They often confuse a batch operating system with running a batch of commands from **DOS**. Although there are some similarities of operation, a quick look at an IBM mainframe manual for a batch operating system would soon dispel any misconceptions about this.

Batch operating systems

The very first operating systems were based on mainframe computers and were originally designed to alleviate the need for time-consuming human intervention by the computer operator (*hence the name 'operating system'*). These early systems were serial in nature in that they undertook just one task at a time. The operating system concentrated on getting as many jobs done as quickly as possible. These operating systems were known as **batch operating systems** because they usually tackled a batch of jobs or programs to be run in the same session. Before the advent of the batch operating system the computer operator spent most of his or her time loading appropriate resources.

Typically, a batch operating system on a university mainframe might have included running several FORTRAN programs for some engineering students, a few COBOL programs for business studies students and some machine code programs for computer scientists. You should realise that these students in the 1970s (of which the author was one!) did not sit down at computers and type in their programs, but prepared the source code on special card-punch machines. The computer operator used to take the batch of cards and place the entire pack into the system's card-reader machine. The computer's operating system would then take over, ensuring that the correct compilers were used for translating the **source code** into the **object code** for the target machine.

The batch operating system is easier to understand when put into this historical context, but modern batch operating systems run on similar principles, and are used extensively in banking, finance, utility billing and government departments like the Inland Revenue.

A batch of jobs to be run on a batch processing system is still very common in the modern mainframe computer environment, and job control languages are still used as outlined below.

The job control language (JCL)

A **job control language** (**JCL**) is used to control a batch of jobs being run. In the early systems described above, job control cards, containing the job control language instructions, were inserted by the computer operator to specify things like the peripherals needed by the job, the beginning and end of the job, what compilers will be needed, and may also be used for accounting purposes. Modern job control languages are still used in the same context, but the commands are now typed into the system from a terminal instead of being submitted on cards as in the earlier systems.

A modern job control language is similar to writing a computer program using a **scripting language**. You can accomplish things like submitting a job to the operating system, request the resources that will be needed to run the job and control how the computer will process the job. Sometimes, for example, a job may be so important that the computer operator will override other factors such as the efficient use of system resources, to enable this important job to be finished more quickly.

You would not be expected to remember the syntax of an actual job control language, but you should appreciate the sort of things it can do and be able to write simple **pseudocode** examples. Typically you would specify the JOB name and the USER ID (the person for whom the job is being run). You might also specify additional parameters like the TIME allowed, in minutes, and whether the USER is to be notified when the job is finished. There are three types of job statements, namely JOB, which identifies the beginning of a job, EXEC, which indicates what is to be done, and DD, or data definition, which identifies the resources needed for the job.

Typically you would specify a job name and a user name. Additionally you might specify a time, in minutes, for which the job is allowed to run, and you can also notify the user when the job is complete. The following is a *grossly simplified collection of JCL statements* which runs a FORTRAN program called ANALYSIS, making use of a file called 'statistics' which is found on a disk called DISKA72 and prints out the results of the analysis on a line printer (a fast-impact printer) called LP3. The program utilises 1 Mbyte of memory and has an error condition that terminates the program if a program error occurs. Note that // denotes the start of a JCL statement and //* is a comment.

```
//JOB ANALYSIS USERID = RAYBRADLEY   //*job name and user ID
//NOTIFY RAYBRADLEY                  //*notify user when job is
                                        finished
//PRIORITY 3                         //*assigns job priority
//FORTRAN                            //*assigns language compiler
//INPUT FILE STATISTICS, DISKA72     //*name and location of input
//LIST LINE PRINTER LP3              //*name and location for
                                        output
//IF ERROR THEN END                  //*terminates program on
                                        error
//INPUT ANALYSIS, DISKA72            //*locate program to compile
//COMPILE ANALYSIS.F99               //*compile FORTRAN 99 source
                                        code
```

Modern mainframe computers, especially those used in banking and the utility industries often make use of batch operating systems.

The current use of batch operating system technology may be confirmed by the abundance of information about job control languages available on the Internet.

You can check out the syntax of a typical JCL by looking at specialist Internet sites.

```
//LOAD ANALYSIS.OBJ          //*load the object code for
                                the job
//RUN                        //*run FORTRAN program
//TIME = 2                   //*maximum time of 2 minutes
                                allowed
//MEMORY = 1024K             //*allocate 1 Mbyte of memory
//ENDJOB                     //*denotes end of particular
                                job
```

There are many other variations on similar themes, but the above example shows some of the typical things that are undertaken during the execution of a job. Once the ENDJOB statement is encountered, the next job in the batch of jobs is undertaken.

A modern example of a mainframe is IBM's eServer zSeries 900 which enables thousands of virtual servers to be run from a single unit. These servers are managed automatically by the operating system, and resources are dynamically allocated to the most demanding tasks.

On a PC a program called the Command Line Interpreter interprets commands typed into a command line operating system.

Modern mainframe computers

Modern mainframes, especially those found in government establishments and universities, are often able to run batches of jobs in the ways described above, but in addition to this are able to support an interactive mode of operation. Thus a batch of jobs may be running, but at the same time many other users may access the mainframe by operating from a computer terminal or a PC pretending to be a computer terminal. A PC is able to work in this mode by running software like Telnet (terminal emulation software), which enables you to run commands as though you were processing them through a terminal connected to a server or the mainframe. Systems where more than one user (possibly thousands in the case of a mainframe) may use the computer at the same time are known as **multi-user systems**.

Specialist software running on a PC is sometimes required to connect to mainframe computers, but others might allow you to use a web-browser connection. Setting up these operations is similar to setting up a **VPN** or **Virtual Private Network** on a standard PC, but once set up, the user is oblivious to the fact that they are connected to a mainframe, and can thus work in an interactive environment similar to that found on their home PC. Indeed, the connection to the mainframe could easily be via their home computer and the Internet.

Students often question the need for mainframe computers in a modern business environment, especially when they experience powerful PCs set up as file servers in their schools, colleges and universities. However, imagine a business which needs several thousand servers set up for 24/7 e-commerce. The space needed by these machines would be huge, and the maintenance of several thousand servers would be phenomenal. All of these servers could be set up as virtual servers and put in the same box that would fit in a single room. They could also be managed more effectively by fewer personnel.

Interactive operating systems

The term **interactive operating system** must be viewed in relation to batch operating systems described above. Historically you had to wait some time to get the results from a batch operating system, and the advent of an operating system where users experience an instant response was remarkable in its time. With modern computers this distinction is no longer made because all users are accustomed to this mode of operation. Nevertheless, the term interactive operating system is still applied to distinguish it from the batch operating systems still in use today. Operating systems like **Windows** and **Linux** are good examples of interactive operating systems.

Real-time operating systems

In the operating systems considered so far, it did not matter too much if a job was delayed or if a task was carried out a few seconds later rather than sooner. However, there are situations in which such a delay would be unacceptable or even fatal. A typical but deadly example of a **real-time operating system** would be found in the embedded-microprocessor systems housed in a guided missile. Suppose, for example, that you happen to be on the deck of a warship which unfortunately is in the path of an incoming missile. You may have just 15 seconds before impact, and you launch your anti-missile missile, which is guided by a real-time operating system. The missile just launched would have to lock on to the incoming missile and destroy it. You would not appreciate the electronics inside the missile dithering for a few seconds while the operating system decided what to do!

The above example is rather drastic but it illustrates the situation in which real-time operating systems are used. However, *real-time does not necessarily mean fast.* Although it is essential to use a real-time system where speed is of the essence, as long as the operating system can respond and process the appropriate data before some outside process could suffer, then you have what is literally a real-time or pseudo real-time system. Suppose, for example, that a computer system was controlling the amount of liquid in a tank. Suppose also that the water valve must be turned off within one minute of a signal being transmitted from the sensor. If the computer system responds within, say, 45 seconds, and the water is safely turned off, then this is a real-time system, even though it is painfully slow. However, it must be said that most real-time systems require a fast response. The majority of real-time operating systems go hand-in-hand with process control such as missile guidance, controlling a power station or controlling a chemical factory etc.

The author has a colleague who served on a Royal Naval vessel in the Falklands war. The scenario outlined in the text saved this person's life. He is therefore eternally grateful for real-time operating systems.

You should appreciate that the definition of a real-time operating system is that the computer responds in an appropriate amount of time, usually to some external event like those found in the process control industry. This may not be extremely fast, but often it is. These are sometimes referred to as pseudo real-time operating systems.

Multiprogramming and multitasking

Multiprogramming is the ability of a system to operate on more than one program at the same time, or apparently the same time. How it does this depends on the type of operating system and the hardware (number of microprocessors) available. If a system gives a small amount of processor time to each task before going on to the next, this would be known as a **time-sharing system**. A system with more than one processor may literally be able to run more than one program simultaneously.

It is the job of the operating system to allocate time to programs and other tasks in a time-sharing environment. Other factors, like the **priority** of the **jobs** (tasks) being undertaken are important too, and often override the requests put in by less-important tasks. The ability of an operating system to handle many tasks or applications at the 'same time' is called **multitasking**. It is this that enables the user to be under the impression that they can download material from the Internet while typing on their word processor. Only operating systems with more than one processor can actually do more than one thing at the same time. Having more than one processor would be called **multiprocessing**.

It is the job of the operating system to assign priorities to jobs so that the maximum amount of work can be done in the shortest possible time. It is also the job of the operating system to ensure that resources like printers and disks are used in an optimum fashion and to ensure that conflicting requests are handled sensibly.

Client server systems

From your AS level work you will appreciate that **LANs** are now common, and special operating systems called **network operating systems** are needed to interface the PCs or **thin clients** to the LAN and to communicate with other computers and the **file servers**. Systems like these, where PCs or terminals are set up as clients on a network, are known as **client server systems**. These systems may be set up to work either locally or from the server or both. Typically a client server system would have a front end which the user will

After reading the material in this chapter you should start to realise the importance of the operating system.

Not only does it provide the user interface, but it has a major management role too.

Add these points to the security and reliability aspects, and you should start to see the fundamental importance of this amazing software development.

see on his or her computer, and a back end running on one or more servers which processes information in the background.

If client server architecture is being used the local machine/s can be optimised for the user interface and the server machine/s can be optimised for processing a particular application. This system therefore makes good use of available resources compared with a time-sharing system in the old **mainframe** environment. The operating system must be able to cope with files spread across multiple clients and servers. The system which copes with this is called a **distributed file system**, and is usually arranged so that the user is under the impression that the files are stored in a single place, when in fact they probably reside on a multiple number of servers, possibly in different locations.

Operating system concepts

An important aspect of operating system design is the **user interface**. For modern PCs the ease of use of operating systems like Windows or Linux underlines the success of the **GUI** or **Graphical User Interface**. Point-and-click devices like mice have made it easy for novice users to drag and drop files from one place to another without requiring any knowledge of the path names or syntax needed to accomplish this. However, remember that other interfaces like the **command line interfaces** typical of DOS, and the **job-control interfaces** typical on IBM mainframes are also just as important.

Most students do not see the power of a command-line or job-control interface because they rarely, if ever, make use of them. On the other hand, a network manager would make extensive use of the command line interface and a mainframe computer operator would make extensive use of a job control language interface. It would not be feasible for a network manager to create hundreds of new users or apply individual permissions to thousands of files on a file server without using the command line interface facilities. Several thousand new users (new students) at a university, for example, could be created by a batch file within a few minutes. The same task, undertaken manually through a GUI environment, might take one person several weeks to accomplish. This is obviously not a feasible use of the GUI interface, and shows the power of a command line interface.

Memory management

If possible, get your network manager to demonstrate how the command line interface may be used with batch files to undertake tedious tasks like creating new users.

Memory allocated to one program must *not* interfere with memory allocated to any other. It is the job of the operating system to actively carry out memory-management techniques. The concept of **memory management** is simple. An appropriate amount of **RAM** must be allocated to a **task**, and when the task is finished RAM must be returned to the system so it can be used by other tasks. It is the job of the operating system to police this memory management process. It does this by splitting the memory up into smaller chunks called **partitions**. These partition sizes may be fixed or variable, depending on how the operating system is organised.

Fixed partitioning

*It is the job of a program called the **command line interpreter** to interpret commands typed into the command line interface.*

Fixed partitioning can be applied to memory management in a complex **multitasking** environment. Appropriate fixed-size partitions may be set up in memory, and the tasks loaded into an appropriate partition when one becomes available. These partitions could all be the same size, or there could be a number of different-sized fixed partitions. The advantage of this system is that the algorithms for allocating users' programs to the partitions are relatively simple. An important point to realise here is that all programs designed to be run in a multitasking system must consist of **relocatable code**. You will recall from reading about machine code in chapter 2, that it is bad practice to write programs that write to specific memory locations. If any program is to run in any partition you should now see why this is important.

The disadvantage of fixed partition-memory is that long queues can build up while at the same time much valuable memory remains unused because many programs do not happen to fit into a particular partition size. Also, the programs that are occupying the partitions might not be doing so efficiently. For example, if the smallest partition size is 500k, then a 20k program will 'occupy' all of this partition, thus preventing 480k of memory from being used effectively during the time that this program remains in memory. Also, by having a finite number of fixed partitions, you are placing an arbitrary limit on the number of tasks that the system can handle at any one time. Due to these limitations, fixed partition systems are not used very often.

Variable partitioning

A better, more complex method of partitioning is to dynamically allocate the partitions as and when necessary. This is called **dynamic memory partitioning**. When a task is loaded it is allocated an appropriate amount of memory, and this is obviously more efficient compared with the fixed portioning described above. However, when a particular task is finished and another task needs to take its place, it is most unlikely that the two tasks will be of the same size. Therefore, a hole is produced in the memory, which starts to become **fragmented**. As time progresses, more holes appear throughout the memory and we eventually get to a stage where the memory is being used inefficiently. Therefore, from time to time, the system has to compact all the tasks by swapping them around until we are back to the situation similar to that at start up.

The major disadvantage of dynamic partitioning is that this compaction process is very tedious and time consuming. You will recall that we are trying to utilise the CPU with maximum efficiency. Clearing out the memory and other housework chores such as compaction do not rate as efficient if they do not contribute to the fast throughput of the system in general.

Example

Explain some advantages and disadvantages of fixed partitioning compared with variable partitioning of memory.

Solution

Fixed partitioning is easier to manage, but can be wasteful of memory space (i.e. too much memory is allocated depending on the partition size). Variable partitioning is more complex to manage but more efficient in terms of memory usage. Memory can become badly fragmented, and considerable housekeeping would have to be undertaken to sort out the variable-size 'holes' created in memory by this variable partitioning system.

Virtual memory

There might not be enough physical RAM available for use by the operating system, and **virtual memory** can be used instead. This is memory, set up on disk, pretending to be RAM. With enough disk space the 'lack of RAM' problem may be completely solved, but the speed of access is very slow compared with conventional RAM-access speeds. The operating system may organise virtual memory by a system called **paging**. The virtual memory can be split up into blocks of a fixed size called pages. Each is mapped onto physical disk space, so data in virtual memory is mapped onto physical memory by the operating system. A special memory-management system carries out this translation (mapping) process.

There are many new operating system concepts described in this chapter covering techniques that cannot easily be experienced directly.

You should attempt to learn these terms as they often crop up in A2 examinations.

There is also an immense spin-off from this virtual-memory method in that each user program can be enormous – they do not have to fit into the available RAM of the computer. Therefore, a computer with an actual 1000 Megabytes of RAM could, for example, be working simultaneously on 30 programs, where each program happens to be 200 Megabytes long, thus giving us a virtual RAM of 6000 Megabytes.

There are, of course, disadvantages when using a virtual memory system. Some of the time the code is executed without any problems, but a branch instruction to some page of code which is not resident in RAM means that the operating system will have to load this new page. However, the operating system is not clairvoyant – how does it know which page to remove from RAM? The page just removed might be the next page that is needed. In virtual-memory systems the worst case scenario is when pages of code are continually being put into RAM and then taken out again. This unfortunate phenomenon is known as 'thrashing'. In bad cases, the virtual-memory operating system can spend more time removing and reloading pages of code than it spends executing the programs!

As you can see from the sections above, the problems of efficient scheduling and memory management are not trivial. Operating systems have become more complex by using combinations of these systems to optimise both resources and CPU time to get the maximum amount of work done in the minimum amount of time. With each new generation of operating system, more efficient algorithms have been developed in a heuristic way with all the benefits of hindsight from the development of previous operating systems. This is just one of the main reasons why computers are becoming so versatile.

Re-entrant code

This is the name given to a system where code may be shared by different programs or tasks using the operating system. Any code, written so that several different programs may use it simultaneously, is called **re-entrant code** or **code sharing**. This method ensures that the same routines do not have to reside in memory many times over. If one program is currently using a piece of re-entrant code, another program may actually interrupt the original program and use the same code. Modern operating systems support code sharing. There are many software routines that reside in the operating system; indeed, the summation of thousands of these routines is the operating system.

Dynamically linked libraries (DLLs)

It is wasteful of memory space if all the routines needed by all programs and tasks are resident in memory simultaneously. Therefore, some routines (called dynamic link libraries by Microsoft) may be called up and executed when needed. These routines, stored on disk as DLL files, may be used as if they were part of the operating system. There are many DLLs provided by other manufacturers, all used for specific purposes. Some DLLs, like those that help the C++ or Visual Basic programmer, for example, are more general in nature. Advanced users may also write their own DLLs with the idea of improving the functionality of their programs.

File management

It is the job of the operating system to manage file space. For example, opened files may be too large to fit into the available RAM, or files that have just been created may be too large to fit into a contiguous disk space due to a fragmented disk. A buffer is often set up to solve these problems. A **buffer** is an area of memory set up to temporarily store data until it is ready to be used.

A buffer may be set up to interface the file 'as seen from an operating system perspective' to the file 'as seen from a hardware perspective'. The hardware, which interfaces the operating system to the disk, for example, will have a physical block size, which does not usually relate in any way to the record size being used by the programmer. A physical block of data would be read from the disk and stored in a buffer. The **operating system** (OS) takes data from this buffer, in a size convenient to it, which usually relates to the logical records used by software. It is the job of the file management software in the OS (**operating system**) to resolve these differences, and make sure that the physical limitations of disks, CD-ROMs and DVDs etc. do not encroach on the programmer's perspective, which is a logical (not physical) view of the data.

In other parts of your A2 course you will also come across a logical and physical view of the same data.

Relational database management systems are a good example of this, where the logical view of the database (records and fields etc.) is not the same as the physical way in which the database files are stored on disk.

Example

Why might programs fill up a disk when the sum of the bytes in each program is considerably less than the disk capacity? How is this affected by the buffer?

Solution

It is likely that the logical block sizes and physical block sizes do not match. Therefore, it is likely that a large part of a physical block is not used when small files store information in the buffer. Much empty space could be saved along with the actual information, thus accounting for the differences described in the question. The larger the buffer, the larger the holes for small amounts of data saved to disk.

I/O management

The operating system provides data in an appropriate form for I/O (Input/Output), but cannot easily cope with the huge variety of dissimilar devices. Different printers, for example, all require data to be in different forms depending on their functionality. Printer **drivers** sort out these features, which are specific to an exact type of printer and OS. Most I/O devices like **sound cards** and **graphics cards** etc. will need specialist drivers to accompany the hardware after it has been installed. Without the correct driver the device probably will not work.

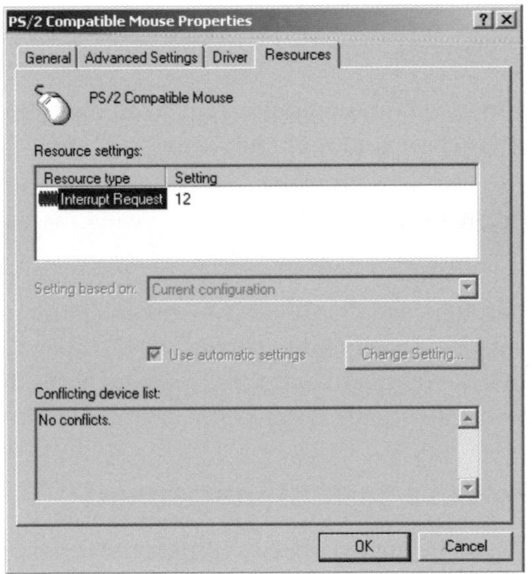

Figure 8.1 Using interrupt request 12

It is the job of the driver to translate the hardware characteristics of the device into what is needed for a specific operating system. The device driver usually handles the direct interface to the device, but additional software routines, often called handlers, may be needed to aid the transfer of data between the device driver and the OS.

Drivers grab resources like interrupts to get attention from the OS. As an example, Figure 8.1 shows a PS/2 compatible mouse connected to a Windows OS using IRQ (Interrupt ReQuest) 12.

If a mouse click occurs, this driver will use interrupt 12 to generate attention from the operating system. The driver will pass the data (regarding which button has been pressed etc.) to the operating system so that appropriate action, like closing a window for example,

Without drivers you would have to have a different version of the operating system for each device! This would obviously be impractical.

Remember that some manufacturers may update their drivers at reasonably frequent intervals.

If you update your hardware drivers then you should experience fewer problems, and this can often be done by using Windows Update if you have the Windows operating system.

can be taken. Devices are interfaced to the OS by the use of drivers, and these will often conflict with each other if the interrupts have not been allocated properly. This could mean that the computer fails to operate in predictable ways, or fails to operate at all. If this sort of problem happens, you may have to use the **BIOS** settings to resolve conflicts before restarting the computer. When set up properly, the interrupts will be handled using the principles discussed above.

Scheduling

Hundreds of **tasks** might be going on inside the computer in a short space of time. It is the job of the operating system to schedule these conflicting requirements to maximise the work done in the shortest possible time whilst resolving possible conflicts. Tasks will be in many different states. A printer, for example, may have run out of paper or a program might be waiting for processor attention. All these processes require the attention of the operating system which can usually do just one thing at a time.

You should realise that an operating system is only as good as the algorithms which are being used to control it.

It is the job of the **scheduler** to make sure that no one process hogs all the attention, that no one process fails to get attention, and the peripherals are used in an efficient way. The operating system copes by considering each process to be in a variety of states. These could be 'waiting for attention', 'using a peripheral', or 'using the processor', for example. The operating system will usually set up a queuing system giving the highest priority to those tasks that need it. Sometimes it is not easy to resolve all the conflicting requirements, and occasionally processes can be **deadlocked** if the scheduling part of the operating system is not operating efficiently.

Example

Why is scheduling important in an operating system that supports both batch and interactive modes of operating?

Solution

If the batch of jobs was carried out with no regard to the priorities of other programs, then the user/s of the system would get no response until the entire batch process was finished. By efficient scheduling, the operating system can interrupt the batch process to give the interactive processes a slice of the action. If done effectively, the interactive processes should notice little degradation in performance.

Process/task/management

The management of tasks (programs) in a multi-programming environment is complex and scheduling, as outlined above, plays an important role in this. Imagine you have just clicked on a program to run it. This is a process (in this case running your program) that must be handled by the operating system. You may request a print job or load up your browser to surf the Internet. All these are examples of processes that are being handled by the operating system. A **process** is, therefore, execution of a particular program, *from the operating system's perspective*.

This concept is useful because it enables the operating system to handle these processes by considering a number of **process states**, enabling the operating system to identify the current state for each process, and therefore take some appropriate action. These states might be 'a program waiting to run', 'a program being run' or 'a program awaiting peripheral attention' like waiting for the printer to be ready. These ideas are shown in the state-transition diagram (Figure 8.2).

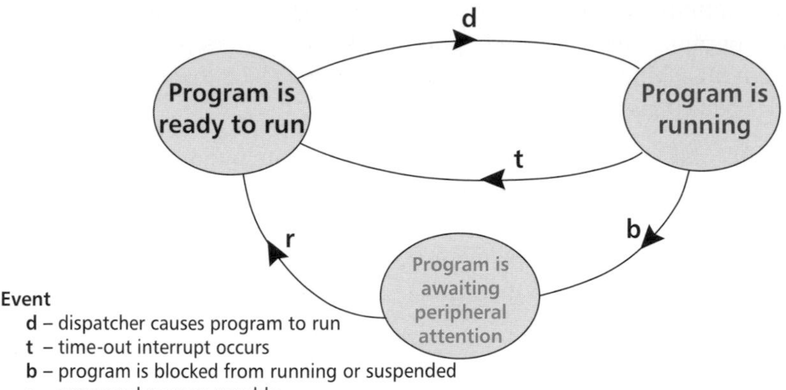
d
Program is ready to run
Program is running
t
r
b
Program is awaiting peripheral attention
Event
d – dispatcher causes program to run
t – time-out interrupt occurs
b – program is blocked from running or suspended
r – program becomes runable

Figure 8.2 A state-transition diagram showing some operating system processes

The concept of tasks, processes and states enable us to understand how the operating system works from a fundamental perspective.

The algorithms that control the overall running of the system are quite complex but usually very effective.

Considering the number of processes being carried out, it is very rare indeed for a computer system to crash, unless there is a hardware or software fault.

This simplified diagram shows how these processes may be managed. It shows the process states in each of the bubbles. A transition occurs, usually under the control of an interrupt, which changes the state of the process. If a program has been running for too long (e.g. your program might be in an infinite loop) then a time-out interrupt (shown by event 't' in Figure 8.2) might cause your program to stop running while the operating system deals with something else. If your program takes a very long time (in computer terms) then it will probably be terminated or suspended by the operating system if it has been set up to do this.

Interrupts have already been covered in detail in chapter 1, and you should recall that if an interrupt occurs, then the **CPU** will process the current instruction, dump the registers onto an area of memory called the stack, and then processes the interrupt. Remember that the operating system is just a complex set of programs, and must therefore run in the same environment as other programs. It is usual for all the processes to have their own stacks.

An event driven system

The term **event** used in Figure 8.2 is important, because operating systems are basically **event driven**. This means that a **process** will run until an event happens to stop it, then another process will run until another event stops that. The operating system will continue in this way, responding to events like those shown in Figure 8.2, and in addition respond to events like mouse clicks, keyboard strokes or data coming in from a modem, for example.

The processes and process states covered here represent what is called the process model, and have been used by operating system designers for a considerable period of time. A process consists of three things, namely the 'executable code being run', 'the data being used by the process' and the 'stack', used when the code needs to call **functions** or **procedures**.

Another way of operating is called the **threaded model**, in which multiple threads of execution, or, more simply, **threads** may be operated within a single system process, and this is known as **multithreading**. It is basically *the ability of different parts of the same program to be operated on at the same time*. Threads are able to share other resources like address spaces and global variables, for example. They are thus far less protected than **multitasking** processes which operate interdependently of each other. Many threads are able to share the same address space (RAM) and this is why they can share resources, unlike other processes that run in different memory address spaces. You should realise that threads also have their own **program counters**, **stack pointers** and registers. Older operating systems were less good at managing multithreading, and this process is therefore relatively recent in the history of operating-system design.

Modern operating systems may switch between threads much more quickly than they can switch between tasks as there are fewer overheads in terms of restoring stacks and other time-consuming activities. Running multiple tasks in parallel on a computer is similar in principle to running multiple threads in the same process.

Self-test questions

1. What is an operating system and why is the operating system important?
2. What are the fundamental differences between a 'batch', 'interactive' and 'real-time' operating system? Give a typical example of where each system would be most useful.
3. Outline two typical scenarios in which a modern mainframe would operate in batch operating system mode.
4. What language is typically used to control a batch operating system on a mainframe? Outline five different things which this language could be programmed to do.
5. Outline what is meant by the terms 'multiprocessing' and 'multitasking' from an operating system perspective.
6. What is meant by the client-server model?
7. Explain the term 'distributed file processing'. Why is this important in modern educational establishments?
8. An operating system must manage many different resources. Make a list of five different things that must be managed in this way.
9. An operating system may use 'fixed' or 'variable portioning' when managing memory. Give one advantage and one disadvantage of each system when compared with the other.
10. What is meant by dynamic memory partitioning?
11. Virtual memory is an important operating system concept. What is it and why is it used?
12. Explain the need for and the difference between relocatable code and re-entrant code.
13. What is a dynamically linked library?
14. A buffer is often used by an operating system to help manage file access. Explain what is meant by the term 'buffer' and outline two typical scenarios in which a buffer might be used.
15. Input/Output peripherals must be managed by the operating system. Describe how interrupts often play a vital role in the management of peripheral devices.
16. Explain why scheduling is needed in a multitasking operating system.
17. What is a 'process' and a 'process state'? How do these concepts help to implement the process model?
18. Operating systems are often said to be event driven. What does this mean?
19. What is meant by a 'thread' in a modern operating system?
20. How does the 'threaded model' differ from the 'process model'. Why was the threaded model not used until much later?
21. A process is typically made up from three different resources. What are they?

Module 4 examination questions

1 (a) The number 0111 0010 1011 1101 is stored in two's complement notation in 16 bits with the most significant 10 bits representing the mantissa and the least significant six bits representing the exponent.

(i) Is this number positive or negative?

....

....

(ii) Estimate the magnitude of this number. Circle the correct answer below.

$>2^{32}$	Between 2^{16} and 2^{32}	Between 2^{2} and 2^{-2}	$<2^{-2}$

(2 marks)

(b) The number 0110 0001 0100 1000 is stored in the **same format**. Convert this number into denary. (3 marks)

....

....

(c) (i) Give one advantage of fixed point over floating point representation.

(ii) Under what circumstances would fixed point representation be used rather than floating point? (2 marks)

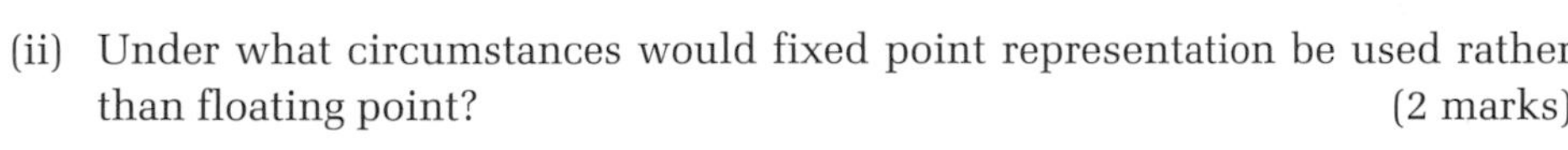

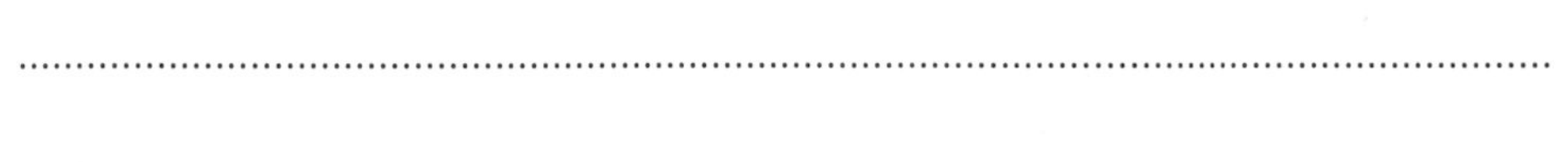

[AQA Unit 4 (CPT4) Processing and programming techniques June 2003 Q(4)]

2 An algebraic expression is represented in a binary tree as follows.

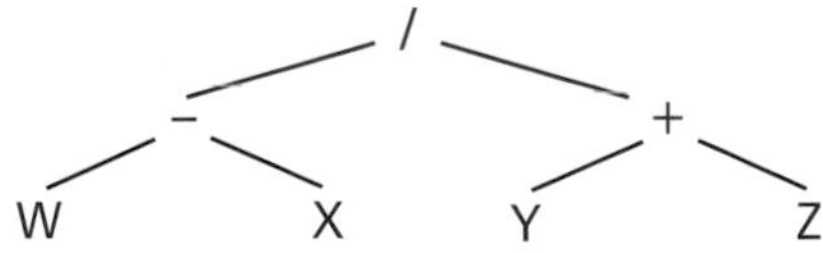

(a) On the above diagram, circle and label the *root* of this tree, and a *branch* and *leaf node*. (3 marks)

(b) In the spaces below, draw the left subtree and the right subtree of this tree.
left subtree right subtree

(2 marks)

(c) What is the result if this tree is printed using in-order traversal? (3 marks)

....

....

[AQA Unit 4 (CPT4) Processing and programming techniques June 2003 Q(8)]

3 A computer design company has produced a design for an elementary computer. It is to be used to teach students about machine architecture, machine operations and the design of an instruction set.

The current instruction register has a length of 16 bits.
The accumulator has a length of 16 bits.
The size of each memory location is 16 bits.
The current instruction register is designed to hold one instruction at a time.
A machine instruction is 16 bits in length.
The most significant eight bits of a machine instruction denote the machine operation.
The least significant bits denote an operand or the address of an operand.
Main memory stores both instructions and data.
The structure of a machine instruction is as follows.

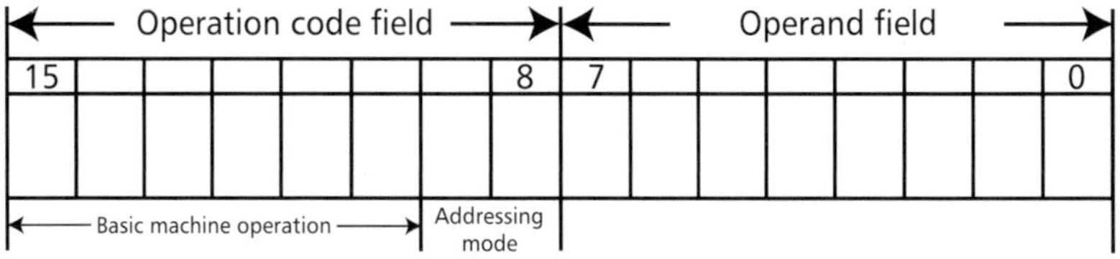

Operation code field								Operand field							
15							8	7							0
Basic machine operation						Addressing mode									

(a) Define the term instruction set. (1 mark)

....

....

(b) With six bits of the operation code reserved to denote basic machine operations, how many basic machine operations may be coded? (1 mark)

....

....

(c) With reference to the operand field of a machine code instruction describe the following addressing modes:

(i) Immediate (1 mark)

(ii) Direct (1 mark)

(iii) Indirect (1 mark)

(d) The following machine operations have their operation codes expressed in hexadecimal.

Machine operation	Addressing mode	Operation code (hex)	Description
LDA	Immediate Direct Indirect	A1 A2 A3	Load accumulator
STA	Direct Indirect	B2 B3	Store accumulator
ADD	Immediate Direct Indirect	61 61 63	Add operand to contents of accumulator, storing result in accumulator

(i) Convert the operation code for the operation STA for indirect addressing from hexadecimal to binary. (1 mark)

(ii) It is required to add the hexadecimal number 6 to the contents of a main memory location whose address in hexadecimal is C1, with the result being stored in another memory location at hexadecimal address AB.

Complete the sequence of instructions, in hexadecimal, to perform this task on the machine above.

A1 06 (4 marks)

(e) For the given machine:

(i) What is the highest memory address that can be addressed by an instruction using direct addressing? (1 mark)

....

....

(ii) What is the highest address that can be addressed by an instruction using indirect addressing? (2 marks)

....

....

[AQA Unit 4 (CPT4) Processing and programming techniques June 2003 Q(9)]

4 In a simple logic processing language, a family group is connected by the following facts and rules.

(1) father(alan, edward)
(2) father(chris, fiona)
(3) father(chris, jane)
(4) father(edward, liam)
(5) mother(barbara, edward)
(6) mother(diana, fiona)
(7) mother(diana, jane)
(8) mother(fiona, liam)
(9) mother(jane, michelle)
(10) grandfather(W,X) IF father(W,Z) AND mother(Z,X)
(11) grandfather(W,X) IF father (Z,X) AND father(W,Z)

Clause (1) says that Alan is the father of Edward.
Clause (10) says that W is the grandfather of X if W is the father of Z and Z is the mother of X.

(a) Use the information above to find Liam's grandfathers, clearly identifying the relevant clauses in each case. (2 marks)

....

....

(b) Two people are cousins if they have the same grandfathers. Write a clause which would define cousin. (3 marks)

....

....

(c) Logic programming is particularly suited to specific types of problem. Give two examples of these. (2 marks)

....

....

[AQA Unit 4 (CPT4) Processing and programming techniques January 2003 Q(7)]

5 (a) How could an operating system allow two files with the same filename to be stored on the same floppy disk? (1 mark)

....

....

(b) Immediately after formatting a new 1.44 Mb floppy disk, the following message appears on the screen:

Bytes free 1 457 664

On checking the properties, the capacity is said to be 1.38 Mb. Give two reasons why all of the disk capacity is not available to the user. (2 marks)

....

....

(c) The *file management sub-system* and the *memory management sub-system* are called when a command is entered to load an executable file from disk. Describe the role of each of these sub-systems in this operation, and state **one** error that **each** might have to deal with.

(i) The file management sub-system. (3 marks)

....

....

Error

....

....

(ii) The memory management sub-system. (4 marks)

....

....

Error

....

....

[AQA Unit 4 (CPT4) Processing and programming techniques January 2003 Q(9)]

6

```
P:\TL01>cd May 2001

P:\TL01\May 2001>dir
  Volume in drive P has no label.
  Volume Serial Number is E04F-F00A

  Directory of P;\May 2001

  .           <DIR>          28/05/01 11.37a
  ..          <DIR>          28/05/01 11.37a
  Seniors     <DIR>          30/05/01 04.16p
  Juniors     <DIR>          30/05/01 04.16p
  Summer      92,160         31/05/01 10.37a
              5 File(s) 92,160 bytes
```

(a) What type of operating system interface is shown above? (1 mark)

(b) What program receives the instructions entered via this interface and analyses them? (1 mark)

(c) Give **two** advantages of this type of interface over alternative types of operating interface. (2 marks)

(d) Give one disadvantage of this type of interface over alternative types of operating system interface. (1 mark)

[AQA Unit 4 (CPT4) Processing and programming techniques January 2003 Q(4)]

7 The list **Days** contains the following representation of the days of the week.

[Sun, Mon, Tue, Wed, Thu, Fri, Sat]

The table below shows some functions which take a list as their single argument and return a result which is either an element of a list, another list, or a Boolean value.

Head(list) – returns the element at the head of **list** (e.g. Head(Days) ⟶ Sun) if list is non-empty otherwise it reports an error.
Tail(list) – returns a new list containing all but the first element of the original list (e.g. Tail(Days) ⟶ [Mon, Tue, Wed, Thu, Fri, Sat]) if list is non-empty otherwise it reports an error.
Empty(list) – returns True if **list** is empty or False otherwise. The empty list is denoted by [].

(a) What result is returned when the following function calls are made?

(i) Head (Tail(Days)) (1 mark)

....

....

(ii) Tail([Head(Days)]) (1 mark)

....

....

(iii) Empty(Tail(Tail(Tail(Days)))) (1 mark)

....

....

(b) Explain why it is faster to access these elements if the above data is stored as a one-dimensional array. (2 marks)

....

....

[AQA Unit 4 (CPT4) Processing and programming techniques June 2004 Q(6)]

8 (a) The Arithmetic Logic Unit (ALU) is that part of the processor which performs operations on the data. *Arithmetical* and *logical* are two different types of operation.

ADD is an arithmetic operation; AND is a logical operation. Both combine two sets of binary digits. What is the difference between their operation? (2 marks)

....

....

(b) (i) In order to process data, a sequence of operations is frequently required. As each of these operations is executed, where are the results stored? (1 mark)

....

....

(ii) Why is it more efficient to store intermediate results in this location rather than in main memory (IAS)? (2 marks)

....

....

[AQA Unit 4 (CPT4) Processing and programming techniques January 2003 Q(6)]

9 Applications and effects

In this chapter you will learn about:

- The application of computers in different contexts
- Different ideas and sources for case studies in each of these application areas
- Reviewing generic packages
- The social, legal and economic consequences of the use of computers
- A case study for the manufacturing industry

Applications of computers in a variety of contexts

The advanced use of computers has revolutionised numerous aspects of everyday life spanning both work and leisure activities. During your A2 course you are expected to extend your knowledge of applications to include several areas which may be taken from **science**, **education**, **manufacturing industry**, **commercial data processing**, **publishing**, **leisure**, **design**, **communication**, **embedded systems**, **information systems**, the **Internet**, **artificial intelligence** and **expert systems**. (The **bold** text is used here to link to typical areas of study shown below.)

You obviously do not have time to study each of these areas, but *all have common threads* in terms of their particular **information requirements** and **communication requirements**. They all raise legal, **ethical** and **moral** arguments, have 'economic' ramifications, and raise a variety of other issues too. A typical case study from the 'education' application area has already been carried out in detail for the first book in this series (chapter 10), where examples of all of these issues were addressed. You are advised to undertake a similar exercise in one or two other application areas in which you are particularly interested (see margin entries). This, together with your knowledge of hardware (see chapter 15 in this book and chapters 17 and 18 in the AS level book), should enable you to answer generalised questions about typical application areas.

There are numerous examples from each category on the Internet. Type some appropriate key words into a search engine and you will be provided with a plethora of useful information.

The research carried out at universities around the world is an excellent source of material which can also be found on the Internet.

The most fruitful way to proceed is by way of a class-based project in which several students give a short lecture on a particular topic. A class-based discussion could then follow.

Videos and TV programmes are also useful.

Typical areas of study

Some examples from each of the above application areas (**shown in bold**) now follow, but there are hundreds of others from which you may choose, and new applications are being developed all the time.

Scientific – **DNA fingerprinting** – This could be used for human identification purposes and for resolving paternity issues. Some systems have a DNA matching probability as good as 1 in 8×10^{10}. The use of DNA ID cards may also be investigated here.
Molecular simulation – This is using force feedback devices to explore molecular structures either on screen or in a **virtual reality** environment. This allows chemists to understand the interaction between complex molecular structures, including getting a feel (*literally*) for the forces involved. These applications enable chemists to test theoretical results and predictions against the results obtained from a simulator.

A force-feedback device enables the user to experience forces generated by the computer. In the case mentioned here, the forces between molecular structures can be experienced by the user as though he or she were a tiny person manipulating the molecules at an atomic level.

Education – **School administrative systems** – Fruitful sources are databases used to hold pupil, staff, parent and general school information. Administrative systems also help with

An example from the manufacturing industry is given later in this chapter.

In this example we show how CNC systems are integrated with CAD packages and networks to build up a modern manufacturing base.

Macromedia Flash is a sophisticated package which enables interactive learning materials to be developed. The interactivity may be controlled by code developed by the designer of the system.

You are likely to live near a facility that makes extensive use of computerisation. It might be possible to get your teacher or lecturer to arrange a visit. However, you must brush up on your chosen industry or you may not be able to ask too many intelligent questions!

timetabling, examination entries, assessments and statistical returns to the government etc. Facility CMIS is a very good example of this system and was covered in detail in the first AS level book in this series.
E-learning systems – These are typically web-based systems used for teaching, analysing progress, examining, marking and reporting purposes.

Manufacturing industry – **CNC systems** – A fruitful source here are the CNC machines linked to CAD packages which make mechanical or electronic artefacts. Typical of the processes undertaken by these machines are grinding, milling, drilling, turning and metal forming. A fruitful area to explore is the aviation industry.
Industrial robots – Look at the computer systems used to control industrial plant like steel manufacture, building cars or controlling production lines. A fruitful area to explore is the automotive industry.

Commercial data processing – **Banking** – A good example here would be the BACS system used to process cheques and make other payments using this secure transaction system.
Stock control – There are many systems which could be analysed here. Major stock-control applications used in companies like retail supermarkets or electronic component distribution are good examples.

Publishing – **Authoring packages** – Applications used to produce material for e-learning. Packages like Macromedia Authorware or Macromedia Flash may be used to generate suitable learning materials.
Electronic books – eBook generators, the software used to produce books electronically that can be read by small computers and **PDAs**.

Leisure – **Computer gaming industry** – Production of a computer game from initial concept through to post production. Fruitful areas of study are the PC gaming industry, Sony's PlayStation, Microsoft's X-Box and Nintendo's GameCube.
Theme parks – The use of computers in the operation of theme-park rides. Good examples here would be control of the Back to the Future simulation ride in Universal Studios or computers used to control the Space Mountain ride at Walt Disney's theme parks. Analyse the effects of computers used in design on leisure activities and the entertainment industry.

Design – **CAD packages** – The use of 2D and 3D CAD packages and their application to the design of artefacts, e.g. look at the automobile or aircraft industries.
Studio animation – The production of a film or cartoon making use of computer animation techniques, e.g. cartoons and generation of special effects.

Communication – **Mobile phones** – The use of computers to program and manage telephone exchanges. Computers used to control telephone exchanges – implications for hacking and terrorism.
Encryption and other security measures – Applications to provide private and secure communication between individuals – implications for hacking and terrorism. There are plenty of moral, ethical and social issues here.

Embedded systems – **TCP/IP enabled devices** – Systems embedded into devices like fridges, burglar alarms and home automation.
Cameras – Analyse the systems embedded into digital video or still cameras. Look at the ways in which these systems have revolutionised the production of complex electronic devices (i.e. the older systems used to be many individual components and chips, now it is a microprocessor running a program in **ROM**.)

Information systems – **Statistical processing** – Analyse systems used to gather and correlate statistics, e.g. the World Health Organization.

Weather forecasting – Analyse the system that correlates the data from around the world to produce national and regional weather forecasts. Analyse the effects that information systems have on the workplace – job losses and job creation.

The Internet – **Video conferencing** – Analyse the systems which enable a number of people to correlate meetings over the Internet. Look at how systems like this could affect the travel industry or people's working habits.
ISPs – Analyse a typical ISP in terms of the facilities it provides and the provision for its customers. Analyse the effects of IRC, newsgroups, e-mail and the web in terms of political, social, moral and ethical issues.

Artificial intelligence – **Speech recognition** – Analyse how systems process and recognise real-time human speech.
Game playing strategies – Analyse systems used to play games against human experts – chess is a good example. Analyse the effects of strong AI on social, moral and ethical issues.

Expert systems – **Language translation** – You could look at systems used to translate one language into another, and then analyse the success or otherwise of the contextual sensitivity of the language translation.
Data mining or **mind mining** – Analyse the systems set up to provide specialist knowledge for companies like oil producers or the stock market. Analyse the effects of expert systems on social, moral and ethical issues.

Generic packages

You need to complete your study of **generic packages** like **databases**, **spreadsheets**, **word processors**, **desktop publishing**, **presentation packages** and **expert system** shells. Apart from the expert system shells, all of these generic packages should have already been covered in the AS course and chapter 11 in the first book in this series should be consulted as a reminder. From your A2 work on Prolog (see chapter 3) you already have a good insight into expert system shells. The only difference is that a professional expert system shell would have a much larger knowledge base and a graphical interface that makes it much easier to use. The idea of an expert system shell containing a knowledge base for animals is outlined in Figure 9.1.

The Expert System Shell shown in Figure 9.1 can be viewed on the Logic Programming Associate's site at www.lpa.co.uk. It can be found under the 'Expert System Shells' section.

If you are good enough at Prolog programming why not try something similar for your A2 project?

Animal Expert System

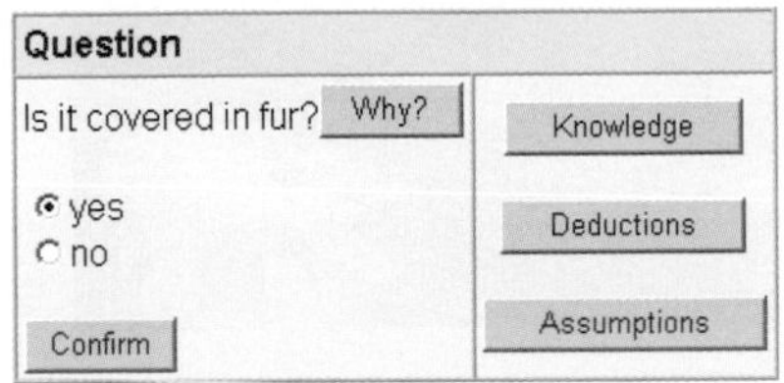

Figure 9.1 An expert system shell from Logic Programming Associates

Social, economic and legal consequences

The AS book in this series has already considered social, economic and legal issues in some depth (see chapter 12 of the AS book). You should already have an appreciation of the difference between ethics and morality, the use of **encryption** technology, and the effects of encryption on privacy. You should know how policies might be implemented in practice, and the role of human rights within this. You should also have a good knowledge of **viruses**, **spam** and legislation such as the **Data Protection Act** 1998, the **Computer Misuse Act** 1990, the **Copyright Design and Patents Act** 1988, and be aware of some other European legislation. For the synoptic element of the A2 course you should consider these issues in the context of your chosen application.

When reviewing the application of computers in a variety of situations remember the ways in which computers have changed everyday life. Fewer workers are now needed in the manufacturing industry because of CNC machines like those shown here.

However, remember that fewer typists are needed because the word processor has replaced the mechanical typewriter, and fewer clerks are needed to add up columns of figures because of the application of spreadsheets.

There are always a large number of social consequences following the introduction of computer applications.

Example

Many young children are now so familiar with the Internet, that they are able to construct sophisticated projects on a range of topics from dinosaurs to obesity. If these projects are undertaken in school, why might most of the children learn very little from using computer technology to find information?

Solution

It is very easy to find, cut and paste material from the Internet with little or no engagement or interaction for the children who are actually constructing these projects. Without direction, guidance, encouragement, monitoring and appropriate feedback from the teacher, little learning occurs unless the children are extraordinarily mature in their attitude to the material they are composing.

An application example from the manufacturing industry

Fifty years ago manufacturing industry relied on machines which were operated by skilled humans turning knobs and dials. If the human operator got tired or made a mistake, expensive components would have to be scrapped. The repetitive nature of some of these jobs often made the human operators bored, and the machines tended to be operated in eight-hour shifts. Gradually **CNC** (**Computer Numeric Control**) machines have taken over the role of manufacturing precision mechanical components, drilling holes in electronic circuit boards and cutting out shapes using laser beams. The human operators still have to be highly skilled, but there are fewer of them because the machines controlled by the computers make fewer mistakes and can work 24 hours a day, seven days a week. A modern factory using CNC machines is shown in Figure 9.2, and a range of CNC machines is shown in Figure 9.3.

Figure 9.2 A factory making use of CNC machines

If you look at the machines you may notice that there is not a conventional-looking PC in sight! However, inside these machines you will find **embedded systems** controlling the devices that form the shapes of the mechanical components. Smaller CNC machines are actually controlled by conventional PCs running operating systems like Windows, but the larger machines shown here have a proprietary operating system, and a proprietary GUI

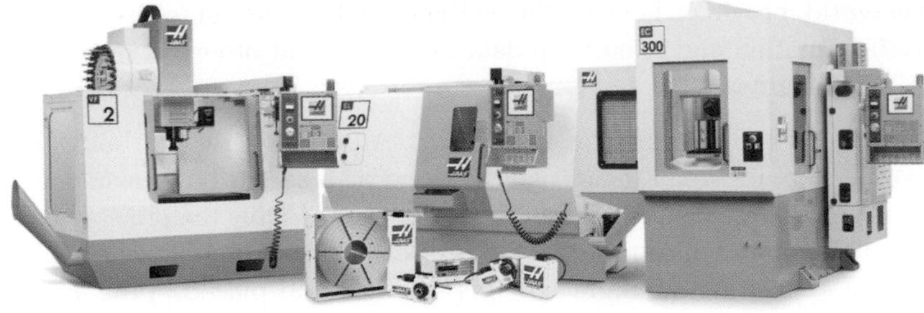

Figure 9.3 A range of CNC machines manufactured by Hass

There are several types of CNC machine.

A lathe will help to manufacture cylindrical components by turning the components in a chuck that goes round, often at very high speed.

A milling machine has a flat bed onto which a component is bolted. A rotating head will hold drills and other special tools which are moved across the surface of the components to shape them into the desired form.

Other CNC machines are special cutters that use lasers or other technologies. These can be used to cut shapes from metal or fabric, and are extensively used in the fashion industry for the mass production of clothes.

depending on the machine being controlled. A typical **user interface** for a milling machine (see margin entry) is shown in Figure 9.4.

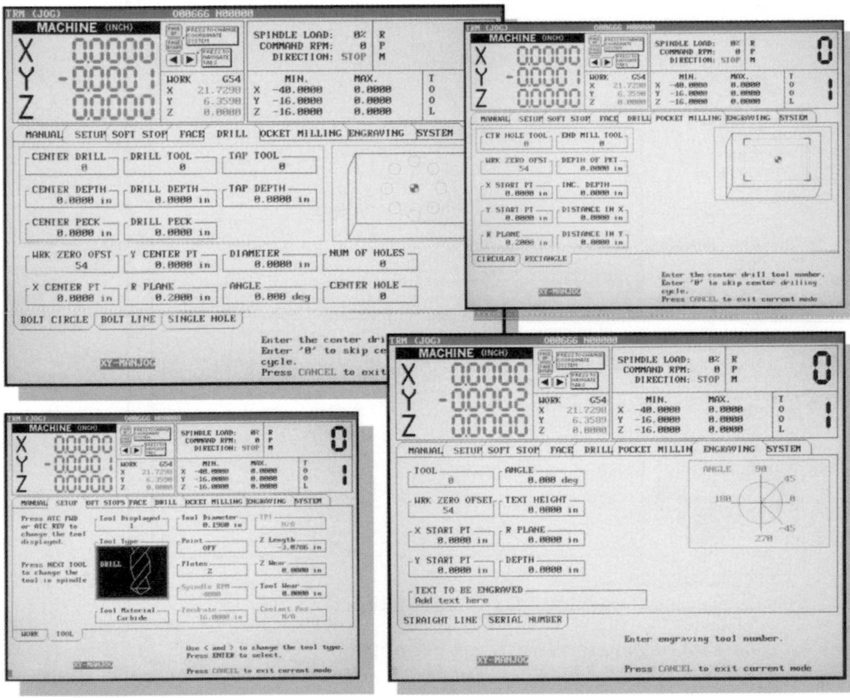

Figure 9.4 The Graphical User Interface (GUI) for a Hass milling machine

Touch-sensitive screens are used but keys and buttons (especially the emergency stop) are placed in a prominent and easy-to-locate position on the actual machine. When considering applications you should look at the special user-interface requirements, and those shown here are very specialised indeed.

Software and sharing manufacturing data

In a large factory like that shown in Figure 9.2, it is very unlikely that the CNC machine would be operating in isolation. The mechanical component being manufactured needs to be designed, and this would be accomplished by people making use of a CAD package in the design office. This office may be in the factory or in some other factory or office somewhere else in the world. Indeed, the design team will probably consist of many people working on the same product, and AutoDesk, one of the leading CAD package manufacturers in the world, provide a host of other software to help design teams manage their projects, share information and export the data to a variety of other packages and systems including CNC machines.

Figure 9.5 shows AutoDesk's Vault, running as an add-on to AutoDesk's inventor software. This is a **client-server** system in which the designs are held on a **server** but downloaded to the **workstation** for processing by a member of the design team. Thus the project managers can have a complete picture of the state of the project at any particular moment in time. All changes to the system are monitored by this software and placed in the Vault. Therefore, a designer in Germany might make a modification to part of a component, which might then be reflected on the file server in the US where the rest of the components are being designed. The project manager, who may be in London, can monitor what is going on by using this software.

Figure 9.5 AutoDesk's software for helping to share design information

The G code shown in Figure 9.6 is for a machine with multiple heads.

There are a variety of tools in each holder (e.g. a 3/8" carbide spot drill and the 8–32 UNC tap (a tool for making threads)).

You can see from Figure 9.5 that every individual component (right down to a nut or washer) is catalogued in the system. With the appropriate CAD-package diagrams, the data needed by the CNC machines (usually in the form of a G code), like that shown in Figure 9.6 for example, can be generated.

Looking at the G code in Figure 9.6 you can see that there is information about the type of tool (drills etc.) needed by the CNC machine, and instructions telling the machine the order in which to do the job. Typically the human operator would place tools like drills, taps (to make threads) and cutters into the CNC machine. They would then place the workpiece at the appropriate location and run the G code program which instructs the machine to carry out the appropriate operations.

Most modern CAD packages can generate the G code (or other code that might be needed) automatically, and the program can then be downloaded from the file server into the CNC machine by means of the **Ethernet** interface on the CNC machine. The server may be located in the factory where the CNC machines reside, or it may be in another part of the world.

The co-ordinates supplied to the machine represent numbers which reflect the position of the tool and the speeds. It also represents changes from one tool to another, and whether to open the door, for example.

In this way the CNC machine is instructed how to make an artefact and to liaise with the human machine operator.

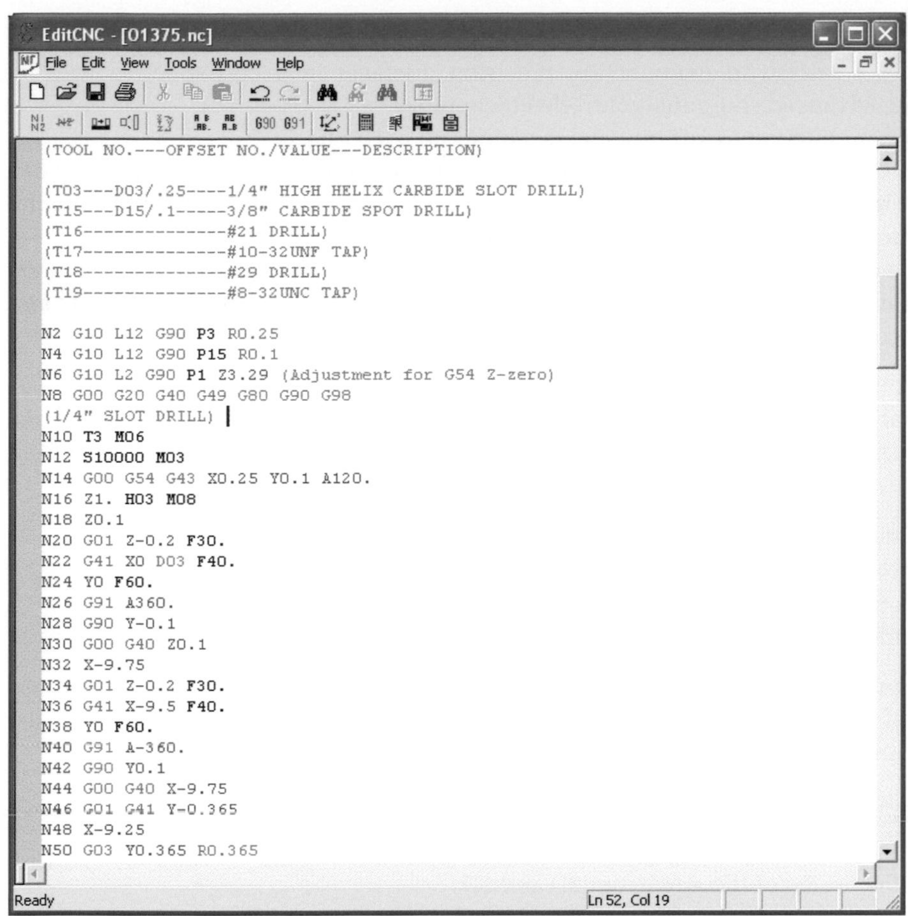


```
(TOOL NO.---OFFSET NO./VALUE---DESCRIPTION)

(T03---D03/.25----1/4" HIGH HELIX CARBIDE SLOT DRILL)
(T15---D15/.1-----3/8" CARBIDE SPOT DRILL)
(T16--------------#21 DRILL)
(T17--------------#10-32UNF TAP)
(T18--------------#29 DRILL)
(T19--------------#8-32UNC TAP)

N2 G10 L12 G90 P3 R0.25
N4 G10 L12 G90 P15 R0.1
N6 G10 L2 G90 P1 Z3.29 (Adjustment for G54 Z-zero)
N8 G00 G20 G40 G49 G80 G90 G98
(1/4" SLOT DRILL)
N10 T3 M06
N12 S10000 M03
N14 G00 G54 G43 X0.25 Y0.1 A120.
N16 Z1. H03 M08
N18 Z0.1
N20 G01 Z-0.2 F30.
N22 G41 X0 D03 F40.
N24 Y0 F60.
N26 G91 A360.
N28 G90 Y-0.1
N30 G00 G40 Z0.1
N32 X-9.75
N34 G01 Z-0.2 F30.
N36 G41 X-9.5 F40.
N38 Y0 F60.
N40 G91 A-360.
N42 G90 Y0.1
N44 G00 G40 X-9.75
N46 G01 G41 Y-0.365
N48 X-9.25
N50 G03 Y0.365 R0.365
```

Figure 9.6 Some G code from the CNC Consulting Company in Canada

Important links with other systems

Notice the variety of economic and social consequences.

The team of people working on this particular project do not have to be in the same factory, indeed, they do not even have to be in the same country, and the manager of the project may be in some remote location.

You should remember the importance of linking the manufacturing base with other systems in the factory. Components required for the design of each artefact need to be sourced and purchased (e.g. nuts, bolts, washers, metal, plastic etc.). These components have already been specified by the designer of the system, and we therefore need to export this information in a suitable form to software packages used by the purchasing department of the company. They would probably use spreadsheets to analyse costs and word processors to send out suitable purchase orders to the suppliers. This would also need to be linked to the stock control software used by the company.

The cost of components needed to make up the artefact should be added to a suitable proportion of the other costs like employee's wages, electricity, maintenance, purchase of new machines and usually a huge variety of other things. This will have to be modelled by the appropriate personnel to arrive at a sensible price for the final artefact given that a suitable amount of profit will need to be made. This would normally be modelled using spreadsheets, and the component information mentioned in the last paragraph would be an integral part of this process.

The information requirements of the manufacturing system

When analysing any system it is important to consider why the system is needed. A list of

The information requirements and the communication requirements of a system were covered in your AS course (see the first book in this series).

The information requirements are basically a list of 'what the system has to do', and the communication requirements are an examination of the user interface.

general objectives (which is not exhaustive) might be as follows:

- to provide a system to manufacture precision artefacts in a cost-effective way by employing advanced computer-controlled technology
- to increase production by running the machines on a 24/7 basis
- to reduce the number of skilled personnel needed to produce quality artefacts
- to import information from the CAD packages which are used to generate and share the design information, often by means of **internetworking**
- to provide an integrated environment such that departments like purchasing, accounts, design and manufacturing may share information by means of using spreadsheets and word processors.

Having looked briefly at CNC manufacturing, you should now be able to start working out the **information requirements** of a typical system. Although the following list is *not* exhaustive, some of the information requirements of the CNC manufacturing system would be:

- import data from CAD packages to the CNC machines
- provide workers with an easy-to-use interface for manufacturing artefacts
- enable workers without knowledge of programming to use the machines
- provide information to the designers and customers about the current state of a project.

The **communication requirements** of the system cover a variety of functions like the ease of transfer of information between users and the user interface. For this system you need to consider individual users such as machine operators, designers and accounts.

Taking the designers of the artefacts as an example, they might typically have the following communication requirements (this list is not exhaustive):

- generate the design of the artefact in 2D and 3D
- produce printed drawings of the artefact
- produce a list of the components needed for the artefact, and hence link to the price-information database
- generate the G code needed for operation of the CNC machines
- liaise with other engineers and designers by means of internet working.

Taking the operators of the CNC machines as an example, they might typically have the following communication requirements (this list is not exhaustive):

- be given a computer-generated schedule of the tasks to be accomplished that day
- be given computer-generated instructions on how to set up the machine for a particular job
- have paperwork which confirms that the tools (drills, taps, cutters etc.) in a particular bin from the machine-tool stores are those required for the particular job in operation
- have an easy-to-use interface on the CNC machine which enables the operator to program the system and to download the program for a particular job from the server.

Example

List four typical communication requirements for personnel in the 'purchase orders' department (i.e. those who order the components that make up the artefacts).

The solutions needed by one company are likely to differ from those needed for another.

Solution

- A link to the design system which specifies the quantity and type of components that are needed for a particular artefact.

- A link to the database that holds the current supplier information, including price.
- The ability to export component and price information to a spreadsheet for further analysis.
- The ability to generate orders (quantities and components) for each of the suppliers.

Always consider the skill requirements of the workforce and the effect that the introduction of new technology might have.

Does the system satisfy the user's needs?

We have considered some of the implications of CNC machines for a large manufacturing company. It is likely that a system of this complexity will easily satisfy the user's needs because other large manufacturers successfully run similar systems. However, the cost of this system might be too high for a small manufacturer, where the price of the artefacts might not be sufficient to recover the high initial financial outlay needed to purchase such a system.

A smaller company might decide not to use the client server model described here, but employ a small stand-alone CNC machine with a conventional PC controlling it. The design information could reside inside the PC controlling the CNC machine.

A smaller company might not have a separate purchasing department, and so the user of the machine might have to generate his or her own component data to work out the pricing for a particular order. Thus the skills that the machine operator would need would be much broader than the skills needed by the machine operator in a much larger company.

What about the economics?

Economics play one of the biggest roles in introducing new technology in the workplace.

If the technology will not pay for itself over a sensible period of time, then the company is unlikely to make a profit from the use of the new technology.

You must never lose site of the fact that most companies exist to make money. Therefore, the economic consequences normally override all others. If the purchase of new technology does not improve productivity and profit, then usually it will not be introduced, no matter how marvellous it might be! On the other hand, with sufficient finance, the purchase of a large new system, together with hiring an appropriate workforce might enable a company to produce high-quality goods more cost effectively than those produced by competitors. In this case the company would have made the right choice, as the competitors would probably lose orders and may go out of business.

The social, legal and ethical consequences

Remember that companies in the industrialised world are often competing with businesses setting up in developing countries where manual labour is cheap, and the workers are prepared to work very long hours indeed, often in dangerous and dirty environments, where health and safety laws do not exist or are flouted.

It may be necessary to retrain workers, some of whom may not want to learn new and complex skills. Some workers may also need to be laid off with the consequence of paying out large sums of redundancy money. Some workers may see the skills that they have possessed for a long time being replaced by an automated machine, and may therefore have negative attitudes towards the introduction of the new technologies.

It will be necessary to convince the workers that there is job satisfaction in acquiring a new set of skills. It will also be necessary to convince people of the need for the new system. Arguments may be based on the following lines:

- there will be a cleaner and safer environment (*compared with using the old manual machines*)
- staff will get the chance to acquire modern skills using computers in the manufacturing

process (*you could convince people they are working more closely with the designers of the system and have valuable input*)
- the increased skill levels will provide an opportunity for better pay and conditions (*this could be financed out of increased productivity with the new machines and methods of working*)
- better job security should result from providing a better product at a lower price (*fewer mistakes are made by the automated machines and lower prices will increase the competitiveness of the company*)
- the new machines are more flexible and adaptable (*the designs for new artefacts can be downloaded quickly and, after the appropriate tools have been loaded, manufacture may proceed immediately*).

The introduction of new machinery and computer systems will not be without legal implications. For example, do the new computer systems conform to the Health and Safety Act 1999 which protects workers from having to undertake unsafe practices? Typically a new risk assessment will have to be carried out, and the workers should be made aware of the new dangers they will face when using the new machinery. This would normally be carried out on an appropriate training course.

There are legal frameworks in operation ensuring that the software which controls the CNC machines is of an appropriate standard to maintain both the safety of the machine and the person operating the machine (*e.g. the machine should not be able to start to drill a hole in itself, or the operator of the machine should not be endangered by the machine starting up when they are working inside it, for example*). Remember that the factory might have to work 24/7. Are there legal frameworks in operation to ensure that the workers do not work excessive hours? Most of the industrialised countries have this legislation in operation already.

Is it successful?

The case study provided here shows just a small part of one system. Your teacher should choose a few other systems and provide a similar analysis. Remember that the Internet provides millions of pages of suitable material.

Inevitably the success or otherwise of a complex manufacturing system will be judged by the profit made by the industry, the reputation of the industry, the quality of the products and the general happiness of the people who work in the system.

It is not possible to communicate the sophistication of these systems in a few pages. Large and sophisticated CNC systems would have the ability to match the job being done to the appropriate machine. They would also be able to calculate the best way to machine a product resulting in the minimum of waste, and even be able to calculate the size and weight of the finished part so that information may be provided for packaging and posting purposes.

Self-test questions

1 **Make a list of five application areas where computers are used in science.**
2 **Make a list of five application areas where computers are used in communications.**
3 **What are generic packages? State one possible ethical and one possible legal implication of the use of an expert system shell.**
4 **List two possible economic consequences of the use of generic application packages in the office environment.**
5 **An embedded system is used to control the security alarm system in an educational institution.**
(a) What is an embedded system?

(b) Outline five typical features this embedded system may provide for the school or college.

6 Computers are used extensively in the leisure industry. Outline three different uses of computers for each of the following parts of the leisure industry.

(a) Computers on board a cruise ship.

(b) Computers at an airport.

7 Computers have been set up to aid air traffic control. List two typical information requirements and two typical communication requirements from the point of view of:

(a) The air traffic controllers.

(b) The pilots.

8 Robots are used in a car production plant.
Write a few sentences outlining the moral arguments for and against the introduction of this technology.

10 Advanced databases

In this chapter you will learn about:

- The basic idea of a DBMS
- Different schema like 'users', 'logical', 'conceptual', 'physical' and 'internal schema'
- Concurrent access to data and access to data via ODBC
- A DDL, DML, Data Dictionary, File Manager and Query Language
- SQL constructs such as 'SELECT', 'FROM', 'WHERE', 'GROUP BY' and 'ORDER BY'
- Aggregate functions and their use with 'GROUP BY'
- Database servers and object-oriented databases

You already have extensive knowledge of database design and implementation from the work covered in your AS level course.

Work on your AS module 3 project will also help to put this chapter into context.

The work in this chapter formalises database concepts and extends your database knowledge into the corporate environment.

You would be well advised to revisit the work you have already covered on databases if you cannot remember very much of it.

Introduction

You studied databases in some detail during your AS year and possibly used a relational database when carrying out the module 3 project. We now take a formal look at databases, and consider the foundations on which a typical database system is built.

The database management system or DBMS

Many modern databases are developed using a three-level architecture. This is shown in Figure 10.1, where the three main levels of architecture are the **physical database**, the **conceptual view** and the **users' view**. The **DBMS** is often referred to as the conceptual view of the system.

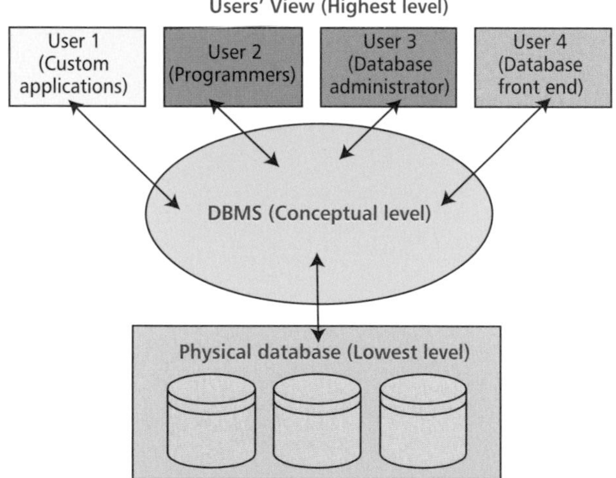

Figure 10.1 Three-level DBMS architecture

The physical database is concerned with how the data is stored. For example, files might be stored and accessed either randomly or serially. You may also be familiar with magnetic disk formats like cylinders and sectors used to store the physical data on the disk.

The **conceptual level** of the database is the way in which the data has been logically organised to gain access to it, and manages the security of the database. You already have a good idea of the conceptual view of a database because you have created **database tables**, written queries and produced reports for your AS course. In this chapter we concentrate mainly on the mechanisms associated with the DBMS.

The highest-level architecture is the **users' view**. Advanced users, such as programmers for example, would be able to access the data in very sophisticated ways, enabling them to process that data in ways limited only by their imagination and programming skills. On the other hand, non-technical users of the system would need simple front ends designed to enable them to process the data in predefined ways. The users' view is also known as the **external view**. A powerful DBMS would allow many users to have completely different views of the system which is built up using the same data.

You should appreciate that advanced DBMS are often the hub of any commercial organisation. The data contained within the database is so important because without this vital information it is unlikely that the organisation would be able to function.

When considering the CNC manufacturing systems in chapter 10, an advanced DBMS would certainly hold much of the valuable information regarding the day-to-day operation of the company.

Different users, like managers, buyers, engineers and designers, would all require very different views of the same data held inside a large database.

Database schema terminology

The views of the database are often referred to as **schema**. You will see terms like the **external schema**, which is the users' view or **users' schema**, the **logical schema**, which is the same as the **conceptual schema**, and the **internal** or **physical schema**, which is the physical database.

If you have used Microsoft Access then you may have used VBA (Visual Basic for Applications) or Excel, for example, to access information contained within an Access database. Figure 10.2 shows how it is possible to do this using a Microsoft Access database.

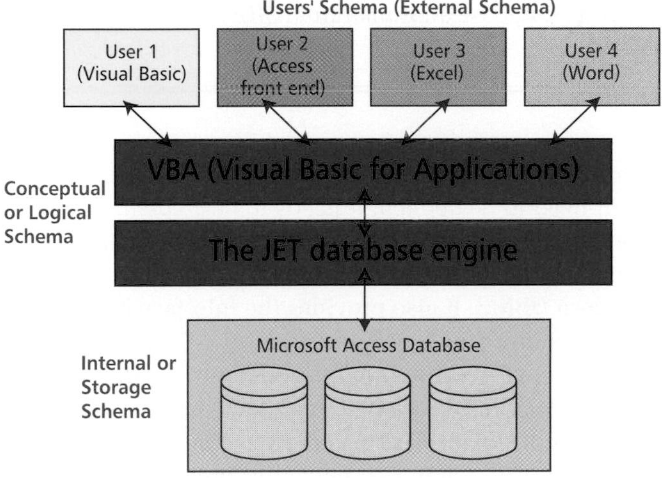

Figure 10.2 Three-level DBMS architecture

Here you can see how applications like Word or Excel, for example, can access the Jet Database engine (the **DBMS**) and hence gain access to data held inside Microsoft Access. Jet stands for Joint Engine Technology.

Concurrent access to data

Many users may access a large database simultaneously. If two or more users are using the same record, then problems can arise with updates. For example, two people could be attempting to book the same theatre seat at the same time. There are a variety of ways to get over this problem, and the DBMS allows the **database administrator** (DBA) to specify which system is currently in use.

An **exclusive lock** can be used to prevent others from locking items until the lock is cleared, usually by closing the record after editing. When different people are using a

Make sure that you understand the difference between importing and exporting data using CSV (Comma Separated Value), and linking to a database using ODBC.

Both databases must support ODBC in order for this to work properly.

database simultaneously, excluding others from being able to update the information within a particular record is a common option. You could open a database by locking the whole lot, as would probably be the case when using a stand-alone PC, but this is not ideal for **concurrent** or **multi-user access**. Record locking or exclusively locking any part of the database will not prevent others from looking at the data, but it will prevent them from updating the data. For **relational tables**, parts of one table related to data being edited, might also have to be locked, or the relational updates will not maintain their integrity.

Accessing data via ODBC

Some databases may be too big for local resources. For example, at the time of writing, Microsoft's Access limits Office 2003 Professional to a 2 Gbyte local database (i.e. a database held on a local hard disk). Larger databases are usually set up on **SQL database servers** (see below), and you can link to these via a Microsoft Access front end. Also, Access and other databases can use what is called **ODBC** or **open database connectivity**. By using this method, you can update (i.e. alter) the records in the remote database from other applications that support this method. This is much more powerful (and potentially dangerous) compared with exporting data from the large database using a system such as **CSV** (Comma Separated Value), for example. The disadvantage of a CSV is that the data is only up to date at the time it was imported or exported. The advantage of ODBC is that the view of the database from any application is current because you are actually editing the data – assuming, of course, that you have been given permission to do so. These security permissions are usually assigned by the database administrator (DBA), who is in charge of setting up and running the databases.

The DBMS in detail

The DBMS should not be new. You have probably used it without realising it when you defined, created, managed, maintained, accessed, interrogated and backed up your module 3 project at AS level.

The only difference at A2 level is that we are formalising these methods and introducing some extra concepts.

The DBMS is basically lots of different items of software which control all aspects of database management. The database will need to be *defined*, it needs to be *created*, efficiently *maintained* and *managed*, and it needs to be *accessed*, *interrogated* and *backed up*. Queries need to be made, from which information can be extracted for reports. These are just some of the functions carried out by a modern DBMS. It also provides the interface between the data and the users. It would probably allow you to create powerful GUI-based systems enabling non-specialist users to enter data very easily into the system or to carry out standard queries. The DBMS allows you to interface a variety of high-level languages via suitable language extensions and provides multiple levels of security etc. You can use the **data query language** (**DQL**) and other aspects of the **SQL** (see below) to provide management with powerful analytical tools that can handle most aspects of their data-processing business because the database literally is their business. The DBMS considered in Figure 10.1 is shown in more detail in Figure 10.3.

As can be seen from Figure 10.3, the DBMS provides the necessary links between the data stored on magnetic disk or other suitable secondary storage medium, and the external software interfaces such as **applications programs** etc. As you can see from the diagram, the database management system also provides an appropriate interface between other applications that might want to make use of the data in the database system. A high-level language, for example, may wish to use the facilities of the DBMS so that it can store and retrieve data for its own particular application. Modern versions of **COBOL**, for example, have been extended to include special commands which deal specifically with databases.

The data definition language (DDL)

The database schema would be modelled by the DBA with the help of a special language called the **data definition language** or, alternatively, the **data description language** (**DDL**).

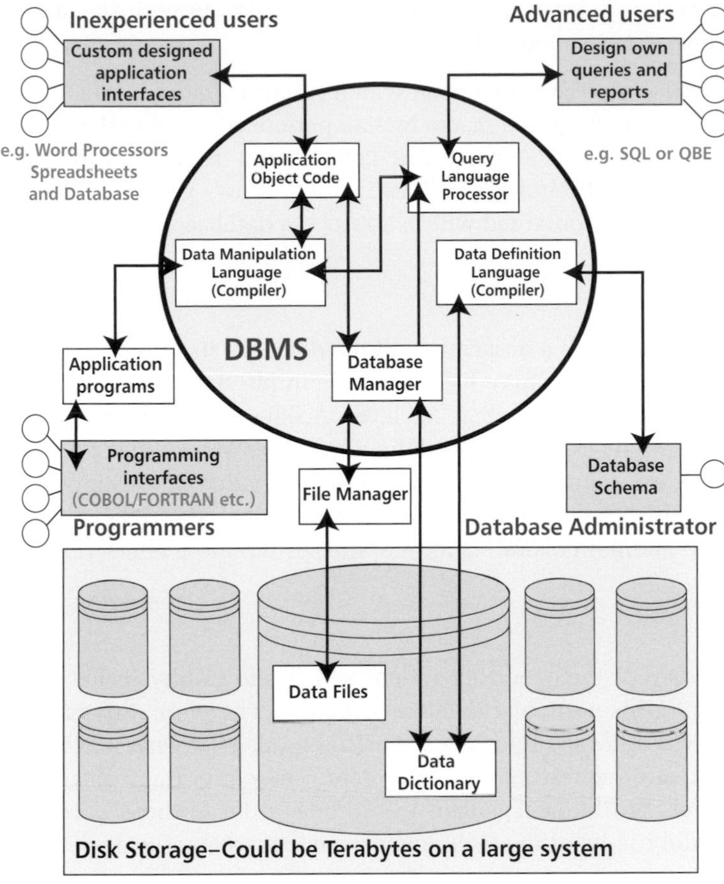

Figure 10.3 Three-level architecture in more detail

The data definition language helps to define the structure of the files. A data definition language is part of SQL, and would help to describe attributes such as record layouts, fields, key fields, and other things such as location of the files. Therefore, the data definition language helps the DBA to define the **logical structure** of and files within the database, which is then used to construct tables that are held in the **data dictionary**.

The data definition language (DDL) and data manipulation language (DML) are both part of a structured query language called SQL.

Some students may have used SQL before, but they probably have not differentiated between the parts of this language that define or manipulate the data.

At A2 level you are expected to be able to differentiate between different parts of the SQL language using the appropriate names.

Data Manipulation Language (DML)

The **data manipulation language** (**DML**) provides a comprehensive set of features to allow modification of the data contained within the database. Some of the facilities provided by the DML are intended only for the DBA, but other facilities such as parts of the **query language** (see below) allow all users to carry out common operations such as retrieving and modification of data (if there is appropriate security clearance). You should realise that large database systems will probably have multiple users, and these conditions usually bring extra problems. For example, different users cannot carry out updates on the same record at the same time. Therefore, a process called record locking is used whereby a record in the process of being updated is not available to other users during this editing period.

There are currently two types of DML supported by some DBMS, and these are related to the procedural (or **imperative**) and non-procedural (**declarative**) languages as explained in chapter 3. You may recall that **4GLs** are typified by non-procedural DML types, and it is these which allow users to access data more easily than writing procedural code. Advanced users may wish to build up their own algorithms enabling them to use the database in innovative ways, but inexperienced users would make do with the simpler aspects of the DML to retrieve data in standard ways.

Programmers or the DBA will write their own code which might calculate statistics, for example, which could then be called up as a macro by inexperienced users of the system. Typically, on a PC running Microsoft Access, you could write routines using **VBA** (Visual Basic for Applications), a subset of Visual Basic which allows very sophisticated processing to be carried out on data contained within an Access database.

The data dictionary

The **data dictionary** can be regarded as a description of the database itself (not the actual data that is held in the data files). You may have created simple database dictionaries when undertaking the module 3 project work at AS level. A data dictionary might typically contain data about the data types used for each field, whether any validation should take place or whether a field is a 'required field' or has a default value, for example. The data dictionary can be thought of as containing data that describes the databases, and therefore enables the DBA to maintain overall control of the system more effectively.

The file manager

The **file manager** would be part of the operating system which allows physical access to the data stored on the disks in this particular database example. Therefore, this manages access to the data at the physical-level sub-schema. The file manager interfaces the data stored on disk with the software requesting particular data. Therefore, the logical structures used at the higher levels of file management would be similar to those covered in your AS course when files and file-handling techniques were looked at in some detail.

The query language

Part of the facilities provided by the **DML** enable the end users to execute queries by using a **query language**. In some systems the DML and the query language is one and the same thing. It is the job of the query processor in the DBMS to take the queries written by the users and to change them into a form that can be used inside the DBMS to interface with the other systems described above. The query processor must also communicate with the DML so that appropriate queries produced from the high-level languages or other applications may be converted into the application code necessary to communicate with the database manager at the appropriate level (see Figure 10.3).

When learning about data definition languages, data manipulation language and query processors etc. it is easy to lose sight of the fact that SQL is really quite simple to use at an elementary level.

Make sure that you have access to a system that uses a SQL language, and then program examples similar to the ones shown in this chapter.

Structured query language (SQL)

The structured query language or SQL (pronounced sequel) is an ANSI standard (a bit like a high-level language) for *creating*, *updating* and *querying* a relational database, and is *the* standard language for relational database management systems. It consists of constructs like 'SELECT', 'FROM', 'WHERE', 'GROUP BY', and 'ORDER BY' etc. to help manipulate the data contained within the database. SQL is much more powerful than the QBE (query by example) methods used when Access databases were covered in your AS year. In fact, the QBE methods generate SQL code automatically, and you can look at the SQL code from Access by selecting a query and choosing the SQL view. This is a good way to learn some SQL and understand Access in more detail. SQL is most easily understood by means of simple examples. Consider the database shown in Table 10.1.

Table 10.1 A database table used to demonstrate SQL code

This table is called 'Books'					
ISBN	**Author**	**Title**	**Publisher_ID**	**Price**	**...**
0-7487-4046-5	Bradley	Computer Science	1	24.00	...
0-7833-8822-7	Farmer	NT 4 Server Secrets	1	39.00	...
0-6324-2817-6	Martin	Radio Techniques	1	36.00	...
0-5834-9921-7	Bradley	Quantum Computers	1	57.00	...
0-3844-8463-8	Bradley	Modulation	2	45.00	...
0-3523-7668-2	Prakash	Java Programming	2	23.00	...
0-6543-9332-8	Burgin	CD-ROM Servers	3	20.00	...

Microsoft Access allows you to create your own SQL code or modify SQL code that has been created using QBE methods.

You should note that the publisher ID is a unique number that identifies a particular publisher.

Some typical SQL code could be written to operate on the above data as follows:

```
SELECT ISBN, Author, Title
  FROM Books
  WHERE Publisher_ID = 1;
```

The above SQL code is quite simple and is explained in detail below.

The **SELECT** keyword is used to retrieve selected data. In the above example, columns 1, 2 and 3 will be selected. The **FROM** keyword is used to identify the 'table name' from which the columns will be retrieved. The table in Table 10.1 is called 'Books', so this name should be used here. Finally, the **WHERE** keyword determines the conditions under which the data will be retrieved. If there are no conditions, then all data from the database will be listed. A typical condition might be 'where Publisher_ID = 1', for example. A generalised form of the above query will therefore be as follows:

```
SELECT "column1"
  [,"column2", "column3"]
  FROM "tablename"
  [WHERE "condition"];
[] = optional
```

The syntax for the conditions varies, but typically the relational operators will be similar to those shown in Table 10.2, which uses the syntax for Microsoft's Access.

From the work just covered you should see how easy it is to write simple SQL code.

You need to remember these keywords because similar tasks are expected in your A2 examination.

SQL code can become extremely complex for large databases containing many related tables.

Table 10.2 Some typical operators for conditions

Example relational operators	Symbol	Examples
'Equals'	=	Teacher = "Bloggs"
'Less than'	<	Name < "Cooper"
'Greater than'	>	Quantity > 3
'Less than or equal to'	<=	Salary < = 50000
'Greater than or equal to'	>=	Tax > = 40
'Not equal to'	<>	Post.code <> "TN4 1JX"
'And'	'And'	(Form = "3a") And (Name = "Tom")
'Or'	'Or'	(Form = "3a") Or (Form = "3b")
'Not'	'Not'	Countries = Not "UK"
'Is like'	'Like'	Like "Brad*"
'Lies between'	'Between'	Date Between #01/01/1999# And #01/01/2000#

The 'order by' property

The **ORDER BY** keyword is used to display the results of a query in some specific order. For example, if we wish to display the same information as before (from the book table in Table 10.1), we could, in addition to the code shown before, add an 'ORDER BY' keyword to display this information in order (alphabetical in this case) by 'Author' using the syntax shown in the following example. If 'ORDER BY' is not used the list of authors would be in the order they happen to appear in the database table.

Example

Using the database in Table 10.1, write some SQL code to display the 'ISBN', 'Author' and 'Title' for books which have a Publisher ID of 2. List the results in order of author.

Solution

The following SQL code should produce the output shown underneath it:

```
SELECT ISBN, Author, Title, Publisher_ID
  FROM Books
  WHERE Publisher_ID = 2
  ORDER BY Author;

ISBN              Author    Title
------------------------------------------
0-3844-8463-8     Bradley   Modulation
0-3523-7668-2     Prakash   Java Programming
```

If you look at the equivalent SQL code from Microsoft's Access then it appears to be more complex. The above SQL code, for example, might appear as follows:

```
SELECT Books.ISBN, Books.Author, Books.Title, Books.[Publisher
ID]
FROM Books
WHERE (((Books.[Publisher_ID])=2))
ORDER BY Books.Author;
```

The 'Publisher ID' field name has a space between the words 'Publisher' and 'ID', therefore brackets have been used to accommodate this. If an underscore is used for the field name (Publisher_ID) then the square brackets would *not* have been used. You could use an underscore if you have several different words in a field name, which is exactly what you would do when building up variables in a high-level language.

When producing SQL queries in A2 examinations you can use the simple syntax shown previously.

In the event of writing a query using more than one related table, you would need to include the name of the table using the methods described here.

The table names also appear *before* the field names because you can have multiple tables. If several tables were involved in an SQL query, then you would have to do this too. Finally, Access uses a few more brackets. These do not need to be put in for the purposes of A2 examination questions where the structure of your SQL code is what is being marked.

Aggregate functions in SQL

Functions, called **aggregate functions**, can be used to operate on data in one or more columns, and typical examples are Avg(), Max(), Min(), Count() and Sum(). These functions are simple to use, as shown in the following example.

Example

Using the database shown in Table 10.1 as an example, write some SQL code that produces the total number of books in the library having a Publisher_ID of 1.

Solution

Note that we have now used the Publisher_ID field name, as suggested above.

```
SELECT Sum(Publisher_ID)
  FROM Books
  WHERE Publisher_ID = 1
  Sum (Publisher_ID);

Sum(Publisher_ID)
-----------------
4
```

This would produce the sum of all the publishers where Publisher_ID = 1. Because there are four publishers satisfying this criteria from Table 10.1, Sum(Publisher_ID) where Publisher_ID = 1 returns the value of four, as shown in the output above.

The 'group by' property

In the previous example we performed operations on an entire column from the table. It is possible to group data, using the keyword **GROUP BY**. This causes them to be displayed by these groups, and we may also perform aggregate functions on each logical group. Below is an example of these techniques.

Example

Using the same database as an example, write some SQL code to select and display the fields 'Title', 'ISBN', 'Author', and 'Publisher_ID' from the Books table. Arrange the data into groups based on 'Author', then 'Publisher_ID', then 'Title' and finally 'ISBN'.

Solution

The output from this query is shown underneath the SQL code.

```
SELECT Title, ISBN, Author, Publisher_ID
FROM Books
GROUP BY Author, Publisher_ID, Title, ISBN;

  Title                  ISBN               Author     Publisher_ID
  --------------------------------------------------------------
  Computer Science       0-7487-4046-5      Bradley    1
  Quantum Computers      0-5834-9921-7      Bradley    1
  Modulation             0-3844-8463-8      Bradley    2
  CD-ROM Servers         0-6543-9332-8      Burgin     3
  NT 4 Server Secrets    0-7833-8822-7      Farmer     1
  Radio Techniques       0-6324-2817-6      Martin     1
  Java Programming       0-3523-7668-2      Prakash    2
```

The output from SQL queries can be controlled in sophisticated ways using the techniques described here.

The red group shows that the authors have been grouped by publisher ID, then title (within Author and Publisher_ID) and finally by ISBN. You would obviously need more data to show all of these logical subgroups.

Notice how the column order is determined by the 'SELECT' statement and the row order is determined by the 'GROUP BY' statement.

The colours used in the example given here are for illustrative purposes only, highlighting how the 'GROUP BY' command is operating on the extracted data.

Using 'group by' with aggregate functions

Both the 'ORDER BY' and 'GROUP BY' key words can be used to sort data, as demonstrated by the above output, but the 'GROUP BY' key word is useful if you want to use an aggregate function on a group rather than the whole column of data. You do this by selecting a group of rows on which to perform the aggregate function as shown in the next example.

Example

Using the database shown in Figure 10.1 as an example, create a simple query which sums how many books have been written by each author.

Solution

The output from this query is shown underneath the SQL code.

```
SELECT Author, Count(Publisher_ID) As Total_Books
FROM Books
GROUP BY Author;
```

```
Author              Total_Books
---------------------------------
Bradley             3
Burgin              1
Farmer              1
Martin              1
Prakash             1
```

The groups have again been shown in colour to help understand the 'GROUP BY' processes. The label 'Total Books' has been constructed using the 'As' keyword at the end of the statement. If this was not used Access would return something like 'Expr1001' at the top which is obviously not as helpful.

Considering the last example, other versions of the SQL language might have slightly different syntax for the production of headings. Typically they might be something like the following:

```
SELECT Author, 'Total Books' = COUNT(Publisher_ID)
FROM Books
GROUP BY Author;
```

If you do not have Microsoft's Access, one of the most popular implementations of SQL is called MySQL and is an open source (i.e. free) implementation of SQL that can be downloaded from the Internet.

Look at www.mysql.com for further details.

As stated earlier, you need to understand the principles and the structure of SQL, and not the exact syntax of any particular implementation. However, actually using some SQL, either from Microsoft's Access or from one of the numerous places on the Internet where you can download a SQL implementation would be extremely helpful.

Creating a database table using SQL

Above we implied that a database could be created by **SQL**. To create the simple database shown in Table 10.1, the keyword 'Create' can be used in the following way:

```
CREATE TABLE Books
(
ISBN            Char(20)    Primary Key,
Author          Char(30)    Not Null,
Title           Char(50)    Not Null,
Publisher_ID    Int         Not Null,
);
```

A command like Insert supports adding the records to the database when entering the data. The number of SQL keywords and things you can do with them is vast. However, the subset shown here should suffice for the A2 computing examination.

Database servers

A good example of a database server is Microsoft's SQL server. This is a client/server **relational database management system** (**RDBMS**). The principles of a DBMS have already been covered, and the ideas were outlined in Figure 10.3. A **database server** is the server on which such a system resides. All the functionality (and a lot more) outlined in Figure 10.3 is available on a typical SQL server.

Microsoft's SQL server integrates with a variety of operating systems including Windows and Unix-based systems. The programming languages supported include all the Visual Studio suite including Visual C++, Visual Basic and Visual J++. It integrates with Microsoft Office applications like the word processor Word, the spreadsheet Excel and the database Access, and third parties provide extra programming languages like Delphi (the Visual version of Pascal) and COBOL.

Most database servers would be fully **ODBC** compatible and support **object linking and embedding** (**OLE**). This is where objects such as pictures, text or other data may be linked to applications like word processors and spreadsheets, where the picture or other data gets embedded in the word processed document, for example. However, unlike ODBC, OLE will need to refer to the source data again if it needs to be kept up to date. OLE is ideal for capturing graphs or other data, for example representing sales figures for a particular month.

At the heart of this database server would be the SQL server engine, which usually has a superset of the ANSI SQL standard, thus ensuring that your SQL code will work only on the proprietary brand of database server! Nevertheless, if you wished you could use a different database as a front end and write your SQL in the syntax of the particular database you are using. As long as you do not wish to use the functionality provided by the superset of SQL, and provided your database is ODBC compatible, it should work very well.

Object-oriented databases

When object-oriented programming methods are appropriately applied to database management you get an OODBMS or object-oriented database management system.

From reading chapter 3 you should be very familiar with object-oriented programming. An **object-oriented database** (**OODB**) is identical in concept, where the data inside the database is represented by objects and can be manipulated by object-oriented programming methods.

The fundamental difference here is that data is actually stored as objects, and thus you need class definitions and methods to access the objects. Instead of the data definition language and the data description languages which are typical of an RDBMS, the same programming language can be used for each. Inheritance is fully supported, sophisticated data structures can be modelled and data can often be found by its type rather than having to search in the conventional way.

An object-oriented database is also ideal for storing multimedia components like music, videos, pictures and sound. Some of these data types are not fully supported in a conventional relational database environment.

Some companies are now using OODBMS in preference to the relational databases covered in this chapter. This is especially true where speed of response to real-time data is important (e.g. on-the-fly analysis of stocks and shares).

The OODBMS model might take over from RDBMS in the future. However, the knowledge and investment currently being made in large RDBMS will ensure that it will take some considerable time to actually achieve this.

Self-test questions

1. What is a DBMS?
2. What is meant by the three-level architecture when considering a DBMS?
3. It is usually arranged so that different types of users have different views of data contained within the DBMS. Suggest three different types of users, and give an example of what each different type of user may require.
4. What is meant by 'concurrent access to data'? Why is concurrent access to data a problem, and what is done to overcome it?
5. Some databases are ODBC compatible. What does this mean? How might data be transferred from one database to another that is not ODBC compatible?
6. What is a data definition language? Give two different examples of things you can do with this language.
7. What is a data manipulation language? Give two different examples of things you can do with this language.
8. What does the file manager in a DBMS do?
9. SQL or (sequel) is one of the most important standards for accessing data within a relational database. List four different things that could be accomplished by the use of some typical SQL commands.
10. Making use of the constructs 'SELECT', 'FROM' and 'WHERE', show how these commands would typically be used in an SQL language to extract data from a table in a relational database. You may choose your own data for the purposes of illustration.
11. What is the function of the 'ORDER BY' command in an SQL language? Give an example.
12. What extra functionality does the 'GROUP BY' command give over and above the 'ORDER BY' command?
13. Using the database in Table 10.1 as an example, write an SQL query to produce the following list.

ISBN	Author	Title
0-3523-7668-2	Prakash	Java Programming

(You should note that there may be several ways of producing this list.)

14. Using the database in Table 10.1 as an example, write an SQL query to produce the following list.

ISBN	Author	Title	Publisher_ID
0-3844-8463-8	Bradley	Modulation	2
0-3523-7668-2	Prakash	Java Programming	2
0-6543-9332-8	Burgin	CD_ROM Servers	3

(You should note that there may be several ways of producing this list.)

15. A database server is needed to implement a large database in a professional way. What is a database server, and how does it relate to the RDBMS?

11 Advanced relational databases

In this chapter you will learn about:

- Database design and the relational model
- Entity-relationship modelling
- The need for normalisation
- First normal form
- Second normal form
- Third normal form
- Boyce Codd Normal Form (BCNF)

Database design – the relational model

The **relational database model** is currently *the* most popular method of database design. To make management of the data efficient, and to prevent undesirable errors, the database has to be designed *very* carefully.

A **database schema** is the 'definition of the tables', and this is what we are trying to perfect when building a relational database. Each table should describe a single **entity**, where an entity is an object within your database. Entities might be books, authors or publishers in a library database. Typically an entity will refer to a **record** or **row** within a **table**. In chapter 10, Table 10.1 shows the books entity or the books table, having seven different examples of the entities books.

We can define **relationships** between various objects or entities. For example, one customer may place many orders, and therefore there is a one-to-many relationship between the entity customer and the entity order. There are four possible types of relationship but only three may be used directly in relational database design. The many-to-many relationship will have to be modelled by using more than one one-to-many relationship, for example. The four basic relationships are as follows:

One to one		*One to many*
Many to one	and	*Many to many*

Relationships may conveniently be expressed by using an entity relationship or **ER diagram**. The entity relationship diagram for customers and orders described above is shown in Figure 11.1, together with some explanatory text in green.

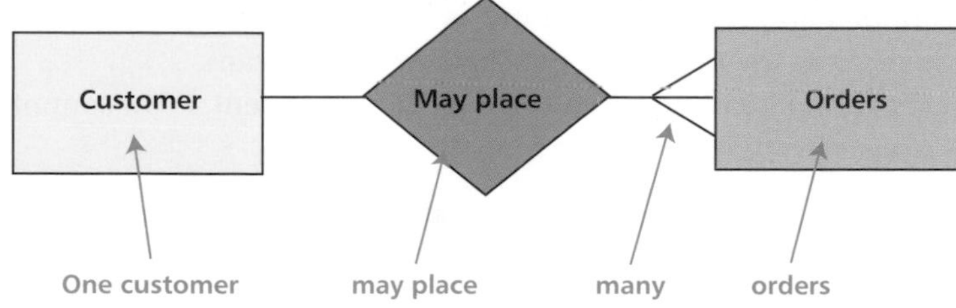

Figure 11.1 Entity relationship diagram

If you are designing a database for your A2 project then the methods covered in this chapter are particularly important.

At AS level it was relatively easy to design a simple relational database without using any formal methods.

At A2 level you would be expected to show that your related tables have been normalised to third normal form.

In your A2 project you are advised to go through the normalisation process even if the data in your tables does not alter. You may lose marks if you do not do this.

Using the shorthand notation to represent relational tables will save you a lot of time.

Use this shorthand method in your A2 project if you are designing a relational database.

Example

When using relational databases, it is not possible to model a many-to-many relationship. How do you think that this might be overcome in practice?

Solution

It is easily possible to model a many-to-many relationship by breaking it down into more than one one-to-many relationship.

Each entity in a table is made up from several **attributes**. The books table shown in Table 10.1 has the attributes ISBN, Author, Title, Publisher ID and Price. Each of these attributes usually corresponds to a **field** within a record. Instead of drawing out the tables as shown in Table 10.1, a convenient way of describing them is by using shorthand notation. Using the Books table again, we get the following shorthand version.

`Books (ISBN, Author, Title, Publisher ID, Price)`

All the attributes representing the entity books are listed, but separated by commas. The **key field** is underlined to emphasise the important role that ISBN plays in the list, but as we shall see below, this is not a particularly good table for describing books!

Normalisation

Normalisation is the name given to the processes that may be followed to achieve an efficient relational database design. There are *three main stages* to normalisation, called **first**, **second** and **third normal forms** respectively. Even if a database is in third normal form, it is still possible to have some redundancy, and so another form, called **BCNF** or **Boyce Codd Normal Form** is also used. It is very likely that data normalised to third normal form is already in BCNF. Designing a database to third normal form or BCNF is common practice and should be used in your A2 projects if appropriate.

When designing a relational database you may use the bullet points on this page as a checklist.

Performing these simple checks at this stage might prevent you from experiencing problems later in the design process when it would be very tedious to change things.

The author knows of students who have had to restart their projects after several weeks of work because they did not pay attention to this advice.

Codd's normal forms are based on a *special organisation of tables* into **relations**. This should not be confused with the term 'relationship', which is used to define the one-to-one or one-to-many connections described above. A relation is a table with the following properties.

- **Each table must have a unique primary key**. You may have to group several attributes (fields), or even introduce a completely new attribute, to form a **composite primary key**. If a table had identical primary keys, then the subject of each table would not be unique.
- **Each row in the table must be unique**. (i.e. no two rows of the table can be identical – it would be a very bad choice of key field if this were the case!)
- **A table should model only one entity**. (We should not have 'books' and 'authors' in the same table – as shown in Table 10.1, for example.)
- **The ways in which the columns and rows are laid out is not important**. The order of the rows in the table or the order of the attributes in each row is irrelevant.
- **All the attribute names (i.e. column headings) in a table must be different**. (You cannot have the same field name appearing twice within a file!)

Before (and during) normalisation it is best to make sure that the above bulleted criteria apply, and that each table applies to only one particular subject (entity). Most databases, like Access for example, will pay no attention whatsoever to the table name, but rely on the primary key alone for the purpose of identification.

Why use normalisation?

Before carrying out some normalisation processes you should be aware of the need to do so. If you designed a database without much thought, you may encounter the following problems.

1 The database might contain redundant data, and this would be wasteful of storage space.

2 When updating the database, other data contained within it might accidentally become corrupted or not get updated.

3 Deleting data in one part of the database might inadvertently cause data to be deleted in another part of the database.

4 Calculated totals may not get updated properly when inserting extra data.

5 Often it is not possible to carry out complex ad hoc queries if the database is built up inefficiently.

Normalisation should get over these and other similar problems and the example below demonstrates these techniques.

Before starting on normalisation more formally, consider the simple database shown in Table 11.1, which will be used as an example of putting this data into **third normal form**.

Students are often reluctant to normalise because, in their eyes, their database works.

The reasons for normalisation on this page demonstrate that this might not necessarily be so!

Hours of 'fun' can be had trying to track down esoteric errors in your database which might be attributed to data that has not been properly normalised.

Table 11.1 An un-normalised table containing items for sale in a computer shop

Order number	Customer ID	Date	Items sold
45799	20063	18/3/2001	1 keyboard, 1 mouse, 2 zip disks
45830	20026	18/4/2001	1 scanner
45701	30087	19/4/2001	10 floppy disks, 3 reams of paper
46333	30003	23/4/2001	2 computer books, 1 magazine
48777	40023	23/4/2002	3 computer games, 1 floppy disk

Always research how your database will be used in practice before designing it.

Already, by the application of common sense alone, we can see that the method for storing data in the 'Items sold' field is particularly awful. The shop would benefit from a numeric code for each product. As it stands we cannot even differentiate between types of computer books or games! You should always work out how the data is to be used *before* designing the database on a computer. In Table 11.1, the primary key is shown in red, and a particular customer order (for customer 20063) is shown in green.

As another example, if there were to be a 'customer address' field, we could put the entire address into this single field, but this is far too restricting. It is better to have separate fields because it is easier to search on 'post code', for example. Again it is all related to the ways in which the data will be used. This is what good database design is about. Normalisation will help make the database efficient but it will not overcome problems regarding lack of research into how the data is to be used in practice.

The address example used here is typical of mistakes that could be made which normalisation would not be able to overcome.

First normal form

Before putting data into **first normal form**, make sure that you have a proper **relation** as shown by the bulleted list at the beginning of this section. To put a table into first normal form we need to undertake the following task:

- Attributes having *multiple values* must be removed so that the rows (records) in a table are *all the same length*.

In other words, you should have no repeating attributes (i.e. different things put into the same field or a variable number of different fields) within a single record.

An example of a *multiple-valued entry* is the 'Item sold' field in Table 11.1. By applying the common sense mentioned above, we can put the database of Table 11.1 into first normal form by arranging the table as shown in Table 11.2.

Table 11.2 A possible first normal form representation for the computer-shop data

Order number	Item number	Date	Customer ID	Quantity	Item ID	Item sold
45799	1	18/3/2001	20063	1	9537	Keyboard
45799	2	18/3/2001	20063	1	7833	Mouse
45799	3	18/3/2001	20063	2	6534	Zip disk
45830	1	18/4/2001	20026	1	8878	Scanner
45701	1	19/4/2001	30087	10	9983	Floppy disks
45701	2	19/4/2001	30087	3	3326	Reams of paper
46333	1	23/4/2001	30003	2	5346	Computer book
46333	2	23/4/2001	30003	1	1122	Magazine
48777	1	23/4/2002	40023	3	1990	Computer game
48777	2	23/4/2002	40023	1	9983	Floppy disk

The examples of putting data into first normal form are designed to be particularly simple to understand.

Much more subtle interactions would cause errors if data were not put into second or third normal form. These are not so easy to understand, and this is one of the reasons for going through the normalisation process.

In this new tabular relation, the order number is no longer unique (it appears several times in the table) and therefore cannot be used as the primary key. To overcome this problem, we introduce a new field called 'Item number'. This composite primary key, consisting of the attributes order number and item number *is* unique, and the **composite key** can be used as the **primary key** (shown in red in Table 11.2). Customer number 20063 now takes up three records and is again shown in green.

Table 11.2 no longer contains attributes with multiple values, it has a unique **composite primary key**, and the rows are all the same length; it is therefore in **first normal form**.

Before going on to put the data into second normal form, let us consider why we have put it into first normal form. When created in an un-normalised way, as shown in Table 11.1, searching the database becomes a nightmare. It would be difficult, for example, to find out exactly how many floppy disks have been sold without doing a detailed search within each of the 'Item sold' attributes; and all because the 'Items sold' attribute has multiple values. Also, searching for floppy disks could create an error because this may not pick up the single floppy disk sold to customer 40023!

Second normal form

Before a relational database table can be put into **second normal form**, it must already be in **first normal form**. Assuming that the table is already in first normal form, to put it into second normal form you would carry out the following task:

- Make sure that all the attributes in an entity are **functionally dependent** (*depend only*) upon the **primary key**.

Remember that the primary key *may* include several attributes, and this functional dependence must be on the composite primary key, not just part of it.

By applying the criteria in the bulleted list shown at the beginning of the section on normalisation, tables should store information about one entity only; this means that every non-key item in a table must now depend only upon the entire primary key. Therefore, you need to analyse each and every non-key attribute and check to see if they are uniquely dependent (i.e. depend totally) upon the primary key. Doing this is actually easier than explaining it, as can be seen from the following example.

We can now put the computer shop database shown into second normal form. Using Table 11.2 as our starting point, and working through the **non-key elements**, we start with attribute 'Date'. Date is *not* functionally dependent on the composite primary key but it is dependent on order number because you *can determine* the date from the order number. Therefore, the date must be taken out of this table and put into another table. Next comes Customer ID; this is functionally dependent on order number only, because we can determine the customer ID from order number alone. Therefore, Customer ID should be removed to another table too. All the remaining attributes in Table 11.2 depend only on the composite primary key (order number, item number). Therefore, we can split Table 11.2 into two different tables as shown below.

A non-key element is simply an attribute that does not form part of the primary key or composite primary key.

For Table 11.2, the non-key elements are 'Date', 'Customer ID', 'Quantity', 'Item ID' and 'Item sold'.

The key elements in Table 11.2 are 'Order Number' and 'Item number' which together form the composite primary key.

Table 11.3 The order table

Order Table (Second normal form)		
Order no.	Customer ID	Date
45799	20063	18/3/2001
45830	20026	18/4/2001
45701	30087	19/4/2001
46333	30003	23/4/2001
48777	40023	23/4/2002

Table 11.4 The items table

Items Table (Second normal form)				
Order no.	Item no.	Stock no.	Qty	Item sold
45799	1	9537	1	Keyboard
45799	2	7833	1	Mouse
45799	3	6534	2	Zip disk
45830	1	8878	1	Scanner
45701	1	9983	10	Floppy disk
45701	2	3326	3	Reams of paper
46333	1	5346	2	Computer book
46333	2	1122	1	Magazine
48777	1	1990	3	Computer game
48777	2	9983	1	Floppy disk

Splitting up tables like the ones shown here is a natural consequence of the normalisation process.

It is unlikely that this process would be undertaken using common sense alone, and this is why relational databases are normalised.

For the purposes of your A2 project, going through the motions of splitting up tables is exactly what is required to achieve the marks.

The attributes shown above are now **functionally dependent** only on the *entire* **primary key** and both tables are therefore in **second normal form**. We now have better ways of storing the data compared with the first normal form Table 11.2. The Date and Customer ID do not have to be repeated, and the database is therefore easier to update.

Third normal form

Before putting the table into **third normal form** it must already be in **second normal form**. If not, we must apply the rules in the previous two sections. To put a table into third normal form means undertaking the following task:

- There should be no **functional dependencies** (*unique associations*) existing between **attributes** (or groups of attributes) that could not be used as an *alternative* to the **primary key**.

In other words, there should be **mutual independence** between all **non-key elements**.

If dependencies exist between non-key elements, situations may arise during updates where dependent information may get left behind or other information gets deleted.

We will now put Tables 11.3 and 11.4 into third normal form.

Looking at Table 11.3, no dependencies exist between Customer ID and Date, and therefore the table is already in third normal form.

From Table 11.4, there *is* mutual dependence between Stock number and Item sold. (*They are the same – you cannot have a stronger dependency than this!*) These items must be taken from the main table and put into another one. By doing this, the data is stored more efficiently. If, for example, you sold many keyboards in many separate orders, you would have to enter both the stock number (9537) and the word 'Keyboard' several times. This extra effort is eliminated by splitting Table 11.4 into two tables as follows.

After going through the normalisation process students are often impressed with the results, but some think that they could have achieved the same by using common sense.

These students are probably right, but many students cannot easily split up tables like this, and the normalisation methods provide the formality required at A2 level and will pick up on any detail that common sense may fail to spot.

Normalise your A2 project databases in the ways suggested, and then apply common sense to see if the results are acceptable.

All tables are now in third normal form, and our entire database now consists of Tables 11.3, 11.5 and 11.7. Remember that Table 11.3 was already in **third normal form**.

Table 11.5 The items table

Order no.	Item no.	Stock no.	Qty
45799	1	9537	1
45799	2	7833	1
45799	3	6534	2
45830	1	8878	1
45701	1	9983	10
45701	2	3326	3
46333	1	5346	2
46333	2	1122	1
48777	1	1990	3
48777	2	9983	1

Table 11.6 A new products table

Stock no.	Product description
9537	Keyboard
7833	Mouse
6534	Zip disk
8878	Scanner
9983	Floppy disk
3326	Ream of paper
5346	Computer book
1122	Magazine
1990	Computer game

The three normalised tables can be written more conveniently by using the shorthand notation developed earlier. These are as follows:

```
ORDER (Order no., Customer ID, Date)
ITEMS (Order no., Item no., Stock no., Qty)
PRODUCTS (Stock no., Product Description)
```

Example

Tables in a database are edited and a 'referential integrity' error occurs. What does this mean? Give an example of what might be causing the problem.

Solution

When linking tables, we may have references to data in both tables. In a library database, there might be a reference to 'Publisher' within a Publisher table, but there might also be a reference to 'Publisher' in a Book table. If we delete a publisher from the Publisher table, then this publisher must also be deleted from the Book table. By not doing this, we have a dangling link, which is a reference to a publisher entry in the book file to a non-existent publisher. This is called a referential integrity error because the integrity of the reference here has been compromised.

BCNF

Most tables, already in third normal form, are probably in **BCNF** or Boyce Codd Normal Form too. If the data can be further normalised into BCNF, some extra anomalies may be avoided. Before attempting to normalise to BCNF, the table must already be in **third normal form**. To put a table into BCNF we make sure that the following statement is true:

- Every **determinant** is a **candidate key**.

A **candidate key** can be used to uniquely identify a record. (It is possible for a record to have several different candidate keys, of which only one is used as the primary key. It is up to the database designer to choose which is used.) Any candidate key that is not used as the **primary key** is called an **alternate key**. Finally, a determinant is an attribute (or possibly a combination of attributes), which is **functionally dependent** (*depends only*) on any other attribute or combination of attributes.

Put more simply, a table is in BCNF if *all the attributes in the table are just facts and nothing but facts about the primary key.*

Example

Is this relational database table in BCNF?

Table 11.7 A BCNF example for some college data

Student ID number	Main course	Tutor
661739	Computing	Bradley
661739	Maths	Evans
234777	Computing	Pinkstone
233338	Computing	Bradley
393362	Maths	Lucas
653349	Physics	Longley
983335	Biology	Belbin
265533	Chemistry	Clugston

Solution

From Table 11.7 we see that the primary key is the pair of attributes (Student ID, Main course). The Student ID is not unique because student 661739 does two different courses.

Look at the determinants. One possibility is the pair (Student ID, Main course). Each pair uniquely determines the tutor. Another possibility is the pair (Student ID, Tutor), which uniquely determines the Main course. Yet another possibility (assuming that the tutor specialises in one course only) is the Tutor uniquely determines the Main course. These are the three possible determinants.

To see if the table is in BCNF, we must check if each of these determinants is also a candidate key (i.e. a possible alternative to the primary key). Now the (Student ID, Main course) and (Student ID, Tutor) pairs are candidate keys, but Tutor (the last of the three determinants) is not; therefore the table is not in BCNF. To overcome this, we split Table 11.7 into two further tables which are now in BCNF.

Some commercial companies deliberately do not normalise their relational databases because they claim that the database is slowed down. However, you would have to design your databases extremely carefully and would need lots of experience to do this. This is not recommended at A2 level.

Part of the problem with normalisation is the unfamiliar terminology that is used.

It is worth making the effort to understand terms like 'determinants', 'candidate keys' and 'alternate keys', because using the correct terminology makes you more confident when undertaking these normalisation processes.

You may also be required to define these terms in an A2 examination!

Table 11.8 The student ID table

Student ID number	Tutor
661739	Bradley
879933	Evans
234777	Pinkstone
233338	Bradley
393362	Lucas
653349	Longley
983335	Belbin
265533	Clugston

Table 11.9 The tutor table

Tutor	Main course
Bradley	Computing
Evans	Maths
Pinkstone	Computing
Lucas	Maths
Longley	Physics
Belbin	Biology
Clugston	Chemistry

Self-test questions

1 Explain what is meant by the 'relational database model'.

2 Explain what is meant by the following relational database terms.
(a) Entity (b) Table (c) Row (d) Column (e) Relationship.

3 (a) There are three possible types of relationship, but only two are usually used when designing a relational database. Name these two.
(b) How is a 'many-to-many' relationship modelled in practice?

4 What is an entity relationship (ER) diagram? Give two examples, one for a one-to-one relationship and one for a many-to-one relationship.

5 What is meant by normalisation when considering a relational database?

6 Give an example of a typical problem that could occur if data in a relational database is not in first normal form.

7 Give an example of a typical problem that could occur if data in a relational database is not put into second normal form.

8 Give an example of a typical problem that could occur if data in a relational database is not put into third normal form.

9 What is meant by the term 'composite primary key'? Why does a composite primary key have to be used on many occasions? Give an example.

10 What is meant by the following relational database terms?
(a) Functional dependence (b) Non-key element
(c) Mutual independence (d) Determinant.

Questions continue on the next page.

11 **The following table shows some data in un-normalised form.**

Table 11.10 Un-normalised data

Order no.	Acc. no.	Customer	Address	Date	Item	Qty	Price	Total cost
7823	178	Chez John	27 The Drive, Tonbridge	16/7/2005	Bakewell Tart Danish Pastry Apple Pie	20 13 45	0.85 0.65 0.95	68.20
4633	563	Harpers	3a High St. Maidstone	16/7/2005	Danish Pastry	120	0.65	78.00
2276	167	Pie Crust	16 High Street, Tunbridge Wells	17/7/2005	Apple Pie Cherry Pie Steak Pie Danish Pastry	130 100 30 20	0.95 1.10 1.55 0.65	293.00
1788	032	Sloggers	17 Maple Av. Maidstone	18/7/2005	Apple Pie Danish Pastry	15 50	0.95 0.65	46.75
7120	289	Dibbles	The Pound, Tonbridge	18/7/2005	Apple Pie Chocolate log	20 3	0.95 2.50	26.50

(a) Express this data in first normal form, writing the tables using the standard shorthand notation.

(b) Express the first normal form tables in second normal form, making use of the standard shorthand notation.

(c) Express the second normal form tables in third normal form, making use of the standard shorthand notation.

12 Systems development

In this chapter you will learn about:

- Methods of gathering information and fact finding techniques
- Reporting techniques, data flow diagrams and EAR diagrams
- Data dictionaries and volumetrics, system flowcharts, the characteristics of users
- Prototyping and designing the user interface
- Object-oriented analysis, class diagrams, association diagram and inheritance diagrams
- Aggregation diagrams and a class diagram example for an A2 project

When undertaking your own A2 projects, make sure that you have a bank of questions written down before you interview your client, and make sure that you take notes during the interview. You could also make use of a tape recorder.

If you gather data by using a questionnaire then this is an example of a direct data source. If you use data gathered by others then this is known as an indirect data source.

Introduction

You covered the **information requirements** and the **communication requirements** of a system when dealing with 'applications and effects' in your AS level module 2 work. The CMIS system was used as an example in the first book in this series, and here we continue with similar themes, looking at the techniques that professionals use for fact finding and gathering information. From your module 3 AS level work you will also be familiar with the **classical system life cycle** which **systems analysts** use to develop a system from conception through to implementation and maintenance. The techniques shown here are essential tools and methods used in industry and commerce.

Fact finding techniques

When developing new systems it is essential to find out as much unbiased information as possible. Interviewing **clients** and **users** of the system is one major technique. Systems analysts would usually make up a list of different categories of people and **interview** them. The interviewees usually know the existing system much better than the analyst does, and much can be learnt here.

Example

When collecting information about possible computerisation it is desirable to conduct interviews to gather important information. Name three other methods of gathering information, giving reasons why you might use them.

Solution

1 If the system is operating manually, or an older system is being updated, then observation is a useful technique. You can make notes about how the current system operates, and think up possible improvements. Making notes about the data flow between individuals or departments is particularly useful as new suggestions can often result in a reduction of the time taken to do things.

2 You can design a questionnaire to conduct a survey. It is important to frame questions carefully so that useful information is obtained and answers are unambiguous.

3 You could review the existing paperwork to see if any of the current methods used are still useful, and see if it is possible to devise ways of improving the existing

system. Useful paperwork includes invoices, filing systems, instruction manuals and ways of communicating between staff. Checks should be made regarding the relevance of particular documentation.

It is important that the interviews are carried out in an appropriate environment and in ways that do not intimidate people. Systems analysts are often viewed in the wrong light if this is not made clear, and interviewees often think that their bosses are trying to check up to see if they are carrying out their job properly!

It is important to analyse the results with the least hassle. What happens if you do not understand an answer to a question? If the respondent is *anonymous*, you will not be able to go back and ask the person to clarify answers. However, if the respondent is *not anonymous*, you may not get the frank answers that you need! The **observation** part of the proceedings can give useful insights. If people have been using a method for years, they do not tend to question existing ways. A stranger observing what is going on can often detect if things can be improved because they are coming into the situation with a fresh mind. A review of existing paperwork, existing manuals or other documentation is helpful. If manuals are available they will list what should be done. It is only by observation that you determine if this is what's actually being done!

The ability to construct a good questionnaire is a skill which few students possess.

You need to ask yourself if the likely answers will provide you with any useful information.

Asking clients a question like, 'Do you like working with the old system?' will only get a 'yes/no' answer which will not provide much useful information.

Asking, 'What is it that you like about the old system?' is much more fruitful because it may provide you with a list of features that you would be ill-advised to change.

Example

Orders are taken by telephone for a company that has no computers. List two things that could go wrong when processing the order, and how a computerised system could help to overcome possible problems.

Solution

If no computerised system is in operation, the person taking the order might lose the piece of paper on which the information is written. This can be overcome by typing the information into a computerised system, which automatically stores and backs up the data.

It is possible, if a manual system is in operation, that an order might get stuck in the system. With the computerised system it is possible for all personnel involved to be aware of the progress of an order because all may have access to the database via a network.

Reporting techniques

After gathering information using a variety of techniques such as **questionnaires**, interviews, observations, and **paperwork reviews**, you need to catalogue the results of your findings in a form suitable for the systems analyst's report. A variety of methods are available to do this, and some are considered below.

Data flow diagrams (DFD)

You have already used **data flow diagrams** in your AS module 3 project. They form a very useful diagramming tool in your arsenal of **systems development** techniques, and you will probably need them in your A2 project too. You are reminded that a data flow diagram is ideal for showing how information moves from one place to another in a variety of computer-based and manual forms. You should recall that there are four different data flow symbols: an arrow for showing the flow of data; a data processing symbol; a source and destination symbol; and a storage of data symbol, in which data can be stored in any form, manual or computerised. The next example makes use of **DFDs**.

Example

Time sheets (showing hours worked) must be processed so that validated data is entered into the computer for the weekly payroll run. By making use of a data flow diagram, show how these forms are likely to be processed during this data-entry phase.

Solution

Remember to question each stage of the manual process. It is no good mirroring an inefficient process. Analyse each stage to see if more efficient ways of solving the problem exist. It is the job of the analyst to see if the existing methods can be improved. Just because something has been done for many years does not mean it is the best way. Data flow diagrams can often highlight inefficient methods, or point to better ways of carrying out the processes.

Figure 12.1 indicates what happens to the time sheets if errors are detected, either by a human operator or by the computer system. Obvious errors, like data omitted, should be detected *before* the data is entered into the system, and can be corrected by passing the time sheet back to the employee. The computer could detect less obvious errors, like an incorrect date, and again the form could be passed back to the employee for rectification.

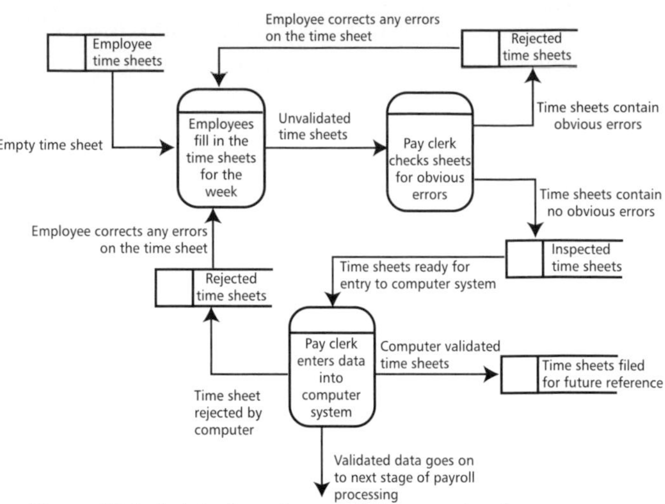

Figure 12.1 A data flow diagram for processing forms

EAR modelling

An **EAR** diagram is an **entity attribute relationship diagram**. You used **ER diagrams** in your AS level course and you may recall that they are particularly useful in helping to build up a model of a **relational database**. An entity is a single thing of interest that is to be modelled. For example, a car, a person or a sales order. An entity is represented on an ER diagram by a rectangular box as shown in Figure 12.2(a). Here the entity 'Person' (the *customer*) 'Likes' (the *relationship*) many cars, where 'Car' is the other entity. Relationships can exist between different entities. Examples might be 'a customer places an order' or 'a person likes a car'. Here the relationships would be 'Places' and 'Likes'.

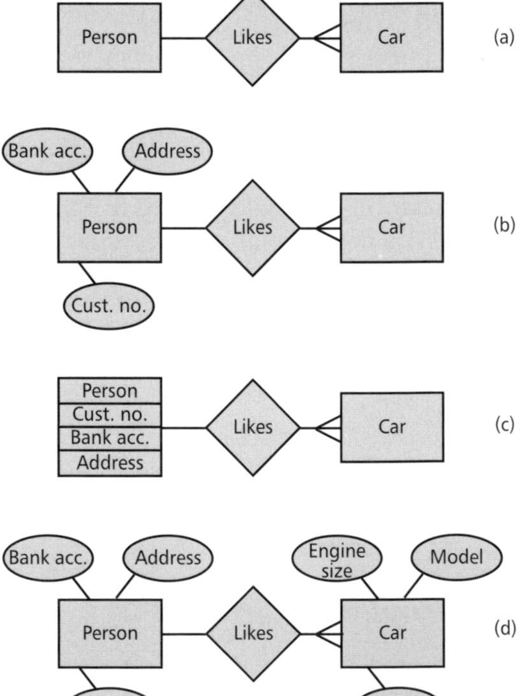

Figure 12.2 An ER or Entity Relationship diagram

An **attribute** describes some property of an entity. If we are modelling a customer who is interested in buying a car, the entity 'customer' might have attributes like 'bank account number', 'address' or 'customer number'. If an attribute is shown on an ER diagram, then it is often shown inside a bubble, and the customer attributes described above are shown in

Figure 12.2b. An alternative is to show the entity inside the rectangular box as shown in Figure 12.2c. The car will also have attributes like 'engine size', 'model' and 'colour', for example, and these are shown in Figure 12.2d.

The relationship 'Likes', shown in Figure 12.2 is a one-to-many relationship, and this is shown by *three lines* going into the car box. Many-to-one relationships, like many orders which may be 'placed' by a customer, can be modelled using a diagram like that shown in Figure 12.3. You should remember from your relational database theory that in all these cases each entity usually refers to a table, of which the individual records are particular instances of the entity, and the attributes usually refer to fields within a record.

Figure 12.3 An ER diagram showing a many-to-one relationship

Example

Students study a variety of courses. Draw a simple EAR diagram showing the relationship 'Studies'. You may assume any suitable attributes for your chosen entities.

Solution

A possible solution is shown in Figure 12.4.

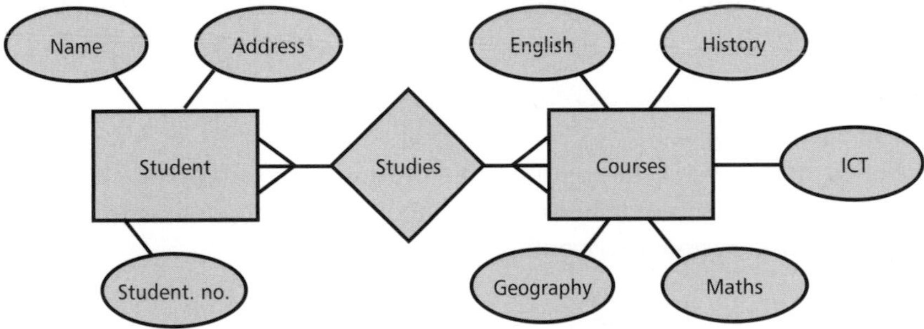

Figure 12.4 An EAR diagram showing the relationship 'Studies'

Data dictionary

A **data dictionary** is data about the data. Important information about managing data for a system can be entered into the data dictionary. Data dictionaries are often associated with

Table 12.1 The idea behind a data dictionary

A simple data dictionary entry	
Name	The name of the data element
Data type	e.g. Integer, long integer, real, date, currency of string etc.
Size	e.g. 4 byte, 256 characters etc.
Domain	This would consist of acceptable values of the data. For example, integers only between 0 and 65 536.
Units of measurement	e.g. Metres, km, feet or miles, etc.
Links	Possible links to other data in a database or on a website for example.
Comments	There may be special situations in which the data can take on some specific meaning.
Etc.	Other attributes may be appropriate for different systems.

relational database management systems but are more general than this. They can be applied to data about any system, computerised or not. Data dictionaries were used extensively when carrying out the module 3 AS project in the AS book, and Table 12.1 will remind you about the sort of data that might be contained in the data dictionary.

It is unlikely that volumetric data would affect projects at A2 level, but in industry it is vital to make large systems work efficiently.

The complexity of systems can vary from simple calculations on estimating the size of a database or file, to estimating the size of a large file server for a corporate organisation, where thousands of Terabytes of data will need to be stored, processed and backed up in efficient ways.

Volumetrics

It is important to have an appreciation of how much data might have to be processed in a given amount of time. A print run of just 100 copies/day would have very different design requirements to a print run containing 1 million copies/day. The hardware required would be very different indeed. A study of the ways in which the project design is affected by the scale of what has to be done is called **volumetrics**.

The characteristics of users

An understanding of the characteristics of users helps us to design a more effective project. You are more likely to get the user interface correct if you understand the people who will use it and the way in which it will be used. The following example shows how this might be achieved by understanding the structure of a company.

Example

Suggest a hierarchy of job descriptions that might exist in a company that develops computer games, and how characteristics of the users in this particular scenario might influence project development.

Solution

Things to consider about the users of the gaming company could be as follows: Who are the line managers? How do individual departments interact? What functions do individual workers within the system carry out?

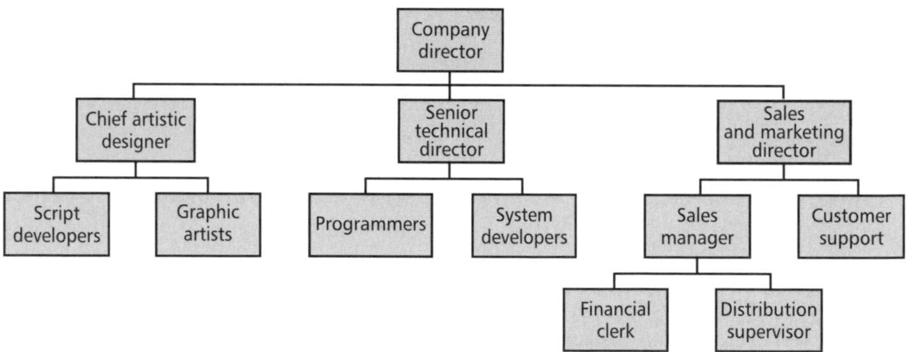

Figure 12.5 A possible hierarchical diagram for a computer gaming company

A hierarchical diagram is useful to describe the hierarchy of authority or areas of responsibility, and data flow diagrams (see earlier in this chapter) can help with interaction regarding the movement of data. A possible diagram for a games software company is shown in Figure 12.5. Three major departments, artistic, technical and sales, are under the control of the company director.

Next we might consider who controls the technical information and the flow of information between the design team and programmers. How is this managed? Who makes sure the projects are on schedule? If a problem exists which customer support cannot handle, how is it passed over to the technical department and dealt with? It is likely that key personnel will have multiple roles, and the analysts must understand this.

Users have well-defined job specifications in larger companies. In a large company it is likely that data entry staff will spend all day typing, and it is easy for the systems analyst to define this role. In a smaller company the financial clerk might also have to carry out the payroll function. The characteristics of this particular user would therefore be complex. It is possible to list job functions and to determine if existing ways of doing things can be improved.

Other characteristics of users would need to be considered by thinking about the end product. Who is the computer game designed for? What age group? What sex? What design characteristics of the user interface are important (see below) from the users' point of view? The characteristics of the users are important but can vary tremendously from system to system.

A good way to understand job functions is to talk to people who work in the computer industry.

This could be integrated with a careers evening, when students and parents can quiz a person who has just given a lecture on a particular topic.

Categories of speakers at the author's school have included those involved in banking, designing computer games, communications, software development and publishing.

Designing a system

Once the information about a system has been collected and analysed, assuming the system is feasible, it is time to start the design, and **system flowcharts** are popular for doing this. Typical system flowchart symbols are shown in Figure 12.6. These flow-chart symbols are, of course, in addition to the conventional **program flowchart symbols** covered in your AS course, which include start and stop boxes and decision-making symbols, for example. You will probably need to make use of system flowcharts in your A2 project.

Systems flowcharts are most easily explained by means of an example.

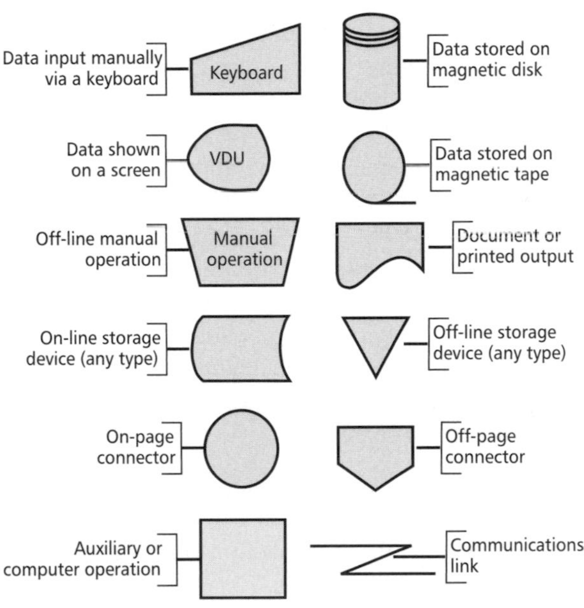

Figure 12.6 Some system flowchart symbols

Example

A company receives customer orders in the post. Making use of a system flowchart, show how a data entry clerk might process these orders. You must include the following processes in your analysis, but you need not consider the routine for the creation of a new customer:

- **validation of customer and order items**
- **rejection of erroneous orders**
- **the creation of a computerised order (transaction file) ready for use with the stock-control system**
- **the creation of a customer invoice to be sent off in the post.**

Solution

A possible system flowchart for processing the orders is shown in Figure 12.7. The data entry clerk picks up the purchase order, enters valid customer details, and creates a new transaction for this order. By referencing the stock database, the order is then processed, any entries with problems are flagged and the purchase order is passed back for correction. If the processing is successful, a customer invoice is printed out ready for sending off in the post.

Prototyping is a particularly good way of showing novice users how the final system may operate.

It is a technique which can be used to good effect in your A2 project if you are designing a database or writing a program.

Remember that it is relatively easy to produce a prototype interface, but it may not be so easy to get the software behind the interface to work properly!

The user interface

User interfaces are particularly important because users expect 'ease of use' and 'consistency across a range of applications'. Microsoft's Office suite is a good example of this, where Word, Excel, PowerPoint and Access have a similar feel to them. Defining 'a similar feel' is not easy, but includes things like the same icon is used for printing or the same icon is used for formatting text or very similar menus are available for loading and saving files. If this were not the case, the user would have to relearn simple operations like how to save a file each time they used a different application. Manufacturers are wise in keeping the interface consistent across a range of applications.

If possible you should develop the user interface in consultation with your users, and the next section on prototyping underlines this.

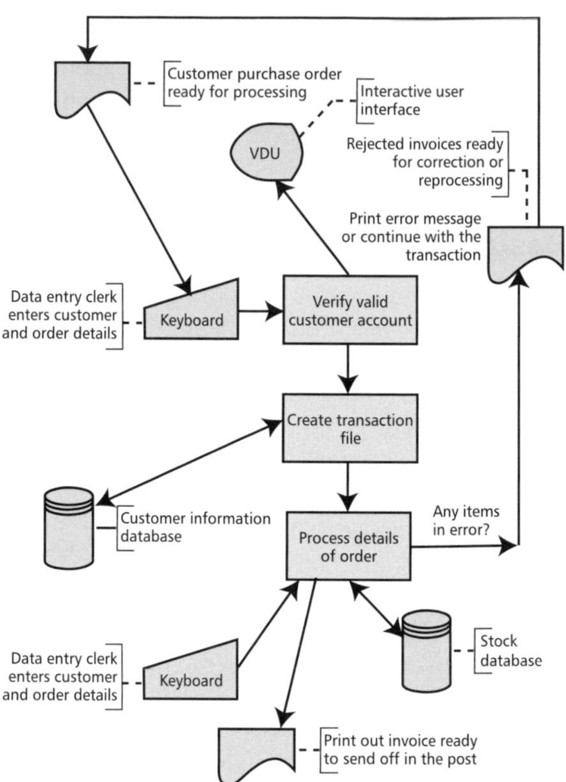

Figure 12.7 A possible system flowchart for the orders sent via the post

Prototyping

Building a mock up (or **prototype**) of a user interface is very useful. Even the best-laid plans can fail if the system does not perform as expected or if the interface is awkward to use. The users may not be able to provide any *effective feedback* if they have nothing concrete on which they can comment.

Consider an interface being designed to control a piece of machinery, like the interface shown in Figure 12.8. The **ergonomics** (the science of designing things to be used by humans in their chosen environment) must be effective or the device might not be efficiently controlled. The ease of use, the layout of the screen, the colours used, and how the information is displayed must all be thought about very carefully. It is usually true that users of the system have the best ideas regarding how things should be arranged. Therefore, a prototype could be set up to test the interface in a simulated environment, and the next example is typical of what might be done to achieve this.

Example

Devise two prototypes for an interface to monitor, control and activate an alarm for the level of drug administered to a patient in an intensive care unit. The display should be easy to use, and life-threatening decisions may be made on the basis of your analysis. Assume that the dosage of the drug is measured and adjusted in units between 0% and 100%, and must be controlled in steps of 0.1%. The nurse controls the system by instructing it to increase or decrease the drug by a set amount. Comment on the relative effectiveness of each user interface in your design.

Solution

To control the dosage in 1000 steps between 0 and 100 some digital input is essential, possibly controlled from a keyboard or possibly controlled with a mouse or a touch screen. Monitoring the level does not have to be done by the user, but we need an instant readout, and an alarm must be activated when urgent action needs to be taken. Possible prototypes are shown in Figure 12.8 and Figure 12.9.

It is very easy to create the screens shown here by using something like Visual Basic or Delphi.

However, the code behind the screen that gets the interface working will require considerable thought and effort!

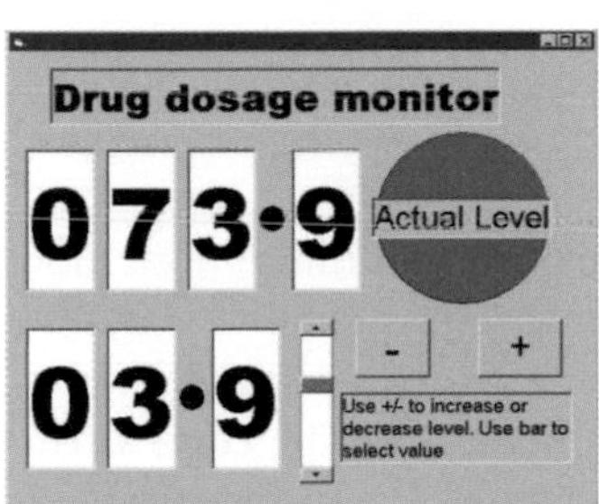

Figure 12.8 A possible prototype for the drug system

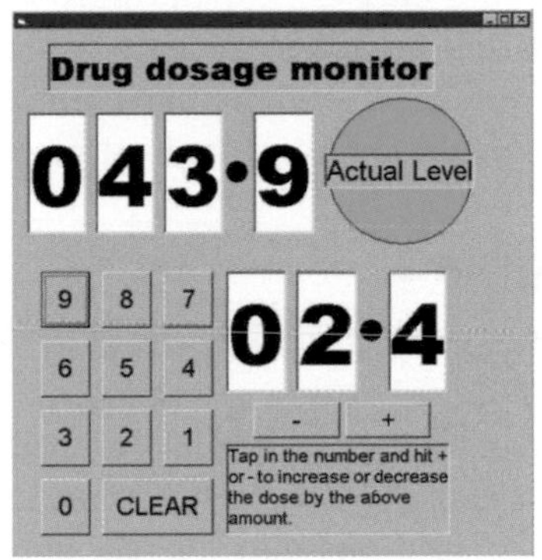

Figure 12.9 An alternative prototype for the drug system

Aspects of the interface can be designed using alternatives, but first concentrate on the entry of dosage. In Figure 12.8, a vertical scroll bar is used to increase or decrease the dose. A touch screen could be used to activate this. The alternative in Figure 12.9 enables the user to input a number directly via a keyboard or touch-sensitive screen. Colour is used to distinguish dangerous and safe doses. An audio alarm is needed to alert medical personnel not watching the screen. We can eliminate the – and + signs, assuming that if the dose is too high the number entered will reduce it, or if the dose is too low the number entered will increase it.

Creating dummy interfaces is quite easy but implementing the real systems could be difficult, because the programming needed might be complex.

The prototypes in the last example can be simulated quickly using an appropriate **visual programming language**. They may represent on-screen displays or act as simulations of a purpose-built hardware display that could be used. It is essential to get feedback from the users of the system and incorporate good suggestions. An appropriate GUI interface is of paramount importance, and you should not ignore even small changes recommended by the users. You should also remember not to promise too much to the users in case you cannot deliver.

Specialist user interfaces

Users might be physically disabled or visually impaired; therefore specialist interfaces

The ease of use of modern computers is a testament to good interface design. Indeed novice users expect it to be easy to use a computer no matter what they are trying to accomplish!

require a lot of thought. The Windows operating system caters for people who are partially sighted by providing very large textual and pictorial keyboards. Braille keyboards are available for people who are totally blind, and the range of input and output devices that can be operated by various parts of the body is extensive. Much psychology goes into the design of a user interface. An entire science has been developed with this in mind. Apple and Microsoft spend millions on perfecting the user interface. Windows, in its various incarnations, is an excellent example. We go from early examples of mice and windows developed at Xerox's Palo Alto research labs, via the commercial use of the GUI systems developed by Apple, to the latest 21st-century editions of Windows.

Object-oriented analysis techniques

From 2006 onwards, if you are using an object-oriented programming solution in your module 6 project, then you will need to make use of a variety of techniques like **class diagrams**, **aggregation diagrams** and **inheritance diagrams** to show the relationships between objects or classes.

New types of object-analysis diagrams are needed to convey concepts like inheritance, dependencies and classes. For the purposes of A2 computing, a subset of the **UML** or **unified modelling language** is used. It would take far too long to explain UML in its entirety here because there are many complex facilities. Many of the techniques used in UML are also highly technical and extremely subtle.

The diagrams shown on pages 170 to 173 will be relevant only if you use object-oriented programming methods in your project in module 6.

Class diagrams

Many students find it difficult to develop **object-oriented** programs and find it even more difficult to explain what they are doing. This makes it hard for teachers to understand the project and hard for the **moderators** to mark it. A **class diagram** shows a pictorial view of the class or classes and the relationships that exist between the classes. The **class attributes** and **class operations** may also be shown on the same diagram. A typical example is shown in Figure 12.10.

You may also see a '#' sign used in addition to the '+' and '–' signs used to denote public and private respectively. The '#' sign relates to protected visibility.

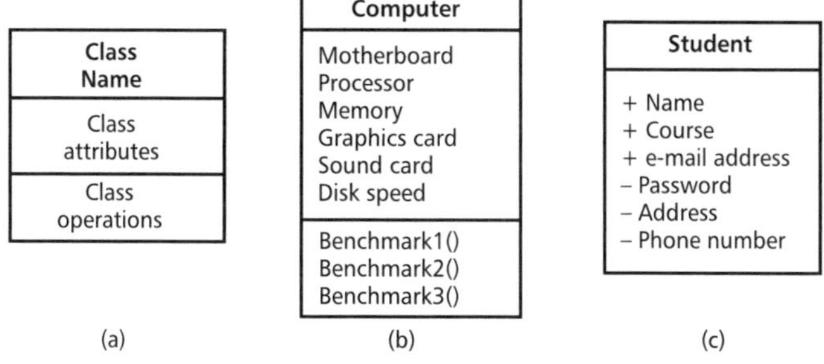

Figure 12.10 Some simple class diagrams

Figure 12.10(a) shows the general idea, and Figure 12.10(b) shows an example of a Computer class which consists of class attributes like Processor, Memory and Graphics card. The class operations are the actions carried out by the class, which in this case works out some benchmarks (numbers that can be used to compare different types of computers).

You will recall from your experience of object-oriented programming techniques (see chapter 3) that some attributes may be visible to other classes and some may not. This is controlled by the mechanisms of **encapsulation** and **inheritance** using keywords like 'public' and 'private'. On a class diagram the visibility of the attributes is indicated by using a '–' for private and '+' for public. Therefore, if we have a class diagram for a 'Student' class with public attributes Name, Course and e-mail address, and private attributes Password, Address and Phone Number, then this could be shown by using the class diagram in Figure 12.10(c). No class operations are shown on the last diagram; therefore only two compartments are needed. The private and public + and – notation may also be used on the class operations.

On complex class diagrams, where the relationships are shown between several classes, we sometimes omit the class attributes too, and hence the class name may be shown inside a single rectangular box. This prevents over-complicating the diagram. This notation (one, two or three boxes as required) is acceptable within the **UML** system.

Association diagrams

An **association** is where a relationship exists between two classes and therefore the classes must interact in some way.

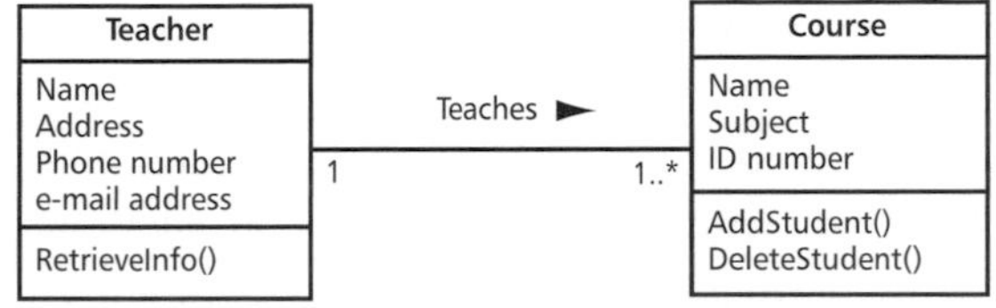

Figure 12.11 A simple association diagram

Associations may be shown on an **association diagram**, and a typical diagram showing the association between a teacher and one of the courses that he or she teaches is shown in Figure 12.11. A *labelled solid line* indicates the association in Figure 12.11, and an arrow may indicate the direction of the association as shown in this case. The notation '1' and '1..*' indicates that one teacher may teach one or more courses in this particular system being modelled. *See the margin entry for other examples of multiplicity.*

There are many UML methods of indicating different types of association, but these diagrams should be kept simple at A2 level.

There are other types of relationships like dependencies, generalisations, realisations and refinements. A **dependency** is a relationship between two elements (like classes or objects) in which one is dependent on the other. A change to the independent element will, for example, force a change in the dependent element. This type of relationship is shown on an association diagram by using a *dotted line with an arrow*, as shown in Figure 12.12, where part of a graphics-drawing system is being designed. A change to an independent class (in this case an Ellipse) causes a change in a dependent (in this case a class called Point).

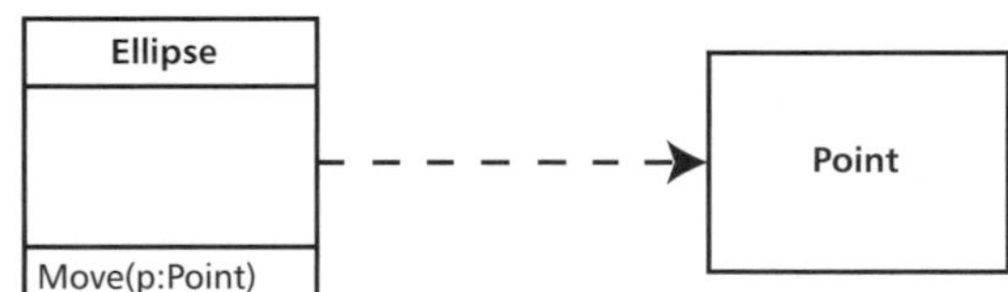

Figure 12.12 A simple diagram showing a dependency relationship

Inheritance diagrams

Inheritance is an example of a 'generalisation' relationship, and an **inheritance diagram** is ideal for this purpose. A simple inheritance diagram is shown in Figure 12.13 where the **generalisation** relationship is shown *as a solid line with a hollow arrowhead on the end.*

From Figure 12.13 you can see that the **subclasses**, consisting of the **classes** Teacher, Student, Administrative Staff and Support Staff may inherit properties like Telephone number, Address and e-mail address etc. from the superclass called People at School.

Generalisations are trying to establish what subclasses have characteristics in common with the superclass. An alternative approach to generalisation is to use **specialisation**, and

Multiplicity notation:

'1' means only 1;

'0,1' means 0 or 1;

'0..*' means zero, or more, or many;

'1..*' means one or more;

'3..4, 6' means the numbers 3 to 4 inclusive or the number 6;

**** may be used to mean 0 or more or many.***

You can also exclude numbers like 3 and 6 by using the following example;

0..2, 4..5, 7..*

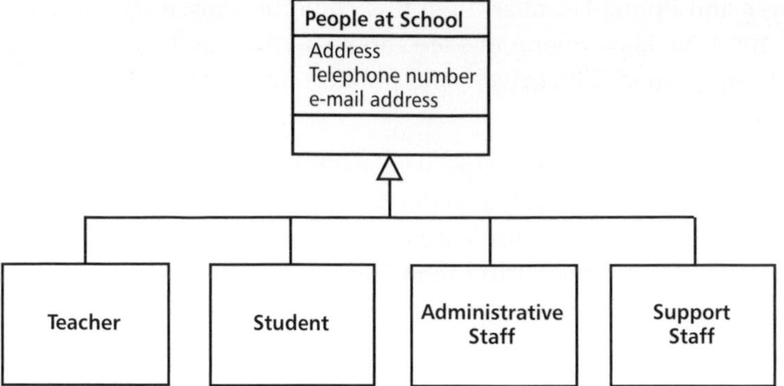

Figure 12.13 An inheritance diagram showing some generalisation relationships

this method splits up a class into subclasses by identification of the objects which have their own special characteristics. Both methods are suitable modelling techniques.

Realisation is a technique that is useful to specify the relationships between an interface and the classes that are used to build it. It is usual to model interfaces in this way, but this technique is more general than this and is used to specify what can be thought of as a 'contract' that exists between two classes in which one class guarantees to carry out the contract specified by the other class. (This also applies to other components and subsystems.) As an example, Figure 12.14 shows part of a project which analyses some code to check its syntax. The software to do this is called a parser. The language being analysed (parsed) is a simplified machine code designed to teach students how to program using machine code. The 'contract' or set of functionalities specified by the 'Simple Machine Code Parser' is actually carried out by the parser.

Figure 12.14 A simple diagram showing a realisation

There are lots of other types of diagrams used in the UML system, with typical examples being statechart diagrams, activity diagrams and deployment diagrams. These may be used in your projects if you think they are helpful, but this is not a requirement of the AQA subject specification.

Finally, a **refinement** is a helpful method to use in your projects where something is specified in more detail than was previously the case. A refinement is also shown by a *dotted arrow with a hollow arrowhead on the end* as shown in Figure 12.15. On a class diagram this could indicate one class at the **analysis** stage and the same class at the **design** stage. Figure 12.15 shows a class called Circle at a further stage of development. The initial box could have been used in a more complex diagram to show how the Circle class is related to other classes in the same project.

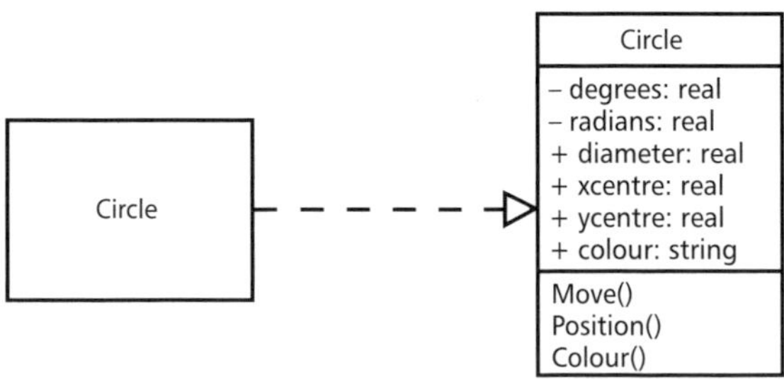

Figure 12.15 A simple diagram showing a refinement

Aggregation diagrams

Aggregation is where an object may be built up from other objects. For example, a theatre production would probably contain many actors. This fact can be shown by linking these two objects (the production and the actor) by using a diamond shape at the end where this aggregation takes place. An example is shown in Figure 12.16.

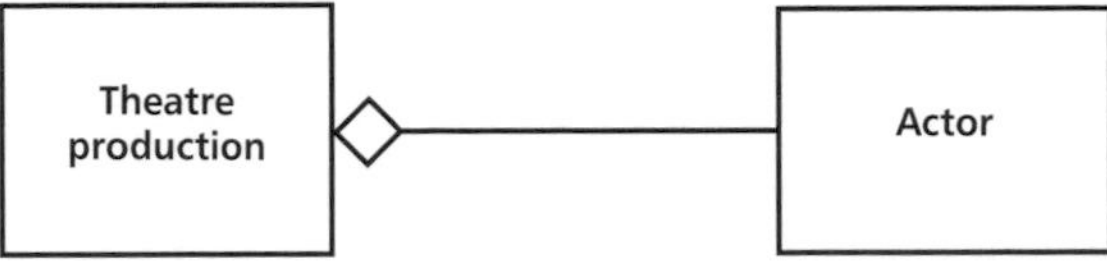

Figure 12.16 An aggregation diagram

Composite aggregation means that one class cannot exist without another, for example an object might be created or destroyed by the action of another object. Typically a transaction in a shop might be created while a customer is being served, but destroyed when a receipt has been printed (i.e. the transaction has been completed). We could arrange for a 'Receipt object' to create and destroy a 'Transaction object'. This type of aggregation is called composite aggregation and is shown on an aggregation diagram by using the filled-in diamond shape shown in Figure 12.17.

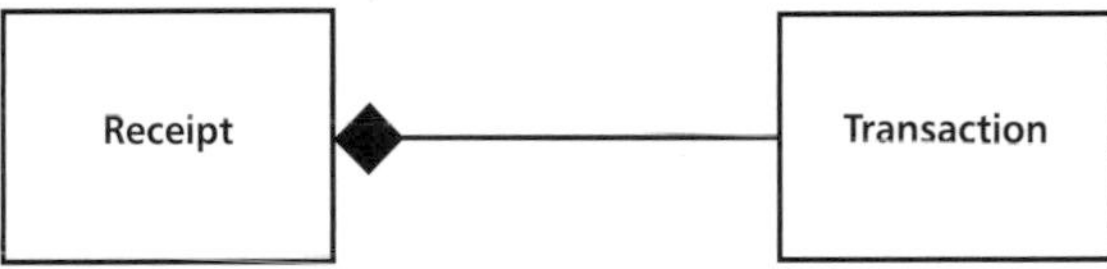

Figure 12.17 A composite aggregation diagram

Whole books are available on the UML diagrams and modelling techniques.

A simple example

A simple example of a combination of the above techniques can be seen in Figure 12.18. It shows part of a system which is designed to process orders of computer consumables.

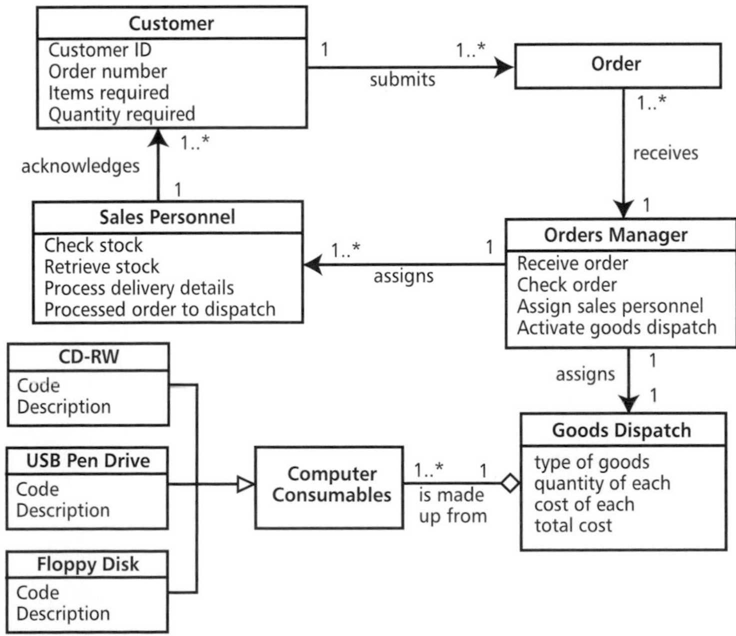

Figure 12.18 A typical class diagram using the UML syntax

The methods shown here are simply a taster and you would be well advised to do some extra research into the use of these diagrams if you are undertaking a complex object-oriented programming problem for your A2 project.

Self-test questions

1 A systems analyst uses a variety of methods for fact finding and reporting. Outline four common methods that may be used for this.
2 Why is observation of the old system usually a good idea before computerisation?
3 Under what circumstances is a data flow diagram (DFD) particularly useful? Draw a possible DFD showing what happens when a cash retail transaction takes place in a shop.
4 Draw a possible system flowchart for booking theatre tickets in a box office.
5 What is meant by prototyping and why is it used? Outline two advantages and two disadvantages of using a prototype.
6 Outline four factors that should be taken into account when designing a user interface.
7 How are the following concepts shown on an object-oriented (UML) diagram?
   (a) An association.
   (b) A dependency.
   (c) A generalisation.
8 Show, by means of a class diagram, the relations between the following classes.
   (a) A college and a department within the college.
   (b) A student who may take up to five examination subjects.

13 Test strategies for the development of a system

In this chapter you will learn about:

- Top-down and bottom-up methods applied to testing strategies
- Unit and integration testing
- Black box testing
- White box testing

Top-down design and testing

From your AS work you should already be familiar with the ideas of **top-down design**, which starts at the highest level of conception (the project) and then splits the project up into major parts, both for functionality and eventual coding. This method can also be applied to **testing** because it splits up the project into manageable sections, all of which may be tested individually. On very large systems, tens of people may work on individual modules each of which may be split up further for testing purposes. This helps allocate tasks to different personnel and enables teams of people to have responsibility for testing major project components. These methods are essential because testing a large and complex system for absolute correctness is an impossible task.

When undertaking your own A2 projects, make sure that you use a variety of the methods shown in this chapter.

You may lose many marks in the 'system testing' section if you fail to do this.

The bottom-up approach

The **bottom-up approach** is useful for developing and testing essential modules which can then be joined together to form larger parts of the system. This is ideal for **object-oriented programming** methods because objects may be defined, tested and evaluated before being joined on to other parts of the system to build up the larger project. Through the strict methods of control like **inheritance**, covered in chapter 3, the tested modules will rarely need retesting because other modules may inherit the properties required without altering the original module. Development time in this environment is thus minimised compared with developing similar modules in a conventional procedurally based language. In a *non* object-oriented programming environment, any modification to any of the sub modules will require these sub modules to be tested again.

The bottom-up and top-down approaches are variations on the same theme, and both involve much planning if the final systems are to operate smoothly.

Unit and integration testing

Most projects, whether designed by the top-down or bottom-up approach, modularise the system into easily identifiable units. **Unit testing** is simply the exhaustive testing of each of these unit modules *before* they are integrated into the larger system. The actual unit testing can be carried out by a variety of methods, including **black box testing** and **white box testing** methods (see below).

If unit testing is used, we join individual units together one by one to form the entire system. If an error is detected in the system after a new unit has been added, then the new unit is probably at fault. There is also the possibility of unforeseen interaction between the rest of the system and the new unit. Either way, it is much easier to identify the new fault than would have been the case with many new units being integrated simultaneously. It is often the case that bugs in some of the original system units may not come to light until other units have been integrated with them. A good testing strategy would therefore be to simulate the addition of the units that will interact with the ones that you are designing when developing your unit testing strategy. In this way, when the real units are added there should be few, if any, problems that have not already been encountered.

Students typically dislike testing. They are usually reluctant to develop suitable testing strategies, and this often leads to problems when designing A2 projects.

When units are joined together in the ways described above, the process is referred to as **integration testing**, i.e. making sure that all the units work when being *integrated* into the entire system. Often more effort goes into unit and integration testing than in the design of the real system. As mentioned above, absolute correctness is a utopian goal unless the system is relatively simple. On a large and complex operating system, for example, it would take an inordinate length of time to exhaustively test all the paths through the system or its interaction with all possible things.

A compromise is to rigorously test the system using black box and white box testing methods, and these are covered below.

It is far easier to develop a test plan when you are designing the system because effectively testing the final system is virtually impossible, and formally testing modules which you have been using for a long time seems to be a pointless task.

You can save yourself a lot of hassle by following the rules shown here.

Black box testing

Black box testing means that you do not require any knowledge of how a particular programming module has been coded. It is therefore quite easy to develop a black box testing method because you are looking at the system as though the coding is hiding inside a black box – hence the name.

As an example, we will test some code which the majority of readers may not have come across. A method, called the bisection method, is used in mathematics to help work out the square root of a number. From our point of view we put a number into a black box, and out pops the square root of the number, as shown in Figure 13.1. If we input 4, we should get the answer 2, because 2 is one of the square roots of 4. Input 9 and we should get 3 out, or input 16 and we should get 4 out etc. Note that only positive numbers have been input because there is no real number that, when multiplied by itself (the idea of a square root), would produce a negative number.

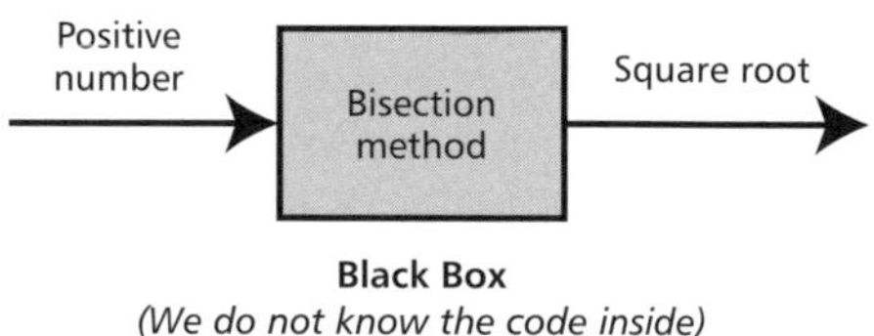

Figure 13.1 The idea of a black box

From Figure 13.1 we see that all inputs (only one in this case) to the system are shown on the left, and the output from the system is shown on the right. The black box representation for this particular system is therefore extremely simple. There is just one input (let us call the positive number N), and one output (we will call it x3 for reasons you will understand a little later in this chapter).

How to proceed with developing a black box test

We already know that we cannot test this routine for all possible input values because it would take too long. Therefore, we have to choose a representative set of input values. If we choose wisely, we can be reasonably confident that other values will work too. We should, for example, consider the *maximum* and *minimum* values that it is possible to present to the system. The minimum is obviously 0 (the lowest possible positive number), but the maximum depends on the compiler being used for the language in which the program is being written. Therefore, the range of the inputs and outputs for this particular algorithm will be:

$0 <= N <=$ Maximum floating point number
0 <= x3 <= Maximum floating point number

Anything outside this range will obviously be beyond the specification of the program. You should take special note of this. If, for example, the maximum floating point number for a particular compiler happens to be 2×10^{60}, then it is not much point trying to find the root of 3×10^{60} in your program. It will not work because you have gone beyond the physical limitations of the system you are using. This is one of the points of testing, and is one reason why the specification of the system ought to be written down very precisely. This is so that the designers and users of the system know the limitations. Bear this in mind when you are attempting to test algorithms in your own projects. You will lose marks if you assume that the program will work under all conditions.

Finally, in your project, it is necessary to build up a table showing all the values which you have used for the black box testing, and the reason why you have chosen the numbers. For our simple system mentioned above, a suitable starting table might be as follows.

Table 13.1 Values used for black box testing

Condition number	Value	Comments
1	0	Smallest possible value of input N
2	Maximum float point	Largest possible value of N determined by the system compiler

When writing up your A2 project you will not have sufficient space to include every single test, and a variety of different tests can be shown to prove that you have undertaken the necessary methods.

The above test cases assume that we will put no negative numbers into the system. To make sure that this is so, a simple routine could be added to the beginning of the code which works out the roots. Next we need to see if there are important numbers between these limits that might cause problems. For example, the nature of square roots means that the root of 1 is just 1, roots of larger numbers get bigger, and roots of smaller numbers (less than one) get much smaller. Therefore, it might be prudent to test for inputs of '1', '<1' and '>1'. Our modified table is shown as follows.

The tabular arrangement shown here is ideal for demonstrating that you have tested your project.

Table 13.2 Modified values for black box testing

Condition number	Value	Comments
1	0	Smallest possible value of input N
2	Maximum float point	Largest possible value of N determined by the system's compiler
3	1	Test to see if the answer is 1 (or as near to it as is described by the accuracy required)
4	0.001	Number less than 1 to test for smaller roots
5	1000	Number greater than 1 to test for larger roots
6	<0	This should generate an error message

As you can see, we have tested for the extremes and have tested important stages inbetween too. The next important part is to document the test procedure. This can be done by constructing another table, similar to Table 13.2, but instead of the comments it will show the actual results of the test produced by the computer during run time. The results of this table would depend on the language you use, the computer on which you run the system, and the compiler being used for the language. Therefore the table is not shown here, but you are advised to include this in your projects if you wish to get maximum marks on testing procedures.

In practice the black box would probably have more than one input, and therefore the number of tests would also have to include salient points for the extra variables in each case. Nevertheless, this is the essence of black box testing. If there is more than one output then we can have a separate black box for each. Therefore, to carry out a black box test on a software module, we do the following:

You may use the bullet points shown here to check your testing methods.

- Make sure that the specification for the module is well written.
- Make sure that the limitations of the system are well understood.
- Determine the inputs and outputs for the software module.
- Draw one or more black boxes labelling the inputs and output.
- Determine salient values for any variables such as maximum and minimum.
- Draw up a table showing the conditions under which the tests have been carried out.
- Provide documentary evidence that the tests have actually been carried out.
- If any mistakes are found, and the code is altered, you must start all the tests again!

Remember that the above black box testing *will not guarantee that the system or module will work*. However, it is reasonable to assume that it does work, and it is the best that you can do using black box testing methods alone.

White box testing

White box testing is usually accomplished by specialist software which is available to professional software designers.

You are advised not to use white box testing methods in your A2 projects as it would take far too long to undertake these methods manually.

We now look at the code for the square-root algorithm already used for **black box testing** above. **White box testing** *requires that we have knowledge of the internal code.* (This is the actual implementation of the program which the black box testing method ignored.) The code for the bisection method of finding the square root of a number is as follows, and you should now be able to see why x3 is used as an output; x1 and x2 have already been used for two previous variables.

```
INPUT N
flag = FALSE
x1 = 1 : x2 = N
x3 = (x1+x2)/2
IF x3*x3 = N THEN flag = TRUE
  WHILE flag <> TRUE
    x3=(x1+x2)/2
    fx1=x1*x1-N:fx2=x2*x2-N:fx3=x3*x3-N
    IF((fx1>0) AND (fx3>0)) OR ((fx1<0) AND (fx3<0))THEN
      IF ((fx2>0) AND (fx3>0)) OR ((fx2<0) AND (fx3<0))THEN
        flag = TRUE
      ELSE
          x1=x3
      ENDIF
    ELSE
      x2=x3
    ENDIF
    PRINT "Guess so far is";x3
    IF ABS(x3*x3-N) < 0.001 THEN flag = TRUE
 ENDWHILE
PRINT "Answer is ";x3
```

White box testing tries to ensure that *all possible paths through an algorithm are tested*. It does this by using the structure of the source code to construct a **flowgraph** which generates a visual indication of the paths that could be taken through the code.

We therefore look at the production of a flowgraph first, as this will be required to carry out the white box testing of the system. The simplest possible flowgraph, applicable to any system, is to have just one entry point and one exit point as shown in Figure 13.2.

Figure 13.2 The simplest possible flowgraph

As you can see from this diagram we have two nodes (the circles). One for the entry point X and one for the exit point Y. Each node is connected by an arc, and the arrow shows the direction of flow from X to Y, hence the terminology flowgraph. The arc represents the flow of the program between the entry point X and the exit point Y, and thus will represent code which could consist of other subprograms and procedures. However, do not do too much manually – special software will make these operations less of a chore, if you are lucky enough to possess it.

To generate a suitable flowgraph for our square-root program we must analyse the code. Split the code up into identifiable parts, each with a specific function but each part having only one entry point and one exit point. Breaking up the code using these criteria, we input a number (N) and then set up a flag and a couple of other variables. Next we have a condition which tests to see if the answer is correct. (This would only occur if N happened to be 1, hence the importance of putting N = 1 as a condition when we undertook the black box testing above.) Next we have a large WHILE loop. (Do not worry about what is inside this loop yet.) Finally, we print out the answers. The following code has been split up to show these entry and exit points more clearly.

The code shown here has been split up into very simple linear sequences.

This is easy to do, and we do not care how complex the code is between these linear entry and exit points.

Note that the routine to deal with numbers <0 has not been included here.

```
                    ENTRY POINT A

INPUT N                                ARC – FLOW FROM A TO B
flag = FALSE
x1 = 1 : x2 = N
x3 = (x1+x2)/2

                          B

IF x3*x3 = N THEN flag = TRUE          ARC – FLOW FROM B TO C

                          C

  WHILE flag <> TRUE                   ARC – FLOW FROM C TO D
    x3=(x1+x2)/2
    fx1=x1*x1-N:fx2=x2*x2-N:fx3=x3*x3-N
    IF((fx1>0) AND (fx3>0)) OR ((fx1<0) AND (fx3<0))THEN
      IF ((fx2>0) AND (fx3>0)) OR ((fx2<0) AND(fx3<0))THEN
        flag = TRUE
      ELSE
        x1=x3
      ENDIF
    ELSE
        x2=x3
    ENDIF
```

```
      PRINT "Guess so far is";x3
      IF ABS(x3*x3-N) < 0.001 THEN flag = TRUE
    ENDWHILE
```

D

```
PRINT "Answer is ";x3                    ARC – FLOW FROM D TO E
```

EXIT POINT E

For the above code, the flowgraph, based on the above analysis, is shown in Figure 13.3.

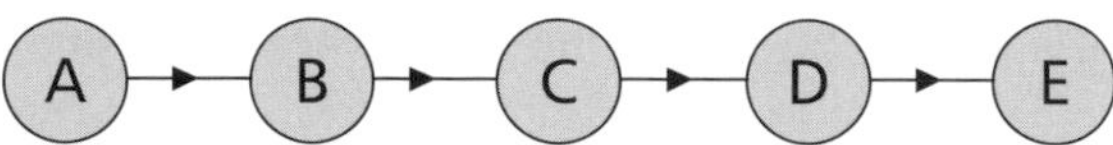

Figure 13.3 A flowgraph based on the above code

The next stage in the production of the flowgraph is to determine if any of the arcs need further analysis. For example, the arc between A and B represents that part of the program which inputs data and sets up some variables. It represents a simple linear sequence of just four instructions – the flow of control through here will move on from one statement to the next, and this arc therefore needs no further flow analysis. For the same reason the arc between points D and E needs no further analysis. However, the arc between points C and D will obviously need further analysis, and the arc between B and C will need a little extra analysis too.

Note how easy it is to build up the flowgraphs using the techniques outlined here.

It is also very enlightening to see all possible routes through the code; this would not be obvious without some sort of structured analysis.

White box testing therefore ensures that all possible parts of the code will be executed, and unusual conditions will be accounted for.

To help understand the next stage in constructing the flowgraph, let us consider the arc between B and C, i.e. arc that represents the single statement:

```
IF x3*x3 = N THEN flag = TRUE
```

There are two possibilities here. Either the condition (x3*x3 = N) is true, in which case the flag is set equal to 'TRUE' and we exit, or it is not, in which case nothing happens and we exit from this statement. Therefore, between the entry and exit points (B and C) for this particular code there are two possible paths. The single arc between B and C shown in Figure 13.3 now needs to be replaced with two arcs, representing the two possible routes. The new situation, showing the next stage of the flowgraph, is shown in Figure 13.4

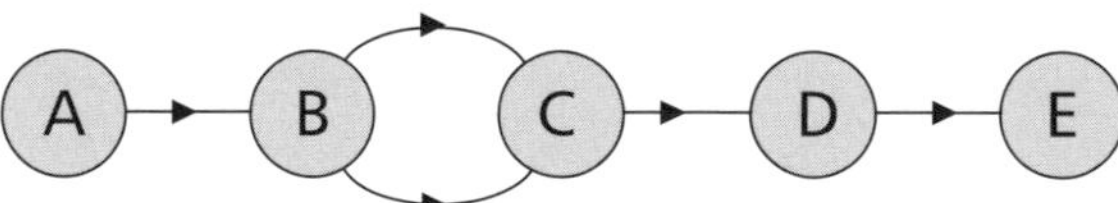

Figure 13.4 The new flowgraph showing additional paths between nodes B and C

If we had multi-line if-then statements, more arcs could be added. For example, for an if-then-else-end-if statement, three arcs would be needed, as we will see in just a moment. For a **case statement**, the number of arcs can also be increased to match – it is a very simple idea.

We now need to investigate the complex arc going from C to D in Figure 13.4. In this particular case, as can be seen from inspection of the code, a 'while loop' has been chosen, but this technique could easily apply to other loop structures with very little modification. Consider the general flowgraph form for a loop shown in Figure 13.5.

As can be seen from Figure 13.5, when implementing a loop structure there are two possible paths. Either it goes around the loop or it does not, based on some test condition on entry to the loop.

For our code, while the flag is set 'true' we go round the loop, or, if the flag is set 'false', we do not go round the loop. Remember that if N = 1, then we do not go round the loop at all, but follow the arc straight from C to D, executing no code. The modified flowgraph showing the large 'while loop' is shown in Figure 13.6.

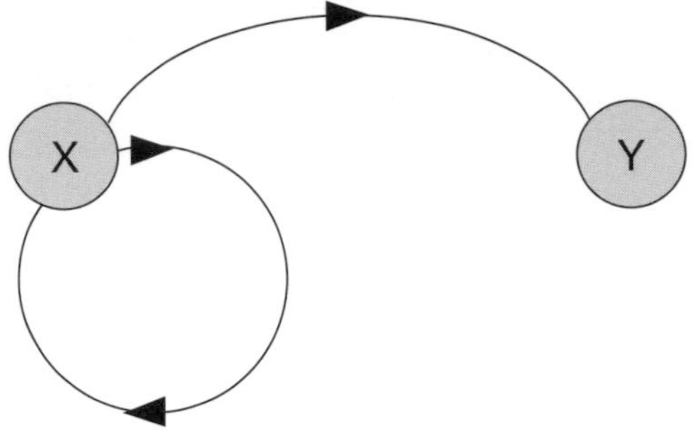

Figure 13.5 A flowgraph used for a loop structure

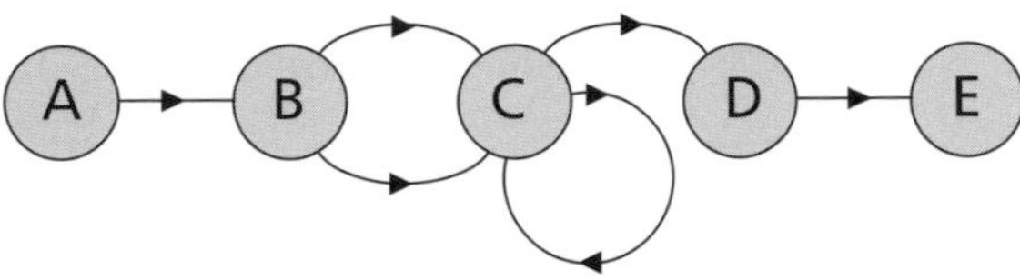

Figure 13.6 A new flowgraph including the while loop from node C to node D

The next stage is to do further analysis within the while loop in this diagram. We can see from an analysis of the code that there are several sections, containing either a simple linear sequence of instructions, or some if-then-else statements, for which we already know the flowgraph structure. Therefore, you already know how to represent this loop with a suitable flowgraph. See if you can get an idea of the new structure before looking at the more detailed analysis of the while loop code that follows.

The analysis is as follows. The while loop is split up, using the techniques demonstrated above, into the following subsections. Remember that *each part can have only one exit and one entry point.*

C

```
WHILE flag <> TRUE
```

```
    x3=(x1+x2)/2                              ARC - FLOW FROM C to F
    fx1=x1*x1-N:fx2=x2*x2-N:fx3=x3*x3-N
```

F

```
                                              ARC - FLOW FROM F to G
    IF((fx1>0) AND (fx3>0)) OR ((fx1<0) AND (fx3<0))THEN
      IF ((fx2>0) AND (fx3>0)) OR ((fx2<0) AND (fx3<0))THEN
 flag = TRUE
      ELSE
          x1=x3
      ENDIF
    ELSE
      x2=x3
    ENDIF
```

G

```
PRINT "Guess so far is";x3            ARC - FLOW FROM G to H
```

H

```
IF ABS(x3*x3-N) < 0.001 THEN flag = TRUE
                                      ARC - FLOW FROM H to D
```

```
ENDWHILE
```

C

The first thing to note is that we have C at the bottom and not D. This might seem unusual at first sight, but remember that we are considering that loop which is going round and round. In other words, the above structure in the flowgraph will replace the 'big round loop' in Figure 13.6 which goes from C to C. We already have the other arc between C and D, which represents the get-out condition, when the flag has been set to 'true'.

We have thus split the while loop into four parts, two of which (the arc from C to F and the arc from G to H) will need no further analysis. Replacing the loop in Figure 13.6 with our four-part split, we end up with the flowgraph shown in Figure 13.7.

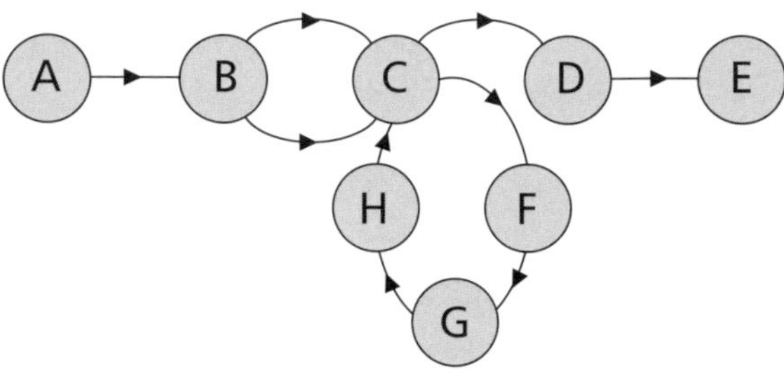

Figure 13.7 A flowgraph based on replacing the loop with four arcs

From an analysis of the 'while-end-while' structure, we can see that arc C to F is only a simple linear sequence of instructions and needs no further analysis. Arc G to H is also a simple linear sequence of instructions. Arc H to C is a simple if-then statement; therefore this arc can be replaced by two other arcs because of the two possibilities being true or false. Arc F to G consists of a more complex if-then else statement, in which one of the loops is nested. Therefore, for the moment, we will draw this as two normal loops, one of which will need further analysis. The second loop will be replaced by the necessary structure for the second if-then-else statement in the next version of the diagram shown in Figure 13.8. Let us not do too many stages at once!

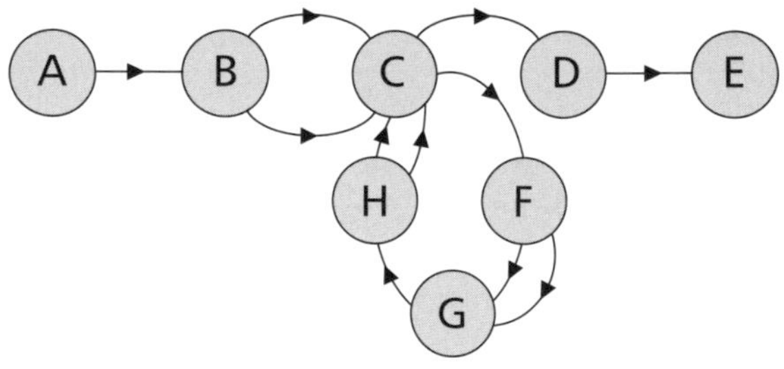

Figure 13.8 A flowgraph based on the analysis so far

Now consider the final part of the code. At the moment we are representing the if-then-else structure between nodes F and G with just two arcs. However, one of these arcs contains a nested loop structure, as shown in the following breakdown of the code.

F

```
IF((fx1>0) AND (fx3>0)) OR ((fx1<0) AND (fx3<0))THEN
                                      ARC - FLOW FROM G to H
```

I

```
IF ((fx2>0) AND (fx3>0)) OR ((fx2<0) AND (fx3<0))THEN
  flag = TRUE
ELSE
    x1=x3
ENDIF
```

J

```
ELSE
  x2=x3
ENDIF
```

G

Therefore, this nested-loop structure needs to be replaced by two nodes called I and J, linked by two arcs, as shown above. Finally, one of the arcs between F and G in Figure 13.8 is replaced by this combination, and our final flowgraph is shown in Figure 13.9.

The actual white box tests

The whole point of white box testing is to ensure that all feasible paths through a software module are executed when the system is being tested. To carry this out in practice we can now make use of the flowgraph we have created in Figure 13.9.

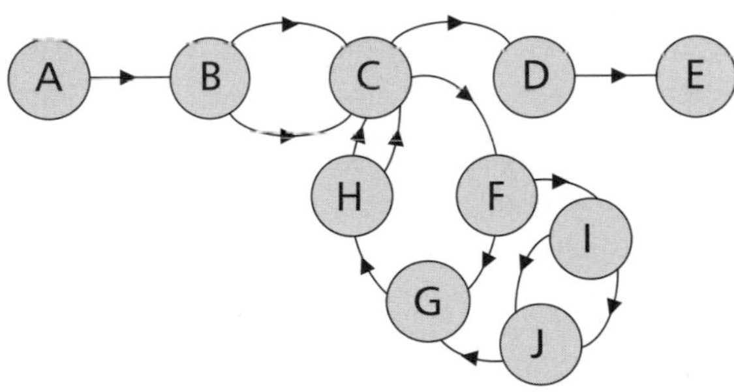

Figure 13.9 The complete flowgraph based on the above analysis

Interestingly enough, the number of different paths that can be taken through a flowgraph can be obtained by counting up how many separate regions there are. (This is not strictly true, but any undergraduate mathematicians who are good at graph theory will realise that it is near enough.) This is identical in principle to colouring in separate regions on a map in a geography lesson. The number of regions for the bisection method flowgraph is shown in Figure 13.10. Therefore, regarding our code, there are *six distinct paths* that can be taken. To indicate the difference between the first two obvious paths, the following subscript notation is used in which the subscript corresponds to the labelling of the arcs in Figure 13.10.

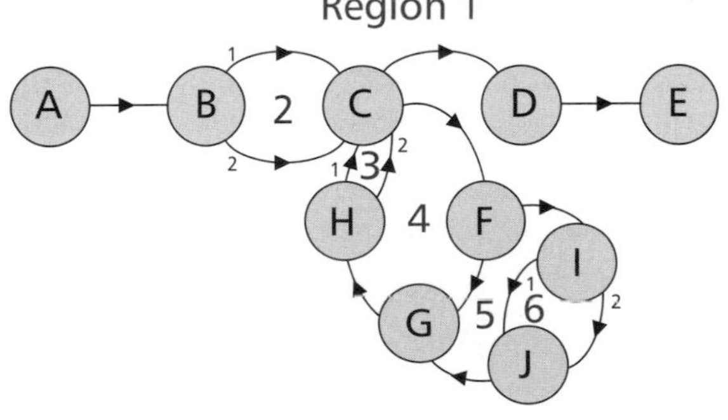

Figure 13.10 A flowgraph based on the final analysis for Figure 13.10

Path 1 $A\text{-}B_1\text{-}C\text{-}D\text{-}E$ Path 2 $A\text{-}B_2\text{-}C\text{-}D\text{-}E$

Therefore, path 1 takes the upper arc from B to C, and path 2 takes the lower arc from B to C. This notation has also been used between the nodes H and C and nodes I and J.

Looking at the flowchart you will probably think that there are many more than just six paths through the program! For example, we could list all the following paths:

Path 1	A-B_1-C-D-E	Path 2	A-B_2-C-D-E
Path 3	A-B_1-C-F-G-H_1	Path 4	A-B_1-C-F-G-H_2
Path 5	A-B_2-C-F-G-H_1	Path 6	A-B_2-C-F-G-H_2
Path 7	A-B_1-C-F-I_1-J-G-H_1	Path 8	A-B_1-C-F-I_1-J-G-H_2
Path 9	A-B_2-C-F-I_1-J-G-H_1	Path 10	A-B_2-C-F-I_1-J-G-H_2
Path 11	A-B_1-C-F-I_2-J-G-H_1	Path 12	A-B_1-C-F-I_2-J-G-H_2

However, consider for a moment what happens when we have tried the first two paths A-B_1-C and A-B_2-C. It is not necessary to try these two combinations again, with all subsequent passes through the program. This would be a waste of time as this path has *already been tested under all possible circumstances*. Therefore, on subsequent passes, we can use A-B_X-C to help identify this; as they have already been completed once for the first two paths, they need not be considered again – it does not matter which of these two paths are taken.

Proceeding with this argument, we can now alter the possible paths to the following:

Path 1	A-B_1-C-D-E	Path 2	A-B_2-C-D-E
Path 3	A-B_x-C-F-G-H_1	Path 4	A-B_x-C-F-G-H_2
Path 5	A-B_x-C-F-G-H_1	Path 6	A-B_x-C-F-G-H_2
Path 7	A-B_x-C-F-I_1-J-G-H_1	Path 8	A-B_x-C-F-I_1-J-G-H_2
Path 9	A-B_x-C-F-I_1-J-G-H_1	Path 10	A-B_x-C-F-I_1-J-G-H_2
Path 11	A-B_x-C-F-I_2-J-G-H_1	Path 12	A-B_x-C-F-I_2-J-G-H_2

We can see straight away that paths 3 and 5, for example, are identical for the purposes of testing the program. Therefore we can eliminate path 5. We can also eliminate path 6, because this would be identical to path 4. Also, path 9 can be eliminated (it is the same as path 7) and path 10 can be eliminated because it is the same as path 8.

Path 1	A-B_1-C-D-E	Path 2	A-B_2-C-D-E
Path 3	A-B_x-C-F-G-H_1	Path 4	A-B_x-C-F-G-H_2
Path 7	A-B_x-C-F-I_1-J-G-H_1	Path 8	A-B_x-C-F-I_1-J-G-H_2
Path 11	A-B_x-C-F-I_2-J-G-H_1	Path 12	A-B_x-C-F-I_2-J-G-H_2

Using the same argument again, once we have tried the paths G-H_1 and G-H_2, we can replace this path with G-H_X in subsequent analysis. Therefore, the paths now become:

Path 1	A-B_1-C-D-E	Path 2	A-B_2-C-D-E
Path 3	A-B_x-C-F-G-H_1	Path 4	A-B_x-C-F-G-H_2
Path 7	A-B_x-C-F-I_1-J-G-H_x	Path 8	A-B_x-C-F-I_1-J-G-H_x
Path 11	A-B_x-C-F-I_2-J-G-H_x	Path 12	A-B_x-C-F-I_2-J-G-H_x

This means that we can eliminate path 8 because it is the same as path 7, and path 12 because it is the same as path 11. The list of paths to check now becomes:

Path 1	A-B_1-C-D-E	Path 2	A-B_2-C-D-E
Path 3	A-B_x-C-F-G-H_1	Path 4	A-B_x-C-F-G-H_2
Path 7	A-B_x-C-F-I_1-J-G-H_x	Path 11	A-B_x-C-F-I_2-J-G-H_x

This gives us the *six paths*, which were predicted by counting the flowgraph regions.

The next stage in the white box testing process is to go through all the above paths using black box testing methods! That is, the programmer should make sure that suitable variables are chosen, and listed in the tables, which will ensure that each of the above paths is executed. However, not all the paths may be feasible due to constraints on the program.

For example, some conditions may never happen in practice. Nevertheless, white box techniques represent a big step forward in ensuring that your code is tested as much as possible.

Applying these methods to your A2 computing projects

In your own A2 project work you should use a liberal sprinkling of the methodologies used in the systems development and testing sections. You need to look at the AQA module 6 mark scheme in general and see how the marks are allocated. If, for example, quite a few marks are assigned to methods of gathering information (they probably will be), then make sure you have used standard methodology like interviews, questionnaires, and shown samples of current data capture forms if they are available. Remember that you could design your own data capture forms specific to your project. The whole point of the methods outlined in the systems development and testing sections is to make you aware of current methods in industry and allow you to apply similar methods to your project work.

Although you are expected to make use of standard methods, you should use your common sense to save you a lot of work. Remember that marks are awarded for methods you have used. You do not usually get marks for repeatedly using the same method. Therefore, make sure you have used an appropriate variety of methods.

Take **white box testing** as an example. You would not really be expected to apply these methods in your project as they are tedious to undertake manually. In industry, more people are usually involved in testing a project than are involved with the original design. You have not got the time or the resources to test your code in this particular way. However, **black box testing** is relatively easy to do, and you should incorporate this at frequent intervals throughout your project testing section.

A large amount of common sense is needed to get maximum marks in your A2 project.

You should pay serious attention to the advice given on this page; it may save you a lot of time and effort when you write up your project.

Self-test questions

1 (a) What is meant by black box testing? (b) What is meant by white box testing?

2 Test data forms an important part of any project design strategy. Outline some suitable test data for:
   (a) Dates in the form 21/12/2005
   (b) Numerical data representing money
   (c) Numerical data representing a person's age.

3 A student has written a program to implement a LIFO or stack data structure in which numeric data between 1 and 100 inclusive may be placed on or removed from the stack. If the stack may hold a maximum of 10 data items, outline a sensible test strategy.

4 A student has written some code for a bubble sort. Outline the methods that need to be put in place for white box testing of this bubble sort project. You do not have to do the white box testing in your explanation.

14 System implementation

In this chapter you will learn about:

- Converting an old system into a new one
- Parallel, direct, pilot and phased implementation strategies
- System testing, acceptance testing, alpha and beta testing
- The need for training
- The installation manual, user manual, operations manual and training manual
- Evaluation
- System maintenance

Converting an old system to a new one

This is the final chapter on system implementation and testing.

It deals mainly with methods, many of which are not applicable to your A2 project.

These methods are mainly used in commercial institutions, and you need to know about them in order to answer questions in the module 5 theory paper.

Once a computer system has been developed and tested (see chapter 13), effort needs to be put into the **implementation phase**. This is a critical phase as customers start to make use of the system in a real-life situation. Techniques, borne out of experience, have been developed over the years, and some of these are outlined in this chapter.

The methods used will depend on whether a new computer system is brand new or an upgrade of an existing system. If it is brand new then life is easier. After testing, a **pilot scheme** could be run before going live. However, if the computerised system is replacing an old one, then problems are quite likely to occur during the changeover.

Conversion

Conversion is moving from the old system to the new. It is inadvisable to throw out the old system on a Friday afternoon and start using a new system on Monday morning. It would be a brave and rather foolish analyst who implemented this particular strategy in a mission-critical system!

Each case is considered on its merits, and the method of implementing a control system in a factory would be different from implementing a stock control and ordering system. However, we can identify some effective strategies which are commonly used on a huge variety of systems, and these are covered below.

Parallel implementation

Running a new system in parallel with the old system is a good option if possible, and this is known a **parallel implementation**. Running new systems in parallel with the old system is the safest method when converting conventional business systems that have been in operation for some time. There are a number of difficulties, including the fact that you have to operate two systems at the same time. This is frustrating for the staff, but does have the advantage that the old system kicks in if the new system fails. A business could be destroyed if it becomes totally reliant on a new system that has not been extensively tested under live conditions and subsequently fails. Vital information such as supplier and customer data may be lost.

During the parallel running phase, any discrepancies between the two systems must be analysed to see if it is the new system or the old system that is at fault. After a period of time, dictated by the volatility of the new system, the old system will be taken off line.

Phased implementation

It might be easier if a new system is implemented in phases. This is called **phased implementation**. If you are computerising a school, for example, reporting, examination entries, admissions and timetable etc. could all be computerised by phasing them in at different intervals. Each phase of the system could be checked and made good before proceeding to the next. For some projects this may not be an option as all parts of the system might have to be operational for it to be of any use.

The personnel implementing a new computer system have an awesome responsibility.

It is up to the systems analyst to determine the best methods, and much money is at stake if the system fails to operate in the intended way.

A number of high-profile systems have failed in the past, including the London Stock Exchange, air traffic control, the .com database for the Internet and the London ambulance service.

Direct implementation

This option means going live all at once. Although risky, extensive **testing** and **prototyping** ensures that the system has few operational glitches. If the system fails then it could be catastrophic, and patches to get the new system up and running would have to be implemented under conditions of extreme stress, with possible damaging consequences to the business relying on the new system.

Pilot schemes

Any important system would not go live without practice runs, and this is where pilot schemes are often used. It is really a trial run of the new system, and once the pilot scheme has proved successful, it can go live by using **direct implementation**. Pilot schemes are often used in very large companies where piloting can be carried out in one division while others continue with the older system. If the pilot proves successful then all divisions of the company may transfer to the new scheme.

System implementation in practice

Implementing a real system is often a combination of the above methods. It depends on the system being computerised, the budget available, and the time over which the system is implemented.

You should never lose sight of the loss of confidence that can result from a system failure. A high-profile example was the London Stock Exchange computer system which failed on 5 April 2000. This meant that traders could not operate effectively, and there was little or no trade until 3.45 p.m. This was embarrassing as it was the last day of the tax year, when investors traditionally tie up all of their investment portfolios. Although very rare indeed, the crash of such a high-profile system, and one in which billions of pounds were at stake, goes to show how much testing is needed on mission-critical systems.

Example

Whizbang.com is to launch a new web site. Whizbang products are stored on a database and clients will be able to access stock levels and order items over the Internet. Items are paid for by credit card. Suggest why direct implementation is the most likely method in this case. What testing and implementation strategies are therefore most appropriate?

Solution

When 'going live' for the first time, the site (i.e. stock control and ordering etc.) must be fully operational. It must work immediately it is launched as real customers will need to use all of the facilities straight away. The project can be modularised. The order system, credit card verification, database and stock-control systems can all be tested as units, and then integrated into the whole. A pilot system could be used for the prototype site, probably via an intranet proxy server, and mock customers can place fictitious orders while the whole system is tested.

Finally, the web site can go live, but with password protection. This means that mock customers, and probably some selected real customers too, can access the real web site on line to check that it all works as planned. With the password-protected part of the site removed, the site is then ready to be launched.

Different phases of implementation

Most users are aware of **beta releases** (pre-release versions) of major software packages on the Internet. Customers can download copies of software like Windows 2003 etc., which are known not to be bug free at that time. The idea is to get hundreds of thousands of people to test the software in a real environment. This pre-release phase of testing is known as **beta testing**. However, users should be aware that the software could prove unreliable. Many beta releases are the norm, until the final version is ready for release. The users can get their hands on the latest versions of software and it is hoped they will report bugs. The bugs are then fixed and another version of the pre-release software is put on the Internet or sent to selected customers.

Before beta testing is carried out there is initial testing of software which is known as **alpha testing**, and often this involves customers visiting the software vendor's site. This takes place after **unit** and **integration testing** (see chapter 13) have been completed. It is usual to involve one or two customers at the alpha testing stage.

Similar ideas are used when in-house software is being developed. After the software has been designed and alpha testing has taken place, in-house beta testing is used to check the system with 'real' data, making use of the personnel who will eventually use the system.

Acceptance testing

After going through all phases of testing it is up to the IT managers in the user's company to officially accept the system. They will do this only when they are completely happy that the system is reliable, is functioning to specification, and will provide an efficient service if used by their clients. There will usually be an official hand-over date when the programmers and analysts will no longer be involved in the day-to-day operation of the system. This is usually a short time after the system has gone live for the first time, but this is not the end of the story – **maintenance** of the system (see below) will then take on a high priority.

Staff training

Training needs to be undertaken by those who will use the new system. From the clerk who enters the data at the terminals, to the IT personnel who will manage the system, all need to be experts in using the new system. Training must take place before the system goes live as personnel involved in day-to-day operations will then be responsible for running the system. Another factor in implementation is to ensure that the new system interfaces correctly with other connected systems. A training schedule should be set up during the development and beta testing phases.

Example

You are to manage staff training for implementation and maintenance of a new computerised system in a large store. Over 100 users, ranging from clerical data entry staff to technical personnel are involved. Comment on the problems that will need to be addressed when this training is undertaken, making specific reference to the likely training needs of different personnel.

Solution

Staff could be split up into different levels of competence. The clerical staff will have very different requirements to departmental managers who are responsible for the day-to-day operation of the system. The IT managers, responsible for the advanced technicalities of the system must also be trained, usually to a much higher level of competence.

Clerical staff can usually be trained during final development. They will need to enter data, be aware of common problems like invalid data, and know how to reset the system if errors occur. Training will usually take no more than a few days, but due to the numbers of staff that may be involved it will have to be scheduled. Staff being trained may also be needed to operate the old system if it is currently still in action in the store.

The departmental managers who look after the data entry clerks (sales staff) in their department will need a higher level of training. They will need to be aware of the objectives of the new system, and be able to troubleshoot non-technical problems that may occur on a day-to-day basis. These departmental managers will probably have access to routines not available to the shop personnel (generation of confidential departmental statistics etc.). These managers must be trained for a longer period of time, and would be actively involved in development and beta testing.

The technical managers who troubleshoot the system will also need to be trained. These few personnel will probably have to be sent on a residential course to the software company. Training may take a few weeks or more and these personnel will need a high standard of computer literacy. As these are key personnel, it is likely that they will be maintaining the old system too and scheduling the entire team at the same time could prove difficult.

Simple system documentation

The **documentation** that accompanies a new system will vary depending on the system in question. Simple documentation such as a **user manual** usually accompanies any new software release like an application package, although paper-based manuals are succumbing to disk-based electronic manuals, usually in **HTML** or **Adobe Acrobat** format. These electronic manuals have a variety of advantages, namely the low cost of distribution and the ease with which they may be searched. Windows-based help files may also accompany the system and these may be specifically designed for PCs.

Technical documentation

The technical documentation might include the following items (it is often long and complex for very large systems):

- the system specifications
- the design of the system
- diagrams like hierarchical diagrams and system flowcharts etc.
- pseudocode
- program listings
- detailed file and data specifications
- modifications made to the system (with dates and author etc.)
- test data with results
- information to help maintain the system.

User documentation

User documentation varies from simple manuals a few pages in length to many volumes depending on the complexity. **User documentation** often consists of **installation manuals**, **user manuals**, **operations manuals** and **training manuals**, all of which are covered below.

Installation manual

If the installation of a new system is complex, an installation manual is needed which specifies how parts of a system are to be installed. This may have to outline different installation procedures for different operating systems, or how to make sure that the latest versions of the drivers and other software such as a Java Virtual Machine or an Internet browser, for example, needs to be installed before the new software can be used.

If a complex system is being installed then technical installation manuals, used by the personnel setting up the system, can be long and complicated documents. These often reflect the huge degree of customisation that can be accomplished. Indeed, these manuals can run to hundreds of pages, with tick lists resembling a pre-flight check plan on a jumbo jet!

At the other end of the scale, a novice user might click on an installation file and the software is automatically installed on the PC with no user interaction whatsoever. In this case the installation manual can be a single paragraph at the beginning of the user manual, which explains how to click on a file. It is now common for a CD to be inserted in the drive, and a program is 'auto run' to set up the system automatically. If all goes well, then this is a superb way of installing software for simple systems.

Essential information in the installation manual would usually include the following:

- operating system
- recommended minimum processor
- the amount of RAM required
- the amount of hard disk space needed
- the type of CD-ROM drive
- the graphics mode
- the versions of applications software with which the new software will work
- other special hardware requirements etc.

Upgrading to new versions of software can sometimes adversely affect other software in the system, and this often has to be upgraded too. For example, Word 2000 has a single document interface, whereas Word 97 has a multiple document interface. This means that Dragon Dictate (one of the speech recognition systems) does not work with Word 2000 unless you upgrade to the new system. Similarly, the 98 version of *Encyclopaedia Britannica* does not work with Internet Explorer 5, and this has to be upgraded to a later version. You can now see why the software vendors love beta testing. It enables tens of thousands of people to test their software in hundreds of thousands of different computer configurations.

The installation of new software is often fraught with difficulty, and **technical help lines** are an essential part of being able to guide the user through many possible things that may need altering.

The Internet comes to the rescue if you need the latest versions of **software drivers** or need to download new versions of browsers or virtual machines. The Internet also has the manufacturers' sites which answer frequently asked questions (FAQs), and many other sites may also be of help including **UseNet user groups** dedicated to getting operating systems or other specialist software up and running. Most technical departments dealing with software installation would not be able to function efficiently without the enormous number of resources now available on the Internet.

User manual

The **user manual** might also contain the installation instructions, but it concentrates primarily on enabling users to make effective use of the new software after it has been successfully installed.

The user manual can often be used for training, but special manuals may be provided for this. It can be used as a reference if the user needs to learn something new or has forgotten how to do something. It is usual for the manual to be extensively cross-referenced and to take the user through virtually every conceivable operation that can be undertaken with the system. It should contain many different examples and have a large variety of screen captures showing the system in operation. It should be easy for non-technical staff to use, and above all it should be simple to find information contained within it.

You are required to produce a section of a user manual when undertaking the A2 project work.

Make a note of the things covered here to see if your particular user manual contains similar information.

The user manual may be split up into many different sections for ease of use. Some of the sections could be as follows:

- Introduction to the system
- Getting started
- Elementary operations
- Tutorials
- Advanced operations
- Reference sections
- Index.

It is likely that electronic versions of the manual will be available to the operators of the system.

The operations manual

The **operations manual** outlines operational procedures such as preparation of data and other manual techniques. It could document what departments are responsible for different parts of the system, and who takes control of particular processes. If the procedures in the operations manual are followed, then the system should run smoothly. These procedures should have been fine tuned during the development stages of the project, but will need to be placed under continuous review in the light of real experience.

Training manual

Specialist training manuals can be provided, either as a stand-alone book or for use with a training course. They are often not the same as the user manual, which is intended to deal with ad-hoc queries on a day-to-day basis.

The training manual could be split into different sections depending on the level of the staff being trained, or be issued as totally separate books. The role of this manual is to provide a comprehensive course taking the users from little or no knowledge about the system up to and including expert level.

The training manual may be accompanied by a simulated system which takes the users through different scenarios, including dealing with problems and other expected errors that may occur. The training manual could be issued electronically on a CD-ROM, or distributed via the Internet where it can be viewed with a conventional web browser. Distance learning techniques and use of a PC at home can easily be accomplished via these electronic methods.

Other training methods

You must not forget also that all the above documentation can go hand in hand with conventional teacher-based training methods. Lectures, demonstrations, discussions, computer-based presentations like PowerPoint, videos and simulated teamwork can all play a role when training. The increased motivation when working with other people on a training course should not be underestimated, and time spent away from the job on training is usually quite productive.

Evaluation

Once a project has been successfully up and running for a few months, it is essential to have an **evaluation**. This evaluation should be attempted sooner if there are pressing problems with the current system.

Feedback from users is essential, and constructive criticism must be taken seriously. Designers of a new system ignore what the users think at their peril, and usually act to alter parts of the project that are not performing well.

Example

A new project has been up and running for a few months. Outline some of the methods which may be used to evaluate the effectiveness of the project.

Solution

A complete audit of the project is necessary to evaluate its effectiveness.

- Are there any errors in the systems that have not yet been corrected?
- Are the users happy with the efficiency of the system, or is it more difficult to operate than originally intended?
- Has extra stress been put on the users, or is the system running smoothly?
- Do people have to work harder or for longer hours to operate the new system?
- Have there been any complaints from customers regarding the new system?

New projects are bound to have teething problems, and they should be identified at first audit and dealt with. If this is not done then the users and customers will become disillusioned, and the business will ultimately suffer. Further audits will be required at longer intervals until the system is running as effectively as possible.

System maintenance

Even if a system is running perfectly, after a period of time the needs of a customer may change, and the system should be able to grow accordingly. If the system has been designed properly then it should be easier to change it at a later date.

The documentation that accompanies a system is important if efficient maintenance is to take place. If the system has been modularised properly then new modules may be added more easily. The object-oriented programming methodology outlined in chapter 3 will also help considerably towards this goal. Ideally, any modular additions or alterations should not affect any other modules in the system, otherwise re-testing may be much more complex than necessary.

If, as is likely, mistakes are discovered some time after the system has been in operation, then the key to sorting out these problems quickly is good **technical documentation**. It is likely that the people who programmed the original system will not be available, and even if they are, they will probably not remember exactly how things work unless they refer to their own technical documentation.

System flowcharts, **structure diagrams**, well-written code with comments, and helpful programmer's notes go a long way to being able to code new modules that will work well with the existing system. Any new modules must undergo the rigorous testing and evaluation to which the original project was subjected.

Applying these techniques to your own projects

The principles outlined here are important. Your A2 project should, for example, contain a sample from a user manual. It is unlikely to be like the user manuals described here. Even so, it should have a section on the system requirements, a 'getting started' section and a 'what to do if errors occur' section. Your technical documentation (i.e. a large part of your module 6 project) should suffice for the technical documentation and system maintenance. It is unlikely that you will need to write an operations manual as these strategically important documents would probably not be appropriate for a project of the magnitude that you will undertake at A2 level.

Although you are not required to implement your system in the detail outlined in this chapter, you would be well advised to take some of the principles outlined here and apply similar methods to your A2 project.

You should appreciate the importance attached to system maintenance when projects are undertaken in the real world. If you complete your module 6 project for a client, you will probably be either in a job or undertaking your degree course by the time systems maintenance is needed on the project that you designed. It is unlikely that you will be available to help sort out problems, unless, of course, you have written the project for a relative or for your parents.

Remember that you should not promise that any part of your A2 project is going to work perfectly forever! As you have seen in this chapter, even the experts cannot do this, and you are much less likely to be able to do so.

Look at the mark scheme for your project in detail, and make sure that you have all the documentation required by the AQA board.

Self-test questions

1 The implementation phase when commissioning a new system is important. What is the implementation phase?

2 When commissioning a new computer system a variety of different methodologies exist depending on the type of system and the circumstances in which the system is being introduced. Explain the following methods relating to the introduction of a new system, giving an example of where each method would be most appropriate.

(a) Phased implementation (b) Direct implementation

(c) Parallel implementation (d) Pilot schemes.

3 Explain the terms 'alpha testing' and 'beta testing'. Why do companies freely distribute beta-test versions of software that would normally cost hundreds of pounds to buy?

4 Staff training may be accomplished in a variety of ways. Outline four possible methods.

5 There are two major types of documentation which may accompany a system. These are 'user documentation' and 'technical documentation'. Explain the purpose of these two different types of documentation.

6 Typically what might be contained in the technical documentation that accompanies a large system?

7 Typically what might be contained in a user manual for a software package?

8 What is meant by system maintenance? Why is system maintenance usually necessary, even after the system has been working well for several years?

15 Hardware devices and output methods

In this chapter you will learn about:

- The role of computer devices in relation to the nature and volume of data
- The role of computer devices in relation to the characteristics of the user
- How the application influences the input method
- Outputs like printed reports and visual displays in relation to the users' needs
- The use of computers where conventional methods cannot be used
- The use of computer output to control machinery
- Some contemporary input and output devices

Introduction

A variety of contemporary **input devices** and **output devices** have already been covered in your AS level course, and you should be familiar with these devices ranging from **MICR** via **touch screens** to **virtual reality helmets**. Therefore, the work covered here will assume that *you know these devices and their characteristics*. Simple methods of data entry have been covered in your AS level course too, and you need to revise the characteristics of these devices if you have forgotten them. At A2 level we concentrate on *data input* and *data output* using a variety of different scenarios, paying particular attention to the needs of the user, the type of data being processed and the **volumetrics**.

It is vital that the work in this chapter is considered as an extension of the work on input and output devices already covered in your AS course.

Chapter 17 in the AS book has already covered much of the work on standard input and output devices.

Computer devices in relation to nature and volume of data

A vast amount of data is collected each day, and innovative methods have been developed making use of a variety of computer-based input and output techniques. As examples, consider collecting data to make a map of Europe, collecting data on the international fight against terrorism, or collecting data which tracks the position of the hole in the ozone layer. How would you go about tracking the routes taken by thousands of birds when they migrate for the winter? All these and thousands of other equally challenging scenarios need data to be collected, processed and output each day using cleverly designed computer systems making use of a variety of **peripheral devices**.

Role of computer devices in relation to characteristics of users

The characteristics of your users should be considered in your A2 project.

You may find the suggestions shown here useful as a starting point.

It is important to consider the **characteristics of the users** in relation to any input devices or output devices. Remember that user characteristics are things like age, gender, physical characteristics, psychological makeup or level of education. So much information is now available that designers of computer systems need to consider how this information should be gathered and presented in order to be effective. **Human computer interaction** and the design of the **human computer interface** are of paramount importance here. A natural keyboard may be ideal for an adult who can touch type, but would be useless as a means of inputting data by a five-year-old who cannot read.

As an example of the characteristics of users, consider the user requirements of artists creating drawings for use in the film industry. Typical of these might be producing animated cartoons like *Toy Story* or *Shrek*. Traditionally, if computer-based methods are *not* used, story boards are made up on which the plot is outlined in some detail. The characters that star in the film are sketched out, and the environment in which the characters will interact is pencilled in as the background. Not too much detail is included in these diagrams because it is the ideas to be conveyed which are important here. Flip charts would also be used, which give the appearance of motion if the artist flips through the pages with their fingers.

Other goals, in addition to cost effectiveness and efficiency may also be important.

Films like* Lord of the Rings *and* Star Wars *made use of computer animation techniques to clone random, but appropriately behaved, figures in major battle scenes. In this way the artist is relieved from having to draw thousands of different characters in different positions.

The aims of computerisation might therefore be to accomplish some special effects which have never been done before.

These traditional methods would involve using pieces of paper, pens, pencils, charcoal or any artistic material that would help the artist to sketch out the plot. Some artists may also work in clay for the production of films with characters like Wallace and Gromit. These artists may not be computer literate, but they *are* highly skilled in the production of quick sketches, model making and the use of all the traditional artistic materials at their disposal. Thus, some of the important characteristics of these users might be 'highly skilled at drawing', 'used to using artistic tools such as paintbrushes and pencils', 'have incredibly good imaginations', 'good communication skills' and 'good model-making skills'. The designers of the hardware to help these users must therefore consider how peripheral devices can be used to mimic and preferably improve on the skills possessed by these people to undertake their day-to-day movie-making tasks more effectively.

Highly skilled craftsmen and craftswomen such as these would need to be convinced of the need for computerisation, and be convinced that it would offer tools which are better than their current ones for making films. However, even these artists would be the first to admit that the production of a full-length feature film like *Snow White and the Seven Dwarfs* takes hundreds of people many months of painstaking work to produce. This particular cartoon was chosen because it was manufactured before computers were advanced enough to be of any help. To convince top-flight artists that a computer will be able to replace their pens, pencils, papers, charcoal and crayons was indeed an uphill struggle, and it was not until the invention of highly sophisticated graphics tablets and impressive Art and CAD packages that this possibility became a reality, as shown below.

How the application influences the input method

Careful consideration needs to be given to the requirements of a particular application with regard to determining the best method of input. If a company like an animation studio wants to make serious use of an Art package like Adobe PhotoShop, for example, then we need to find out if the users will be creating artistic pictures manually. For the film animation artists mentioned above, this is definitely so, and a **graphics tablet** with a **pressure-sensitive pen** would be infinitely preferable to struggling to draw pictures using an ordinary mouse.

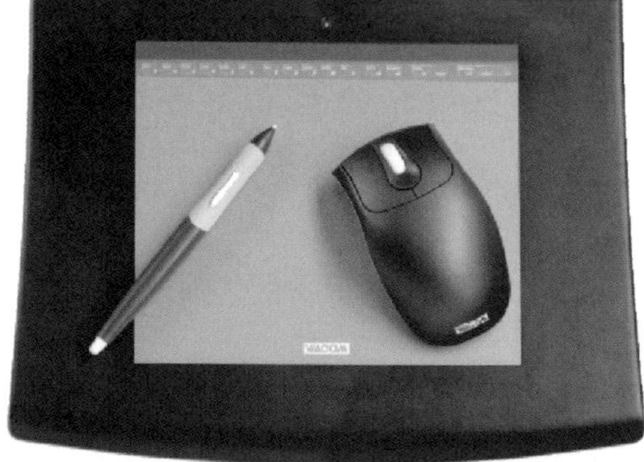

Figure 15.1 A Wacom graphics tablet with pressure-sensitive pen and 4D mouse

A graphics tablet with pressure-sensitive pen and a 4D mouse is shown in Figure 15.1. This system is ideal for creating computer-generated drawings and paintings, and for creating and editing CAD drawings. It also gives control over video editing, including pan and tilt and a variety of other functions.

Artists make use of pencils and paintbrushes which react very differently according to the amount of pressure exerted by the artist. It would be very frustrating if this pressure sensitivity was not available on the computer input device used for drawing. The Wacom pressure-sensitive pen shown in Figure 15.1 has *1024 different pressure levels*, which is easily enough to cope with the needs of the most discerning artist. Indeed, artists who make use of high-quality graphics tablets soon get used to drawing in this way, and feel comfortable making use of this sophisticated technology.

The technology described here is now so pervasive that it is becoming less likely that a full-length feature film would be drawn out by hand.

Film goers are also used to the 3D effects which are more easily achievable with computerised technology.

When evaluating the outcome of computerised systems, the end user is often neglected in favour of more measurable objectives which appear in the design **specification**. Never underestimate the importance of how the users feel about any new technology that has been introduced. The new equipment should be better than the system it replaces or there is no point in introducing it! The majority of artists working in films are completely happy to draw cartoons, paintings and other styles making use of graphics tablet technology, which is often much larger and more sophisticated than the system shown in Figure 15.1. They do feel that it is as good as using a pen or a paintbrush, and when coupled with the advanced editing capabilities of the software into which the drawings are entered, the system really is extremely powerful. This is especially true in the animation film industry where cartoons used to be drawn out by hand on many different pieces of paper or acetate.

Geographic information systems

At the start of this chapter you were asked to consider how you would gather data to make a map of Europe. You may be wondering why anybody would want to map information about major parts of the world when we already have maps! However, the latest trend in geographic information systems (GIS) is to be able to *superimpose information from other systems* (like police database information) onto these maps. This is ideal for planning services in a large city, for dealing with emergencies like a terrorist attack, or for dealing with natural disasters like an earthquake. GIS systems are also used a great deal in less dramatic circumstances, like forest management, helping civil engineering companies to manage projects, and to help map archaeological sites. Here we will use the GIS system as an example of **hardware devices** and input and output methods, but first we need to look at the **GPS system**, which is one of the ways used to input data into a GIS system.

Data input methods – the global positioning system

The GPS or global positioning system is already well established. This system, based on satellite technology and appropriate software, enables data about the location to be distributed to computers with the appropriate **peripheral equipment**, and to other suitably equipped devices (e.g. hand-held GPS navigation systems). The GPS system is able to collect individual *points* or *areas*. These and many other **attributes** can be collected and stored in a **data dictionary**, which can then be linked to a suitably designed **database**. This makes the collection of spatial data particularly effective, especially for import into a typical GIS system.

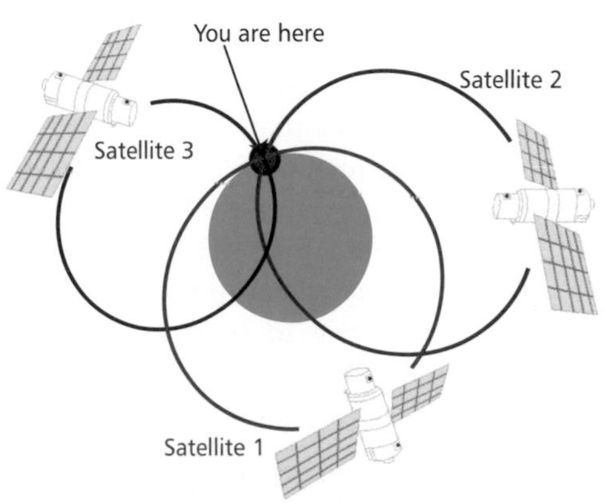

Figure 15.2 A simplified GPS representation

The GPS system works by using a system of 24 satellites, arranged in a constellation around the earth which ensures that about six satellites are always in view for any user. Using these satellites, of which just three are shown in Figure 15.2, you can estimate a position of latitude and longitude by calculating how long it takes radio signals from three or four different satellites to reach the receiving device. This time interval, together with the known position of the satellites (radio signals travel at the speed of light) can be used to triangulate your position in 3D (height too). Using the civilian version of the equipment (the military have access to more accurate systems) you can estimate your position to within 10 or 15 metres if the reception conditions are favourable.

How the application influences the output method

The computer-based output needed to display GPS information depends on the application. This could be as simple as a hiker wanting a typical hand-held portable device of the sort shown in Figure 15.3, or very complex systems providing central command with positional information linked to a GIS emergency planning scheme as shown in Figure 15.4.

A lot of technology and applications are based around the GPS and GIS systems, ranging from in-car satellite navigation to plotting courses for cruise ships.

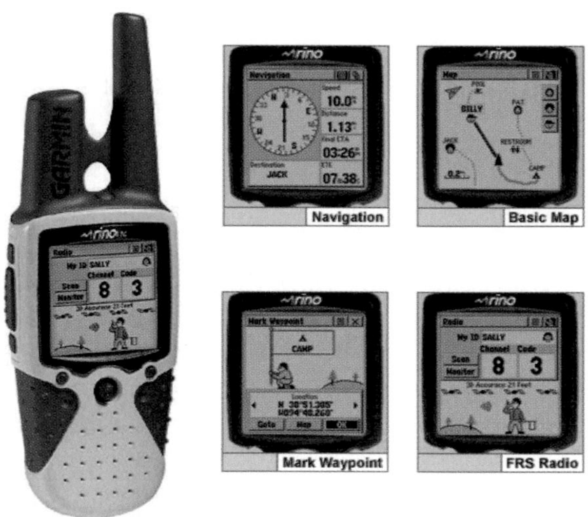

Figure 15.3 A Garmin Rhino 110 integrated GPS/radio system

From Figure 15.3 you can see that the output is tailored to the needs of the users who, in this case, are hikers. The system is waterproof and so can be used in adverse weather conditions. Co-ordinates of users can be beamed to other users with the same system, thus promoting co-operation between teams of hikers. Individual users can have unique IDs, like Sally and Billy shown in Figure 15.3. It is ideal for users on skiing and camping trips. The hardware requirements are an **embedded system**, portability, sufficient battery life, clear and easy-to-use displays, and integrated radio and GPS. Users should realise that their communications may be heard by anyone else using the same channel (and hence the same radio frequency). Therefore, this unit would not be suitable for users such as the military or for people who wanted to communicate in private. Much more expensive units that use **encryption** are employed by the military for this purpose. People making use of radio-based peripheral equipment connected to a computer or other hand-held device might need a licence to operate at particular radio frequencies, and the Rhino 110 GPS/radio system is no exception. A license may be obtained from the appropriate authorities.

The **special needs** of some **users** will need to be considered when using radio-based computer peripherals and communication equipment. Users fitted with pacemakers (an electronic aid implanted into a person to regulate their heartbeat) or hearing aids must not use this device within about 15 cm of the pacemaker or hearing aid to prevent possible interference with the device.

Emergency planning teams might use an integrated **GPS/GIS system**, and have conventional PCs displaying suitable information. Figure 15.4 shows a GIS system which is currently displaying a map of the city of Moorhead in Minnesota, US. The flood level is currently being displayed and you can choose a depth of flood by selecting the flood stage in a dropdown menu.

Many systems set up for emergency planning have dual uses, for example use by the utility companies to map out services such as water and electricity supply. They could also be used to predict the consequences of a flood or a hurricane. Thus emergency teams could act out practice exercises using the real equipment and software.

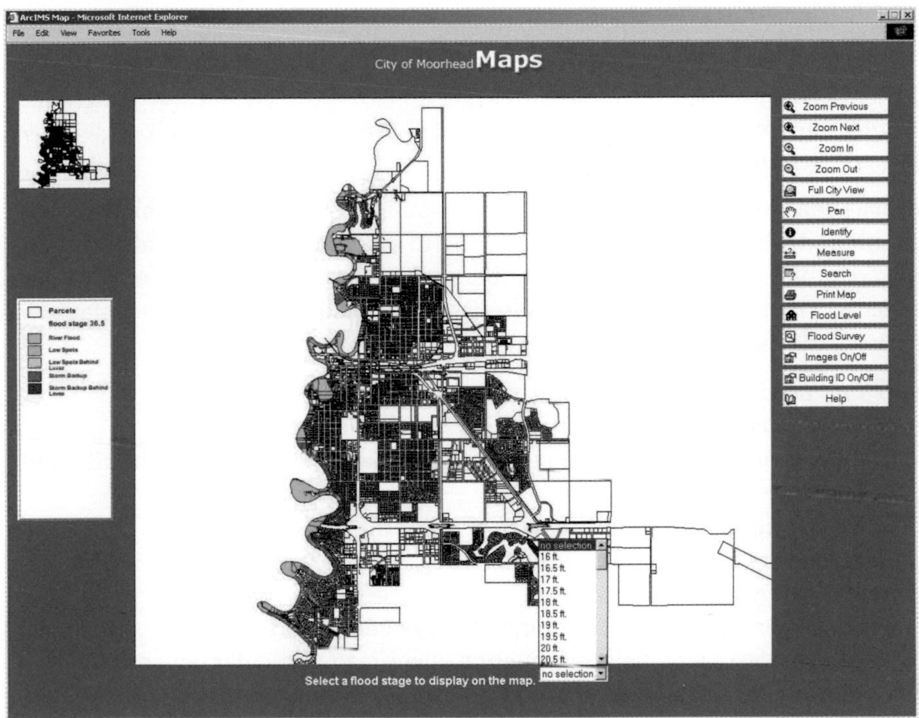

Figure 15.4 Emergency planning at Moorhead in Minnesota, US

Example

An emergency planning team is based in a major UK city. They intend to set up a central headquarters for use in an emergency such as an oil spillage, flood or chemical accident.

(a) Suggest five characteristics of these users which are important.

(b) Name three different computer devices and suggest how each might play a role in your proposed system.

(c) If a toxic chemical spillage occurred, suggest a suitable computer device to capture the data. How might this be utilised?

(d) List six items of hardware that might be needed in the central operations room.

Solution

(a) The users involved in this system would be trained professionals like the police, fire and ambulance services. Five requirements of these users might be as follows:

(i) require up-to-date information in real time

(ii) each department might want different information from the same map
(iii) automatic data logging facilities for inputting data are required
(iv) automatic routing of data to personnel in the field is necessary
(v) summary statistical information may need to be printed out.

(b) The following computer devices could be useful:
(i) A graphics tablet with a mouse or a puck (a device on which cross-hairs locate position accurately) could be used by personnel at the centre to interact with the GIS system to map out dangerous areas.
(ii) A large computer projection system (preferably back projection) could be used by the planners to get an overall picture of the situation at any particular moment in time.
(ii) Mobile units with two-way radio and GPS information will probably be needed by personnel in the field.

(c) Appropriate sensors (depending on the type of spillage, e.g. a gas cloud might need to be monitored) should be available connected to mobile devices. Typically a portable computer would be needed, together with an antenna, a special receiver and a data logger. The portable would run software which helps to co-ordinate data transfer with the main centre.

(d) The hardware needed in the main control room might be as follows:
(i) A network to connect the main computers in the control room.
(ii) A file server on which to store data and the software needed to run the GIS and GPS systems.
(iii) Printers to print out statistical reports or other information.
(iv) Radio receivers to receive data from data loggers and personnel who wish to communicate with the centre.
(v) A proxy server and firewall to connect the system to the Internet.
(vi) Database servers which hold information specific to particular departments. The information on these servers could be superimposed on the main map (e.g. electricity supplies, water supplies, roads, rail, waterways etc.).

Output of computer data

A large amount of thought needs to be put into ensuring that data, either displayed on a screen, printed on a printer or output to some other device, meet the needs of the users. Specialised output might be needed for users with a differing range of disabilities, for example. You should remember that output may also be in the form of computer-generated speech, sound which has been sampled or synthesised by the computer, multimedia-based output and perhaps some **virtual reality** systems too.

We are so used to data being displayed as text on a screen or a piece of paper that we forget that some users might not be able to make use of this. A navigation system in a car, shown in Figure 15.5, is likely to be dangerous if the driver has to concentrate on a small screen for instructions. It would be far better to have computer-generated voice output, which would be able to speak commands like 'turn left at the next junction' or 'traffic jam ahead, rerouting to avoid'.

A typical in-car navigation system from Pioneer is shown in Figure 15.5. On-screen map information is displayed, but computerised voice output directs the driver for safety. There are other modes of operation too, in which the roads can be displayed as on a conventional map or in 3D.

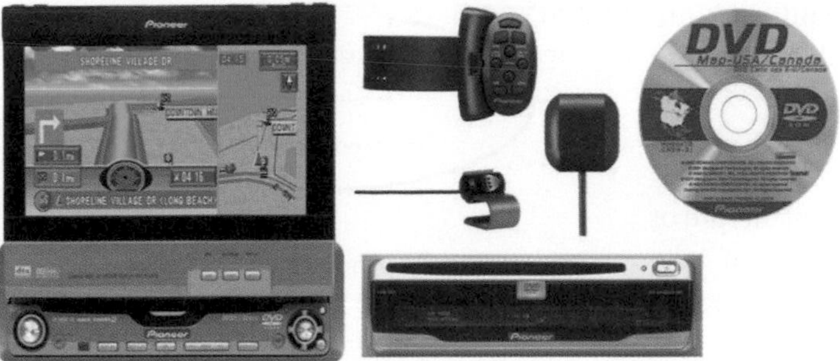

Figure 15.5 A voice-controlled in-car satellite navigation system with voice output

3D projection systems

You should already be familiar with **projection TVs** for projecting two-dimensional images. However, combine several of these projection systems in a suitable environment and you have the capability to visualise data in three dimensions. Japan's National Institute for Fusion Science uses this form of computer output to research data using three-dimensional images. Figure 15.6 shows a scientist in this environment wearing special goggles to interact with multiple computer projections. Although Figure 15.6 is only two-dimensional, you can easily imagine walking around in this virtual-reality environment. The phenomena being investigated making use of this method at the time of writing this book are nuclear fusion plasma, molecular dynamics, fluid dynamics etc.

Figure 15.6 A scientist at Japan's National Institute for Fusion Science investigating magnetic fields

Computer science students usually need no prompting to keep up with the latest developments in technology.

You may be able to use your knowledge of contemporary devices to help answer questions at A2 level.

I would suggest that you read appropriate magazines, look at relevant TV programmes and keep an eye on scientific journals to expand your knowledge of contemporary devices and new techniques.

The system, called CompleXcope, is controlled by a supercomputer. The computer output system makes use of 10 ft square rear projection screens and a floor display mounted from a projector on the ceiling. A magnetic tracking system is used to detect real-time spatial position and direction. The user can interact with this system via a portable computer with buttons and a **joystick**.

The use of computer output to control machinery

Computers are used extensively to control a variety of machines ranging from robots via nuclear power stations to in-car management of fuel systems. Although this sounds complex, several principles will make it seem a lot easier.

Any control system can be split up into three parts, namely **sense**, **decision** and **action**, as shown in Figure 15.7. Very simple systems may not have all these elements, but most computer-based systems will incorporate the important principle of **feedback**. Feedback means that you take note of what is happening by sensing the environment (e.g. is it too hot or too cold?), deciding what to do (e.g. if it is too cold then you need some heat) and, finally, acting on the decision (e.g. turning a heater on). Remember that feedback in most of these systems is continuous. After a heater is switched on it will eventually get too hot, and when this happens the decision to turn the heater off will need to be made.

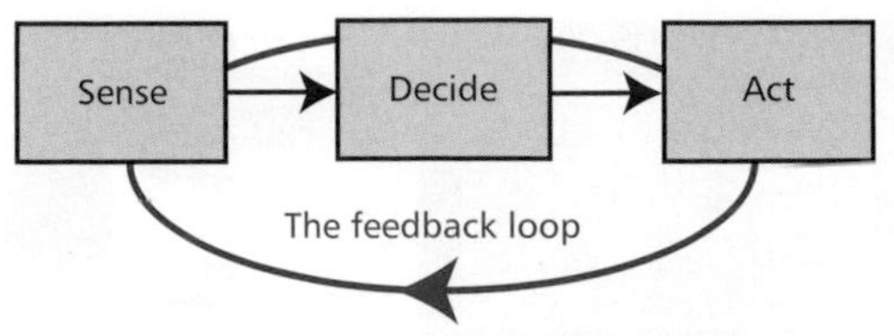

Figure 15.7 A simplified control system

A control system will typically be going around the loop shown by the red arrow in Figure 15.7. The decision-making element is either a computer running software written for the purpose, or an **embedded microprocessor system**.

The ability of a computer to sense its environment is due to the enormous variety of **sensors** available which convert physical quantities into electrical signals, and the huge variety of control equipment and actuators such as relays and valves etc., which can be used to switch external devices on and off, or cause things to move. In these systems it is the computer or microprocessor which acts as the decision-making element under the guidance of a set of instructions or program which controls the process. There is much to be considered here in terms of the sensors, feedback systems and interfaces, but one should not forget the important role played by the operating systems when computers are used in control. This has already been considered when real-time operating systems were covered in chapter 8.

Transducers

A **transducer** is the name given to any device that converts energy from one form into another. Therefore, a motor is an example of an **output transducer** which converts electrical energy into rotary motion. A light bulb would be an example of an output transducer which converts electrical energy into light. **Input transducers** are equally important, for without them the computer system would have no idea of what is actually going on. These input transducers are the eyes and ears of the computer system, and typical examples would be heat sensors which convert temperature into an electrical signal, or alternators and generators which convert rotary motion into electrical signals.

Interfacing

Signals from the input transducers must be converted into a form that the computer can process. Similarly, signals from the computer must be converted into a form suitable for driving (operating) any particular output transducer. Occasionally the signals coming from or going to the computer are compatible with the transducers, but most often it is necessary to have extra electronic circuits which perform the necessary conversions. These electronic circuits are called **interfaces**.

Sensing the environment

Many quantities to be measured are analogue in nature, and a small selection of typical sensors is shown in Table 15.1.

Analogue and digital signals are covered in the first book in this series.

Table 15.1 A selection of input transducers or sensors

Resistance	Voltage	Current	Temperature	Pressure
Light intensity	pH	Sound intensity	Colour	Humidity
Rotational speed	Time	Radiation	Capacitance	Inductance
Magnetic field strength	Strain	Wind speed	ECG monitor	EEG monitor

Remember that analogue signals are continuously variable between some maximum and minimum, and digital signals are discrete values.

As you can see from Table 15.1, input transducers are available, ensuring that computers may be fully integrated into virtually all scientific, industrial and medical processes. Transducers convert appropriate quantities into **analogue** signals which can then be fed into an **A to D converter** so that the **digital** values may be fed into the computer.

All signals need to be converted into digital form to be processed by a computer or embedded microprocessor system.

Controlling the environment

Although many types of control system can be accomplished by wiring together a few electronic components, making use of a **microprocessor** or using a computer gives us the ability to solve more complex problems in ways which are extremely cost effective. Also, the behaviour of the systems can be modified more easily as software changes are inevitably easier than rebuilding parts of the electronic circuits (hardware). Most modern installations of any complexity make use of programmable systems as the decision-making element within the complete control system environment. Many quantities which may be measured are analogue in nature, and just a small selection of typical output transducers which are available are shown in Table 15.2.

Table 15.2 A small selection of output transducers or actuators

Motors	Light bulbs	Loudspeakers	Valves (liquid control)	Hydraulics
Stepper motors	Linear motors	Switches	Relays	Heaters
Coolers	Infrared devices	Ultraviolet devices	Ultrasonic devices	Buzzers

It is very easy to say that a digital signal can switch an electric motor on and off, but an interface will be needed in virtually all scenarios. Although the computer is supplying the signal to switch on the motor, it obviously cannot supply the required current (and hence power) needed by the motor. Therefore, an external power supply (or battery) must be used. We effectively use some electronics to interface the low-power output from the computer to the higher-power required for the motor as shown in Figure 15.8.

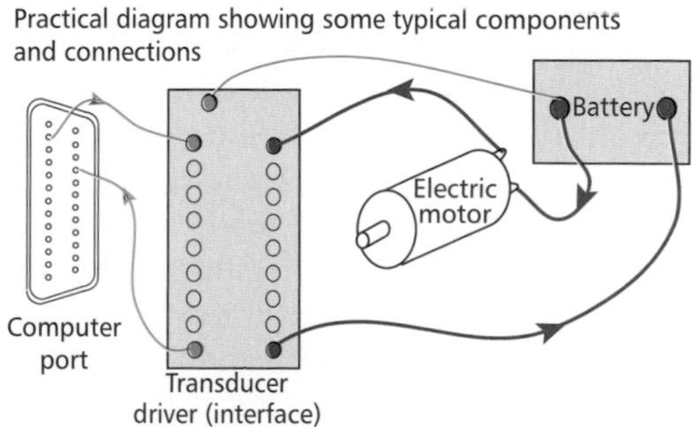

Figure 15.8 A system for controlling an electric motor

The conceptual model, shown at the top of Figure 15.8 shows the output from a typical **computer port**. The signal from here would be very low power, and so a

The software being considered here is very similar in principle to the software used to switch control systems on and off (see masking in chapter 2).

Many embedded microprocessor systems would be controlled directly from assembly language programs. Others would use proprietary programs developed especially for electronic systems, and PIC programming is an example of this.

transducer driver or interface is used to boost the signal so that it can be used to power the electric motor. The transducer driver shown in Figure 15.8 gets its power from a battery, but mains operation is available for larger motors. For very large industrial plant, huge motors may be controlled in this way with an appropriate computer interface.

Control software

It is the job of the software inside the computer or **embedded microprocessor system** to form the decision-making element of the control system. There is nothing difficult about this, and the majority of readers of this book should be able to write suitable software. This assumes, of course, that you have an appropriate high-level language or low-level language which can be used to monitor signals from, or output signals to, a suitable port on the computer. As an example, consider the case of the temperature-control system shown in Figure 15.9. A chamber (enclosed space) is to be kept at just the right temperature, defined by the controlling program inside the computer or embedded microprocessor system.

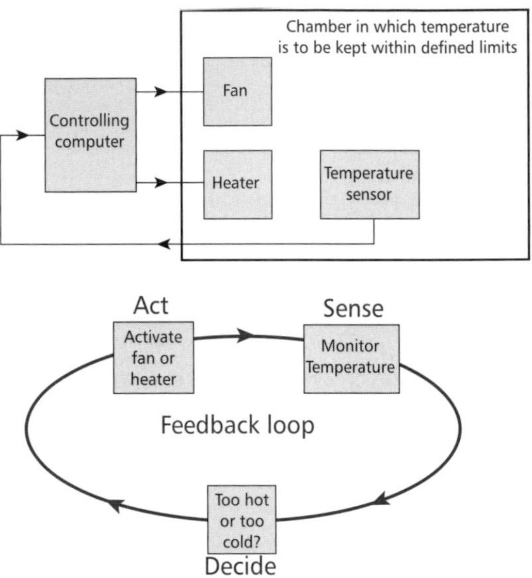

Figure 15.9 A simple computer control system with feedback

Most of the time would be spent going round loops and checking for certain conditions, as described by the feedback loop in Figure 15.9. If it is too cold then the heater will be switched on, or if it is too hot then the fan will be switched on. If the temperature is OK, then both the fan and the heater are switched off. You are already familiar with designing similar systems, and the assembly language covered in chapter 2 would be ideal for this (see margin entry).

There may be some conditions under which the control system cannot cope. For example, if the chamber being monitored gets damaged, then it might not be possible for the heater to heat up the chamber to a sufficient temperature, even if the heater is on all the time. Under these conditions it would be possible to activate an alarm if the temperature does not reach a desired level in a set period of time. An alarm can easily be connected to a third output from a suitable port of the computer.

Most control systems, no matter how complex, are variations on the simple themes described above. Feedback is constantly being monitored to provide the necessary data for the control system to be able to make decisions. Alarms can be activated or systems shut down if continuation of a particular process would be unsafe. Real-time clocks (usually the one set up inside the computer system) can be used in conjunction with the data to provide further analysis. Statistics may be produced such as a graph of temperature against time at five-minute intervals throughout the night if this was thought to be necessary. Salient points at which the fan or heater was brought into play could be plotted on the graph too. You are limited by your imagination only.

Contemporary input and output devices

You are reminded that you should be aware of a range of contemporary input and output devices. These have already been covered extensively in your AS level course, and you should be prepared to integrate these into your A2 work.

Example

Suggest one suitable input device and one suitable output device for each of the following scenarios. For each of your chosen devices, say why you think that it is useful for the given situation.

1. **Controlling a robot used to deactivate bombs.**
2. **Controlling a wheelchair for a disabled person who has no movement in their arms or legs.**
3. **Controlling a variety of devices around a house in which different devices are attached to a network and have different IP addresses.**

Solution

1. The video camera is an essential input device here so that the operator of the system can see what he or she is doing. A robot arm with pressure-sensitive grips may be used to manipulate wires or use tools such as screwdrivers or a spanner.
2. Assuming that the user is able to move his or her head, a suitable input device would be a joystick which is mouth operated. A suitable output device would be a solenoid to operate the brakes on the wheelchair.
3. Suitable input devices here would be a conventional keyboard and mouse so that settings on devices like fridges or ovens can be programmed from a networked computer. A suitable output device would be a conventional computer monitor on which the state of each of these devices could be observed. E.g. the oven might be programmed to come on at 8.00 p.m. at 200° Celsius for half an hour.

Self-test questions

1. It is important to match peripheral devices to the 'characteristics of the users'. In each of the following, suggest suitable peripheral devices, giving reasons for each choice.
   (a) Animation artists producing a film
   (b) Gathering data from a Formula One car on the move.
2. What is a sensor? Suggest a sensor for monitoring radiation.
3. What is a transducer? Suggest a transducer for controlling water flow.
4. Feedback is an important concept when dealing with computers controlling machines. Explain what is meant by feedback and how it is typically used.
5. Suggest suitable transducers, sensors and other hardware that could be used to help build a computer-controlled coffee machine.

16 Networking

In this chapter you will learn about:

- Baseband and broadband networking
- Synchronous data transmission and time division multiplexing
- Circuit switching, packet switching, datagrams and the virtual circuit
- Asynchronous transmission mode (ATM), standard protocols
- TCP/IP, protocol stacks and sockets
- Types of cable and network topology, including star, ring, bus and tree
- Switched Ethernet and hubs
- Network segmentation and bridges, peer-to-peer networking, contrasting LANs and WANs
- IP addressing, the IP address format, network IDs, host IDs, different classes of networks

*The term **Broadband** is used in two distinctly different ways:*

1 as the correct technical term for transmitting multiple signals simultaneously;

2 as the term for a faster Internet connection compared with a dial-up modem.

As it is possible to use the telephone at the same time as using the Internet, definition 2 does entirely agree with definition 1, but make sure you do not get mixed up when answering questions in an A2 examination.

Baseband and broadband networking

Baseband technology transmits only one signal at any one moment in time. When transmitting, no other machine on the network may do so. If an attempt is made during this time, a clash would occur and the signals would need to be retransmitted later (often in just a few milliseconds). This is how the **Ethernet** network operates. Signals are transmitted if the line is free, but if a clash occurs then the system waits a small random moment in time and tries again. Slow networks (10 Mbit/sec) can be inefficient where there is a large number of users as many clashes may occur. Faster networks (e.g. 100 Mbit/sec) would be better as the information is sent more quickly.

Broadband networks send different signals at the same time along the same wire or wireless link. This is because different **carrier frequencies** are used which do not interfere with those used by other computers. An example of a broadband system is Nortel's Reunion broadband wireless access network, shown in Figure 16.1. A base station transmits a radio frequency (called a **carrier signal**) which carries the computer information by a suitable **modulation** method. Other customers may send and receive other signals using different carrier frequencies. In this way many signals may be sent *simultaneously*.

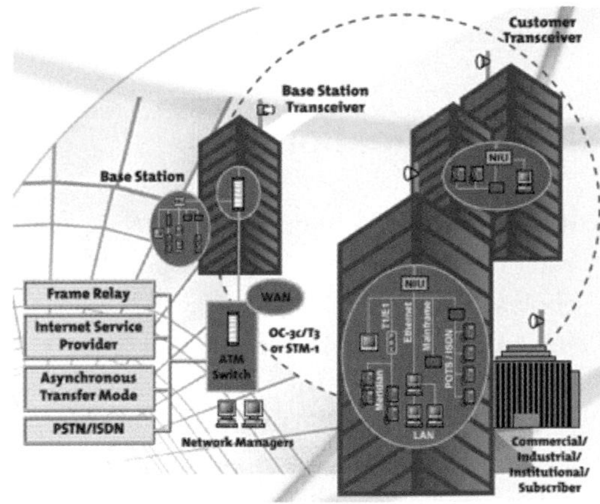

Figure 16.1 Nortel's broadband network

Multiplexing

Multiplexing is the name given to sending different signals over the same link. If signals are sent at different times it is called **time-division multiplexing**, or if different frequencies are used it is called **frequency-division multiplexing**. Time-division multiplexing is easy to understand; it is identical in principle to the **time-sharing** systems covered in chapter 8 when operating systems were considered. Each signal is given a tiny slice of time so that other users may receive information during their time slices too. Users may not realise that others are using the same link because time slices come round very rapidly, and not all users may be transmitting at the same time.

Frequency-division multiplexing transmits signals at exactly the same moment in time but on different carrier frequencies. It is identical in principle to FM radio, where many different stations send out signals over the airwaves simultaneously.

Example

Distinguish between baseband and broadband networks, giving examples of where each system might be used. Give typical examples of baseband and broadband systems.

Solution

Information is transmitted over a baseband network using a single frequency and a system operating time-division multiplexing. Only one signal can be transmitted at any one moment in time. The other signals have to wait until there is a free moment during which data may be transmitted. Clashes occur if two signals transmit simultaneously.

A broadband network can transmit more than one signal simultaneously, often by using a different carrier frequency, which is then transmitted over the same cable or wireless link. The signals have to be demodulated at the other end to extract the information signal. Ethernet, used in LANs, is a good example of a baseband network; a wireless access network like Blue Tooth is an example of broadband linking computers via wireless signals.

Radio-based networks are now extremely important because of the extensive use of mobile phones and wireless Ethernet.

Many campuses now have wireless Ethernet access points enabling students to connect to networks using a suitably equipped computer.

A student with a portable computer and a wireless Ethernet card would be able to connect to the network from anywhere within range of the wireless access point.

Circuit and packet switching

Figure 16.2(a) shows a dedicated communication line between two people or computers. It could be a direct link or routed via a telephone exchange. This line is used for the duration of the call, irrespective of whether any information is actually being transmitted or not. This is an example of **circuit switching**.

Circuit switching is inefficient for computers as the line is tied up when no useful information is being sent. If data is sent as a single message, then it could go via different routes, as indicated in Figure 16.2(b). This is called **message switching**. To prevent large messages hogging the line for long periods of time, messages are spilt up into smaller parts called **packets**. Sending a message in this way is called **packet switching**. With packet switching you do not 'own' the same line for the duration of the call, and are therefore said to have a **virtual circuit**. The packets would obviously have to be reassembled into the correct order at the receiving end.

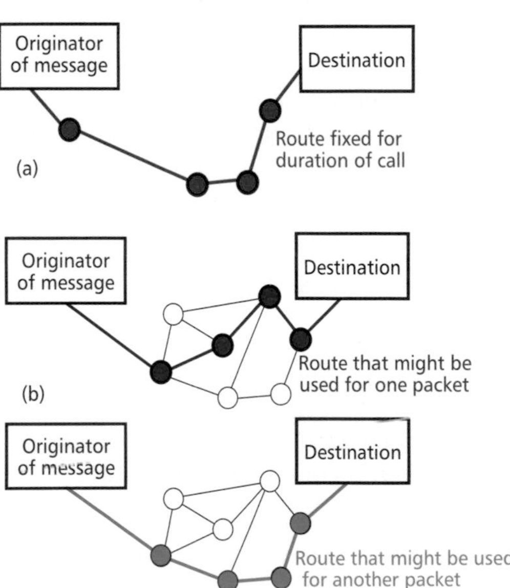

Figure 16.2 Circuit and packet switching

Layering communication systems

Communication between machines is often arranged in **layers**. Hardware or software can interface to its own layer without affecting the others. Before the **International Standards Organisation** (**ISO**) established the layered approach, communication between computer systems was virtually impossible. One model is the **ISO Open Systems Interconnection** or **ISO OSI model** shown in Figure 16.3. This model enables different computer systems to communicate effectively with each other via different networks such as LANs and WANs. Specifically the **physical layer** provides the specification for the mechanical connections and basically defines the hardware. The **data link layer** splits up the signal into frames needed to be sent over the hardware link, and also provides for synchronisation and error checking.

An often-quoted way to remember the order of the layers in the ISO OSI model is to use 'All People Seem To Need Data Processing'.

Before the advent of sets of rules to transfer data via a network it was impossible for different computer systems to communicate with each other.

It was common practice for information to have to be manually re-entered into a different computer system.

The use of the Internet shows how far we have come from these early days, and all because of the layered communication model.

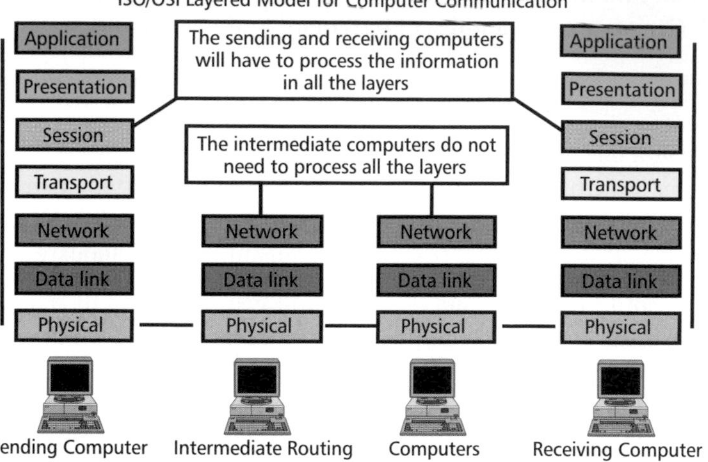

Figure 16.3 The ISO OSI layered model for computer communications

The **network layer** assembles the data into packets for transmission over a variety of different networks, and copes with the conversion needed to transmit data over different network types. The **transport layer** establishes a reliable point-to-point connection and assembles packets into the right order. It can also determine the most cost-effective route given the quality of service that is required, like video, voice or computer data, for example. The **session layer** deals with logging on and off, and establishing and terminating connections between the host computers. The **presentation layer** helps to maintain compatibility with different coding methods and file types used on different computer systems. Finally, the **application layer** has the job of servicing the communication requirements of **application software**.

The anatomy of an Ethernet packet

A **packet** contains the data to be transmitted, but it also contains information like **ID**, **source** and **destination** of the packet, and some error checking too. It corresponds to **layer 3** of the **ISO OSI model**. The exact form of the data depends on the system being used, and proprietary systems have their own names for the different protocols corresponding to the different layers of the ISO OSI model.

When a packet of data is sent, along with the delivery information like the destination address, it is then known as a **datagram**. Typically an Internet datagram might be made up of several lower-level packets, together with the destination address. This is so that the datagram can arrive at its destination without any reference to other information. An Ethernet packet has been assembled in Figure 16.4.

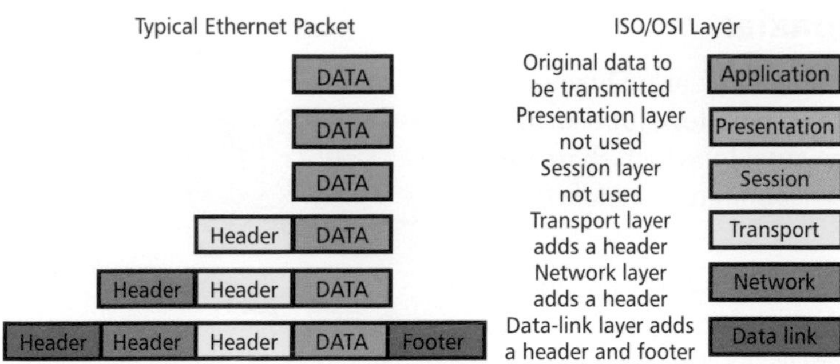

Figure 16.4 Building up the layers for an Ethernet packet

Example

Explain what physically has to be done to connect a stand-alone PC to an Ethernet network. Give an example of the typical hardware and software needed and explain the role played by the ISO OSI layers 1, 2 and 3.

Solution

Layer 1 is the physical layer. It consists of the connections and network hardware. You install an Ethernet card (NIC) to enable it to be connected to an Ethernet network.

Layer 2 is the data-link layer. This is the software driver for a particular Ethernet card. This driver interfaces the card to the operating system, and implements the software needed to change the data into the frames to send over the Ethernet hardware.

Layer 3 is the network layer. Software which supports IP is installed (or activated from the operating system). Higher-layer protocols (TCP representing layer 4) may be installed at this stage on the client machine. TCP/IP would usually be installed at the same time.

Different LAN configurations

A **local area network** or **LAN** can be set up in a variety of ways according to the type of technology being implemented. The most popular LAN is Ethernet, which can be split up into several types depending on the speed of communication required. Each proprietary network uses a different type of cable, and typical ones are covered below.

Types of cable – twisted pair

Twisted pair cable is where two insulated wires are twisted together, as shown in Figure 16.5.

Twisting helps prevent electromagnetic interference, and shielding gives further protection. Many cables do not use extra shielding as twisting is effective for preventing noise corrupting the signals. Twisted pair cable is common in 100 Mbit/sec Ethernet.

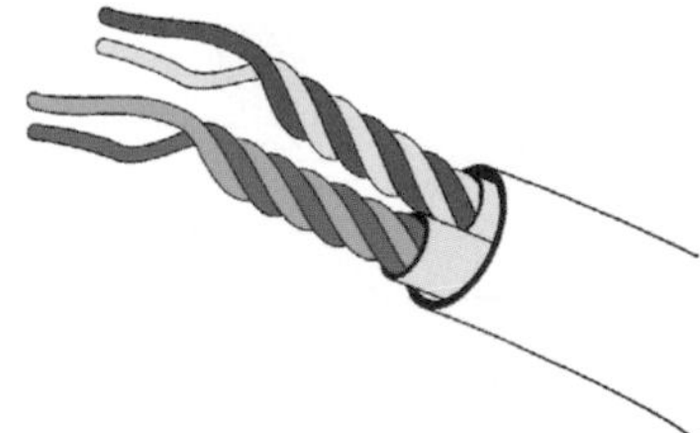

Figure 16.5 Twisted pair cable

Many homes now have more than one computer, and a number of people are establishing simple peer-to-peer networking in their domestic environment. This enables them to share resources like printers and the Internet, and to play games over the network.

The example given here is typical of what has to be done to connect a PC to the network, and makes the theoretical layered system much easier to understand.

If possible, get your network manager or teacher to show you how a computer may be connected to a network.

It is possible to use twisted pair in 1 Gbit/sec Ethernet configurations, but the distance over which this faster signal will travel is much shorter compared with the same cables being used for 100 Mbit/sec Ethernet.

Types of cable – coaxial

A **coaxial cable** and connector are shown in Figure 16.6. This has two conductors (one in the middle and one around the outside) which share the same axis. Coaxial cable is common in 10 Mbit/sec Ethernet systems.

There are different types of coaxial cable for different purposes, such as baseband Ethernet, cable TV or broadband wireless signals. As different types of coaxial cable are used for each of these applications, it is not as versatile as the other media and is not usually used in new network installations.

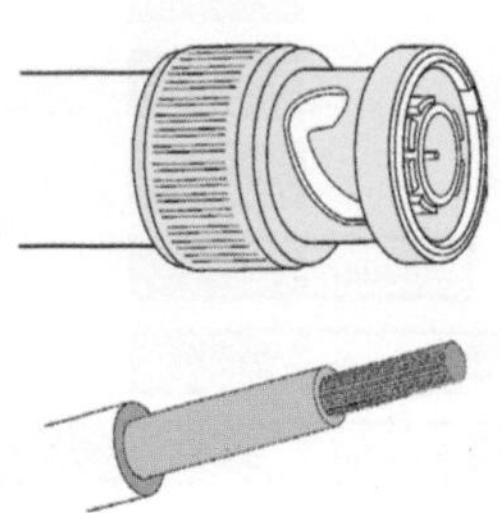

Figure 16.6 Coaxial connector and cable

*Cables must conform to a particular standard; they have to be terminated properly with the right connectors, and then installed without damage to ensure that the theoretical **bandwidth** is actually achieved in practice. These are called **CAT standards**.*

Fibre optics

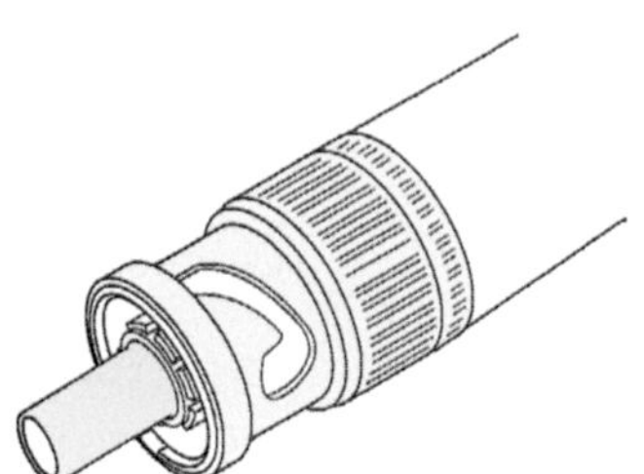

Figure 16.7 A fibre optic connection

Twisted pair and coaxial cables are examples of copper-wire connections. **Fibre optic connections** are made out of glass or plastic and transmit optically instead of electrically. This means they make use of light instead of electricity, although the light signals are obviously converted back to electrical signals to be interpreted by the electronics inside the computer.

Fibre optics suffer less from interference and are easily capable of transmitting at 1 Gbit/sec or more. They are used for backbone connections, but as speeds increase, they will probably connect workstations too. A fibre optic connection is shown in Figure 16.7. Fibre optic cable is much more difficult to install than twisted pair or coaxial cable. The ends of the cable have to be finely polished, and the connections must be of an exceptional standard for it to work properly.

10 Gbit/sec Ethernet is now available, and this has brought new challenges, even using fibre optic cables.

Network topologies

Network topology refers to the ways in which the cables connect the machines together.

A **star-network** topology is shown in Figure 16.8. Each workstation has a unique connection to the central computer, ensuring maximum security and no shared bandwidth.

As the speed of networks increases, engineers are challenged to extract every ounce of performance out of the existing technology.

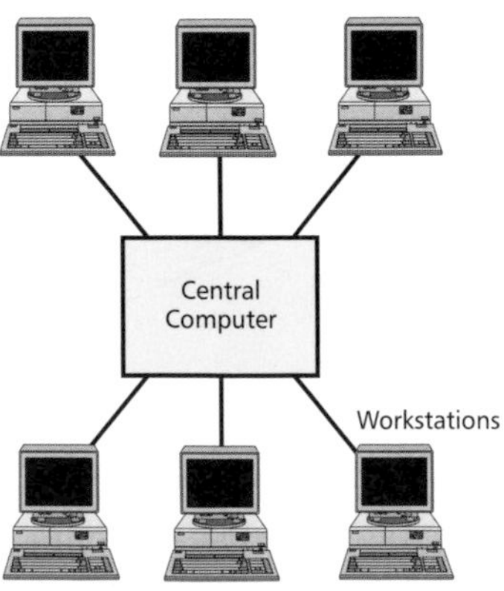

Figure 16.8 Star network topology

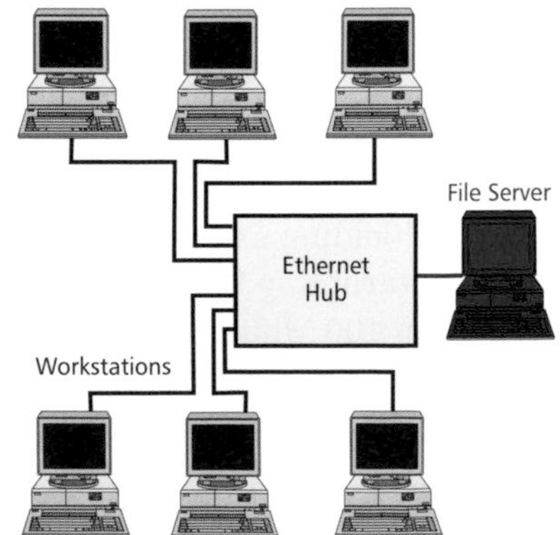

Figure 16.9 A tree network topology

A similar system (at least visually!) can be implemented by using a **hub**, but the bandwidth advantage is lost because the connection on the other side of the hub is shared, as can be seen in Figure 16.9. Security is also lost if a hub is used, and this connection should more usefully be called a **tree network** rather than a **star network** because it is like a tree, especially if other hubs are used too. As the hubs contain a bus network inside, it is also sometimes called a star bus network.

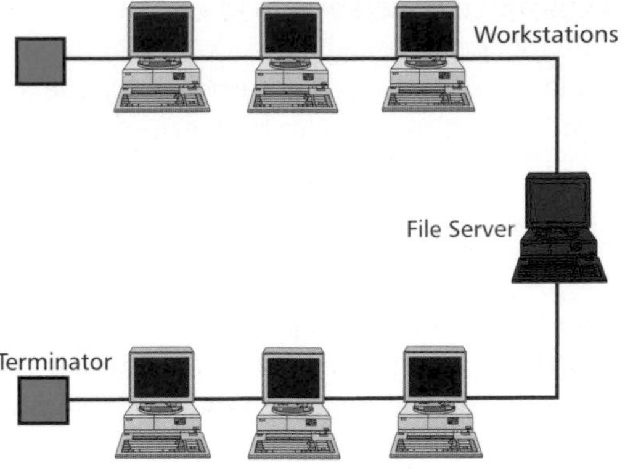

Figure 16.10 A bus network topology

A **bus network** is shown in Figure 16.10. Messages for one machine have to pass by other machines, and so the security of this system is lower than that of a true star network. A bus network is terminated at each end to prevent unwanted reflections of signals. Large bus networks are uncommon as the bandwidth of the network is not used efficiently.

It is better to split up networks into smaller **segments** by the use of **bridges** (see below) or some other means. If this is done, traffic destined for one part of the network does not interfere with traffic for another. If arranged like this it is called segmentation. Without proper segmentation and planning, the performance would be unsatisfactory for all but the smallest of networks.

Another network topology is the **ring network**, as shown in Figure 16.11. The particular system shown in Figure 16.11 is a **token-ring network**. An **electronic token** is passed around the network and grabbed by a machine for a limited period of time. During this time no other machine can transmit information, and thus there is no possibility of collisions, as with the Ethernet system. Don't associate all base-band systems with clashes, because the token ring overcomes this problem.

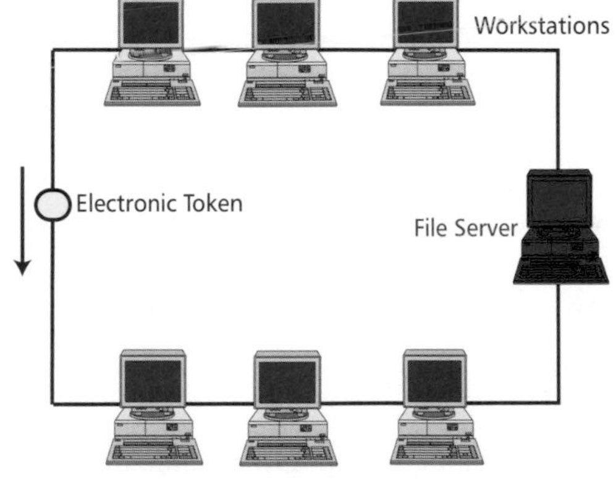

Figure 16.11 A token-ring network topology

Peer-to-peer versus server-based networking

A minimal network can be set up between several PCs without the use of a **file server**. It would be up to the users to share their drives with each other, and for the user with the printer attached to share this printer so that others on the network may make use of it. Security on this type of network would be low, and backups of important work may not be done properly if it is left up to the users. This type of network is called a **peer-to-peer network** because it has been established between your peers who manage and control their own machine.

On larger networks it is not efficient to organise the management in this ad hoc way. If a file server is used instead, it is called a **server-based network**. It is more sophisticated because dedicated server software gives managers access to facilities in terms of security and accounting (see chapter 6 where the security of operating systems was covered).

On large Ethernet networks the network manager would probably prevent users from setting up peer-to-peer networks.

Doing this would prevent students in a school or college from playing unauthorised network games, and prevent communication between computers that could not be monitored or controlled.

Typically file servers with ultra-fast disk drives operating in a **RAID** configuration are suitable for server-based networks. In larger LANs there could be entire **server farms**. Nothing (other than the security imposed by the system managers) stops clients on server-based systems setting up peer-to-peer networks. Managers do not like this as low security and loss of important data can often result from such action.

Example

You have set up a simple network for three computer users. There is one machine with a printer, which needs to be used by all three people. What is the simplest and cheapest way to do this? You may assume that there are three PCs running a recent version of Windows.

Solution

The simplest way is to use peer-to-peer networking. This involves putting an Ethernet card in each machine and connecting them via a hub, in ways identical to those shown in the AS level book. Next you would install the drivers for each of the cards, set up **TCP/IP** and set up shared resources. The printer would need to be shared so that the people who do not have a printer attached can use the shared one. Some folders on each of the disks may need to be shared so users may transfer data using the network.

Managing a complex network of networks

The distance along a network that a signal may travel before degrading is limited. The higher the transmission rate, the less distance can be travelled. A range of different devices help manage these problems and help with the routing too.

Repeaters are simple devices to boost signals so they can travel over longer distances. **Bridges** may also be used to boost the signal so that you end up with a longer physical network. **Intelligent bridges** are used to pass packets from one network to the next or to filter packets so preventing them from using up valuable bandwidth on parts of the network that do not need to be affected.

Example

LANs are being set up in a science department. Chemistry, Biology and Physics wish to run their own network so that traffic does not interfere with any other or with the main school network. They sometimes need to connect to each other, via the school backbone, and the Physics Department is also a long distance from Chemistry and Biology. Show how this network may be implemented using *bridges and repeaters only*.

The decreased price and increased sophistication of Ethernet switches means that they are becoming the norm for management of large Ethernet networks.

Solution

Figure 16.12 shows a possible configuration making use of bridges as a filter. If Physics had a spare bridge available but no repeater, then a bridge (which is set up to let all the traffic through) could have been used instead of the repeater.

In more sophisticated systems, intelligent **switches** could be used instead of bridges. As switches become more cost effective they are becoming popular. A switch performs a similar function to a bridge in that it can either block or let through traffic. However, unlike a bridge, a switch can route a single input to a single output, it can route a single

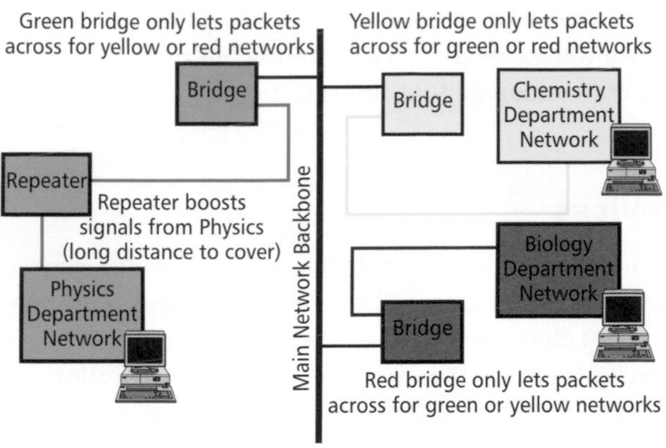

Figure 16.12 Bridges used as a filtering mechanism

The functionality of some of the more sophisticated switches is quite remarkable, and now includes security measures like MAC address filtering, for example, which helps to prevent unauthorised machines from connecting to the Ethernet networks.

input to multiple outputs, or it can concentrate multiple inputs into a single output. The switch boxes may also be programmed from a remote computer via the network. A typical switch interface running in an Internet browser at the author's school is shown in Figure 16.13. It is called a switch because it performs the switching operations described above. Think of it like a telephone exchange which makes connections on demand. It can also be used to connect different computers to maximise the bandwidth.

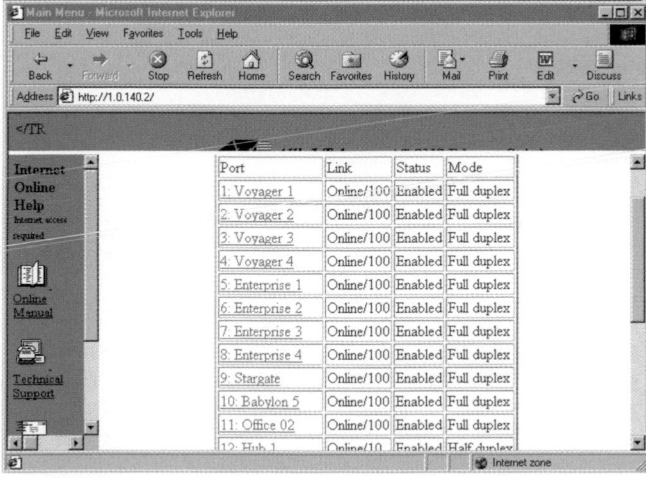

Figure 16.13 Programming a switch

Routers and gateways

Routers provide much functionality and can be implemented either by hardware (special boxes) or **software** (e.g. a **proxy server**). Routers are often used to connect LANs to **WANs**. i.e. they can route Internet requests from multiple users on a LAN, via a **proxy server** to a WAN, for example.

The **TCP/IP protocol** (transmission control protocol/internet protocol) is a good example of sending information via a router. Routers have to communicate with each other to establish how many hops would be needed to get from one part of the WAN to another. If you are in London and type in a Las Vegas hotel website address, then you may be routed via New York, Chicago and Denver to connect to Las Vegas. The routers decide the best available route at the time based on geographical location, availability, current traffic and quality of service. The Internet itself is formed as a vast interconnection of networks, and the computers which help to join these interconnected networks together are known as **gateways**. They often perform protocol conversion so that information may go over many different network links.

The difference between devices

Students are often confused about the terms repeaters, bridges, routers, switches and hubs. This is not surprising, as you will encounter terms like 'hubs', 'managed hubs' and 'switching hubs'. Even experts argue about these definitions, and at the time of writing, consultation of the Usenet newsgroups for networking confirms this. The definitions of these devices have changed over the years, and with the introduction of new technology the functionality of most of these components becomes ever more pervasive. A summary of current usage of this technology is shown in Table 16.1 together with the main ISO OSI levels at which the device operates.

Computing is a very dynamic subject and networking is particularly prone to major advances in new technology.

The definitions shown here should be suitable for examination purposes, but you can expect new components (like the sophisticated switches) to take over the roles played by some of the devices shown here.

You should also realise that networks are usually in place for many years, and all these devices are still in common use today.

Table 16.1 A summary of typical uses for network devices

Gateway	The name often used for computers on the Internet which connect the different parts of the network. These form the glue by which the Internet is constructed. They can also carry out protocol conversion.	These are often computers, and operate at layers 4 and above of the ISO OSI model.
Router	Used to connect the same or different networks. Used on the web to route traffic, or for the connection of a LAN to a WAN. Some routers can handle interconnecting LANs of differing architectures, whether or not they use the same protocol.	This device operates at the network layer (layer 3 of the ISO OSI model).
Switch	Can perform the same function as a bridge, but the box has much more sophistication and can deal with many segments.	This device operates at the data-link layer (layer 2 of the ISO OSI model).
Bridge	Used to block or let through signals. Can be used as an expensive repeater. Depending on type, some bridges are only able to handle the same protocol but others can handle different protocols. For example, Ethernet and token ring. (See Figure 16.12.)	This device operates at the physical layer and data-link layer (layers 1 and 2 of the ISO OSI model).
Repeater	Used to boost signals over longer distances.	This device is related to the physical layer (layer 1 of the ISO OSI model).
Hub	A device allowing many computers to share a network. Here the bandwidth is shared between the computers connected to the hub. (These devices have been covered in the AS level course.)	Depends on the types of hub. E.g. simple, switched, managed etc.

Example

Show how a switch might be used to manage communication between four different computer rooms and a file server, ensuring that the bandwidth is maximised to each room.

Solution

Figure 16.14 shows how the switch manages the connection via a four-port network card. The bandwidth is shared out efficiently according to the traffic in each room.

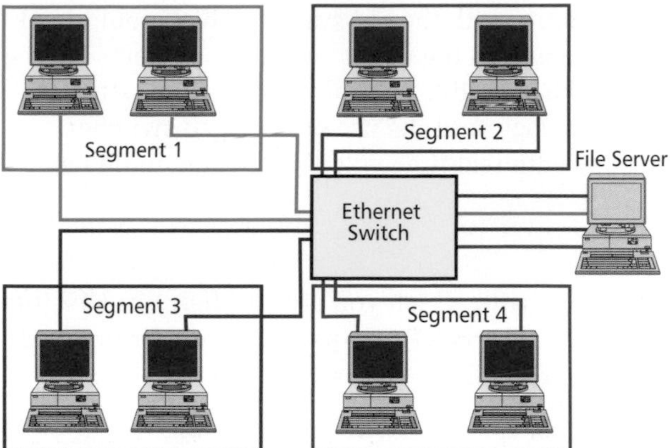

Figure 16.14 A switch used to connect the computer rooms

ATM is a very popular network, especially for use over the Internet, but also for use in LANs.

Although Ethernet dominates the LAN environment, you must not be under the impression that this is the only system available.

You will need to be able to answer questions about ATM in your A2 examinations.

ATM

ATM stands for **Asynchronous Transmission Mode**. Unlike most other networks, this is designed with simultaneous transmission of computer data, **real time voice**, **real time audio** and **real time video** data. It is thus ideal for **multimedia** communications and **videoconferencing**. **Wideband ATM** now allows transmission at just less than 1 Gbit/sec.

ATM is widely utilised in both the LAN and WAN environment. ATM utilises a continuous stream of cells, some of which may actually be empty. This allows the telecommunications companies to manage bandwidth more effectively because ATM is ideally suited to situations in which bursts of transmission may occur.

The telecom providers can also manage the system effectively, providing a **guaranteed bandwidth** down a particular line, even though the line may be used simultaneously by other lower-bandwidth users. This guaranteed bandwidth is essential for real time voice, real time audio and real time video otherwise these systems would not work properly. It also means that the telecommunications providers can charge for the amount of data sent rather than charge for the connection time. ATM is defined by the level 1 and 2 protocols in the ISO OSI model. The **ATM adaptation layer** does the conversion of the audio, video and voice data into the computerised form needed for transmission over the ATM networks. In the ATM network, the basic computer unit is called a cell, and this is a unit of 53 bytes which contains 48 bytes of data, together with a 5 byte header.

Conversion between ATM and Ethernet

Special switches are available to switch between the popular Ethernet network and ATM. Thus PCs working on an Ethernet LAN can make use of the ATM networks, which often provide the high-bandwidth links for the ISPs (internet service providers).

Example

A university is upgrading its existing 100 Mbit/sec Ethernet networks to ATM. Explain why this is not as easy as upgrading to a faster Ethernet technology. Comment on the arguments in favour of upgrading to a faster Ethernet system.

Solution

ATM is a radically different technology to Ethernet, and there is no easy upgrade path. Both systems are incompatible with each other, although it is simple to link Ethernet to ATM (via a suitable switch). It may be more cost effective for the university to upgrade to a faster Ethernet system because of compatibility with the old system, which could work in parallel with the faster Ethernet. It all depends on the use to which the systems will be put, and special consideration of guaranteed bandwidth for multimedia use may be important. With the appropriate network topology, and the use of managed switches, Gigabit Ethernet should also be able to cope with real time voice, video and audio data.

The port number can be tagged on to the end of a standard URL. This is done by writing the port number after a colon. Thus, accessing port number 900 on an e-mail server located on the web called 'mymail.org' i.e.

www.mymail.org

would be done by using a colon and 900 as follows:

www.mymail.org:900

If the server has an IP address of 130.221.67.20, for example, then the same socket can be accessed using

130.221.67.20:900

Note that this is not a 5 byte IP address, but an IP address followed by a colon, followed by the port number.

The TCP/IP protocol stack

The **TCP/IP stack** incorporates many protocols with which you are familiar, like **FTP** (file transfer protocol), **telnet** (terminal emulation) and **SMTP** (simple mail transfer protocol). Over 100 different protocols are supported in the TCP/IP suites.

The TCP/IP stack is a set of **protocols** (layered as a stack), which work together to help machines communicate over a typical network like a LAN and the Internet. The operation is based around **port numbers** on the client machine, which are set up to deal with each different protocol like telnet or FTP. There are 65 535 port numbers that can be assigned to different functions, with port 80 being used for the popular **http protocol**. A port number ensures that the computer sends information to the right software inside the machine so that it can be dealt with without getting mixed up with other information using other protocols. An **IP address** (e.g. the address that identifies a computer on a network) together with a port number, is called a **socket**. (See margin entry.)

Wide area networks

The topologies and methods considered so far typify hardware for a LAN. A **WAN**, or **wide area network**, makes use of the public communication systems. If you are using the phone system to connect to the Internet, then you are using a WAN. Using WANs opens up new possibilities, of which the resources available on the world wide web are just one example, and these are covered in the next few chapters, but first let us see how LANs and WANs may be integrated by using the IP addresses mentioned above.

IP addresses in detail

From the AS work on computing (see the first book in this series) you will appreciate that computers on a LAN may be connected via proxy servers to the Internet (see chapter 18). You will also appreciate from reading this chapter that the *same computers* may simultaneously connect to the Internet, a local **intranet** or to a variety of **services** (applications like **web servers**, **ftp servers** or **telnet**, for example) running on servers either locally, on the Internet or both. All routing is made possible because of clever allocation of IP addresses.

The format of an IP address

The current format for an IP address is four **bytes** separated by dots, as shown in Table 16.2. Thus the theoretical range of addresses are 0.0.0.0 to 255.255.255.255 (shown here in decimal), but some addresses may be allocated for special purposes (see the next margin entry on the next page).

Table 16.2 The IP address format

The format of an IP address – four groups of eight bits separated by dots																																		
1st byte									2nd byte									3rd byte									4th byte							
0	0	0	0	0	0	0	0	.	0	0	0	0	0	0	0	0	.	0	0	0	0	0	0	0	0	.	0	0	0	0	0	0	0	0

Different classes of network IP addresses are an efficient way of organising networks both locally (using a LAN), nationally and internationally (using a WAN). This is accomplished by making use of the available IP addresses in different ways by allocating different ranges of IP addresses to different classes of network. Each class of network has a specific use, and the classes in common operation are Class A, B, C, D and E, as outlined below.

Class A network addresses

A **class A network** address is one in which the first bit of the first byte in the IP address is set to '0', as shown at the top of Table 16.3. In addition to this requirement, the first byte is reserved for the **network IDs** and the remaining three bytes are reserved for the **host IDs**. The network ID determines the number of different networks (sub-networks) and the host ID determines the number of computers (hosts) you may place on a particular network. This helps with **segmentation** and switching organised by the routers and network switches.

Table 16.3 Class A network address

The format of a class A network IP address																																		
1st byte									2nd byte									3rd byte									4th byte							
0	0	0	0	0	0	0	0	.	0	0	0	0	0	0	0	0	.	0	0	0	0	0	0	0	0	.	0	0	0	0	0	0	0	0
The theoretical range of IP addresses for a class A network																																		
Network IDs									Host IDs																									
0	0	0	0	0	0	0	0	.	0	0	0	0	0	0	0	0	.	0	0	0	0	0	0	0	0	.	0	0	0	0	0	0	0	0
0	1	1	1	1	1	1	1	.	1	1	1	1	1	1	1	1	.	1	1	1	1	1	1	1	1	.	1	1	1	1	1	1	1	1

From the bottom half of Table 16.3 we can see that one byte is assigned to the network ID, but the top bit of this should remain zero. Therefore, we have a theoretical maximum of 00000000 to 01111111 or 128 possible different networks using a class A IP address. We also see that three bytes are reserved for the host IDs, and this gives us a possible range of 00000000 00000000 00000000 to 01111111 11111111 1111111 or $2^{24} = 16\ 777\ 215$ hosts (networked computers) per network!

Class B network addresses

A **class B network** address is one in which the first two bits of the first byte in the IP address is set to the bit pattern '10', as shown in the top half of Table 16.4. In addition to this requirement, the first two bytes are reserved for the **network IDs**, and the remaining two bytes are reserved for the **host IDs**.

From the bottom half of Table 16.3 we can see that two bytes are assigned to the network ID, with the top two bits having a pattern '10'. Therefore, we have a theoretical maximum of 10000000 00000000 to 10111111 1111111 or 16 383 possible different networks using a class B IP address. We also see that two bytes are reserved for the host IDs, and this gives us a possible range of 00000000 00000000 to 01111111 11111111 or $2^{16} = 65\ 536$ hosts (networked computers) per network.

Not every IP address is utilised in the ways described in these tables. Network ID number 127 in a class B network address, for example, is used for testing purposes.

Therefore the theoretical maximum number of network IDs or host IDs is never quite reached. However, the figures given in the examples here are good indications of the approximate number of network IDs and host IDs that may be used with a particular class of IP address.

Table 16.4 Class B network address

The format of a class B network IP address						
1st byte		2nd byte		3rd byte		4th byte
1 0 0 0 0 0 0 0	.	0 0 0 0 0 0 0 0	.	0 0 0 0 0 0 0 0	.	0 0 0 0 0 0 0 0
The theoretical range of IP addresses for a class B network						
Network IDs				Host IDs		
1 0 0 0 0 0 0 0	.	0 0 0 0 0 0 0 0	.	0 0 0 0 0 0 0 0	.	0 0 0 0 0 0 0 0
1 0 1 1 1 1 1 1	.	1 1 1 1 1 1 1 1	.	1 1 1 1 1 1 1 1	.	1 1 1 1 1 1 1 1

Class C network addresses

A **class C network** address is one in which the first three bits of the first byte in the IP address is set to the bit pattern '110', as shown in the top half of Table 16.5. In addition to this requirement, the first three bytes are reserved for the network IDs, and the remaining one byte is reserved for the host IDs.

Table 16.5 Class C network address

The format of a class C network IP address						
1st byte		2nd byte		3rd byte		4th byte
1 1 0 0 0 0 0 0	.	0 0 0 0 0 0 0 0	.	0 0 0 0 0 0 0 0	.	0 0 0 0 0 0 0 0
The theoretical range of IP addresses for a class C network						
Network IDs						Host IDs
1 1 0 0 0 0 0 0	.	0 0 0 0 0 0 0 0	.	0 0 0 0 0 0 0 0	.	0 0 0 0 0 0 0 0
1 1 0 1 1 1 1 1	.	1 1 1 1 1 1 1 1	.	1 1 1 1 1 1 1 1	.	1 1 1 1 1 1 1 1

A subnet mask (or address mask) is often used to separate the network IDs from the host IDs.

Subnet is the name given to a network that is part of a larger network.

From your work on machine code (see chapter 2) you already know about masking. Therefore, a subnet mask like 255.255.255.0 could be used to 'look' at the first three bytes but mask out the last byte.

Note that the format is the same as the IP address, and the 'OR function' is used with the actual IP address to let through or pay no attention to particular subnets.

From the bottom half of Table 16.5 we can see that three bytes are assigned to the network ID, with the top two bits having a pattern 110. Therefore, we have a theoretical maximum of 11000000 00000000 00000000 to 11011111 1111111 11111111 or 2 097 151 possible different networks using a class C IP address. We also see that one byte is reserved for the host IDs, and this gives us a possible range of 00000000 to 11111111 or $2^8 = 256$ hosts (networked computers) per network.

Class D and E network addresses

A **class D network** address is one in which the first four bits of the first byte of the IP address start off with the pattern 1110. These are used for multicasting, which enables network managers to clone many machines at the same time. A **class E network** is one in which the pattern of the first four bits of the first byte of the IP address starts off with the pattern 1111. These networks are used for experimental purposes, and from reading this you can now appreciate why not all theoretically possible addresses are actually used.

Self-test questions

1. What is the difference between baseband and broadband techniques of transmission?
2. How might multiplexing be used to enable more than one signal to be sent simultaneously?
3. Explain the difference between circuit switching, message switching and packet switching. What is meant by a virtual circuit?

4 Typically communication systems on a computer system are layered. What is meant by this statement and why is layering used? Give an example of a layered communication system.
5 Outline some scenarios in which twisted pair, coaxial and fibre connections are used.
6 Explain four different types of network topology, giving a typical use for each.
7 Explain how an intelligent switch may be used to increase effective network bandwidth on a large LAN. How might this help with the security of the system?
8 Explain what is meant by the terms 'router', 'hub' and 'repeater'.
9 What advantage, if any, does ATM have over Ethernet?
10 Suggest a type of network and any additional hardware that would be most applicable for the following Ethernet network setups.
   (a) Two computers linked at home to play a computer game.
   (b) Three computers linked at home to share a common printer and Internet connection.
   (c) 100 computers linked together in an office environment.
   (d) 1000 computers linked together on a large school campus.
11 A server has an IP address of 140.234.1.25.
   (a) What class of network is this and why?
   (b) What is the host ID?
   (c) What is the network ID?
12 A client with extensive computing facilities is setting up a LAN and needs to segment it into 15 000 different networks, but will need no more than 200 computers on each segment. What type of network class should be used?

17 Wide area networks

In this chapter you will learn about:

- Electronic data interchange (EDI), public and private networks, value added networks
- On-line service providers and Internet service providers (ISPs)
- Connecting with leased lines, ISDNs, cable modems, dial ups, ADSL and VDSL
- CODECs, inter-networking, routers and gateways

Wide area networks

Local area networks (LANs) were covered in chapter 16. In this chapter we concentrate on wide area networks or WANs.

The Internet is obviously the biggest example of a WAN, but this is such a vast topic that using the Internet is covered separately in chapter 18.

A wide area network or WAN makes use of the public (and private) communication systems provided by companies such as BT. They enable users to send computer data, video, voice and audio data over a *wide geographical area*. This chapter concentrates mainly on the topics associated with WANs and the Internet.

EDI

EDI is Electronic Data Interchange. EDI uses special formats for exchange of information electronically. This could be in the form of invoices or other special documents. An example is the system used by exam boards. Instead of using **OMR** forms (covered in your AS course), the school enters exam marks via a computer. This is convenient as data is in electronic format when it arrives at the board. The board will send special files to the school and data from the school administration system can be transferred across to the EDI files which are then sent back to the board.

EDI is also used in businesses where companies exchange information electronically between themselves or with their customers. Many companies have their own proprietary systems, but the EDI system should be easy to use (via a suitable front end), provide facilities for converting the data into a suitable format, and provide for automatic logging of documents that have been transmitted and received. In this way customers can be confident that the information has been processed properly.

Not many students will have experience of using EDI because they use the Internet for other purposes.

You should appreciate the EDI is a very important tool for many businesses and provides bespoke facilities for different types of transactions.

Private networks

A **private network** is typically set up using a **leased line** (covered in your AS course), or is privately owned and installed by a company. It is available 24/7 without dialling a number, and typical services provided include low band, voice band or wideband. This should *not* be confused with a **virtual private network** or **VPN**, which makes use of the Internet, **encryption** and the **point-to-point tunnelling protocol**. A VPN is like having a private network but it is achieved by using a public network. This important topic is covered below.

Value added networks

A **value added network** or **VAN** is a network in which additional functionality (over and above just carrying your data or voice) is provided. A company providing a value added network service may hire out facilities like the provision of additional security and mailbox facilities (e.g. holding and then forwarding mail and similar documents). In addition to this some companies might provide access to sensitive business information. Up-to-date stock market information (in real time) or specialist databases that may be of benefit to solicitors, doctors, lawyers or other similar professions are also typical examples.

A VAN is ideal for a company that does not want to provide the complex infrastructures (e.g. **web servers**, **mail servers** and **database servers** etc.) that other companies may have set up using the Internet or their own **intranets**. You should contrast a VAN with similar functionality that can be provided by the world wide web.

On-line service providers

An **on-line service provider** is a company such as AOL and CompuServe who provide a huge number of on-line services for their customers. In *addition* to providing Internet access, these companies have huge databases, which their users can access for a variety of services. Typically, services provided by CompuServe are education, business, money, travel and sport etc. Most on-line service providers are also Internet service providers.

Many Computer Science students use the Internet so often that they think they do not have to learn very much about this topic.

Nothing could be further from the truth, as questions about VANs and EDI, for example, reveal!

Internet service providers

An Internet service provider or ISP, also called an **Internet access provider** or **IAP**, provides you with a connection to the Internet. These companies do not have to provide a whole host of other facilities like the added value databases given by the on-line service providers, but the distinction between these two is blurred to say the least. Technically an Internet service provider is someone who provides a connection to the Internet. This means that you dial up (or use a permanent connection), load your browser and away you go.

Whatever method of connection is used, the phone call is usually charged at the same rate as a local call, and connects you to a **point of presence**, which is simply the *equipment* (modems etc.) to connect your phone line to the Internet (see the example below).

Example

You connect to an ISP via a dial-up connection and modem. Draw a diagram showing a typical route between your PC and the ISP network file servers which provides the eventual Internet connection. Make sure that you include a mail server and news server in your diagram, and explain why the ISP might sometimes be busy.

Solution

The modem is connected to one of the ISP's modems via the public telephone network. The connections might be via dial-up connections, as shown in Figure 17.1, or other methods like ISDN, ADSL or a leased line. At the ISP end the terminal server multiplexes your signal on to the ISP's LAN.

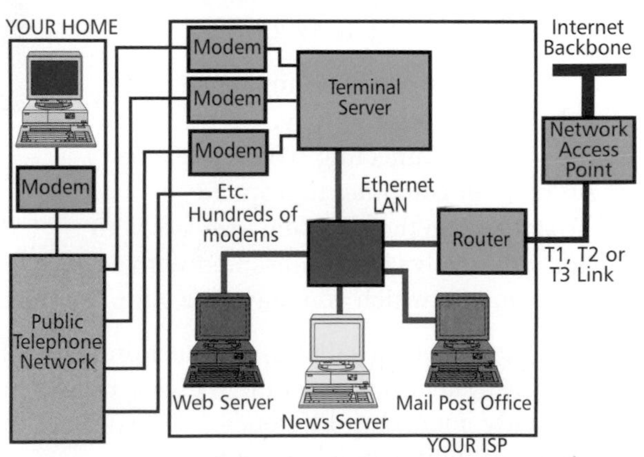

Figure 17.1 Possible methods of connection to your ISP

The web server verifies you have permission to log on and also undertakes any accounting necessary. There is a news server and post office which handles the mailboxes for all of the ISP's customers.

Any request for a web site not cached by the ISP is sent via the router into the Internet backbone via the ISP's NAP or network access point. Large ISPs will have very fast links into the Internet. A T4 line (274.176 Mbit/sec) or even better is typical. An ISP has only a limited number of modems (and telephone lines). When all of these modems are in use you will get a message saying that the line is busy.

As ISPs get busier, larger numbers of modem banks have to be provided to enable a reasonable service. The bandwidth to the Internet backbone might need upgrading if the number of customers becomes very large. Also, when the Internet itself becomes clogged, the response from your ISP, irrespective of the speed of connection, will be slow.

Dial-up connections

For the purpose of A2 examinations, a leased line or ISDN line are the only permanent connections.

Dial-up modems and ADSL are regarded as temporary connections.

A **dial-up connection** is the conventional connection from home, using a **modem**, via the public telephone system, as shown on the left-hand side of Figure 17.1. However, Internet connections are just one use of dial-up. If you have two computers running a recent version of Windows, then you could set up your own peer-to-peer networking via your modems, telephone system and dial-up networking. Dial-up networking would allow you to access a company intranet site via a virtual private network and is ideal for the new breed of road warriors (sales people on the move who need office connectivity). You should realise that this type of connection is *not* regarded as a permanent connection, even if you end up in the unlikely scenario of being constantly connected by dial-up for weeks on end! A dial-up connection is still regarded as a *temporary connection* to the Internet.

Example

A dial-up connection is to be established between two computers in different places. Outline the equipment needed to do this. What software has to be set up using this dedicated connection? (You are not to make use of an ISP for this connection.)

Solution

Both computers will need a modem, a terminal adaptor or some other suitable link. As far as the computer is concerned, the process is virtually identical to connection to an ISP. All you have to do is supply your colleague's phone number as shown in Figure 17.2.

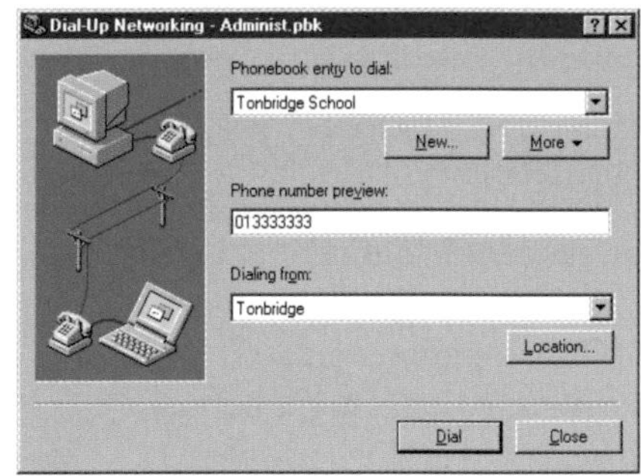

Figure 17.2 Setting up a dial-up connection

The phone book entry can be any name that you wish, but will preferably reflect the place to which you are connecting. Your colleague must set up their computer to respond appropriately when their modem answers your call. This will involve being presented with a log-on screen, into which you may type your user ID and password.

The act of logging in via a dial-up connection is no different from logging in via a network. The system can be set up to give access to the drives that you would see via a LAN. The only noticeable difference is the speed of the connection, which could be quite slow compared with networked connections.

ISDN lines

This is a faster connection called an **integrated services digital network**. Unlike a conventional analogue connection, which needs a dial-up modem to convert the digital signals from the computer into an analogue form, an ISDN connection is digital, although carrier signals obviously still have to be used.

Telecom companies like BT usually provide an ISDN line, and the bandwidth of the line is 64 Kbit/sec. It is a **full-duplex** line, which carries either voice (the normal phone) or data. It is thus ideal for computer communication for use in the home, where the consumer wishes to use the same line for a telephone conversation. ISDN2, which is, in effect, two 64 K ISDN lines, is quite popular. This has the advantage that one line can be used for computer communication while the other line is simultaneously being used for voice. Alternatively you can use both lines for computer data and get an effective bandwidth of 128 Kbit/sec. The number of ISDN lines may be increased above three. ISDN32 would, therefore, be 32 ISDN lines. This is typical of the Internet connection that might be established in an educational organisation like a school or college, for example. ISDN32 would give you a bandwidth of 16 × 128 Kbit/sec (for ISDN2), which is about 2 Mbit/sec. However **ADSL** and **DSL** (see below) may now be more cost effective.

Cable modems

Many homes have cable TV, and Internet connection via this particular method is becoming popular. There are various methods in operation, but it is possible to receive computer data and TV at the same time by assigning a TV channel to computer data.

The advantage of the **cable modem** provided by the TV company is that you do not have to use dial-up connections – you are on-line 24 hours a day, seven days a week (called 24/7) and the connection is instant. Expect between 500 and 1000 Kbit/sec, but also expect to share bandwidth with your neighbours! In practice this means a considerable drop in performance. Sometimes cable companies will remotely program modems to limit the speed with which data can be accessed. There are also one-way cable modems, where the data from the ISP comes in very fast, but the data from the computer is transmitted by the conventional telephone system. Obviously this is less satisfactory than the cable modems described above.

ADSL

ADSL is an **asynchronous digital subscriber line**. It is obviously a digital system, and the asynchronous part means that the data you can receive is at a different rate to the data you can transmit. Usually the send data rate is 256 Kbit/sec, and the receive data rate can be anything up to a few Mbit/sec depending on the cable used and the distance from the telephone exchange. Typically the receive rate would be 500 Kbit/sec or 1 Mbit/sec, but faster speeds are available. BT launched the ADSL service for consumers in June 2000, but not all exchanges were ready.

The asynchronous nature of the **full-duplex communication** is quite favourable for normal web surfing where information transmitted by the client is usually trivial in comparison to the data received. It would obviously be less useful if you are intending to send as much information as you receive. It is not recommended that you host a web site by this method. Fortunately, ADSL is ideal for home and office use, and is now becoming the norm. Faster ADSL connections are also popular in education.

ADSL is now a popular method of connection for those who live near to an appropriately equipped telephone exchange.

For those who live in areas not served by ADSL, an ISDN line will provide similar or better bandwidth, but at a cost!

If ADSL is not available in your area, satellite links may also be possible, but again at some considerable cost.

DSL and VDSL

DSL stands for **digital subscriber line** and uses technology similar to that used by ADSL, but it offers the same uplink bandwidth as opposed to ADSL which offers a slower **uplink** speed. The speed of DSL at the time of writing is between 128 Kbit/sec and 8 Mbit/sec depending on your telecom provider and the amount you are prepared to pay for the connection. The next generation of ADSL is **VDSL**. This stands for **very** *high-speed* **digital subscriber line** or **very** *high bit rate* **digital subscriber line**. Assuming that you are close enough to a quality connection (i.e. near enough to a suitably equipped telephone exchange) the speed of connection can be anything up to 22 Mbit/sec.

Example

A department in a school has asked your advice on the merits of ISDN compared with ADSL. They already have a 128 K ISDN line serving 25 machines on a network, and too often it is painfully slow. They need to know if switching to an ADSL line will give better performance. Outline the pros and cons of each case, explaining why fast connections may actually be quite slow on occasions, and what might be happening in practice in the classroom to slow down this network connection.

Solution

A 128 K ISDN line would normally be quick enough for a single user under optimum conditions. If the site they are trying to use is very busy, then any fast link will be slow because access to this particular site would be dictated by the response of the server hosting it. It also depends on how many people share bandwidth at the exchange end.

A 128 K ISDN line shared between 25 users may well be satisfactory under some conditions, but the response could be slow if an individual on the network is downloading a large file. As an example, Service Pack 2 for Windows XP professional contains a file of about 250 Mbytes! Even at 128 Kbits/sec, this download would theoretically take 16 384 seconds, or about 4.5 hours, but it is likely to take longer in practice, even assuming that one student hogs all the available bandwidth. If selfish students do this frequently, then the response will be slow.

Assuming that the line is used only to surf the net, i.e. not to host a web site or send thousands of e-mail messages, an ADSL line should give much better performance because of the increased bandwidth from the ISP to the school. Even with the significant increase in bandwidth offered by the ADSL line, you may have to share the bandwidth to get onto the Internet backbone.

To sum up, the ADSL should give a significant increase in performance unless the local telephone exchange to which you are connected cannot cope. In this case you may need to consider a leased line, as described below.

Leased lines are popular for large institutions and for Internet service providers.

Fast lines are expensive, but are extremely reliable and available 24/7.

Leased lines

A **leased line** connection is a *permanent connection* to your ISP. The speed of this type of connection varies enormously, but you obviously have no phone bills to pay. A leased line is also known as a dedicated line, and these typify the sort of connection used by universities and large commercial organisations. Table 17.1 shows typical connection speeds for different leased lines at the time of writing. The second column gives the multiples of 64 Kbit/sec. Thus a T1 line is 24 × 64 Kbit/sec = 1536 Kbit/sec.

Table 17.1 Typical data transmission rates of leased lines

Line type	Multiples	Transmission rate (Bit/sec)
T1	24 × 64K	1.536 Mbit/sec
T2	4 × T1	6.312 Mbit/sec
T3	28 × T1	44.736 Mbit/sec
T4	6 × T3	274.176 Mbit/sec

Leased lines are expensive but would speed up Internet access. They are for large institutions that can afford tens of thousands of pounds each year. As new technologies such as ADSL, DSL and VDSL come on stream, and if the number of Internet users continues to rise at its present pace, the demands on the bandwidth of the **Internet backbones** and **file servers** will be enormous. Fortunately the telephone infrastructure is being continually upgraded, and digital connectivity is now largely completed in the UK. Cable and satellite companies are providing extra bandwidth too, and companies like CISCO are striving to keep the communication nodes up to speed.

There is a constant struggle between the available bandwidth and the facilities which people expect from the net. There are now hundreds of radio stations and some TV stations broadcasting over the net and even people with low-bandwidth links expect these services to work efficiently! As soon as the bandwidth is raised, the technology and software moves on, and video phones, free telephone calls anywhere in the world, live pop concerts on the net and a whole host of other activities will ensure that the bandwidth needs to be increased still further.

CODECs

The term **CODEC** stands for **coder/decoder**, which could be an electronic device or a piece of software for converting digital signals (like audio and some video) into digital form enabling them to be transmitted over a digital communication link or processed in some way by a computer. Part of the requirement for **ATM**, for example, would be to generate voice signals, which are obviously analogue in nature (covered in the AS book), and change them into the appropriate form to send over an ATM communication network. In this way the system can replace conventional analogue voice and video connections. The modern trend is to record video onto MPEG2, which is already in digital form so that it may be broadcast over a digital link (see margin entry).

CODECs are under continuous development to keep up with the latest audio, video and other multimedia standards.

There are several web sites where you can download a large number of CODECs for free, and these enable you to keep your computer up to date quite easily.

Software CODECs are used extensively to compress and decompress data such as sound and images when being transmitted over networks like the Internet. Typical examples of these CODECs are MPEG and WMA Audio.

Internetworking

The term **internetworking** means connecting two or more different networks together. The Internet (i.e. the world wide connection of networks) is the largest example of internetworking. We have already seen how disparate networks can be connected together from a LAN point of view, and the principles are very similar indeed for a **WAN**. A good example of internetworking would be **JANET** (the **Joint Academic Network**), or **SuperJANET** as it has now become, set up for the British higher education system. It links universities like Edinburgh with Newcastle, Leeds, Nottingham, London, Southampton, Bristol, Birmingham, Oxford, Cambridge, Exeter and Cardiff to name but a few. The London area is an internetworking system in itself, linking UCL, Imperial College, South Bank and the University of Greenwich plus others, and the Manchester area has a vast internetworking system too.

The Internet is *not* managed by anyone, and can be regarded as thousands of individual networks connected together, where each network is connected, owned, managed and run by hundreds of different public and private companies and individuals. We have already seen the importance of **protocols** and the ISO OSI model, and as long as everybody agrees on these and any new standards that may come to light (like DSL and VDSL, for example) then it should all work together as a network of networks quite effectively. The Internet obviously takes internetworking to its ultimate limit, and chapter 18 concentrates on some of the management structures imposed on the Internet by a variety of international and national standards organisations.

Self-test questions

1. **Define the terms 'WAN', 'EDI' and 'VAN'.**
2. **What is the difference between an on-line service provider and an Internet service provider or ISP?**
3. **Explain the terms 'analogue dial up', 'leased line', 'ADSL' and 'cable connection'.**
4. **What is a CODEC?**
5. **What does the term 'internetworking' mean?**
6. **DSL and VDSL are recent extensions to the ADSL technology. What extra functionality do DSL and VDSL provide?**

18 The Internet

In this chapter you will learn about:

- The world wide web, Internet registries and Internet registrars
- The client/server model of the Internet, http protocols and hyperlinks
- Web sites, web page construction, the organisation of pages on a web site
- FTP, Telnet, the role of URLs in the retrieval of web documents
- Internet search engines and web browsers, Java, applets and active server pages
- E-mail, usenet, Internet relay chat, video conferencing, on-line shopping and banking
- The moral, ethical, social and cultural issues arising from the use of the Internet
- Security on the Internet, firewalls, encryption and digital certificates

The world wide web

The Internet is a vast network of networks communicating with each other making use of the TCP/IP protocol. The IP protocol ensures that data, in the form of **packets**, is *sent to the right destination* (see below) and the TCP protocol makes sure that the *packets are assembled in the right order* (see **packet switching** in chapter 16). At the heart of the Internet lie the high-speed backbones, which link the **node computers**, and **routers** which manage computer data by routing it around the world, sending it to and from the computers connected to the Internet.

To be technically correct, if Internet is spelt with a 'capital I' it refers to the world wide network of networks, but if it is spelt with a 'lower case i' it is simply a term for a 'network of networks', which may not actually refer to the Internet itself, but a smaller network of networks.

It is common practice in the press to use either a capital I or a lower case i to mean the same thing, but in an examination, if you are asked about the difference between the Internet and an internet, you need to provide the above explanation.

An 'upper case I' has been used throughout this book to refer to the Internet.

IP addresses

Each computer connected *directly* to the Internet (i.e. not hiding behind a **proxy server**) needs a unique ID. This is so that packets may be sent to the right destination. This unique ID is given by numbers called Internet protocol address or IP address. IP addresses have already been covered in great detail in chapter 16.

Routing devices make use of IP addresses, but humans prefer a user-friendly system making use of **domain names**. If, for example, you access Tonbridge School's web site, the full domain name, including the protocol, is given by http://www.tonbridge-school.co.uk. After it is typed into the browser, this would be converted into the 32-bit number (four lots of eight binary octets) or, in decimal, 81.91.108.5, which at the time of writing is the IP address for this particular subsection of the '.uk' **domain**.

The domain name system

The Internet is organised hierarchically by the **domain name system** or **DNS**. At the top level are domains like .com or .org, for example. We have one unique name for each individual domain; therefore, www.widget.com may be a different company from www.widget.co.uk. We are rapidly running out of domain names, and so new domains like .web, have been developed. The .com names are still *the* most prestigious.

Internet registries

A **registry** is a **database**, held on computers placed at strategic points on the **Internet**, so domain names can be used. A **name server**, also called a **host**, is needed to perform the function of converting the domain names into the IP addresses. These are provided by ISPs (Internet service providers) such as CompuServe and AOL, for example. The registry itself contains only the domain names, IP numbers and server names. At the top of this hierarchy are **root servers** that contain authoritative data for the .com, .net, .fr and .uk etc. domains, and these are located in the US, UK, Sweden and Japan.

Students who have set up their own web sites (not as part of the package often provided by an on-line service provider) will have registered their name and site with one of the Internet registrars.

Once a unique name has been chosen, and the appropriate sum has been paid, the registrar will register the site and it should be available for use in about a day or so, once the new information has been uploaded to the Internet registry held by root servers. This information is then propagated to the name servers in due course.

Internet registrars

Internet registrars are organisations that register domain names for individuals and companies with the **primary domain name servers**, like '123 Domain Names UK' for example. Many different companies are licensed to act as Internet registrars.

The client server model of the Internet

You are already aware of the **client server model** from a LAN point of view, i.e. many different servers providing a range of functions such as application delivery, database access and other information. You can imagine the entire Internet operating on this strategy too, with millions of servers and hundreds of millions of clients connected. The **domain name servers** deal with routing requests, root servers organise the system world wide, and millions of other **servers** host individual sites.

The HTTP protocol

The **HTTP**, or **hypertext transfer protocol**, is one method by which pages are transferred from **web servers** to the **browser** on your local machine. It is thus a **client server model** making use of the TCP/IP protocol. As an example, the **URL** (uniform resource locator) for NatWest's on-line banking at the time of writing is https://www.nwolb.com/secure/default.asp. The http protocol is being used, and the 's' at the end of https stands for '**secure**', which in this case allows for 128-bit encryption through a **secure port** to NatWest Bank's computer. The resource being run is the default **active server page**, which interacts with NatWest's database to control the session. Each time you log on a different ID number is generated. This would typically be something like the following, which together with the time and date provides a unique ID: https://www.nwolb.com/secure/default.asp?refereridentt=10175525.

URLs are considered in more detail later on in this chapter.

Data like 'customer number' is entered in the boxes (fictitious data is shown in Figure 18.1), and, if successful, the next screen will prompt you to enter three characters from your PIN and three characters from your password. If this is successful too, you will gain access to your account, enabling you to look at balances, transfer money, manage debit and credit cards and perform a variety of other useful functions.

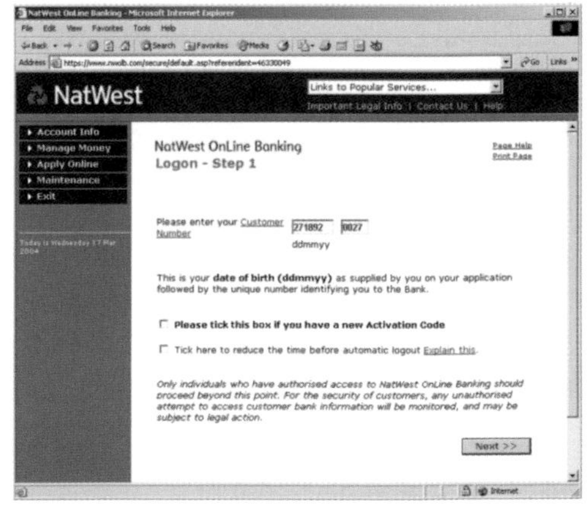

Figure 18.1 An active server page log on

The structure of a web site

To construct a good web site you need to define a hierarchical structure. As an example, consider the web site designed by the author for the Computer Science department at

Tonbridge School. The **main page** is shown in Figure 18.2.

The author's intranet site has been chosen because the structure is very easy to see from the main page. It consists of information about the department, getting help, academic, resources, ICT library, timetable/booking, site map, school maps, school links and other links.

Each subsection on the main page links to other pages, and the academic page can be seen in Figure 18.3. The academic page also has links to other pages like Careers and Computing Courses etc. Click over the Computing Courses link and you are diverted to the computing courses pages for each year in the school, including AS Computing and A2 Computing.

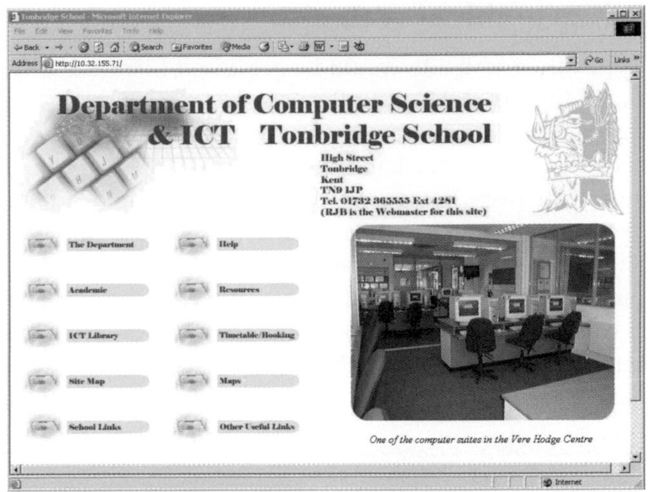

Figure 18.2 The author's departmental intranet site

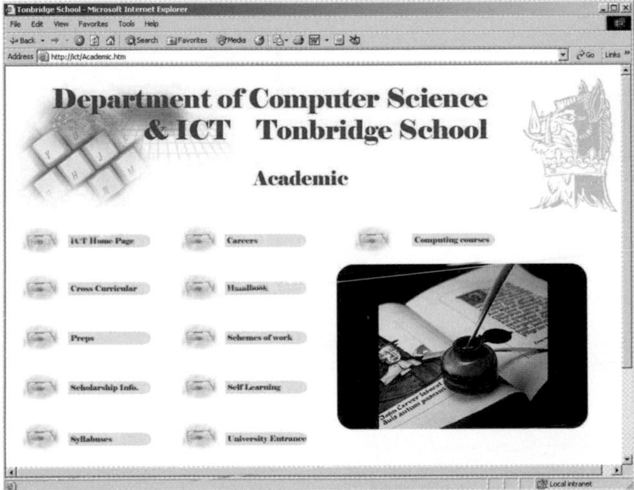

Figure 18.3 The academic section of the author's site

There is always an ICT home page button (shown in red), which returns you to the main page shown in Figure 18.2 if you get lost. A search engine is available from the main page to navigate through the site without making use of the hierarchical structure. There are over 35 000 pages of information on the author's intranet site, and a well-structured site is needed to manage this information in an effective way.

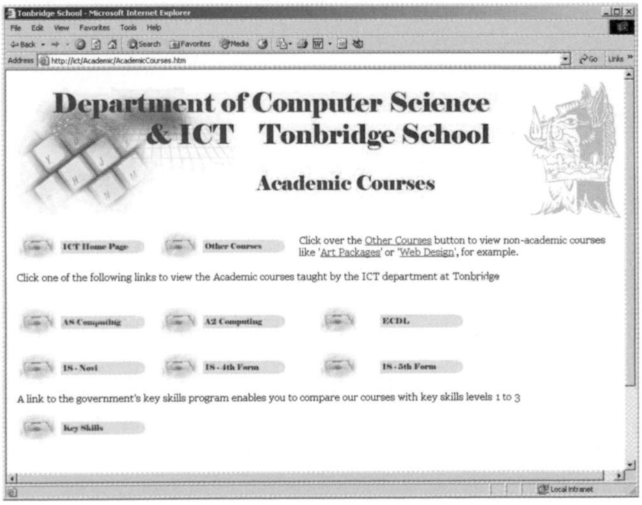

Figure 18.4 The detailed courses section

Designing a web site makes a good A2 project only if it links to a database or some other similar functionality.

The static pages demonstrated here would not be sufficient for an A2 project, even if all 35 000 of these pages were to be submitted!

For an A2 project, interaction with the user would be required, and the part of the author's site which does this is the on-line booking system enabling resources to be booked from the LAN or via the VPN from home.

The booking system part of this site uses Active Server pages, and therefore makes an ideal A2 project.

A hierarchical web site structure

Typically a web site would be organised hierarchically, with the main page being called index.htm and placed in the root folder. Figure 18.5 shows Macromedia's Dreamweaver MX suite being used to edit the page which explains about the computers at the author's school. On the right-hand side of Figure 18.5 you can clearly see the structure of the web site. The page being edited is inside the folder called Department, and has a name TonbridgeSchool.htm. This particular page is an interactive map of a diagram which shows the interrelations between the administrative and academic departments, the computer centre, the boarding houses, the virtual private network and the students' homes. If a web site is not organised hierarchically, and if resources like diagrams, mouse over buttons and PDF files etc. belonging to a particular section of the web site cannot be found easily, then a large site like this one would become unmanageable.

It makes life considerably easier if you design a web site making use of a special-purpose application package like Macromedia's Dreamweaver MX.

Learning HTML code to the standard required for the production of a professional web site is not necessary at A2 level, and the facilities of these packages help to design a WYSIWYG site quite easily.

However, you do need to know what HTML code is, and understand the structure of a simple set of typical HTML commands. These are covered a little later in this chapter.

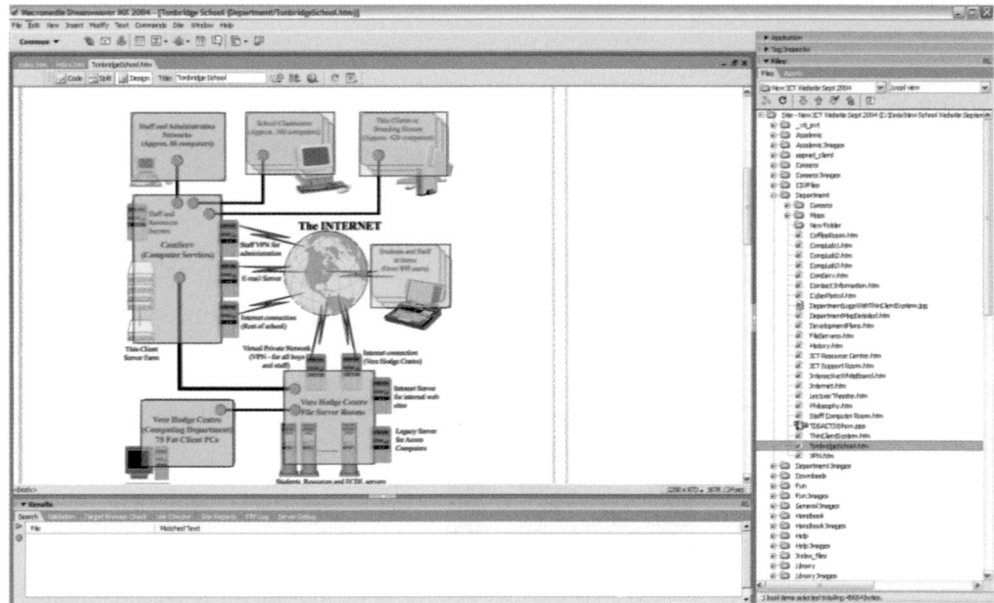

Figure 18.5 The structure of the author's web site being displayed in Dreamweaver

The rectangular boxes are visible only in editing mode, and they represent the areas over which the user may hover the mouse, and then click to go to the appropriate page which explains these different parts of the diagram in more detail.

Example

Suggest a web site structure for a shop selling electrical goods from washing machines to video recorders. You must consider that customers may make on-line purchases.

Solution

The goods customers buy can be categorised into main sections. The following is typical:

1 Household (washing machines etc.)
2 Sound and Vision (video recorders etc.)
3 Personal Electrical (shavers etc.)
4 Computers (PCs, printers etc.)

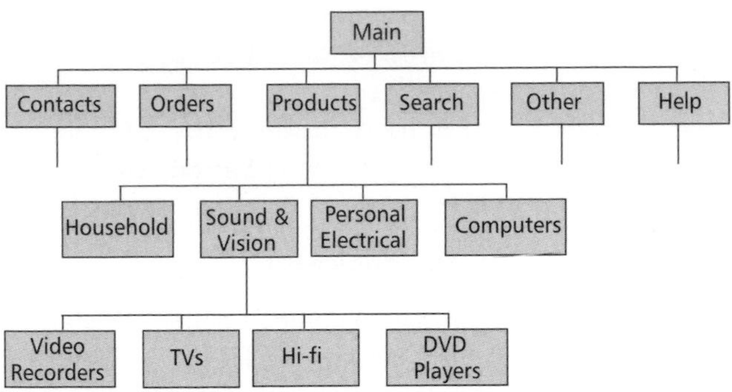

Figure 18.6 A possible web site structure for the shop

In practice there may be other categories, but the above is suitable for illustration. Each of the above categories has subsections. The Sound and Vision category could be split up into video recorders, TVs, hi-fi, DVD players etc. Each section could have a picture of the devices, together with general information and price, and a hyperlink on which you can click to add the device to your order. However, it might be preferable to split these sections further. The TV section could be split into portable, conventional and wide screen. The ordering system itself would be a major subsection. It could consist of the typical shopping-trolley idea, into which customers can put their order. The customers would have to be confident with the system, and secure transactions using a credit card would need to be implemented. You also need help, contact addresses and store information etc. if the shop has more than one branch. Therefore, the following are typical of the main categories that need to be added to those considered above.

1 Secure ordering system
2 Help system (use of site, place an order)
3 Company contact (address + telephone number + e-mail)
4 Search engine (a means of searching the site for specific information)
5 Other information (e.g. special offers or new lines etc.)
6 Branch information (locate the stores within this group)

The original markup languages were used to help university researchers find information quickly.

A universally acceptable language enabled people to find information more easily via wide area networks, and the Internet started from these basic ideas.

Constructing web pages

The main language used to construct a web site is called **HTML**, or **hypertext markup language**. A web page is an HTML file, usually with extra graphics and maybe other resources like JavaScript (see below). The file is made up from text-based HTML commands. A markup language is used to control the layout of a page. Any web site can be constructed using a *simple* **text editor** like Microsoft's Notepad. Simply type in the **HTML commands** and you can construct a satisfactory site. The *structure* of an extremely simple site, containing the word 'Hello', and displayed in an Internet browser in Figure 18.7, could be as follows:

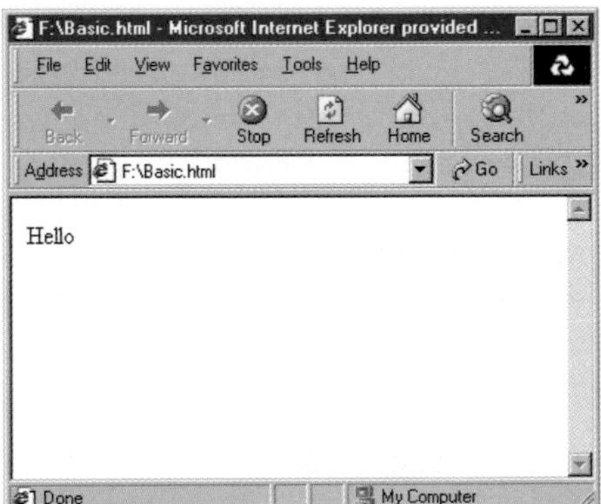

Figure 18.7 A very simple web site

```
<HTML>          This marks the opening of an HTML document.
  <HEAD>        This is the head of the document. A title and
  </HEAD>       other information could go here.
  <BODY>        This is the main body of the HTML document. It
    Hello       contains all the things which get displayed in
  </BODY>       the user's browser.
</HTML>         This marks the end of an HTML document.
```

HTML commands are contained within <tags>, many of which come in pairs. The start of the HTML document is given by <HTML> and the end is given by </HTML>. No heading information is used in this example, and the body consists of the single word 'Hello'. The comments, shown in green text (*not* part of the HTML document) are to help understand the use of the tags on the left-hand side. Sophisticated sites can be constructed like this – it is easy as long as you learn all the HTML commands.

The hyperlinks

Hyperlinks can be placed anywhere on a page, and 'href' commands provide links between the current position and the destination document, another HTML page or some other resource. The code for the 'Academic web page' in Figure 18.3 now follows:

```
<td colspan="4"><a href="Index.htm"
onMouseOut="MM_swapImgRestore()" onMouseOver="MM_swapImage('Home
Page','','Main%20Menu%20Images/HomePageWhiteButton.jpg',1)"><img
name="Home Page" border="0"
src="Main%20Menu%20Images/HomePageBlueButton.jpg" width="126"
height="20"></a></td>
          <td> </td>
          <td> </td>
          <td colspan="4"><a href="Careers/Careers.htm"
onMouseOut="MM_swapImgRestore()"
onMouseOver="MM_swapImage('Careers','','Handbook%20Images/Careers
WhiteButton.jpg',1)"><img name="Careers" border="0"
src="Handbook%20Images/CareersBlueButton.jpg" width="126"
height="20"></a></td>
          <td> </td>
          <td> </td>
          <td colspan="4"><a href="Academic/AcademicCourses.htm"
onMouseOut="MM_swapImgRestore()" onMouseOver="MM_swapImage
('Academic Courses','','/Academic%20Images/ComputingCourses
WhiteButton.jpg',1)"><img
name="Academic Courses" border="0"
src="/Academic%20Images/ComputingCoursesBlueButton.jpg"
width="126" height="20"></a></td>
```

One of the links (the button with ICT home page shown in red) takes you back to the main page shown in Figure 18.2. The main page is 'index.htm', and the href for this link (`href="Index.htm"`) is shown in the above code. The code looks complex because this link is not simple text but an image which changes to another one (simulating a colour change) when you hover over it with the mouse. Two other references `href="Careers/Careers.htm"` and `href="Academic/AcademicCourses.htm"` make links to the Careers page, and the Academic courses page, an HTML page called

AcademicCourses.htm. You should note that all these href commands are *relative* to the **root directory** of the site, which contains the Careers and Academic directories.

These tabulation commands like `<td colspan="4">` make the HTML code appear to be much more complex than it actually is. They are simple in themselves, and control a tabular layout. Also, all the **hyperlinks** refer to information within the author's intranet web site. Hyperlinks will also need to point to other web sites, and this will involve using the full **URL** as described earlier in this chapter.

Always use relative path names and never use absolute path names. If a site is subsequently moved to a new place, the relative path names will always work. Never use links to local resources because these almost certainly will not be available when you publish the web site either on an intranet server or on the Internet (i.e. do not use links like `"C:\index\subject"` ***which would work only on the local machine on which the web site was created.***

WYSIWYG HTML editors and web site creation tools

Web site design is much easier with a **WYSIWYG HTML editor**. Instead of a text editor like Microsoft's Notepad, you can use a purpose built **HTML editor** like Arachnophilia. This enables you to create web sites much more easily than coding in HTML directly. Figure 18.8 shows the Arachnophilia front end. A colour menu is currently being displayed, which helps the user considerably.

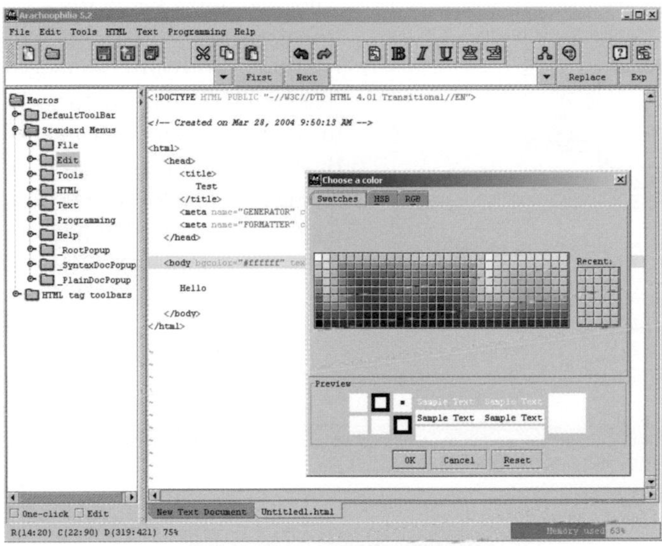

Figure 18.8 An HTML editor being used to change some colour

Just like the visual program development environments covered in the AS level course, similar functionality is provided specifically for helping with web site design. At the time of writing, the most sophisticated of these development systems is Macromedia's Dreamweaver, which is shown helping the author to develop his site in Figure 18.5.

Make sure you appreciate the difference between transferring files (with ftp or mail attachments) and viewing information via a web browser.

The FTP protocol

The **FTP** (**file transfer protocol**) allows users to *transfer files* from one computer to another in a client server network. It is ideal for transferring files on LANs and WANs which make use of the **TCP/IP** protocol. It is an ideal mechanism for transferring files that would be much too large for most e-mail attachments, for example. (Most ISPs provide limits on the size of attachments that you can send.) Some **FTP file servers** (see margin entry) enable users to log in anonymously so that they can download files from the server (most web servers can be set up to support FTP). The **user ID** is often anonymous and the **password** is often the user's e-mail address.

FTP is currently *the* most common way to publish a site because files can easily be uploaded to an **FTP server**. Using CuteFTP software is one way of doing this, as shown in

You may not appreciate the need for FTP if you have not tried to transfer large files using these other methods. A file server must be set up appropriately and have the ftp protocols installed for this to work.

In addition to Telnet you can also use VNC for remote administration.

To remotely administer a server in a GUI environment you may use software like VNC (this establishes a Virtual Network Connection). Assuming that the VNC client and server software have been set up on the appropriate machines, you can VNC into the server (or indeed another client) and remotely administer their machines. This would enable you to run any software on this machine as though you were actually sitting at the remote machine.

Figure 18.9. If you have designed a simple site making use of the relative path names suggested above, have used a suitable directory structure, and have a main HTML file labelled 'index.HTML' in the root directory, it is probably ready to be published.

From Figure 18.9 you can see that the site, constructed and saved on the hard disk, is identified by CuteFTP and displayed in the left-hand window. You then run a Wizard, into which you type information regarding your ISP, a label to identify the site, the address of the FTP server, a default directory from which to obtain the site, and, most importantly, a **user ID** and **password**, which will be used to help manage the site. The files to upload are shown on the left of Figure 18.9. The uploaded files would be shown on the right after the wizard has processed the information. Once you have made the FTP transfer your site is up and running. Software packages like CuteFTP also enable you to manage your site effectively. You can make a change to one or just a few pages without having to upload the entire site again.

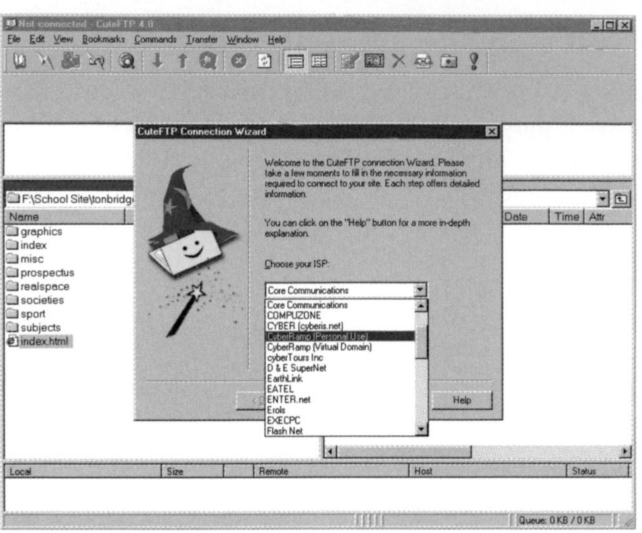

Figure 18.9 Using CuteFTP to upload a web site

Telnet

Telnet is a **protocol** enabling users to *manage a remote computer* connected to the Internet. A typical **Telnet terminal** is shown in Figure 18.10. After logging on, assuming that you have the appropriate privileges on the remote computer, it is as though you are sitting at the keyboard of the remote computer. The Telnet console operates in a very similar way to a conventional DOS-based window. Web servers may be remotely administered by using Telnet (see margin entry above).

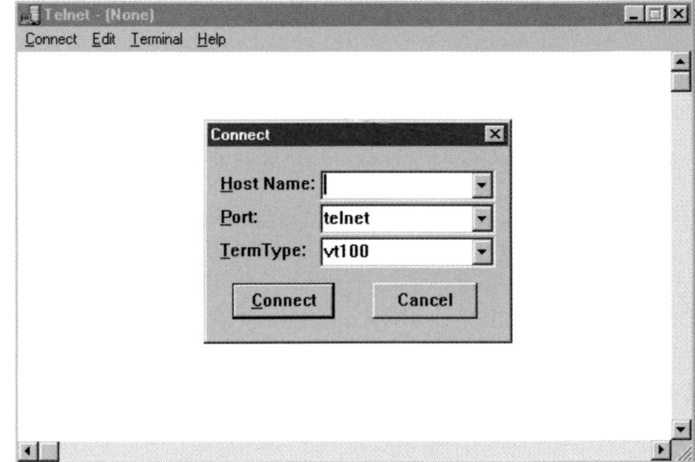

Figure 18.10 Logging on for a Telnet session

Internet search engines

To locate information on the web we make use of a **search engine** like Google, for example. This popular search engine is shown in Figure 18.11. It offers options to search the web for images, newsgroups and general news etc. The http://www.google.co.uk version of the engine also gives you the option of searching for pages in the UK, which is particularly useful if you are shopping.

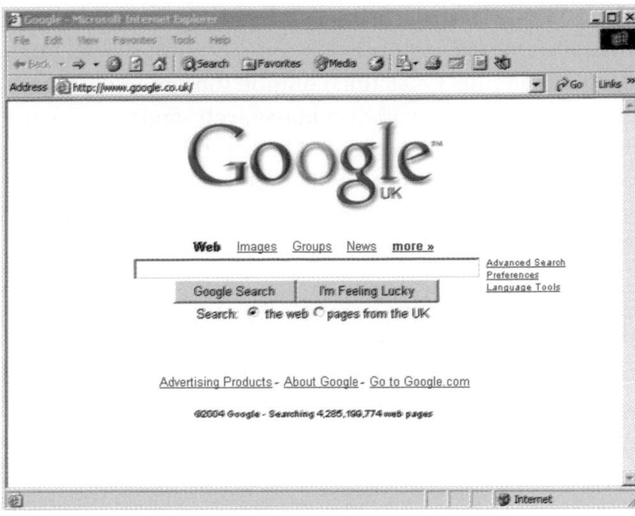

Figure 18.11 The Google search engine

As an example of a simple search, to find the CuteFTP software used to upload a web site in Figure 18.10, we simply type 'CuteFTP' into the Google search engine, which, at the time of writing this book, got the results shown in Figure 18.12. You can see that Google returned the appropriate references to the CuteFTP site in 0.32 seconds. There are also 327 000 references to CuteFTP! Without search engines the Internet would be extremely hard to use. The search engines make finding information relatively easy, but you will need to learn some appropriate techniques if you wish to get relevant information in an efficient manner.

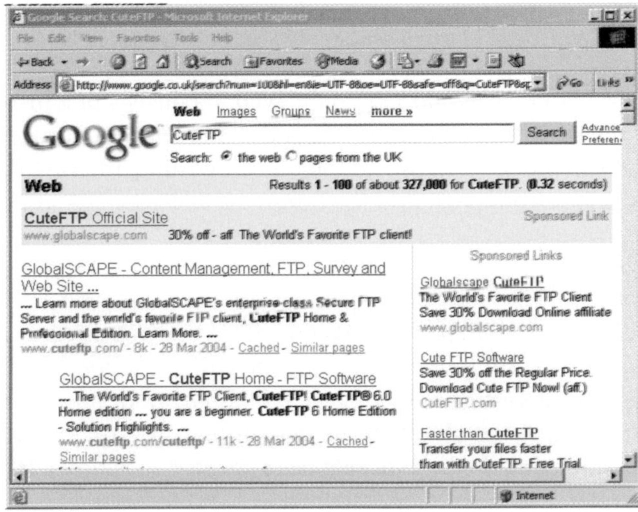

Figure 18.12 Searching for the CuteFTP software

Different search engines have slightly different ways of operating, but this is an advantage, otherwise identical results may be returned by them all! It's unlikely, for example, that you would know that 'CuteFTP' is one word unless you were familiar with this software. Therefore, searching for 'Cute FTP' would probably give you all the references to 'Cute' and to 'FTP', whether or not they occur together! To overcome this problem most search engines would have an intelligent default, and might come up with a message like 'Did you mean CuteFTP?' Most search engines allow the user to enter search strings like 'Cute FTP' or 'Cute + FTP', but the syntax varies from one search engine to the next. The best advice is to learn how the search engine operates.

Top-of-the-range search engines like Google permit a huge variety of search techniques.

You could, for example, search only for pdf documents created in the last three months on a specific web site!

Using facilities like these, in combination with the usual Boolean operators, for example, gives very powerful search parameters indeed.

Learn these techniques and you could save a lot of time when using search engines.

Search techniques

You should refine your search techniques and use the **Boolean operators** like **AND**, **OR** and **NOT** when necessary. Also, make use of the + signs for inclusion and the – sign for exclusion. Remember that most search engines have advanced search options and help. Make use of this if you are not sure of the syntax for a particular engine. When performing

It's usually obvious if you have clashed with another use of one of your key words while conducting a search, and other search strings can easily be built up if you inadvertently hit on your words being used in a different context.

Remember the international nature of the Internet. Searching for a term like 'football' is likely to bring up 'American football', so, if you were interested in the British or European game, then searching for the term 'soccer' might be a better alternative.

a search you are not actually searching the entire web, you are searching a database or several databases compiled by one or more search engines. There are basically two types of search engine. Ones that compile their own databases and ones that search other search engines which are called **meta-search engines**. Dogpile is an example of a meta-search engine. The search engines that compile their own databases do so by employing electronic robots called **bots**, which go trawling the web pages and then compile lists of key words. It's also possible to submit the address of your own site to be added to particular search engine database.

Example

Using appropriate syntax for a search engine with which you are familiar, suggest a search string for each of the following search criteria. You must ensure that only the appropriate sites are listed, eliminating unwanted possibilities.

(a) Search for the computer programming language called Python.

(b) Search for the Python reptile.

(c) Search for Monty Python.

Solution

The following are suggested syntax for finding the above information quickly.

(a) Python –Monty –Snake (b) Python +Snake (c) Python +Monty

URLs in more detail

A **URL** is a **uniform resource locator**, which is an address on the web. It consists of a **protocol** like http or FTP, the name of the server on which the site is hosted, and perhaps the path name of the particular HTML document of interest. At the time of writing, the HTML document representing the *Sunday Times* front page is at the following address:

http://www.sunday-times.co.uk/news/pages/times/frontpage.HTML

http is the hypertext transfer protocol. The web server on which the site resides is //www.sunday-times.co.uk. The individual HTML page is located within the web site hierarchy at /news/pages/times/frontpage.HTML. By typing in a complete URL for a document you can go straight to a specific page of interest on a specific site, *but individual pages do change frequently as sites are restructured*. Remember that the default port for http is port 80, not shown here, but described in more detail when **sockets** were covered in chapter 16.

Web browsers

To surf the net you need an **Internet browser** or **browser**, and a typical one is shown in Figure 18.11. The two most popular browsers are Microsoft's Internet Explorer and Netscape's Browser. Both provide a similar degree of functionality, enabling users to surf the net, compile lists of favourites, print or save web sites, manage secure transactions using strong encryption techniques and provide a history of what you have done etc. Browsers organise and store a large amount of information, and Figure 18.13 reveals information about User ID (which can be set as an alias to prevent junk mail from sites you are visiting), **newsgroups**, push databases, **e-mail** records, histories, URL windows, **cookies**, favourites, caches and start documents.

Things like sites you have visited and what you do on a day-to-day basis leave a trail of information which can easily be stored. Figure 18.13 also shows the cookies directory, containing 51 different cookies stored from recently visited sites. A cookie is information, placed there by the server, when a user surfs a particular site. The browser can use customised information, which does not have to be re-entered if the site is revisited. You can view cookies on your system by looking at the text file in notepad, but they are usually a set of numbers that are meaningless to the user.

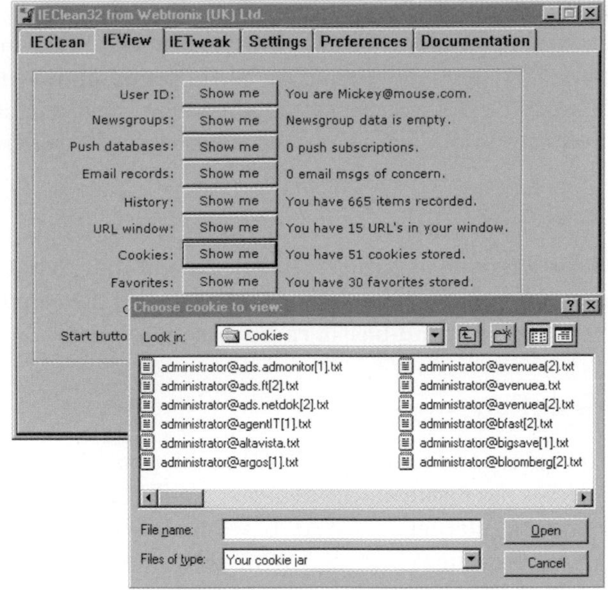

Figure 18.13 Some information stored by a browser

You can instruct your browser to accept or reject the cookies, or to warn if a cookie is about to be saved to your disk. However, it is annoying if you have to keep responding to these messages. As with the **history database information**, you can delete your cookies at frequent intervals if you do not want them. However, be prepared for some sites to ask you to type in a lot of set-up information if you do this, and this can be annoying too. If you have **on-line banking**, then deletion of a cookie belonging to this can cause you to enter quite a lot of extra data, as though you have never logged on before.

It is possible for forensic scientists to analyse a computer to extract a huge amount of information about what the computer has been used for over the last few months or years.

Special software (not shown here) may be used to image a disk such that the investigative techniques do not compromise the information stored on the original computer disk.

Most criminals do not realise that electronic trails of what they have done are usually traceable, and the browser information shown here is just a small part of this.

WAP enabled browsers

Other browsers exist, like the **micro browsers** for **WAP** enabled mobile telephones. WAP stands for **wireless access protocol**. It is a standard enabling devices to access digital services via mobile phones and other portables.

PCs use HTML, but **WAP** devices use **WML**, which stands for **wireless markup language**. This is similar in principle to HTML, but is tailored for the small screens that are found on portable electronic devices. Just like HTML, WML commands are included between tags, and some examples of WML commands are as follows:

```
<img>, <anchor>,<big>,<card> and <input>
```

A WAP enabled mobile phone is shown in Figure 18.15. This particular shot shows an e-mail being constructed, but you can

Figure 18.14 A mobile phone credit card interface in use

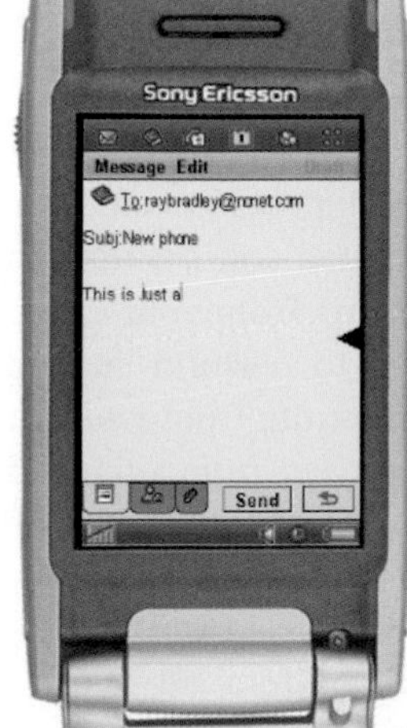

Figure 18.15 A WAP enabled phone from Sony Ericsson

also surf the net, take still and moving video images and send these via the wireless network. This particular phone also acts as a **PDA**, and you can synchronise your diaries, calendars and address books with **personal information management software** like Microsoft's Outlook. Many mobile phones have a micro browser, and some phones have a credit card interface for on-line transactions, as shown in Figure 18.14.

Example

Write a couple of paragraphs on some of the advantages and disadvantages of WAP enabled mobile technology compared with the conventional HTML browsers operating on a PC via a land-based, radio or satellite link.

Solution

The obvious advantage for WAP enabled mobile technology is portability. However, you do have the disadvantage of a very small screen and fewer facilities. Nevertheless, when using the Internet on a WAP-based mobile phone, you are unlikely to use it in the same way as on your PC. Special WML web sites present the information in ways convenient for a small screen, and this is ideal for looking up text-based information such as share prices, who is top of the pops, or for finding telephone numbers for example.

Devices like third generation mobile phones are ideal for statistical information on the move, but conventional Internet browsers and PCs are more suited to a rich Internet experience (i.e. full-size screens, lots of text on a single page etc.) or finding more copious amounts of information. It is currently not possible, for example, to download large computer programs, print out web pages, scan information to be transmitted over the net or add attachments to your e-mail via your mobile phone. No doubt some of these facilities will be available in the near future.

Java Applets

Extra interactivity can be added to a site if it is capable of being viewed in a Java-enabled browser. A **Java Applet** is a Java program that can be referenced by the HTML language, then downloaded and run on the client's machine. The user can then interact with the site in special ways. Interactive games can be played, and the user can interact with utilities such as calculators or customised financial portfolios.

Running Java Applets from an untrusted source can be dangerous. It is for this reason that Java Applets are not allowed to be as powerful as applications written in the **Java** language. Java Applets are not allowed to carry out some operations on the user's machine for security reasons, and are restricted to running inside set boundaries. Java **Servlets** allow the programs to be run on the web server instead.

To increase what an applet may do we use a **digital signature** (see below). Applets from trusted sources may then perform operations such as writing information or running programs from your computer. Applets from other, unknown, sources should not be permitted to perform such operations. Examples are on-line banking, shopping or setting up accounts from well-known commercial organisations. A Java Applet running in a secure browser from a trusted source can be seen in Figure 18.16. The user is being prompted to enter a Global Key Code to log on to a NatWest One Account. Note that the https (secure) protocol is being used, the padlock is being displayed at the bottom right-hand side of the window to confirm the secure link, and the message 'Applet App started' is displayed in the bottom left-hand side of the browser window (see margin entry).

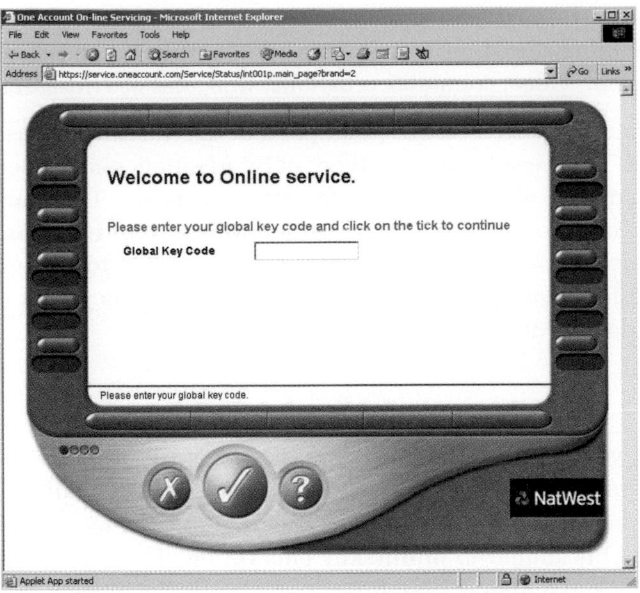

Figure 18.16 A Java Applet has been started

Functionality similar to that obtained with Java Applets can be achieved by using ***Active Server Pages****. These help to create dynamic HTML pages in which the user can interact with the web server. Active Server Pages are used on Microsoft's servers when running* ***Internet Information Server****, Microsoft's web server technology. Figure 18.16 shows the log-on screen for a NatWest current account making use of an Active Server Page.*

E-mail

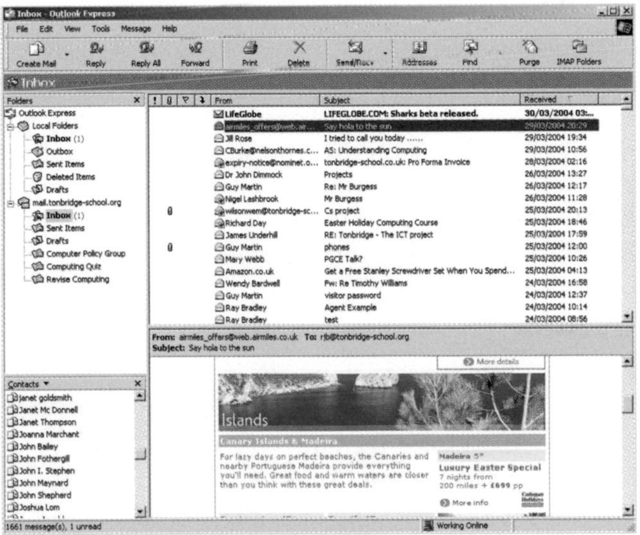

Figure 18.17 Microsoft's Outlook Express e-mail client

E-mail is electronic text or other files, sent from one system to another via networks such as LANs or WANs. Facilities available depend on the device you are using. A WAP enabled mobile phone will have limited e-mail capability compared with a PC. E-mail is compiled by the sender and sent to a **mail server** where it is distributed to another server which hosts the recipient's e-mail account. When the recipient logs on to their system and downloads e-mail, the text or other files get transferred from their **mailbox** into their local computer. If on a LAN, then a local mail server will probably handle contact with the ISP's mail server. The e-mail can be viewed when a user logs on to the LAN. Some typical e-mail software is shown in Figure 18.17, with the address book (bottom left), the e-mail folder (top left), the e-mails in the main window and an e-mail being read (bottom right).

Here you can see **icons** representing an inbox, an outbox, sent items, deleted items and drafts. A list of e-mails appears in the top right-hand window, and a particular e-mail is displayed in the bottom right-hand window. You can usually read and create e-mail off-line. This saves paying phone charges on dial-up connections while constructing or reading text. You can have multiple e-mail accounts, all of which can be downloaded automatically by the software.

One advantage of using e-mail on a computer is that you can send an **attachment**. This is a computer file of any form. Anything stored on a computer can be sent via an e-mail attachment including pictures, sound, video, computer programs, web sites or viruses!

E-mail was originally designed for text-based messages, and parts of the Internet still use **ASCII** making use of the **parity bit**. This messes up other types of information, often coded in more sophisticated ways making use of the parity bit for other purposes. There are several encoding methods that overcome this problem, of which **MIME (multi-purpose Internet mail extensions)** is a particular example. These encode information to be sent making sure the parity bit is used for its original purpose. A MIME encoded document is therefore larger than the original document.

Preventing forgery

At the time of writing the Verisign company manages over 30 million ***digital identities*** *in over 300 different languages.*

One problem with e-mail is that you can never be sure that it is from the person who appears to have sent it. One way round this is to make use of a digital identity or **digital ID**, and software like Outlook Express works in conjunction with digital IDs allocated by the appropriate bodies. A digital ID is similar to **public-key encryption**. There are *three parts* – a **public key**, a **private key** and a **digital signature**. If you put a digital signature with your e-mail message then the combination of the public key and digital signature is called a **digital certificate**. This can be obtained from companies such as Verisign or other independent certification authorities. The recipient of e-mail uses the digital signature as a verification mechanism, and your public key is used to encrypt messages they send to you, as described in detail in your AS course.

Do not post illegal material to Usenet newsgroups or create an illegal Usenet newsgroup of your own, even if you are doing this for a joke!

The above is useful for e-mail and for other aspects of e-commerce where confidentiality and authentication are essential. Anyone who uses a digital signature or certificate can be easily traced and made responsible for any of his or her actions. When you receive an e-mail which has been digitally signed, software like Microsoft's Outlook Express automatically contacts the company holding the digital certificate to see if it is still valid or has been revoked. The help files in Outlook Express show how digital signatures and other security features are set up and work.

Usenet

Police departments regularly trawl through these groups to find information on paedophiles, drug users and terrorists.

As anybody can post anything to any newsgroup, legal but unmoderated groups often contain unsuitable material posted there by unscrupulous people who do not obey the rules.

Usenet is similar to a **bulletin-board system** where users read material placed there by others. Anybody can post material to Usenet groups. The **Usenet user groups** are often unregulated, and therefore any sort of material can be found. At the time of writing there are over 85 000 newsgroups on many of the **news servers**, and topics range from changing light bulbs, through support groups to finding technical details on a variety of subjects. A large number of these groups contain absolute rubbish, and

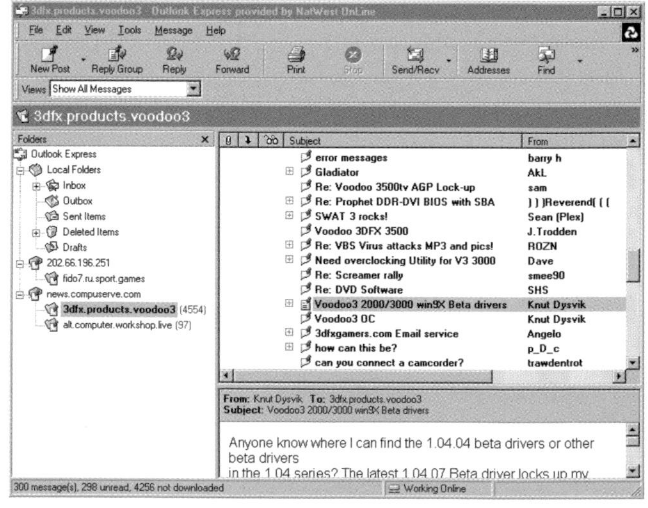

Figure 18.18 Viewing a Usenet Newsgroup

much of the material is illegal. Fortunately, there are an even larger number of sites with essential and useful information. To access newsgroups you need a news server. At the time of writing, CompuServe's server can be found at 'news.compuserve. com', but only CompuServe members can make use of this.

In Figure 18.18 you can see Outlook Express accessing a Voodoo3 graphics-card newsgroup. There are 4554 messages, most about topics for graphics cards! You can see just one of these messages displayed, which is a request from a user about beta versions of graphics-card software. People often use news groups to request help from other like-minded people, and this is the whole point of Usenet. If your ISP does not have a news server, many public news servers are available.

Internet relay chat (IRC)

The Usenet user groups are passive in that you could be reading messages that have been posted months or even years ago. Google, for example, has 20 years of Usenet messages available on-line. When using Usenet, people may never actually read your particular posting! **Internet relay chat** provides a real-time experience where you can chat to people who are currently on-line and logged on to an IRC server.

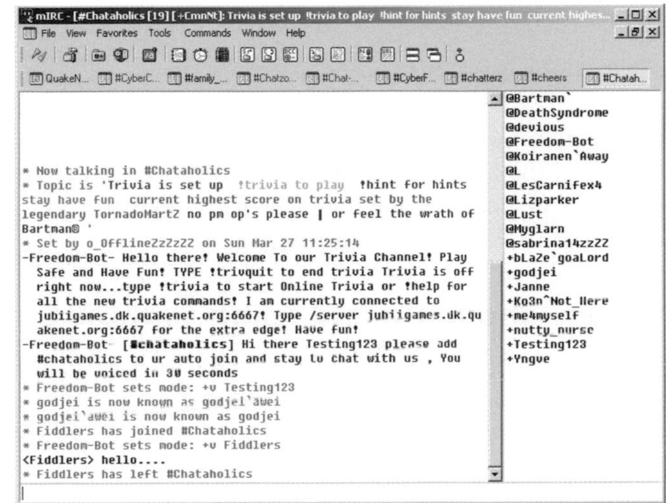

Figure 18.19 Using Internet Relay Chat

Messages can be exchanged interactively if you have appropriate software on your machine. Figure 18.19 shows some mIRC software during a session in which users are chatting about how to use the mIRC software! At any one time there will be a variety of IRC channels in session, and you can join in by selecting an appropriate one.

Be careful if you are allowed to make use of Internet relay chat rooms.

People will often masquerade as others, and you can never tell if someone is being truthful about their age or sex.

A lot of good things go on in some of these chat rooms, and people will often find solutions to their problems or make new pen friends with similar interests.

Video conferencing

This is software that enables real time video, real time audio and computer data links to be used to interact with others at remote locations. This is typically used for board meetings, but is also useful for a variety of other purposes, developing electronic resources with a company that is based overseas, for example. It would be possible to provide complete specifications, but it is far easier to set up a video conferencing facility with the software developers. You can see and hear each other, as well as share an interactive white board. It is possible to use an A4 graphics tablet, and what you draw on this tablet appears on a window on the developer's computer overseas. It is then possible to add annotations to the diagrams that are being produced interactively over the video conferencing link.

Internet banking

On-line banking entails using the Internet to carry out transactions that would normally be conducted in a conventional bank. It is popular for people with computers, WAP enabled mobile phones, and Internet-ready TVs via satellite or cable.

If you make use of Internet banking, then make sure that your Internet security software is up to date.

The author uses a program called Pest Control but many others are also available.

Without protection like this, a hacker might hack into your computer, install some key logging software, and may even be able to determine your password and PIN.

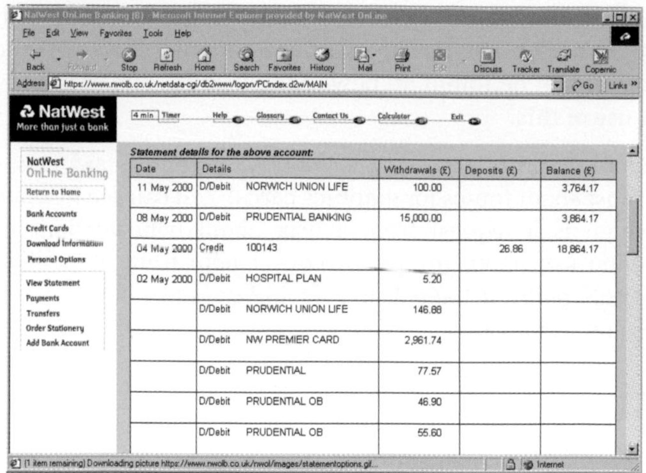

Statement details for the above account:

Date	Details		Withdrawals (£)	Deposits (£)	Balance (£)
11 May 2000	D/Debit	NORWICH UNION LIFE	100.00		3,764.17
08 May 2000	D/Debit	PRUDENTIAL BANKING	15,000.00		3,864.17
04 May 2000	Credit	100143		26.86	18,864.17
02 May 2000	D/Debit	HOSPITAL PLAN	5.20		
	D/Debit	NORWICH UNION LIFE	146.88		
	D/Debit	NW PREMIER CARD	2,961.74		
	D/Debit	PRUDENTIAL	77.57		
	D/Debit	PRUDENTIAL OB	46.90		
	D/Debit	PRUDENTIAL OB	55.60		

Figure 18.20 Typical on-line banking facilities

The most sophisticated service is available via a **secure web browser** and a PC. For example, you could display your monthly bank account statement, as shown in Figure 18.20. This statement shows direct debits (regular monthly payments), a transfer of £15 000 into a different Internet bank account and a deposit by cheque of £26.86 etc. However, the facilities available are much more sophisticated than this. You can display **credit card** accounts, or download information into a **spreadsheet** for further analysis. **Hard copy** may be obtained for any of the information that can be viewed, and requests may be made to the bank for new cheque-books or paying-in books. About the only day-to-day thing that cannot be done via the Internet is depositing cash.

On-line shopping and using shopping agents

Bots or Robots are also examples of agents which search the web for the user. Systems like AIRbots, short for Autonomous Intelligent Robots, use software agents to help users find information from health care to transportation.

You should not confuse a shopping bot or agent with these other bots and agents that are used for advanced research purposes!

A free copy of Copernic Agent Basic can be obtained from Copernic's web site.

Virtually anything from a house to a mouse can be bought via the Internet. As long as you have some valid plastic (a credit card) and a suitable credit limit, you can purchase goods on-line which will normally be delivered to your door within a matter of days. Major companies, like www.2checkout.com have been set up to enable on-line retailers to provide a comprehensive service to the customers. Facilities such as secure-site checks, on-line point of sales, e-mail receipts, consumer billing, credit-card processing, and credit-card

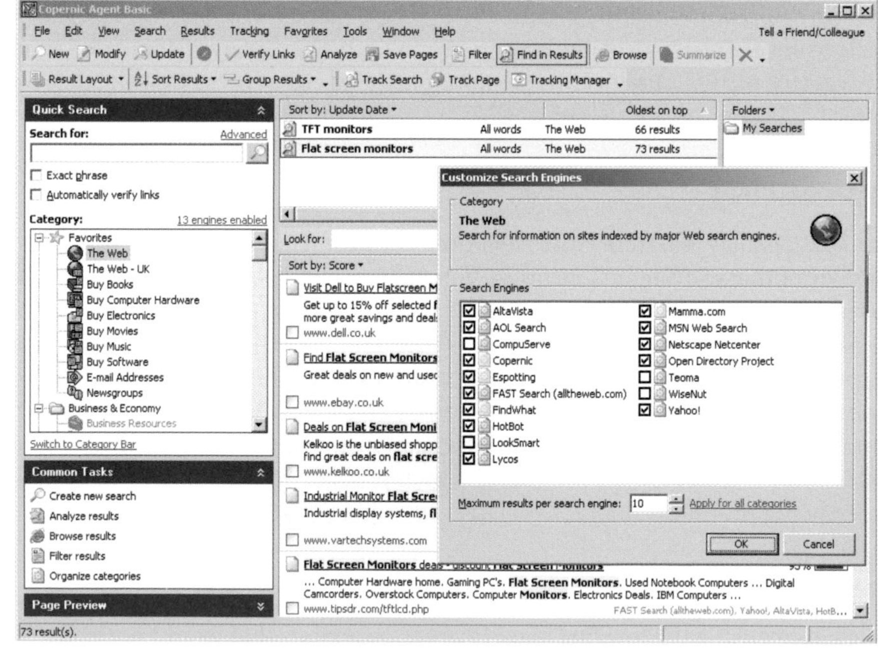

Figure 18.21 Using a general-purpose search agent called Copernic

checking facilities form just a part of a comprehensive on-line retailing system provided by www.2checkout.com and other similar companies.

As far as *shopping on the Internet* is concerned (see margin entry on previous page), an **agent** is a program to search for information on the Internet. There are many specialist and general-purpose agents, like the shopping agent called BargainDog. BargainDog is an example of a **specialist agent**, set up to enable shoppers to hunt for bargains. Although selective, a shopping agent can present the user with a good range of bargains, usually at the lower end of the price range.

Agents can also be general purpose. An example of a general-purpose agent is Copernic, and this is shown in Figure 18.21. Here you may type in a request, but rather than direct it to a *particular* search engine, you may search many search engines. Figure 18.21 shows Copernic searching search engines, starting with AltaVista, AOL Search and Copernic. However, there is more to an intelligent search engine than this. An intelligent agent like Copernic will also correlate results, eliminate duplicates and give other facilities such as restricting searches to areas like Newsgroups or e-mail addresses etc.

On-line security

The security of on-line transactions is important. 128-bit **encryption** has already been covered, and shopping channels may use the https protocol too. Other methods, like the digital certificates used with e-mail, ensure the authenticity of the person at the other end of the line. However, **e-commerce** is open to fraud, and unscrupulous companies can set up bogus web sites to sell sub-standard goods or goods that do not exist at all. If credit card details are to be given over the net, then the company hosting the site should make use of the **secure http** or **SSL (secure sockets layer)**, one of the **protocols** for secure transactions.

Example

A user wishes to find information on DVD players for sale at less than £100. Suggest how he or she could make use of the Internet, from initial research, through to purchase of an appropriate device.

Solution

A search engine can be used to find sites with information about DVD players. The search string would have to contain the word player or many sites selling DVD media may be selected instead. After finding a list of suitable machines and numbers, the user could log on to the manufacturer's site and download the specifications of each machine. Reviews of the machine may be found on other web sites, like those sponsored by the hi-fi magazines. People's opinions could also be solicited from the UseNet newsgroups. Having decided on a machine within the appropriate price bracket, a shopping bot (agent) can be used to find the cheapest source of supply. If, after a suitable amount of research, www.bigsave.com was found to be the most cost-effective source, the user could log onto the bigsave site as shown in Figure 18.22.

If the user is happy with the price, clicking on the 'buy me' icon would access the secure credit card transaction service, assuming that the user had already registered with www.bigsave.com. When the item is added to the shopping trolley, it is possible to go back into other areas of the site to add other items, and then pay for them all at the checkout using a secure transaction facility.

If individuals purchase items on the Internet it is essential to use a credit card.

A credit card will give you protection if the goods do not arrive or if they are faulty. This will usually last for a period of three months after the date of the credit card transaction and applies to goods that cost more than £100.

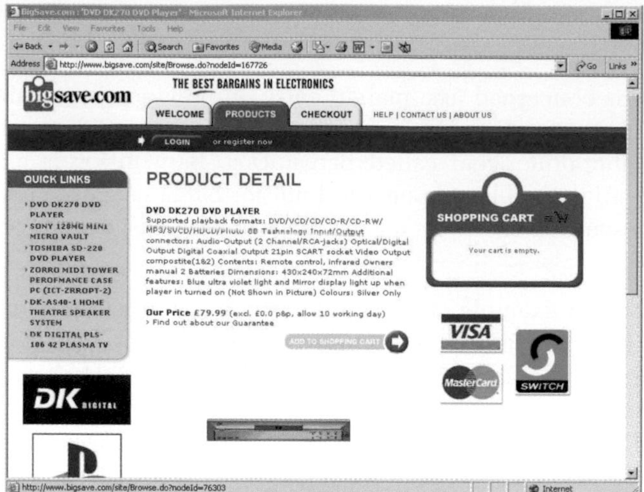

Figure 18.22 Using a shopping agent

Firewalls may be implemented in hardware or software.

Sometimes a separate computer or piece of hardware may be used, but software can also be installed either on a file server or a stand-alone machine connected to the Internet or an intranet.

MAC address filtering is another common way of preventing unauthorised access. Each machine has a unique Media Access Control (MAC) address of the form 00-OA-C4-16-35-D6. Machines not within the defined MAC-address range would not be allowed to connect to the system.

Firewalls and intranets

Many companies and educational institutions allow access to internal LANs (intranets) from the outside world. Figure 18.23 shows a school, but these ideas apply to any organisation including commercial institutions which sell goods on the Internet. Teachers, pupils, parents and hackers (unauthorised users) are trying to access the system, but the **firewall** (a machine placed between the Internet and the school LANs) helps prevent unauthorised access (see margin entry).

All communications, either from the Internet to the school's LANs or from the school's LANs to the Internet, are routed via the firewall, which is effectively a proxy server set up to decide if the messages coming in or going out are safe to pass. Any message deemed to be unsafe is blocked, as are particular machines which are not authorised. When a user has passed through the firewall, they are allowed access to resources from inside the school site, going through the normal authentication routines by logging onto the school's file servers. Without the firewall, hackers from outside the organisation could damage the companies' resources or get access to information that might be commercially sensitive.

Virtual private networks

When set up in the ways described in Figure 18.23, authenticated users from the outside world are using the Internet as a virtual extension to the company's LAN. Used in this way the system is said to be a **virtual private network** or **VPN**.

Many people may want to connect to the system simultaneously, and the

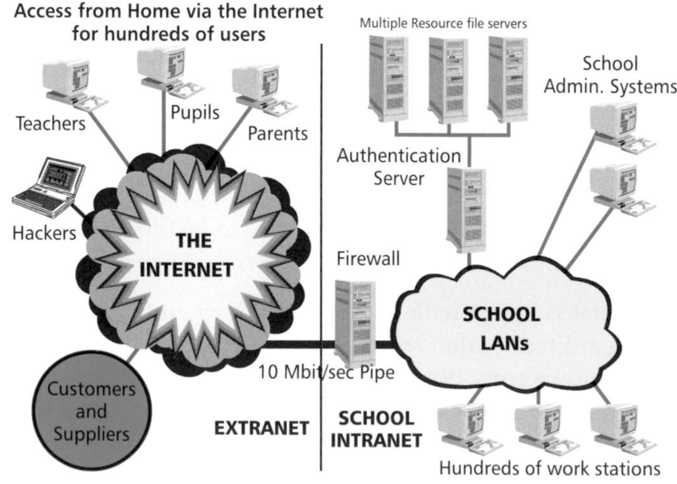

Figure 18.23 Connection to a VPN via a firewall

local school or college will probably not have many telephone lines free. Therefore, access to the pipe (ISDN, ADSL or some other link) is usually made via an ISP. Users log onto their ISP, who is able to deal with many telephone calls simultaneously. The ISP then routes requests down a single high-bandwidth line, which connects the ISP to the school or college using **point-to-point tunnelling protocol** (**PPTP**). The appropriate software, security protocols and a number of settings must be set up on the client machine before a VPN can be successfully utilised.

Moral, ethical, social and cultural issues

The Internet is all powerful and cuts across cultural and social boundaries causing a large number of problems. Conventional authorities like Customs and Excise, the Inland Revenue and the Police have little control over what people are allowed to buy, see or do on the Internet. On the other hand, you have freedom of speech and the ability to communicate with others. Unfortunately drug barons, terrorists and pornographers abuse the system to distribute illegal material, or make use of encryption and e-mail for criminal activities. Legal systems in most countries lag a long way behind the current pace of technological change, and not enough knowledgeable people are available to police the system.

The Internet is also a major source of **viruses**, which can easily be spread via e-mail, downloading software and other material. A whole industry has evolved to protect innocent people from the extremes of material that can be found on the net. It would be an irresponsible parent, for example, who allowed their underage child freedom to access uncensored information from any part of the web. Teachers also have a legal responsibility to supervise children who use the net from their schools.

Software solutions

Software like SurfControl or NetNanny provides filtering for a range of sites containing pornographic, racist, violent or other material deemed to be unsuitable. However, the Internet is a dynamic entity, and hundreds of new sites are set up each day. It's unlikely that anything (short of not letting a person use the net) will deter a person with enough time and knowledge from finding material which others may deem to be unsuitable, and this is why policies like those covered in your AS course are put into action. It is easy for people to become addicted to material on the net, from illegal sites to more innocent games. They may also become addicted to Internet relay chat or spend so much time surfing that they become obsessed to the detriment of other day-to-day activities.

International boundaries

There is a significant amount of religious or government influence in some countries, and the Internet can be an unwelcome catalyst for change. Even material innocent in the eyes of a westerner might be totally unacceptable to some cultures in the Middle East, for example, where alcohol is banned. Some books and publications would also be banned, and reading western newspapers is frowned upon in some societies. Laws in different countries define what is or is not decent, inflammatory, illegal or tolerated. Because servers may be accessed from all countries, the situation becomes complicated, and material which can be viewed in one house might be illegal in another house just a few hundred yards down the road across an international border.

Educational and other organisations have taken a serious look at how their pupils and employees make use of e-mail and the web during working hours. Issues include illegal activities like accessing unauthorised material or stealing software.

Remember that you should have knowledge of current legislation such as the Data Protection Act 1998, the Computer Misuse Act 1990 and the Copyright Designs and Patents Act 1988. This legislation was covered in your AS level course, and copies may be downloaded from the Internet.

Self-test questions

1 Explain the format of an IP address. For what purpose is an IP address used?
2 What is meant by the terms 'domain name', 'top-level domain name', 'Internet registry' and 'Internet registrar'?
3 Consider the following URL:
https://www.doctorwho.med.pro/patients/bloggs/medicalhistory.htm
(a) What does 'https' mean?
(b) What is the name of the HTML document that will be loaded?
(c) What is the top-level domain name?
(d) What is represented by /patients/bloggs/?
(e) Why do you think that https has been used for this site?
4 When designing web sites it is important to create a structure. Outline why this is important, giving very brief references to setting up a web site for a college.
5 A web site can be created in a variety of ways from making use of a simple text editor to using a special-purpose application package enabling WYSIWYG operation. Give two advantages of a WYSIWYG system compared with a text editor, and two advantages of a text editor compared with a WYSIWYG system.
6 Typically what processes need to be undertaken to publish a web site? How might you maintain your web site effectively (i.e. change pages etc. once it is published)?
7 What is Telnet?
8 Why are search engines important? Comment on the different search facilities available when searching for specific information on the Internet.
9 What is a web browser? Web browsers have become particularly sophisticated over the last few years. Outline three things that a modern web browser does which 'helps' users surf the net more efficiently.
10 The Internet can now be surfed using a mobile phone. What protocol has made this possible and what differences does the user experience compared with a normal browser?
11 What is a Java Applet?
12 E-mail provides a lot of additional functionality for the user over and above being able to send a message from one person to another. Name five things you can do.
13 Comment on the difference in use between UseNet newsgroups and IRC.
14 Outline the software and hardware that would be needed for video conferencing.
15 On-line shopping is becoming an increasingly important part of retail in the UK. What is a shopping agent and how do shopping agents help consumers?
16 Internet banking is becoming popular. Why is this so? Are there any disadvantages?
17 What is a VPN?
18 Extra problems have been caused by the introduction of the Internet. Among these problems are easy access to pornography, viruses being transmitted to computers and junk mail or spam filling up e-mail boxes. Outline what counter measures may be taken in each of these situations.

Module 5 examination questions

1 The UK's National Health Service was created to provide health care to the nation through:

- hospitals
- health centres/GPs' (doctors') surgeries
- pharmacies (chemists).

The UK government is proposing to computerise and network the entire National Health Service (NHS) so that it will be possible to have on-line *access to the system at a level of security relevant to their status* for anyone who:

- works for the NHS
- uses its services
- works at a branch of government responsible for the NHS.

Patient records will be stored in multi-user distributed relational databases managed by *Database Management Systems* (DBMS).

- Every person in the UK has a unique numeric key, the patient reference number, and is assigned for primary health care to a doctor in a health centre or a GPs' (general practitioners' or doctors') surgery.
- A person's doctor may, if necessary, arrange for the person to see a specialist doctor in a hospital.
- Drugs prescribed for a person by their GP for the treatment of an illness are obtained from a pharmacy.
- Every computer in the NHS will be interconnected *in local area networks* (LANs) and the local area networks will be interconnected by a *wide area network* (WAN).

(a) Which network type is most appropriate, WAN or LAN, within a health centre of GPs (doctors)? Justify your choice. (2 marks)

....

....

(b) Explain **one** way in which the networked NHS can benefit each of the following. Each benefit must be different.

(i) The patient (1 mark)

....

....

(ii) A health centre/GPs' (doctors') surgery (1 mark)

....

....

(iii) A pharmacy (1 mark)

....

....

(iv) The UK government. (1 mark)

....

....

(c) (i) What level of the architecture of a DBMS allows the NHS system to be designed to permit on-line access to the system at a level of security relevant to status for anyone who works for the NHS? (1 mark)

....

....

(ii) Explain **one** method that DBMSs use in a multi-user system to avoid losing updates to records that are accessed concurrently (at the same time). (2 marks)

....

....

(d) For each of the following, give **one** reason why large-scale software systems such as this NHS system could fail. Each reason **must** be different.

(i) Perform as its users expect (1 mark)

....

....

(ii) Work at all (1 mark)

....

....

(iii) Be completed on time. (1 mark)

....

....

[AQA Unit 5 (CPT5) June 2003 Q(7)]

2 Software is used extensively in the control and monitoring of systems that have the potential to cause loss of life if the system fails.

(a) Briefly describe **two** different aspects of control or monitoring software which could endanger life if they fail. (2 marks)

....

....

(b) A software system failed shortly after entering service with the customer even though it passed all phases of testing successfully including *acceptance testing*.

(i) What is meant by acceptance testing? (1 mark)

....

....

(ii) Excluding testing, design flaws or hardware failure, give **another** possible explanation for the failure of this software system. (1 mark)

....

....

(iii) Name **one** type of testing that could have been applied to the developed system to discover potential problems. (1 mark)

....

....

[AQA Unit 5 (CPT5) June 2004 Q(2)]

3 A company wishes to replace its existing data processing system with a more up-to-date system. After consultation, two alternative methods for converting from the old to the new system are proposed, parallel and phased.

(a) What is meant by:

(i) Parallel conversion? (1 mark)

....

....

(ii) Phased conversion? (1 mark)

....

....

(b) State two tasks that may have to be carried out when converting from the old to the new system. (2 marks)

....

....

(c) The company wishes to assess how maintainable the new system will be. Give three questions for the company to put to the developers of the new system to help with this assessment. (3 marks)

....

....

[AQA Unit 5 (CPT5) June 2003 Q(4)]

4 An international charity provides humanitarian aid to areas which suffer a disaster such as an earthquake. It has the following generic software:

- database
- word processing
- spreadsheet
- desktop publishing
- presentation package
- expert system shell.

(a) Describe **three** different ways in which computer systems using these packages could assist the international charity in achieving this task. Each way should use a different package. (3 marks)

....

....

(b) Data produced by one of the above generic packages may be integrated with or shared by another package. How could two of the above packages be used in this way to assist the international charity in its work? You must state which packages are used. (2 marks)

....

....

[AQA Unit 5 (CPT5) June 2004 Q(6)]

5 A local area network (LAN) connects a host with host name fido and an application server name neptune as shown in Figure 1.

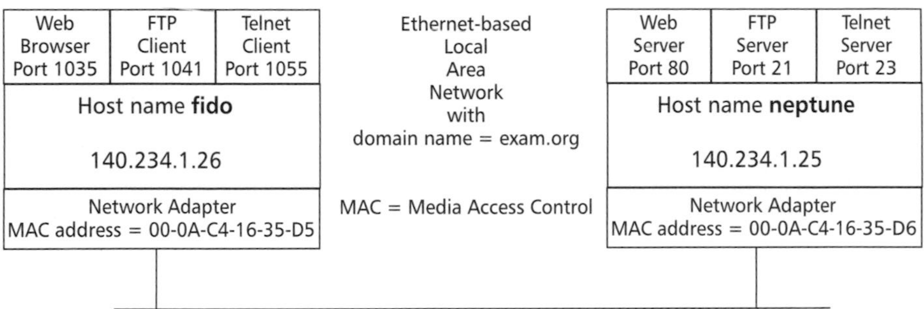

Figure 1

The application server is executing three services:

- Web server
- FTP server
- Telnet server.

The host fido is executing three applications:

- Web browser
- FTP client
- Telnet client.

Figure 2 shows a part of the graphical user interface generated on fido's VDU by one of the applications executing on fido.

Figure 2

(a) (i) What application, executing in **fido**, generated the graphical interface shown in Figure 2? (1 mark)

....

....

(ii) Complete the following simplified Ethernet frame that will be sent to the server when the URL shown in Figure 2 is requested.

Table 1

Source Port no.	Destination Port no.	Source IP Address	Destination IP Address	Source MAC Address	Destination MAC Address
		140.234.1.26	140.234.1.25	00-OA-C4-16-35-D5	00-OA-C4-16-35-D6

(b) IP addresses consist of Network ID and Host ID.

(i) What is fido's Network ID? (1 mark)

....

....

(ii) What is fido's Host ID? (1 mark)

....

....

(c) Figure 3 shows a Telnet session initiated by fido. Table 2 shows the output from a command **netstat**.

```
C:\Telnet 140.234.1.25
neptune login: aqa
password:
logged into neptune 12/05/2004 10:23am
neptune $>ls
home/cgi-bin/index.html www/mail.fromChil/
```

Figure 3

Table 2

Protocol	Local Address	Foreign Address	State
TCP	140.234.1.25.23	140.234.1.26.1055	Established
TCP	*.23	*.*	Listening

(i) At which computer was the netstat command run? Justify your answer.
Computer (1 mark)

....

....

Justification (1 mark)

....

....

(ii) For the established Telnet connection, what is the socket address used by the:
A. Telnet server? (1 mark)

....

....

B. Telnet client? (1 mark)

....

....

(iii) State one purpose that Telnet may be used for. (1 mark)

....

....

(d) The LAN www.exam.org.uk is connected to a wide area network (WAN) so that examination documents may be transferred between hosts on the organisation's Chilean branch's LAN and hosts on the UK branch's LAN as shown in Figure 4.

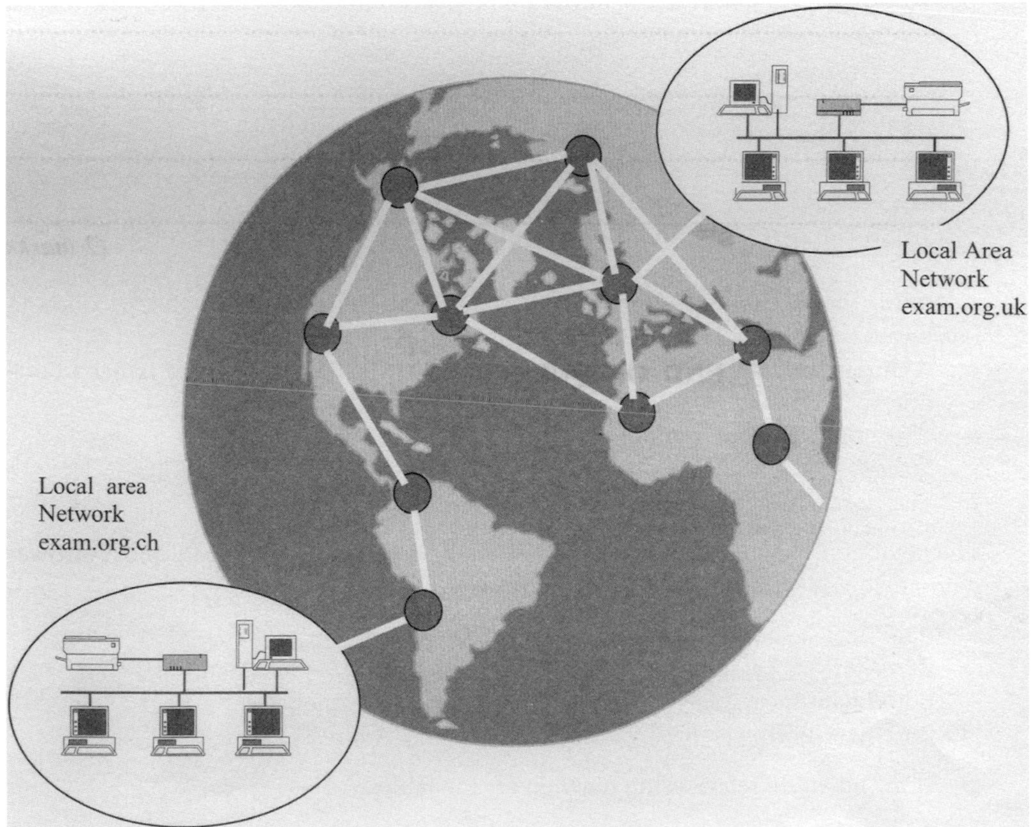

Figure 4

(i) What is the most appropriate protocol to use on a host in the Chilean LAN for transferring exam documents from the Chilean LAN to the formChil folder on the UK server neptune? (1 mark)

....

....

ii) Each LAN is connected to an access point on the WAN using a copper link provided by the local telephone company.
Name one type of connection from the LAN to this access point that could be used for data transmission rates in excess of 100 Kbit/sec. (1 mark)

....

....

(iii) The WAN operates in Asynchronous Transmission Mode (ATM). Explain why an ATM WAN behaves more like a circuit-switched network than a packet-switched network. (2 marks)

....

....

[AQA Unit 5 (CPT5) June 2004 Q(10)]

6 A lending library uses a relational database to record details of books, book loans and borrowers.

- A unique International Standard Book Number (ISBN) is assigned to each book title such as *The Art of Passing Computer Examinations*.
- The library assigns a unique Accession Number to each copy of a book in the library.
- The library assigns a unique Borrower Number to each borrower.

The relational database uses four tables Book, BookCopy, BookLoan and Borrower with attributes (primary key is underlined) as follows:

Book(<u>ISBN</u>, AuthorName, Title, NumberOfCopies)
BookCopy(<u>AccessionNumber</u>, ISBN, DateAcquired, ReplacementCost)
BookLoan(<u>AccessionNumber</u>, BorrowerName, DateDueBack)
Borrower(<u>BorrowerNumber</u>, Surname, Initials, Address)

(a) Draw an entity relationship diagram for the tables:

(i) Borrower and BookLoan (1 mark)

....

....

(ii) Book and Borrower (1 mark)

....

....

(b) Using the SQL commands SELECT, FROM, WHERE and any others considered appropriate, write SQL statements to query the database tables for each of the following:

(i) The title of the book with ISBN 1-57820-082-2. (2 marks)

....

....

(ii) The name of the author and ISBN of a book with Accession number 1234 (4 marks)

....

....

(c) By linking the database with a word-processing package, overdue book reminder letters can be generated when copies of books on loan to borrowers are overdue. What is this process called? (1 mark)

....

....

[AQA Unit 5 (CPT5) June 2003 Q(8)]

19 The practical project – introduction

In this chapter you will learn about:

- The nature of A2 project work
- Choosing a suitable project
- The all-important mark schemes for the module 6 project
- Keeping a project diary
- Developing professional methods of working

Introduction to the A2 project work

Always consult your teacher or lecturer before starting your A2 project.

If your project does not conform to the mark scheme you may waste a lot of valuable time.

At A2 level you are required to produce a practical working solution to some *real problem* which can be chosen from a huge variety of possible areas. This is often the most exciting part of the course, because *you get to make the decisions about what you would like to do.* The skill lies in making sure that your chosen project will conform *exactly* to the mark scheme. The project must be agreed between you and your teacher/lecturer, and then it is marked at the centre, and finally moderated by the board.

One major advantage of this coursework is that candidates have complete control over what they are doing. Start early, work hard to produce a good system tailored to the mark scheme, and you have a recipe for very high marks in this component of the course. At the author's school a number of pupils have scored 100%, and the project exemplar to be developed in the next few chapters is one of them. Unlike the written examinations, *you have complete control over what you actually do – do not waste this marvellous opportunity.*

Thinking that they have many months to work on their project, some candidates put off starting work until much later in their A2 course. This is *usually* a mistake. I would suggest that you start thinking about possible projects immediately after the AS examinations. If possible, *spend a few weeks discussing possible projects* with your A2 teacher or lecturer. You can then spend time over the summer holidays finding a **client** (see below) mapping out what you will probably do, and learning any package or language that you might need. In September at the start of the A2 year you will then be in a position to start work on your module 6 project having done a lot of the time-consuming ground work.

Choosing a suitable project

After working through a possible project with your teacher or lecturer, see if the likely method of solution is one with which you are happy. If it is not, then choose a different project.

Never choose a project which is likely to lead to a method of solution with which you are not happy. If, for example, after the AS project you are fed up with **databases**, then do not choose a project which is likely to need a database for its solution. Similarly, if you are *not* very good at programming, then do not choose a project which is likely to be solved by using a programming language. Databases *and* programming *are the two scenarios most likely to result in a project that fits the mark scheme exactly.*

Do not choose a web site *unless* the project contains a sufficient programming element. For a web site this can easily be achieved by linking one or more of the pages to a database. If you choose a static web site (no interaction with the users) *you will not be able to score many marks* on the project because it *does not conform to the criteria*, which includes inputting data, processing the data in some way and then outputting data.

It is essential that you find a suitable client. This is a person (or *people*) for whom you are designing the project. Without a client you will not be able to do the project properly. Your client is usually somebody who acts in a professional capacity, like a teacher, parent or relative who will be able to interact with you (*often in written form*) throughout the duration of the project. He or she will help you to produce a **design specification**, will help to design the **user interface**, and will make suitable comments when you have to **appraise** your project. *Few students are able to make it appear that they have a client when they do not!* The language used in supposed communications with their clients is often not written in the right style, and students cannot usually fake professional headed paper very well!

Make sure that your client knows what they are letting themselves in for. Make sure they are available when needed (**e-mail** communications are very effective) and ensure that they appreciate that they will need to write several formal letters.

Spend some time over the summer holidays finding a suitable client.

Some clients might be under the impression that you will produce a professional, fully working solution to their problem. This is unlikely to be the case due to time constraints, possible technical difficulties or your ability to solve problems. *Make sure that your client understands that this is an exercise for your A level project, and not a commission to produce a fully working solution tailored exactly to their specification.* You may find that you have to modify what you will offer a client because they sometimes get carried away when they realise what you might be capable of.

If your client does not wish to help you in the ways suggested here then choose a different project.

If your client is your parent or a relative, by all means produce a very large, fully working project if you wish, but *this is not the requirement of the A level course*, and you may be making a rod for your own back.

Never promise your client too much. If they get a fully working solution to their problem at the end of your course then that is a bonus, not a requirement.

Criteria for the project

It is important to carry out your project exactly according to the **mark scheme**. There is nothing worse than working hard for several months, only to find that no marks are awarded for large sections of your project because the project you chose did not make use of certain techniques. To ensure that you make a wise choice, the AQA board have produced the following module 6 project criteria, which you can use as a tick list for the project you intend to do. The necessary criteria are shown in the following list.

- Is it a real situation that the candidate can investigate?
- Is there a user whose needs can be investigated and taken into account when designing the solution?
- Does it conform to the specification requirements, i.e. will the finished product be a tailored solution which allows interaction between the user and the computer system with input, storage and manipulation of data and output of results?
- Is it of advanced-level standard?
- Is it within the capability of the candidate to complete in a reasonable time?
- Are the necessary facilities available to the candidate?
- Is it a subject that the candidate has knowledge of or an interest in?

If the answer to *any* of the above questions is *no*, then choose another project.

Your teacher or lecturer will be able to advise if your project is or is not of a suitable standard.

They will also be able to advise if your project will take too long.

The mark scheme

It is vital that you get a copy of the mark scheme *before* starting your project. If you know how the project is to be marked, then you can tailor the write up to conform exactly to what the **moderator** is expecting. This will help you to modularise your project, and help your teacher and the moderator to find important information within your project.

The total marks for this module changed from 60 to 65 in the 2005 specification

The 4000-word limit was also thankfully removed.

Mark schemes and methods are likely to change over time.

Make sure that you have downloaded the mark scheme applicable to the year when you will be completing your A2 examination.

Remember that the methods used will vary depending on your chosen solution.

A web site or object-oriented programming solution require different sorts of analysis needing different types of diagrams or methods. However, they all share a common theme of analysis, and this is what is important here.

Pay attention to those parts of the mark scheme that are applicable to your particular project.

The 2005 mark scheme is slightly different to the one shown here. The marks have gone up from 60 to 65 and there are some other minor changes too.

A copy of the mark scheme for the A2 project can be found in the AQA subject specification. Download a copy of this from the Internet (www.aqa.org.uk) and print out the relevant pages. In brief, the 2004 mark scheme is split into the parts shown in the sections below. *It is important at this early stage to have a mental picture of what you are trying to achieve.*

Introduction to the analysis of the problem

The **analysis** section is particularly important; it is *the* section in which you agree what needs to be done by consulting with your client. The mark scheme for this section of the project is summarised in Table 19.1. The **objectives** of the project are a list, preferably containing *quantitative* elements, against which the project will eventually be judged, i.e. if you have achieved everything in this list of objectives then your project works perfectly! Your client needs to appreciate at an early stage that if he or she wishes to change any of these objectives later on, this could cause considerable problems, and may not be possible given the time available.

Table 19.1 Analysis of the problem

Section	Marks	Brief explanation
Analysis	12	• Background identification of the problem • Identification of prospective users • Identification of users' needs and acceptable limitations • Realistic appraisal of feasibility of potential solutions • Justification of chosen solution • Data source(s) and data destination(s) and DfDs (existing system and proposed system) and ER model where relevant • Objectives of the project

It is unlikely that any student will come up with a perfect list of objectives at this stage, and some modification might need to be made as the project proceeds. This is what happens in real life, and you should make a note of the valid reasons why things might have to differ from your original plan. *You will not lose marks for this.*

Introduction to the design of the problem

The **design** section is one in which *critical decisions are undertaken*. The efficiency with which you have undertaken the design will drastically affect how you implement the solution. Wrong decisions made here could mean that you might have to start some sections again. Work hard on this section and get it right *before starting the project*. Some brief explanations are given in Table 19.2.

You are reminded that a *representative sample* of the above is needed in your project. You will gain no extra marks for showing the same methods of validation twenty times! *You should also note that not all subsections of the design are applicable to all projects.* As an example, you are unlikely to need an ER model if you are not designing a database.

Introduction to the technical solution

The **technical solution** of the project is the part which most students like doing best: using the computer to make the project work. The mark scheme is different for students who undertake projects using an **applications package** like a database, or undertake projects making use of a high-level language like Visual Basic or C++ (see margin entry).

Table 19.2 Designing the solution

Section	Marks	Brief explanation
Design	12	• Overall system design • Description of modular structure of the solution (not detailed algorithm design) • Description of data requirements, such as input and output data types and formats • Identification of appropriate storage media and format • Identification of suitable algorithms for data transformation (not detailed algorithm design) • Identification of any validation required • User interface design including input/output, forms and reports • Sample of planned data capture and entry • Sample of data validation, illustrating the operation of error messages • Description of record or database structure • Sample of planned valid output • File organisation and processing • Database design including ER model • Description of measures planned for security and integrity of data • Description of measures planned for system security (access control) • Overall test strategy

Table 19.3 The technical solution

Section	Marks	Brief explanation
Students are expected to undertake the project by: • writing a suitable program or suite of programs; or • using a standard package to produce a tailored solution; or • a combination of the above.		
Technical solution	12	• Annotated listings of programs • Annotated listing of macros • Samples of annotated design screens showing details of package-generated forms, reports, queries, buttons, cross tabulations etc. • Any other reported evidence showing how the implementation was achieved.

If you choose to code the solution to your project using a programming language, then the **code listing** or **program listing** should be shown in an appendix which accompanies your project. If you need to refer to the same code a number of times, refer to the code in the appendix instead of having multiple copies in your project report.

Introduction to system testing

System testing demonstrates that your project works. Unless you work through a convincing test strategy (*worked out during the design section*), you will not gain many marks here. Some ideas are shown in Table 19.4.

Table 19.4 The system testing phase

Section	Marks	Brief explanation
System testing	6	• Design of test plan • A minimal set of test data and expected results for typical data and erroneous/extreme data that is clearly cross-referenced to the test plan • Annotated hard copy of actual test runs showing actual results for typical and erroneous/extreme data cross-referenced to the test plan

Far too many students start on the technical solution before attempting to design the project.

This is usually a bad move, because writing the design section after you have completed the project is notoriously difficult to do.

The moderators are usually very competent at spotting students who have gone via this route. This is often obvious where tell-tale screen shots of finished projects have been used in the design section!

If you are using an object-oriented programming solution then a variety of diagrams exist to help with your analysis and design including object-analysis diagrams, association diagrams, aggregation diagrams and class diagrams.

Use of these diagrams makes your object-oriented analysis and design easier to follow, and these diagrams will be required for OOP solutions from the 2006 subject specification onwards.

Hard copy is particularly relevant when dealing with reports output from a database. The AQA board prefers hard copy to screen captured images for the output in this and similar situations.

You should note that screen shots are often *not acceptable* as evidence of testing the system if hard copies of test runs are easy to produce. The evidence for these can also be shown in an appendix which is referred to in your project report.

Introduction to system maintenance

System maintenance is useful if the system ever needs updating (*most systems will require updating as the needs of the customer change or errors occur*). Much of the documentation already produced goes a long way to satisfying these system maintenance requirements, especially if you have used a high-level language-based solution to the problem. The requirements for system maintenance are shown in Table 19.5

Table 19.5 The system maintenance phase

Section	Marks	Brief explanation
System maintenance	6	• A very brief summary of the features of any package used • A sample of detailed algorithm design using a recognised methodology • Annotated listings of program code or macro code and details of package tailoring. Samples of annotated design screens showing details of package-generated forms, reports, queries, buttons, cross tabulations etc. may be included • Procedure and variable lists/descriptions for programs or list of package items developed, e.g. tables, forms, reports, buttons, macros etc. • Samples of annotated design screens showing details of package generated forms, reports, queries, buttons, cross tabulations etc.

A good test of your system maintenance section is to give your project to another student and ask them to modify it.

The system maintenance documentation should enable someone of similar technical competence to you to modify the project.

Any non-trivial project which cannot be maintained effectively will become useless over a period of time as the needs of most users will inevitably change with time.

Introduction to the user manual

The user manual is a 'stand alone' non-technical document (from the point of view of containing no analysis, design or technical implementation about the project) intended for the user of the system. It should not be long, but it should include what the system does, and enable the user to get the project up and running from the point of view of minimum hardware and software requirements, and enable them to recover from typical errors that might occur in the normal running of the project. The user manual should be kept quite brief, normally running to no more than half a dozen pages, and some ideas are shown in Table 19.6.

Table 19.6 The user manual phase

Section	Marks	Brief explanation
User manual	6	• A brief introduction describing the overall function of the system, but only one section of the system needs to be described, which includes the following: (a) Samples of actual screen displays to illustrate the interface (menus, data input forms, sample data, expected output) in situ with good explanations (b) Samples of error messages/error recovery procedures

Introduction to the project appraisal

The **project appraisal** is a critical analysis of what you have done. No project is perfect, and with the benefit of hindsight all of us can do better. Your client should also be critical of your project, and if your client is your parents then this is sometimes quite difficult! There is always something that can be improved, and this is where critical feedback from your client is important. Some ideas are shown in Table 19.7.

Table 19.7 The project appraisal

Section	Marks	Brief explanation
Appraisal	3	• Comparison of performance against objectives • Possible extensions • User feedback

In the 2005 mark scheme, 5 marks are awarded for the appraisal.

More marks are awarded for constructive criticism, and few if any marks are awarded for bland statements like, 'The project works perfectly'. Even if your project does work perfectly, you should go through the appraisal comparing the outcome with the **design specification** as outlined in the analysis phase. The user feedback should preferably be in the form of a formal letter on company headed notepaper and signed by your user.

Do not rush your project – make sure that you have time to proofread it.

Introduction to the quality of communication

The **quality of communication** marks are very easy to get if you have produced your project in a logical fashion, clearly arranged all the sections with an index, and run the spelling and grammar checking utilities. The only way that you will lose marks here is if you have rushed your project or your English is terrible.

Many people are not good at proofreading what they have written themselves because they are used to their own style and read what should be there rather than what actually is there!

Table 19.8 The quality of communication

Section	Marks	Brief explanation
Quality of communication	3	• Relevant information is clearly organised • Good use of English – continuous prose, with good use of grammar, punctuation and spelling

It is always best if you get someone else to proofread your report for typos etc.

Keeping a project diary

It is essential to keep a **project diary**. It enables you to remember the stages you have been through when solving particular problems. It is very easy to get so engrossed in your project that you forget the route by which you arrived at some impressive solution! Few students will hit on the perfect way to solve complex parts of a problem with little or no thought; the project diary outlines the main points that you have covered to arrive at your chosen solution. At the author's school we use the project diary format shown in Figure 19.1.

This time sheet is available to students at the author's school and is downloadable from the school's intranet site. Students e-mail it back to their teacher as an attachment when the appropriate entry has been filled in. A bad entry is shown in Figure 19.2, and a good entry is shown in Figure 19.3.

The entry in Figure 19.2 is not really any use because *it contains no detail that will help either the student or the teacher*. It appears that a couple of hours have been put into interviewing the candidate's client, but nobody can prove they have done this! A better diary entry, from the *same candidate doing the same project* is shown in Figure 19.3.

Department of Computer Science & ICT Tonbridge School

A2 Project Time Sheet

Name		House / Date	

Attach a new sheet and send it by e-mail to your teacher once per cycle. (Week number is in the calendar.)

Notes: You do not have to fill in each box, but you should have enough detail to indicate what you are doing – Use the examples as a guide.

Calendar information		Detailed progress made
Week Number		
Date		
Hours put in		
Calendar information		**Detailed progress made**
Week Number		
Date		

Figure 19.1 Part of an A2 project time sheet used at the author's school

Few students regret writing up the actual project as soon as they make a start.

It is soul destroying to be faced with a major project write up as you are approaching the project deadline, attempting to get your project working and also trying to revise for important A2 examinations.

Starting the write up very early will ensure that you are less likely to be in this situation.

You will not regret learning a CAD package like Adobe Illustrator, for example, to produce your project diagrams. You should allow a number of hours to learn the necessary techniques.

Calendar information		Detailed progress made
Week Number	1	I had an interview with my client to formalise what we will be doing for my A Level Project.
Date	5/9/02	
Hours put in	2	
Calendar information		**Detailed progress made**
Week Number	2	I had a second interview with my client to sort out many of the details.
Date	10/9/02	
Hours put in	4	

Figure 19.2 An example of a time sheet which is *not* acceptable

Calendar information		Detailed progress made
Week Number	1	I had an interview with Mrs. Smith, which was recorded on audio cassette. We talked in general terms of what was required for the project, and I have written this up into a brief memo. A copy has been sent to Mrs. Smith to check. I have saved a copy onto my X drive.
Date	5/9/02	
Hours put in	2	
Calendar information		**Detailed progress made**
Week Number	2	I had a second interview with Mrs. Smith, who altered some of the things which I thought we had agreed; this was a little annoying so I have made more detailed notes about this interview. I have also come up with a much tighter specification, and have explained that it will be difficult to alter once I proceed. The specification has been fully written up and saved on my X drive. I have also backed this up onto Zip.
Date	10/9/02	
Hours put in	4	

Figure 19.3 A much better entry showing the same information as Figure 19.2

The information in Figure 19.3 is better *because it can be verified*. It also points to other resources like audio tapes and interview notes which help during the project analysis and design phases, and verification that the work done so far has been backed up.

Develop a professional method of working

You are expected to use a word processor to write up your project report. *You should write up the project as you go along*. This means understanding and implementing the following advice from day one when you start writing up the analysis section of your project.

- **Develop a consistent style.**
  - Use a font size of about 10 or 12 pt. Do not go larger than this because it will look like the report has been written by a primary school pupil.
  - Use a different style of heading for each major section and major subsections.
- **Use headers and footers.**
  - The header information could contain the project title and the sections.
  - The footer could contain your name and the page number. It is also useful to insert the candidate number and centre number as a precautionary measure.
- **Number your diagrams and refer to them.**
  - A diagram which is not referred to in the text may not be looked at!
  - Use figure numbers and captions, like those used in this book for example.
- **If possible create your diagrams using a suitable CAD package.**
  - This will make your diagrams easy to follow and read.
  - Make sure you can use the CAD package to create suitable program flowcharts and systems flowcharts, hierarchical diagrams, ER and EAR diagrams, DfDs (Data Flow Diagrams) and class diagrams etc.
  - Create all the symbols you need and reuse them in different diagrams, or make use of a library of symbols if you have one. Once you get used to this it is much quicker.
  - Do not wait until the last moment to create your diagrams, do them as you are going along.
- **Make sure that your project has an index** with all sections like 'analysis', 'design' and 'appendices' etc. clearly marked.
- **Do not leave the write up until the last minute.** If you do this it will take up many hours of your time which you could spend more profitably on revision.

What have other people done for projects in the past?

It is often enlightening to get some ideas of the appropriate standard by looking at what other students have done in the past. Remember that most ideas have been used already; therefore it is unlikely that you will come up with something unique. As long as you do not copy the work of others there is no harm in doing things that have already been done. Some of the projects undertaken at the author's school are as follows:

Once you have chosen a suitable project you would be well advised to check it against the AQA criteria for success outlined earlier in this chapter.

- A relational database for a jeweller's shop (programmed using Microsoft Access)
- An electronic reporting system for teachers for a school in Hong Kong (programmed using Access and Excel)
- An automatic report-generation and profiling system to produce ICT reports and profiles (programmed using Access)
- A web-based electronic glossary for Computer Science (programmed using PERL)
- A microprocessor simulation and teaching aid (programmed using Visual Basic)
- A statistical analysis program for Post Office closures based on demographic data from a post-code database (programmed using Visual Basic)
- An advertising package to show business clients the facilities that can be hired at Tonbridge School (programmed using PowerPoint with VBA extensions).

What next?

The remainder of this book concentrates on the analysis, design, technical solution, system testing and system maintenance, producing a user manual, critically appraising and ensuring good project style. A real AQA project is used as an example.

Self-test questions

1 The AQA board outlines criteria which candidates should follow. Name five different criteria to be considered before starting your A2 project.
2 Why should you download a copy of the mark scheme before starting your project?
3 A web site may not be sufficient for the purposes of satisfying the AQA A2 project criteria.
   (a) Why would a static web site fall foul of the mark scheme?
   (b) What particular criteria would not be satisfied in this case?
   (c) What would you have to do about it to rectify the situation?
4 The AQA board splits A2 projects into a number of important sections. What names are given to these sections?
5 What is the purpose of the system maintenance section of your A2 project?
6 Why is it a good idea to keep a project diary?
7 The write up for your project should be produced using a word processor. What other package do you need to learn to use for the purposes of your project write up? Why do you need to learn how to use this package early on in your course?
8 The style of write up is important. Apart from looking professional, suggest five other things you should do to help ensure that your project is more easily managed and more easily marked by the moderator.

20 The practical project – analysis

In this chapter you will learn about:

- The exemplar project which illustrates analysis for A2 project work
- Identification of the current and potential solutions and methods
- Identification of the users, users' needs and acceptable limitations
- A range of feasible solutions and identifying the best solution
- Producing a list of objectives for the project

Introduction

Having decided on a suitable project and found a client (see chapter 19), you can now proceed with the analysis, which involves writing about what your client wants your project to do. Remember from reading chapter 19 that the mark scheme *is all important*, and the part of the mark scheme dealing with the analysis (for 2004) is reproduced in Table 20.1.

Table 20.1 The mark scheme for the project analysis section

Section	Marks	Brief explanation
Analysis	12	• Background identification of the problem • Identification of prospective users • Identification of users' needs and acceptable limitations • Realistic appraisal of feasibility of potential solutions • Justification of chosen solution • Data source(s) and data destination(s) and DfDs (existing system and proposed system) and ER model where relevant. • Objectives of the project

The author is very grateful to Ivan for permission to use his project as an example in this book.

Ivan started thinking about his project after the AS level exams and got the project approved by his teachers before the summer break.

Ivan started work on the analysis of his project in September of his A2 year.

An exemplar project

It is far easier to develop a *real project*, and the example used here is a *real AQA project* undertaken at the author's school. The student, Ivan, scored 100% for this project.

A chat with your teacher or lecturer will usually result in a useful source of projects.

Databases have already been covered extensively in your AS level course, and a real AQA database **practical exercise** was used for the module 3 AS project work. Advanced databases, relational **database design** and **normalisation** are also covered in chapters 10 and 11 of this book; because of this, a project involving programming in a high-level language has been chosen. Remember that *databases and high-level language solutions are the two methodologies that fit most easily to the AQA mark scheme.*

If you are interested in other subjects like languages or physics, for example, then talk to those teachers too, but make sure they understand the requirements of the mark scheme.

We must differentiate between 'help and advice from the author', and 'work undertaken by the student', i.e. his actual project write up. All work undertaken by Ivan and reproduced here has a green line down one side of it. Ivan's diagrams have been redrawn in the style of this book, and given figure references to help students follow the material. Screen captures are the real screen captures used for Ivan's project.

Introduction to Ivan and his A2 project

Ivan is a competent Visual Basic programmer and therefore wanted to undertake a project in which the most likely method of solution would be to write a program. He asked his teacher for some ideas for a suitable project, and he suggested a teaching aid for computing at A level (*this is a rich source of projects*). It was decided that a system for the traversal and maintenance (*adding and deleting nodes*) of binary trees would be suitable. The teacher suggested an interactive teaching aid for in-order traversal, pre-order traversal, post-order traversal and insertion and deletion of **nodes** in a binary tree structure. The following shows how Ivan carried out the background identification to the problem, analysed the current solution and identified prospective users.

Background identification of the problem

When Ivan's project was written in 2003, the books referred to here were in current use. They have now been replaced by the following five resources:

1. Understanding AS level computing for AQA
2. Understanding A2 level computing for AQA
3. The Ultimate Computing Glossary for A Level
4. Understanding Computing Interactive (AS Level electronic resources)
5. Understanding Computing Interactive (A2 Level electronic resources)

Tonbridge School is a boarding school situated in Tonbridge, Kent. It has about 760 pupils, all of whom are boys. A large computer department teaches ECDL to the lower school and AS and A2 computing in the A level years.

After talking with Mr Bradley, our computing teacher, we decided that it would be a good idea to produce a teaching aid to help A level computing students understand important concepts. After investigating many different possibilities, I decided that I am going to develop a study aid to help teach traversal and maintenance of binary trees, by using pre-order, in-order and post-order traversal. At present these concepts are taught using conventional methods which are described below.

The current solution

At A level, we have two computing teachers: Mr Bradley and Mr Davis. They usually teach by using an OHP or an interactive whiteboard. First, they explain the basic concepts, e.g. what a binary tree is and why it is used. Then, they put an example on the board and make sure that everybody understands it. We are, of course, welcome to ask any questions. Then, they set another example, but this time we have to solve it. When they think they have spent enough time on the topic, they move on to the next, harder concept of the same topic, or teach a new topic.

Traversing binary trees

You can traverse a tree in three different ways; **Pre-order traversal**, **In-order traversal** and **Post-order traversal**.

These methods refer to the position in which the **node** is visited. Consider the simple tree shown in Figure 37.1.

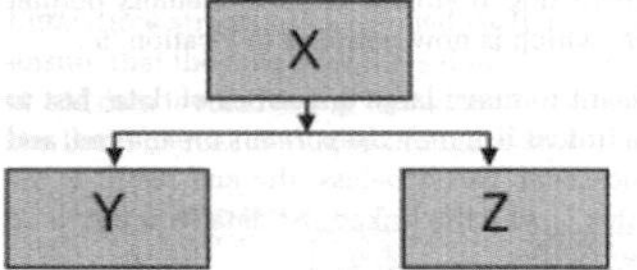

Figure 37.1 Tree for traversal methods.

By observation of Figure 37.1, we can see that the node data would be listed in the following ways, for each traversal mechanism.

(a) **Pre-order traversal** (visit root first, then left sub tree, then right sub tree) X, Y, Z

(b) **In-order traversal** (visit left-hand sub tree first, then the root, then the right-hand sub tree) Y, X, Z

(c) **Post-order traversal** (visit left-hand sub tree, then the right-hand sub tree, then visit the root) Y, Z, X

Always do the left-hand sub tree before the right-hand sub tree.

If the tree structure is larger, then the sub trees must be treated as though you were starting the problem again, even though you are in the middle of traversing a larger tree. You will recall that the process, where you can solve a smaller identical problem, by applying the same algorithm, whilst in the middle of a more complex problem is called **recursion** (see unit 39). You can see recursion in operation in the following example.

Example

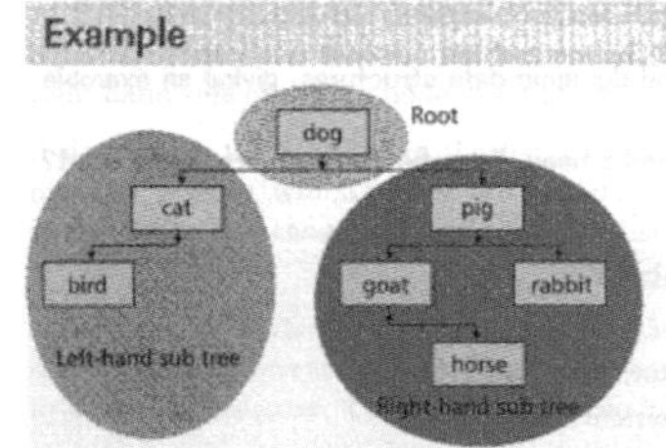

Figure 37.2 Example tree structure.

Consider the tree in Figure 37.2.

List the data in this tree by applying the following traversal mechanisms.

(a) Pre-order traversal
(b) In-order traversal
(c) Post-order traversal

Figure 20.1 Ray Bradley's study guide

In addition to the teachers there are books. In fact, we use two books: *Understanding Computer Science for Advanced Level* and *Understanding Computer Science for Advanced Level the Study Guide*, both written by Ray Bradley, our teacher. They both have good diagrams and an example of the study guide is shown in Figure 20.1. This particular example explains how to traverse binary trees, and it is this that I am hoping to make more interesting by using a computer-based solution.

Identification of the prospective users

The prospective users of this system are the teachers of computing and students who are undertaking the AS and A2 level computing courses. These students are 17 or 18 years old, and both students and teachers have a high degree of computer literacy. I will be making this project for Mr Bradley, and he will distribute it to whoever he wants, but in actual fact the real users will be Tonbridge School Computing students, at A2 and AS level, starting from the year 2004. Mr Bradley might even choose to give it to some GCSE students who want to see what AS computing is like.

It is vital that you describe the potential users of your project. Unless you do this the moderator will not appreciate the people for whom the project is being designed (e.g. their standard of computer literacy, age, sex etc.).

Feedback from the author

Always explain the environment in which your proposed system will be used. Ivan has painted a picture of Tonbridge School from the perspective of the computer department, but you will have to paint a picture of your prospective users and the business, educational or other environment in which they operate. For example, you could be developing a program for young children in a local primary school, building a database for a small business consisting of half a dozen people, or creating a web site for a sports club run at the local community centre. It is easier for the **moderator** to mark your project if they know the environment in which it will be run, because *this helps them to visualise the needs of your users*.

Ivan has explained what he is attempting to do. The moderator should now have a clear understanding of the scope of what is to be achieved, but has no idea of the way in which it might be accomplished or any limitations that will be imposed on the system that Ivan will design.

You should note that you do not have to mirror the exact titles from the AQA mark scheme as Ivan has done, but the moderator needs to find information quickly, and the titles used here will enable him or her to do just that.

The next two sections show how Ivan identifies the needs of the potential users, outlines acceptable limitations which were agreed with his client, makes a realistic appraisal of the feasibility of potential solutions and justifies his chosen solution.

Identification of the user needs and acceptable limitations

In general, the users will want some or all of these things to be included in the project:

- A user-friendly interface, so that they do not need to spend too much time adapting to it, but can get straight to work.
- A well-designed help facility, so that even if they are not sure what to do, they can look it up.
- Enough depth to cover the AS and A2 syllabuses in the chosen topics in the project.
- Clear and simple information so that it is easy for them to grasp the concepts. There is no point in designing a project which makes the concepts harder to understand than Mr Bradley himself or his book. It has to be a useful tool as a supplement to the books and the teacher.
- The users will want some interactive aspects of the project, so that they can experiment with it and try out different scenarios and combinations etc. This will mean that they can use it again and again but in different ways (e.g. using different node data and different trees).
- The teachers are looking to save time, to help students who may have been absent, and to provide extra interest.
- The students are looking for extra practice, more variety and a revision aid.

In terms of limitations, there are almost none in our school. In terms of software, we have Microsoft Office, Adobe Photoshop, Macromedia Dreamweaver and many other useful programs, but even if I wanted to use something we do not have, the school would not mind buying at least one copy of it, according to my teacher. The programming languages available are Visual Basic, Pascal, C++ and PROLOG. The operating system in use at the school is Windows 2000 Professional.

In terms of hardware, the current computers have the following specification

Athlon XP 1.8 GHz	256 MB DDR RAM	32 MB graphics card
100 Mbit/sec Ethernet	Multiple file servers	Broadband Internet links

The computers are fast enough to run all the software with acceptable speed. The hardware would only be a limitation if I was going to do some video editing or video rendering or something similar, but as this is unlikely to be the case in my project, I can pretty much say that the limitations are minimal.

Feasibility of potential solutions

Ivan wanted to write a programming solution and has given reasonable evidence for doing this. Remember that time constraints, your current knowledge and interests are all important factors in determining the final solution.

Macromedia Flash is one possibility that Ivan could have mentioned here. An authoring package is another, but these would not fit the mark scheme as well as writing a program.

There are many ways in which computers can be used to achieve the described task. On the lowest level, I will have to decide whether it will be interactive or not (e.g. writing a text document). However, one of the identified user specifications is interactivity because they already have a non-interactive solution (the book) and even one interactive one (the teacher).

Having decided that my project has to be interactive, there are still many different alternatives:

- **A PowerPoint presentation** A PowerPoint presentation would be an aesthetically pleasing solution as PowerPoint has many templates with pictures, sounds, animations and other similar aids. There are some animations and sounds and even videos, but on a basic level – it is only flipping pages one by one. I have seen this and done this, but that is not to say that real interaction between the users and the presentation cannot be made. But, for that to happen, one needs to know VBA (Visual Basic for Applications). I do not know VBA, and this means that I would have to spend some time learning it because my project will be quite complex to program.
- **A web page** The biggest advantage of a web page is that the students can access it from home any time they want. Another advantage is that the web page can be updated regularly without the user having to do very much (e.g. downloading updates, patches etc.). The problem is that I would have to learn how to use a web design package (e.g. Dreamweaver), and also learn a language which I do not know such as JavaScript or VBScript. I know some HTML, but nothing powerful enough for what would be needed.
- **An executable program** A different solution is to make a program in a programming language. The advantage of this is that it can be very flexible. You can make whatever you want; you dictate your own rules and can customise it to the exact needs of the user, and if an executable program is made the user does not need to have a copy of the programming language used to create it.

If, after the initial analysis, you are unhappy with the way that your project is progressing (method of solution or interests etc.), you should choose a different one.

Chosen solution and its justification

From my current analysis, I have concluded that an executable program is the best solution for my problem. All I have to decide now is what programming language to use. As I have said, any language can be made available to me, so availability is not a limitation. Possible languages include C++, Pascal or Visual Basic. C++ is a very powerful language and would be excellent for the job. Pascal is another powerful language. Visual Basic is also powerful, and as I know a lot of it already I will not need to learn too many new things.

I also know QBASIC which is even simpler, but it can only be used in DOS. The obvious language to use is Visual Basic. It has everything I need (it is a third-generation declarative language, with loops and arrays etc.), more than powerful enough for what I need to do.

If you get this far and cannot justify using a method with which you are completely happy, then change your project now! It is not going to be any fun spending months learning a system which you dislike or are not interested in.

Feedback from the author

Ivan has made an excellent attempt at identifying the needs of his users, from both the teachers' and pupils' perspectives. A realistic appraisal of potential solutions has been carried out, which includes looking into each solution in a little detail. (*It is no good if you simply list some of the alternatives – you need to explore each of them like Ivan has done above.*)

He has justified his proposed method. Remember that *familiarity with a particular system* (like Visual Basic programming) is a *good reason* to use that language rather than any other system which might be available to you, like the object-oriented language C++, for example. Familiarity with a particular language might enable you to solve problems more easily.

You will recall that Ivan wanted to undertake a project using Visual Basic, and his teacher knew from the outset that this would be an acceptable method of solution. *Skilful choice of project in the first place should ensure that you end up with a project which interests you and which uses a method of solution with which you are totally happy.*

In the next few sections Ivan compares his project with the manual methods used at the school to ensure that he is on the right track, he will identify the data sources and destinations, and produce the all-important list of objectives against which his project will be judged when he comes to write up the appraisal (see chapter 23).

My project compared with the current solution

Ivan has an exceptionally good list of reasons why the project will be useful.

You should have a number of good reasons for doing your project, otherwise there is not much point in undertaking it!

There is no point in making a program if it will be no better than what we already have in school to teach the students those topics. First, we will look back at the section on the current solution at the beginning of the analysis. There are many ways in which my solution to the problem could be better than the current solution, and I will try to list most of them:

- The program will break the monotony of everyday school life. It introduces variety. It will be something different from a teacher and a book, which are used in most lessons. It will generate interest, enthusiasm and a desire to learn. Hopefully an example of this would be the interactivity in my program.
- The program is less likely to make mistakes than teachers. Teachers can get distracted, and if they are not concentrating they could make silly mistakes on the board (e.g. add an extra 1 in a binary number) or as they talk (e.g. say something they did not mean).
- The program can make many examples available to students. In a book, there might be only two or three examples of how to traverse a binary tree, and the teacher can only do a few examples in class. The program could have a random number generator, so that the students can have an infinite amount of examples. They can keep practising until they get it right.
- An advantage of my program over a teacher is that it can be used at any time and also at home. A teacher is only available during the lessons (and only during the school day).
- This is a relatively cheap improvement for teaching. All the students need is a computer. Other teaching aids might be much more expensive.

Ivan's data sources and destinations are quite simple in that any string of characters is acceptable for data input, and his program is a tightly controlled environment.

Your data sources and destinations might be considerably more complex than his.

Data sources and destinations

The data for my project will come from the individual users of the program. For example, if they want to specify what data is contained in each node or how many nodes there will be, this data will be input via a keyboard, and the program will accept it via a text box.

The program will then process the data, and output some other data using a text box, or by drawing rectangles (for binary trees) or opening another window. There is another form of data that the users can specify as well, and these will be the different options in the program (e.g. do the users want help or not?). This data will be processed as well, but the computer will have no direct output, it will just alter the way data entered by the user (as in the first example) is processed. The user will mainly use the mouse for this input, as the computer will accept this data using radio boxes or check boxes.

Objectives of the project

After this analysis of the project has been done, it is time to make some decisions about what exactly I need to do. Therefore I have conducted some extra interviews with my client, Mr Bradley, which you can see in the appendix of the analysis and design.

The appendices referred to in this text are not shown in this book but are available in the A2 Understanding Computing Interactive CD.

The *agreed* objectives for this project are as follows.

- There are three basic modes of operation:
  - Adding data
  - Deleting data
  - Tree traversal
- The system must be able to correctly draw a binary tree and let the user choose what data to put in it or take out of it.
- There needs to be an option that will traverse the tree in three different ways:
  - In-order
  - Pre-order
  - Post-order traversal.
- There should be an option to clear all the data and start again.
- There should be an option to generate a random binary tree so the user does not have to type in lots of data to generate the tree. Ten nodes should be sufficient for this.
- There should be a time delay so that the user can see what's happening in slow motion.
- There should be an automatic mode (used in conjunction with the time delay) which draws the binary tree for the user.
- There should be a user interactive mode in which the user can interact with the system to add and delete nodes manually.
- There should be a system to help the user to learn how to use the program, and this help should be easily available.
- The user should also be able to delete nodes from the tree, and the tree should maintain its binary tree structure.
- The user should be tested on a variety of tasks. If he or she wants to add a node to the tree, the user should be prompted to click on the appropriate space in the tree where the node should be added.
- To delete the nodes, the user should be prompted to select the node to be deleted and then click on the nodes indicating where they should be moved to, and which nodes should be removed and added again. In this way the user should be tested on everything that needs to be done in order to delete a node.
- When using the program in the appropriate mode the user should be prompted to click the nodes in the correct order of traversal.

- The program should be visually appealing to the user. For example, when looking at and comparing the nodes they should be different colours, and the user should receive feedback about what the program is doing. For example, if a node is being added, as the value of the node is being compared with other nodes, the nodes could change colour and some sort of status box could tell the user what is happening.
- The speed of the program should be variable. We know that the program can perform all the instructions almost instantly (since they are in Basic), and so the user will not be able to follow everything that is happening. So, it should be possible to slow down the program. When it is not slowed down it will still be useful, for example if the user needs to check the answers and does not care about the explanations.
- The binary tree will need to be up to six levels deep.

Finally, a system flowchart has been drawn to make the process of choosing the options more clear.

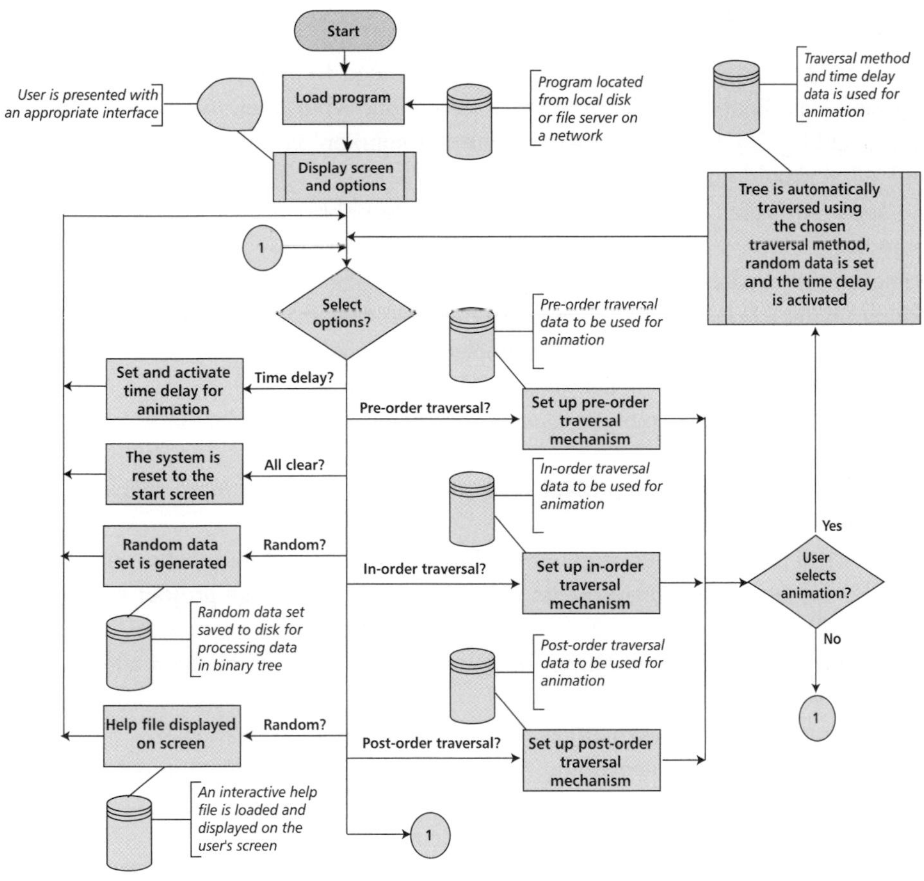

Figure 20.2 The system flowchart for automatic mode

The mark scheme suggests that ER diagrams and DFDs be carried out, but in Ivan's case a simple systems flowchart is a better option.

You need to choose the best options for your project, but do check with your project supervisor before making any decision.

The system flowchart showing the automatic mode is shown here.

There is another system flowchart showing manual mode, where the user can add or delete nodes, but this is not shown here.

Feedback from the author

Ivan has diverted slightly from the format suggested in the mark scheme by including a section about why his project should be better than the current manual methods. Do not hesitate to add extra information if you feel that this will enhance your explanation. The information given in this section clarifies the needs of the users considerably.

Remember that your project will be considerably different from the one shown here.

Databases, procedural programming (Ivan's chosen method of solution), object-oriented programming and web site design will all need to be explained using very different techniques.

Nevertheless, it is still very useful to see how previous students have interpreted the mark scheme for their projects. You will need to take advice from your teacher or lecturer about your particular project.

The data sources and destinations are very simple in this project because they are generated by the user of the program. Often this section can be quite large, especially if you are designing a database or customising some business process. You will be lucky to get away with a minimalist section like Ivan has here, but as mentioned in chapter 19, *not all projects require information from all sections.*

Ivan's project does not need ER diagrams, but a DFD diagram or system flowchart is essential here because it simplifies some complex information briefly outlined in the objectives. It is quite difficult to construct a DFD because there is minimal movement of actual data. A system flowchart is more appropriate for this project because it enables you to show the proposed interaction between the user and the system more effectively. A DFD could be produced, but it would be difficult not to write things like 'Pre-order has been chosen' or 'Clear all data' etc. which is not really the flow of data but actions undertaken by the user.

Self-test questions

1 When designing an AQA A2 Computing project you need to produce some 'Background identification of the problem' information. What does this mean?
2 What is meant by the 'current system' or 'current solution' in terms of your project design? What should you do if there is no current system?
3 Outline some attributes which are important when describing the 'users' for your A2 project.
4 All projects need to identify acceptable limitations. Suggest some acceptable limitations on the following two projects. (Remember that these are being tackled by an A2 student, they are not professional implementations.)
   (a) A database for managing meals for patients in a hospital.
   (b) Developing a simple assembly-language interface for teaching low-level language programming.
5 There is no point in designing a project unless it solves a problem more efficiently than is currently the case.
   (a) Suggest two possible improvements for the hospital project in question 4.
   (b) Suggest two possible improvements for the assembly-language project in question 4.
6 When considering feasible alternatives for your project you must suggest alternatives which would work quite well.
   (a) Suggest two ways of implementing the hospital project in question 4.
   (b) Suggest two ways of implementing the assembly-language project in question 4.
7 Project objectives are of paramount importance; why is this so?
8 (a) Suggest two objectives for the hospital project in question 4.
   (b) Suggest two objectives for the assembly-language project in question 4.
9 It is important to consider data sources and destinations when designing a project.
   (a) Suggest two data sources and destinations for the hospital project in question 4.
   (b) Suggest two data sources and destinations for the assembly-language project in question 4.
10 (a) Suggest two suitable diagram types for the hospital project in question 4.
   (b) Suggest two suitable diagram types for the assembly-language project in question 4.

21 The practical project – design

In this chapter you will learn about:

- Designing the binary tree traversal and maintenance project
- How to tackle project design using appropriate diagrams
- Calculation of storage requirements and selecting appropriate storage media
- Creating a suitable user interface and prototypes, data integrity and data security
- Devising a suitable test plan

Introduction

In the previous two chapters you have been introduced to the practical project work at A2 level. A real AQA project at the author's school was chosen as an example, and this involved producing a teaching aid for the traversal and maintenance of binary tree structures. The analysis of this project has already been undertaken in chapter 20, so we now continue work with the same project, but this time concentrating on the **design**.

This chapter continues the project work started in chapter 20. Make sure that you read chapters 19 and 20 first, or you may not understand the material in this chapter.

The design section covers how the user interface will look, the organisation and processing of any data structures or files, any data validation that will be needed and the procedures needed to implement the project. The mark scheme for the design section (for the 2004 subject specification) is shown in Table 21.1 (see margin entry).

Note how we make use of the real AQA mark scheme to construct the sections for the project. This is not cheating; it ensures that you have a tick list to check off the things that need to be done.

Make sure that you have downloaded a copy of the mark scheme for your year. It may not be exactly the same as the one shown here.

Table 21.1 The mark scheme for the project design section

Section	Marks	Brief explanation
Design	12	• Overall system design • Description of modular structure of the solution (not detailed algorithm design) • Description of data requirements, such as input and output data types and formats • Identification of appropriate storage media and format • Identification of suitable algorithms for data transformation (not detailed algorithm design) • Identification of any validation required • User interface design including input/output, forms and reports • Sample of planned data capture and entry • Sample of data validation, illustrating the operation of error messages • Description of record or database structure • Sample of planned valid output • File organisation and processing • Database design including ER model • Description of measures planned for security and integrity of data • Description of measures planned for system security (access control) • Overall test strategy

An introduction to design

It is important to realise that a project should be designed *before* any work on the computer is undertaken. It is rare for most students to do this properly, but your project write up must make it look as though you did! A combination of wanting to start the actual work on the computer and learning new packages or new techniques in your chosen programming language are too tempting for most; but the design of the project *really is easier if you do it first*. Unfortunately, most students find themselves getting into a complete mess before they realise this! Even most experts cannot design a project completely without some sort of prototype or the odd procedure or two being checked out first, but the documentation needs to be written as the mark scheme suggests, or it is very difficult for your teachers, the **moderator** and even you to follow it. Below are some snippets of work that Ivan covered for the design of his system.

The modular structure of the system

As you have seen from the analysis of the system, there will be three basic parts to the project:

1 Addition of data
2 Traversal of the nodes
3 Deletion of the nodes

In addition, there will be two modes of operation.

1 User Mode OFF
2 User Mode ON

This means that I will effectively need to split my program into five subsections, and a simple hierarchical diagram of the system is shown in Figure 21.1. Because the deletion part is the most complex of all, it can be split into more subsections where the node to be deleted has no subnodes, right subnodes only and left subnodes. If a node has left subnodes, once it has been deleted, the tree can be left with a gap or without a gap. If it has a gap, a further problem needs to be solved. This will all become clear once I explain the algorithms used in the solution.

The diagrams have been relabelled using the conventions in this book to make it easier for the reader to follow.

Ivan has decided on a design limitation, namely the use of alphanumeric data instead of having both string and numbers. He has gone on to say why he has imposed this limitation.

This is a good example of something that was not thought about at design time, but is now agreed with Ivan's client.

You will not lose any marks for sensible limitations like this which you have agreed with your client, even if the moderator could think of a way around your problem.

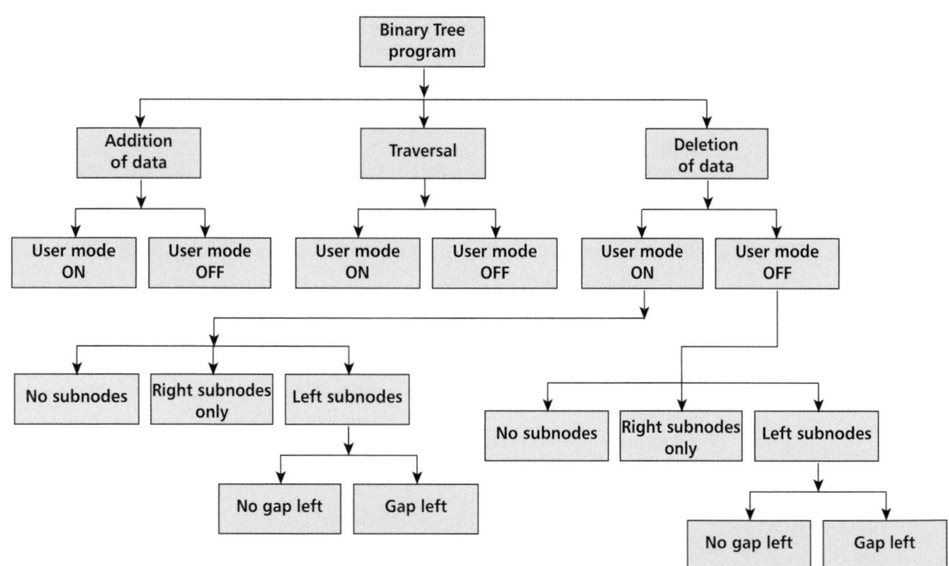

Figure 21.1 The hierarchical nature of the binary tree project

Definition of data requirements

The data to be used in the binary tree could be either numerical or alphanumerical. However, it cannot be both at the same time. I could therefore decide to use one of them, or maybe have a radio box so that the user can select what data to use. Obviously, it would be better for the user to choose what data to use, but I do not think that it would work easily in Visual Basic. This is because the variables have to be specifically defined at the beginning of the program (if we want it to work correctly). If the data type of a variable is changed suddenly, I am almost certain that the same code will not work for the new variable. Therefore, I would have to create new code for another mode of working, and this would mean that I will have 12 parts to my system, not six. Because of my time limitations, I have decided to use only one data type: alphanumerical (or string as Visual Basic calls it). This was decided because when teachers introduce binary trees, they work with words not numbers (at least I was taught like that). In addition, strings are easier to work with in Visual Basic as the captions of objects (buttons, rectangles etc.). I have not yet decided what to use as a tree node.

Storage media, format, file organisation and processing

The project will be stored on the school network during the development. This means that the files will be on one of the servers in the school. The school backs up their servers on a daily basis, and I will be backing up my project on a zip disk on a regular basis. Once the project is finished, the users can choose where they want to store it. I guess as most of the users are students from the school, they will either copy it to their network or access it from the resources server (Mr Bradley will put it there so that anybody can access it once I finish it). Of course, they could also take it home on a floppy disk or a zip disk.

I can estimate how large the project will be. I have created an empty project with one blank form and the size was 1.09 Kbytes. When I added one object to it (a command button) the size was 1.34 Kbytes, and when I entered one line of code for it with a comment as well, the size was 1.46 Kbytes. If I assume that for every object I add, 0.25 Kbytes will be added, and for every line another 0.12 Kbytes, then a reasonable estimate for the size of the project would be 1.09 + 150*0.25 (I will have no more than 150 objects on the page (64 nodes, 64 lines to join the nodes and some buttons/text boxes/radio buttons/tick boxes)) + 1000*0.12 (I will not have more than 1000 lines of code) = 125 Kbytes. So, I do not expect the actual Visual Basic program to be bigger than 125 Kbytes. When it is compiled, this number should come down (because all the comments are erased and machine code is used), but not too much, so I do not think it will be bigger than 100 Kbytes (this includes the icon, which is about 10 Kbytes). Finally, the help file will be no bigger than 1 Mb (it will be quite large because it will contain photos). Therefore, the total size of the project will be (I will distribute the source code with it as well): 125 Kbytes + 100 Kbytes + 1 Mb = 1.25 Mb. This is a nice size as it will fit on a floppy disk.

You should always say how you will back up your data and make an estimate of the amount of disk space needed for your project.

Ivan made a few prototypes using Visual Basic to estimate the likely file size.

The final size (compiled into an .exe file) of Ivan's project is about 88 Kbytes (this does not include the help file).

During the development, the program will be in the Visual Basic format. After I have finished, it will be compiled and will use a normal executable file format (.exe). The user manual will be in another format.

I could develop the user manual just as a Word document, but I do not think that is professional enough. On the other hand, I think that it would be too complicated and unnecessary for me to use a proper help file format. Creating .hlp files is as complicated as using a programming language, and unfortunately I do not have any time to learn it. So a good compromise is a web page. It will look professional because I can put links in it to take the user to the relevant sections on the page, similar to how FAQs are designed on the Internet: the user clicks on a question, and the screen scrolls to the appropriate section. However, if I do it as an HTML page, the pictures (screenshots) will have to be in separate files, probably in a separate directory. That is why I have decided to use a .mht format, which is a web page archive, i.e. everything it needs is contained within one file. A summary of file types and formats is shown in Table 21.2.

If you use unusual file formats like .mht, explain what they are for and why you will be using them.

Table 21.2 The file formats to be used in the binary tree project

File type	Description
Visual Basic Project (.vbp)	Stores data about the project and its components
Visual Basic Form (.frm)	Stores data about any forms in the project
Visual Basic Standard Module (.bas)	Stores data about any modules in the project
Executable File (.exe)	Used for the compiled version of the project
Web Page Archive (.mht)	Used for the user documentation

The flowcharts shown here are not for the design of the detailed algorithms. They are macro flowcharts suitable for use at the project design stages for helping to develop the detailed algorithms and the user interfaces.

Some of the material shown here would have been more appropriate for the 'technical solution' section. However, as long as the moderator can find information you will get marks for it.

Remember that the methods used in your project may be significantly different to those shown here. It is up to you to decide the best way to communicate your design ideas to the moderator.

Identification of suitable algorithms for data transformation

I will explain each modular section of my project and which algorithms will be used to solve them. Figure 21.2 shows a macro flowchart for addition of data in User Mode OFF.

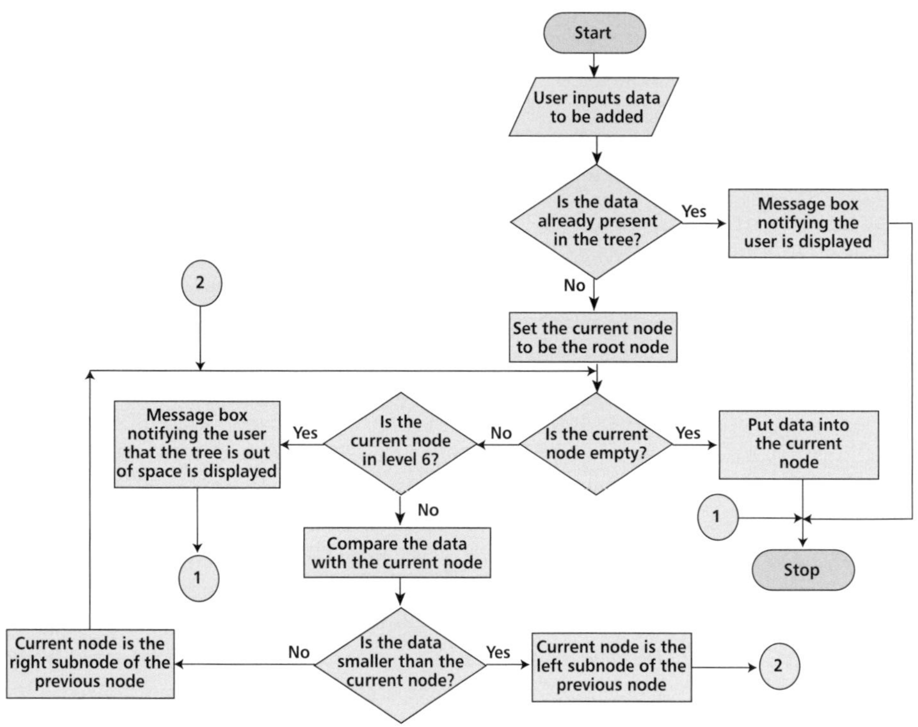

Figure 21.2 Flowchart showing addition of data in User Mode OFF

Addition of data in User Mode ON

To use a binary tree, it first needs to be created. It is created by adding data to it. To maintain a binary tree structure, given any node, its left subnode (if it exists) needs to be smaller than the node and the right subnode (if it exists) needs to be bigger than the node.

The flowchart in Figure 21.3 describes how this will be achieved. Its basic principle is that when a node is added, it will travel down the tree, and based on its value, it will move left or right. When it reaches an empty node, this is where the node is added. To prevent ambiguity between small and capital letters, any small letters will be converted to capital.

Ivan has done well to notice patterns pertinent to his implementation of the project that will simplify some of the algorithms that may otherwise have been necessary.

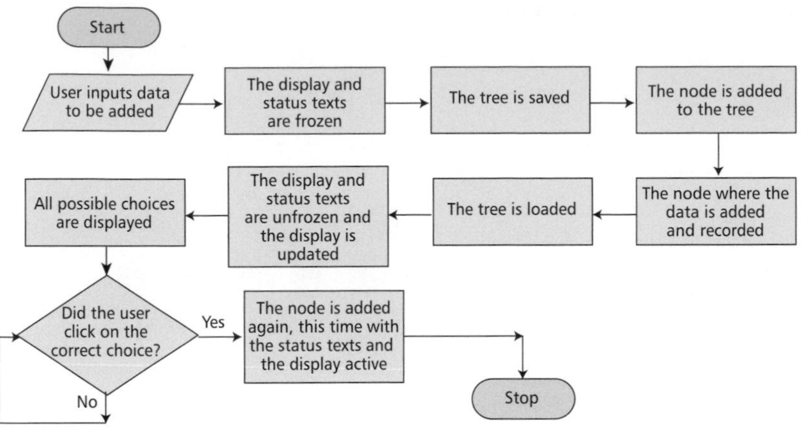

Figure 21.3 Flowchart showing addition of data in User Mode ON

Traversal of data in User Mode OFF

The traversal of the data is quite complicated when a proper general algorithm is used (like for the data addition), and the flowchart is shown in Figure 21.4.

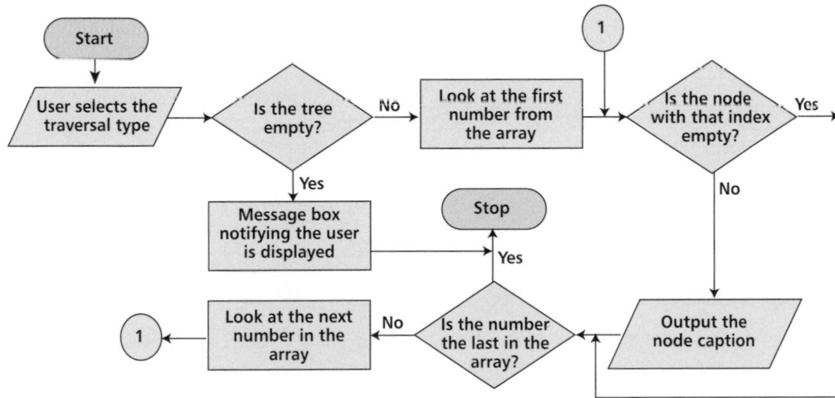

Figure 21.4 Flowchart showing traversal of data in User Mode OFF

I have noticed that no matter how big the tree is, and no matter what its shape is, traversal of the nodes is essentially the same, just with some nodes skipped. Let me explain. Imagine a tree which is completely full, all 64 nodes are taken up. When I do a traversal of the nodes on the whole tree, I will have 64 answers. However, if I remove some nodes from the tree, and do the traversal again, the order of the nodes that were not removed does not change, the only difference is that the nodes that do not exist are skipped. I will use this fact to devise an easier algorithm for tree traversal. For example, let us say that the results of a traversal are ALSD, KJSHD, SAJKD, NDKA and ASDD (this is just for illustration purposes). Then let us say that I delete the node SAJKD; then the result of traversal will be ALSD, KJSHD, NDKA and ASDD. The nodes are in the same order as before. So, I decided to label each node in my tree, and perform a large traversal of the tree and put the result in an array. I will label the nodes in VB by using the Index property. I will tailor the labels so that the in-order traversal is simply given by the nodes with consecutive indices. Let us say the tree will look like Figure 21.5 (with numbers in the nodes representing the indices).

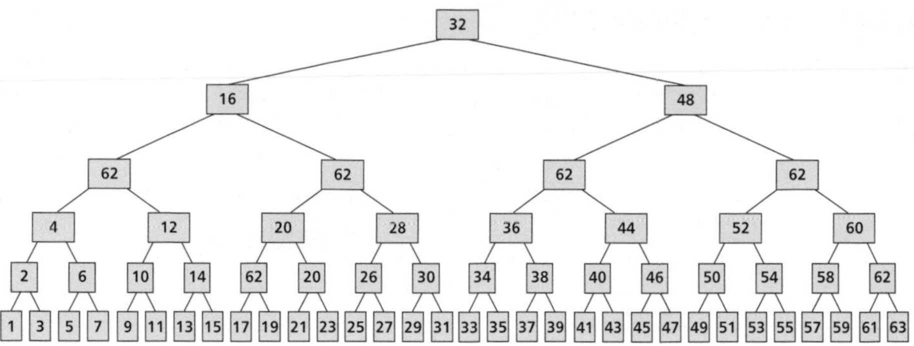

Figure 21.5 A full binary tree

Now, the in-order traversal of this tree is simply given by:

1,2,3,4,5,6,7 ... 62, 63.

The post-order traversal will be given by:

1,3,2,5,7,6,4,9,11,10,13,15,14,12,8,17,19,18,21,23,22,20,25,27,26,29,31,30,28,24,16, 33,35,34,37,39,38,36,41,43,42,45,47,46,44,40,49,51,50,53,55,54,52,57,59, 58,61,63,62,60,56,48,32.

And the pre-order traversal is given by:

32,16,8,4,2,1,3,6,5,7,12,10,9,11,14,13,15,24,20,18,17,19,22,21,23,28,26,25,27,30, 29,31,48,40,36,34,33,35,38,37,39,44,42,41,43,46,45,47,56,52,50,49,51,54, 53,55,60,58,57,59,62,61,63.

It is not necessary for you to read and understand all of this material in detail.

What is being conveyed here is that Ivan has produced a design section for each of the boxes outlined in the hierarchical diagram of Figure 21.1.

As you should have modularised your project, you should be able to produce similar sections appropriate to object-oriented programming design, database design or website design, for example.

The examples shown here are appropriate for procedural programming solutions.

So, I will just put all of these numbers in an array and use the algorithm from the flowchart to come up with traversal results.

Traversal of data in User Mode ON

Since all the results of the traversal are predefined in the array, the tree does not need to be hidden from the user like in the addition. The user simply needs to click on the traversed nodes, and the order is checked using the array. The flowchart for this is shown in Figure 21.6.

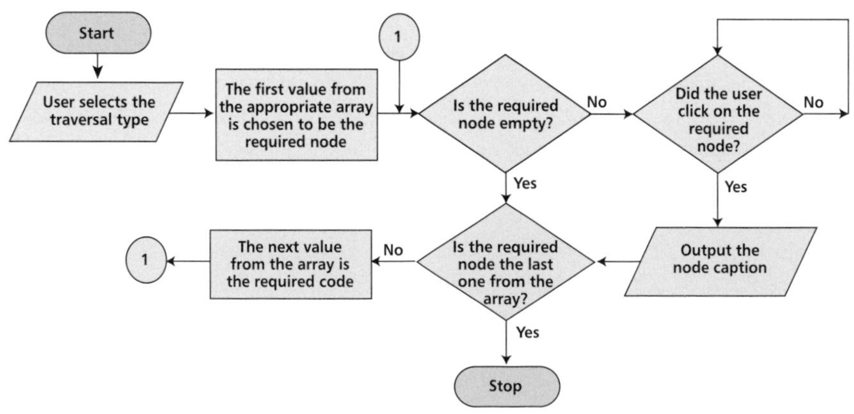

Figure 21.6 Flowchart showing traversal of data in User Mode ON

Deleting data in User Mode ON

If the node has no subnodes, then it is really easy to delete the node as it is simply removed (deleted). If it has only right subnodes, then it is removed again, but the problem is that the tree will have some gaps in it, so it is not a binary tree any more. I will deal with this later. If the node to be deleted has left subnodes, then it needs to be replaced with another one from the tree. The replacement node is found using an algorithm in which you go along the tree by going to the left subnode first, and then to the right subnode if there is one, and then to the right again, and again, until there are no more full right nodes to go to. This is all shown on the flowchart of Figure 23.7. The replacement node is the last right node you visited (if there were no right nodes, then it will just be the left node of the deleting node) before you came across an empty node, or the end of the tree. Then, the deleting node is replaced with this node, and deleted.

In the above way, the binary tree structure is preserved (there might be some gaps in it however) without moving any of the data. Then, in a real tree, the pointers could be altered so that no other nodes need to be moved. However, I am not using pointers, and I can get the same tree as if I changed the pointers by adding the nodes under the gap, if there is one, to the tree again (just after deleting them), so that is what I will do. I will probably have two separate procedures in the program, one for finding a replacement node and one for removing a gap from the tree. The two of them will be used to delete the node in another procedure.

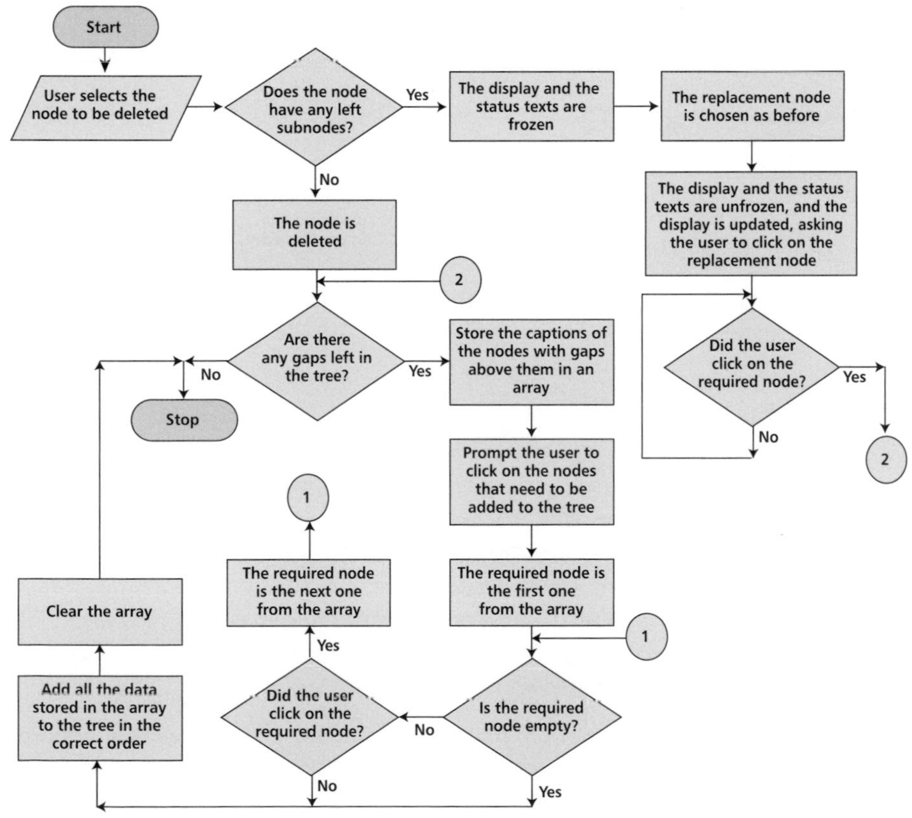

Figure 21.7 Flowchart for deleting data in User Mode ON

Notice how Ivan has modularised each section and explained his strategy for solving each problem by the production of suitable diagrams.

Notice also how much time it takes to read the solution that somebody else has produced. You should now appreciate how your teachers feel when they have to mark a class set of projects!

You should also be able to appreciate the difficult and tedious role the moderator has, and begin to understand the need to keep things clear, concise, and to the point.

Finally, you should appreciate the important role of diagrams in the design section.

Deleting data in User Mode OFF

This will be quite a challenge, probably the most complicated algorithm in the program. Firstly, if the deletion of the node is trivial (i.e. it just needs to be removed), then the user does not need to do anything, the node will be deleted automatically. However, if a replacement node needs to be chosen, then the display will be hidden away from the user, just like with the addition of the data, until the node is chosen. After that, the user will need to click on the replacement node and the nodes will get replaced. Then, if there is a gap, it needs to be sorted out. The display will be frozen again and the nodes that need to be added to the tree will not be added to the tree but to an array. Then, the tree will be reverted back to what it was just before the picture was frozen. Then, the user will have to click on the nodes that need to be added in the correct order, dictated by the array, just like the traversal arrays.

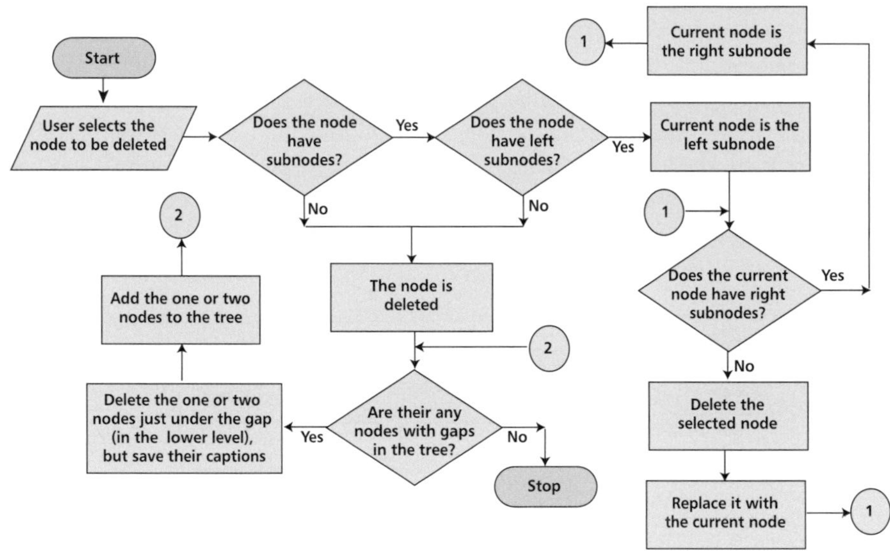

Figure 21.8 Flowchart for deleting data in User Mode OFF

As this is the design section it is perfectly normal not to have all the details that will be needed when the system is implemented.

It is quite appropriate that Ivan does not know all the procedures that will be necessary to support the main design at this particular stage.

Other procedures

Of course, these six tasks will not just be there by themselves, there will be many other procedures which I will produce separately to make the above procedures easier to work. For example, there will be a procedure that checks if the tree is empty, and a procedure that updates the display by showing only the nodes that have captions. There will be another one that will add 10 random nodes to the tree. Another procedure will display text on the screen telling the user what is going on (see the user interface). However, I do not know yet which procedures I will need, so I cannot write a full list. They will be developed as I go along to make the main procedures work.

The main procedure that I have not mentioned yet is the one for creating delays between events. Well, when the program adds or deletes or traverses the nodes by itself, it will all happen very fast. So, I will slow the program down. Between each step in the events, I will add a line of code for the program to pause for a certain period, so that the user can see what is happening. There will be three time delays: no delay, one, two and three seconds' delay.

Feedback from the author

There are an unusually large number of flowcharts here, but this is one of the easiest ways to explain what is happening and will make the Visual Basic programming much easier to understand (see the technical solution in chapter 22). It is quite difficult to understand exactly how things will pan out from the list of objectives alone, and the flowcharts help with this. Ivan has also spotted many patterns that will help him to make use of simpler methods, and these have been outlined in the design. He realises that some parts of this project will not be easy to do, and has put in some sensible limitations that have been agreed with his client.

Program flowcharts were the easiest method for development of the algorithms here, but you may find that other methods, likes system flowcharts, ER diagrams, pseudocode or hierarchical diagrams, work best for your project. Flowcharts worked well for Ivan because of the nature of the problems he was trying to solve.

The worst case scenario is having no diagrams in your design section at all. If your project ends up without diagrams then the design is probably not written in an appropriate manner. Check with your teacher or lecturer if you cannot find suitable diagrams because there definitely will be something that is suitable. Next is Ivan's design section.

Identification of any validation required

As I will be working with alphanumerical strings, there is nothing the user can type in that will not be handled by the program. However, to prevent ridiculous entries, I will limit the length of the strings typed to 100 characters. This is because even though the actual rectangles on the screen representing the nodes can correctly show only about eight characters, when the user drags the mouse over a node, its caption will be displayed in the status box (see user interface). The status box will have a limit as well, and I think that it should be about 100 characters, to get a decent font size. So, if the user enters a string longer than 100 characters, the program should reject it and notify the user of the 'mistake'.

These prototypes have no code behind them. They were used to test the user interface.

User interface design

This might be the hardest part of the program as there are so many ways of designing an interface and there are no right or wrong answers. The interface design needs to be simple, functional and user friendly. The first dilemma I had was whether to do everything on one screen or have a start-up screen like a switchboard in a database, where the user decides what to use. A screen shot of the prototype of the start-up screen can be seen in Figure 21.9. From here, the user will go directly to the tree. In the case of data addition, the tree will be empty, and the user will be asked to add some nodes.

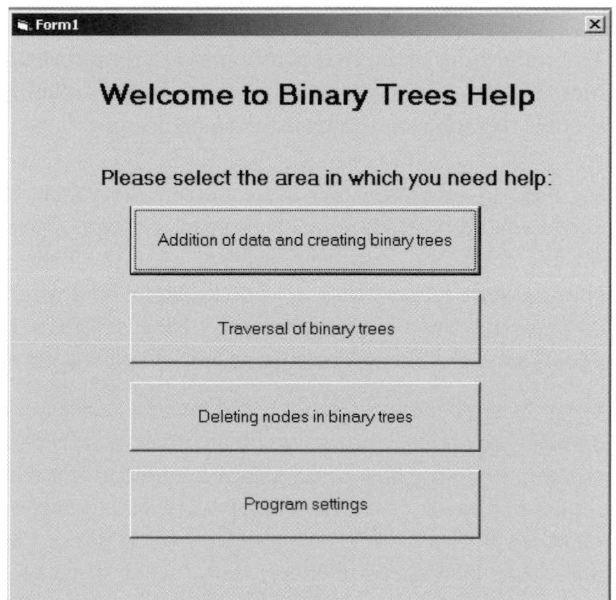

Figure 21.9 A possible user interface for the help section

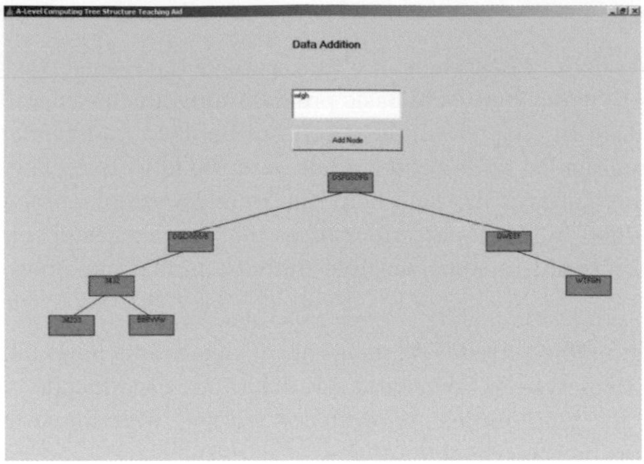

To save space Ivan's interface prototype screens have been made quite small; in his real project they took up a lot more space.

These smaller figures are sufficient to show what the interface is likely to be.

Figure 21.10 A possible user interface for the help section

The interface for displaying the tree could be something like that shown in Figure 21.10.

In the case of traversal and deletion, the tree will be randomly generated and filled with data, so that the user can concentrate on deleting or traversing nodes, and a typical interface is shown in Figure 21.11.

Feedback from the author

Ivan had a number of screen shots similar to those shown in Figures 21.10 and 21.11. His client decided that it might look better if he had a single-screen interface with the option choices shown on the same page. This would limit the number of nodes that could be displayed, but the estimated 64 nodes capable of being displayed on a single page are sufficient for teaching purposes.

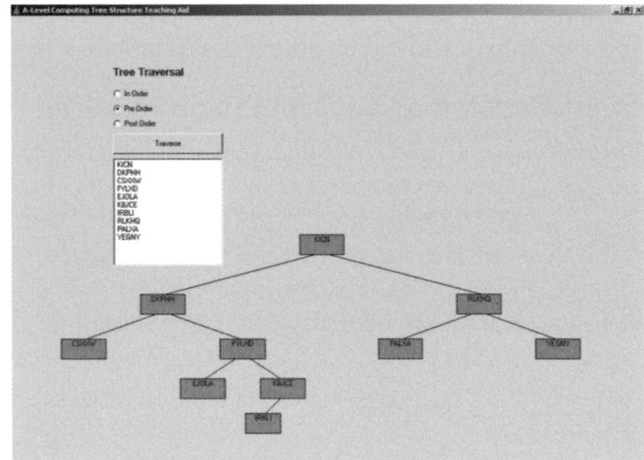

Figure 21.11 A possible user interface for the help section

The remainder of the first prototypes are therefore not shown here. Keep all your development work, even though it might not appear in your final project folder. Below are Ivan's second thoughts on the user interface design.

Don't forget that different methods need to be considered at the design stage.

My second prototype will try to cram everything on one page. Everything that a user needs will be here. However, the disadvantage of this prototype is that it is not as neat as the first one. But, the problem with the first one is that the user cannot quickly change what he wants to do. For example, on a given tree, the user can either add nodes, or traverse them or delete them. I have conducted a small survey, and eight out of 10 people said that they liked the second solution better.

There is another problem with the interface design. If the last level of nodes (level 6) will contain 32 nodes, how do you fit all of them on the screen? I thought of having a scroll bar but was not sure how to do this. So I posted a message on a forum for VB, and got some replies. However, their solutions were too complex for me. One of them mentioned a Viewtree Active X command, and this would help if I wanted the tree to look like a directory structure in Windows Explorer, but I want it to be more graphical. I want to be able to colour the nodes a different colour if I want to, not to mention that I would have to learn all the specific commands for that Active X control. I tried to improvise a little myself using a normal form as an MDI child to an MDI form. The MDI form has a scroll bar.

However, I discovered that the MDI child form has a width limit that is just a bit bigger than the screen. A screen shot of this new interface prototype is shown in Figure 21.12.

It is very likely that your project will develop as you consider the user interface design in more detail and consult with your client.

Do not delete anything to do with your project, even if you will not use it in your final report. It would be ideal if you kept this work in a different directory.

Remember to make entries in your project diary (see chapter 20) so that the stages you have been through can be documented. This should also include aborted attempts at trying to solve a problem in a particular way.

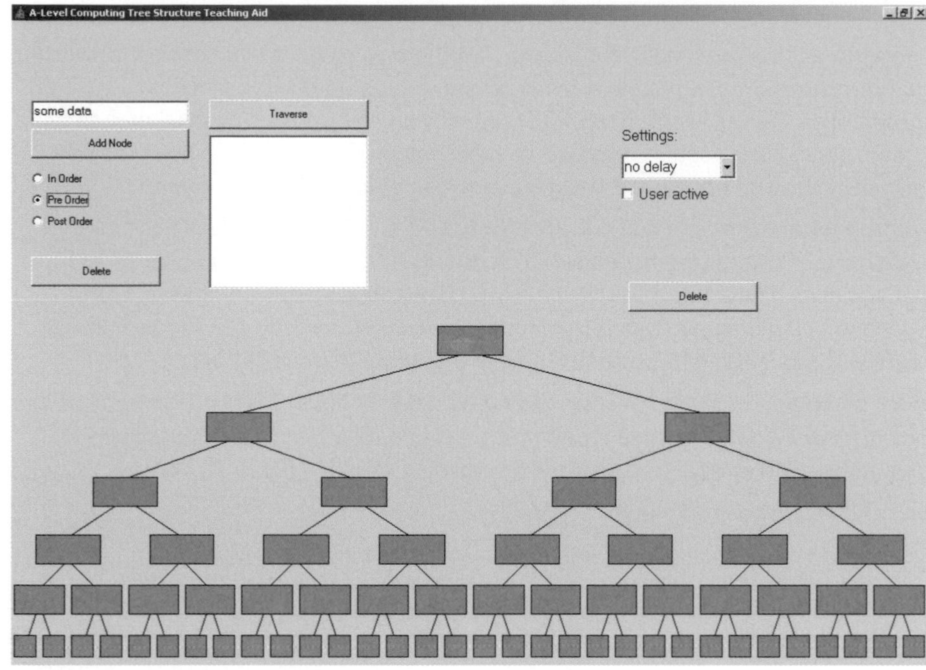

Figure 21.12 The mark II interface for the binary tree project

So, in the end, I have decided to make the nodes in the bottom row smaller so that they can fit. When a user drags the mouse over a node, its caption will be shown in the status box. Apart from the tree (drawn using rectangles and lines), and the buttons for addition and traversal, there will be certain other objects on the form and these are shown in Figure 21.13.

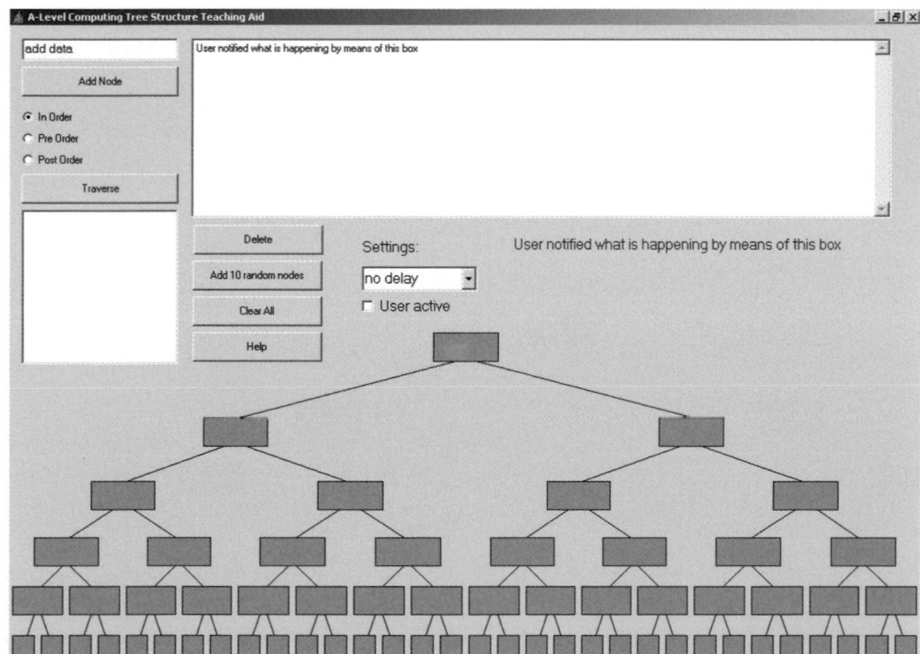

Figure 21.13 The mark II interface for the binary tree project with extra buttons

Ivan has shown how the final interface here has been developed in consultation with his client. A bulleted list like that shown here or the use of 'Callouts' (a function of Microsoft Word) placed at strategic positions on your user interface diagrams would be ideal.

You should treat your database interface, object-oriented programming interface or web site interface design diagrams in a similar way.

- A text box for the user to enter data.
- Three radio buttons for the user to select the traversal type.
- A combo box containing the results of traversal (the captions of the nodes).
- A large list box acting as a status indicator. The user will have to be notified of what is going on. For example, when a node is being added (let us say 'TTR'), the status indicator will read: 'TTR is smaller than QUR so moving to the left subnode' and so on. At the same time, the nodes involved will be highlighted. The list combo box will store messages like this, and not delete them so that the user can look at them.
- A label acting as another status indicator. Only this time, it will hold only the last status. If the user drags the mouse over the nodes, it is here that the caption will appear. If the user drags the mouse over any button, an explanation of what that button does will be displayed. But if the mouse is dragged back to the background of the form, it will just show the last status from the large status list box.
- Three more command buttons. One for adding 10 random nodes to the tree so that the user does not have to waste time creating a tree, one for resetting the program to what it was when it was started, and one for opening the help file.
- A combo box for the user to choose the delay.
- A tick box for the user to choose whether the User Mode is ON or OFF.

You will notice that there is no button for deleting the data. This will be done by right clicking on the node that needs to be deleted.

Sample of planned data capture, entry and planned validation

The data will be captured using the text box and the 'Add Node' button. It will be validated by checking that it is no longer than 100 characters. For example, IVAN will be allowed, but KANFNSAKFLANSKFDNSKDNF<MNVCNVZ VCZVM<ZDMFRL LSDFKLSFD XLKLAKSF <DSF DSMFSD>SADMFMSA DFMASD>FMSADTLWLER:LD DSLFM SADFGLLSMG will be not allowed.

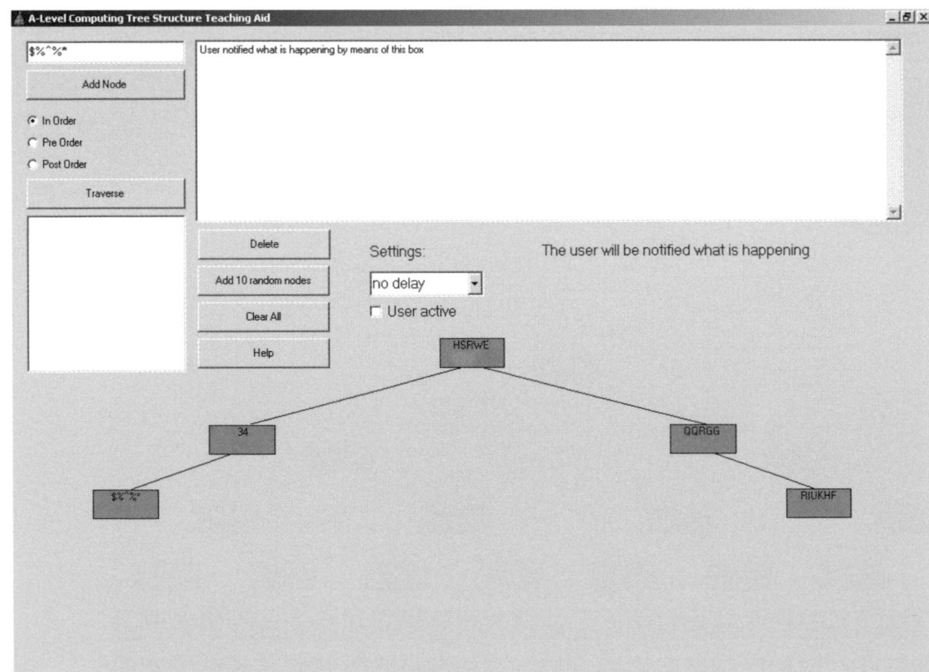

Figure 21.14 A sample of planned valid output

Sample of planned valid output

If the user inputs the following data to the tree: 'HSRWE', 'QQRGG', 'riukhf', '34' and '$%^%*', the expected result is shown in Figure 21.14 (the captions were edited manually to produce the screen shot shown in Figure 21.14.)

Description of measures planned for security and integrity of data, as well as system security

As I am not making a database, the data does not need to be kept secure from hackers or anyone else. Everybody will be welcome to try the program. The only threat to the integrity and security of data is a virus or a system failure. However, this can easily be solved by having a copy of the program on a zip disk stored somewhere safe. Not even a backup is needed because the data is not changing. The same holds true for the system security. The school will keep a safe copy in the file server room.

The security measures in your program are likely to be more complex than those shown here.

Most programs will need password protection at least.

Feedback from the author

Ivan made the **prototypes** shown above in Visual Basic with *no code behind the screens other than that of displaying the boxes and nodes* etc. If you are undertaking a programming project then it is relatively easy to present your client with a variety of scenarios which can be assembled quite quickly.

Ivan asked his fellow students (the most important users of the system) which type of interface they preferred, and got important feedback from potential users. Always try to do things like this if you can, it makes your system more lifelike. It is not until the prototype has been produced that you realise that there may need to be a few more buttons. This is not bad initial analysis but good design, identifying places in your project which need to be tweaked before the project is implemented.

Below is part of Ivan's vital test-plan strategy. Not all procedures have been considered.

Overall test strategy

As with the whole project, the test plan will be split into parts. There will be two main parts. First, I will test all the independent parts of the program, and then the program as a whole.

Ivan has modularised his solution to the problem and testing each module is covered here.

Independent procedures

As my program consists of procedures, I will have to test each independent procedure separately. The other more complex procedures which make use of many other small and independent procedures will be tested afterwards, as part of the full program. Since most of the procedures I will be testing are used by other procedures, they cannot be tested directly from my user interface. That is why I will have to make certain modifications to the program. For example, an extra button that calls that specific procedure. This is the design of my test plan in a bullet pointed form:

Some procedures are difficult to test in isolation from others, and Ivan has identified where dummy data will be used to test a particular part of his project.

- **Subnodes**
  This procedure will need to return the correct values of the indexes of the subnodes of a given node. For example, if the value 32 is passed to it (this is the root node), it should return the values 16 and 48. I will call the function on these nodes:
  - A node with two subnodes
  - A node with only one subnode
  - A node without subnodes
  - A node (without subnodes) in level 6 (the last level)

This is an unusually comprehensive test plan and yours may be simpler. Note that this is only an outline of what he will do to test the system.

- Call the function on an empty tree.

- **Update**
This procedure will need to remove the nodes without a caption. I will just remove the captions from some of the nodes and call the procedure and see if they are removed correctly.

- **Delay, cmbDelay_Validate and cmbDelay_Change**
These procedures are all to do with the time delay in the program used for the User Active mode. This is how I will test them:
  - For the delay procedure I will make a separate procedure that will display something on the screen before calling the delay procedure and then displaying something else on the screen after the delay has finished. I will change delay times and see if they work correctly.
  - cmbDelay_Validate is used when the value for the delay is changed in the delay combo box. So I will change it and see if the delay time has really changed.
  - cmbDelay_Change is easy to test. All I have to do is attempt to change the value in the delay combo box manually, and I should not be able to.

Remember that you need not understand the technical detail of material shown here, but you do need to produce similar modularised test procedures for your own project, be it a database, object-oriented programming or a web site.

- **Status**
The status procedure needs to put the text into the status box. I will just make a text box where I will enter some text and press a button to call the procedure and see if the text has been added to the status box.

- **Highlight**
The highlight procedure will need to change the colour of a certain node into a certain colour for the duration of the time delay. I will simply try to highlight one of the nodes, expecting the colour to change.

- **Default**
The default procedure will need to colour the nodes in their default colour (orange). I will colour the nodes in a different colour using another procedure and see if the default procedure returns them to their original colour.

- **Record and load**
These two procedures are very important in User Mode ON. If a tree is recorded, then it is effectively saved as an array and can be retrieved later. So I will record a random tree and then add and delete some nodes. Then I will load the tree and see if it is the same as the original.

- **Choices**
This is another procedure used in the User Mode ON. It will need to correctly display the empty subnodes of the current nodes in the tree. This is how I will test it:
  - Test it on a random tree
  - Test it on a second random tree
  - Test it on an empty tree (only the root node should appear).

- **checkifempty**
This procedure simply needs to correctly identify if the tree is empty or not. I will test it out in the following cases:
  - With an empty tree
  - With only the root node
  - With more nodes.

- **findindex**
This procedure will correctly find the index of a given node caption. Beside a button I will also need a text box to enter the caption name. I will test the procedure on three random nodes from a random tree.

- **cmdhelp_Click**
  This procedure should load the help file when the Help button is clicked. I will simply click the button and expect the help file to be opened.
- **txtInput_GotFocus**
  This procedure should remove the 'Enter data to be added' text from the text box for adding data when the box is clicked on. I will just click on it and see if the text is erased.
- **addfromarray**
  This procedure should add the data in it to the tree until an empty value is reached. This will be hard to test actively, and I think that I will have to write some code to manually add data to the array and then run the program. The data in the array should be added to the tree. I will change the values added from a few nodes to between about 10 and 30 and see if they are added correctly and chronologically.
- **inorder**
  This procedure will be tested extensively in the second part of the testing as part of tree traversal. Here I will just check the in-order traversal of one tree and see if it is correct and the list of traversed nodes is correctly displayed in the traversal box.
- **postorder**
  Same as inorder.
- **preorder**
  Same as inorder.
- **cmdAdd_MouseMove, cmdRandom_MouseMove, cmdReset_MouseMove, cmdTraverse_MouseMove, Form_MouseMove and Node_MouseMove.**
  All of these procedures are supposed to be controlling what appears in the small status box when the mouse is moved over an object. The things I would expect to appear are shown in Table 21.3.

Table 21.3 Expected results of user interaction

Mouse moved over	Expected message	Procedure responsible
'Add Node' button	'Enter data to be added to the tree above and click here to add it'	cmdAdd_MouseMove
'Add 10 random nodes' button	'Click here if you just want to add some data in the tree'	cmdRandom_MouseMove
'Clear All' button	'This will reset the program to what it was at startup'	cmdReset_MouseMove
'Traverse' button	'Select the type of traversal above and then click here to perform it'	cmdTraverse_MouseMove
Anywhere on the form	Last status message (e.g. last added node confirmation)	Form_MouseMove
Any node	The caption of the node	Node_MouseMove

If I have missed any parts of the program, then this is because either they are trivial (e.g. putting values into the arrays for tree traversal) or because they will be tested as a part of the whole program.

Detailed testing

Although I would have tested everything by now I still have not tested the code, just the output. However, it would be impossible to test the code in detail for every possible

Only a sample of Ivan's procedures have been shown here to demonstrate a suitable amount of detail when outlining a test plan.

You are likely to have fewer procedures than Ivan because he is attempting a complex problem.

Ivan wanted to do a complex project which would be useful for the Computer Department at his school. You will get away with considerably simpler problems for the purpose of the A2 project.

Ivan realises that it is going to be impossible to test that the entire program works under all conditions, and he will consider salient points only.

Remember that marks are awarded for a comprehensive test strategy, and not proof that every conceivable possibility is tested, which will probably be impossible with the resources that you have at your disposal.

situation. That is why I will do just two tests in detail: one adding a node in User Mode ON, and one deleting a node in User Mode OFF, as these are the two most complicated processes in my program. I will generate some random tree, and add a new node. I will have breaks in the code to check the variables occasionally. The same process will be used to check deleting the nodes. However, as I have not developed the code yet, I cannot give more details on this test.

Feedback from the author

Ivan's testing strategy is unusually comprehensive. Remember that these are *not* the actual tests but the methods for undertaking the tests, i.e. what you intend to do to make sure that each section is working.

Many students find it hard to devise a suitable test strategy during the design section. *One of the worst things you can do is to implement your project, get it working and then try to devise a suitable test strategy*. It is far easier to devise a test plan before you have implemented your project because you have nothing to test yet! This forces you to go through the correct mental processes of modularising the tests and thinking about sensible test data. If your project is working well, it is very difficult to think up a test plan retrospectively, and you will probably lose marks because your plan does not look very effective and falls into the trap of looking like it has been designed as an afterthought.

It is particularly easy to design comprehensive test plans for programming exercises because of the modular nature of the system. Test plans for testing a database are slightly different in their approach and were covered comprehensively in the AS book in this series when the module 3 exercise was undertaken using a Microsoft Access Database.

Self-test questions

1 Many students attempt to 'get the project working' on a computer before they attempt the project design section. Why is this normally a bad way to proceed?

2 When designing a system it is common practice to develop a diagram which outlines the modular structure of the system. What type of diagram is most frequently used for this?

3 When designing a system it is vital that you think about data types and formats. What is meant by this statement?

4 When designing a project you should consider what algorithms might be suitable for data transformation. How does consideration of this aspect of your project differ from the detailed algorithms that you might use in your implementation section?

5 If it is possible to validate data on entry you should do so. What must be carefully considered at design time with respect to validation of data?

6 (a) The design of the user interface must be considered very carefully. What techniques are available at design time to help your client visualise what the user interface would be like?

(b) What dangers are present for a student who has implemented his or her project before designing it?

7 It is important that the user is able to understand why data entered into your system has failed. What is usually done to accommodate this? Give an example.

8 Sometimes it might be necessary to design a data-capture form. What is this? Give an example of a situation in which a data capture form might be needed.

9 When designing a project the user will be particularly interested in how data output from the system is to be displayed. Outline what sort of information is typically needed from your user to produce some planned data output.

10 You should plan for the security and integrity of the data controlled by your project.

(a) What is data integrity?

(b) What is data security?

(c) Outline three different measures which may be used to ensure data integrity.

(d) Outline three different measures which may be used to ensure data security.

11 It is important to design suitable test strategies early on in your project. Why is it easier to design the tests now rather than wait until the system has been implemented?

22 The practical project – solution and testing

In this chapter you will learn about:

- Implementing the technical solution for a programming project
- Annotated code listings and good programming style
- Making the work easier to mark by the moderator
- Carrying out comprehensive unit and integration testing

This chapter continues the project work started in chapter 20. Make sure that you read chapters 19, 20 and 21 first or you may not understand the material in this chapter.

Note how we make use of the real AQA mark scheme to construct the sections for the project. This is not cheating; it ensures that you have a tick list to check off the things that need to be done.

Make sure that you download the correct mark scheme for the year in which you take the A2 examination. It may be different from the one shown here.

Introduction

In the previous three chapters you have been introduced to the practical project work at A2 level. A real AQA project at the author's school was chosen as an example, and this involved producing a teaching aid for the traversal and maintenance of binary tree structures. The analysis of this project has already been undertaken in chapter 20, and the design of the project has been carried out in chapter 21. We will continue to work with the same project, but this time concentrating on the technical solution.

The technical solution section shows how you *implemented your project*, and the mark scheme (2004 subject specification) is shown in Table 22.1.

Table 22.1 The mark scheme for the project analysis section

Section	Marks	Brief explanation
Students are expected to undertake the project by: • writing a suitable program or suite of programs; or • using a standard package to produce a tailored solution; or • a combination of the above.		
Technical solution	12	• Annotated listings of programs • Annotated listing of macros • Samples of annotated design screens showing details of package-generated forms, reports, queries, buttons, cross tabulations etc. • Any other reported evidence showing how the implementation was achieved.

The technical solution is *intimately connected* with the design, and many of the following procedures have already been outlined in principle. Other procedures are also added to fill in details like controlling what is displayed in a text box, for example.

Ivan has about 40 procedures in his project, some complex and others trivial, and about 20 public variables passed between them. When teachers and moderators are marking a programming project *it is important that they can find information about procedures and variables quickly*. The moderator is likely to zoom in to a particular procedure and have a detailed look to check for code which is unlikely to work. Therefore, Ivan has produced an alphabetical list of the procedures with a description of what each procedure does and how it interacts with other procedures. Ivan has also produced a list of public variables, their data types and a description of what they do.

These two tables are shown below.

The technical solution to the binary tree project

There are a number of procedures and function calls in this project, and an alphabetical list of the function or procedure calls is shown in Table 22.2.

Table 22.2 An alphabetical list of procedures/functions used in the binary tree project

Procedure/function	Description	Other procedures called from it
addfromarray	This procedure will add the data from ArrangeArray (a variable – see next table) in the appropriate order and erase the contents of the array.	addnode
addnode	This procedure will add a node to the tree based on the passed string.	status, update, subnodes, default, highlight, record, load, choices
arrange	This is a module that is called when the program is loaded. It is used to load the traversal arrays with data. Also, it declares the Sleep function from the kernel to pause the program for a certain number of milliseconds.	status, record, load, addnode, findindex
checkifempty	If the tree is empty, this function will return a True value.	delay, status
chkUser_Validate	When the user checks the User Active checkbox, the variables have to be set up again based on whether the User mode should be on or off.	
choices	This procedure is used in the User Active mode when adding data. It will display the empty nodes below the nodes with data in them because the user will have to choose an empty node to put the data in.	subnodes
cmbDelay_Change	Just in case the user tries to manually input the time delay, this procedure returns the value of the combo box to 'no delay'.	
cmbDelay_Validate	Once the data in the delay box is validated, or accepted, the appropriate action takes place, by changing the value of the Timedelay variable; the number represents the delay in milliseconds.	
cmdAdd_MouseMove	'Enter data to be added to the tree above and click here to add it' is displayed in the status label.	
cmdhelp_Click	This procedure will load the help file, help.mht, using a shell command ShellExecute.	ShellExecute
cmdRandom_Click	This procedure adds 10 random five-letter words to the tree.	
cmdRandom_ MouseMove	'Click here if you just want to add some data in the tree' is displayed in the status label.	
cmdReset_Click	This procedure simply sets all the variables to defaults, and the display to what it was at start up.	
cmdReset_ MouseMove	'This will reset the program to what it was at start up' is displayed in the status label.	
cmdTraverse_Click	When the user clicks the Traverse button, based on the selected traversal, the appropriate required node is selected if the User Active mode is on, or if it is not, it calls the procedure to do the traversal automatically (see figures 5 and 6).	default, status

Ivan could have produced a hierarchical diagram showing a pictorial interaction between these procedures.

I would advise other candidates to do this as it makes the project easier to mark.

Please note that some of the Figures referred to in the Tables appear in the student's project but are not reproduced here.

Table 22.2 *(Continued)*

Procedure/function	Description	Other procedures called from it
cmdTraverse_ MouseMove	'Select the type of traversal above and then click here to perform it' is displayed in the status label.	
default	This procedure sets all nodes to their default colour.	
delay	This procedure stops the program for a certain period of time based on the Timedelay value, in milliseconds.	Sleep, Refresh (internal)
delete	This procedure will delete the node with the index that is passed to it (see figures 7 and 8).	subnodes, status, delay, default, update, arrange, replacenode
findindex	This function returns the index of a given node.	
Form_Load	When the form loads, all the variables are set up.	status, update, arrays
Form_MouseMove	Last status message (e.g. last added node confirmation) is displayed in the status label.	
highlight	This procedure colours a certain node for a set period of time, and then returns it to its original colour.	delay
inorder	This subroutine outputs the in-order values of the nodes, based on their Index.	status, highlight
load	This procedure loads the saved state of the tree in the recording array.	
lstTraversal_Click	If the user selects any number in the lstTraversal (this list holds the indexes of traversal results) then the appropriate node will change colour to illustrate this.	
Node_MouseMove	The caption of the node is displayed in the status box.	
Node_MouseUp	This is the routine which decides what to do when the mouse is pressed on the nodes. If the User Mode is on, the user could be asked to click where the node is to be added, or if performing traversal, the user would need to click on the next node to be traversed, or the user could be asked to click on the replacement node in the deletion process, or the user will need to click on the nodes in the order in which they should be added to erase the gap. If the User Mode is off, then if the user clicked with a right button on the node, then that node would be deleted (see figure 9).	delay, status, addnode, choices, default, update, addfromarray, delete
postorder	Outputs the post-order values of the nodes.	status, highlight
preorder	Outputs the pre-order values of the nodes.	status, highlight
record	This procedure records the current state of the tree in the recording array.	
replacenode	This routine will find the node that needs to be deleted and replace it with an appropriate one. The old node will be deleted.	status, subnodes
status	This procedure displays the string passed to it in the txtStatus and lblStatus.	update
subnodes	This subroutine will give back the values of the two subnodes of a given node.	
txtInput_GotFocus	This is used the first time the user clicks on the input box; its contents get erased.	
update	All the nodes that do not have a value are hidden.	

You do not have to understand what these procedures do. The point of this section is to illustrate that your project should have documentation detailing the modularisation of the problem, together with details about what each of the modules does.

A list of the major public variables used in my program is shown in Table 22.3. I have not made a list of the variables used locally to control loops or perform other trivial functions, but have ensured that their names will not clash with those listed below.

Table 22.3 A full list of the public variables used in the binary tree program

Name	Type	Description
Addingdata	String	Index of the node that needs to be added.
ArrangeArray(1 To 63)	String	This array stores the order in which the nodes need to be added in order to erase any gaps in User Mode ON.
CurrentNode	Integer	Used in procedures 'addnode' and 'replacenode' as a general node to be experimented with.
CurrentStatus	String	The current message that is displayed on the screen.
DeletingNode	Integer	Index of the node that needs to be deleted.
Disablepopups	Boolean	Used in the 'addnode' procedure; if it is false, the popups for no space and duplicate values will not appear.
LeftNode	Integer	Index of the left subnode used in the 'subnodes' procedure.
NoSpace	Boolean	If the 'addnode' procedure cannot add a node because there is no space in the tree, then NoSpace will be true.
Position	Integer	The position is used to mark where the user came up to in the ArrangeArray in User Mode ON.
postorderarray(1 To 63)	Integer	This array contains the indexes of the nodes in the correct order for post-order traversal.
preorderarray(1 To 63)	Integer	This array contains the indexes of the nodes in the correct order for pre-order traversal.
recording(1 To 63)	String	This array stores all the captions from nodes so that they can be retrieved later.
Replacement	Boolean	If the value is true, then the user should click on the node that needs to be replaced in delete mode.
RequiredNode	Integer	Index of the node that the user needs to click in User Mode ON.
RightNode	Integer	Index of the right subnode used in the 'subnodes' procedure.
Secondgo	Boolean	In the User Mode, when data is being added, the addnode procedure needs to be executed twice; if the SecondGo is True, this means that it has been executed the first time already.
Selection	Integer	Index of the selected node on a mouse click.
Timedelay	Integer	This is the time delay in milliseconds used for the 'delay' procedure.
Traversal	Boolean	In the User Mode, if Traversal is true, this means that the user is in the middle of doing a traversal.
User	Boolean	Used to set the User Mode.
UserArrange	Boolean	If the User Mode is on, and the user deleted a node and left gaps, then he will need to select the nodes in the order in which they should be added to erase the gap; in this case, UserArrange will be true.

Tabular arrangements are shown here but a variety of diagrams would also be suitable.

All of this has been explained in the comments. The algorithms for the major operations are already given in the design section (see chapter 20). The only explanation that I think is missing is the one for the Node_MouseUp procedure. It happens when the user clicks on a node (when the button is released actually). Please look at Figure 22.1. You should note that these flowcharts do not follow the code exactly but show the principles.

If, like Ivan, you forget to do part of your design, do not put it in the technical solution section; put it in the design section with the other flowcharts to make your project easier to follow.

You will not lose marks if the moderator can find the information, but it makes it easier if you put the material where it belongs. You also run the risk of the moderator not being able to find the information.

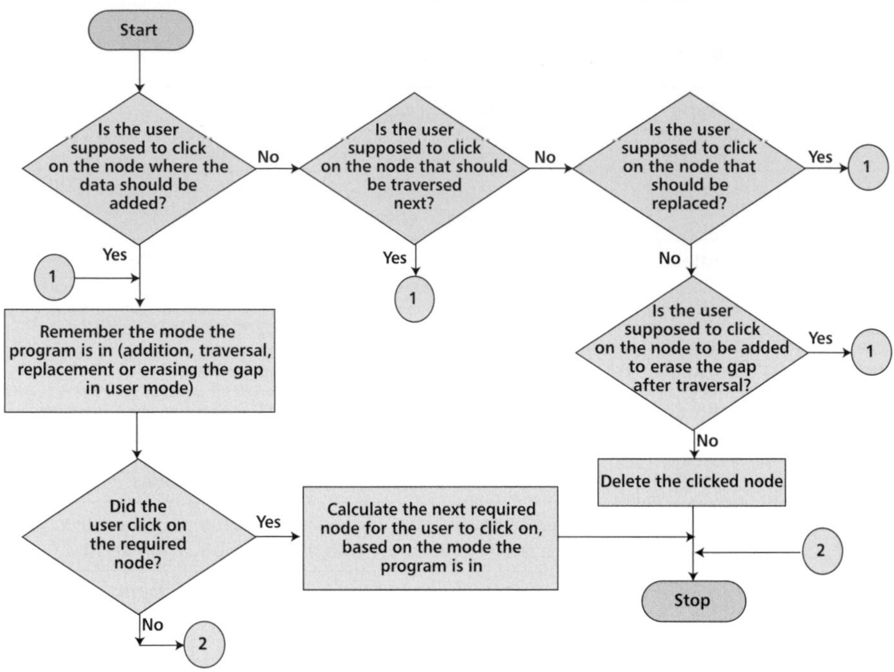

Figure 22.1 Flowchart showing what happens when a user clicks on a node

Feedback from the author

A complete listing can be found on the Understanding Computing Interactive A2 CD-ROM.

Detailed flowcharts have already been given in the design section, but Ivan would have benefited from using a hierarchical diagram showing the interaction between the large numbers of procedures in his project. Just a small part of Ivan's Visual Basic code now follows. The entire listing will not be given because this would more usefully be put in an appendix to the project, and *not included* in the page count. The dimension statements where the variables are declared at the beginning of the program listing are now shown. The comments have been highlighted in green, but the program statements are black to make the code easier to read. The following is only a sample of the code used for declaring the variables (*see margin entry*).

Always produce the full program listing of any programs you write in an appendix to your project.

You should note that the code for the program is not included in the word count for your project.

```
Private Declare Function ShellExecute Lib "shell32.dll" Alias
"ShellExecuteA" (ByVal hwnd As Long, ByVal lpOperation As String,
ByVal lpFile As String, ByVal lpParameters As String, ByVal
lpDirectory As String, ByVal nShowCmd As Long) As Long 'This
makes the shell command, ShellExecute, available from the
shell32.dll library'
Dim CurrentNode As Integer           'used in procedures "addnode"
and "replacenode" as a general node to be experimented with'
Dim CurrentStatus As String          'the current message that is
displayed on the screen'
Dim LeftNode As Integer              'index of the left subnode
used in the "subnodes" procedure'
Dim RightNode As Integer             'index of the right subnode
used in the "subnodes" procedure'
Dim Selection As Integer             'index of the selected node
on a mouse click'
```

```
Dim Addingdata As String               'index of the node that needs
to be added'
Dim RequiredNode As Integer            'index of the node that the
user needs to click in User Mode on'
Dim DeletingNode As Integer            'index of the node that needs
to be deleted'
Dim ArrangeArray(1 To 63) As String 'this array stores the order
in which the nodes need to be added in order to erase any gaps in
User Mode ON'
Dim Timedelay As Integer               'this is the timedelay in
milliseconds used for the "delay" procedure'
Dim User As Boolean                    'used to set the User Mode'
Dim Secondgo As Boolean                'in the User Mode, when data
is being added, the addnode procedure needs to be executed twice,
if the SecondGo is True, this means that it has been executed the
first time already'
Dim Traversal As Boolean               'in the User Mode, if
Traversal is true, this means that the user is in the middle of
doing a traversal'
Etc.
```

Make sure that any code you write is well documented, modularised, uses helpful comments, and has a meaningful name.

Feedback from the author

Put yourself in the position of the moderator. They will not have seen the program working, and therefore do not have the advantage that your teacher or lecturer has. The moderator will obviously be impressed with the standard of work here, but *will not have time to check or even read most of the code*. They are relying on the integrity of your teacher and lecturer to know that it works, but *they will almost certainly perform some random checks to see if what you are doing is sensible.*

If the author were moderating this project, he would pick two or three variables at random from the declarations shown above, and check that they were considered at design time! Ivan's list of variables is actually in the technical implementation section (it would have been better in the design section) and looking at the variables 'UserArrange', 'DeletingNode' and 'Secondgo' confirms that they have been considered and their purpose is stated.

Below is Ivan's technical solution; a small selection of the easier-to-understand modules are shown as examples. This is how you should organise your technical solution if you are undertaking a programming exercise.

The following function, 'checkifempty', is designed to return a true value if the tree has no data in it. The tree is checked by the 'for to next loop' to see that all 63 nodes are null. If this is true then the function is exited without the Boolean variable being set.

```
Private Function checkifempty() As Boolean
  'If the tree is empty, this function will return a True value'
  For X = 1 To 63
    If Node(X).Caption <> "" Then Exit Function
  Next X
  checkifempty = True
  status ("The tree is empty.")
  delay
End Function
```

Table 22.4 Information about the checkifempty function

Function	Description	Other procedures called from it
checkifempty	If the tree is empty, this function will return a True value	delay, status
Extra information		
checkifempty	Boolean	
status	A **procedure** to which a string is passed to display the status information	
delay	A **procedure** which is used to slow down the running of the program	

The 'findindex' function returns the index (the number representing) a given node. The subscripted variable Node(X) is assigned by this function call.

```
Private Function findindex(Data As String) As Integer
'This function returns the index of a given node'
For X = 1 To 63
    If Node(X).Caption = Data Then
        findindex = X
        Exit Function
    End If
Next X
findindex = 0
End Function
```

Feedback from the author

It would serve no purpose to give a complete listing of Ivan's code. The above few procedures show that he made use of modularisation, good programming style, and comments to help the moderator.

Note that you do not have to include evidence that every single thing in your project has been tested, but you need to include a representative sample which gives a good indication that extensive testing has been carried out.

Make sure that you use the appropriate mark scheme for the year in which you take the A2 project.

The next important stage in the technical solution section is to show that your program works by using a series of screen captures of the actual project in operation. However, many of these screenshots are shown in the section on testing, and they will therefore *not* be repeated here. If you already have screenshots of your working project in a testing section, then you do not need to have the same screenshot elsewhere. However, remember that the screenshots in the design section must *not* be those used for the completed project. This is because they could not possibly exist at that stage!

System testing

We now take a look at a sample of Ivan's system testing, the mark scheme for which (2004 subject specification) is shown in Table 22.5.

Table 22.5 The system testing phase

Section	Marks	Brief explanation
System Testing	6	• Design of test plan • A minimal set of test data and expected results for typical data and erroneous/extreme data that is clearly cross-referenced to the test plan • Annotated hard copy of actual test runs showing actual results for typical and erroneous/extreme data cross-referenced to the test plan

Independent procedures – testing

As my program consists of procedures, I will have to test each independent procedure separately. The other, more complex procedures, which make use of many other small and independent procedures, will be tested afterwards as part of the full program. Since most of the procedures I will be testing are used by other procedures, they cannot be tested directly from my user interface. That is why I will have to make certain modifications to the program, like an extra button that calls the specific procedure. This is the design of my test plan in a bullet-point form:

- **Subnodes**
  This procedure will need to return the correct values of the indexes of the subnodes of a given node. For example, if the value 32 is passed to it (this is the root node), it should return the values 16 and 48. I will call the function on these nodes:
  - A node with two subnodes
  - A node with only one subnode
  - A node without subnodes
  - A node (without subnodes) in level 6 (the last level)
  - Call the function on an empty tree.
- **Delay, cmbDelay_Validate and cmbDelay_Change**
  These procedures are all to do with the time delay in the program used for the User Active mode. This is how I will test them:
  - For the delay procedure, I will make a separate procedure that will display something on the screen before calling the delay procedure and then displaying something else on the screen after the delay has finished. I will change delay times and see if the delays are correct.
  - **cmbDelay_Validate** is just used when the value for the delay is changed in the delay combo box. So I will change it and see if the delay time has really changed.
  - **cmbDelay_Change** is easy to test. All I have to do is attempt to change the value in the delay combo box manually, and I should not be able to.
- (MUCH MORE FOLLOWS IN IVAN'S ACTUAL PROJECT)

Ivan did not need to remind the moderator about the test plan that has already been covered in the design section.

This would have made the project longer than is necessary. All you need to do is cross-reference the test plan in the design section with the actual test runs in the implementation section.

When carrying out the actual test runs you need only give a good sample of the tests you have carried out in your write up.

Feedback from the author

Ivan's testing strategy is comprehensive, and mirrors that strategy outlined in the design section (see margin entry). Ivan realises that unit testing should be carried out on each module, and has even gone as far as modification of the user interface to achieve this.

Test runs – the subnodes procedure

To test this procedure independently, I had to add a separate button which will call the procedure, and perform it on the selected node. A node can be selected by clicking on it. A screenshot of the temporary user interface set up for testing purposes is shown in Figure 22.2.

The code behind the 'subnodes button' is as follows:

```
Private Sub cmdsubnodes_Click()
subnodes (Selection)
If Selection <> 0 Then Print Node(Selection).Caption
If LeftNode <> 0 Then Print "Leftnode = " +
Node(LeftNode).Caption
If RightNode <> 0 Then Print "Rightnode = " +
Node(RightNode).Caption
End Sub
```

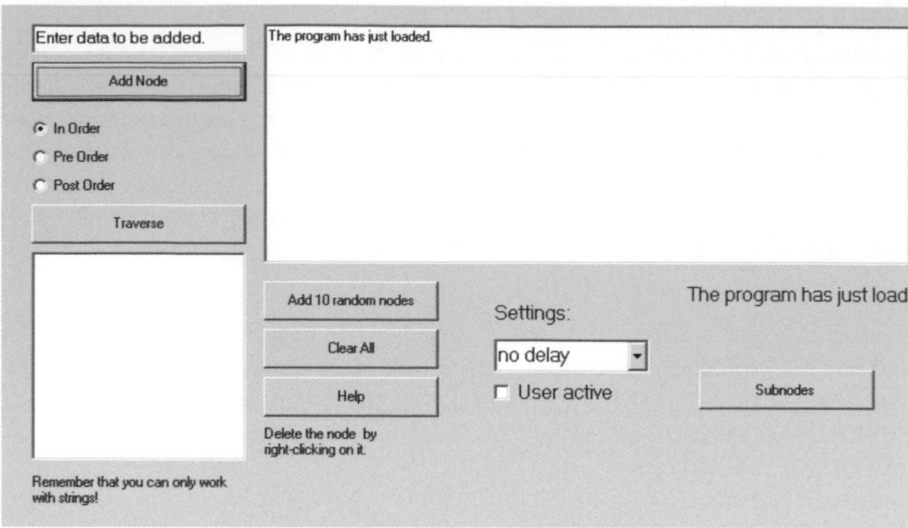

Figure 22.2 A slightly modified user interface for testing purposes

When I select the node to be tested and click the button, the program should print the subnodes of the test node in the top left corner. If the node has no subnodes then blank nodes should be printed, or if the node is in level 6, just the name of the node should be printed. Now let us do some testing. A random tree is shown being generated in Figure 22.3.

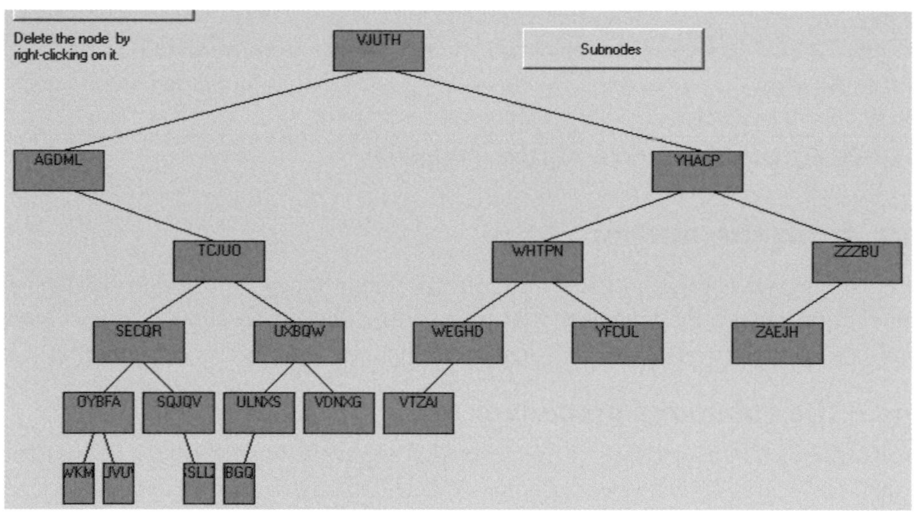

Figure 22.3 A random tree being generated for testing purposes

My test nodes will be TCJUO (two subnodes SECQR and UXBQW), AGDML (one subnode TCJUO), YFCUL (no subnodes) and LWKMT (a node in level 6 with no subnodes). I will click on each of them and then click on subnodes and see what the program prints. This is shown in Figure 22.4.

Many projects at A2 level may be tested using more conventional black box testing which was covered in your AS level course.

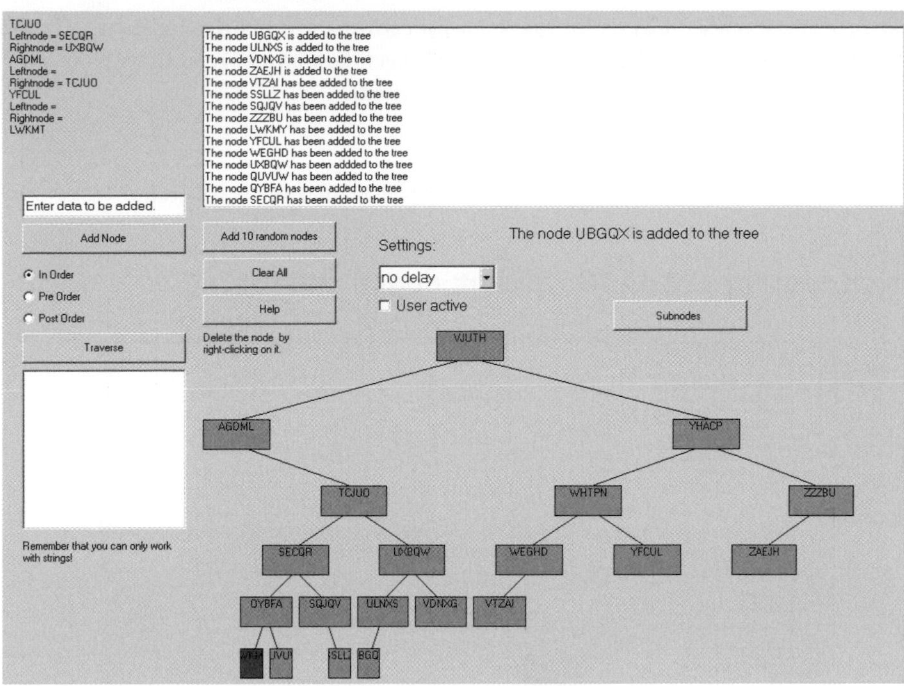

Figure 22.4 Testing which nodes have been added to the tree

So the test was successful. Now I will check that the program does not crash when the tree is empty. This will also check that the program does not crash if no nodes are selected and that the program correctly identifies an empty tree. I restarted the program and clicked the subnodes button, and the result is shown in Figure 22.5.

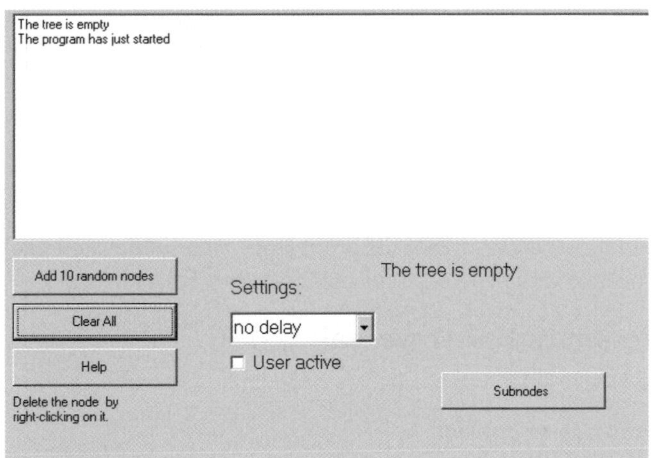

Figure 22.5 A slightly modified user interface for testing purposes

A good selection of comprehensive testing is required.

Although you would test your entire project to see that it works properly, your project documentation does not have to reflect all tests actually carried out, just a reasonable selection.

Feedback from the author

Ivan went on to test the other procedures in a similar way. *Remember that you do not have to provide documentary evidence of every single procedure and every single test,* especially if the tests are similar in nature. A moderator will not give you 20 times the marks awarded for one test procedure, especially if the next 19 procedures are nearly identical! Having convinced the moderator that extensive unit testing has taken place, Ivan then went on to prove that integration testing has also been accomplished.

General program operation

Now my program has been unit tested, I will test the project as it is intended to be used by the users.

Integration testing – 'Add 10 random nodes' button

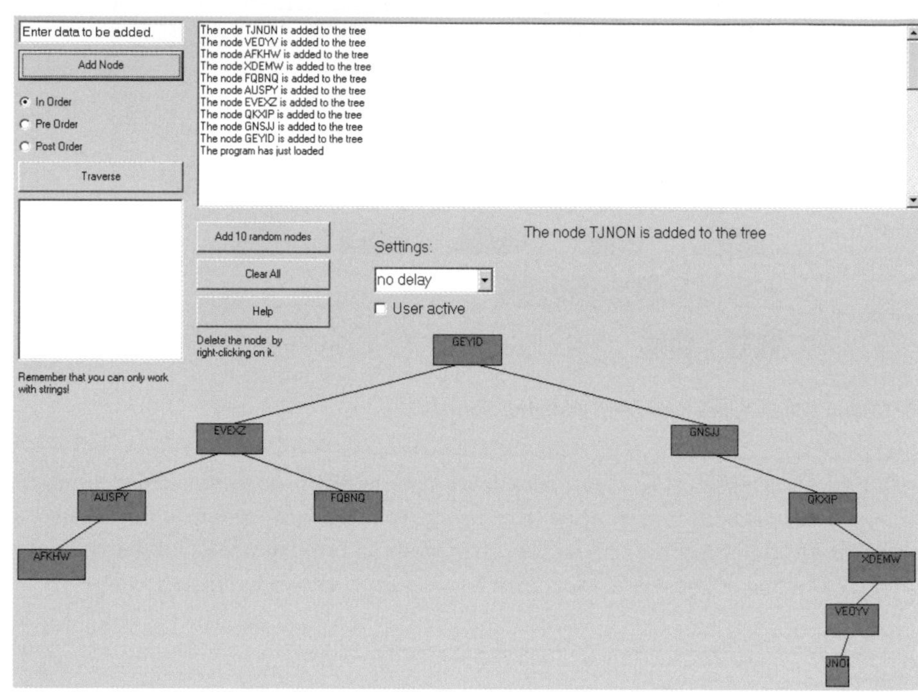

Figure 22.6 Testing the 'Add ten random nodes' button

Feedback from the author

Ivan produced several more screenshots to show that different trees were generated each time the 'Add 10 random nodes' button was pressed. We continue with Ivan's work.

Integration testing – data entry and traversal

These are the problems associated with data traversal that need to be tested:

- **The result of the traversal might not be correct**
  Of course, the most important thing is that the output of the traversal is correct. The order of nodes should be correct, and no empty nodes should be listed. I will test the traversal with a small tree, a medium-sized tree and a large tree.
- **Extreme situations**
  There are some situations that may be a bit tricky for the program to deal with. For example, if there is only one node in the tree or if all the nodes form one branch (e.g. if 'A'; 'AA'; 'AAA'; 'AAAA' etc. are added). I will test both of these situations.
- **Program bugs**
  There should be no crashes during any of these operations when attempting to traverse an empty tree.

Figure 22.7 shows the screen for adding some extreme data.

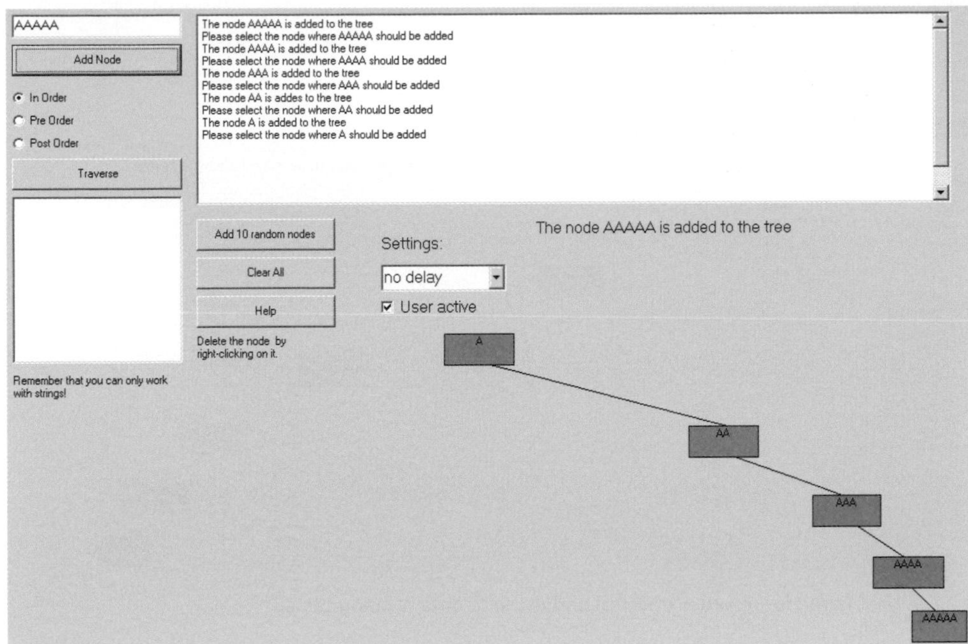

Figure 22.7 Testing for some extreme data conditions

Now would be a good time to test the 'Clear All' button, and this is shown in Figure 22.8.

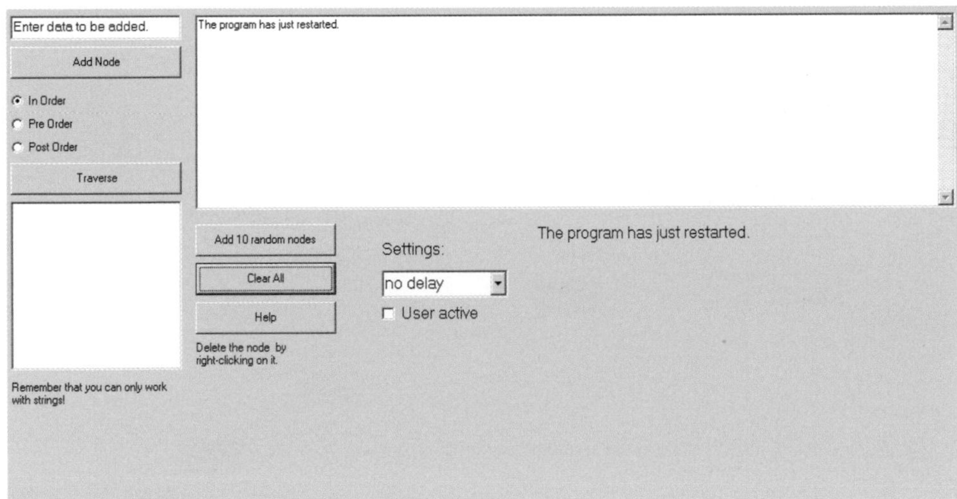

Figure 22.8 Testing the 'Clear All' button

The same extreme data was added, but this time user mode was selected, and the user was invited to click on the node in the correct order to carry out an in-order traversal. Figure 22.9 shows the user half way through clicking over the nodes to carry out the in-order traversal process. They have successfully established that 'A' and 'AA' come first and second respectively, and the program message 'Well done – that is the correct node, now choose the next one' is displayed at the top of the tree area and confirmed in the window which records the user actions. Remember that the other entries in the top window show the tree being created. You cannot traverse a tree that does not exist.

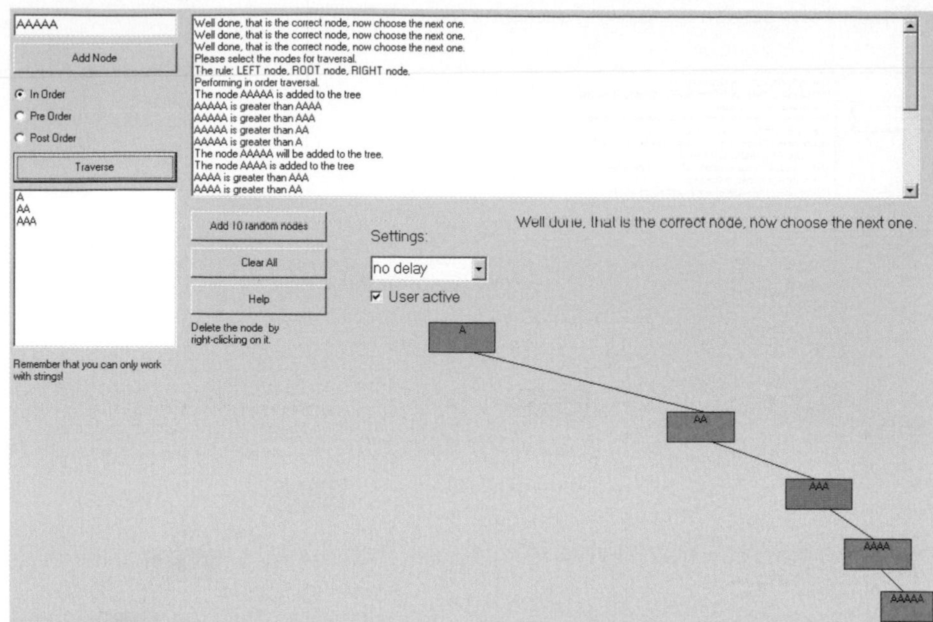

Figure 22.9 User mode for in-order traversal and extreme data is being tested

Next the user will make a mistake by clicking over a node that is not 'AAAA', and thus an error message should appear. This is shown in Figure 22.10.

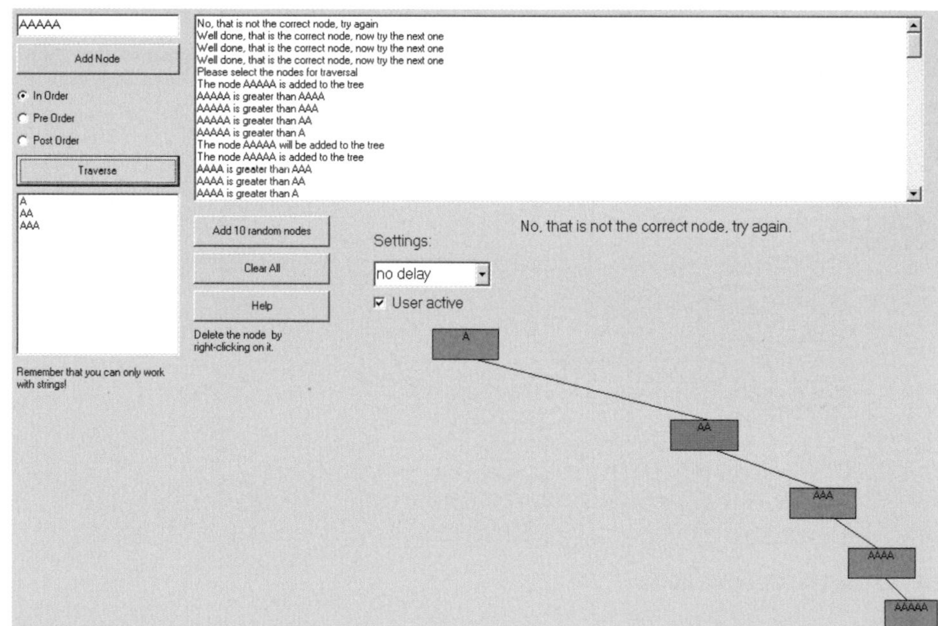

Figure 22.10 The user has made a mistake

The error message 'No, that is not the correct node, try again' is displayed at the top of the area where the tree has been generated and is also reflected in the top window.

Integration testing – testing the help system

When the user clicks over the help button a help system should be displayed. This loads a '.mht file' which is displayed in an Internet browser. The screenshot of this is shown in Figure 22.11.

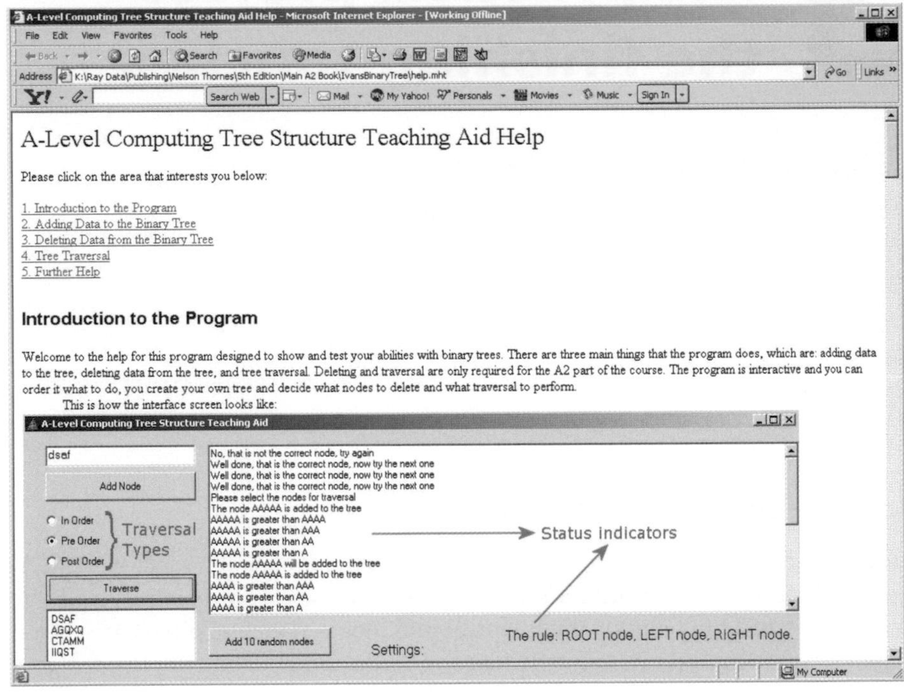

A-Level Computing Tree Structure Teaching Aid Help - Microsoft Internet Explorer - [Working Offline]
A-Level Computing Tree Structure Teaching Aid Help
Please click on the area that interests you below:
1. Introduction to the Program
2. Adding Data to the Binary Tree
3. Deleting Data from the Binary Tree
4. Tree Traversal
5. Further Help
Introduction to the Program
Welcome to the help for this program designed to show and test your abilities with binary trees. There are three main things that the program does, which are: adding data to the tree, deleting data from the tree, and tree traversal. Deleting and traversal are only required for the A2 part of the course. The program is interactive and you can order it what to do, you create your own tree and decide what nodes to delete and what traversal to perform.
This is how the interface screen looks like:
A-Level Computing Tree Structure Teaching Aid
Add Node
In Order
Pre Order
Post Order
Traversal Types
Traverse
Status indicators
The rule: ROOT node, LEFT node, RIGHT node.
Add 10 random nodes
Settings:

Figure 22.11 The help system for using the program has been activated

If you are comprehensively testing a relational database then you should look at the chapters in the AS book where the module 3 exercise was undertaken.

The ways in which the database was tested are very similar to the tests you need to carry out if you are undertaking a database for an A2 project.

Feedback from the author

Ivan carried out many more tests, showing screenshots of each one, to prove that the project works properly. The large number of screenshots included in the project report together with extensive analysis, design and code listing prove that Ivan's program works. Ivan made sure that he included erroneous and extreme data conditions as well as normal data. You will lose marks if you do not do this. It is not possible to say if it all works perfectly, and there will inevitably be some bugs which the testing did not address. It is not possible in the time available at A2 level to exhaustively test a program of this complexity. Ivan also carried out a range of beta testing on his peers and the computer staff, and gained useful feedback regarding the operation of the project.

When you are completely happy that your project works, it is a good idea to give it to your client who should test it for you.

This was particularly easy to do as Ivan's end users were his peers.

Self-test questions

1. What annotation should accompany the technical solution to a programming project?
2. What annotation should accompany the technical solution to a database project?
3. What is the difference between 'testing' in the design and implementation sections?
4. What important role is played by 'screenshots' in your implementation?
5. Why is it important to show evidence of both unit and integration testing?
6. You have carried out alpha and beta testing. What does this mean?

23 The practical project – the finishing touches

In this chapter you will learn about:

- Producing the system maintenance documentation
- Creating an effective help system and user manual
- Undertaking a project appraisal
- Ensuring good-quality communication
- Finishing your project to an appropriate standard – sections, index and cover sheet

Introduction – system maintenance

This chapter continues the project work started in chapter 20. Make sure that you read chapters 19, 20, 21 and 22 first or you may not understand the material in this chapter.

Note how we make use of the real AQA mark scheme to construct the sections for the project. This is not cheating; it ensures that you have a tick list to check off the things that need to be done.

Make sure that you are using the mark scheme for the year in which you are undertaking the A2 examination. It may be different from the one shown here.

In the previous four chapters you have been introduced to the practical project work at A2 level. A real AQA project at the author's school was chosen as an example, and this involved producing a teaching aid for the traversal and maintenance of binary tree structures. The analysis of this project has already been undertaken in chapter 20, the design of the project has been carried out in chapter 21, and the technical solution was undertaken in chapter 22. This chapter continues to work with the same project, but this time concentrating on the system maintenance, user manual and evaluation phases.

The system maintenance section should show enough information to enable somebody else to carry on with or modify your project at a later date. The mark scheme for this section (2004 subject specification) is shown in Table 23.1.

Table 23.1 The mark scheme for the maintenance part of your project

Section	Marks	Brief explanation
System maintenance	6	• A very brief summary of the features of any package used • A sample of detailed algorithm design using a recognised methodology • Annotated listings of program code or macro code and details of package tailoring. Samples of annotated design screens showing details of package-generated forms, reports, queries, buttons, cross tabulations etc. may be included • Procedure and variable lists/descriptions for programs or list of package items developed, e.g. tables, forms, reports, buttons, macros etc. • Samples of annotated design screens showing details of package-generated forms, reports, queries, buttons, cross tabulations etc.

If you have carried out the design and technical solution as shown in this book, *you will have little, if anything else to do* for the maintenance sections!

In the case of Ivan's project, he already has detailed flowcharts showing how the system is implemented, he has detailed annotated listings (this is another reason why extensive comments are useful) and he already has procedure descriptions, listings of variables and many screenshots showing how the program functioned when it was tested.

Ivan also gave a brief summary of why Visual Basic was used for this project (*you will have to add a brief summary of the facilities within any packages you have used*), and the features of VB that he has used.

No extra information is needed to maintain the project, and therefore all the marks awarded for system maintenance can be obtained by using the material that is already in Ivan's project portfolio. If this is the case in your project, then remember to put a 'system maintenance' section into the report and say so. *Do not just leave it blank.* If you do, a kind moderator will probably award the marks anyway, especially if you have a good project write up with all the necessary things present and easy to find.

Marks for different sections can be awarded for material covered earlier. If you have an effective design and technical solution section, you are unlikely to need any extra material for the system maintenance documentation.

Introduction – user manual

The user manual should be non-technical (from the point of view of not containing any technical information about the way that the system has been implemented).

Table 23.2 The mark scheme for the user manual part of your project

Section	Marks	Brief explanation
User manual	6	• A brief introduction describing the overall function of the system, but only one section of the system is needed, which must include the following: (a) Samples of actual screen displays to illustrate the interface (menus, data input forms, sample data, expected output) in situ with good explanations (b) Samples of error messages/error recovery procedures

Feedback from the author

The user manual is normally a four- or five-page document which is *separate from your main project*. It should normally be placed in an appendix to your project or tucked into your main folder, and it is *not* included in the word count.

An electronic help file activated from a Visual Basic program has been set up for our exemplar project, and this is covered below. If you create an electronic help file, remember to print out the contents and include it in an appendix – otherwise the moderator will not see it!

The format of the help file has been altered to make it fit this book, and you should note that there are hyperlinks in the original system to help the user navigate. A screenshot of this help system in operation has already been shown in Figure 22.11, when the help system was being tested. The hyperlinks are shown here in green so that they stand out and make the text easier to read.

A level computing tree structure teaching aid help

Please click on the area that interests you below:

1 Introduction to the program
2 Adding data to the binary tree
3 Deleting data from the binary tree
4 Tree traversal
5 Further help

Always include the user manual as a separate document. Here it is shown as a searchable and easy-to-use electronic resource.

Introduction to the program

Welcome to the help for this program, which has been designed to show and test your abilities with binary trees. The program does three main things:

- It adds data to the tree

- It deletes data from the tree
- It carries out tree traversal.

Deleting and traversal are only required for the A2 part of the course. The program is interactive and you can therefore tell it what to do, create your own trees and decide what nodes to delete and what traversals to perform. The screen interface is shown in Figure 23.1. The big indicators (white areas) show the past and present actions, and the smaller indicator shows the current action, the name (data) of the node that the mouse is over, or a description of the button that the mouse is currently over. This can be useful if the node is not large enough to hold its name (data).

The author has made minor grammatical corrections to make this help file (user manual) easier to read, and has added the captions to the diagrams to fit in with the style of the rest of this book.

The user manual has also been reformatted to fit the layout of this book more effectively.

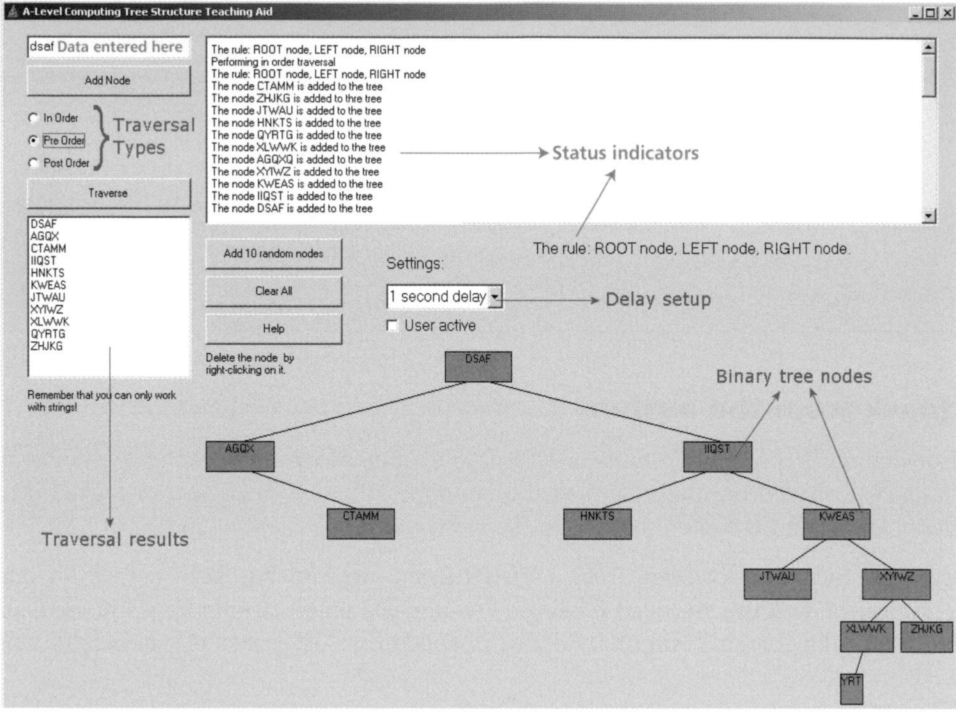

Figure 23.1 The screen interface

The program only works with strings, i.e. you can input numbers, so 20 will be bigger than 100 because the program is treating the number as a string. There are two settings you can adjust:

- The time delay between the processes
- Whether you want to take an active role in the program or not.

The time delay

The time delay, shown in Figure 23.2, determines how fast the program runs. With no time delay, due to the speed of the program you cannot see what is happening to the nodes, and you will see only the final tree structure, for example, after a node has been deleted. The only way for you to find out what has happened is to scroll down the status indicator and look at the previous actions. This is why a delay can be added. It has three settings: no delay, one second, two seconds and three seconds.

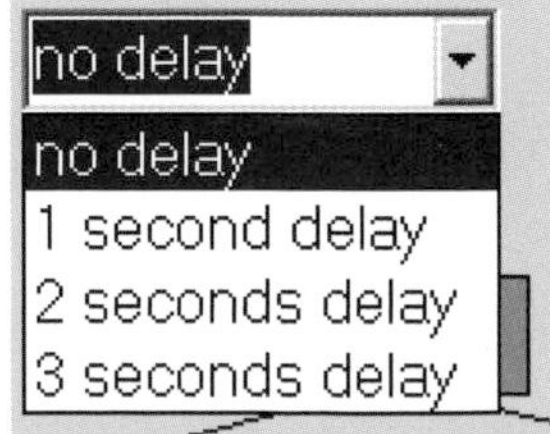

Figure 23.2 Setting the time delay

If a time delay is selected, then the program will run more slowly so you can see what is happening. You can also simultaneously read the status indicator and look at the nodes.

User active and automatic modes

When the 'User active' checkbox is unchecked, see Figure 23.3, the program does everything automatically. This is useful for generating exercises, but it is not so useful for active learning because you are not actively involved.

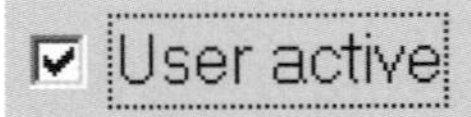

Figure 23.3 Setting user active mode

If you check the 'User active' checkbox, the program will go into User Active Mode. It will then prompt you and lead you through certain tasks by getting you to click on the relevant nodes. See more detail on the specific tasks below.

Back

Adding data to the binary tree

There are two ways to add data to the tree: manually and automatically. To add the data manually to the tree, all you have to do is enter the data to be added in the text box above the 'Add Node' button and then press the button; this is shown in Figure 23.4.

Figure 23.4 Adding data manually

The automatic way is simply to click the 'Add 10 random nodes' button (see Figure 23.5). The program will then add 10 random five-letter words to the tree. However, as this can take a long time; if all 10 nodes are not added after a certain amount of time, the program will stop adding nodes.

Figure 23.5 Adding data automatically

Adding nodes in the User Active Mode

When 'User Active Mode' is selected, the program will display all the children of the current nodes in the diagram, and you need to click on the correct child where the node should be added. An example of this is shown in Figure 23.6, where the user instructions are shown at the top right-hand side of the screen.

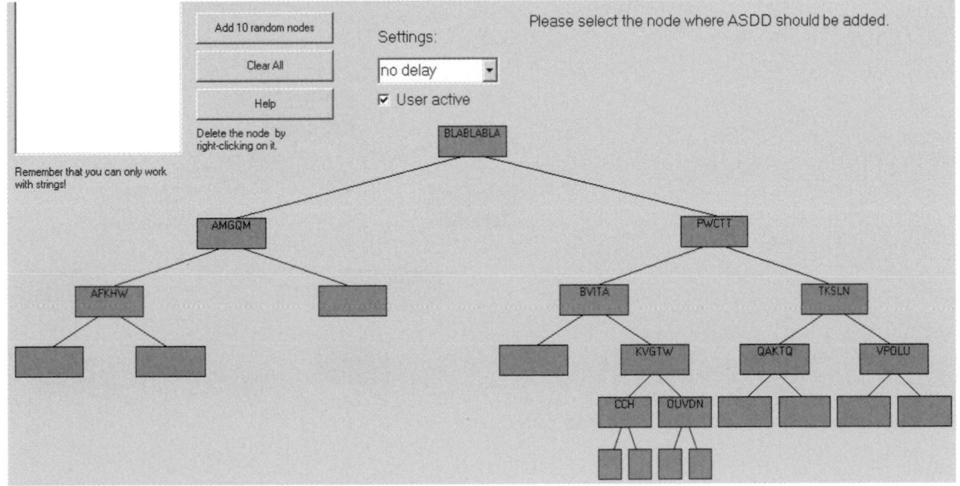

Figure 23.6 Adding nodes in User Active Mode

If the nodes are being added automatically, you cannot use 'User Active Mode' as the automatic insertion of nodes is meant to save time and be as fast as possible.

Back

Deleting data from the binary tree

A node can be deleted by right clicking on the desired node. If processes are going on at that moment, the click will act in an identical way to a left click (e.g. if the program is asking you to select a node).

There are three types of node deletion.

1 Deleting a node with no children

If a node has no children it is simply removed. As an example, the node ASDD will be removed as shown in Figure 23.7.

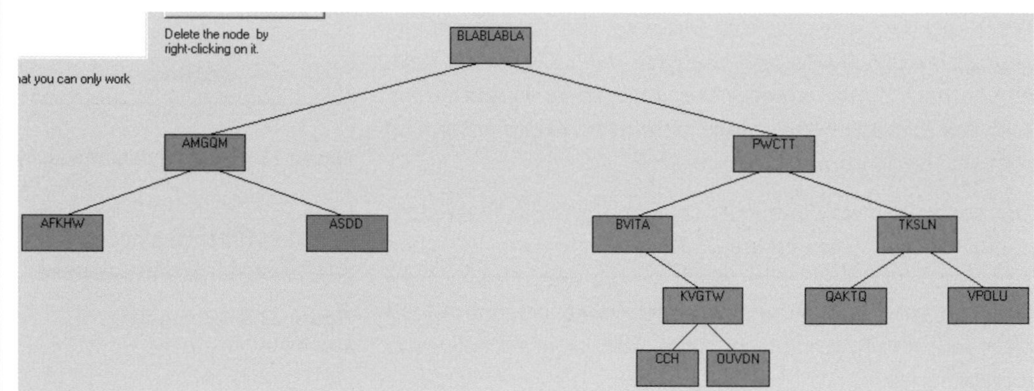

Figure 23.7 Deleting a node with no children

2 Deleting a node with only right children

As an example, the node JJRTU will be deleted as shown in Figure 23.8.

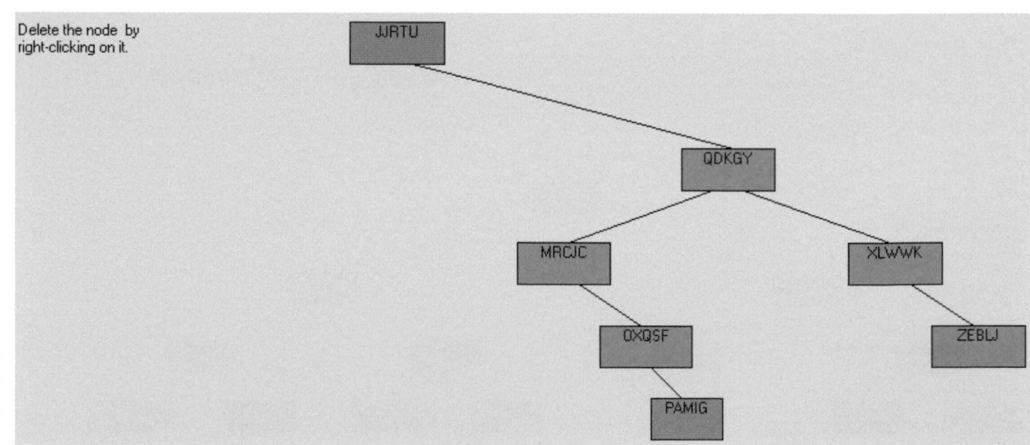

Figure 23.8 Deleting a node with right children only

JJRTU has only right children, so it will be removed straight away, and the remaining nodes need to be sorted into the correct order. This is done by adding them in the following order: QDKGY, MRCJC, XLWWK, OXQSF, ZEBLJ and PAMIG. This way, the tree will maintain its structure; the final result of these operations is shown in Figure 23.9.

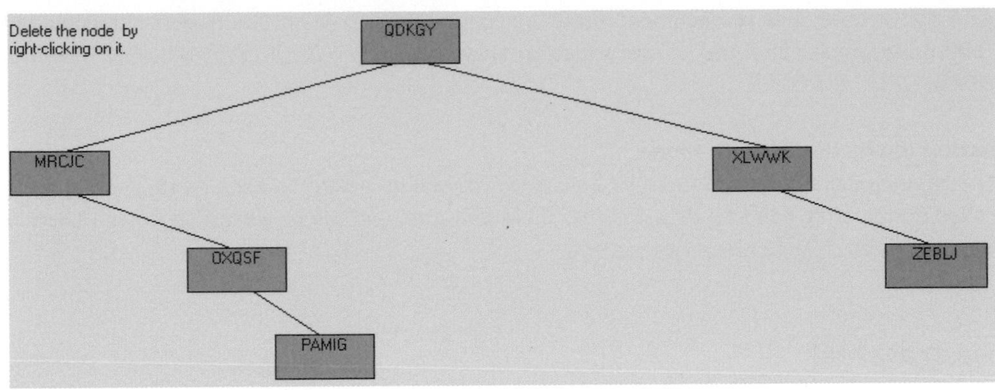

Figure 23.9 The result after deleting the node JJRTU

3 Deleting a node with left (and right) children

If a node has left children, then when it gets deleted we replace it with another node from the tree. Consider the example shown in Figure 23.10.

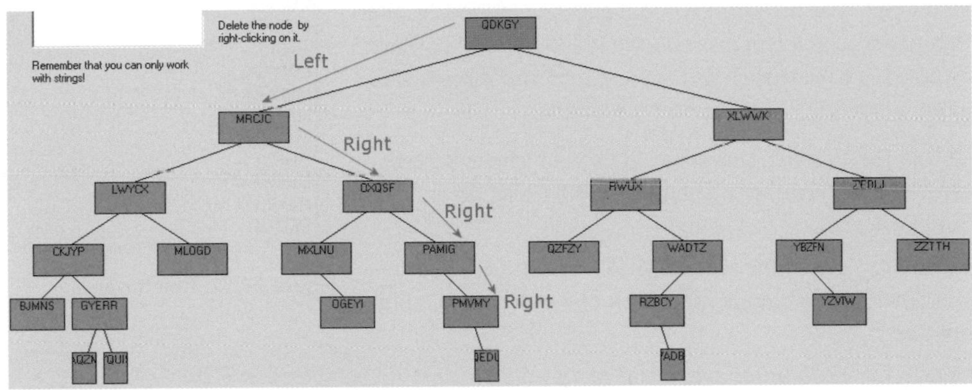

Figure 23.10 Example of a node with left and right children

If QDKGY needs to be deleted, the replacement node is searched by going left from the node once, and then all the way right until there are no more nodes to be looked at, as shown by the green annotation on this diagram. In this case, the replace node is PMVMY. If there are any gaps left in the tree when the node is replaced, the nodes under the gaps are added in a way so that they preserve the structure (as before). In this example, only the node EDU will be added. If, when searching for the replacement node, we find that there is only one left node to go to and no right nodes, then the replacement node would be the first left node in the tree as shown in Figure 23.11.

Maintenance of binary tree structures is a complex topic, especially when certain nodes in the tree have to be deleted.

See chapter 4 for a detailed explanation of these binary tree maintenance algorithms, but Ivan has chosen to implement things differently in this situation.

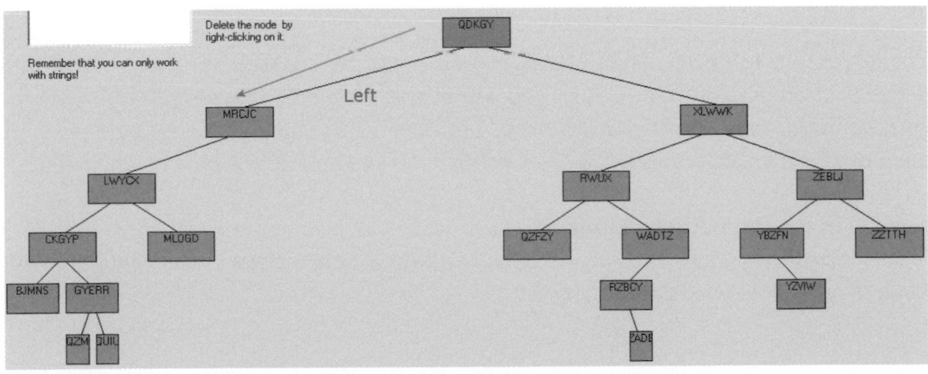

Figure 23.11 Demonstration that the replacement node will be MRCJC

In the above case, the replacement node would be MRCJC. When the nodes get replaced, all the nodes under the gap will be added in this order: LWYCX, CKGYP, MLOGD, BJMNS, GYERR, QZM, and OUIS.

Deleting in the User Active Mode

If the replacement node needs to be selected, you will be asked to click on it. Then, for any further nodes that need to be added to fill in the gap, you will be asked to select them in the order in which they should be added.

Back

Tree traversal

Tree traversals are used to parse (or walk around) the tree. There are three types of traversal:

- In order
- Pre order
- Post order.

Figure 23.12 Tree traversal

Given a tree, the program will output the nodes in the correct order, using the area shown in Figure 23.12. There are three rules for traversing a tree, and the simple tree used in Figure 23.13 is used as an example.

- The rule for 'in order traversal' is to visit the left node, then the root node, and then the right node, so it would be A, B, C.
- The rule for 'pre order traversal' is to visit the root node, then the left node, and then the right node, so it would be B, A, C.
- The rule for 'post order traversal' is to visit the left node, then the right node, and then the root node, so it would be A, C, B.

Traversing binary trees is a good example of using recursive techniques.

Recursion is code that is able to call itself, and traversing subtrees is a good example of this.

Recursion is covered in several parts of this book.

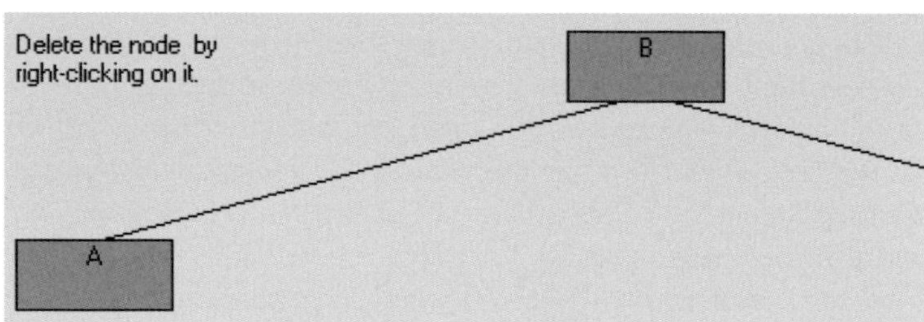

Figure 23.13 A simple tree used to demonstrate traversal

If the tree structure is larger, then the subtrees must be treated as though you were starting the problem again, even though you are in the middle of traversing a larger tree. This might be hard to understand at first, but the best thing is to experiment. The significance of the in order traversal is that it outputs the nodes in alphabetical order.

Tree traversal in the User Active Mode

In the User Active Mode you will simply be asked to click on the nodes in the required order for the type of traversal you have selected.

Back

Further help

You can always look at your Computer Science textbook for help on the theory of binary trees. In addition, here are some good web sites on binary trees:

http://www.ibr.cs.tu-bs.de/lehre/ss98/audii/applets/BST
http://www.csse.monash.edu.au/~lloyd/tildeAlgDS/Tree/
http://www.cs.nyu.edu/algvis/java/bst.html
http://www.cs.nyu.edu/algvis/java/Examples.html#Insert

If you still have any questions/suggestions, you can contact me at:

bilickii@tonbridge-school.org

Back

The e-mail address was Ivan's e-mail address when at school. However, he has left now and his account has therefore been deactivated.

Feedback from the author

We now go on to the two final sections of the module 6 project work. *You and your client should critically appraise the project.* It is unlikely to be perfect, and with the benefit of hindsight you should be able to think of a number of things that could be done better. The mark scheme for the project appraisal (2004 subject specification) is shown in Table 23.3.

It is essential that you have feedback from your client.

A formal letter, written on company headed paper, is essential.

Even if a parent or your teacher has acted as your client, a degree of formality should exist at this stage.

Table 23.3 The mark scheme for the appraisal part of your project

Section	Marks	Brief explanation
Appraisal	3	• Comparison of performance against objectives • Possible extensions • User feedback

The author of this book was Ivan's client and he wrote a letter which was added in an appendix to Ivan's project report. It was placed with other letters written at various stages of the process, starting with the original request to make a teaching aid on binary trees.

Your client must not say things like, 'What a wonderful project, I think it is marvellous and does exactly what I wanted', even though this may be true. It is far better to say things along the following lines.

You must compare what your project actually does with the original objective worked out in the analysis section.

- Ivan has produced a useful teaching aid which has been tested and welcomed by his peers (see the user feedback in the appendix).
- I am impressed with the on-line help system which is convenient to use because it can be called up electronically from the program and navigated easily.
- Producing a .exe file has made the program very easy to use, and students may take a copy home on a floppy disk, or e-mail it to themselves as an attachment.
- The project conforms to the specification and has exceeded our expectations in several respects, especially with the interactive messaging systems which can be scrolled through and analysed by the teacher.
- With the benefit of hindsight, the 'add random nodes' system would have been better to choose a random selection of real names, like Tom, Dick and Harry, for example, because this would make the trees easier to use than the current KJDLK, KDTER and IEGDF methods. This is not hard to do and should have been thought about at the analysis of design stage.
- Ivan's project is complex enough already and we decided that working with numeric variables would add extra complexity. However, a message emphasising that numeric input will be treated as a string could be displayed when the user enters numeric data.

Picking up marks for Appraisal and Quality of Communication should be relatively easy. Do not throw marks down the drain by failing to perform these essential tasks at the end of your project – it could cost you an A level grade.

Feedback from the author

Make sure that you are using the appropriate mark scheme for the year in which you are taking the A2 examination.

Finally, the quality of communication should be good if you have organised your project according to the mark scheme and run spelling and grammar checks. Remember that the spell checker should be run many times, mainly because students tend to make so many alterations that typos are inevitable. You will not lose any marks for the odd spelling or grammatical error, but you will lose most if not all of the marks if your project contains bad English and is full of spelling errors. The mark scheme for the quality of communication (2004 subject specification) is shown in Figure 23.4.

Table 23.4 The mark scheme for the quality of communication

Section	Marks	Brief explanation
Quality of communication	3	• Relevant information is clearly organised • Good use of English – continuous prose, with good use of grammar, punctuation and spelling

Self-test questions

1 Assuming that you have designed a programming project, outline five things that should accompany the project to enable effective system maintenance to take place.

2 Assuming that you have designed a database project, outline five things that should accompany the project to enable effective system maintenance to take place.

3 A separate user manual should usually accompany any project.
(a) What is this?
(b) What information is usually contained in the user manual?

4 It is now common practice to produce a user manual in electronic form, and the following are typical ways of doing this:
(a) A pdf document.
(b) An HTML document.
(c) A Windows help file.
Outline an advantage/disadvantage for each of these electronic forms of documentation. Which is the hardest to produce and which is the easiest?

5 Screenshots form a common part of the project implementation and write up.
(a) What may be added to screenshots to help with the project documentation?
(b) Explain how this may be done by using an art package or a word processor.

6 There are three important stages for the 'Project appraisal'.
Comparison of performance against objectives
Possible extensions
User feedback.
(a) What techniques could you use to compare the current performance with the original objectives?
(b) Why is it unlikely that you could think of no possible extensions to your project?
(c) What sort of feedback should be given by your client?

7 Quality of communication provides three relatively easy marks. You should make sure that you gain these.
(a) What electronic resources are available to ensure the good use of English?
(b) Why is method (a) not foolproof?
(c) What else can you do to ensure that errors are minimised?

Full answers to all end-of-chapter self-test questions

Complete answers are given to virtually all self-test questions. In many cases *extra material*, not covered in the main book, is added to produce hundreds of comprehensive answers to the questions posed.

Chapter 1 – The microprocessor and its register set

1 (a) **Microprocessor** – This is a single chip which lies at the heart of a microcomputer. It contains the CPU, registers set and associated bus systems.

(b) **Fetch-execute cycle** – This involves fetching an instruction from memory, decoding it and then carrying out (executing) the particular operation.

(c) **ALU** – this is the Arithmetic Logic Unit. It carries out arithmetical (+, – etc.) and logical operations (AND, OR, NOT etc.).

(d) **Register** – This is a small electronic storage device inside the microprocessor used for temporary storage of data.

(e) **Program counter** – This is a register, the contents of which help to keep track of the next instruction to be obtained from memory.

(f) **Address bus** – A group of parallel conductors along which the numbers representing the addresses in memory or of some peripheral device may travel to the microprocessor.

(g) **MAR** – The memory address register holds the number representing the address currently being accessed for a read or write operation.

(h) **MDR** – The memory data register holds the data which was either read from or written to memory the last time this happened.

(i) **CIR** – The Current Instruction Register holds the instruction currently being decoded and executed.

(j) **Data bus** – A parallel group of wires along which the data travels to and from the microprocessor.

(k) **Control bus** – A group of wires which carry control signals like whether the memory has to be read or to write data, for example.

(l) **Internal bus** – The bus systems which are inside the microprocessor.

2 **Machine code** is the pure binary digits representing operations that may be carried out by a microprocessor. **Assembly language** is the mnemonics representing machine code instructions. There is a one-to-one relationship between an assembly language instruction and its machine code equivalent.

3 A wider data bus, wider address bus, faster clock speed and faster memory would all make a program run faster.

4 **Clock speed** alone is insufficient to determine the comparative speed of a computer because the data bus and address bus widths may be different in each machine.

5 A special purpose register is assigned to a specialist task like that of examining the status of the flags, for example. A general purpose register may have its function assigned by the programmer. For example, it could be used for temporary storage or for maintaining a index.

6 The **stored program concept** was invented by von Neumann and describes the process where a program is stored in memory, and each instruction is fetched, decoded and executed sequentially.

7 There is no real difference because the peripheral devices are mapped onto memory. Writing to a peripheral device is therefore no different from the point of view of the microprocessor.

8 The function of the **clock** is to provide the electronic signals which provide the timing to enable the microprocessor to go through the fetch-execute cycle. The type of electronic signal output from the clock is a square wave whose frequency is measured in GHz.

9 A **memory map** is a picture of the computer's memory usage, showing how different parts of the memory are allocated to different tasks.

10 A microprocessor cannot tell the difference between data and program instructions. It is up to the programmer to make sure that the program is correctly written so that instructions are interpreted as such.

11 Assume the numbers are in memory locations 100 to 104 inclusive. Assume the answer is to be placed in memory location 105. Assume that the accumulator register is denoted by (A). The following instructions are typical of what is needed.

```
LOAD, A [100]   ;Load acc. with contents of
                ;memory location 100
ADD, A [101]    ;Add contents of location 101
ADD, A [102]    ;Add contents of location 102
ADD, A [103]    ;Add contents of location 103
ADD, A [104]    ;Add contents of location 104
STORE, A [105]  ;Store contents in location
105
```

12 An **interrupt** is something that requires the attention of the microprocessor. To process a simple interrupt the contents of the registers are dumped onto a LIFO stack and the PC is used to point to the place where the interrupt handler resides. After handling the interrupt the contents of the registers are pulled off the stack, the PC returned to its original contents and the main task can be reinstated.

13 A **LIFO stack** is useful because data placed onto the stack is the first to be needed after an interrupt has been serviced. A LIFO stack is thus ideal for nested interrupts too.

14 A **vector** is used to point to the place in memory where the actual interrupt routine resides. This means that it is possible to alter both the size and position of the interrupt handling routine without altering any other part of the calling program.

15 The bit inside the **flag register** is usually set if an interrupt occurs, and reset after the interrupt has been processed. Details (numbers) inside the **interrupt register** instruct the processor as to the type of interrupt that has just occurred and the place in a table where the interrupt handler address may be found.

16 **Interrupt priorities** are usually assigned a number which relates to their importance. Higher-priority interrupts are processed first, but the operating system must make sure that low-priority interrupts are eventually serviced.

17 The following table shows what would happen.

Interrupt	Process	Comment
–	MMM	Main process being carried out
3	333	M suspended, 3 being serviced
2	222	3 suspended, 2 being serviced
–	333	2 finished, 3 reinstated
–	MMM	3 finished, main task reinstated

Chapter 2 – Assembly language

1 For small embedded devices like cameras and video recorders, there may not be an **assembler** available for the **microprocessor** contained inside them, thus **machine code** may need to be used.

2 Assembly language is unique to a particular type of microprocessor. It will not run on another type of machine because the **instruction set** is different.

3 (a) A **label** is used as a reference to some point in an assembly language program. It is often used as a point to which you can jump.
(b) An **operation code** is the mnemonic used to represent an assembly language program. ADD or XOR, for example.
(c) **Operands** usually describe the source or destination of data in an assembly language instruction.
(d) **Comments** aid the readability of an assembly language program.

4 Different modes of addressing are encountered, mainly because of the addressing range offered by each mode. **Immediate addressing** is where the data appears immediately after the operation code. **Direct addressing** is where a specific memory location is referred to. **Indirect addressing** is where the operand after a register holds the location of the item of data. **Indexed addressing** is where a number in one register is usually combined with another (like an index register) to give the location where the data may be found.

5 Two numbers may typically be added together as follows. We assume that the numbers are generated by using immediate addressing.

```
mov al, 20    ; Get 20 into the al register
mov bl, 10    ; Get 10 into the bl register
add al, bl    ; Add al to bl and store the
              ;result in al
```

Each number must be such that the sum is not greater than 255, the maximum that can be stored in 1 byte.

6 The logical OR operation could be used together with the following **mask**.

```
7 6 5 4 3 2 1 0 Bit number
0 0 0 1 1 1 0 0 Mask
```

In this way, the top three bits and the bottom two bits will remain the same, but bits 2, 3 and 4 would be set to '1' because of the 'OR' operation.

7 A **logical shift** is movement of the register contents left or right with zeros filling the vacating spaces. An **arithmetical shift** preserves the sign (two's complement) by making sure that positive numbers have the most significant bit remaining zero and negative numbers having the most significant bit remaining a one.
For the register contents shown in the question, the answers are as follows.

(a) 1 0 0 0 0 1 1 1 1 0 0 0 0 0 0 0
(b) 1 0 0 0 0 1 1 1 1 0 0 0 0 0 0 0
(c) 0 0 1 1 1 1 0 0 0 0 1 1 1 1 0 0
(d) 1 1 1 1 1 0 0 0 0 1 1 1 1 0 0 0

8 Logical operations like 'AND' and 'OR' operate in bitwise mode. This means that bit number 7 in one register, for example, is paired with bit number 7 in the other register. As an example, consider the 'OR' operation being carried out on the A register and B register with the result being put in the C register as follows.

```
A register  0 1 1 0 0 1 1 0
B register  1 0 0 1 0 1 0 0
C register  1 1 1 1 0 1 1 0 (A OR B)
```

9 (a) An **assembler** is software which converts assembly language source code into machine code.
(b) Four possible advantages are as follows.
  (i) Mnemonics may be used instead of the machine code.
  (ii) Labels may be used so that relative jumps may be made very easily.
  (iii) The assembler will check for any syntax errors.
  (iv) The assembler may be able to be used to help debug a program by single stepping through it.

10 (a) **Source code** is the term given to the original assembly language mnemonics and comments etc.
(b) **Object code** is the name given to the machine code program that is ready to run on the target machine.
(c) Typical stages would be:
  (i) Create the source code in a typical text editor.
  (ii) Assemble the source code.
  (iii) Correct any syntax errors (go back to (i) if necessary).
  (iv) Link with any libraries and run the code (go back to (i) if errors occur).
  (v) Check the logic of the program, then go back to stage (a) and alter the source code if necessary.

11 A **debugger** is a system in which there are facilities to single step through a program and examine register contents etc. This can be helpful when trying to find errors in the logic of your program.

12 An **assembler directive** or **pseudo operation** is an instruction to the assembler that does not form part of the actual assembly language program.

13 There are many routines that may be called from the operating system. These routines save the assembly language programmer the hassle of having to write their own routines to do the same thing. Typically this might involve reading characters from the keyboard, printing out characters to the printer or saving characters to a file on disk, for example.

14 One possible assembly language program to test to see if the 16-bit accumulator is zero and then jump to the given labels is as follows.

```
cmp   ax, 0       ;compare the 16-bit acc.
                  ;with zero
jz accumzero      ;jump to 'accumzero' if
                  ;true
jmp accumnonzero  ;jump to 'accumnonzero'
...

accumzero    ;routine for zero accumulator
```

```
...
accumnonzero ;routine for non-zero accumulator
...
```

Chapter 3 – Programming concepts

1 A **natural language** like English, for example, is context sensitive and sometimes ambiguous. Any computer language must be unambiguous and completely logical, and this is an example of a **formal language**.

2 A **programming paradigm** is the name given to the main methodology used for a programming language. The **imperative** programming paradigm typifies giving sequences of instructions (imperatives) which explain to the computer how a particular problem is to be solved.

3 The **procedural programming** paradigm helps split up problems into sub-problems by the use of procedures. This makes the problems easier to tackle and also enables teams of people to work on different parts of the same problem.

4 Three different languages which typify the **procedural programming paradigm** are FORTRAN, BASIC and COBOL.

5 (a) A **function** is a call to a routine and may have parameters passed to it, and one value is returned from it.

(b) Typically a **functional programming language** is based around calls to different functions (mathematical and otherwise). Function may be defined recursively or called from within other functions.

(c) It is less likely that variables will get inadvertently messed up compared to a procedural language. Some of the code is also much more efficient due to the heavy dependence on recursion.

6 **Logical** and **functional programming** paradigms both belong to what is called **declarative programming**.

7 When solving a problem using a **logic programming** paradigm you create a knowledge base by defining facts and rules. You then interrogate the knowledge base by asking questions.

8 Three advantages of logic programming over procedural programming are:

(i) There is a very close relationship to mathematical logic, and this is useful for programming expert systems.

(ii) We are able to concentrate on the solution to the problem rather than the steps necessary to get to the solution.

(iii) Programs written in a logical programming language are usually considerably smaller than their procedural equivalents.

9 (a) A **fact** is something that is incontrovertibly true.

(b) A **rule** is the condition that must be applied for something to be regarded as being true.

(c) A **list** in Prolog is something that consists of a head and a tail, both of which may be empty.

(d) A **head** is the item at the beginning of a list.

(e) The **tail** is the remainder of the list after the head has been taken away.

10 For a programming language to be considered fully object oriented it must support **objects**, **classes**, **polymorphism**, **encapsulation** and **inheritance**.

11 (a) A **class** is an abstract data type which can be regarded as a blueprint or plan for an object.

(b) An **object** is an instance (example of) a class. An object can be any physical or abstract thing that the programmer cares to dream up.

(c) **Encapsulation** means encapsulating both the methods and data associated with an object. This method enables us to hide the internal workings from other parts of the program.

(d) **Inheritance** is a useful mechanism whereby attributes of a derived class may be inherited from the base class in a controlled way. This is useful because it allows us to reuse code without altering or inadvertently interacting with the original code.

(e) **Instantiation** means creating an instance of a class, i.e. creating an actual object.

(f) A **base class** is a class from which derived classes may inherit attributes in a controlled way.

12 **Object-oriented programming** methods have proved popular because they help to minimise development time on large projects. They do this by eliminating the need to alter code that has already been tested and certified correct. New classes and objects do not inadvertently mess up ones that have already been written. Objects also mirror the real world rather conveniently.

13 **Polymorphism** means many forms. Typically in an object-oriented programming language this refers to derived classes inheriting properties from a common base class. For example, we could create a base class called transport. We could then have derived classes called 'aircraft', 'cars', 'bicycles', 'boats' etc. all of which would share common properties, like the ability to carry people on a journey, for example. The derived classes are different forms of the common base class, and this is one example of polymorphism.

14 The following is a possible class definition of 'Teapot' using the syntax of the object-oriented programming language C++.

```
class teapot
{
  public:
  void teapot();       //declares a function which
                       //accepts and returns no
                       //arguments (parameters)
  int spout;           //The number of spouts
                       //maximum of three!
  int handles;         //Number of handles -
                       //maximum of two!
  string name of teapot;
  string colour of teapot;
  string theme of teapot;
  string value of teapot;
};
```

15 A derived class called 'teapot_and_stand' inherits all the attributes from the base class teapot using the following C++ syntax.

```
class teapot_and_stand : public teapot
{
  public:
  void stand();       //declares a function which
                      //accepts and returns no
                      //arguments (parameters)
  int legs;           //The number of legs
                      //maximum of six
  string name of stand;
  string shape of stand;
};
```

Chapter 4 – Data structures

1 A **data structure** is a way of modelling things like queues, linked lists and arrays, for example. Each abstract data structure enables the computer to process the data contained within it very efficiently.

2 A **linear list** is an ordered set of elements. **Pointers** are numbers which enable items in a list to be identified. Typically a subscripted array 'like A(22)' might be used where 22 is a number which acts as a pointer pointing to the twenty-second data item in the list.

3 A **tree structure** is a hierarchical data structure which has a root node at the 'top'. Other nodes, which contain data, branch from this root in the form of a tree. Tree structures are important in computer science because they mirror a huge variety of hierarchical structures encountered in real life, and enable these data structures to be processed very efficiently.

4 A typical **tree structure** is as follows.

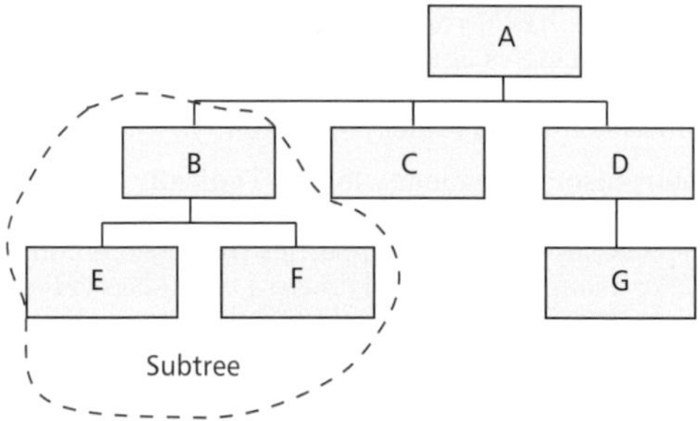

All of the boxes are examples of **nodes**. The **root node** is box A. Examples of **child nodes** are B, C, D, E, F and G. Examples of **parent nodes** are A, B and D. Examples of **leaf nodes** are E, F, C and G. There are a number of **subtrees**, and one is shown in red on the diagram.

5 Each node in a **tree** may have many children. In a **binary tree** each node may have a maximum of two children.

6 (a) An **ordered binary tree** is one in which the data has been used to build up the tree in some particular order. A common example is 'alphabetical order' (see (7) below).

(b) **Ordered binary tree** structures are important because you can insert new items into an ordered list without having to move all the other data items. You can also delete old items without moving data.

7 For alphabetical order, the data to be inserted into the tree is compared with data at the root node. If the data to be inserted is greater than the data at the root then the 'right-hand path' is followed. Otherwise the left-hand pointer is followed and the data compared with the next node. We continue in this way until an empty node is found, and the data is inserted here.

8 A **LIFO** is a Last In First Out data structure. This means that the last data item to be placed onto the stack is the first data item to be removed from the stack. A **FIFO** is a First In First Out data structure where the first item to be placed in the queue is the first item to be removed from the queue.

9 (a) The alternative name is a **stack**.

(b) The alternative name is a **queue**.

10 The pointers used to implement a queue are the **start pointer** (or **header**) indicating the start of the queue and the **end pointer** (or **footer**) indicating the end of the queue. A stack is managed by a single **stack pointer**, which usually indicates the top of the stack.

11 A **static data structure** is one which cannot be altered during the execution of a program. An array is a good example of a static data structure, whose dimension (size) cannot be altered unless the program is stopped and modified.
A **dynamic data structure** is one in which the size can be altered during the execution of a program. A good example of this is a file whose size is allowed to get smaller and larger during the execution of the program.

12 A **linked list** is a data structure where one item is linked to the next item in the list by a pointer. The pointer is usually stored along with the node data. A start pointer indicates the start of the list and an end pointer indicates the end of the list. A free space pointer is used to denote the places where extra data may be stored when needed. The data inserted in the free space then becomes part of the linked list.

13 A **two-way linked list** is a linked list in which two pointers are stored along with the node data. A forward pointer points to the next item in the linked list and a backwards pointer points to the previous item in the linked list. In this way it is possible to traverse the list in both directions. A simple example of the use of a two-way linked list would be the position of a football team in a league. It would be possible to see which team is ahead or which team is behind a particular team very easily.

14 A **stack** is a LIFO data structure, but a **heap** is an area of memory used for the purposes of temporary storage. Blocks of data may be assigned to the heap in a random fashion.

Chapter 5 – Further data structures

1 (a) The node data for **pre-order traversal** are:

a, b, d, h, i, e, j, k, c, f, l, m, g, n, o

(b) The node data for **in-order traversal** are:

h, d, i, b, j, e, k, a, l, f, m, c, n, g, o

(c) The node data for **post-order traversal** are:

h, i, d, j, k, e, b, l, m, f, n, o, g, c, a

2 This question is a mini-project and depends on your chosen language. The **pseudocode** to build up a binary tree is shown in this chapter on pages 75, 76 and 77.

Chapter 6 – Sorting and searching algorithms

1 The **insertion sort** is the simplest of all sort algorithms. The first item in the unsorted list is taken and placed in the sorted list. The next item from the unsorted list is considered, and this is compared with each element in the sorted list and inserted in the appropriate place. The process continues in this way until all elements from the unsorted list have been inserted in the sorted list.

2 The **bubble sort** is as follows:

(a) Start by comparing the first pair of numbers in the list to be sorted.

(b) If first number > second number swap and set a flag.

(c) Go on to the next pair of numbers and repeat stages (a) and (b). If a swap took place reset the flag and start again; if no swap took place the list is sorted.

3 A **linear search** means searching for an item of data by examining each item in the list of data to be searched until the item is found, or found not to be in the list.
A **binary search** means splitting an ordered list into two

parts. If the item to be found is in the lower 'half' of the list then this lower half of the list is searched by using the binary search again. This recursive process continues until the item of data is found, or found not to be in the list.

4 Using the binary search method, a list of two elements would require just one comparison. A list of four elements

Number of elements	Maximum comparisons
2	1 (2^0)
4	2 (2^1)
8	3 (2^2)
Etc.	
1024	10 (2^{10})

would, at worst, require two comparisons. A list of eight elements would require three comparisons etc. The patterns established are shown in the above table. Therefore, for a list of 1000 data items, no more than 10 comparisons would be needed.

5 **Recursion** is the technique of an algorithm being able to call itself. The binary search is a classic example of a recursive algorithm.

Chapter 7 – Data representation in computers

1 A **number base** is the name given to a system of counting. Denary, or base ten, uses the digits {0, 1, 2, 3, 4, 5, 6, 7, 8, 9} and column headings 100, 10, 1 etc. and is the system familiar to all. The binary (or base two) system uses the digits {0, 1} and column headings 16, 8, 4, 2, 1 etc.

2 (a) (i) 10 (ii) 40 (iii) 255 (iv) 1339
(b) (i) 11011 (ii) 10000000
(iii) 110 001 0101 (iv) 11111 11111 111111

3 (a) AB (b) F0 (c) 9954

4 (a) 10110 0000 (b) 10011 11001
(c) 1111 1111 0110 0000
(d) 1111 1011 1111 1111

5 (a) 0.01 (b) 0.00001 (c) 1.1 (d) 1111.011
(e) 1100.000001

6 **Two's complementation** is a system for representing positive and negative binary numbers. It is based on a mechanical counter that goes either forwards or backwards. Any number starting with a zero is positive and any number starting with a one is negative. The system is useful for binary because subtraction may be undertaken by adding the two's complement of the number being subtracted.

7 (a) 11111100 (b) 11110011
(c) 10111011 (d) 10000101

8 (a) 1100 00010 . 1100 (b) 1110 1110 . 0110
(c) 1000 1110 . 1101

9 **Normalisation** is needed otherwise there is a plethora of exact representations for the same number, and the precision with which you can express a number may be lost.

10 The **mantissa** is the part of the floating point number which represents a binary fraction, usually in two's complement form. The **exponent** is an integer number which moves the binary point in the mantissa either right or left according to whether it is positive or negative respectively.

11 (a) An **eight-bit integer register** is not capable of storing fractional numbers, and is limited to 256 different numbers, either 0 to 255 if positive numbers are used, or −128 to +127 if two's complementation is used.
(b) An **eight-bit fractional register** is not capable of representing integers, (except, of course, −1).
(c) An **eight-bit fractional mantissa** determines the precision with which the integer or fractional numbers will be represented. The **four-bit exponent** is not capable of extending the range beyond moving the binary place seven places right or eight places left.

12 For a **12-bit register**:
(a) Maximum positive number is 011111111111 = +2047
(b) Minimum positive number is 00000000001 = +1
(c) Smallest-magnitude negative number is 111111111111 = −1
(d) Largest-magnitude negative number is 100000000000 = −2048

13 For the register * . * * * * * * * * *
(a) The maximum positive number is $0.111111111 = 1 - 1/2^9 = 0.998046875$
(b) The minimum positive number is $0.000000001 = 1/2^9 = 0.001953125$
(c) The smallest-magnitude negative number is $1.111111111 = -1/2^9 = -0.001953125$
(d) The largest-magnitude negative number is $1.000000000 = -1$

14 As normalisation is now being used:
(a) The maximum positive number is $0.111111111 \| 0111 = (1 - 1/2^9) \times 2^7$
(b) The minimum positive number is $0.100000000 \| 1000 = (1/2) \times 2^{-8}$
(c) The smallest-magnitude negative number is $1.011111111 \| 1000 = -(1/2 + 1/2^9) \times 2^{-8}$
(d) The largest-magnitude negative number is $1.000000000 \| 0111 = -1 \times 2^7$

Chapter 8 – Operating systems

1 An **operating system** is software that controls virtually every aspect of the computer system. It controls the security and the user interface and controls which tasks are being run and when. Without the operating system the computer would be extremely difficult to use.

2 A **batch operating system** is designed to run a batch of jobs, one after the other, under the control of a job control language. This is typical of the systems found running utility billing in major companies like water and electricity.
An **interactive operating system** is typified by the modern Windows operating system running on a PC. This operating system allows the user to be in control of what is happening by interacting with the operating system through the mouse or the keyboard.
A **real-time operating system** is usually found in the process-control industry or embedded inside electronic systems. The response from a real-time system must be such that processes requiring the operating system's attention get dealt with in a suitable time span (hence the

name). Typically this would be very fast, but real time also applies to systems where the response time is adequate, like booking an airline ticket, for example, which is called a pseudo real-time operating system.

3 Two scenarios might be BACS, the Bank Automated Clearing System where millions of cheques are cleared each day, and the analysis of millions of census returns for a country.

4 The language to control a batch of jobs is called a job-control language. Typically you can program when a job is run, what resources are needed, evaluate how much the job will cost, where the beginning and end of a particular job occurs and what peripherals or compilers, for example, are needed by the job.

5 **Multiprocessing** means having more than one processor in the system so that more than one thing may be done at the same time. **Multitasking** means the ability to run more than one task on the same processor. It usually happens so fast that you think that you are able to do more than one thing at a time.

6 This is a term applied to operating systems running on networks. A **client machine** (either a thin client or a fat client connected to a network) interacts with a **file server** on the network. This is a form of distributed processing, and can be quite complex when hundreds of clients and many servers are involved.

7 **Distributed file processing** is a term used where the files being worked on by a particular system may be obtained from a huge variety of sources including locally or from network file servers or other machines on a network. It is important for educational establishments because this enables pupils and staff to work on the same files throughout an organisation, or for all staff to use the same school or college database, for example.

8 Examples of resources that must be managed by an operating system are memory, peripherals, security, time allocation and the user interface.

9 **Fixed partitioning** is easier to manage but more wasteful of memory compared with variable partitioning. **Variable partitioning** is more efficient in terms of memory allocation, but the memory will become fragmented at some stage, reducing the efficiency of the system compared with fixed partitioning.

10 **Dynamic memory partitioning** is allocating memory on the fly (i.e. as and when needed by the operating system).

11 **Virtual memory** is a technique enabling you to run programs or load files that would require more physical RAM than is actually present in the system. It does this by swapping pages of memory between RAM and disk.

12 **Relocatable code** is code that may be run anywhere in memory. All references within the code are relative to the other parts of the same code, and no absolute memory references are used to call any of the program. **Re-entrant code** is code that can be used by more than one process simultaneously.

13 A **dynamically linked library** (or dll) is a routine that is called up at run time by a particular application. Many applications may use the same dll, and this library system is therefore more efficient than compiling these common routines and embedding them with each application that needs it.

14 A **buffer** is the name given to memory used as temporary storage, often to interface one system to another. A printer, for example, may have a buffer inside it so that information to be printed can be sent to the printer more efficiently than sending it to a printer without a buffer. Also, a disk might have a buffer to interface the disk hardware to the operating system, overcoming the different sizes and formats used to store information on the disk and the way in which data is stored in the file from an operating system perspective.

15 Most peripherals operate using **interrupts**, e.g. a printer might run out of paper or a disk might be full or a CD-ROM may not be spinning at the right speed yet. The operating system must be interrupted from sending information to a peripheral that is not ready to receive it, or a key might have been pressed on the keyboard requiring action from the operating system to display the character on the screen.

16 **Scheduling** is an important part of the functioning of the operating system which ensures that tasks are carried out in an appropriate order to maximise the efficient use of resources like memory and peripheral access, and making sure that everything in a multitasking environment gets some attention. Typically the OS will make sure that no one task hogs all the processor time, and if a task needs to print and the printer is available then this will get a high priority.

17 A **process** is the execution of a program from the point of view of the operating system. The **states** that a process may be in are typically 'program waiting', 'program being run' or 'program awaiting peripheral attention', for example. The **process model** manages the processes by analysing and acting on the process states. This technique is fundamental to the design of an operating system.

18 An **event** is something like a mouse click, a key being pressed or a user plugging in a PDA, for example. Typically these events, created by the user, will cause events to happen which the operating system will service. Thus, in an event-driven system the user is in control of what the computer does.

19 A **thread** is the name given to a part of a much larger program being run by the operating system. A thread is far less protected than a task, which operates more independently than a thread.

20 The **threaded model** allows different parts of the same process to be run at the same time, and is therefore harder to manage than the **process model** which does not allow this to happen. More complex modern operating systems are therefore needed to support multithreading.

21 The three resources associated with a **process** are the executable code being run, the data being used by the process and the stack used by the process.

Chapter 9 – Applications and effects

1 Five possible application areas of computers used in science are:

(i) Weather forecasting.
(ii) DNA mapping (the human genome project).
(iii) Monitoring the environment.
(iv) Simulations of scientific experiments.
(v) Creating computer life forms.

2 Five possible application areas of computers used in communications are:

(i) The control of telephone exchanges.
(ii) The provision of Internet services for mobile phones and PDAs.
(iii) Application of computers for the visually or aurally handicapped.
(iv) Managing switched ethernet networks.
(v) Communicating with artificial intelligence.

3 A generic package is the general name for applications software like word processors, spreadsheets, CAD packages and databases, for example.
A possible ethical issue could arise when deciding the use to which an expert system might be put. If an expert system is built up for bomb-making, for example, then the person who programmed the system is probably in serious breach of the ethical code for his or her profession. Ethical issues arise frequently, and professionals like doctors, scientists and computer scientists usually subscribe to a set of ethical values laid down by the professional society to which they belong.
A possible legal implication of using an expert system shell is that you are relying on the knowledge base that is programmed into the system. If the system has incorrect information in it or if incorrect inferences are drawn, then the conclusions drawn will be wrong. This could lead to litigation unless a disclaimer is made by the producer of the system. (It probably will be!)

4 Two possible economic consequences of the use of generic packages in the office could be:
(i) Greater productivity means that fewer staff are likely to be needed.
(ii) The use of e-mail could reduce the cost of communicating in-house and with other employees throughout the world.

5 (a) An **embedded system** is a microprocessor-controlled computer which is built into a machine like a camera, CNC machine or a data logger.
(b) Five possible features that an embedded security alarm system may provide are:
(i) Automatically ringing a telephone number and calling the police in the event of a break in.
(ii) Producing a printed copy of the events that cause the alarm to go off.
(iii) A control panel may have lights which indicate if there are windows or doors open before the system is armed.
(iv) It is possible to activate different zones independently of others so that some areas may be armed and others not. (e.g. an evening class might use only one block and not the rest of the school).
(v) Faults in the system might activate a maintenance request so that an engineer can be called automatically.

6 (a) Computers on board a cruise ship could be used for the following things:
(i) Monitoring faults with the systems throughout the ship.
(ii) Controlling the engine management system.
(iii) Helping to present information from the GPS navigation satellites.
(b) Computers at an airport could be used for the following things:
(i) Controlling the security scanners which X-ray bags and other goods.
(ii) Linking security with national databases to check details on passports and immigration documentation.
(iii) Managing the baggage handling system by reading the labels on the luggage and directing the baggage to the appropriate aircraft or conveyor belt.

7 (a) For air traffic control, two typical **information requirements** might be:
(i) Splitting up the air traffic space into manageable sections for each controller.
(ii) Presenting the managers of the system with statistics about near misses.
From the point of view of air traffic control typical **communication requirements** might be:
(i) Presenting the controller with an instant picture of the aircraft to include information about height, speed and ID.
(ii) Give access to the flight plans for a particular aircraft.
(b) For the pilots, two typical **information requirements** might be:
(i) Provision of information regarding the correct flight path to take.
(ii) Display of information regarding height, direction and ETA.
From the point of view of a pilot typical **communication requirements** might be:
(i) Presenting the pilot with the appropriate frequency with which to communicate with air traffic control.
(ii) Updating the pilot with any new headings in terms of speed, directions and height.

8 A **moral argument** for robots might be as follows. People sometimes work in dangerous or unpleasant environments. Typically this might be where conditions like excess radiation, danger from explosions or other similar conditions exist. The use of robots in these circumstances enables this dangerous work to be carried out without risk to human life.
A **moral argument** against robots might be as follows. Robots are undertaking tasks that used to be accomplished by skilled and unskilled workers in the manufacturing industry. Many people are now unemployed because of the introduction of this new technology. This has had a disproportionate effect on those workers that have few skills and were employed in undertaking repetitive tasks in factories.

Chapter 10 – Advanced databases

1 A DBMS is a **database management system**. It is the conceptual view of the database, and contains software to help database administrators create, manage and interrogate the database.

2 A typical DBMS architecture has three different levels, mainly the **user's view** (the highest level), the **conceptual level** (the software to create, manage and interrogate) and the **physical level**, which is how the actual data is stored on the system.

3 There are usually several types of different **users** when considering a database. These fall into categories like non-technical users who need only enter and edit data, technical users who may need to create their own queries or reports, and administrative users who have the ability to change the structure of the database to alter the functionality.

4 **Concurrent access** to data occurs when two or more users are trying to access the same data simultaneously. This is not a problem for read-only data, but two people obviously cannot update the same record at the same time.

Therefore, record locking (or putting an exclusive lock on the record) is carried out to overcome this problem.

5 **ODBC** stands for open-database connectivity. It allows data contained in one database to be updated from data contained in a separate database if both databases are ODBC compatible. The only way to get data from one database into another without this feature is to export it using CSV or similar. However, doing this means that the data is only valid at the time that the export took place.

6 A **data definition language** is a language used by the DBA to build up the database. Typically you could create tables and an index on a particular field, for example.

7 A **data manipulation language** allows the user to modify data already in the database. Typically this might be the addition or deletion of data, for example.

8 The **file manager** in a DBMS has the same role as the file manager within the operating system. Namely it interfaces the physical storage of the files with the ways in which the files are used by the software, which in this particular case is a database. From the database perspective a file might be viewed as a relational table, but from the physical perspective it is viewed as a collection of records stored on disk. The file manager helps control these two interfaces. On a modern relational database many tables may be stored in the same database file.

9 Some typical **SQL commands** are 'SELECT', 'FROM', 'WHERE' and 'ORDERBY'. SELECT enables us to choose the fields, FROM specifies the table from which the fields are taken, WHERE determines under which conditions the selection is made and ORDERBY determines the order in which any criteria matching the selection will be displayed.

10 A **database** containing information about animals in a zoo might have the following SQL code.

```
Select Name, Animal type, Location
  From Animals
  Where Location = 23;
```

This would give a list of the names, types of animal and location where location = 23 is true.

11 The **ORDERBY** key word in the SQL language enables us to order the data selected from a query. Using the same database as shown in question (10), the animals at location 23 in the zoo could be listed alphabetically in order by the following sequence of SQL commands.

```
Select Name, Animal type, Location
  From Animals
  Where Location = 23
Order By Animal type;
```

12 The extra functionality of the **GROUPBY** command is that it enables data to be ordered in groups instead of operating on the whole column of data, as would be the case with ORDERBY.

13 The following **SQL code** would produce the required output.

```
Select ISBN, Author, Title
  From books
  Where Author = Prakash;
```

14 The following **SQL code** would produce the required output.

```
Select ISBN, Author, Title, Publisher_ID
  From books
 Where Publisher_ID =2 OR Publisher_ID =3
  Order By Author;
```

15 A **database server** is a file server running a database, probably created in SQL, for example. Very large and complex databases are often accessed by thousands of different people simultaneously (e.g. the Google search engine), and a client-server system is the only way to cope with this demand. If the database is relational, then it is probably running an RDBMS.

Chapter 11 – Advanced relational databases

1 The **relational database model** models a database by the production of a series of related tables. Each table represents a 'file', with rows representing records within the 'file' and columns representing fields within a record. Relations like 'one-to-one' or 'one-to-many', for example, link the tables. On a modern database lots of tables may be placed in the same logical file.

2 (a) An **entity** is a particular thing that is being modelled by a relational database table. Typical examples might be a book, car or student.

(b) A **table** is a relation in a relational database. A table must conform to rules like 'it must model one entity only', 'must have a unique primary key' and so on.

(c) A **row** in a table represents a record.

(d) A **column** in a table represents a field.

(e) A **relationship** is a mapping from one table to another like 'one-to-one' or 'one-to-many' etc.

3 (a) The two relationships used to model a relational database are 'one-to-one' and 'one-to-many'.

(b) Many-to-many relationships are usually modelled by using a number of 'one-to-many' relationships.

4 An ER diagram is a pictorial way of expressing the relationships between entities. Typical examples for a 'one-to-one' and 'many-to-one' relationship are as follows:

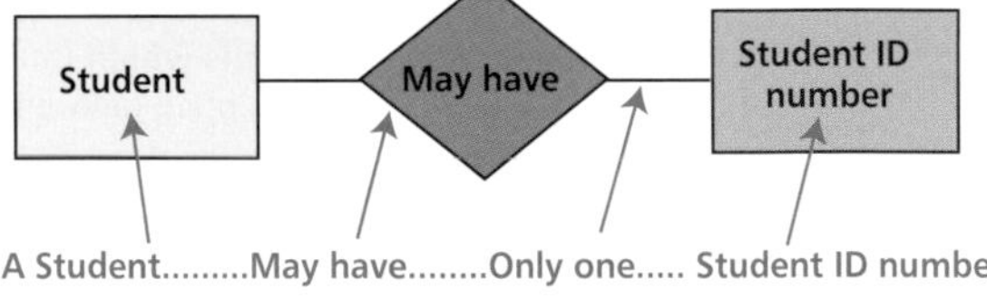

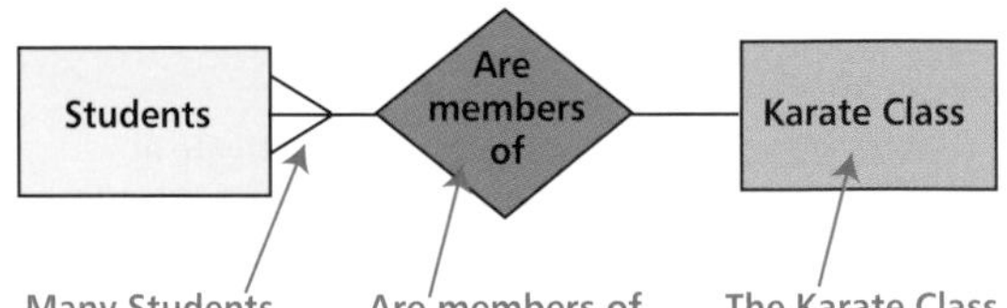

5 **Normalisation** is a set of rules, developed by Codd, called normal forms. If these rules are applied then the data is usually stored in a form where errors are less likely to be made.

6 If data is not put into **first normal form** then it is possible that the records are not all of the same length. If this happens it is much more difficult to search for items of information. Each item really needs its own field which can be indexed for fast searching if necessary.

7 If data is not put into **second normal form** then it is possible to have multiple entries containing the same data and this could lead to further errors when updating the database.

8 If data is not put into **third normal form** then it is possible that you may have to enter several items when the same information could have been altered with a single item. Thus the data is stored even less efficiently and there is more likelihood of an error.

9 A **composite primary key** is one in which two or more fields are combined to produce the primary key. A primary key must uniquely describe the data in a record, and sometimes a combination of order number and item number, for example, might be used to uniquely describe the item for a particular order. Order number or item number alone would not be able to do this.

10 (a) **Functional dependence** means that there is a unique association between two data elements (e.g. stock number and stock description are different ways of describing the same thing, and they are therefore functionally dependent on each other).

(b) A **non-key element** is the name given to an attribute that is not part of a primary (or composite primary) key.

(c) **Mutual independence** means that there are no unique associations between attributes in a database.

(d) A **determinant** is the name given to an attribute that is dependent on another attribute (or group of attributes). A stock number, for example, will determine the description of an item and the description is therefore a determinant.

11 (a) For data to be put into **first normal form**, the items in the list of data contain repeating values. The data may be split into two tables, one for the 'Orders' and one for the 'Items Purchased' as follows.
Orders(<u>Order no.</u>, Acc no., Customer, Address, Date, Total Cost)
Items Purchased(<u>Order no.</u>, Item, Quantity, Item Price)

The order number is used to relate the two tables. As there are no repeating keys, the tables are in first normal form.

(b) For data to be put into **second normal form**, all attributes in the entity must depend only upon the primary key. Therefore the primary key must uniquely identify each attribute; if this is not the case the attribute must be removed to another table.
The customer and customer address are not functionally dependent on order number, but are functionally dependent on account number, because the account number is a unique reference for the customer and his or her address. Therefore, the Customer's table has been created to remove these attributes to get
Customers(<u>Acc. no.</u>, Customer, Address)
This leaves the order number, data and total cost in the Orders table as follows:
Orders(<u>Order no.</u>, Acc no., Date, Total Cost)
We have therefore dealt with the original Orders table from part (a) above.
We now have to deal with the Items purchased table from part (a) too, and this is done as follows.
The item price is functionally dependent on item but not on order number. Therefore we can build up an Items table as follows.
Items(Item, Item Price)
We are now left with the Order number, Quantity, and Item. (Item is needed to relate the Items table to whatever we have left.)
The quantity and the item are not uniquely associated with order number, but if we choose a composite primary key of Order number and Item, then the quantity (i.e. a particular number of a certain item) would depend only upon this primary key. To distinguish this table from the Orders table, it is called 'Part Order' as follows.
Part Order(<u>Order no., Item</u>, Quantity)
To sum up, the following is one possible representation of the tables in second normal form:
Customers(<u>Acc. no.</u>, Customer, Address)
Orders(<u>Order no.</u>, Acc no., Date, Total Cost)
Items(Item, Item Price)
Part Order(<u>Order no., Item</u>, Quantity)

(c) **Third normal form** states that there should be no unique associations between attributes that could not be used as an alternative to the primary key.
In the Customers table, all attributes could be used as an alternative to the primary key. Therefore, this is in third normal form already. The Orders table has no alternatives that could be used as the primary key, therefore we have to check that there are no unique associations between any of these. There are not, so this is in third normal form too. By similar arguments, all the remaining tables are in third normal form too. Therefore, the tables in third normal form are as follows:
Customers(<u>Acc. no.</u>, Customer, Address)
Orders(<u>Order no.</u>, Acc no., Date, Total Cost)
Items(Item, Item Price)
Part Order(<u>Order no., Item</u>, Quantity)

Chapter 12 – Systems development

1 Four common methods used by **systems analysts** are interview, questionnaires, observation and review of existing paperwork.

2 It is often the case that observing day-to-day operations will reveal methods and techniques that are useful for the new system. Often you will find that people do not follow the existing manuals, but have developed better methods which are worthy of consideration in the new system design.

3 A DFD is useful for showing the flow of data between computerised or manual systems. Data can be represented in any form, and can be associated with a variety of things from paper-based information to people having information inside their head!
One possible DFD for the shop transaction is as follows:

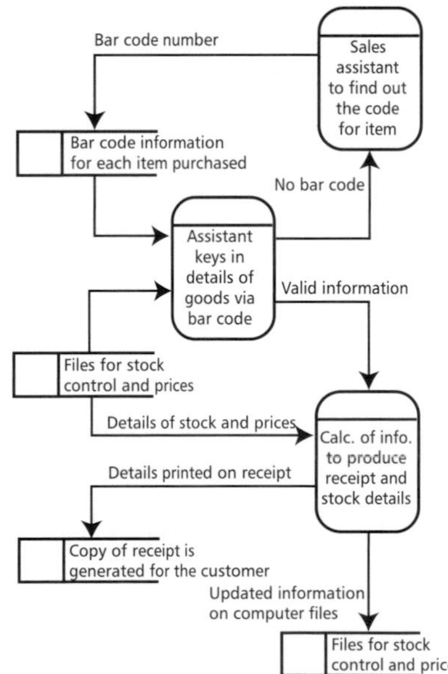

4 A possible system flowchart is as follows:

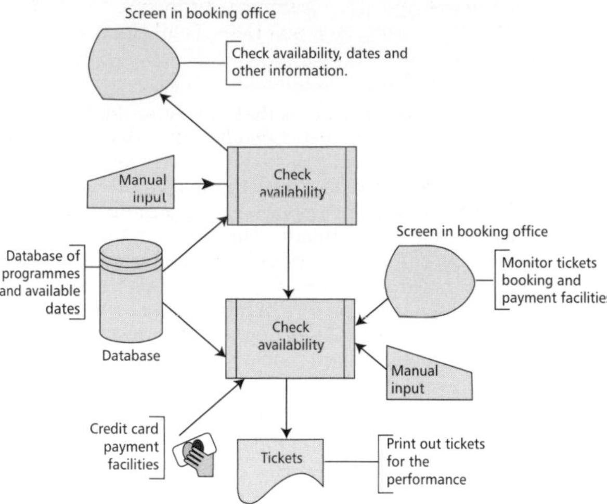

5 **Prototyping** means building up a simulation of the real thing. It will not have all the code to carry out the actual project, but will have most if not all of the functionality of the real user interface. A prototype is used to give potential users an idea of what the real system will look like. Two advantages of prototyping are: enabling the users to have a better idea of what the system will be like and getting important feedback from the users before the actual system is built. Two disadvantages are: the users' expectations may become unnecessarily unrealistic and the actual system may not reproduce what is promised by the prototype.

6 There are many factors that should be taken into account when designing the **user interface**, but four possible factors are the experience of the users, the age of the users, any special needs of the users and special peripheral devices that might help with data entry.

7 (a) An 'association' is shown on a UML diagram with a labelled solid line. An arrow indicates the direction of the association and a 'multiplicity notation' is used to show quantities, like '1..*' meaning '1 or many'. An example is shown in the following diagram.

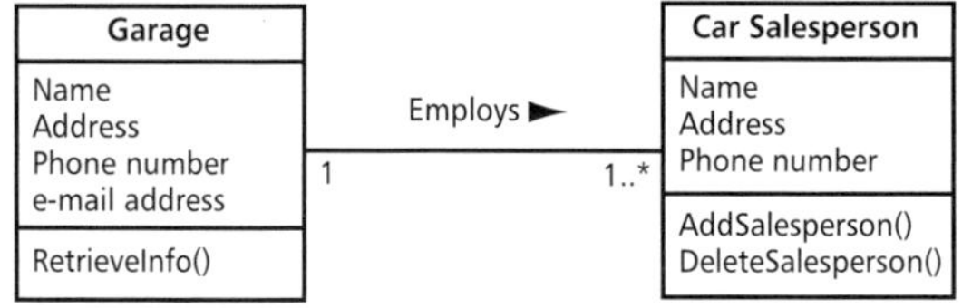

(b) A dependency is shown on a UML diagram using a dotted line with an arrow head. An example is shown in the following diagram.

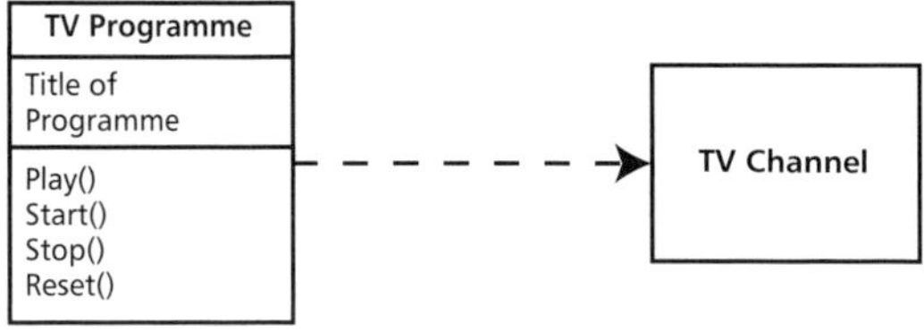

(c) A generalisation is shown on a UML diagram using a solid line with a hollow (not filled in) arrow head. An example is shown in the following diagram.

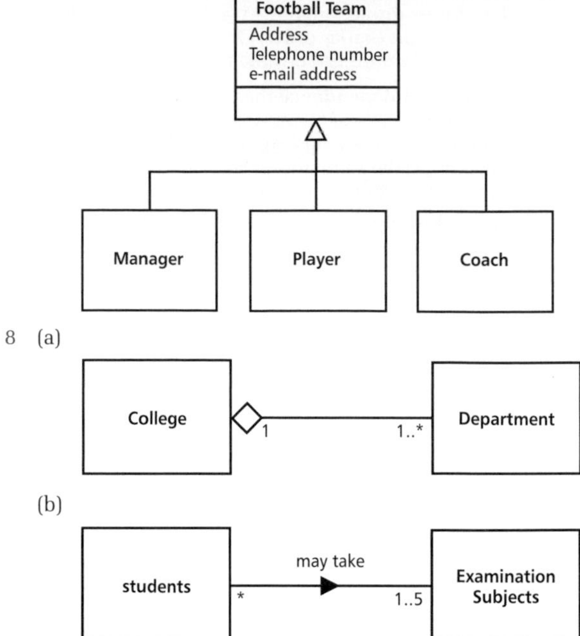

8 (a)

College ◇ 1 ——— 1..* Department

(b)

students * ——— may take ▶ ——— 1..5 Examination Subjects

Chapter 13 – Test strategies for the development of a system

1 (a) **Black box testing** involves producing a suitable set of inputs which have known output conditions. You do not need any knowledge of how the program or system does this. It is usual to test for normal, erroneous and extreme data input conditions. A table of values with expected outputs should be completed when the actual testing has taken place.

(b) **White box testing** involves identifying possible paths through the system. Special software exists to do this, but we can use flowgraphs to accomplish this manually. Once the paths have been identified, black box testing methods are used on each path.

2 (a) The following table shows how to test for a valid numerical date format.

Conditions	1	2	3	4	5	6
Date is numeric	N	Y	Y	Y	Y	Y
1 <= month <= 12	–	N	Y	Y	Y	Y
1 <= day <= 31	–	–	N	Y	Y	Y
month = 9, 4, 6 or 11	–	–	–	Y	–	–
day = 31	–	–	–	Y	–	–
leap year	–	–	–	–	Y	N
month = 2	–	–	–	–	Y	Y
day > 28	–	–	–	–	–	Y
day > 29	–	–	–	–	Y	–
Actions						
Reject date	X	X	X	X	X	X

The table shown here is called a decision table, and outlines the conditions under which a date is rejected. For condition (1), if a date is Not numeric (N), the Action taken is to reject the date (X).
For condition (3) If a date is numeric (Y) AND the month is between 1 and 12 inclusive AND the day is outside the range (1 to 31 inclusive) then the date is rejected (X).

(b) Limit the numerical data type to two decimal places. Limit the maximum range depending on the application. E.g. a domestic electricity bill is unlikely to be higher than £10 000, for example.

(c) Limit the age to a sensible range given the application. As an example, for a secondary school in the UK, the age range is likely to be between 11 and 18 inclusive.

3 Non-numerical data should be rejected. Data outside of the range 1 <= data <= 100 should be rejected. Normal data within the range should be checked. Extreme data (1 and 100) should be checked. Ten valid items should be placed on the stack and an attempt made to add an eleventh. A message saying 'The stack is full' should be displayed. Attempts should be made to remove data from an empty stack. A message saying that 'The stack is empty' should be displayed.

4 For **white box testing** the code that the student has produced for the bubble sort will need to be analysed and split up into identifiable sections, with entry and exit points to these sections labelled with a letter.
A linear flowgraph may then be constructed, with labelled circles representing the entry and exit points and the arcs representing the code.
The arcs need to be analysed in more detail, and more detail needs to be added to the flowgraph. When all identifiable paths have been listed, black box testing needs to be undertaken on each path. Suitable data must be identified for each black box test.

Chapter 14 – System implementation

1 The **implementation phase** is the name given to the part of commissioning a system in which the system is installed at the customer's premises. A team of people including a commissioning engineer will ensure that the system is operating smoothly before being handed over to the customer.

2 (a) **Phased implementation** means parts of the system are introduced in phases. If considering a school, then the examination administration system could be introduced independently of the timetabling system.

(b) **Direct implementation** means that the whole system goes on-line at the same time. This is sometimes the only way to implement a system because all parts depend on all the other parts. A brand new shop, for example, would need all of the system operational from day one.

(c) **Parallel implementation** is running the new system in parallel with the old one until the new system takes over entirely. This may mean entering data twice, but provides a fail-safe mechanism if the new system fails. This can obviously only be used if there is an old system, but it is used if failure of the new system might result in a catastrophe. Air traffic control would be a good example of this.

(d) **Pilot schemes** are schemes set up to test the reaction of users to the new scheme, to provide staff training or as a test bed to see if the new system works as expected. In large companies this is often an option if one particular department tries out the new system.

3 **Alpha testing** is an early stage of testing and involves selected people (often potential customers) testing the system to provide useful feedback to the company manufacturing the system. It is often done in-house at the company's headquarters.
Beta testing is where software is freely distributed to the public for the purposes of detecting bugs and getting further feedback. A company may distribute beta test versions of software via the Internet in the hope that users will provide additional feedback. This is useful because of the vast testing base involving thousands of users having computers that are configured in innumerable ways running a whole host of different hardware and software not encountered at the vendor's headquarters.

4 Staff may be trained by making use of videos and DVDs, by attending lectures, by using CAL (computer aided learning) software or by training on the job (i.e. a different user explains what to do).

5 **User documentation** is intended for the people who will use the system on a day-to-day basis. These manuals are non-technical (from the point of view of the system implementation) and contain things like screenshots of the system or what to do in the event of something going wrong, for example.
Technical documentation is intended for people who will maintain or modify the system. There should be information about how the system was designed and implemented, and enough technical detail to enable a person with the appropriate level of technical skill to maintain the system long after it has been implemented.

6 The **technical documentation** would typically contain the specification of the system, hierarchical diagrams, data flow diagrams, program and system flowcharts, program listings, data and file specifications, test data with test results and modification to the system with date and authors etc.

7 The **user manual** might typically contain the following information: introduction to the system, a getting started section, an elementary operations section, tutorials, advanced operations, a reference section an index, and how to fix error messages.

8 System maintenance means fixing any bugs after the system has been installed at the user's site. A patch is usually made available to correct any bugs or security loopholes. However, even if the system has been working perfectly for years, the changing needs of the users usually demand that some form of system maintenance takes place.

Chapter 15 – Hardware devices and output methods

1 (a) Artists creating animation movies require a simulation of pencils and paintbrushes. This can be achieved with a pressure-sensitive touch pad working in combination with a suitable art package. It is also possible that virtual reality input devices like a 'helmet' or 'data glove' might enable the artist to interact in more natural ways with the environment they are creating.

(b) To gather information from a Formula One car on the move requires a variety of sensors. Typically these might be temperature sensors for the engine or level meters for the fuel level. These would need to be transmitted remotely from the car to the pits via a radio link. Software inside the computers back at the pits could monitor the sensors and mechanics could relay information back to the driver via a radio link. Data over the link might need to be encrypted to stop others determining race tactics.

2 A **sensor** converts physical quantities into an electrical signal. A **sensor** suitable for monitoring radiation would be a Geiger counter.

3 A **transducer** converts electical energy into a physical quantity. A **transducer** suitable for controlling the flow of water would be a valve.

4 Feedback is when information, derived from the output of a system, is fed back into the system for control purposes. Thus, the colour of a piece of toast might be used on a computer-controlled toaster to determine if the cooking cycle is finished.

5 Valves would be needed to control the water, milk and sugar. A heating element would be needed to heat the water, and some sort of motor system would be needed to dispense the cups. Water-level meters would be needed to make sure that not too much liquid is put in the cup. A specialist keyboard would be useful to choose the combination of milk and sugar etc.

Chapter 16 – Networking

1 **Baseband** is a method of transmitting information using a single carrier frequency. Thus only one signal may be transmitted at any moment of time. **Broadband** is a method of transmitting information in which multiple signals may be sent simultaneously. As an example, different carrier frequencies may be transmitted at exactly the same moment in time without interference.

2 **Multiplexing** can be used to send more than one signal simultaneously if frequency division multiplexing is employed.

3 When a line is dedicated for the duration of the communication between two devices then you have a dedicated circuit and this is an example of **circuit switching**. Speaking to someone on a conventional telephone line is an example of this.
Message switching is when a dedicated connection is available for the duration of a message. If a different message is sent, it might be sent via a different line.
To prevent very large messages clogging up the system **packet switching** was developed. This is where small defined packets are sent via whatever route is available and then they are reassembled in the right order at the other end. This is an example of packet switching. With packet switching, parts of the same communication may be sent by very different routes. When you have this condition it is called a **virtual circuit**.

4 A **layered communication system** (e.g. the ISO OSI model) defines the hardware and the software and protocols needed to interface the hardware with operating systems and applications.
A computer communication system is **layered** to prevent the need to replace the entire communication system at the computer end if a change is made to the hardware or software inside the computer. As an example of the layered system, you may change your network card but will only have to change the software needed to interface it to your operating system.
The **TCP/IP** is a good example of a layered system.

5 **Twisted pair** cable is commonly used in 100 Mbit/sec Ethernet and Gigabit Ethernet. **Coaxial cables** are used for 10 Mbit/sec Ethernet, and **fibre** optic links are used for Gigabit Ethernet and 10 Gigabit **Ethernet**. Fibre optics are also used for LAN and WAN backbone connections.

6 Four different types of network topology are **bus**, **ring**, **star** and **tree**. Typically a bus network is used on 10 Mbit/sec Ethernet making use of coaxial cable. A ring topology is used on networks like Cambridge Ring or Token Ring, and star topologies are used where security of communications may be an issue (i.e. direct connections to a server). The tree topology is used where multiple hubs are used to implement a switched Ethernet network. (Note that a tree topology is sometimes referred to as a star topology. This is because the hubs act as though they are the star connection; however, in this configuration security is no different to a tree network.)

7 On large networks, packets would be transmitted to all computers on the network. It is possible to put an **intelligent switch** into the system which prevents traffic from local parts of the network straying unnecessarily onto the backbone or other parts of the system unless it needs to (by making use of the IP addresses).
It is possible to block unauthorised IP addresses, and this means that it is possible to prevent communication with certain machines. (Note: It is actually quite easy to change IP addresses, and so Mac address filtering could be used instead if greater security is required.)

8 A **router** is a device which can be used to connect similar or dissimilar networks together. Typically it might be used to connect a WAN with a LAN, for example.
A **hub** is a device which connects two or more computers on an Ethernet network. All computers share the same bandwidth. Typically a hub connects between four and 25 computers. Hubs may be daisy-chained to make more connections.
A **repeater** is simply a device to boost signals so that a greater distance may be achieved between two computers on a network.

9 **ATM** was designed with simultaneous communication of computer data, video data and audio data. It is possible to have a guaranteed bandwidth if ATM systems are used. However, as Ethernet becomes faster (e.g. Gigabit and 10 Gigabit Ethernet) the Ethernet systems are able to cope with the real-time demands of audio and video signals.

10 (a) The simplest way to connect two computers at home is by making use of a single cable between them.
A crossover cable is used if both computers have an Ethernet card.

(b) To link three computers to share common resources a hub would be needed.

(c) To link 100 computers in an office environment a 100 Mbit/sec Ethernet network should be sufficient. It would be preferable if intelligent switches or hubs were used to keep local traffic within a department. Hubs would also be needed to link the computers, and file servers would need to be set up to provide common resources, backups and enable the network to be managed effectively.

(d) For 1000 computers, the system would need to be segmented effectively. There would probably be many file servers, hubs and switches, and Gigabit Ethernet would be needed for adequate bandwidth on the backbone to the system.

11 (a) The IP address 140.234.1.25 has the decimal number 140 representing the first byte of the IP address. Thus, the binary pattern for the first byte is 10001100. It is thus a Class B network, because it starts off with the first two bits being 10.

(b) Being a Class B network, in which the first two bytes are reserved for the network ID, the host address is 1.25.

(c) Being a Class B network in which the first two bytes are reserved for the network ID, the network ID is thus 140.235.

12 A Class B or C network is ideal for this company.

Chapter 17 – Wide area networks

1 A **WAN** is a wide area network. This is the term given to a network, usually spreading across a wide geographical area, making use of the public or private telecommunications systems.
EDI is Electronic Data Interchange. This is a form of electronic documentation in which businesses and their customers agree on a standard format to exchange information such as orders and invoices electronically. Customers can fill in information which then gets sent back and processed by the business.
A **VAN** is a value added network. Extra functionality is provided over and above basic services like transmission of data or voice. Typically, a company that provides a VAN will give other companies access to specialist databases or services like e-mail and extra security services. VAN functionality can be set up using the Internet, but it is often more cost effective for a business to use these facilities provided by others because they do not need their own infrastructure.

2 An **on-line service provider** is a company which simply lets you have access to the Internet. Few if any bells and whistles are provided. These companies basically rent out their high-speed Internet connections between their customers.
An **Internet service provider** is a company like AOL, CompuServe or MSN, which not only provides you with an Internet connection, but will also provide web hosting, e-mail and newsgroup servers, for example. There are also a whole host of other value-added databases which distinguish one company from another.

3 An **analogue dial-up** connection uses a conventional analogue modem. Typically the connection speed would be up to 56 Kbit/sec. It is normal for users to pay a telephone charge while they are connected to the system, usually at a local rate.
A **leased line** is a permanent connection to the Internet, and a router is normally used for this as businesses usually have more than one computer. The speed of the line varies from 64 Kbit/sec (128 Kbit/sec if you do not use the voice facilities) and varies in multiples of 128 K to speeds in excess of 250 Mbit/sec.
An **ADSL** connection is also a dial-up connection, even though you can be connected 24/7 without incurring phone charges. ADSL stands for Asymmetric Digital Subscriber Line, and means that the download speeds are significantly faster than the upload speeds. The equipment needed is an ADSL modem or router, and the phone connection needs to be upgraded to provide this service.
A **cable connection** is usually provided by a cable television or telephone company. A cable modem provided by the telecoms company provides the connection to the computer.

4 **CODEC** is simply the name given to a coder/decoder. This means that information is coded into some particular form (e.g. music or videos changed into a form to be downloaded and played over the Internet) and then decoded to be used in some particular software package or utility on a computer. There are hundreds of different CODECs, but MPEG, MP3 and Wav are typical examples.

5 **Internetworking** means the connection of two or more networks. The Internet is the largest connection of networks that exists, and is therefore the biggest example of internetworking.

6 **DSL** is a symmetric version of ADSL in which the upload speed is the same as the download speed. This is more suited to users who wish to host their own web sites or run VPNs.
VDSL is much faster than **DSL** and hence much faster than ADSL with all the advantages of DSL.

Chapter 18 – The Internet

1 An **IP address** is a set of four binary numbers called octets because they consists of 1 byte (or 8 bits) each. They are usually represented as four decimal numbers like 82.62.189.202, where each decimal number has a maximum of 255 (the largest number that can be represented with a byte). The purpose of an IP address is to route information to and from different computers connected to a LAN or a WAN like the Internet.

2 (a) A **domain name** is a name used to help humans specify a web site without having to use the IP address system used by the routers.

(b) A **top-level domain name** refers to the .com, .uk or .fr parts of the domain name. These usually refer to a country or particular type of business or organisation.

(c) An **Internet registry** is a list of valid (registered) Internet domain names. It is managed by a number of companies who offer Internet registration services. This list is used to translate valid domain names into the IP addresses needed to route the information.

(d) An **Internet registrar** is the name given to a company that registers Internet domain names.

3 (a) **https** is the secure hyptertext transfer protocol system. It is the http system with 128 bit encryption for extra security.

(b) medicalhistory.htm is the name of the HTML document that will be loaded.

(c) The top-level domain name is 'pro'.

(d) This is a hierarchical directory structure showing that 'Bloggs' is a subdirectory of 'Patients'.

(e) https has been used because confidential information is being transmitted about medical records.

4 It is vitally important to have a hierarchical web site structure. Different directories may be used to contain different information. Typically for a college, there might be different departments, the student's union, general information about the college, enrolment and so on. Without a suitable structure, information would be difficult to organise, and finding information on very large sites would be almost impossible.

5 Two advantages of using a **WYSIWYG** system are you can see mistakes as you are designing the site and you do not have to know any HTML code to use it. Two advantages of using a simple text editor are it is inexpensive and the HTML code is more concise.

6 Assuming you have a server on which to publish the site and a domain name which is registered, you need to transfer the site to the server connected to the Internet. This is normally done by using the ftp protocol. The home page is usually placed in the root directory of the site and called index.htm. Effective uploading and maintenance of the site may be undertaken by using software like CuteFTP. Once the site has been published, this software will allow you to make changes to individual pages without having to upload the whole site again. You can sometimes remotely manage the site if your host allows you to do so.

7 **Telnet** is a protocol which allows you to remotely control a computer on which this has been set up. Typically a server may be remotely administered from another machine by this method.

8 There are billions of pages of information on the Internet and finding things would be virtually impossible without using one of the **search engines**. Typically you may search for any word or an entire phrase. Words could be in any order or in the exact order. You can reject a certain word or change the context of the search by rejecting combinations of words. Boolean operation like 'AND', 'OR' and 'NOT' are usually available, and you can often restrict your search to the UK only or even a specific Internet site, for example, giving you very powerful search facilities.

9 A **web browser** is software that is used to surf pages on the Internet or on an intranet. Typically a web browser will enable users to store and organise their favourite web sites, will store cookies enabling easier log on to some sites, and will enable a user to track the history of sites they have visited recently.

10 **Mobile phones** may be connected to the Internet using the WAP protocol, assuming that the phone is modern enough to support this. Typically a micro browser would be used because of the nature of the small screens which most mobile phones have. Although it is theoretically possible to surf the Internet in its entirety, special sites written with mobile phones and PDAs in mind will give the user of the system a much better experience than attempting to surf sites designed for full-size browsers.

11 A **Java Applet** is a small Java application that can run in a suitably equipped web browser. It typically gives the user a lot of extra functionality which is provided by the application. This functionality can be anything dreamed up by the designer of the site, but might, for example, enable the user to use a calculator or play a virtual musical instrument via the browser.

12 **E-mail** systems allows you to attach files, encrypt messages, create groups of people to whom you can send the same e-mail, provide evidence of authenticity of the sender and search for old e-mails between particular dates, for example.

13 **Newsgroups** are like bulletin board groups created by individuals to which others may post or read entries. Tens of thousands of these groups exist on all conceivable topics. Material posted to these groups may never be read by others, and it is a very passive experience. **IRC** or Internet relay chat is a real-time chat room in which people respond to postings provided by others.

14 To make use of a **video conference** facility you would need a computer, video camera, microphone, USB ports (usually needed to connect modem equipment) and possibly a graphics tablet that could be used for input to a white-board facility. Of course, you will also need a fast Internet connection – the faster the better. The simplest software available is Microsoft's MSN messenger, but this only works with the latest operating systems. Larger, more professional software is available for real business conferencing where multiple camera feeds and audio feeds may be routed through the system.

15 A **shopping agent** is a special Internet site which is set up for searching for bargains in particular areas. There are many sites dedicated to particular areas of shopping like electrical goods or clothes, but others are more general, allowing the user to select the categories. A shopping agent will usually get a good guide price with which to compare other sites.

16 **Internet banking** is popular for those with computers at home and an Internet connection because it enables them to manage their accounts on a 24/7 basis from the comfort of their home. Some people without access to the Internet are disadvantaged, and less-used bank branches are closing down at a significant rate.

17 A **VPN** is a virtual private network. It allows users to connect to their LAN via the Internet. Special encryption makes this relatively safe to do.

18 Access to pornography may be made more difficult by installing filtering software. Most **viruses** will be prevented from being installed on a computer by the introduction of anti-virus software that is kept up to date. Spam can be prevented by the introduction of anti-spamming software, although this is often quite tedious and difficult to set up effectively.

Chapter 19 – The practical project – introduction

1 (i) Is it a real situation that the candidate can investigate?

(ii) Is there a user whose needs can be investigated and taken into account when designing the solution?

(iii) Does it conform to the specification requirements, i.e. will the finished product be a tailored solution which allows interaction between the user and the computer system with input, storage and manipulation of data and output of results?

(iv) Is it within the capability of the candidate to complete in a reasonable time?

(v) Is it a subject about which the candidate has knowledge or an interest?

2 You should consult the mark scheme before starting your project because it outlines the structure of what you need to do. You should write up your project according to the mark scheme.

3 (a) A static web site would be unsuitable because there would be no interactivity with the user of the system, i.e. the specification requires that there be input, output and processing, and a static web site would not provide this.

(b) There would be no input from the user which could be processed to produce some particular output.

(c) A link to a database from a form on the web site could rectify the situation if there were a sufficient amount of input/processing and output capabilities.

4 The sections into which an AQA A2 Computing project is split up are: Analysis, Design, Technical Solution, System Testing, System Maintenance, User Manual, Appraisal and Quality of Communication.

5 The System Maintenance section should enable a user of similar competence to the designer of the system to modify the system at some later stage.

6 Keeping a project diary is a good idea because it enables you to remember important decisions that you have made at salient points throughout your project. These diaries often help when you are completing the final write up.

7 Besides making use of a word processor, it is essential to learn how to use a suitable CAD package. This often takes a considerable number of hours, so you should make sure that you have mastered what you need (creation of flowcharts and DFDs etc.) before any project deadline is looming.

8 Other things that will help to make your project more manageable are page numbers, use of an index, splitting the project up into suitable sections, creating numbered

diagrams which are referred to in the text and developing a consistent style by using appropriate headings and an appropriate font and font size.

Chapter 20 – The practical project – analysis

1 The production of background information means deciding the context in which your project is going to be used. This would mean describing the organisation for which you are producing the project and the people who will use it.

2 Your project will solve a particular problem. The 'current solution' is the way in which the problem is currently being tackled. This might be by a computer or it might be by some manual methods. If there is no current solution at the moment (i.e. your project is doing something which is not currently undertaken), then you should say so in your report. It is unlikely that anything of importance is not currently being tackled in some way, so watch out here!

3 Attributes of users which might be of importance are age, competence using computers and the experience of the users etc.

4 (a) Acceptable limitations for the hospital project could be the number of patients, the frequency of the meals, the variety of food, the information about nutritional content of the food and the number of special diets etc.

(b) Acceptable limitations for the assembly-language simulator could be the number of machine code instructions, limitations on the number of addressing modes, a very limited register set and a limitation of 100 characters in the comment field etc.

5 (a) Possible improvements for the hospital database could be: Patients are less likely to be given the wrong food because the database could flag any dietary requirements; and an electronic record of what a particular patient has eaten can be called up very easily.

(b) Possible improvements for the assembly-language simulator could be a very simple instruction set which is easy for beginners to use; and unlike a real assembler the machine will not crash if the program goes wrong.

6 (a) Two feasible alternatives for the hospital project would be a database (probably accessed via a browser at the patient's bed) and a high-level language running a program written specifically for this purpose.

(b) Two feasible alternatives for the assembly-language project are a high-level language program or an interactive Flash animation.

7 Project objectives are important because the success (or otherwise) of your project is measured against them.

8 (a) Two possible project objectives for the hospital database could be fewer errors in the production of meals and less time needed to produce the instructions for the kitchen staff.

(b) Two possible project objectives for the assembly-language project could be a less intimidating interface compared with a real assembler and more interactive help for an A2 student.

9 (a) Two data sources for the hospital project might be the patient entering choices and the doctors entering data about patient's dietary needs. Two data destinations for the hospital project might be hard copy for the menus and the database table that holds nutritional information.

(b) Two data sources for the assembly-language project might be the students typing in the source code and pre-prepared programs from the teacher on disk. Two data destinations for the assembly-language project might be the source code listing and the simulated register contents on the computer screen.

10 (a) Two suitable types of diagram for the hospital project might be a data flow diagram and an ER diagram.

(b) Two suitable types of diagram for the assembly-language project might be a system flowchart and a hierarchical structure.

Chapter 21 – The practical project – design

1 It is bad practice to try to implement a project before it is designed properly because many costly mistakes could be made. For students this normally involves trying to redesign a project by bodging it at a later stage, and this normally takes longer than if the project had been done properly in the first place.

2 A hierarchical or structure diagram is normally used to describe the modular structure of a project.

3 Data types and formats reflect a deeper level of thought applied to how you might store or process particular data. For a database this might be the choice of data type for a particular field like long integer or Boolean, for example, or for a programming language it might be the type of variable that you use like string or array, for example. The data types used in your project should be explicitly stated in the design section.

4 At design time you may identify that names, for example, need to be sorted into alphabetical order. Therefore, at design time you could specify that a sort algorithm would be needed. However, when it comes to the implementation of your project, you could choose between a bubble sort and an insertion sort, for example.

5 You should think up the rules that need to be used for validation of data and state them explicitly in your data dictionaries.

6 (a) You need to draw sketches of the user interface for your client. CAD packages may be used for this, or you may use an application like Microsoft Access or a high-level language like Visual Basic to produce some prototypes which you can show to your client.

(b) Some students produce screen captures of the finished project for this design section! This is silly because these screens do not exist at design time. If you do this you will lose marks.

7 When data is rejected due to the data validation process, the designer of the system usually produces a context-sensitive error message. E.g. if age for entry into a secondary school was being undertaken, and 21 instead of 12 was entered, a message saying that only ages between 11 and 18 are acceptable should appear.

8 A data-capture form is a sheet on which data is entered manually, usually with the idea of putting the data into the computer system at some later stage. The results of a survey might be gathered in this way.

9 The data to appear on the form should be outlined, including any data that is conditional on some particular process (e.g. some items on an invoice may incur VAT and other items may not). The positioning of the data is

important, as is the layout used, the fonts and any other information like logos or registered numbers etc.

10 (a) Data integrity means ensuring that no preventable corruption of the data has occurred as a result of your project not doing appropriate checks.

(b) Data security means ensuring that the data is not deliberately sabotaged by people with malicious intent or accidentally corrupted.

(c) Three different ways to ensure data integrity are validation, verification and techniques like CRCs etc.

(d) Three different ways to ensure data security are passwords, anti-virus software and locking rooms etc.

11 At the design stage you are familiar with what the system should do in some considerable detail. It is easy, making use of the data dictionaries in your design section, to suggest ways of black box testing the system. This includes normal data, erroneous data and extreme data. When the project is fully working, students find it difficult to think up test strategies because they think that the project already works, and they find it difficult to modularise the tests.

Chapter 22 – The practical project – solution and testing

1 Typically your code should be modularised, with each procedure being accompanied by a suitable bank of comments. You should use meaningful variable names, and parts of the code should be commented where necessary. Ideally the program code should be cross-referenced with the design diagrams and algorithms that produced it.

2 Typically the database printout of the database tables, the linking between the tables and the types of relationship set up, the design of the reports and the queries (or SQL code) etc.

3 In the design section you design a test plan, but in the implementation section you carry out the test plan and demonstrate that the testing works. There should be detailed evidence that the tests have actually been successful, or that code was altered until the tests were successful.

4 Screenshots will demonstrate that your project is working. Together with hard copy and the statement made by your teacher, this is all the moderator has to prove that your project is actually working.

5 Unit testing will show that you have tested each of the modules referred to in your hierarchical design, and integration testing will show that you have tested the project in its entirety. Both types of testing are needed in order to get full marks in your project.

6 Alpha testing is the unit and integration testing, carried out by using black box (and maybe white box) testing methods. Beta testing is when you give your project to somebody else to try out. Hopefully you will use the feedback gained to improve the project if there is sufficient time to do this.

Chapter 23 – The practical project – the finishing touches

1 Five different things that would help to effectively maintain the program are an annotated listing, hierarchical diagrams showing the modularisation, a list of the variable names and functions, detailed system and/or program flowcharts and other details of algorithm design like pseudocode or English statements etc.

2 Five different things that would help to effectively maintain the database are data dictionaries, details of each database table, the relationships between the tables, the processes gone through for normalisation and a list of the queries and reports etc.

3 (a) The user manual is a non-technical manual explaining how to operate the new system.

(b) Typically the user manual would contain sections detailing what type of computer hardware and software are needed, what type of operating system and peripherals are needed, screenshots showing the system in use, what to do if the system goes wrong, common errors, how to backup the system etc.

4 (a) A pdf document is very easy to distribute either on disk or via a network like a LAN or a WAN. You need only to download a free reader to read it, and the formatting of the document depends on nothing else inside your computer (e.g. you do not need access to different fonts etc.).

(b) An HTML file is quite easy to produce and distribute as most people have access to a browser even if they do not have access to the Internet. Although it is easy to produce links in a pdf document, people are more familiar with an HTML document running in a web browser, and many other functions (like animation etc.) are possible.

(c) A Windows help file is the most professional context-sensitive help available, but it needs to be embedded into your application to be most effective.
The HTML document is the easiest to produce, with the pdf document being the next easiest, but you will need Adobe Acrobat to produce the document. A Word file may be dragged and dropped into Adobe Acrobat.
It would be very hard for a student to produce a Windows help file, and the author would not recommend using this method for an A2 level project.

5 (a) Annotation may be added to a screen capture to point, for example, to a specific area of interest.

(b) This annotation may be added via an art package (use a different layer so you do not mess up the original) or a word processor (by using callouts, for example, from Word).

6 (a) You should compare the list of objectives produced in the design section with the results of tests etc. in the implementation section. If your database validates for age between 11 and 18 inclusive, and if you have tested your database with typical, erroneous and extreme data, then this, for example, has been met. You should also attempt to compare objectives like 'less time taken to do X or Y with the new system' by comparing it with the old system.

(b) If you have designed a project which is of A2 level standard and if you have spent several months doing this then, with the benefit of hindsight, it is very unlikely that you could not think of extensions or things that you would do differently. Even if you have met all your objectives, you should still be able to think of some others. Remember that you will not have to implement these.

(c) Typically your client should provide critical feedback; they should not say things like, 'Your project is wonderful', but should constructively criticise what you have done. You will get more marks for constructive criticism.

7 (a) Spelling and grammar checking utilities.
  (b) These are not infallible on modern computers.
  (c) Get your parents and friends to help read through your project. It is usually much easier for others to find your mistakes.

Index